# RAOUL WALLENBERG

LUND UNIVERSITY PRESS

# Raoul Wallenberg
## Life and legacy

ULF ZANDER

*Translated by Arabella Childs*

Lund University Press

Copyright © Ulf Zander 2024

The right of Ulf Zander to be identified as the author of this work has been asserted in accordance with the Copyright, Designs and Patents Act 1988.

Lund University Press
The Joint Faculties of Humanities and Theology

LUND
UNIVERSITY
PRESS

P.O. Box 192
SE-221 00 LUND
Sweden
https://lunduniversitypress.lu.se

Lund University Press books are published in collaboration with Manchester University Press.

British Library Cataloguing-in-Publication Data
A catalogue record for this book is available from the British Library

Lund University Press gratefully acknowledges publication assistance from the Thora Ohlsson Foundation (Thora Ohlssons stiftelse)

ISBN   978-91-985578-0-0   hardback

First published 2024

An electronic version of this book is also available under a Creative Commons (CC BY-NC-ND) licence, thanks to the support of Lund University, which permits non-commercial use, distribution and reproduction provided the author(s) and Lund University Press are fully cited and no modifications or adaptations are made. Details of the licence can be viewed at https://creativecommons.org/licenses/by-nc-nd/4.0/

The publisher has no responsibility for the persistence or accuracy of URLs for any external or third-party internet websites referred to in this book, and does not guarantee that any content on such websites is, or will remain, accurate or appropriate.

Typeset
by Cheshire Typesetting Ltd, Cuddington, Cheshire
Printed in Great Britain
by TJ Books Ltd, Padstow, Cornwall

History must be re-created, re-evaluated, re-written, because it does not comprise permanent truths but is subject to the erosions of the present and the shifting time perspectives highlighted by research. Darkness and light alternate across the stage according to our place in the stalls or in the third row, not only according to our differentiation between genuine and false documents.

*Per Wästberg*

# Contents

| | |
|---|---|
| *List of plates* | *page* x |
| *Preface* | xi |

**1 Raoul Wallenberg: an evolving history** — 1

| | |
|---|---|
| Life and legend | 4 |
| The historiographical dilemma | 8 |
| Raoul Wallenberg between the historical and the practical past | 17 |
| Historical studies in flux | 19 |
| Communicating history | 22 |
| Raoul Wallenberg and Oskar Schindler as role models | 25 |
| Raoul Wallenberg: a saviour and a spy? | 33 |
| Raoul Wallenberg in and outside the archives | 37 |
| Myths and meanings | 40 |
| About this book | 44 |

**2 Raoul Wallenberg, the War Refugee Board, and the Holocaust in Hungary** — 49

| | |
|---|---|
| From antisemitism to extermination | 52 |
| The United States and the creation of the War Refugee Board | 58 |
| Raoul Wallenberg's mission | 60 |
| Raoul Wallenberg in Budapest | 63 |

**3 The Scarlet Pimpernel: from the French Revolution to the 1970s in Chile** — 66

| | |
|---|---|
| The Scarlet Pimpernel: literary role model and screen hero | 69 |
| Pimpernel Smith: an updated version of the Scarlet Pimpernel | 74 |

|   |   |
|---|---|
| Pimpernel Smith, Svensson, and Raoul Wallenberg | 85 |
| From black to 'red' Pimpernel: Harald Edelstam as an emulator of Raoul Wallenberg | 93 |

## 4 Raoul Wallenberg and Sweden: from bone of contention to brand — 102

|   |   |
|---|---|
| Trying to understand the Holocaust | 106 |
| In the shadow of Folke Bernadotte | 111 |
| Neutrality as an ideal | 113 |
| Raoul Wallenberg in the wake of the Second World War | 119 |
| The failure of diplomacy | 125 |
| Rudolph Philipp and the Wallenberg campaign | 141 |
| Raoul Wallenberg and Henry Kissinger | 158 |
| Quiet diplomacy as a contentious domestic political issue | 161 |
| Is Raoul Wallenberg still alive? | 171 |
| The Gulag in the Swedish cultural debate | 177 |
| Continued quiet diplomacy | 185 |
| The Swedish effort measured by US standards | 188 |
| The new Russian openness and Raoul Wallenberg | 192 |
| Innocently imprisoned then and now | 199 |
| In memory of Raoul Wallenberg | 206 |

## 5 The Americanization of Raoul Wallenberg — 210

|   |   |
|---|---|
| An emerging international interest | 216 |
| Raoul Wallenberg and the mass media | 228 |
| Wallenberg as a television series | 232 |
| Raoul Wallenberg between fact and fiction: the reception of the television series | 263 |
| A Swedish Wallenberg film for an international audience | 268 |
| The businessman as the role model of a new age | 274 |
| Raoul Wallenberg in moving images: universalism, Americanization, nationalization | 279 |

## 6 The immortalized Raoul Wallenberg — 287

|   |   |
|---|---|
| Holocaust memorial places and non-places | 290 |
| Holocaust monuments and Wallenberg statues | 293 |
| Wallenberg as a snake killer | 296 |
| 'A monument never without flowers' | 300 |
| *The Snake Killer*'s return | 309 |
| Reconciliation, but with reservations | 312 |

|   |   |
|---|---|
| A helping hand | 316 |
| Art, monument, or both? | 320 |
| **7 The history-cultural Raoul Wallenberg** | **325** |
| Raoul Wallenberg: a role model in and for our times? | 333 |
| Tragedy, trauma, triumph | 336 |
| *Bibliography* | 338 |
| *Index* | 377 |

# List of plates

1 *Hope – a monument to Raoul Wallenberg*, by Gustav and Ulla Kraitz. Photo: Ulf Zander.
2 *The Snake Killer*, by Pál Pátzay. Photo: Wikimedia Commons.
3 *The New Raoul Wallenberg Monument*, by Imre Varga. Photo: Wikimedia Commons.
4 *Hommage à Raoul Wallenberg*, by Kristin Ortwed. Photo: Bengt Oberger, Wikimedia Commons.
5 *R. W. Briefcase*, by Gustav and Ulla Kraitz. Photo: Ulf Zander.

# Preface

This book is about histories that give us no peace: in part the Holocaust and in part Raoul Wallenberg's much-discussed deeds and his still unclear fate in the Soviet Union. In particular the focus is on the encounter between these hard-to-deal-with histories and posterity's attempts to understand, interpret, process, and represent them in all kinds of ways.

The origins of the book can be found in the research project 'The Holocaust and European History Culture', which took place between 2001 and 2007. I would like to express my sincere thanks to the members of the project. With Klas-Göran Karlsson, the research director, I already had a well-functioning and friendly collaboration. This is still ongoing, as are the always valuable and welcome exchanges of ideas with Kristian Gerner, Kerstin Nyström, Barbara Törnquist-Plewa, and Oscar Österberg. Oscar has also been helpful to me at his current workplace, the Living History Forum, in obtaining permission for me to rework for this book *Förintelsens röda nejlika: Raoul Wallenberg som historiekulturell symbol* (The Scarlet Pimpernel of the Holocaust: Raoul Wallenberg as history-cultural symbol), published in 2012 in the Living History Forum's publication series.

At an early stage I exchanged ideas and texts with art historian Tanja Schult. I have greatly benefited from Max Liljefors and Patrick Amsellem's extensive and in-depth knowledge of monuments and the politics of memory. With Tommy Gustafsson and Erik Hedling I have conversed over a number of years about how history is communicated in moving images. The always equally welcome meetings with Pelle Johansson, who works at Kulturmagasinet in Helsingborg, never fail to lift my spirits and broaden my horizons.

My warmest thanks also go to Bengt Jangfeldt, Magdalena Smidova, Omi Söderblom, Cecilia Åhlberg, and Olle Wästberg, who have generously shared their knowledge of Raoul Wallenberg and how his memory has been preserved in Sweden. My gratitude goes to Andrea Pető and Borbala Klacsmann for their willingness to share their knowledge about the perception of Raoul Wallenberg in Hungary and Hungarian history culture with a particular focus on the Second World War and the Holocaust. Thanks to Dag Blanck, Jill Seaholm, Dave Garner, Wendy Hilton-Morrow, Taddy Kalas, and many others at Augustana College, Rock Island, Illinois, who helped me gain new insights into US history, politics, and memory culture during a memorable three months in the spring of 2016 and on several occasions thereafter. I would also like to express my appreciation to the two anonymous peer reviewers who provided insightful comments.

The staff at Lund University Library, the Swedish Government Offices Archives and Library and the National Archives in Stockholm, the Yad Vashem Archives in Jerusalem, the New York Public Library, the Thomas Tredway Library at Augustana College, and the British Film Institute Archives and Library in London have been very helpful. Special thanks go to Sean Delaney at the last-mentioned institution. Under the motto 'Your wish is my command' he has gone far beyond the call of duty in the search for relevant Wallenberg material. Jenny Langkjaer at the Swedish Government Offices Archives also deserves a special mention for her friendly and professional assistance.

Lund University Press could not have had a better editor than Marianne Thormählen, whose great expertise and commitment have contributed to making the publication process a true pleasure. I am also grateful for the efforts of David Appleyard and Rachel Evans of Manchester University Press in the process of turning the manuscript into a book.

This book is dedicated to my wife Helén. Her wholehearted support has been crucial in enabling me to realize this project.

# Chapter 1
# Raoul Wallenberg: an evolving history

It is unusual for announcements from the Swedish Tax Agency to attract international attention. When officials there announced in October 2016 that Raoul Wallenberg had been declared dead, more than 71 years after his disappearance, the news was widely reported. His relatives emphasized that a key reason for their application was that they wanted to let him rest in peace. The memorial ceremony they had held for him at Kappsta on the island of Lidingö outside Stockholm, where Wallenberg had spent much of his youth, was a way of mourning the fact that he had almost certainly died prematurely and that he, who had saved so many, had not been rescued from his own captivity. For the relatives, finally applying for an official declaration of death was a way of dealing with a grief and trauma they had lived with for decades. This is not to say that the mystery of what had happened to him had been solved. In the relatives' application to the Swedish tax authorities, they had stressed that questions remain about the Soviet death certificate according to which Wallenberg allegedly died of a heart attack in Moscow on 17 July 1947.[1]

The difficulties in reaching a conclusion on this matter had once again become obvious some months before his death was declared. At that time, Vera Serova had spoken out in the Swedish press. During renovation work in 2012, she had discovered two suitcases hidden inside a wall. Their concealment was in all likelihood due to the fact that the documents they contained came from her grandfather, Ivan Serov. He had held a high position in the Soviet

---

1 Martin Eriksson and Martin Töpffer, 'Raoul Wallenberg begärd dödförklarad', *Expressen*, 29 March 2016; Eduardo Eurnekian and Baruch Tenembaum, 'What really happened to Raoul Wallenberg?', *The New York Times*, 4 November 2016; 'Raoul Wallenberg officially declared dead, 71 years after disappearance', *Haaretz*, 31 October 2016.

security service, the NKVD, and had then become the first head of its successor, the KGB, from 1954 to 1958, whereupon he led the military intelligence service, the GRU. Serov, who was awarded the title Hero of the Soviet Union, repeatedly demonstrated his prowess, which amounted to ruthlessness. He was a driving force during the construction of the White Sea Canal in the early 1930s, during which tens of thousands of Gulag prisoners died. In the 1930s and 1940s he organized liquidations, deportations, and forced relocations of Ukrainians, Poles, Balts, Volga Germans, Chechens, and Crimean Tatars, which also resulted in thousands upon thousands of deaths. After the Second World War, Serov organized the establishment of the East German security service, the Stasi, played a central role in quashing the 1956 Hungarian Uprising, and was a key figure during the 1962 Cuban Missile Crisis, before falling out of favour in the ensuing power struggle. He was forced to resign as head of the GRU in 1963, lost his membership of the Soviet Communist Party two years later, and subsequently played no political role until his death in 1990.

What made the discovery of Serov's notes interesting in 2016 was that he, who had not been involved in the arrest of Wallenberg, had been commissioned by Joseph Stalin's successor, Nikita Khrushchev, to investigate the matter. According to Serov's investigation, the Soviets had been prepared to hand Wallenberg over to Sweden, but reports that he had been a US or German spy had led to his continued Soviet captivity. For Stalin and Minister of Foreign Affairs Vyacheslav Molotov, Wallenberg could fulfil a function in the run-up to the Nuremberg Trials. In exchange for eliminating what were, for the Americans, sensitive questions about the financial dealings between the US and Nazi Germany, in which the Wallenberg family was alleged to have been involved, the Americans would be prepared to rule out questions, troublesome to the Soviets, about the secret supplementary protocols that were part of the Molotov-Ribbentrop Pact of 1939. After the Nuremberg Trials Wallenberg had lost his value, with the result that Molotov proposed that he be killed. Serov's investigation indicated that 17 July 1947 could well have been Wallenberg's last day of life. The cause of death was not natural; it was the result of a poison injection administered by Grigory Mairanovsky, the head of the security service's toxicology laboratory and a specialist in lethal injections, who, as a result of his 'speciality', was nicknamed 'Doctor Death'.

Swedish and foreign commentators alike found this information interesting, but almost all of them added that it was impossible to establish the documents' credibility. A critical assessment of them, and of how they could have been hidden for decades, raised more questions than answers.² Once again, it was impossible to reach a clear-cut answer about Raoul Wallenberg's fate.

The mystery surrounding the Swedish diplomat's disappearance has been a significant feature in both the news coverage about him and the books written about him. Author, translator and Russia expert Bengt Jangfeldt and journalist Ingrid Carlberg were the first to write comprehensive biographies of Raoul Wallenberg, both published in 2012 to mark the centenary of his birth. Looking back, Jangfeldt noted that there was a clear pattern in the way many writers had approached the Swedish diplomat:

> A quick review revealed that almost everything written about him focused on his six months in Budapest, his disappearance in the Soviet Union and the Swedish government's handling of the so-called Wallenberg issue. His 32 years before Budapest were mostly covered by a few obligatory words along the lines of: 'He came from a very rich and influential family.'³

That many of his biographers have made similar choices may be explained by the fact that while they certainly wanted to supply as comprehensive a description as possible, in the process, some aspects of his life story were toned down while others were enhanced, primarily to contribute psychologically plausible explanations for his actions in Budapest in 1944–1945. Consequently, their main focus was not on his upbringing in the powerful financial family, his training as an architect in the United States in the 1930s, or his activities as a banker and businessman in South Africa, Palestine, and Central Europe in the late 1930s and early 1940s. Instead, it is his efforts to help Jews escape one dictatorship – that of Nazi Germany – and his own downfall in another totalitarian regime – that of the Soviet Union – which have shaped posterity's image of him, and these aspects have repeatedly been linked. In retrospect, his arrest and imprisonment on unclear grounds became an example of the cruelty and arbitrariness of the Soviet system under Joseph Stalin's rule. It was particularly bitter that

---

2 Jonas Gummesson, 'Hemlig dagbok: Wallenberg avrättad av "Doktor Död"', *Svenska Dagbladet*, 6 June 2016; Neil MacFarquhar, 'In a Dacha wall, a clue to a Cold War mystery', *The New York Times*, 7 August 2016; Gudrun Persson, 'En bra rysk story – om vi bara kunde lita på den', *Utrikesmagasinet*, 9 September 2016.

3 Jangfeldt, *En rysk historia*, p. 432.

'a man, who like the Jews he failed to save disappeared into the "night and fog" of Nazi extermination camps, had himself vanished into the "night and fog" of the Soviet Gulag'.[4]

## Life and legend

The word 'legend' stems from the Latin word *legendus*, in the sense of 'something which ought to be read'. The meaning of 'legend' is similar to that of 'myth', but while a myth need not have any historical basis, a legend can be traced back to an actual person and their deeds. In this way, a legend may be said to occupy a position between myth and historical fact. This reasoning may be applied to Raoul Wallenberg, with a particular focus on his efforts during his six months in Budapest. Many Jews in the city perceived him as their foremost benefactor. Looking back, a few decades later, one survivor stated that the Swedish diplomat was 'the only one real hero, the one who risked his life for us every day', while another survivor said he was 'the greatest hero of my life' and 'a great leader, friend and brother to all of us who had the privilege to know him and work with him'.[5]

During the autumn and winter of 1944, Wallenberg's image spread like a light in the darkness as an almost superhuman, saint-like figure who offered the persecuted and vulnerable the hope of rescue.[6] The legend about him began forming even as his endeavours to help were still underway. Not only was a march dedicated to him; at Christmas 1944, the art-loving Wallenberg was honoured by a humorous poem about 'The Protective Passport in Art History', supplemented with a kind of history of the protective passport illustrated with watercolours, including a motif of a figure in a Byzantine mosaic floor. In the halo around his head are the words 'Wallenbergus sanctus', the holy Wallenberg, 'who embodied St George for us', as one of the authors explained afterwards.[7] Similar symbolism was

---

4 Werbell and Clarke, *Lost Hero*, p. x.
5 Lynn Simross, 'Holocaust survivors record acts of heroism: Eyewitness recalls Raoul Wallenberg's exploits during the war' (interview with Tibor Vayda), *The Los Angeles Times*, 7 April 1985; Adachi, *Child of the Winds*, pp. 23–24.
6 Lajos, 'Raoul Wallenberg i muntliga källor', pp. 252, 256–261.
7 'Raoul Wallenbergs gärning', *Judisk Tidskrift*, 1946:7, 216–218; Villius and Villius, *Fallet Raoul Wallenberg*, pp. 46–47; Staffan Rosén, 'Raoul Wallenbergs porträtt målades under blodigt kaos', *Skånska Dagbladet*, 24 April 1971; Carlberg, *Raoul Wallenberg*, pp. 334–335.

applied in Sweden on St George's Day, 23 April 1945, when he was praised as a modern equivalent of the dragon-slaying saint.[8] Some three years later, writer and journalist Mia Leche Löfgren argued that Wallenberg's actions revealed a man characterized by order, consideration, and the use of constructive and unconventional solutions that made him appear an 'organizational and somewhat of a diplomatic genius'. Her admiration for him shone clearly as she affirmed the fusion of his life and legend:

> It is as if the radiance emanating from this saintly legend without a saint would shine more brightly the longer one looks at it. But because the uninitiated can scarcely comprehend the terrible conditions under which he worked, his labour of love will probably always be surrounded by a shimmer. What a rare instrument of the Powers of Light was this 'man from the North', who could guide people's minds like streams of water and around whose figure the magic words 'Wallenberg is here!' resounded like a quiet murmur of hope wherever he appeared in ghettos and prisons.[9]

It was not only in Budapest in 1944–1945 and in the Swedish press in the years after the end of the war that the legend of Wallenberg took shape. Art scholar Tanja Schult has identified a persistent pattern in biographies of Wallenberg, dating back to the first biographical sketches of him in the second half of the 1940s, in which his heroic actions featured prominently. Motifs familiar from traditional heroic narratives were often applied to him, ranging from his birth with a caul through his love of challenges and his willingness to stand as a solitary warrior against a brutal regime and its henchmen, to the tragic end when he faced death, still young and abandoned by his own people. Like Joseph Campbell in his *The Hero with a Thousand Faces*, Schult assumes that heroic narratives may display much internal variation, but that this need not entail any unfavourable consequences, concluding that: 'The classical hero patterns are extended by finding suitable terms that ... fit the Wallenberg narrative as well as our contemporary understanding of the hero concept'.[10]

---

8 'Wallenberg kämpade med S:t Georgs vapen', *Göteborgs Morgonpost*, 24 April 1945.
9 Mia Leche Löfgren, 'Dubbelbottnad avsikt' (review of Jenő Levai, *Raoul Wallenberg – hjälten från Budapest*), *Göteborgs Handels- och Sjöfartstidning*, 8 June 1948.
10 Schult, *A Hero's Many Faces*, pp. 51–60, quotation p. 60. See also Campbell, *The Hero with a Thousand Faces*, pp. 19–20.

It is therefore no surprise to find that Wallenberg's road to Hungary has been described from different points of view. One Wallenberg scholar wonders what factors might account for his transformation from the low-key persona of a quiet businessman 'into a powerful general'.[11] One former acquaintance argued that Wallenberg's years in the early 1930s, studying architecture at the University of Michigan in Ann Arbor, contributed to the transformation. After his return from the United States, the 'new' Raoul moved like a whirlwind as he tossed around bold ideas and suggestions.[12] Looking back, others have chosen to emphasize continuities and have hence sought to find recurring character traits from his early years through adolescence and adulthood until he arrived in Budapest at the age of 31. One Jewish helper portrays a man who was well suited for the job he was sent to do, but who excelled himself once there: young, adventurous, passionate, humanistic and with a great belief in justice, who often appeared troubled.[13] His half-sister Nina Lagergren spoke without reservation, explaining that 'no coincidences steered Raoul towards Hungary and the rescue of the Jews. Raoul had all the qualities needed to succeed in his difficult and dangerous mission'.[14]

In the early 2010s, Carlberg and Jangfeldt set out to write the first comprehensive biographies. In their books, the early years of Wallenberg's life were given far more attention than in previous biographies, and their approaches were similar: essentially chronological and detailed accounts from the cradle up to the unclear location of his grave, and the aftermath of his disappearance. The content thereby became largely overlapping – detrimentally so, in the view of some reviewers.[15] The considerable attention paid to the early years of Wallenberg's life was welcomed by all except a few persons. Swedish journalist Nils Schwartz preferred popular

---

11 Neuman, 'Wallenberg? Which One?', p. 77. See also Handler, *A Man for All Connections*, pp. 7–9.
12 Sjöquist, *Raoul Wallenberg*, p. 17.
13 Adachi, *Child of the Winds*, especially p. 24.
14 Lagergren, 'Still, We Cannot Close This Chapter', p. 8. See also King, 'In Tribute to Raoul Wallenberg', p. 6; Rosenfeld, *Raoul Wallenberg*, pp. 17 ff. and Schult, *A Hero's Many Faces*, p. 65, where she writes: 'In retrospect, Wallenberg's upbringing appears as the optimal precondition for becoming a universal hero.'
15 Nils Schwarz, 'Dubbelarbete', *Expressen*, 3 June 2012; Lennart Bromander, 'Hjältesagans slut', *Aftonbladet*, 23 June 2012.

historian Alex Kershaw's book (recently translated into Swedish), called *To Save a People: The Epic Story of Raoul Wallenberg and His Mission to Save the Last Jews of Europe* (2010), which was reminiscent of earlier biographies of the Swede. Instead of Carlberg and Jangfeldt's 250-page presentations of Wallenberg's childhood and youth, Kershaw had summed up the Swede's life until he arrived in Budapest in 1944 along familiar lines and in a few pages. This focus placed the spotlight on Wallenberg's heroic deeds, which was to be preferred, as was the fact that Kershaw was British. Without elaborating on how he reached this conclusion, Schwartz argued that this guaranteed that the depiction was objective. The implication was that this ideal was something that Swedish writers were unable to embrace when writing about their world-famous compatriot.[16]

The response to both the Swedish and the international biographies was generally favourable. The issue of how they dealt with 'life' in relation to 'legend' was repeatedly discussed, and most commentators expressed relief that the books had found a balance and thereby avoided succumbing to declaring Wallenberg a saint.[17] The biographies differed in a few respects, in that Jangfeldt contributed a solid overview written by a good stylist with a great knowledge of Russia and the Soviet Union. Carlberg's journalistic background was most evident in her preference for interview material, her narrative and engaging prose style, and the fact that she devoted much space to details while also presenting more and larger contexts than Jangfeldt at the expense of writing a concentrated biography. In a review that included both biographies, Budapest-born British journalist Monica Porter devoted far more space to Carlberg's book, because her 'approach is altogether more forensic and she has unearthed a staggering amount of details'.[18] The scope also impressed British historian Joanna Bourke, who has written

---

16 Schwarz, 'Dubbelarbete'.
17 Bromander, 'Hjältesagans slut'; Patrick Salmon, 'Raoul Wallenberg bortom helgonbilden', *Respons*, 2012:4, 49–52; Ulf Zander, 'Dubbelt upp om Wallenberg', *Populär Historia*, 2012:11, 64–65.
18 Monica Porter, 'Review: Raoul Wallenberg', *The Jewish Chronicle*, 23 February 2016. See also Per Svensson, 'Outsidern som blev en hjälte', *Sydsvenskan*, 7 June 2012; Jan-Olov Nyström, 'Raoul Wallenberg i dubbel belysning', *Skånska Dagbladet*, 7 June 2012; Disa Håstad, 'Nya spår i fallet Wallenberg', *Axess*, 2012:5, 75–76; Zander, 'Dubbelt upp om Wallenberg'; Lesley Chamberlain, 'Schutzpass', *Times Literary Supplement*, 15 August

several acclaimed works on the histories of war and killing, fear and rape; but she felt that the rich portrait 'contributes too much to the cult of personality' while failing to touch the reader deeply, mainly because Carlberg was not able to connect the history of the past with the problems and challenges of the present.[19] In other words, the voluminous biography was not an example of a living history.

## The historiographical dilemma

In his overview *The Holocaust in History*, Michael R. Marrus discusses the events in Budapest in the autumn and winter of 1944–1945. He explains that the German efforts to 'solve the Jewish question' in Hungary resulted in feverish diplomatic activity. Thanks to the efforts of representatives of Switzerland, Spain, Portugal, and the Vatican, thousands of Jews were saved from the ongoing genocide. Marrus particularly stresses the Swedish efforts, 'energized by Raoul Wallenberg, a businessman turned diplomat'. The Swede's ability to use 'bribery, bluff, and deception' distinguished him from other rescuers: 'There is scarcely a better example of how an intrepid, strategically placed individual could capitalize on the standing of a neutral power to effect large-scale rescue.'[20]

As Marrus points out, Wallenberg's status as a role model today is based on the extraordinary nature of his deeds in Budapest. This does not exclude the fact that they have been and still are a matter of debate. Soon after the end of the war, information began circulating that some 100,000 Hungarian Jews owed their lives to Raoul Wallenberg. This figure has survived and is still quoted even today in a variety of contexts, from encyclopaedia articles and official websites to books starring him, written for children

---

2014; Steve Donoghue, '"Raoul Wallenberg"' tells the story of the bureaucrat who fooled the Nazis', *The Christian Science Monitor*, 24 March 2016; Tony Moriarty, 'Raoul Wallenberg by Ingrid Carlberg: Review', *The Irish Times*, 14 May 2016; Neil Robinson, 'Book review: Raoul Wallenberg: The biography', *The Irish Examiner*, 21 May 2016; Rafel Medoff, 'Raoul Wallenberg's journey from grocery salesman to Holocaust hero', *Haaretz*, 30 August 2016.
19 Joanna Bourke, 'Enigma of the lost hero', *The Daily Telegraph*, 27 February 2016.
20 Marrus, *The Holocaust in History*, p. 178.

and young adults, to politicians' opinion pieces.[21] However, this information has repeatedly been challenged. Historians such as William Rubenstein, Andrew Handler, and Paul Levine argue that the number of people rescued is greatly exaggerated. In the gigantic maelstrom of the Holocaust, Wallenberg was 'a minor diplomat' who made a contribution in one city for a brief period as the Nazi genocide was coming to a close. Levine argues that the scant empirical evidence has contributed to many misconceptions about Wallenberg, but that more research into what he actually did under difficult circumstances 'will show that he deserves his place among history's heroes'.[22] By extension, one conclusion of this argument is that Wallenberg's actual achievements were not commensurate with his heroic reputation.[23] It is therefore of the utmost importance to distinguish the actual historical events from later myths and legends.

It should be emphasized that there are good grounds for revising the number of people whom Wallenberg saved. However, difficulties arise if the scholarly aspects of the past, whether related to Raoul Wallenberg or any other individuals, events, or processes, are accorded monopoly status. Nevertheless, the symbolic implications of his story are virtually impossible to avoid, even when the aim is to record 'hard' historical facts in order to clarify 'how things really were'. The challenge of contrasting true historical facts with created legends and false myths can be illustrated by three books about Raoul Wallenberg in Budapest, written by historians who have been or are working in Sweden. In their studies, the three authors, Attila Lajos, Paul Levine, and Klas Åmark, of whom the first two have passed away, present new and valuable research

---

21 See e.g. Lichtenstein, *Raoul Wallenberg*; Nicholson and Winner, *Raoul Wallenberg*; Hillary Rodham Clinton and Carl Bildt, 'Wallenberg's life-giving legacy', *The New York Times*, 16 January 2012; *The International Herald Tribune*, 17 January 2012 and, in Swedish, 'Vikten av att inte vara likgiltig', *Svenska Dagbladet*, 18 January 2012.
22 Rubenstein, *The Myth of Rescue* pp. 191–194; Handler, *A Man for All Connections*, p. 109; Levine, *From Indifference to Activism*, pp. 248, 277. See also Schult, *A Hero's Many Faces*, p. 42.
23 Levine, 'Raoul Wallenbergs uppdrag i Budapest', pp. 269–271, quotations pp. 269, 271. See also Paul Levine, 'The myth has obscured the reality of his heroism', *The Washington Post*, 7 January 2001, also published as 'The Wallenberg myth: Swedish diplomat was certainly a hero but his deeds and stature have been distorted by time', *The Montreal Gazette*, 17 January 2001.

findings about the situation in Budapest in 1944–1945. Alongside other historians who have studied the Holocaust in Hungary, they stress that Wallenberg and other diplomats at the Swedish Legation were far from alone in making important efforts to save Jews from the Holocaust. Based on archival material from Hungarian government authorities, Lajos concludes in *Hjälten och offren: Raoul Wallenberg och judarna i Budapest* ['The hero and the victims: Raoul Wallenberg and the Jews in Budapest'] that the Hungarian government tried to assist foreign rescue operations up until the autumn of 1944, when Admiral Horthy was forced to resign. Like their Swedish counterparts, Hungarian politicians realized that a German defeat was inevitable. Lajos's analysis of the Hungarian sources is a welcome and well-documented contribution to Wallenberg scholarship. So is Levine's *Raoul Wallenberg in Budapest*. Levine's aim is to complement a previously one-sided focus on the Swedish diplomat with information about the rescue work done by other people in Budapest. He also seeks to paint a picture which agrees better with that presented in the Swedish press in 1945, namely that Wallenberg was one person in a diplomatic team effort at the Swedish Legation. According to Levine, the Swedish diplomats should be characterized as 'desk-based rescuers'. Via personal appeals, meetings, letters and so on, they tried to stop the 'desk-based killers' in the SS.[24]

One of the many merits of Åmark's contribution is his careful and balanced review of the many different rescue efforts that occurred. The result is insightful discussions of individual efforts and how they related to one another. Åmark's approach has points in common with those of the other two scholars, but it is both broader and deeper. Lajos discusses Wallenberg mainly in relation to the concurrent rescue efforts by Jews, while Levine focuses on Wallenberg in relation to the other Swedish diplomats at the Swedish Legation and the Red Cross operations of Valdemar and Nina Langlet. Åmark also includes the efforts of other individuals and aid organizations and goes into depth with a careful and consistent source-critical approach. Among others, he singles out the papal envoy Angelo Rotta, the Italian Giorgio Perlasca and the Swiss diplomat Carl Lutz for their rescue efforts in Budapest.

---

24 Levine, *Raoul Wallenberg in Budapest*, p. 291. See also Carl Johan Gardell, 'Hur mycket hjälte var Wallenberg?' (interview with Paul A. Levine), *Upsala Nya Tidning*, 17 April 2010.

Lutz in particular has received international attention, but only rarely have his endeavours been compared to the Swedish rescue efforts. Åmark's study reveals that the collaborations were far from unproblematic and in several cases led to open conflicts and broken-off relations. This becomes especially clear when Raoul Wallenberg's efforts are treated in the same way as those of other actors. There is no doubt that Wallenberg made significant contributions and worked extremely hard, but Åmark also emphasizes things that did not work, such as the system of transactions that Wallenberg never managed to make operational in a satisfactory manner.

The discussion about Wallenberg's money transactions and the bookkeeping associated with his rescue efforts is one of many examples of Åmark's skilful handling of sources. He often discusses this subject in a dialogue with previous research. On a number of occasions, Åmark points out how many of the people who have tackled this topic either failed to pursue their initial arguments when the sources became too few or fell completely silent. In other cases, the favourable preconception about Wallenberg's achievements led to the inclusion of hard-to-confirm information in the narrative about him without closer critical scrutiny. Åmark notes that in line with this, there is a tendency, especially in the biographical literature, to exaggerate Wallenberg's administrative skills. Åmark's close reading of the sources reveals that Wallenberg was far from having the meticulous control over his operations and organization that was often emphasized in earlier works about him.

The Swedish historian Klas-Göran Karlsson has developed a model for uses of history. One important aspect illustrated by this model is that history has been and is being utilized by various groups. Uses of history are based on different needs and interests. The model illustrates that history is used on distinct levels, ranging from its existential use, which is linked to the meaning-making of individuals, to the need of intellectuals and politicians for rehabilitation, rationalization, and legitimization in those cases where history is used morally, ideologically, and politically. These uses of history are often in sharp contrast to the scholarly use of history. The latter's practitioners, mainly historians and history teachers, work to discover and reconstruct the past in order to interpret the research results and label them true or false. According to proponents of the scholarly use of history, only people who work according to the scholarly system of rules may be said to be seriously engaged with history. In other words, this use is the only reasonable one, while other uses of history are tantamount to misuse. Karlsson notes 'that history can and is in fact being used in several different ways, of which the scholarly use is only one. It is not superior to the others, but nor is it subordinate'.[25]

In academic contexts, however, a distinction has often been made between myth and legend. While the former is essentially a symbolic way of expressing events that did not necessarily happen in order to explain difficult-to-understand aspects of existence and to contribute a moral to a story, legends are based on actual people and circumstances. Over time these are romanticized, and the role models who were the subject of the legend become heroic larger-than-life characters. Another feature of traditional historical scholarship is that myth stands in opposition to truth with a capital 'T'. It is therefore crucial to debunk a myth and replace it with solid knowledge based on a foundation of historical science.

I agree with the conclusion that it is very important to strive to clarify what Raoul Wallenberg actually did during his time in Budapest, whom he met there, and how many Jews he managed to save.[26] It is striking that it is also precisely in such classic historical-scholarly contexts, in which historical contextualization and source criticism are at the forefront, that Lajos, Levine, and Åmark come into their own. In line with the above reasoning about uses of history, problems arise when other uses of history than the scholarly kind inevitably become part of the analysis. For example, Lajos challenges a commonly expressed view of Jews as passive victims. He argues that this explanation has taken hold owing to the dominance of the heroic depictions of Wallenberg. While Wallenberg's active, heroic efforts have been increasingly emphasized, the actions of Jews have been overshadowed.[27] A fundamental problem with this conclusion is that Lajos assumes that Wallenberg was trying to help the Jews not only for their sake, but also – and above all – as a means of building up his own heroic status, which he knew would be useful after the end of the war. The result is an unjustified downgrading of Wallenberg's achievements, as there is nothing to suggest that he had such ulterior motives.

---

25 Karlsson, 'Historiedidaktik', p. 58. See also Karlsson, 'The Holocaust in European Historical Culture', pp. 431–433 and Karlsson, 'The Uses of History and the Third Wave of Europeanisation', pp. 46–54.
26 Levine, *Raoul Wallenberg in Budapest*, p. 27.
27 Lajos, *Hjälten och offren*, pp. 57–63, 93–99, 177–227.

# An evolving history

The difference here is striking when compared with the case of another Swedish role model, Folke Bernadotte, who actively contributed to the creation of his own heroic image by publishing several books in the wake of the Second World War.[28] Bernadotte's posthumous reputation has alternated from acclaim to questioning, as his own efforts to polish his heroic halo at the expense of other actors have repeatedly been a matter of debate.

Given the opportunity, Wallenberg would emphatically have rejected being called a hero because he was merely doing his duty, argued commentators soon after the end of the war.[29] Against this background, it is not reasonable to 'judge' Wallenberg on the basis of the heroic status he was given after the Second World War in a process over which he had no influence whatsoever.[30] However, it is important to note how the image of a selfless man driven by a humanist conviction easily melds with existing heroic ideals. Another aspect worth pointing out is that unlike many of the great figures of the twentieth century, Wallenberg was not fighting for 'his own kind'. He did not strive to stop genocidal murderers in the ranks of the Nazis and Arrow Crosses in order to save 'Swedes in Hungary, or Jews in Sweden, but rather fought for Jews in Hungary'. He is, continues cultural journalist and author Ricki Neuman, 'thus a genuine international hero, a true citizen of the world. This makes him all the more important as a role model.'[31]

Lajos argues that Wallenberg did not act heroically enough in Budapest. Eating dinners and bribing Germans and Arrow-Cross

---

28 See Lomfors, *Blind fläck*, pp. 27–32; Zander, 'To Rescue or be Rescued', pp. 361–365.
29 See e.g. Philipp, *Raoul Wallenberg*, p. 13; Hugo Valentin, 'En partisan i mänsklighetens tjänst: Anförande vid Konserthusmötet den 11 jan. 1948', *Judisk Tidskrift*, 1948:1, 5; Isak Klasson, 'Raoul skulle inte vilja kallas hjälte' (interview with Wallenberg's assistant in Budapest 1944–1945, Gabriella Kassius), *ETC*, 15 March 2009; Linnéa, *Raoul Wallenberg*, p. 145; Lévai, *Raoul Wallenberg, hjälten i Budapest*, pp. 8, 190–191. However, the last-mentioned was not consistent, because in the same text he described Wallenberg as 'the fairy-tale hero', p. 259.
30 Krister Wahlbäck, 'Alltför ivrig nedskrivning av en hjälte', *Svenska Dagbladet*, 25 April 2004; Fredrik Lindström's review in *Scandia* 2004:2, 330–331; and Ulf Zander, 'Wallenberg: Man and Myth', *The Hungarian Quarterly*, Summer 2006, 166–168. See also George Z. Bien, 'Remembering Raoul Wallenberg', *The Washington Post*, 16 January 2001.
31 Ricki Neuman, 'Raoul Wallenberg – en hjälte värd ett eget museum', *Svenska Dagbladet*, 27 August 2016.

members to achieve his goal was not only unorthodox but also contradicts the definition of heroism advocated by the author. According to that definition, Wallenberg should have acted in clearer opposition to the prevailing power structures, of which he instead took advantage.[32] One obvious problem is that Lajos judges Wallenberg according to an ideal-typical definition of heroism that the Swedish diplomat had never heard of and therefore had no reason to conform to. Had he done so, his tale would soon have been over. Openly challenging the German and Hungarian rulers was not a realistic option. That conclusion had already been reached at the time. A number of Palestinian Jews made efforts to be allowed to fight on the battlefields of Europe. Hanna Szenes, one of the better-known members of this group, was airdropped by the British into Yugoslavia, her mission being to make her way to Hungary in order to save as many as possible of that country's Jews. The British had their doubts about the wisdom of such actions. Those doubts were not only, or even primarily, due to British fears that success in these endeavours might strengthen Jewish hopes for an independent state in what was then British-administered Mandatory Palestine. The British commanders most probably believed that Szenes did not have much chance of success. The doubters turned out to be right. She was captured and executed in Budapest in November 1944.[33]

The distinguished Holocaust scholar Yehuda Bauer has reasoned along similar lines. He has established that while a number of successful rescue operations were indeed carried out in Hungary, including the one led by Wallenberg, the grim truth is that the majority of the country's Jews perished anyway. That this mass murder was so effective can be explained by the fact that the German and Hungarian authorities were in almost total control, 'and no American, British, Russian or Jewish rescue team, no bombing of Auschwitz even, could have changed the overall picture'.[34]

Attila Lajos's study illustrates the problem of unilaterally starting from an ideal-typical and ahistorical concept of the hero. Paul Levine's book shows that a stereotypical understanding of myths can lead to an unintended and paradoxical hollowing-out of the historical research findings that the author wishes to liberate

---

32 Lajos, *Hjälten och offren*, pp. 309, 315.
33 See Morse, *While Six Million Died*, p. 361.
34 Bauer, 'Conclusion: The Holocaust in Hungary', p. 207.

from mythmaking. Studies of individuals like Wallenberg, who performed extraordinary feats in extremely difficult situations, must take account of the historical and social circumstances in which these people operated, as well as of the factors and processes underlying the creation of their status as legends. Accordingly, a unilateral challenge to the myths about Wallenberg, which first reveals the false premises that led to their creation and then replaces them with historical truths is indeed supported by traditional historical scholarship, but it is insufficient when studying the history of effects. In an assertive argument, which dismisses earlier research as 'simplistic' or 'hagiographic', Levine contrasts his own research findings with the prevailing mythmaking.[35] One problem in this context is that in his eagerness to puncture the heroic legends, he is himself guilty of over-simplification by lumping all myths together. The truth-seeking historian may well argue that Raoul Wallenberg was not the Scarlet Pimpernel in a new guise.[36] However, such an assertion leads nowhere, as it does not help to explain why there have been and still are strong associations drawn between the fictional hero the Scarlet Pimpernel and the actual role model Raoul Wallenberg. Like Lajos, Levine seeks to topple Wallenberg from his pedestal through 'revelations' of less appealing characteristics, such as his lack of a disavowal of Nazi racial policies prior to his appointment in 1944 and his ongoing business activities in Budapest concurrent with his rescue operations there. Several reviewers have pointed out that many of these conclusions are far-fetched because they are based on a one-sided utilization of materials.[37]

When Klas Åmark's *Förövarna bestämmer villkoren* ['The perpetrators determine the conditions'] was reviewed in the Swedish press, the reactions were generally benevolent, including the hard-to-surpass verdict that it was 'a brilliant study, a textbook example

---

35 Levine, *Raoul Wallenberg in Budapest*, p. 8.
36 Levine, 'Raoul Wallenberg Was a Real Life Hero', p. 33.
37 Ingrid Carlberg, 'Hjältestoryn trampar fel', *Dagens Nyheter*, 14 April 2010. For a similar critique, see Schult, 'Whose Raoul Wallenberg is it?', pp. 781–783 and Schult's reviews in www.H-Soz-u-Kult.de, 20 May 2010 (accessed 5 June 2010) and in 'Myter om mannen bakom myten', *Judisk Krönika*, 2010:3, 12. See also Georg Sessler's critique of Levine's interpretation of Wallenberg's business dealings, with a starting point in the source material 'Myter kring myten Raoul Wallenberg' and Levine's reply in 'Vilseledande om en sann berättelse', both in *Judisk Krönika*, 2010:6, 38–39.

of serious research efforts'.[38] The fact that Åmark was accustomed to 'treading on morally mined ground' was also a great advantage, as was his ability to separate fiction from reality.[39] This was praise he is probably happy to endorse. In the first chapter of the book, he commits himself to writing a historical account that focuses mainly on source handling and 'a more active critique of sources than modern historians normally tend to apply'.[40] His discussion ends in the conclusion that the historian's main task should be to find and interpret sources that are as close as possible to the historical event.

However, skilled as Åmark is as a source critic, he is equally unskilled as a myth researcher. Like Lajos and Levine, Åmark argues that myth and history are concepts that are clearly at odds with each other. Because he never makes any attempt to distinguish one myth from another or to investigate the contexts in which they have taken shape, the result is that he consistently dismisses myths as being the opposite of serious (meaning source-critical) research. The problem is not lessened by his treatment of the US television series – which he erroneously refers to as 'the film' – *Wallenberg: A Hero's Story* (1985) as if it were any other printed source material. However, along with several popular written books about the Swedish diplomat the television series was produced not with the aim of establishing 'how things really were', but to link to commonly held beliefs that were sometimes of a mythological and hero-exalting character. In other respects, too, perspectives from the history of effects are conspicuous by their absence. Among other things, this means that limited space is given to the international interest in Wallenberg. During the presidencies of Jimmy Carter and Ronald Reagan, the missing Swede became the personification of a tragic hero who fought with considerable success against one dictatorship in order to save the innocent victims of its lethal racial politics, only to fall victim to another brutal dictatorship. In Åmark's version, the great significance which this US interest in Wallenberg acquired, particularly from the late 1970s onwards,

---

38 Niclas Sennerteg, 'Omvärdering av Raoul Wallenbergs insatser', *Borås Tidning*, 29 March 2016. For similar assessments, see Ola Larsmo, 'Klas Åmark: Förövarna bestämmer villkoren: Raoul Wallenberg och de interrnationella hjälpaktionerna i Budapest', *Dagens Nyheter*, 29 March 2016 and Annika Borg, 'Inte ensam hjälte', *Axess*, 2015:5, 83–84.
39 Fredrik Persson-Lahonen, 'Raoul Wallenberg var ingen hjälte', *Aftonbladet*, 3 April 2016.
40 Åmark, *Förövarna bestämmer villkoren*, p. 31.

is merely fuel for further myth-making. Such political interests certainly helped to perpetuate exaggerations about Wallenberg's achievements. However, the meaning-making mythologizing and legend-creation that formed part of the interest in Wallenberg also contributed to a renewal of interest in both him and the Holocaust.

## Raoul Wallenberg between the historical and the practical past

The approach of the above-mentioned historians fits well with philosopher Michael Oakeshott's description of people who are proponents of the historical past. The implication is that past and present are clearly separated. Past events and phenomena can only be accessed through scholarly analyses, developed and applied by professional historians who are also the ones who can – and should – decide what is history.[41] Interpreting Oakeshott's argument, the historian Hayden White underlines that the historical past is 'a theoretically motivated construction' that can only be found in books and articles written by professional historians. Proponents of the historical past regard knowledge of the past as an end in itself, since the main tasks are to reconstruct past events and processes and to reinterpret old sources or find new ones that can contribute to a better understanding of established views, or of revisions to them. One premise is that there is a correct set of conclusions that can be reached, because historians view the past 'from the vantage point of a future state of affairs', which means that they 'can claim a knowledge about the past present that no past agent in the present could ever have possessed'.[42] Historians may justly claim to be able to provide guidance to the past. However, they rarely contribute analyses conducive to a greater understanding of the present, and of connections between then and now. Nor do they tend to supply arguments by which it is possible to predict the ways in which the actual state of things may affect the future.

The practical past is of a different kind. Oakeshott likens this didactic or 'living past' to objects in a warehouse with no supervisor and in a disorderly state. Many of these objects remain forgotten while others have been well known for a long time, remembered in the form of symbolic characters, mythical figures, and living legends. Still others are activated because they are serviceable

---

41 Oakeshott, *On History and Other Essays*, pp. 15–21.
42 White, *The Practical Past*, pp. xiv, 9–10, 42–46, quotation p. 10.

'for their present usefulness'. Thus, the practical past is a recent term for *historia magistra vitae*. According to Cicero, this type of history should be 'the teacher of life' and is existentially significant because it is directly linked to existence in the here and now. It is based on perceptions that most people carry with them in the form of memories, mental constructs, fragments of information, associations with historical persons and events, hearsay, symbols of various kinds, exemplary or detestable objects of contrast, and more or less detailed ideas about the past and present state of affairs. More often than not, dramatic and transformative events are what brings history to life. It is hence not surprising that this book focuses primarily on the shadows of history. The German philosopher of history Jörn Rüsen argues that it is precisely examples of dramatic and turbulent history, termed *borderline events*, which fundamentally influence the manner in which human beings interpret history, make sense of the present, and predict the future. Consequently, boundary-setting events in the form of crises, wars, disasters, revolutions, genocides, and persecutions certainly contribute to new ways of relating to traditional scholarly approaches to tradition and continuity; but they also raise existential questions about victim and perpetrator positions, responsibility, guilt, and, possibly, reconciliation.[43]

There have long been discussions about the pros and cons of the ongoing professionalization of historians, which has often led to a widening gap between history as a scholarly pursuit and history as something closely connected to a world of life and experience. In historical research, the concept of text has slowly but surely expanded to include both words and images, although there remains a preference for studying historical museum objects rather than contemporary art, and documentary films rather than feature films.[44] Perhaps this is due to an unfamiliarity, or even unwillingness, on the part of many professional historians to recognize that all history-making is documentary in the sense that whether the past is brought to life in scholarly texts or in works of art, no matter how historically accurate and credible or ahistorical and anachronistic they may be, they always bear traces of the time in which they were created. Looking backwards activates and mobilizes both individual and collective knowledge, experiences,

---

43 Rüsen, 'Holocaust Memory and Identity Building', pp. 252–269.
44 See Berkhofer Jr, *Fashioning History*, pp. 133–213.

and memories. As we shall see later, there are intricate connections between the actual history of Raoul Wallenberg and recent representations of him as a person, his deeds, especially those in Budapest in 1944–1945, and the still-uncertain end of his life in Soviet captivity. When his story is conveyed, it rarely, if ever, only involves the extent to which the representation is historically correct. The ideal of professional historians has long been to free themselves from the values prevailing in their day, but even they are influenced by their times. For the recent musician, visual artist, or film director, the approach is different, as they usually start from the vantage point of 'the present'. Although many similarities can be identified in the portrayals of Raoul Wallenberg and his deeds, the different choices made and approaches taken reveal how the view of him has changed over time. Similarly, these depictions raise questions about what significance they acquire in cases when their impact is so great that an artistic interpretation or a fictional event complements or out-competes a previous scholarly interpretation of a historical course of events.

Nevertheless, the differences between the accounts of history provided by historians and by the general public are rarely as clear-cut as the division between a historical and a practical past would suggest. The findings of historical research may launch or modify debates in the public sphere, just as past individuals, events, and processes may gain new topicality and lead to scholarly studies in the wake of a novel, a film or television series, a work of art, or a piece of music that arouses strong public reactions. Unsurprisingly, the ways in which history is handled in various contexts has become the subject of study, not least among experts in visual studies. In recent decades, there has been a growing interest among those researchers who construct historical perspectives in how history is manifested in monuments and museums; how past times are conveyed in schools, in film and theatre, and in art, music, and computer games; how the past is utilized and becomes meaning-making; and how we orientate ourselves in time and space. In such contexts, the distance between a historical and a practical past, between history as a science and the world of life and experience, is no longer substantial and perhaps not even relevant.

## Historical studies in flux

We both *are* and *create* history. We are products of the developments that preceded us, but we also help to influence our situation in the present, and we have expectations for the future. The impact of changing conditions in the present on our views of both the past and the future is evident in various history-cultural contexts. On the one hand, many producers of history consciously look backwards, towards established perceptions of the past, while remaining firmly anchored in the present. On the other hand, a unifying feature on the part of many of those who criticize, and have criticized, the fact that the Holocaust has to some extent become everyone's property is that they represent a traditional scholarly use of history that stands in sharp contrast to other ways in which history may be utilized and understood. Further, it is now clear that the history that is conveyed via popular culture has a large impact unmatched by any product of historical scholarship. Exploring the broader interest in history therefore requires a different approach from the conventional ones. Historians mostly focus on explaining the causes of a historical course of events and, in historiographical contexts, on how history is produced by historians. History-cultural studies also attach great importance to the effects of the past and to the history of effects, as well as to the fact that social factors of various kinds influence the shaping of historical products, both within and outside the academy. In this way, questions about how history appears as awareness, memory, and myth, as well as in monuments, museums, music, television, and computer games and on film, are central to history-cultural studies. In such contexts, it is important for the history-cultural researcher to recognize that different types of historical narrative are involved. The requirements and starting points are not the same when the narrative is presented in a museum, as a monument, on the film screen, or in a history thesis. Filmmakers who produce moving images in historical settings are aware of the importance of linking to the actual history, but the audience's sense of recognition is of even greater importance. Recent visual depictions of past times must somehow reflect influential trends and values rather than show 'how things really were'. In this way, successful films become a litmus test for the contemporary world and its view of historical events. Since history is constantly in flux, the same historical event is bound to be depicted in different ways in films from different eras.[45]

The dual perspective of *both* knowing the importance of understanding history on its own terms *and* realizing the relevance

---

45 Zander, *Clio på bio*, pp. 11–39.

# An evolving history

of each era's posing new questions to the past is essential when studying how producers of history relate to history itself, as well as to the ways in which history is connected to the present. In the present context, however, that dual perspective is more than a tool: it is a fundamental analytical starting point for this book. In traditional historical scholarship, the aim was to find out what was behind a particular historical development, or the emergence of certain scholarly ideals in the discipline. Posterity's view of history – the effects – was hence undervalued. In historiography – that is, the scholarly analysis of historical research and the communication of history – the research of professional historians has more often than not been the given, and rarely problematized, starting point. In addition, the work of the historian has often been presented as if it were isolated from the surrounding society and its development. Furthermore, the second part of the definition of historiography – the communication of history – has frequently been neglected, which is why there is a dearth of studies of interest in the past within a broad social context, and of conditions affecting this type of history communication. In other words, it is important to study the facts of the past, but it is also necessary to consider the significance of the present for the interpretation of the past. The view that looks backwards from the present is just as important as the view that starts out from a specific point in history. From this reasoning, it follows that later interpretations and additions are indispensable given that all forms of history, whether we confront it *in situ* or read, see, and hear representations of it from a distance, are devoid of value in and of themselves. Historical representations and places derive their meaning from present-day issues, problems, and perspectives that help us to bring a dead past to life.[46] A historical construction cannot be created on its own; it must take established historical facts into account. The research that helps us gain greater clarity about the past is certainly important, but we must also be aware that those who produce history are dependent on economic and political situations, cultural patterns, social institutions, and other structural conditions. As a result, some aspects of history are highlighted while others are gradually forgotten. The writing of history is thus always the result of a process of selective choice: in order to remember something, we must always discard something else.

---

46 Gerner and Karlsson, *Folkmordens historia*, p. 95.

## Communicating history

In most previous studies of Raoul Wallenberg, the given starting point has been texts of various kinds: archival documents, recorded testimonies, newspaper and magazine articles, books and articles about him. Such sources are important in the present study, too, but even greater importance is attached to monuments, films, and television series based on Wallenberg. This book places such expressions of cultural history within a history-cultural context. A history-cultural approach is applied to a study of the contexts within which history is communicated and the different meanings that this communication acquires in various forums. In this sense, 'history culture' is a term used to describe the places in society, particularly in the public sphere, where history is communicated, discussed, and used.[47] A tripartite division can help to shed light on how we can examine and analyse history cultures. This tripartite approach is based on the need to study history as such, the conditions of history production, and the channels of communication and aspects of conveyance. Such a study involves analysing texts and images on their own terms while simultaneously placing them in social contexts. History culture has been one of the central concepts in an extensive Swedish research project on how and why the Holocaust has been utilized in post-war Europe, Israel, and the United States.[48] The treatment of the Holocaust after 1945 is of interest in this book as well, not least because the post-war ebbs and flows of the Holocaust complex are to a large extent correlated with waves of interest (and lack of it) in Wallenberg. More specifically, I focus on the chains of communication through which narratives about Raoul Wallenberg were conveyed and the actors of these communication processes: senders, conveyors, and recipients. It is primarily the first two categories that will be discussed in this book.

---

47 Rüsen, *Historische Orientierung*, pp. 211–213, 219–225.
48 The project 'Förintelsen i den europeiska historiekulturen' is presented in Karlsson, *Med folkmord i fokus*. See also Karlsson, 'The Holocaust as a Problem of Historical Culture', pp. 9–58; Karlsson, 'The Holocaust as a History-Cultural Phenomenon', pp. 85–96; Karlsson, 'The Holocaust in European Historical Culture', pp. 427–440. Usage aspects of Holocaust images are discusssed in Zander, 'Den slingrande vägen från Auschwitz', pp. 283–319. The American perspective is often cited in the project, above all in conjunction with Martin Alm's comparative article 'Holocaust Memory in America and Europe', pp. 494–524.

History culture can be analysed in terms of both process and structure. The core assumption of the processual perspective is that the conditions under which history is conveyed differ in different times. Both form and content have changed from the time when history was mainly communicated via school education to today's online learning opportunities. The symbolic meanings and functions that monuments possessed at the turn of the twentieth century are not in evidence today. The great impact of the media is also likely to have influenced people's perceptions of what distinguishes individuals who are placed in exalted positions. At a fundamental level, there is much to suggest that heroic narratives in predominantly oral cultures are about preservation over time: the role model must remain relevant for future generations. With the introduction of a book-based culture, the hero category expanded to include writers and politicians, whose expertise and strategic skill were as valuable as classical qualities such as strength and courage. And just as a printed story can be read over and over again, it can also easily be rewritten to suit the values and needs of new generations. Media scholars argue that both the oral and the printed hero were real historical figures. Conversely, the role model of our own time is an individual who exists in the present and was created by a kind of media attention that is increasingly rarely accorded to historical models. It is becoming more and more difficult to draw a clear line between legendary status and celebrity adulation, but such a distinction does still exist. For while those people who find themselves in today's spotlight are exposed on an unprecedented scale, their celebrity is rarely based on heroic deeds.[49]

The attention still being paid to Raoul Wallenberg and others proves that legendary figures can still fulfil a function. As discussed later, even his elevated position has been heavily dependent on media attention, in the form of both traditional press coverage and products of popular culture. In an account of the emulable efforts made by his former counterparts, the diplomat Richard Holbrooke argues that there is a wide gap between fact and fiction. In an example of the latter, the character Rick (Humphrey Bogart) in the classic film *Casablanca* (1942) hands over his visa to a persecuted freedom fighter, in consequence of which action he himself faces an uncertain future. Such conduct, writes Holbrooke, is rare in

---

49 Drucker and Cathcart, 'The Hero as a Communication Phenomenon', pp. 2–8; Strate, 'Heroes', pp. 15–23.

real life.[50] Nonetheless, the ideal actions of fictional role models are of great importance to our perception of what it means to be heroic. Not least in modern media, it is very important for the hero to be 'marketable'. In the British-American film *Hero*, also called *Accidental Hero* (1992), the plot revolves around the idea that a grand and selfless act is no guarantee of being elevated to the status of a role model in today's society. The role model must also meet a number of other criteria in order to be presented as worthy of emulation to the general public. Failure to do so may produce the outcome experienced by the amoral petty thief Bernard 'Bernie' Laplante (Dustin Hoffman). In the wake of a plane crash, he sees a new opportunity to steal, but he also performs a selfless act in rescuing passengers from the wreckage. The latter action guarantees him the status of a hero, but that role is better fulfilled by the handsome and media-savvy John Bubber (Andy Garcia).

The fact that history is communicated in different ways in different countries forms the basis of the structural perspective in historical research. The social structures of the countries at the core of this book – Sweden, Hungary, and the United States and, to a more limited extent, the Soviet Union/Russia, Great Britain, and Germany – have been and remain dissimilar. In concrete terms, this means that the view and the use of history differ in each country as a result of the emergence of dissimilar political systems and social structures, but also because concrete historical developments have led to dissimilar history-cultural traditions. That Sweden was not a belligerent during the Second World War and remained outside the Cold War bloc formations has probably resulted in a more distanced attitude to history than in Hungary, the Soviet Union/Russia, Britain, and the United States. In addition, the fact that Hungary was part of the Soviet-dominated Eastern bloc, while the last two belonged to the West, has also influenced the view of the past in each respective country.[51]

A unilateral focus on national starting points is not sufficient or desirable when, as in this book, the discussion encompasses phenomena and concepts that can occur in national contexts while simultaneously also being transnational. The comparative endeavour which lies at the heart of the Sweden-Hungary-United States analysis is inspired by entangled history and *histoire croisée*.

---

50 Holbrooke, 'Defying Orders, Saving Lives', p. 135.
51 See Karlsson, 'Historiedidaktik: begrepp, teori och analys', pp. 37–43.

My approach has been to study similarities and differences with regard to views of the Holocaust and of Raoul Wallenberg in both national and transnational contexts, starting from the premise that 'historical entities are not naturally given but dynamic phenomena subjected to [a] process of exchange and negotiation'.[52]

## Raoul Wallenberg and Oskar Schindler as role models

The reasoning described above invites the conclusion that history is not merely, or even primarily, a string of individuals, events, and processes that lie along a timeline. When history is communicated, it always happens within a particular context. In a discussion of the communicative characteristics of history culture, Klas-Göran Karlsson explains that the producers of history '[choose] the history and interpretations they find worth remembering, preserving, and disseminating on various grounds, whereas consumers choose what they want to hear, see, and learn on various grounds'. This is not to say that all producers and consumers necessarily agree on how the past should be portrayed. In turn, this fuels a struggle over history that has consequences for our perceptions of the present and our expectations, or trepidation, about the future. The respective showcasing and downplaying of historical individuals, events, and processes are thus often the results of conscious choices and expressed needs.[53]

By extension, we can conclude that it is not necessarily a question of *either* memory and attention *or* neglect and obscurity. The highlighting of some aspects and downplaying of others are the result of several factors. It depends partly on what has been preserved for posterity in the form of sources and miscellaneous remnants and partly on the questions asked by the researcher – what he or she finds worth knowing and important. This evaluation may vary over time, as historians find new and previously untested starting points.[54] The history-cultural insight is that role models only remain immortal as long as society encompasses interests in keeping them alive.[55]

In addition, the extent to which a person or an event is remembered or forgotten may vary at the same time and in the same place.

---

52 Karlsson, 'The Evil Twins of Modern History?', p. 12.
53 Karlsson, *Europeiska möten med historien*, pp. 15–36, quotation p. 35.
54 Österberg, *Tystnader och tider*, pp. 34–35, 204–207.
55 Asplund, *Tid, rum, individ och kollektiv*, p. 33.

For example, in Sweden in the mid-1980s there were two diametrically opposed views about Raoul Wallenberg's status. In 1985 one commentator asserted, without supplying any evidence, that former UN Secretary-General Dag Hammarskjöld was a revered Swedish hero, while both Folke Bernadotte and Raoul Wallenberg were fading away.[56] In an interview the following year, the influential cultural debater, critic, and publicist Olof Lagercrantz expressed a totally different interpretation. According to him, Wallenberg was the unwilling victim of a cult, an example of moral hypocrisy of monumental dimensions that had a particularly strong hold in Sweden:

> Year after year the heroization of this man continues, streets are named after him, statues of him are erected, the keys of cities are presented to his shadow. Is it to keep the memory of the Holocaust alive? Certainly not! The sole purpose of all this is to keep the hatred of Russia alive. History is full of heroes. Was there no one who tried to stop the bombing of Dresden or Hiroshima? Let him or her come forward![57]

Besides contributing to the almost continuous, and infected, Swedish debate over East versus West during the Cold War, Lagercrantz's statement indicates frustration that so much attention was paid to Raoul Wallenberg while others received little or none. Since the late 1970s, the Swedish diplomat has attracted considerable international attention, which, as already indicated, has contributed to the fact that it has been difficult for others who made great efforts to save Jews from the Holocaust to take their place alongside the Swedish role model. For while Wallenberg was just one of many named in Swedish newspaper reports from 1945, he subsequently became a humanitarian fixed star with a luminescence that still has considerable power, not least among politicians and diplomats. In various late twentieth-century and

---

56 Stig Hadenius, 'Hur blir man en hjälte? Varför är Folke Bernadotte nästan bortglömd?', *Arbetet*, 22 August 1985. On a list from 1974 of 30 world-famous Swedes, Hammarskjöld was one of those selected, in contrast to Folke Bernadotte and Raoul Wallenberg; see Inga-Lill Valfridsson, '30 svenskar som blev kändisar i hela världen', *Aftonbladet*, 5 May 1974. Like Hadenius, Shelley Emling does not supply evidence that Folke Bernadotte is now *A Forgotten Hero*, to cite the title of her biography.
57 Erik Åsard, 'Jag ser mitt liv som ett långsamt uppvaknande' (interview with Olof Lagercrantz), *Tiden*, 1986:3, 146; also published in Olof Lagercrantz, *Vårt sekel är reserverat åt lögnen*, p. 466.

early twenty-first-century contexts, the UK's former Prime Minister Gordon Brown, former UN Secretary-General Kofi Annan, former Swedish Liberal Party leader Lars Leijonborg, and his fellow countryman, the Swedish diplomat, UN mediator, and former Foreign Minister Jan Eliasson, have thus cited Raoul Wallenberg as their primary role model, a man whose actions in Budapest in 1944–1945 have inspired and guided them.[58] Eliasson's American colleague Richard Holbrooke, whose efforts to negotiate a peace after the civil wars in the former Yugoslavia attracted much attention, has also repeatedly stressed the importance of Raoul Wallenberg and Folke Bernadotte's efforts to save lives. According to Holbrooke, the two Swedes – into whose lives he gained insight partly because his wife, Kati Marton, wrote biographies of them – were worthy of emulation despite the high price they paid in falling victim to Soviet security men and Israeli terrorists respectively.[59]

Perhaps the most important indication of Wallenberg's central position in the post-war era is that he has long been an accepted point of reference. There has been no shortage of people with similar credentials; diplomats are common among those who saved people from the Holocaust, mainly because they were able to achieve more owing to their immunity.[60] But none of them has

---

58 Brown, *Courage*, pp. 65–88; 'Kofi Annan on public service', *The Christian Science Monitor*, 8 June 1998; Annan, 'Introduction by Kofi A. Annan', pp. 13–15; Leijonborg, *Kris och framgång*, p. 300; Jan Eliasson, 'Inte en timme att förlora: Raoul Wallenberg angrep ondskan instinktivt och tveklöst', *Dagens Nyheter*, 18 January 1995; Svante Lidén, 'Sju frågor till Jan Eliasson', *Aftonbladet*, 5 October 2009; Eliasson, *Ord och handling*, p. 27. It may be added that Holbrooke mentions Wallenberg in the same breath as Folke Bernadotte and that it is regularly pointed out that Kofi Annan is married to Raoul Wallenberg's niece, the lawyer and artist Nane Lagergren; see e.g. Matthias Nass, 'Der Mann, den Madeleine wollte', *Die Zeit*, 1996:52; Barbara Crossette, 'Salesman for unity: Kofi Atta Annan', *The New York Times*, 14 December 1996; Barbara Crossette, 'How U.N. chief discovered U.S., and earmuffs', *The New York Times*, 7 January 1997; Dagmar von Taube, 'Die Frau an Kofi Annans Seite', *Die Welt*, 9 December 2001; Warren Hoge, 'Annan, at U.S. urging, seeks special U.N. Session to mark liberation of death camps', *The New York Times*, 19 December 2004.
59 Holbrooke, *To End a War*, p. 147. See also Richard Holbrooke, 'The Road to Sarajevo', *The New Yorker*, 21 and 28 October 1996 and Richard Holbrooke, 'Defying orders, saving lives: Heroic diplomats of the Holocaust', *Foreign Affairs*, June 2007, 137.
60 Lundgren, *I hjältens tid*, pp. 21–26.

been able to match the Swedish role model. When other rescuers have received media attention, often after being forgotten for decades, their names have not been considered to have sufficient lustre, sometimes not even among the officials from the Swedish Foreign Office (Utrikesdepartementet, UD) tasked with investigating what happened in Budapest in 1944–1945.[61] Instead, other diplomats have been described as Denmark's, Poland's, Portugal's, Spain's, Hungary's, or China's Wallenberg.[62] Wallenberg's media dominance has occasionally led to chronological adjustments. As a number of scholars have pointed out, the work of rescuing Jews did not begin with Wallenberg's arrival in Budapest on 9 July 1944 but was already underway 'well before that date'.[63] The fact that the Swiss had begun handing out protective passports as early as 1942 has accordingly been overshadowed by the concentration on Wallenberg as an individual, a man whose tireless actions in Budapest 'rubbed off' on others – both Swedes and people of other nationalities – who were present in Budapest.[64] Observers interested both in the work done by Jews assisting their unfortunate brothers and sisters and in the relief efforts of other actors have expressed frustration that such people have been overshadowed by Lutz, Schindler, and Wallenberg. However, they have also voiced their hope that the individuals who at long last do have their portraits drawn alongside these already established great personages will

---

61 Giorgio Perlasca, an Italian who, like Wallenberg, made great efforts to save Jews in Budapest in 1944–1945, was clearly unknown to some of the people at the UD who were working on the Wallenberg case when Perlasca contacted Swedish authorities on at least two separate occasions; see e.g. K. O. Stefanson, 'Till Kungl. Maj:ts beskickning i Rom', 25 April 1951 and Stellan Ottosson, 'Raoul Wallenberg – Perlasca', Memorandum, 21 January 1982, RKA, Raoul Wallenberg, UD2001/00009, Vol. 16.
62 See e.g. Reese Erlich, 'World War II Holocaust hero's honor caught up in politics', *The Christian Science Monitor*, 4 September 1986 (on Aristides de Sousa Mendes, the Portuguese consul in Bordeaux); Judith Weintraub, 'Hero refused to turn away from persecuted Holocaust: After more than four decades of obscurity, Giorgio Perlasca has been honoured for protecting thousands of Jews in Budapest', *The Los Angeles Times*, 22 November 1990; Roman Freud, 'De okända rättfärdiga', *Judisk Krönika*, 1991:4, 12–13; Gerhard Gnauck, 'Die "polnische Wallenberg"', *Die Welt*, 31 January 2004; Klein, *Jag återvänder aldrig*, pp. 69–100; 'Portugals Wallenberg hedras stort', *Göteborgs-Posten*, 21 October 2021.
63 Barany, 'The Current Stage of Research on Raoul Wallenberg', p. 569.
64 See e.g. Morse, *While Six Million Died*, p. 364; Tschuy, *Dangerous Diplomacy*, p. 7.

posthumously receive recognition that extends beyond previous sporadic and geographically limited acknowledgements of their contributions.[65]

Wallenberg may have lost some of his international star power over the past decade or so. When his life was presented in the form of a musical in New York in 2010, one of the organizers argued that an important reason was to rescue him from oblivion in the United States, where he had until only recently been a central figure.[66] This may be partly due to a shift in the amount of attention beginning to be paid to Oskar Schindler. For several decades after the end of the Second World War, Schindler received scant attention outside the circle of those he had rescued. It was only with Thomas Keneally's 1982 fictionalized biography *Schindler's Ark*, and even more with Steven Spielberg's 1993 film *Schindler's List*, that his name became world famous.[67] As we shall see later, recent fictionalizations of historical figures and events are characterized by a constant negotiation between historical recognition and the values of 'the present'. In the case of *Schindler's List*, argues British historian Tim Cole, the fusion of the protagonist's historical deeds and cinematic actions has resulted in a Christ-like, humanist icon. In Spielberg's version, Schindler also possessed qualities that have been highly relevant following the fall of the Berlin Wall. While Wallenberg was linked to both 'the Cold War and the "Holocaust" [in an American context], Schindler speaks both of capitalism and the "Holocaust"'. Cole's conclusion before the turn of the millennium was therefore that Oskar Schindler has 'in some ways … eclipsed Raoul Wallenberg'.[68]

The popularity of *Schindler's List* is not the sole indication of such a shift. Prior to the unveiling of Phillip Jackson's statue of Wallenberg in London in 1997, *The Guardian* newspaper ran a major feature on this 'Schindler of Budapest'.[69] When Kjell Grede's

---

65 Ben-Tov, *Facing the Holocaust in Budapest*, p. 388; Paldiel, *Saving One's Own*, pp. xix–xxi; Camargo, 'Preface', p. 7.
66 Ted Merwin, '"Wallenberg", the musical', *The Jewish Week*, 19 October 2010; Steve Lipman, 'Spreading Wallenberg's legacy', *The Jewish Week*, 10 March 2006.
67 Crowe, *Oskar Schindler*, pp. 542–563; Zander, 'Oskar Schindler and Raoul Wallenberg', pp. 459–462.
68 Cole, *Selling the Holocaust*, pp. 80–81.
69 Alan Travis, 'Could Raoul Wallenberg still be alive?', *The Guardian*, 18 February 1997.

*Good Evening, Mr. Wallenberg* (1990) was distributed on DVD in the US by First Run Features in the early 2000s, it was presumably not only the fact that it was a relatively unknown film in the US that prompted marketers to write on the cover: 'Schindler Saved Hundreds, Raoul Wallenberg Saved Thousands.'[70] Along the same lines, it was claimed from a British perspective some ten years later that most people who had made great efforts to save Jews had ended up in Schindler's shadow. Wallenberg, who was accordingly called 'Hungary's Schindler', was one of them.[71] In the name of history-cultural consistency, some of those who saved fellow human beings from genocide have thus come to be categorized as the Schindlers of Brazil, Japan, Britain, China, Taiwan, and Rwanda. Bertold Bietz, a German citizen like Schindler, was simply referred to as 'the other Schindler' in Germany. In line with the great interest in Schindler during the 1990s, Wallenberg has been referred to as 'Der Schindler von Budapest', 'the Swedish Schindler', or occasionally before that as 'Sweden's other Folke Bernadotte'.[72]

The conclusion drawn from the preceding discussion is that the Sudeten-German Schindler has become at least as well known internationally, and as self-evident a history-cultural reference

---

70 DVD cover of *Good Evening, Mr. Wallenberg*, First Run Features (2002).
71 Guy Walters, 'Hungary's Oskar Schindler: He saved thousands of Jews from the gas chambers, but Raoul Wallenberg is now an almost forgotten figure', *The Sunday Times*, 21 November 2010.
72 Gösta von Uexküll, 'Wer hat zuletzt Raoul Wallenberg gesehen? Schwedens zweiter Folke Bernadotte in sowjetischen Gefängnissen verschlossen', *Die Zeit*, 12 April 1956; Gert Sundström, 'Sugiharas List', *Judisk Krönika*, 1996:4, 21–23; Stewart Ain, 'The lost history of the Holocaust', *The Jewish Week*, 13 November 1998; Tony Paterson, 'Berlin plaque pays tribute to "Schindler of Stourbridge"', *The Independent*, 25 November 2004; Jake Wallis Simon, 'Revealed: The Hungarian "Schindler" who saved George Soros from Nazi death squads during the occupation by hiding him behind a cupboard' (about Miklós Próhaszka), *The Daily Mail*, 26 November 2018; Gary Shapiro, 'The Brazilian Schindler', *The New York Sun*, 13 December 2004; Judith Miller, 'Searching for an Arab Oskar Schindler', *The New York Sun*, 7 November 2006; Michael Streich, 'John Rabe, the Oskar Schindler of China', www.suite101.com, 28 September 2011 (accessed 28 June 2015); Matthew Day, 'Raoul Wallenberg: Holocaust heroes', *The Telegraph*, 1 September 2011; Heinz W. Koch, 'Der Schindler von Budapest', *Badische Zeitung*, 10 July 2012; Gillian Brockell, '"A Japanese Schindler": The remarkable diplomat who saved thousands of Jews during WWII', *The Washington Post*, 27 January 2021. See also Wiesen, 'Overcoming Nazism', pp. 201–202.

# An evolving history

point, around the turn of this millennium as Wallenberg was from the late 1970s and for at least the following decade. It is in the nature of history-cultural analysis that status is changeable and varies over time. In conjunction with the 2012 commemorative year marking the centenary of Raoul Wallenberg's birth, plus Nina Lagergren's visit to Washington D.C. two years later to receive the Congressional Medal of Honor bestowed on her half-brother, the global spotlight was once again focused on the missing Swede. The great attention paid to him at that time has certainly faded now, but nor is Oskar Schindler invoked as often as in the early 2020s. As pointed out above, new events in our time create new selections from the past and thus new role models. This does not amount to saying that Wallenberg and Schindler are in danger of being forgotten in the foreseeable future. They are by now 'institutionalized', with their names not only on streets and buildings but also attached to institutions and organizations whose mission is to reward civic courage and counter racism. Moreover, they have become politically and educationally useful as their actions have been seen as worth emulating and invoking in present-day contexts. In conjunction with the re-release of *Schindler's List* in US cinemas in 2018, 25 years after its 1993 premiere, the particular importance of young people watching the film was cited as being a possible countermeasure to the decline in knowledge among younger people and the rise in antisemitic views in virtually all age groups.[73] Another illustrative example is the Raoul Wallenberg calendar published during the 2012 commemorative year, a publication filled with brief stories about people who had acted in his spirit. Day by day, the contents highlighted the principle of history as the teacher of life, since both Wallenberg the role model and all of his successors had acted in an exemplary manner.[74] In other cases, the Swede's exemplary deeds have been invoked to shine a spotlight on political shortcomings and wrong decisions, both past and present. For example, Wallenberg's historical example has functioned as an alternative to a more restrictive Swedish refugee policy after 2015. Similarly, his actions have been sharply contrasted with Ireland's similarly restrictive refugee policy in the 1940s and with

---

73 Stephen D. Smith, '"Schindler's List" more relevant than ever', *The Detroit News*, 7 December 2018.
74 The 2013 Raoul Wallenberg calendar has been highlighted by e.g. Danielsson Malmros, 'Den historiska berättelsen i teori och praktik', p. 185.

the absence of any recent critical debate about the pervasive silence in Israel when the civil war in neighbouring Syria claimed hundreds of thousands of lives, a situation that prompted the question 'Where is Israel's Raoul Wallenberg?'[75]

Because of Schindler and Wallenberg's latter-day fame, they have also been employed in comparisons between them and other individuals who made heroic contributions during the Second World War but only gained recognition afterwards. When the Romanian-Swede Constantin Karadja, whose efforts as a Romanian diplomat in Berlin and Bucharest saved tens of thousands of people from the concentration camps, received belated recognition in recent years, he was mentioned in the same breath as Wallenberg.[76] The Swedish businessman and diplomat Raoul Nordling has been recognized for his efforts in 1944, particularly in France. As the Allies approached Paris, Hitler ordered the destruction of the city, but Nordling went to considerable lengths to persuade the German military on the ground to ignore the Führer's orders. In addition to being awarded a French medal, having a square in the French capital and a street in Neuilly named after him, and being portrayed on the screen by Orson Welles and André Dussollier in *Is Paris Burning?* (1966) and *Diplomacy* (2013), Nordling, too, has ended up in the shadow of his namesake. In connection with the latter film, he was described as 'the lesser-known Raoul', with Wallenberg as the obvious object of comparison.[77] One of many people who made major contributions during the Second World War but received limited recognition is the Latvian Janis Lipke, who managed to hide more than 50 Jews with virtually no resources and few contacts. Despite this, Lipke has

---

75 Pär Frohnert, 'Så blev flyktingmottagandet en svensk paradgren', *Dagens Nyheter*, 15 October 2015; Klas Åmark, 'Så kan Raoul Wallenberg hjälpa oss att göra rätt val i flyktingpolitiken', *Dagens Nyheter*, 20 June 2016; Stephen Collins, 'State did nothing to save Jews, says Shatter', *The Irish Times*, 13 September 2012; Aluf Benn, 'Facing atrocities in neighboring Syria, where is Israel's Raoul Wallenberg?', *Haaretz*, 15 December 2016.

76 Langer and Berglund, *Constantin Karadja*, pp. 16, 69, 88, 153, 193. See also Per Wästerberg, 'Hjälten som Sverige har glömt bort', *Svenska Dagbladet*, 15 December 2016.

77 Mikael Forsell, 'Ny film om svensk krigshjälte', *Göteborgs-Posten*, 10 May 2013. The director of *Diplomacy*, Volker Schlöndorf, dedicated the film to one of Wallenberg's admirers, Richard Holbrooke; Lara Marlowe, 'Low-key diplomacy saved Paris from Hitler's wrath', *The Irish Times*, 26 March 2014.

received scant recognition, not least in his old home country, where interest in him is nowhere near that in foreign role models such as Schindler and Wallenberg.[78]

### Raoul Wallenberg: a saviour and a spy?

The great interest in Raoul Wallenberg has come about despite, or possibly because of, the fact that much of what has been written about him and the Holocaust in Hungary is characterized by unanswered questions rather than clarifying answers. Another distinctive feature is that, barring a few exceptions, it took a long time for professional historians to begin to take an interest in the Swedish diplomat and his activities in Hungary. Recently, new evidence has been published about his and other rescuers' activities in Budapest in 1944–1945, but there are still knowledge gaps pertaining to the extent and effects of Wallenberg's activities in the Hungarian capital, both in real numbers and in comparison with other, concurrent rescue operations. Furthermore, there is disagreement as to whether Wallenberg left Budapest in the autumn of 1944 for some kind of secret mediation mission in Stockholm. One explanation put forward for his abduction by Soviet security officials is that he had accessed documents from investigations done in 1943, documents which proved that the Soviet security services were behind the mass murder of Polish officers, clergy, and intellectuals in Katýn.[79] However, this is only one in a long line of speculations about why Soviet forces abducted Wallenberg and his Hungarian-Jewish driver Vilmos Langfelder in January 1945. More than 60 years later, the last years of their lives are still shrouded in mystery. Multiple shelves of books, many based on the testimony of people who claim to have spoken to or seen Wallenberg in Soviet prisons and detention centres, exist in the biography sections of libraries.

Among the 'cloak-and-dagger' actions attributed to Raoul Wallenberg are reports that the company he worked for in the early 1940s, Mellaneuropeiska, was part of the Swedish government's

---

78 Janis Lipke was highlighted in the 1990s by Per Ahlmark, who compared Lipke only with Wallenberg; see Per Ahlmark, 'Vilken historia skriver balterna?', *Expressen*, 25 January 1992; Ahlmark, *Det öppna såret*, p. 377. In his autobiography, the comparison is extended to also include Schindler; see Ahlmark, *Gör inga dumheter medan jag är död!*, pp. 385–395.
79 Ungváry, *The Siege of Budapest*, p. 341–342.

official Economic Defence Readiness programme and was an important part of a scheme of collaboration between representatives of the Wallenberg family and the section of the Swedish intelligence service known as C-byrån [the C Bureau]. One possibility is that Wallenberg was carrying out secret missions for the Swedish state even before he arrived in Budapest in 1944, but no conclusive evidence that this was the case has been presented.[80] According to one allegation, he worked closely in Budapest with the US Office of Strategic Services (OSS), but this is also disputed. When a large number of US Second World War documents were declassified in the mid-1990s, US commentators suggested that Wallenberg was probably 'the only reliable man in wartime Budapest'. The Swedish side was not prepared to go that far. Jan Eliasson, then Secretary of State for Foreign Affairs, went so far as to admit that Wallenberg had been an 'asset to the United States'. Per Anger was not willing to go to such lengths. He laconically stated that he had not seen Wallenberg, whom he kept close to on a daily basis, perform any intelligence work whatsoever. Besides, both he and Wallenberg had definitely been 'busy doing other things than spying for the United States'.[81]

According to a report presented by a Russian-Swedish working group in 2000, the 'other things' in which Anger and Swedish intelligence officers in Budapest were involved were contacts with the Hungarian Resistance. At the same time, it was established that Iver Olsen, who was one of the driving forces behind the decision to send Wallenberg to Budapest, was an OSS agent, unlike the Swede. This did not rule out the possibility that the Americans had considered recruiting Wallenberg, but they appear to have been satisfied with being informed of the contents of his reports.[82] That Wallenberg was posted at the request of the Americans, and that there was a person close to him who worked for US intelligence, remained a secret in Sweden for most of the Cold War. It is quite possible that Wallenberg knew nothing about Olsen's connection

---

80 See Susanne Berger and Vadim Birstein, 'Raoul Wallenberg and Mellaneuropeiska – Swedish economic "agents" in World War II', www.birstein.com (accessed 5 December 2021); Hardi-Kovacs, *Hemligast av alla*, pp. 228–229.
81 'WWII savior of Jews reportedly spied for U.S.', *The Los Angeles Times*, 5 May 1996.
82 Palmklint and Larsson (eds), *Raoul Wallenberg*, pp. 40–45. See Pierrejean and Pierrejean, *Les secrets de l'Affaire Raoul Wallenberg*, pp. 261–263.

with the OSS, but it is highly probable that Soviet intelligence knew that the Swede's employer was an agent, which probably helped to convince them that Wallenberg, too, was secretly working for the Americans.[83]

Although it is unlikely that Wallenberg did act as a spy, language related to such a theme has been common. When a Swedish official White Paper on the Wallenberg case was published in 1957, a journalist observed that the disappearance of the Swedish diplomat was a tragedy akin to those of the ancient world, but also a fateful thriller. According to a fellow prisoner, Wallenberg had spent time waiting on slow trains in the final stages of the war, writing a spy novel based on his own experiences. Such a manuscript was likely to reveal many exciting episodes. It would also have been explosive material for the Soviet security officers who arrested him and who may have found it difficult to separate fact from fiction, since Wallenberg was *de facto* accused by the Soviet security services of being a German or American spy.[84] Similar arguments were repeated in 1980, when the UD released seven volumes of material from the 1940s on the Wallenberg case. It was not least the 'exciting reading involving Nazi and Communist agents, Hungarian nightclub dancers, and Finnish cheque fraudsters' that, together with the handling of the case by Swedish diplomats, attracted media attention.[85] According to one of Wallenberg's colleagues, the diplomat in charge of sifting through the material was well suited to the 'James Bond' elements found in the Wallenberg dossier.[86] Agent 007 reappeared as an object of comparison with the publication of Ingrid Carlberg's biography of Wallenberg in 2012. She modelled her protagonist on Ian Fleming's hero of novels and films, but with the important difference that while Bond had a licence to kill, 'the real Wallenberg was an agent with a mission to save lives'.[87]

Soviet intelligence telegrams between Stockholm and Moscow had been deciphered from the 1940s to the 1970s by British, US,

---

83 Agrell, *The Shadows around Wallenberg*, p. 4. See Smith, *Lost Hero*, p. 160.
84 Gunnar Müllern, 'Wallenberg föll offer för sitt namn!', *Aftonbladet*, 8 February 1957. See also 'Beskylld för spioneri: "Ni är ett politiskt fall"', *Dagens Nyheter*, 8 February 1957.
85 Disa Håstad, 'UD:s rafflande volymer ger delvis fog för kritik', *Dagens Nyheter*, 1 February 1980.
86 Leifland, 'Lars-Åke Nilsson', p. 447.
87 Kristian Gerner, 'Helgon och agent', *Judisk Krönika*, 2012:4, 23.

and – from the 1950s onwards – Swedish intelligence services. In the early 2000s, they were analysed by Swedish historian and intelligence researcher Wilhelm Agrell. His book about what was named the Venona project portrays Vilmos Böhm, a Hungarian who had been forced into exile after serving as Foreign Minister in Belá Kun's short-lived Communist government from 1918 to 1919. Böhm came to Sweden in 1938; and along with Willy Brandt and Bruno Kreisky, among others, he was a member of the international group of democratic socialists that is sometimes referred to as the 'Little International'. After the end of the war, Böhm became Hungary's ambassador to Sweden, a post he left after the Communists came to power in 1948. Not least because of his language skills, he had become a valued member of the British intelligence service's Press Reading Bureau during the war years, with special responsibility for monitoring events in Hungary. In this capacity, Böhm informed Wallenberg about suitable collaboration partners in Budapest prior to the latter's departure for the Hungarian capital in 1944. After Wallenberg's disappearance, Böhm claimed on several occasions that the Swede had died in Hungary. That information was already known. However, a new dimension has been added by the analysis of the Venona material: according to Agrell, Böhm had been recruited in 1942 as a paid spy for the NKVD under the code name Orestes, and in that capacity he had contributed to Wallenberg's arrest by Soviet personnel in January 1945.[88]

The book sparked intense debate. On the one hand, Agrell was praised for his skills in source analysis.[89] On the other hand, critics were doubtful or dismissive of what they saw as 'serious accusations on ... loose grounds, as incompletely deciphered spy telegrams do after all constitute'.[90] More fuel was added to this exchange of views when members of Böhm's family, who survived him, sued Agrell for damages, claiming that his statements amounted to libel. In the trial, during which two history professors acted as expert witnesses, Agrell was acquitted. The verdict was based on the

---

88 Agrell, *Venona*, pp. 295–301; Wilhelm Agrell, 'Raoul Wallenbergs vän förrådde honom', *Dagens Nyheter*, 12 May 2003. See also Agrell, *The Shadows around Wallenberg*, pp. 177–178.
89 See e.g. Kim Salomon, 'Det kalla krigets hemliga värld', *Sydsvenskan*, 3 June 2003.
90 Ingemar Lindmarker, 'Levandegjord spionhistoria', *Svenska Dagbladet*, 15 June 2003. See also Lennart Lundmark, 'Med hjälp av gamla telegram', *Dagens Nyheter*, 31 May 2003.

# An evolving history

observation that the material from the Venona project proved what Böhm had actually done. Agrell's conclusion that Böhm had been a Soviet agent was therefore reasonable, because it was consistent with the political ambitions for Hungary expressed by Böhm during the last years of the war.[91]

A further aspect of the spy theme is that the initially meagre efforts of the Swedish authorities to clarify Wallenberg's fate may have been a consequence of a note handed over to the Swedish government in August 1947, signed by Soviet Minister of Foreign Affairs Andrey Vyshinsky. It stated that the information that Wallenberg had been arrested by representatives of the Soviet security services on 17 January 1945 could not be confirmed, and that the Soviets had no knowledge of what had happened to the Swedish diplomat or his possible whereabouts. He had probably died during the final battle for Budapest or been captured by Hungarians loyal to the government, was the official Soviet position. A recent conclusion is that this note was not written in connection with Wallenberg's possible death in a Soviet prison on 17 July 1947, but was mainly intended to provide counterfire to allegations that Soviet citizens, including embassy staff, had conducted espionage activities in Sweden.[92]

## Raoul Wallenberg in and outside the archives

The view that the truth about Raoul Wallenberg has not yet come to light, but is hidden in Russian archives, has repeatedly been expressed.[93] In recent years, this argument has been supported both by former KGB agents and by researchers familiar with Soviet and Russian archival collections. They claim that the files with the relevant information had indeed existed but had been destroyed, or

---

91 Gerner, 'Fallet Raoul Wallenberg, Vilmos Böhm och Stalin', p. 76.
92 Matz, 'The Konnov/Mikhailov/Barourskii espionage crises', pp. 30–51.
93 See e.g. (Örjan) Berner, 'Wallenbergaerendet', 6 September 1989, RKA, Raoul Wallenberg, UD2001/00008, Vol. 34; Andrei Sacharov, 'The fate of Raoul Wallenberg', *Moscow News*, 1987:37; Åke Gustafsson, 'Sanningen om Wallenberg', *Svenska Dagbladet*, 22 August 1979; Harald Wigforss, 'Den förnekade fången', *Upsala Nya Tidning*, 29 May 1982; Ricki Neuman, 'Ny bild av Raoul Wallenberg', *Svenska Dagbladet*, 20 April 2007; 'Nytt material kan ge ledtrådar om Wallenbergs öde', *Expressen*, 2 August 2011; 'Formal request to the Swedish government and archival authorities on the Raoul Wallenberg case', 26 March 2018, www.rwi-70.de/documents/the-swedish-catalogue (accessed 29 March 2022).

that they still exist but that the material which has been released is 'harmless'. If there is information among the documents that would place the Soviet rulers of those times in a bad light, it will never be made public.[94] Dmitri Volkogonov drew a similar conclusion on the basis of his many years of studying Soviet archives. A colonel-general and head of the Soviet Union's psychological defence department, Volkogonov had become increasingly critical of Stalin's rule and of the Marxist-Leninist social system. This is evident in the books he wrote about Lenin and Stalin, relying on extensive archival research. In his voluminous biography of Stalin, he was able to provide – with references to archival material – examples of preserved correspondence referring to well-known non-Russian figures, many of whom were taken into custody by Soviet troops. Despite his comprehensive archival searches, he had not found a single document in the Soviet archives relating to Wallenberg's fate.[95]

In a study of how the Soviet bureaucratic system handled Wallenberg's case, with a focus on the Soviet Ministry of Foreign Affairs and the Soviet security services, Swedish political scientist Johan Matz notes that there was little information within these organizations in the immediate post-war years about the reasons why Wallenberg was arrested and the places to which he had been taken. To date, there is still no unambiguous evidence regarding the motives behind Wallenberg's arrest. One starting point to work from is that Stalin wished to neutralize Wallenberg. The question of what lay behind this wish has been explained in various ways over the years, but it still awaits a definitive answer. The fact that this question remained unanswered even within the Soviet administrative apparatus contributed to a collision, as representatives of

---

94 Sudoplatov and Sudoplatov, *Special Tasks*, p. 286; Brent, *Stalins arkiv*, pp. 190–193; Roginskij and Ochoton, 'Die Archive des KGB', pp. 54–55; Magnusson, 'The Search for Raoul Wallenberg', p. 184. See also Björn Lyrvall, 'Samtal med Arsenij Roginskij och Nikita Petrov i RW-ärendet', 21 April 1994; RKA, Raoul Wallenberg, UD2018/05505, Vol. 11; Björn Lyrvall, 'Ryske riksarkivarien Pichoja om RW-ärendet', 8 February 1995, RKA, Raoul Wallenberg, UD2018/05505, Vol. 12.
95 Volkogonov, *Stalin*, p. 500. However, in a conversation with Ambassador Sven Hirdman, Volkogonov did not rule out the possibility that documents about Wallenberg could still surface, since new revelations had indeed emerged from discoveries in the archives after the fall of the Soviet Union; (Sven) Hirdman, 'Wallenberg-ärendet', 9 February 1995, RKA, Raoul Wallenberg, UD2018/05505, Vol. 12.

the security services were trying – with increasing desperation – to conceal a murder, while those working on foreign affairs were trying to understand why it had been committed.[96]

The information that has nevertheless been unearthed in the Russian archives has not provided any clear answers either. Over the past twenty-plus years, a joint Swedish-Russian enquiry and a Swedish government commission of enquiry have been conducted, but the investigators have not been able to establish with certainty when, where, and how Wallenberg died.[97] As will be seen below, the stories of both former prisoners and prison guards have received considerable public attention, but following scrutiny by UD officials, they have been dismissed in a number of cases as being based on vague, inaccurate, outdated, or untrue information. In addition, when former KGB agents put their memories on record after the collapse of the Soviet Union, it turned out that scant new information emerged about the Cold War's most high-profile cases, including that of Wallenberg.[98] In fairness, it should be said that despite all the obstacles, the greater opportunities for investigation following the Soviet Union's collapse have not merely led to far-ranging speculation. The extensive preparatory work that resulted in the Russian-Swedish working report examined both old testimonies and material previously hidden in the Russian archives. As a result, doubts were sown among Russian investigators as well as to the reliability of the death certificate asserting that Wallenberg died in 1947. In conjunction with the late 1980s' interest in Stalinist terror, and in coming to terms with it, Russian lawyers and journalists began taking an interest in Wallenberg's fate and in the various Soviet versions of it that had culminated in the publication of the death certificate in 1957; but that did not provide answers as to why Wallenberg and Vilmos Langfelder had been arrested. However, uncertainty about the document's authenticity and contradictory Soviet versions of what had happened to the Swede did not go so far as to result in any official

---

96 Matz, *Stalin's Double-Edged Game*, pp. x, 304–305.
97 Palmklint and Larsson (eds), *Raoul Wallenberg*, especially chapter 14; Eliasson et al., *Ett diplomatiskt misslyckande*. See also Martin Hallqvist, 'Aide-mémoire' 2 October 1997, RKA, Raoul Wallenberg, UD2018/05505, Vol. 16.
98 See e.g. Björn Lyrvall, 'Samtal på SVR i RW-ärendet', 6 February 1995, RKA, Raoul Wallenberg, UD2018/05505, Vol. 12; Knight, 'The Selling of the KGB', pp. 16–23.

Russian reassessment.[99] Nevertheless, the publication of previously unknown source material did lead to a number of questions being answered. As Wilhelm Agrell observed, the answering of existing questions, together with the discovery of new sources, has led to the raising of new questions.[100]

This book does not shed any new light on the question of how many Jews Wallenberg saved or what happened to him in Soviet captivity. My starting point is, at least in part, a different one. The story of Raoul Wallenberg is not confined to questions of what he did and how he did it. Over time, his life, in particular the time he spent in Budapest plus his subsequently largely unknown months and years in Soviet captivity, has been filled with new meaning and been transformed into a legend charged with symbolism. The encounters between life and legend form the core of this book.

## Myths and meanings

'He has remained forever young. His honour and his calling have not let him grow old', said Hungarian President Árpád Göncz when he inaugurated the Wallenberg exhibition in Budapest in 1992.[101] However, questions about exactly which factors made Wallenberg eternally young and relevant remain to be answered. Accordingly, in order to explain the change from the emphasis in 1945 on the collective efforts of the Swedish Legation to the strong focus on Wallenberg in recent decades, other factors than the actual historical ones must be taken into account and other types of material must be analysed. For example, monuments, films and television series, postage stamps, operas and symphonies, musicals, plays, and novels are essential elements within the larger narrative about him. These and other kinds of history products about Wallenberg have been conveyed through different channels and by different groups, whose impact has varied over time.

---

99 The material dealing with the Russian-Swedish working group fills a large number of volumes in the previously classified materials in the Swedish Government Offices' archive. For the Russian doubt about the death certificate from 1947, see further in RKA, Raoul Wallenberg, UD2018/05505, Vol. 36. See also Mikael Holmström, 'Raoul Wallenberg kan ha överlevt angiven dödsdag', *Svenska Dagbladet*, 23 December 2000.
100 Agrell, *The Shadows around Wallenberg*, p. 1.
101 Árpád Göncz quoted in Lundvik, 'My Undertaking Began On a Grey Autumn Day 1960', p. 15.

# An evolving history

On a more general level, the French historian Henry Rousso reminds us that nations and other massive entities are created by many different sources. In his study of how post-war France has dealt with the problematic legacy of the Vichy regime, he states that signals are transmitted via various carriers of collective memories. These include people who were directly involved in the historical events and who wish to set up links between personal and collective memories. In this book, that category is mainly covered by Wallenberg's relatives and the diplomats who served with him in Budapest. Rousso has also identified scholarly carriers who seek factual information and credible conclusions. 'Looked at it in this way', Rousso writes, 'a work of history is a carrier of memory like any other and subject to the same changing influences.' Yet another category is cultural carriers. These operate at many different levels in society, most notably in the media in a wide sense, including literature, film, and television. Characteristically, their messages are implicit rather than explicit. As we shall see, media and history products have had great impact as effective carriers of Raoul Wallenberg, and new generations have passed on his story. Rousso points out that official carriers are of great importance for the creation of collective memories. These carriers are not people, but ceremonies and monuments. Events and statues often express unity but are in fact products of compromise, as the road to the end result is long and lined with competitions, meetings, and debates.[102] This is also true of most of the events and monuments dedicated to Wallenberg.

The concept of *Wirkungsgeschichte* (history of effects), coined by the German philosopher Hans-Georg Gadamer, deals with types of impact that are the consequences and effects of a historical course of events. It also refers to the ways in which a work or an individual has been received and processed in retrospect in various times and places. It is mainly in the latter sense that this term has been employed. With the help of such an 'after-history' it is possible to answer questions about when Wallenberg went from being a vanished and little-noticed Swede to being a world-famous symbol, what led to this change, and what the motives are behind the still-frequent use of him as a role model. These aspects of the history of effects are at the heart of the analysis in this book of how official Sweden has handled Wallenberg's actions and disappearance, his

---

102 Rousso, *The Vichy Syndrome*, pp. 219–221, quotation p. 220.

importance as a pawn in the Cold War game between the US-led Western bloc and the Soviet-dominated Eastern bloc, and the many media narratives in words and pictures about him. To put it another way, I start from history-didactic questions about where, when, how, and why Raoul Wallenberg has been remembered and utilized. What factors explain why he was rarely celebrated by Swedish politicians for a long time, whereas he was exalted as a larger-than-life hero abroad, especially in the United States? What actors have paid attention to him, and what have their motives been? What symbols and other forms of expression have been used in order to portray him in the post-war period? How does his image agree with and deviate from those of other historical role models?

Correcting misconceptions and inaccuracies is, of course, a historian's job, but legends and myths are rarely, if ever, built and perpetuated by lies and fabrications alone. Arguably, it is also an essential task for a historian to explain how and why some stories of dubious veracity gain traction and influence while other, more credible, narratives fall by the wayside. In this vein, one reviewer (who is also a historian) of Swedish books on Raoul Wallenberg has argued that a historical text that deals with both the Holocaust and the Stalinist terror was 'too serious a matter to be left to myopic professional historians of the source-fetishist type, those who cannot see the wood for the trees and believe that there are "facts" that "speak for themselves" and that the specific sources they have used contain all the "facts"'.[103] A colleague came to a similar conclusion when he championed the perspectives made possible by the 'second wave of Wallenberg literature', arguing that 'nowadays both the historical and the mythological Wallenberg are realities that we must be able to relate to simultaneously'.[104]

A closely related insight is that the power and the meaning-making functions of myths must be taken seriously instead of being dismissed out of hand. In history-cultural studies, the phenomenon of the myth, including its components and functions, is of great interest, as is the close connection between myth and hero worship. Myths have existed in all civilizations. The objects and

---

103 Kristian Gerner; 'Helgon och agent', *Judisk Krönika*, 2012:4, 22.
104 Wilhelm Agrell, 'Den andra Raoul Wallenbergvågen: levnadsteckningarna, källkritiken och mytologin', *Historisk tidskrift*, 2013:1, 74. See Zander, 'Oskar Schindler and Raoul Wallenberg', pp. 453–454.

ritual acts through which they have been expressed have varied, but 'the motives for mythic thought and mythic imagination are in a sense always the same'.[105] In its original sense, a myth is the story of a divine event which explains and imparts meaning to human existence. However, the starting points of myths are not only religious; myths have been used in many other meaning-making contexts, too. One reason why they contribute meaning is their transhistorical nature; they can be constantly adapted to new circumstances and places. The same holds true in key respects for saints and heroes. Hagiography originates as a literary and religious genre that describes saints and their cults. Hero worship is closely related but has also been described as a secular religion, and in countless cases heroes are indeed the protagonists of secular mythological narratives. Like the myth, both hagiography and the hero narrative are idealized and simplified. It is not the life a person has lived, but rather the selections from their life that are thought to be particularly memorable, relevant, and appropriate starting points for identity creation, that lie at the heart of the saint, legend, and hero narratives.[106]

Accordingly, unlike the ideals of historical scholarship that prevailed from the beginning of the twentieth century and stayed strong through the decades after the Second World War, the present enquiry is not a matter of exposing and breaking down myths that contradict established historical facts. In recent years, scholars have emphasized that myths continue to serve important functions in explaining how the world works, our place in it, and our image of 'the others'. We may not recognize these myths, though, as they are sometimes hidden behind established concepts. Even so, studying the popular expressions of myths may constitute a way of accessing their components and analysing their functions and purposes. Political scientist Cynthia Weber argues that fictional films about international relations which deliberately create links to modern myths contribute to making real-life contacts between world leaders more understandable. This cross-fertilization can be extended to other aspects and helps to build bridges between the political and the popular, and between the large scale and the everyday.[107]

---

105 Cassirer, *The Myth of the State*, p. 51.
106 Wecter, *The Hero in America*, pp. 5–10; Schult, *A Hero's Many Faces*, p. 28; Schult, 'Whose Raoul Wallenberg is it?', pp. 771–772.
107 Weber, *International Relations Theory*, pp. 4–10, 178–188.

On the basis of similar material and starting points, I draw attention to and analyse the hero-myths of Raoul Wallenberg in different times and places, as well as the ways in which they have contributed to attempts to find some kind of meaning in the Holocaust by focusing on one individual who tried to stop the madness.

As has been established by research on identity creation, individuals want to be part of larger contexts. One way to achieve this is to link their own time-limited life stories to the history of a nation or some other large entity that extends over time. In troubled times and unsafe places, this connection is forged by linking past heroes and heroic deeds to present-day issues and to expectations of a future, and safer, society.[108] At a time when the lessons to be learned from the Holocaust are accorded high priority, it is therefore hardly surprising that a person like Wallenberg is held up as a role model over and over again. Consequently, specific historical selections from his life – as well as the myths, legends and heroic notions with which he is associated – have occasionally had to be adapted to new conditions in time and space. Such processes of history-cultural adaptation are at the focus of this study.

## About this book

Most history-cultural studies have so far been based on the type of history that has been conveyed within a broad social context. Using Raoul Wallenberg as an example, Tanja Schult has shown how books about him, often written in a popular-science style, have influenced both the form and the content of other representations of the vanished Swede and his actions.[109] As I have explained, history in the public sphere – via press debates, monuments, films, and television series, as well as intertextual connections between various types of history products with a focus on Wallenberg – is also of central importance in this book. It is complemented by another important aspect of the Wallenberg case, namely the diplomatic game behind the scenes and the interplay between covert diplomacy and the open public sphere. Anyone who follows the history of Raoul Wallenberg over time will soon become aware of his significance

---

108 Shalit, *The Hero and His Shadow*, pp. xv–xvi.
109 Schult, *A Hero's Many Faces*, p. 119; Schult, 'Whose Raoul Wallenberg is it?', pp. 777–778.

An evolving history 45

to the politics and diplomacy of several countries. Another factor that stands out for anyone looking back from the early 2020s is the new forms that this diplomacy has assumed. For decades, secrecy, hush-hush dealings, and negotiations away from the public spotlight have been complemented by public diplomacy, according to which foreign relations are part of the brand of a nation. The more attractive something is, the more reason there is to refer to old and new role models. Applied to this study, one question begs to be answered: what traces have the secret negotiations concerning Wallenberg's disappearance at the highest political and diplomatic levels – particularly in Sweden, the Soviet Union, and the United States – left in the public sphere, and, conversely, in what ways have high-impact history-cultural products influenced foreign policy and diplomacy?

I have sought many of the answers to the above questions in the archives of the Raoul Wallenberg Committee, and even more in the documents on Raoul Wallenberg that UD staff have collected over decades. This material, amounting to some 140 volumes, is stored at the archives and library of the Swedish Government Offices in Stockholm. The fact that a small part of the material, totalling some 230 pages, is still classified information has been questioned in recent years, not least because no clear explanation has been given for the non-publication of these documents.[110] For a long time, virtually all of the UD's material on Raoul Wallenberg was kept secret. Documents in the case, which date up to 2018 and total 170,000 pages, have twice been made available to researchers, most recently in 2019 when 66 volumes were made public. More than 70 volumes had previously been made available to the independent commission of enquiry, whose members published *Ett diplomatiskt misslyckande: Fallet Raoul Wallenberg och den svenska utrikesledningen* ['A failure of diplomacy: The case of Raoul Wallenberg and the Swedish Foreign Office'] in 2003. Their work was the result of a compromise between Sweden's then Social Democratic government, which had proposed that a number of researchers investigate the matter, and the centre-right opposition, which wanted a commission of enquiry. The task of the investigators was twofold: to

---

110 See e.g. (Christian Democratic member of the Riksdag) Mikael Oscarsson's parliamentary proposal for the publication of the materials that are still classified: Offentliggör all information om Raoul Wallenberg Motion 2019/20:2813 av Mikael Oscarsson (KD) – Riksdagen (accessed 1 December 2021).

report on Wallenberg's mission in Budapest and its outcome, and on the actions of the Swedish foreign-policy leadership following his disappearance in January 1945.[111]

The enquiry was thus an investigation undertaken in order to clarify, as far as possible, the actual course of events in the Hungarian capital while the Second World War was still happening and to examine the actions of Swedish diplomats in the Wallenberg case during the first few years after the war. By its very nature, a history-cultural analysis starts from dissimilar questions and draws attention to other aspects than those highlighted in the extensive work of the commission of enquiry. For this study, I have drawn on the wealth of books and articles about Raoul Wallenberg, as well as on diaries and autobiographies written by diplomats and politicians who have worked on or had insights into the Wallenberg case, plus material in other archives in Sweden, the UK, Israel, and the United States. In addition, I have followed the discussions about Raoul Wallenberg in newspapers, magazines, and radio and television programmes from the initial post-war years up to the present day, mainly focusing on Sweden and the United States. In this rich material, articles, opinion pieces, interviews, and reviews in newspapers and magazines have played an important role, above all when they relate to Wallenberg being the subject of plays, opera performances, monuments, television series, and feature films.

In analysing the history-cultural products dedicated to Wallenberg, I have endeavoured to overcome the limitations long associated with divisions between the traditions of different disciplines. Historians have been considered to have a good eye for the bigger picture, but their longstanding concentration on textual interpretations has resulted in flawed and insufficient analysis of concrete objects and images of various kinds. Conversely, art historians have been praised for their close readings of individual works by recognized artists, but they have been criticized for a lack of interest in placing their findings in larger social contexts. Similarly, for much of the twentieth century, art historians have been rather uninterested in the collective and popular art movements of preceding centuries, such as the monumental tradition and historical painting. Another objection has been directed against the dominant interest

---

111 Eliasson et al., *Ett diplomatiskt misslyckande*, pp. 43–44; Eliasson, *Jag vet var jag kommer ifrån*, pp. 296–297.

on the part of art and film studies in avant-garde artists and film directors, who have come to be known as auteurs. Proponents of auteur theory have argued that these moving-image equivalents of art's solitary geniuses could be extracted from the collective process that filmmaking almost always entails. The result has often been neglect of monuments and of feature films and television films produced for mass audiences. In recent decades, however, more researchers have been paying increased attention to the image productions of popular culture.[112]

It is worth stressing that the divisions outlined above have by no means been universal. Recent decades have seen a number of collaborations and fruitful borrowings across old disciplinary boundaries and divisions. In line with this development, my aim has been to study both the form and the content of images of Wallenberg, my starting point being that images often require other methods and approaches than studies of the printed word. Similarly, different kinds of questions are relevant for the different aspects of Raoul Wallenberg that are discussed in this book. It is, for instance, highly relevant to apply the classic type of source analysis, focusing on determining when the source was created and for what purpose, and to study tendentious elements in connection with discussions of Wallenberg's deeds and how he has been treated in all kinds of secret and public contexts in the post-war period.

Other parts of my analysis are based on materials that have been produced with different aims than that of shedding new light on Wallenberg and on recent reactions to his disappearance. Here, too, other methodological approaches are required. To be sure, questions of origins and purpose are still of interest to anyone studying a monument, a television series, or a feature film, but discussions that start out from the question of whether these are true or false, or have a tendentious content, will lapse into absurdity. Nor is it enough to study the design and symbolic meanings of individual monuments. The history of their creation and their placement within urban or cultural landscapes are of crucial importance, too. It is also essential to consider films and television productions on the basis of their specific conditions and circumstances. Focusing unilaterally and exclusively on how moving images reflect political and ideological trends and values tends to be misguided. The choice

---

112 See further Andersson, Berggren, and Zander, 'Bilden som källa' and literature they refer to there.

of director and actors, marketing efforts, and viewer reactions are indispensable elements in the analysis of films and television programmes. These types of considerations have guided my close study of visual works dedicated to Raoul Wallenberg, while my aim has been to place him and his actions within the political, ideological, and history-cultural context of the post-war period.

## Chapter 2
## Raoul Wallenberg, the War Refugee Board, and the Holocaust in Hungary

As the preceding chapter stated, the purpose of this book is not to provide (yet) another biography of Raoul Wallenberg, but rather to show how knowledge about his life has influenced the formation of legends about him and to examine the effects that his elevation to the status of a role model have had on the selection of particularly significant events in his life. From this reasoning it follows that certain episodes from his life, especially those linked to his activities in Budapest in 1944–1945, are also discussed in subsequent chapters. The account presented here therefore makes no claim to be a comprehensive depiction of his life from the cradle to the (unknown) grave. Instead, it contains three main elements, one of which consists of some important milestones in his life. The other two deal with developments in Hungary in the half-century preceding the disaster there in 1944–1945 and with the US initiative known as the War Refugee Board, which, together with the Swedish Foreign Office (Utrikesdepartementet, UD), was Wallenberg's sponsor and funder.

As was pointed out above, the story of Raoul Wallenberg is one with no definite conclusion. Its beginning, though, is well known – a childhood and adolescence as a member of one of Sweden's most prominent families. In the second half of the nineteenth century, André Oscar Wallenberg had made the Wallenberg name famous in the world of finance. Before that, the family had left a mark on the activities of the Swedish Lutheran State Church. Shipping had been another family activity ever since Jacob Wallenberg's service as a ship's chaplain in 1769, an experience he wrote about in *My Son on the Galley* (1781, English translation 1994).

In the early twentieth century it was the turn of Raoul Wallenberg's father, Raoul Oscar Wallenberg, to sign on. On 18 March 1910, two days before the second lieutenant was due to embark on a long sea tour, he plucked up his courage and paid a visit to the famous neurology professor Per Johan Wising and his wife Sophie Benedick. He had spent quite some time with their young and beautiful daughter, Maj Wising, and had fallen in love. His feelings were reciprocated and the young couple received her parents' blessing. The marriage took place on 27 September 1911. Less than a year later, on 4 August 1912, young Raoul was born.

Raoul Oscar Wallenberg, however, never saw his son, having died of cancer three months earlier. As a single parent, Maj played a major role in her son's upbringing and education, as did his maternal grandmother and his cosmopolitan paternal grandfather, Gustaf Wallenberg. Following a family quarrel Gustaf had left the banking business, which instead came under the influence of his brothers. The alternative for him was diplomacy, and he spent a long career serving in China, Japan, and Turkey. The great geographical distances did not prevent Gustaf from maintaining continuous contact with Raoul through letters.[1]

In 1918 Maj Wallenberg married Fredrik von Dardel, who was head of the Swedish medical board, and the family was blessed with Raoul's younger half-siblings Nina and Guy. Raoul grew up in central Stockholm, which was bustling with activity in the late 1920s. The many new buildings, especially in the central parts of the city, sparked his interest in architecture.

After completing school and his military service, Raoul began his great adventures. In letters to his grandson, Gustaf Wallenberg repeatedly stressed the great importance of perspectives and experiences from abroad, particularly because they could function as good alternatives to the Swedish 'laissez-faire' system that belittled 'the individual resilience of men, especially the young, exposing them to temptations that are mathematically certain to have disastrous consequences'.[2] Raoul took his grandfather's advice and was well served by his linguistic talent. He studied in the south of France, but on the advice of his grandfather then headed west. The United States, which Gustaf had visited in the late nineteenth century, was very different from the Old World. In Sweden, his grandfather asserted, education was militaristic and archaic.

---

1 von Dardel, *Raoul*, p. 107; Lagergren, 'Still, We Cannot Close This Chapter', p. 7; Böhm, 'Raoul's Childhood and Youth', pp. 30–32; Schult, *A Hero's Many Faces*, pp. 53–54.
2 Letter from Gustaf Wallenberg to Raoul Wallenberg, 30 October 1934, in Söderlund and Wallenberg (eds), *Älskade farfar!* pp. 130–131.

Young people were forced into compartments early on and told to wait their turn 'to give or take whatever circumstances might call for'. The result was that Swedes as a people learned to march at a moderate pace, always retaining their place in line. The contrast with the United States was striking, Gustaf argued. There, young men were expected to take the initiative and make the best of a situation, whatever the odds, and this led to a healthy curiosity and an unfailing go-getter attitude. These were qualities he wanted Raoul to have the opportunity to acquire – not at one of the finer universities but at the 'people's' university in Ann Arbor, Michigan, where Raoul studied from 1931 to 1935.[3] The grandson's impressions did not quite match his grandfather's experiences at the end of the previous century, mostly because the technological and economic differences between the two countries were no longer as marked. This did not preclude Raoul from understanding that Gustaf's intention for his grandson's visit to the United States was not to learn how to build skyscrapers, but 'to acquire a desire to build them!' and to get a taste of the 'American spirit' that lay behind the nation's many successes.[4]

After returning from the US, the 23-year-old Raoul Wallenberg followed his grandfather's advice and went to South Africa, where he represented the Swedish African Company. For seven months he travelled around the country selling all kinds of goods. His insights into South African society led to reflections on nature, culture, and ethnic tensions.[5]

The next stop on his journey was Haifa in Palestine, where he worked in a bank. The atmosphere between the bank manager and the employees was tense. Raoul sided with the latter, who felt they were being exploited, but he still received a good reference from the bank management. During his time in Haifa, he came into contact with Jews who had fled Hitler's henchmen. Through their stories he received detailed descriptions of what was happening in Nazi Germany. It was an experience that would become significant to his future.

---

3 Letters from Gustaf Wallenberg to Raoul Wallenberg, 28 July 1929 and 18 May 1932; the quotation comes from the latter, in Söderlund and Wallenberg (eds), *Älskade farfar!*, pp. 34–35, 60–62.
4 Letter from Raoul Wallenberg to Gustaf Wallenberg, Ann Arbor, 7 November 1931, in Wallenberg and Söderlund (eds), *Letters and Dispatches 1924–1944*, p. 38.
5 Raoul Wallenberg, 'Sydafrikanska intryck', *Jorden Runt*, 1936:11, 590.

After his stay in the Middle East, Raoul once more returned to Stockholm. Gustaf Wallenberg died in 1937, and the international banking career he had planned for his grandson had not yet been realized. Raoul's architectural training was not valid in Sweden, and he had no plans to return to university studies. He began working at the Wallenberg-owned Enskilda Bank, but to his great frustration no offer of permanent employment materialized. His setbacks in the banking world do not appear to have affected his social status in Stockholm in the late 1930s and early 1940s, though. He was known as a good host who liked to arrange 'small' social gatherings. One visitor described one of these events as more of a 'splendid dinner', not least owing to the fine wines that were served.[6]

Idleness seems not to have been an option for Raoul, and he soon moved on from banking. Through the agency of his paternal uncle and godfather, Jakob Wallenberg, Raoul obtained a post with a company called Mellaneuropeiska Handels AB, which specialized in food imports from France and Hungary and was owned by Kálman Lauer. As a Hungarian Jew, Lauer could not move freely in Central Europe, and so Raoul had to make many trips there.[7]

## From antisemitism to extermination

While the persecution of Jews in Hungary had long been well known, it had not always existed. Antisemitism has deep roots in much of Europe, but from the late nineteenth century until the end of the First World War, Hungary had been something of an exception, although antisemitism did persist alongside more or less successful attempts to curb it. At the times when there was broad support for social inclusion, that attitude helped encourage both Christian and Jewish Hungarians to view Hungarian national identity favourably. One way to further strengthen this identity was by helping minorities to become part of a Hungarian community. A concrete result of this manifest political desire was that many Jews were assimilated, and the Jewish religion was accorded equal status with other faiths.[8] At the same time, secularized Jews – especially

---

6 von Platen, *Resa till det förflutna*, p. 187; Milles, *Ensamvargar*, p. 206.
7 Sjöquist, *Raoul Wallenberg*, pp. 18–19; Schult, *A Hero's Many Faces*, pp. 35–36.
8 Száraz, 'The Jewish Question in Hungary', pp. 18–30; Patai, *The Jews of Hungary*, p. 359; Deák, 'A Fatal Compromise?', p. 218.

in Budapest, with its Jewish population of more than 20 percent – worked in various ways to be accepted as fully fledged Hungarians. Some of their Christian compatriots did not look kindly on such initiatives. In the second half of the nineteenth century, conservatives in Hungary argued that Jewish emancipation was a threat to national homogeneity and cohesion. Another argument was that commercially successful Jews – in some parts of the Hungarian countryside, the word 'shopkeeper' became synonymous with 'Jew' – were representatives of capitalism, which by its very nature was harmful and incompatible with traditional Hungarian national values. According to this view, the Hungarian nation was particularly vulnerable in the capital, which was considered 'too Jewish'. This belief resulted in an antisemitic play on words, as the first part of the capital's name was replaced by the German word 'Jude' to create 'Judapest'.[9]

Antisemitism in Hungary was fuelled by the collapse of the Habsburg Empire after the First World War and in the wake of the Armistice of November 1918. The deterioration of the Jews' situation was particularly marked in Eastern and Central Europe, where the ensuing years saw continued strife in the form of territorial conflicts, often combined with Communist offensives to the west. The ultimate goal of the revolutionary troops was a world revolution, affirmed Leon Trotsky, organizer and leader of the Red Army. The presence in the ranks of the Red revolutionaries of Jews such as Béla Kun, the leader of the short-lived Hungarian Soviet Republic of 1919, helped to fuel antisemitic sentiments. The loss of large parts of Hungary's population and territory under the Treaty of Trianon in 1920 added to the crisis. One 'solution' to the problem, supported across the political spectrum, was a renewed belief in 'Christian values' as the foundation of the nation. These were on a collision course with continued Jewish assimilation, and together with Communists, Jews became scapegoats in a radicalized social climate. In 1920, Hungary became the first nation in Europe to introduce anti-Jewish laws after the First World War.[10]

---

9 Gluck, 'The Budapest Flâneur', pp. 1–22; Berend, 'The Road toward the Holocaust', pp. 32–33; Ranki, *The Politics of Inclusion and Exclusion*, pp. 58–60.
10 Sachar, *Dreamland*, pp. 6–15, 64–65, 108–109; Braham, *The Politics of Genocide*. Vol. 1, p. 30; Hanebrink, 'The Memory of the Holocaust in Postcommunist Hungary', p. 263.

Valdemar Langlet had been living in Hungary since the early 1930s. In a book about the country, written for a Swedish audience and published in 1934, he depicted the heightened ethnic divisions of the interwar years in a single sentence: 'For the Jew, opposition to Christians is a religious matter; for most Magyars, by contrast, it is a racial issue.'[11] With this in mind, it is scarcely surprising that the Hungarian government, inspired by the German Nuremberg Laws of 1935, introduced three sets of anti-Jewish laws in the period 1938–1941. Under these laws, Jews were not allowed to exceed 20 percent of employees in a long list of business activities; criteria were established for what constituted a Jew; and finally, marriage between Jews and non-Jews was banned.[12]

When Germany attacked the Soviet Union in the summer of 1941, in what was codenamed Operation Barbarossa, Hungary fought alongside the Germans. Afterwards, some 16,000 Jews who had no record of Hungarian citizenship were deported. They were shot dead in Ukraine by soldiers of the SS and the Hungarian army. About 2,000 Hungarian Jews who had also been deported managed to escape and returned to Hungary, where they spread information about the genocide taking place in the German-occupied areas of the Soviet Union. In January 1942, units of the Hungarian army massacred Serbs and Jews in Novi Sad, located in a part of Yugoslavia occupied by Hungary. In addition, tens of thousands of Hungarian Jews were forced to serve unarmed in work units, often in the immediate vicinity of battlegrounds. Diaries written by Hungarian officers and soldiers rarely referred to these Jews but when they did, it was often in the context of what antisemitic propaganda termed 'Judeo-Bolshevism'. The main argument was that most Jews were Bolsheviks, that is, they were allies of the Soviet enemy.[13] In all likelihood, this and other antisemitic ideas contributed to the difficult conditions of the Hungarian-Jewish forced labourers on the Eastern Front. Over 40,000 of them perished in the Soviet Union, and 4,000 died as forced labourers in Serbian copper mines. The 5,000 or so who survived and were sent back to Hungary also spread the word about the mass murder occurring on the Eastern Front. Similar information was passed on

---

11 Langlet, *Till häst genom Ungern*, p. 331.
12 Herczl, *Christianity and the Holocaust of Hungarian Jewry*, pp. 81–169.
13 Pihurik, 'Hungarian Soldiers and Jews on the Eastern Front, 1941–1943', p. 74.

by Polish-Jewish refugees, who were given sanctuary in Hungary in 1942–1944. However, as Yehuda Bauer and others have noted, willingness to listen was very limited, mainly because many Jews were Hungarian nationalists who could not imagine that anything similar to what was taking place in the Soviet Union could ever happen to Jews in Hungary. Another factor was serious divisions among Jews in Hungary, but the awareness that their position was extremely vulnerable mattered more than anything else: 'They were caught on an island in shark-infested waters, and they had no boat. If the island was flooded, they were doomed.'[14]

Despite the obvious antisemitism in Hungary, the Horthy regime under Miklós Kállay, who was Prime Minister from 1942 to 1944, refused to agree to German demands – supported by hard-line Hungarian antisemites – for 'the final solution to the Jewish question' by deporting the nation's Jews to extermination camps in Poland. The Hungarian government's reluctance to give in to German demands was reinforced by the reversal of the fortunes of war after several German military defeats in 1942–1943, the most notable being the Battle of Stalingrad. Adolf Hitler's dissatisfaction over Hungary's failure to do enough in the 'crusade' against Communism was made very clear at a couple of meetings between the two leaders in 1943–1944. Another stumbling block was the German leader's view that the Hungarians were not cooperating sufficiently on 'the Jewish question'. The result was that German troops entered Hungary, paving the way for a form of control similar to that in Norway. This involved the installation of a government that was pro-German, fascist, and comprised of local members.[15]

The British historian David Cesarani argues that the German takeover of Hungary was not primarily and directly due to 'the final solution of the Jewish question'. Nor should the attacks on Hungary's Jews be seen as the result of an irrational hatred that took resources away from the German war effort in an already strained situation. There were several strategic reasons for the Germans to militarily 'secure' Hungary. In addition, the Hungarian peace overtures, launched after several of the nation's leaders became convinced that Germany was losing the war, were no secret

---

14 Bauer, *Rethinking the Holocaust*, p. 226.
15 Sakmyster, *Hungary's Admiral on Horseback*, pp. 303–333; Åmark, *Att bo granne med ondskan*, p. 560.

to Berlin. Preventing the Hungarians from following the Italian example, with the aim of reaching a separate peace with the Soviet Union or otherwise withdrawing from the war – perhaps after a British airborne landing – was therefore a high-priority German objective. The Jews 'represented untapped potential', as they could first be plundered and then become a welcome partial solution to the ever-increasing need for slave labour.[16] German researchers have stressed that the incorporation of Hungary and the subsequent persecution of Jews were motivated by military priorities but even more by economic ones. The extent of the German seizure of Hungarian Jewish assets and the impact of the loss of Jewish labour on the Hungarian economy have been a point of contention between German and Hungarian scholars in recent years.[17]

Whatever the German reasons behind the invasion of Hungary, the result was devastating for Hungary's Jews. A new Hungarian government was formed, and its ministers included a number of well-known right-wing politicians who were also outspoken antisemites. Within days, the strongly antisemitic Arrow Cross movement was legalized. SS officer Adolf Eichmann only commanded about a hundred men in the *Sondereinsatzkommando* (special taskforce) he led. They were certainly experienced and had a reputation for being 'effective', but without active Hungarian help their mission could not have been carried out. They were strongly supported by Hungarian politicians in the new government as well as by the Hungarian police. Soon after the transfer of power, stricter anti-Jewish legislation was passed, making it compulsory for Jews in Hungary to openly wear the Star of David. A further step was the appointment of two explicitly antisemitic secretaries of state, who paved the way for the German extermination policy. By the beginning of April, work on rounding up Jews was in full swing. It was motivated on the Hungarian side by a conviction that the confiscation of Jewish property would improve matters, as the fact that it had not been done before was one important cause of the nation's previous economic difficulties.[18]

During the spring and summer of 1944, the Germans and their Hungarian allies transported hundreds of thousands of Jews to

---

16 Cesarani, *Becoming Eichmann*, pp. 161–162. See also Agrell, *Shadows around Wallenberg*, pp. 153–154.
17 Ferenc Laczó, 'From Collaboration to Cooperation', pp. 530–555.
18 Blomqvist, 'Local Motives for Deporting Jews', pp. 673–704.

ghettos and extermination camps.[19] The work was done systematically province by province, and exceptions were few. Only Jews with hard-to-replace jobs or skills were permitted to stay. The guidelines also included rules for replacing deported Jews with other workers as quickly as possible, so as not to hamper the war effort.[20]

Horthy explained to one of his colleagues in the summer of 1944 that he had little use for Jews and Communists. It did no harm for them to be deported, with a few exceptions because some Jews were also good Hungarians.[21] These were clearly not numerous, however, as the Regent did not act to stem the deportations of Jews in the first few months. At first he seems to have been reluctant to acknowledge the news about what was happening in the Hungarian countryside, and he emphasized that those already deported were unharmed. When the Vrba-Wetzler report was delivered to Horthy at the end of May 1944, he could no longer live with such a delusion. Trying to assert himself in relation to the German occupiers, and under pressure from foreign leaders – who included Franklin D. Roosevelt, Britain's King George VI, and Sweden's King Gustaf V – Horthy ordered an end to the deportations in early July, by which time an estimated 430,000 Jews had already been taken to the death camps.[22]

After the Hungarian leader negotiated a ceasefire with the Soviet Union in October, he was forced to resign and was taken to Germany. The new Hungarian government was dominated by men from the Arrow Cross movement. Persecution of Jews intensified almost immediately. While the Red Army troops slowly but surely closed their ring around the Hungarian capital, 38,000 Jews were murdered. In addition, Eichmann was given willing permission by the Arrow Cross to resume deporting Jews from Budapest in the autumn of 1944, which led to some 80,000 being taken to slave-labour or extermination camps. This was the final phase of a scheme

---

19 Kádár and Vági, 'Rationality or Irrationality?', pp. 32–54; Deák, 'The Holocaust in Hungary', pp. 50–65; Szita, *Trading in Lives?*, pp. 27–42.
20 László Baky, 'The Royal Hungarian Minister of Interior. No. 6163/1944. res. Re: The Assignment of Dwelling Places for Jews', in Levai, *Eichmann in Hungary*, pp. 72–73.
21 Herczl, *Christianity and the Holocaust of Hungarian Jewry*, p. 220. See also Deák, *Essays on Hitler's Europe*, pp. 150–151.
22 Levai, *Eichmann in Hungary*, pp. 122–124; Fenyo, *Hitler, Horthy, and Hungary*, pp. 194–195; Cornelius, *Hungary in World War II*, p. 307; Deák, *Essays on Hitler's Europe*, p. 156.

of deportation that in every way exceeded previous measures, including the extensive actions in the summer of 1942 when large numbers of Jews in Warsaw were sent to the death camps. From mid-May onwards, some 12,000 Jews were transported by train, mainly to Auschwitz-Birkenau. Eichmann and his closest associates made full use of their logistical skills, which ultimately led to more than 437,400 Jews being loaded onto 150 trains.[23]

Eichmann's continued goal to kill as many Jews as possible was on a collision course with SS leader Heinrich Himmler's new position on 'the Jewish question'. At this time, discussions were being held about releasing Hungarian Jews in exchange for lorries and petrol. Eichmann was one of the negotiators, but Himmler was in the background monitoring the process. One possible explanation is that the SS leader wanted to use the discussions as a smokescreen for peace talks with the Western Allies. Continued mass murder would make such negotiations more difficult.[24] The deportations also ran counter to the wishes of other leading Nazis to use Hungarian Jews as slave labour. In fact, in the Hungarian operation, the Germans selected only between 10 and 30 percent of the arriving Jews for labour. At the same time, more people were being killed in Auschwitz-Birkenau than before. An estimated five to six times as many people as before were mass-murdered in the camp between March and November 1944. This brutal extermination policy led to a reduction in the number of Jews in Hungary from around 750,000 in 1941 to 140,000 in 1945.[25]

## The United States and the creation of the War Refugee Board

Following Germany's attack on the Soviet Union in the summer of 1941, reports circulated at irregular intervals of an ongoing war of extermination against Jews and other groups not included in the Nazis' national, or, as they put it, people's community. One difficulty was that claims about millions of people being subjected to systematic persecution and mass murder seemed implausible, even

---

23 Lozowick, *Hitler's Bureaucrats*, p. 253; Cesarani, *Becoming Eichmann*, pp. 159–199.
24 Bauer, *Jews for Sale?* pp. 167–168; Fleming, *Auschwitz, the Allies and Censorship of the Holocaust*, p. 236.
25 Braham, 'The Holocaust in Hungary', pp. 27–40; Dwork and van Pelt, *Auschwitz: 1270 to the Present*, pp. 342–343.

to representatives of Jewish communities in countries that were at war with Germany or neutral. It was commonly thought that such depictions were greatly exaggerated propaganda products, like those that had circulated during the previous world war.

Such notions, combined with the virtual impossibility of obtaining visual evidence of an ongoing genocide, meant that even people with first-hand knowledge of what was going on found it difficult to be heard. Polish resistance fighter Jan Karski had witnessed German atrocities and claimed to know what was happening in the Bełżec extermination camp. Once in Britain and then in the United States, he met with Polish politicians, representatives of the World Jewish Congress, and representatives of the British and US governments, including Anthony Eden, Franklin D. Roosevelt, and Felix Frankfurter. During one meeting the last-mentioned, a judge of Jewish birth and a member of the Supreme Court, stressed that he did not believe the information, which was not the same as accusing Karski of being a liar: 'I did not say he was lying, I said I did not believe him.'[26]

Other holders of high-ranking positions in the United States also either had difficulty accepting the information or chose to ignore reports of an ongoing mass murder in Europe. However, the US Holocaust whistleblower Josiah E. DuBois Jr had little difficulty convincing his boss, Secretary of the Treasury Henry J. Morgenthau Jr, of what was going on. In the First World War, the latter's father had personally witnessed the horrific consequences of the Young Turks' genocide of the Armenians. Even before the outbreak of the Second World War, the son had feared for the safety of European Jews, though he could not foresee the extent of 'those terrible eighteen months' during which reports poured in that Jews in Eastern Europe were being murdered or left to starve to death.[27]

During much of 1943, a political game was played in which DuBois managed to persuade Morgenthau not to adhere to the formal channels via the State Department, where there were people who were delaying plans to assist the Jews of Europe. Instead, the Secretary of the Treasury should try to persuade President

---

26 Felix Frankfurter's statement is cited in e.g. Hanna Kozlowska, 'How a Polish courier tried to tell the world about the Holocaust', *Foreign Politics*, 24 January 2014. See also Breitman, *Official Secrets*, pp. 142–154, and Åmark, *Främlingar på tåg*, pp. 72–77.
27 Blum, *The Morgenthau Diaries: Years of War 1941–1945*, pp. 207–223.

Roosevelt personally to take action. Once the President had become convinced of the need for an immediate rescue effort, the War Refugee Board was established on 22 January 1944.[28] Its purpose was clear from the outset: to take all available measures as soon as possible 'to rescue the victims of enemy oppression who are in imminent danger of death and otherwise to afford such victims all possible relief and assistance consistent with the prosecution of the war'.[29] Despite this ambitious goal, the organization received rather limited support from the President. It remained closely tied to the Treasury Department, which in turn cooperated with a number of Jewish organizations in both the United States and Europe. Estimates suggest that measures involving staff of the War Refugee Board saved some 200,000 Jews from the Holocaust, 120,000 of whom were in Budapest.[30]

## Raoul Wallenberg's mission

In the UK there were many critics of the War Refugee Board because it was founded on the assumption that Jews were a specific category of victims. On the basis of such reasoning, there was a danger that it 'was following policies that put saving the Jews before the universalistic goal of winning the war'.[31] As a neutral state, Sweden was not inherently opposed to saving Jews on the one hand and winning the war on the other, and this type of objection continued to fall on deaf ears in Sweden. Cooperation between the Swedish government and the War Refugee Board proceeded without any major complications.

One result of the new Swedish policy was the endeavour to save as many of Hungary's Jews as possible. In May 1944, the American attaché in Stockholm, Iver Olsen, began to search for a Swede who could work for the War Refugee Board and act as a foreign, neutral observer in Hungary. The situation was urgent. Now, in the eleventh hour of the war, 'the Jews of Hungary must also set out upon that path of horror along which millions of European Jews have already walked during this war', read the April 1944

---

28 Medoff, *Blowing the Whistle on Genocide*, pp. 53–69; Rosen, *Saving the Jews*, pp. 346–347; Erbelding, *Rescue Board*, pp. 49–64.
29 JDC and the US War Refugee Board (1944–1945) in JDC Archives (accessed 2 February 2022).
30 Wyman, *A Race against Death*, p. 12.
31 Kushner, *The Holocaust and the Liberal Imagination*, pp. 198–199.

issue of *Judisk Tidskrift*.[32] Information about what was happening also reached Swedish government members and diplomats. It was increasingly clear to them what the outcome of the war would be, and that a new world order was at hand after Germany's increasingly predictable defeat. One problem was that in the same month, Olsen had reported to the US Deputy Secretary of the Treasury that Swedish banks and companies were continuing to help the Germans to obtain large amounts of neutral currency. If the Swedes ceased such activities, it would have a favourable effect on the US view of Sweden. The same would be true if Sweden chose to comply with US requests for Swedish representation on the ground in Hungary.[33]

A proposal for Sweden's state Lutheran Church to appeal to its Hungarian counterpart met with sympathy at the Swedish Bishops' Conference but was not considered feasible.[34] The other concrete proposal was to find a suitable Swede who could lead a rescue operation in Hungary. Marcus Ehrenpreis, rabbi of the Stockholm synagogue, asked Lauer if he knew of anyone capable of carrying out such a mission. Lauer recommended Raoul Wallenberg. At first Ehrenpreis appeared to doubt Wallenberg's suitability, but he was soon convinced that Wallenberg was the right person for the job. Lauer arranged a meeting between Wallenberg and Olsen. The War Refugee Board made a formal request to Wallenberg, who accepted it. The proposal also won almost immediate support from diplomats in Stockholm and Washington.[35] Representatives of the War Refugee Board initiated discussions with Sweden's State Secretary for Foreign Affairs, Erik Boheman, as did Wallenberg, who announced in a letter of 19 June that he was 'making my services available to meet the UD's needs'. Neither the representatives of the War Refugee Board nor Swedish UD staff expected any

---

32 Kurt Stillschweig, 'Judarna i Ungern', *Judisk Tidskrift*, 1944:4, 127.
33 Eliasson et al., *Ett diplomatiskt misslyckande*, pp. 103–112. See also Susanne Berger, 'Pengar och politik omgav fallet Wallenberg', *Svenska Dagbladet*, 11 December 2007. For Olsen's activities in Stockholm, see Agrell, *The Shadows around Wallenberg*, especially pp. 11–19, and Hardi-Kovacs, *Hemligast av alla*, pp. 277–285.
34 Koblik, *The Stones Cry Out*, pp. 87–94, 106–119; Einhorn, *Handelsresande i liv*, pp. 170–171.
35 Letter from Raoul Wallenberg to Gustaf Wallenberg, 6 July 1936, in Söderlund and Wallenberg (eds), *Älskade farfar!*, p. 204; Rudberg, *The Swedish Jews and the Holocaust*, pp. 217–220; Rosenberg, *Rabbi Marcus Ehrenpreis obesvarade kärlek*, pp. 374–376.

formal obstacles from the Hungarian government, since Wallenberg was not going to engage in any business activities but was to concentrate on rescue efforts in Budapest. If the Hungarians were to cause problems, Boheman promised that the Swedish government would expel the Hungarian chargé d'affaires in Stockholm, while his colleague Sven Grafström stressed that 'any [hostile] intermezzo with the authorities [in Hungary] should of course be avoided'.[36] In turn, the Americans promised to ensure that the funding from the War Refugee Board reached its destination.[37]

In Budapest Wallenberg's arrival was eagerly anticipated. Valdemar Langlet was ill, and the rest of the Swedish Legation was overwhelmed with work.[38] Wallenberg immediately began gathering information about the ongoing genocide in Hungary.[39] Like representatives of the US State Department and the War Refugee Board, the UD was receiving continuous information about the increasingly acute situation of the Jews in Hungary. During the summer of 1944, it became clear to both US and Swedish officials that the Germans and their Hungarian allies had already murdered most of the Jews in the Hungarian countryside, whereas the majority in the capital were still alive. These reports included the testimony of two young Slovak Jews, Rudolf Vrba and Alfred Wetzler, who had managed to escape from Auschwitz. Their detailed report revealed what was happening in the Auschwitz-Birkenau extermination camp. After his arrival in Budapest, Wallenberg received similar, albeit less detailed, witness statements on several occasions.[40]

---

36 Letter from Raoul Wallenberg to Erik Boheman, 19 June 1944; (Sven) Grafström, 'Ang. R. Wallenberg', 6 July 1944; Sven Johansson, 'Handlingar om Raoul Wallenbergs tillträde i Budapest 1944. Promemoria', 3 January 1997, RKA, Raoul Wallenberg, UD2018/05505, Vol. 14.
37 Herschel Johnson, 'Department of State, DMH-502', Stockholm, 21 June 1944, RKA, Raoul Wallenberg, UD2018/05505, Vol. 1.
38 (Per) Anger, Telegram i chiffer från Kungl. Maj:ts Beskickning, 7 July 1944, RKA, Raoul Wallenberg, UD2018/05505, Vol. 14.
39 Sjöquist, *Raoul Wallenberg*, pp. 13–23; Schult, *A Hero's Many Faces*, pp. 53–54.
40 See e.g. 'Ang judefrågan' and 'Auschwitzrapporten'; Raoul Wallenberg, 'P.M. beträffande de ungerska judeförföljelserna', published in Schattauer (ed.) *Räddningen: Budapest 1944*, pp. 47–111 and 148–152; Herschel Johnson, 'The American Legation, No. 2412', Stockholm, 1 July 1944; (Cordell) Hull, 'Amlegation, No. 1349', Stockholm, 6 July 1944, RKA, Raoul Wallenberg, UD2018/05505, Vol. 1. See also Einhorn, *Handelsresande i liv*, pp. 169–170.

## Raoul Wallenberg in Budapest

The Hungarian capital, in which Wallenberg arrived in 1944 for the third time, was marked by conflicts with no end in sight, alliances of highly uncertain duration, and shifting loyalties.[41] The fact that there were many cases of links between rescue operations and intelligence activities in Hungary contributed to the climate of uncertainty.[42] Sweden intensified its efforts to rescue the persecuted. From Stockholm, Gösta Engzell of the Swedish Foreign Affairs Council worked to help Jews in Hungary. On the ground in Budapest, Ivan Danielsson and Per Anger had been busy for some months assisting as many people as possible who sought help at the Swedish Legation, located in Buda. Wallenberg threw himself headlong into the work. At first his time in the Hungarian capital was characterized by the calm before the storm, in what has aptly been called Budapest's 'Indian summer'. However, the situation soon worsened and in early June, Ivan Danielsson reported that the situation for the city's Jews was 'becoming more alarming day by day'.[43]

A month later, Admiral Horthy broke off his government's cooperation with the Germans and ordered the deportations to be halted. For the majority of Jews in the Hungarian countryside this measure came too late, but the decision entailed a reprieve for those living in the capital's ghetto. Both at this time and later, Wallenberg engaged in intensive negotiations with German and Hungarian officials as well as with Jewish organizations. Like Danielsson and Anger, he wrote reports to the UD in Stockholm in which he repeatedly highlighted the plight of the Jews.[44] A few weeks after his arrival, Wallenberg changed his strategy and decided that most of the funds at his disposal would no longer be used for bribes and tickets out of the country. Instead, he and Valdemar Langlet began to spend more money on acquiring housing that could function as safe houses. In total, Wallenberg rented more than 30 buildings in Budapest, including hospitals and soup kitchens, from which Swedish flags were hung to mark that the people in the buildings were Swedish citizens. Tens of thousands of Jews lived in these

---

41 Andrew, *A Man for All Connections*, p. 54.
42 Agrell, *The Shadows around Wallenberg*, passim.
43 Telegram no. 157 from (Ivan) Danielsson to the UD in Stockholm, Budapest, 2 June 1944, in Schattauer (ed.), *Räddningen*, p. 44.
44 Levine, *Raoul Wallenberg in Budapest*, pp. 129–245, 250–253.

buildings under Swedish protection, and hundreds of them worked for Wallenberg.[45]

American goodwill remained at a high level. Advice was conveyed via Secretary of State Cordell Hull on how Hungarian refugees could be smuggled out of Budapest by barge or rail, to areas close to those controlled by Yugoslav partisans. Hull was aware that these proposals were difficult, if not impossible, to implement but showed great confidence in Wallenberg's ability to rescue as many people as possible. Representatives of the War Refugee Board agreed with this assessment. They were impressed by Wallenberg's ability to act intelligently and discreetly while taking full advantage of the circumstances prevailing at the time.[46] Like his Swiss colleague Carl Lutz, Wallenberg worked doggedly to produce identity documents that would protect Jews, who, once in possession of such a document, would instantly change their nationality and thereby come under the protection of a neutral nation.[47]

In October 1944 the situation deteriorated drastically after the openly antisemitic Arrow Cross Party came to power. Wallenberg was originally due to return to Sweden in September 1944, but he remained in Budapest as the political situation grew worse. The months following the Arrow Cross takeover proved to be the worst and the most dangerous, both for the persecuted Jews and for Wallenberg and others who were trying to help them. Things came to a head in October, as Wallenberg described in his reports to Stockholm. The one dated 12 October was marked by cautious optimism. Jews with Swedish passports were being released from internment and labour camps, and the Germans had promised to leave them in peace. A mere ten days later, however, the situation had become much more alarming. The Arrow Cross Party intensified its persecution of Jews and no longer allowed any exceptions.[48]

In the last few months of 1944, Wallenberg accomplished many of the deeds that would later form the basis of most accounts of his important work in Hungary, as evidenced not least by the

---

45 Carlberg, *Raoul Wallenberg*, p. 230.
46 (Cordell) Hull, 'War Refugee Board, Amlegation, No. 1353', 26 June 1944; Herschel Johnson, 'Department of State, MAE-910', Stockholm, 29 June 1944, RKA, Raoul Wallenberg, UD2018/05505, Vol. 1.
47 Carlberg, *Raoul Wallenberg*, pp. 233–238.
48 Herschel Johnson, 'DCG-449', Washington, 30 October 1944, RKA, Raoul Wallenberg, UD2018/05505, Vol. 1.

tales of survivors.[49] Everyone with insight into the work realized the danger of the situation. Eichmann wanted to 'get the Jewdog Wallenberg' out of the way, but the assassination attempt failed. Wallenberg slept in different houses every night. He was under the protection of police officer István Parádi, who also fended off several Arrow Cross attacks on Jews.[50] The greatest threat was from the ever more desperate Germans and Arrow Cross members, who increasingly questioned or ignored rules and exceptions. This led to raids on safe houses and to Jews being forced on death marches instead of being deported by train. As soldiers under Eichmann's command and Arrow Cross members continued their antisemitic operations to the bitter end, no Jew was safe in Budapest.[51]

As the Red Army slowly but surely broke down the stubborn resistance in and around Budapest, it became clear that the staff of the Swedish Legation would be forced to travel to Sweden via the Soviet Union. Both Lauer and Wallenberg believed this would almost certainly be a physically arduous and bureaucratically complicated journey home. In the last days before he was arrested by Red Army soldiers, Wallenberg was unsure whether the Soviet authorities perceived him as friend or foe, but there is no indication that he or anyone else foresaw what was to come.[52]

---

49 Yahil, 'Raoul Wallenberg – His Mission and His Activities in Hungary', p. 36; Levine, *From Indifference to Activism*, p. 260; Levine, *Raoul Wallenberg in Budapest*, pp, 290–317; Schult, *A Hero's Many Faces*, p. 57. See Anger, *With Raoul Wallenberg in Budapest*, pp. 49–51, 57–58, 61–72.
50 Ungváry, *The Siege of Budapest*, p. 316.
51 Carlberg, *Raoul Wallenberg*, pp. 303–306; Jangfeldt, *The Hero of Budapest*, pp. 202–207.
52 Letters from Koloman Lauer to Jacob Wallenberg, 29 September 1944 and 19 December 1944, in Nylander and Perlinge (eds), *Raoul Wallenberg in Documents, 1927–1947*, pp. 100, 104. See also Levine, 'The Unfinished Story of a Swedish Hero', p. 57 and Levine, *Raoul Wallenberg in Budapest*, pp. 352–356, 368–370.

## Chapter 3
## The Scarlet Pimpernel: from the French Revolution to the 1970s in Chile

As we have seen, it was not until the early 2010s that the first biographies of Raoul Wallenberg were published which also paid significant attention to his pre-Budapest years. It also took a long time before scholars seriously began to examine the formation of legends about him and the ways in which the figure of Raoul Wallenberg has been adapted to old and new heroic ideals. Unlike the biographies, which focus on the principles behind the historical past, these studies of legends examine the conditions under which history is mediated as a practical past. In the latter case, the focus is on how the figure of Wallenberg has been adapted to traditional perceptions and values, and how various types of narratives about him have helped to change the image of what characterizes a world-war legend and hero.[1] There are good reasons to examine the history-cultural implications of the creation of a mostly uniform narrative of Raoul Wallenberg's journey from a rather insignificant figure in an influential Swedish family to a renowned international hero. One aspect of this journey that is worth investigating is what ideals and idols Wallenberg himself praised. This topic will be discussed with special reference to the Scarlet Pimpernel as literature, theatre, film, and symbol.

Two of Wallenberg's role models were particularly active during and after the First World War in helping refugees and people in need. He admired the Norwegian explorer Fridtjof Nansen, who, as a representative of the newly founded League of Nations, did much in the early 1920s to repatriate prisoners of war and refugees. As a

---

1 See e.g. Ulf Zander, 'Wallenberg: Man and Myth', *The Hungarian Quarterly*, Summer 2006, 166–168; Zander 'Heroic Images', pp. 126–135; Schult, *A Hero's Many Faces*, passim; Schult, 'Whose Raoul Wallenberg is it?', pp. 770–796.

token of his admiration for the Norwegian, Wallenberg named his reconstruction plan for post-war Budapest the Nansen Plan.[2]

Another of his role models was the Swedish nurse Elsa Brändström, who was born in St Petersburg. She made a name for herself during the First World War working in Siberia to improve the situation of German and Austrian prisoners of war interned there. Her efforts were much appreciated and earned her the appellation 'the Angel of Siberia'. Maj von Dardel, whose sister married into the Brändström family, was a great admirer of Elsa, who continued her humanitarian work in the following decades. 'An admiration for Elsa Brändström was inculcated in Raoul and [in] Maj's other children from an early age', writes Bengt Jangfeldt. He adds that many years later in Budapest, Wallenberg stressed neutral Sweden's proud tradition of helping the vulnerable with the help of two concrete examples: Brändström's efforts in Russia during the First World War and the Russian Revolution, and the work of her fellow nurse Asta Nilsson in the service of the Red Cross during the First World War and on behalf of orphans in Hungary during the Second World War.[3]

A third role model is fictional: the Scarlet Pimpernel. Nina Lagergren has said that in 1942 she and Raoul saw the film *Pimpernel Smith*, shown in US cinemas as *Mister V* (1941), at a private screening in Stockholm; the film was banned in Sweden at the time. After the film, Wallenberg told his sister that the hero's efforts to help refugees escape the Nazis so inspired him that he would like to do this type of rescue work himself. This statement, which is widely referenced in the literature, invites a cause-and-effect reasoning in which fiction both precedes and inspires actual developments.[4] This thought process reached its apex when the British Embassy in Stockholm hosted a screening of *Pimpernel*

---

2 Lévai, *Raoul Wallenberg, hjälten i Budapest*, pp. 7, 255; Derogy, *Fallet Raoul Wallenberg*, pp. 180–183, 254; Sjöquist, *Raoul Wallenberg*, p. 20; Linnéa, *Raoul Wallenberg*, p. 27; Schult, *A Hero's Many Faces*, pp. 54–55.
3 Jangfeldt, *Raoul Wallenberg*, pp. 36–37, 337, quotation p. 36.
4 The information comes from Nina Lagergren and is mentioned in e.g. Bierman, *Righteous Gentile*, p. 29; Aldgate and Richards, *Britain Can Take It*, p. 63; Monika Tunbäck-Hanson, 'Kreativitet går inte att styra', *Göteborgs-Posten*, 21 October 1997; Wästberg, *Om Raoul Wallenberg*, pp. 5–7; Schult, *A Hero's Many Faces*, p. 55, Philip French, 'Philip French's screen legends. No. 68: Leslie Howard 1893–1943', *The Observer*, 30 August 2009; Kershaw, *The Envoy*, p. 59; Eforgan, *Leslie Howard*, p. 160;

*Smith* in 2018. In a panel discussion after the screening, Ian Haydn Smith, editor of *Curzon Magazine*, described the film as 'a time capsule' through which a modern audience was given an illustrative example of a British propaganda film from before the United States entered the Second World War. He said it was particularly interesting because of the link between the film's protagonist, played by Leslie Howard, and Raoul Wallenberg – a connection that the former 'would have been proud to have been associated with'.[5]

In a 2009 interview with Nina Lagergren by Danish-American film scholar Richard Raskin, she confirmed that her brother had indeed been influenced by Howard's film hero. However, he had not referred to Pimpernel Smith in any subsequent conversation with her, nor had he expressed any desire to perform any rescue mission until the opportunity presented itself in 1944. The direct link that so many have wished to make is thus not evident. Even so, Raskin stresses that the film can nonetheless be seen as 'the catalyst that first set Wallenberg's plans in motion', since there are a number of obvious similarities between Howard's portrayal of the role and Wallenberg's mode of operation in Budapest. There are good reasons to believe that once committed to his mission at the Swedish Legation in Hungary, Wallenberg found in *Pimpernel Smith* a role-model he could adapt to the situation at hand when facing down Nazi and Arrow guards and snatching prisoners from their grasp.[6]

While agreeing with Raskin's conclusion, I would add that from a history-cultural perspective, there are also other aspects to be extracted from Raoul Wallenberg's delight in the Scarlet Pimpernel character and the ways in which Wallenberg was influenced by Leslie Howard's film hero. Indeed, the story of this literary and cinematic hero reveals much about the interwar ideal of the hero and why he was clearly a role model for many more people apart from Wallenberg. Let us therefore consider the reasons behind the success of *The Scarlet Pimpernel* and *Pimpernel Smith*.

---

Kaj Schueler, 'De livsviktiga hjältarna', *Svenska Dagbladet*, 9 January 2012; Hannes Lundberg Andersson, 'Filmen som förändrade Raoul Wallenberg', *Expressen*, 23 February 2018. Lagergren confirmed this in an interview with the author of this book on 29 April 2008.
5 'Ian Haydn Smith on the Pimpernel Smith', www.britishcouncil.se (accessed 10 November 2021).
6 Raskin, 'From Leslie Howard to Raoul Wallenberg', pp. 11–12.

## The Scarlet Pimpernel: literary role model and screen hero

In the early 2000s, a Swedish cultural debater categorized *The Scarlet Pimpernel* (1934) as 'counter-revolutionary'.[7] In support of such a view, it can be argued that *The Scarlet Pimpernel* showcases good English governance in contrast with French revolutionary hysteria. Portrayed in sharp contrast to Britain's upstanding nobility are the power-hungry leaders of the French Terror, the unshaven Revolutionary Guards, and the bloodthirsty women of working-class and peasant origin. The women sit knitting busily, only allowing interruptions when it is time for yet another group of the French upper class to lose their heads to Madame Guillotine. But English aristocrat Sir Percy Blakeney's secret rescue missions to save French noblemen and women from the guillotine in the Paris of the French Revolution are not primarily about whether the overthrow of the *Ancien Regime* was right or wrong; they are a protest against indiscriminate terror. That is why the tale of the Scarlet Pimpernel has become an oft-cited role model for subsequent rescues of victims from bloodthirsty regimes, not least that of the Nazis.

*The Scarlet Pimpernel* was originally a stage play. When first performed in 1903, however, Baroness Emmuska Orczy's play was not a success. Given that the French Revolution was a very popular subject in British history culture, a new attempt was made in 1905 with a rewritten final act. Looking back, a Swedish writer noted that although many critics had predicted 'a rapid wilting of the scarlet flower', the outcome had in fact been different.[8] The new premiere was a success, not least because in the figure of the Pimpernel, the Hungarian baroness had managed to capture the perfect representation of the quintessential English gentleman. Soon after the London premiere, Orczy adapted the play into a novel, which also enjoyed great success in Britain and abroad. By the time the story was made into a film in the mid-1930s it had already been performed at least 4,000 times in theatres in Britain, and there were thousands of performances of it elsewhere in the West. She continued to write novels about the Scarlet Pimpernel, his family, and fellow rescuers until 1940, but none of them could rival her first-born creation

---

7 Åsa Linderborg, 'Jag köper inte det här' (opinion piece about Sofia Coppola's film *Marie Antoinette*, 2006), *Aftonbladet*, 21 November 2006.
8 'Bovarna på Parnassen', *Dagens Nyheter*, 25 August 1935.

in popularity. Its protagonist came to be a long-lived role model for the twentieth-century hero – especially during the interwar period, when a series of popular-culture heroes were conceived on the basis of the Scarlet Pimpernel's dual identities. The better known of these include Scaramouche, Zorro, and Superman.[9]

Contributing to the Scarlet Pimpernel's continued successes was the fact that interwar radio and film versions of the tale 'created an emotional climate in support of war, while moving towards a democratisation of the myth'. Sally Dugan's account of these successes emphasizes the contradiction between Orczy's persona and her private life. During the interwar period she lived a comfortable life on the French Riviera, although this became complicated during the Second World War when she came under first Italian and then German occupation. Regardless of her external circumstances, she was a strong proponent of continued privileges for the upper strata of society in a world becoming increasingly characterized by middle-class values. In contrast, during that same time period her foremost hero, the Scarlet Pimpernel, underwent an adaptation that would also make him viable on the US side of the Atlantic.[10]

This goal was very much present in the 1934 film version. It was directed by Harald Young, assisted by Lajos Biro and the brothers Alexander and Vincent Korda, who, like Orczy, can best be described as Hungarian-born Anglophiles and admirers of the British Empire. For Alexander Korda in particular, the film adaptation was an old dream come true. He had begun a career in the film industry during what has been described as the first golden age of Hungarian cinema, which occurred during the last years of the First World War. Like other Hungarian Jews in the film industry, he was frightened by the white antisemitic terror that followed Béla Kun's short-lived Communist Republic. Korda fled to France, where he continued his work as a critic and film producer before moving to Britain in 1932.[11]

The films he produced in his early years in London included both successes and failures. It was after one of the latter that he went in for doing the film adaptation of *The Scarlet Pimpernel*. Some people were sceptical about a film version of the popular novel, but

---

9 Melman, *The Culture of History*, pp. 29–91, 247–277.
10 Dugan, *Baroness Orczy's* The Scarlet Pimpernel, pp. 181–191, quotation p. 181.
11 Frey, *Jews, Nazis, and the Cinema of Hungary*, pp. 29–32.

he refused to listen to them. For a book that had sold five million copies, the odds were good for a big-screen success. Orczy's novel was already packed with some of the primary characteristics of motion pictures: movement and intensity. In addition, it was full of adventure and drama and was hence perfect for the world of film. *The Scarlet Pimpernel* was a big hit, and it was widely appreciated by critics of the time. The reviewer in *The New York Times* went so far as to say that thanks to this film, the British could 'recover some of their recent losses in cinema prestige'. Audiences also loved the film. It was high on the list of most popular titles, grossing over half a million pounds in its first few months of release in Britain alone.[12] The Scarlet Pimpernel lived on for at least another decade as a romantic ideal for women attracted by the way in which the brave, ingenious hero hid behind the facade of an effete buffoon.[13]

That the Scarlet Pimpernel already held almost iconic status in Britain is clear from the debate over who would play him in the film. Alexander Korda's first choice was Charles Laughton, who had won an Oscar the previous year for best male lead in *The Private Life of Henry VIII*, but the proposal met with stiff resistance. Leslie Howard was the next to be considered. Orczy objected, arguing that he was literally too small for the role and was therefore unable to carry the film, especially in the scenes in which he confronted the Scarlet Pimpernel's arch-enemy Chauvelin, portrayed by the stately Raymond Massey.[14]

Her objections fell on deaf ears, however, and the lead role did go to Leslie Howard. He had been born in London in 1893 to a British-Jewish mother and a Hungarian-Jewish father. After working as a bank clerk, in the 1920s and early 1930s he had made a name for himself on both sides of the Atlantic. On stage and on the film screen, he was praised for his ironic and humorous roles. His Central European background was downplayed as part of the very deliberate image-creation process favoured by the film companies. In the official version, both in his private life and on stage, like

---

12 Tabori, *Alexander Korda*, pp. 152–154; Melman, *The Culture of History*, pp. 264–265, 270–272; Perry, *The Great British Picture Show*, pp. 68–69; Andre Sennwald, 'Leslie Howard as the Scarlet Pimpernel in a fine british screen version of the famous novel', *The New York Times*, 8 February 1935. See also the review in *Variety*, 12 February 1935 and Stig Almqvist, 'Bränningar', *Vecko-Journalen*, 1935:10, 10.
13 See e.g. Maj Lorents under the heading 'Mitt hjärtas val', *Idun*, 1945:50, 39.
14 Dugan, *Baroness Orczy's* The Scarlet Pimpernel, p. 185.

the Pimpernel of the play and the novel, he appeared as the quintessential noble Englishman: intelligent, refined, gentlemanly, sophisticated, and sensitive, 'the thinking man as hero', which for many moviegoers – and not only those in the UK – amounted to the personification of 'the Englishman's Englishman'.[15]

Howard had had fearful experiences as a soldier in the British Army, and he had returned from the battlefields in 1916 severely traumatized.[16] There are no traces of this legacy in *The Scarlet Pimpernel*, though. When Blakeney is in the company of his co-conspirators, he pooh-poohs the risks involved. Like the ideally portrayed heroic British soldiers who had fought on the battlefields of the First World War two decades earlier, the film's Scarlet Pimpernel compares wars and perilous rescues to gentlemanly sporting events.[17]

At that time, Americans claimed that their nation's role models often tended to be entertainers, whose heroic status was based on different and less edifying qualities than those found in their own and other countries' historical heroes and martyrs.[18] This belief is reflected in the Swedish assessment of Leslie Howard's performance. According to one description he was the personification of 'a modern hero', being the knight, the dandy, and the tender lover all in one person. This was the polar opposite of other types of cinematic role models that prevailed in the interwar period, such as 'the tough guy', 'honest Joe', and the 'Latin lover'.[19] For example, Clark Gable, Howard's counterpart in the epic blockbuster *Gone with the Wind* (1938), was a cowboy type: 'brutal, nonchalant, hungry for women and gunshots, whiskey, and raw red meat'. In contrast to this vulgar American brutality born of a violent settler tradition was Howard's English refinement, elegance, and modernized heroic ideals. 'It was like wild strawberries and champagne after the raw beef and whiskey', one Swedish fan enthused.[20] Another Swede stressed that Howard's 'real weapon was not the

---

15 Aldgate and Richards, *Britain Can Take It*, pp. 44–46, 53, 55.
16 Eforgan, *Leslie Howard*, pp. 17–29. See also French, 'Philip French's screen legends. No. 68: Leslie Howard 1893–1943', *The Observer*, 30 August 2009.
17 See MacDonald, *The Language of Empire*, pp. 21–22.
18 Klapp, 'The Folk Hero', pp. 17–25.
19 Aldgate and Richards, *Britain Can Take It*, p. 53.
20 Ilja, 'En modern hjälte', *Idun*, 1943:30, 11. For a similar distinction between the English 'cultured individual' and 'the hearty he-men of American films',

revolver or the sword, but ... the finesse, the imagination, the wit, the culture'.[21]

The British actor also embodied a redefined view of masculinity, a view in which style, glamour, and sensibility operated alongside the classic male cult of physical adventure and risk-taking. These were qualities that attracted both men and women, albeit for different reasons. Against this background and despite Orczy's doubts, Howard was perfect in the lead role in *The Scarlet Pimpernel*. No one could match him in portraying Sir Percy's dual character. On the one hand, he displayed a 'feminine' interest in fashion combined with a dismissive attitude to political issues. On the other hand, Howard's lightning-fast shifts in facial expression and body language show that Blakeney's supposed feebleness and snobbery have nothing in common with his action-orientated and courageous alter ego. Using modesty and a deliberate rejection of valued 'manly' qualities – to avoid detection, Blakeney and his team are prepared to suffer the indignity of being dismissed as unmanly, uninteresting, and egocentric upper-class boors – they elude the ruthless and determined French chief of police time and again. Blakeney likens the Scarlet Pimpernel to a simple roadside flower. As a symbol it is associated with signalling meetings, preferably clandestine ones like those in *The Scarlet Pimpernel*.[22]

---

see Georg Svensson, 'Leslie Howard', *Bonniers Litterära Magasin*, 1943:6, 438. This distinction is problematized in a later analysis. From a masculine perspective, Rhett (Gable) is the hero of the drama, because, unlike Ashley (Howard), he undergoes a transformation in a humanist direction in *Gone with the Wind*. True, Ashley's status changes, from plantation owner to manufacturer, from bachelor to widower, but he is basically the same at the end of the film as at the beginning, as noted by Trice and Holland in *Heroes, Antiheroes and Dolts*, pp. 20–27.

21 Arne F, 'Dyre prins godnatt!', *Biografbladet*, 1942:25. However, in the obituary in *The Manchester Guardian*, 4 June 1943, his English image is described as not always an advantage. While it benefited him in the Pimpernel films and *Pygmalion*, it was 'exactly that same all-enveloping Englishness and phlegm which came between him and the big romantic and classical parts which were his ultimate ambition as an actor'.

22 Bergström, *Den symboliska nejlikan i senmedeltidens och renässansens konst*; pp. 12–86; Marion Dixon, 'The dashing Lord Percy and his little scarlet flower', *The Christian Science Monitor*, 7 November 1987.

## Pimpernel Smith: an updated version of the Scarlet Pimpernel

After war broke out in 1939, it was not uncommon for people to use historical events to comment on current developments. For example, several British and American film productions referred to Queen Elizabeth I's resistance to Spain's lust for conquest in the sixteenth century, with the implication that the successor to Spain's King Philip II was Adolf Hitler. Like many of his fellow actors on both sides of the Atlantic, Leslie Howard offered his services to his country. For him, this led to propaganda work – that is, film production under new conditions. For Howard, though, that did not involve producing propaganda under the guise of history. He was worried by conversations he had with refugees from Nazi Germany and German-occupied countries and by reports of prominent individuals in Germany who had disappeared or been murdered. These contacts with refugees from Germany also inspired a sequel to *The Scarlet Pimpernel*. Set in Howard's own times, it was the first British-made war film of the Second World War: *Pimpernel Smith*. A possible source of inspiration was the British-German Jew Wilfrid Israel, who managed to bring 8,000 Jews from Germany to Britain after the pogrom in November 1938. When Israel and Howard met, the latter is said to have declared Israel a living Scarlet Pimpernel.[23]

Although it was set in a time 150 years before the era of *Pimpernel Smith*, *The Scarlet Pimpernel* was still highly relevant to twentieth-century troubles. In it, the heir to the British throne has to accept that if the French run amok within their country's borders, the scope for direct British intervention is limited. This observation held true both for 1792 and for 1934, when developments in Germany were taking an ominous turn. The film's central theme of refugees could be used to highlight the vast difference between the Germany of the First World War and the same country under Hitler's rule. From 1914 to 1918, intellectuals and artists had remained in the country and supported the German cause in various ways. Now the situation was different. Many had fled Germany to support the Allied war effort.[24]

Leslie Howard, who was in Hollywood when the storm clouds were gathering over Europe, did not hesitate to return to his homeland. A press release, marked by the tense situation

---

23 Shepherd, *Wilfrid Israel*.
24 Murphy, *British Cinema and the Second World War*, pp. 46–47.

and with nationalistic tones, again stressed that the actor was 'typically British' and would not hesitate to offer his services to his country without reservation, as 'every true Britisher' would.[25] Convinced that Franklin D. Roosevelt was on the side of the British, Howard strongly advocated more efforts by British writers, actors, and cultural figures who could help sway US opinion in a pro-British direction. He worked on a plan to shoot documentary and information films, and he spoke on radio broadcasts about German racial policies before putting other work aside to concentrate on a sequel to *The Scarlet Pimpernel* set in his own times.[26]

Sir Percy's replacement in *Pimpernel Smith* by the seemingly equally confused and ineffectual archaeology professor Horatio Smith was shaped by Howard's impressions from radio broadcasts from Poland before it surrendered to German and Soviet supremacy. The artist Alfons Walde, whom Howard had met on a skiing holiday in Kitzbühel, contributed harrowing tales of his friends being killed by the Nazi regime's henchmen. Howard soon began to consider how these narratives could be turned into a film that could help boost British morale. His friend the Scottish writer Archibald Gordon Macdonell contributed the frame story of an archaeological expedition to Germany and the suggestion of creating 'a modern Pimpernel'. Howard embraced the idea. He did not want to include 'Pimpernel' in the title, but on that point he had to give in.[27]

Trying to turn real-life tragic circumstances into a comedy that employed humour as a sharp weapon aimed at Hitler and his followers was no guarantee of success in the years around 1940. *The Great Dictator* (1940) was Charles Chaplin's greatest commercial success, and Ernst Lubitsch's *To Be or Not to Be* (1942) has long been considered a classic, but both films were harshly criticized for their subject matter. After watching *The Great Dictator*, Roosevelt's only comment to Chaplin was that the film had led to Argentinian protests. Confusion comedies with Hitler in the lead role also caused other critics in the US and Britain to object. They included representatives of the British upper classes and US isolationists who regarded Hitler as a legitimate ruler, albeit with

---

25 Howard, *A Quite Remarkable Father*, p. 263.
26 Howard, *A Quite Remarkable Father*, pp. 268–269, 281; Eforgan, *Leslie Howard*, pp. 140–141, 170–175.
27 Ronald Howard, *In Search of My Father*, pp. 63–64, 77–78; Eforgan, *Leslie Howard*, pp. 141–151, 160.

extreme political views. Howard harboured no such illusions; he regarded the German Führer 'as a vicious madman who had blighted a nation'.[28]

One main reason why Howard's film escaped the kind of criticism that befell these other two wartime films was that the Pimpernel character was already well known and loved. Like his noble predecessor, Smith is a master at helping regime opponents escape the reign of terror. The change of setting from 1790s' revolutionary France to contemporary Nazi Germany is emphasized in the film. A black-clad SS man's assertion that in Nazi Germany, no one can hope to be saved, very clearly sets the tone. So does the contrast between the 'Come to Romantic Germany' promotional poster featuring a beautiful woman in a pastoral landscape and the soundtrack's gunfire volleys as well as Hitler's aggressive speeches. The protagonist's basic humanist attitude also contrasts sharply with the prevailing German ideals. Smith makes it clear that he hates violence. He believes it is paradoxical and uncivilized to kill a man when it is possible to convince him by reasoning that there is another and better path to choose.

### On a secret mission in Nazi Germany

In 1939 Smith and his students embark on an expedition to Nazi Germany under the guise of a scientific expedition. Their official reason is to discover traces of an Aryan civilization in Central Europe. The professor uses various disguises, but the best one is his own behaviour. The Nazis are searching for a man of action. On the surface, Smith is anything but. One of the individuals he rescues is unaware that the professor is his benefactor, remarking that, unlike his bold liberator, such people are no 'men of action'. The archaeologist does nothing to correct this impression. His chief weapon is that he appears to be a person who blends in with his surroundings and behaves in a very low-key manner. Even his surname Smith signals ordinariness. However, his first name tells a different story. Horatio – the first name of one of Britain's greatest heroes, Admiral Nelson – signals that other qualities are hidden behind the quiet facade. Smith's feigned confusion makes him

---

28 Annette Insdorf, *Indelible Shadows*, pp. 64–68; Avisar, *Screening the Holocaust*, p. 102; Rosenfeld, *Raoul Wallenberg*, pp. 209–244; Zander, 'Modernitetskritik i svart-vitt', pp. 222–224; Eforgan, *Leslie Howard*, p. 157.

seem like a person of no account. By combining this deceit with courage, cunning, planning and – when necessary – also physical disguises, he manages to rescue political prisoners from jails and concentration camps. During the excavations in Germany, he plans to rescue Sidmir Koslowski (Peter Gawthorne), a Polish intellectual with knowledge valuable to the Allies, who is imprisoned, accused of espionage. In the long run Smith is unable to fool his students, especially the American one, who is not very studious but is all the more enthusiastic and enterprising. After discovering an injury sustained by Smith during one of his missions, the students confront their professor, who admits that he is Pimpernel Smith. They then close ranks behind him, and he somewhat reluctantly accepts their help.

In *The Scarlet Pimpernel*, Blakeney is a married man. However, the marriage has cooled because of his knowledge that his wife has betrayed a noble family. It is only after the reason for her betrayal – a wrong committed against her – has been revealed, and after she proves willing to sacrifice herself to save the Scarlet Pimpernel, that happiness smiles on the couple again. In *Pimpernel Smith*, romance is absent for a long time, but Professor Smith's lack of interest in women, which almost takes on misogynistic overtones, eventually proves to be another of his deceptions. He implies that his ideal woman is the statue of Aphrodite, but a woman of flesh and blood soon wins his heart. SS General von Graum, who in Francis Sullivan's masterful portrayal bears a resemblance to Hermann Göring, blackmails Kowalski's beautiful daughter Ludmilla (Mary Morris). To save her father's life, she must spy on and, if necessary, seduce Smith, who von Graum suspects is none other than Pimpernel Smith. The archaeology professor does not fall for the trap, but he realizes that Ludmilla, with whom he has fallen in love, is the victim of German blackmail.

As in *The Scarlet Pimpernel*, the qualities that were most associated with Howard's character – gentlemanliness, wit, humour, and irony – are also abundantly present in *Pimpernel Smith*. In both films, these qualities are presented as specifically English, and they stand in sharp contrast to the Germans' total lack of humour. The message is reinforced by von Graum's concern about the English people's secret weapon: their sense of humour. In both Pimpernel films, the dictatorships' minions try to expose the hero while he is attending a ball. Balls also function as convenient gatherings for the filmmakers in their efforts to bring out the differences between the British on the one hand and the French and Germans on the other.

Thus, when the British in *Pimpernel Smith* jokingly declare that the theme of this year's Nazi Nuremberg Days is peace, the irony totally escapes the Germans. By contrast, von Graum, after a few seconds of reflection, does understand the meaning of Smith's line 'I was looking for Jekyll but I found Hyde'. He seems not to appreciate it, though, particularly when the archaeology professor stresses that it was not meant as a joke. Conversely, the German fails to understand Smith's ironic observation that life in Nazi Germany reminds him of Alice's adventures in Wonderland. von Graum does not comprehend the reference to Lewis Carroll's tale of a surreal, upside-down world; for him, the Third Reich is literally a fairyland made real.

Such exchanges of opinion in the film repeatedly highlight the fact that the British characters are educated to a completely different level than the German ones. For example, Smith is willing and able to recite poems by the English poet Rupert Brooke. He does remain silent when the general asserts that German ersatz coffee is superior to the coffee, brewed from real beans, served at the British Embassy. However, Smith wins the final battle. When von Graum argues that German scholars have once and for all proved that William Shakespeare was German, Smith retorts with lightning speed: 'You must admit that the English translation is most remarkable.' This scene is typical of the film, in which the Nazis are consistently portrayed as culturally inferior. One reviewer thus noted that this very obvious propaganda should be seen as 'good-natured mockery of Nazi pomp and hyper-seriousness'.[29] After the war, one Swedish critic categorized *Pimpernel Smith* as a textbook example of the 'anti-Nazi state of innocence' that had prevailed in the early stages of the war.[30] To be sure, there was a danger in such an image, but it was a case of wishful thinking – 'nice to indulge in and anxiety-reducing to participate in', to quote the film scholar Leif Furhammar and the author Folke Isaksson.[31] The presence of humour should also be regarded as an expression of the need to laugh in dark times, as is demonstrated by the fact that the ukulele-playing film comedian George Formby was the

---

29 Anonymous, '"Röda nejlikan" och Gestapo', *Dagens Nyheter*, 18 August 1941.
30 Georg Svensson in *Bonniers Litterära Magasin*, 1945:6, 517. This state of innocence also appeared after the war, see e.g. 'Humorn är det starkaste vapnet', *Filmjournalen*, 1945:23, 10–11.
31 Furhammar and Isaksson, *Politik och film*, p. 308.

highest-grossing actor in Britain from 1939 to 1943.[32] At the same time, both *The Scarlet Pimpernel* and *Pimpernel Smith* had serious contemporary relevance. 'Leslie Howard did not play *The Scarlet Pimpernel* as a historical adventure film. Today's deadly serious struggle for human dignity permeated the role, and that struggle continued in ... "Pimpernel Smith"', observed the writer of a Swedish obituary of the actor.[33]

The inferior technical quality of *Pimpernel Smith* is obvious to viewers today. At the time of the film's release, its tight budget – manifested in the backdrop-like backgrounds and the scarcity of true outdoor scenes – was not remarked on. The film did encounter objections from critics who called for a more 'realistic' portrayal, but realism was by no means the only valid criterion for good entertainment at that time. The reviewer in *The New York Times* noted that the film was a representation of 'absurd derring-do' which followed a 'routine pattern', but said that these criticisms should not detract from Howard's 'causal direction' and from the 'consummate ease and the quiet irony of his performance'. Referring to the recent devastating British defeat, he noted that 'Singapore may fall, but the British can still make melodramas to chill the veins'.[34] The reception of *Pimpernel Smith* was broadly in line with this view, and the critics were not alone in being pleased with it. *Pimpernel Smith* attracted large audiences and was one of the most successful films during the Second World War.[35]

One contributing factor was that the film was a propaganda product which drew on various types of mythological elements. On one level, both Pimpernel films are successful updates of the classic tale of the quick-witted hero who fools the mighty villain. The hero's efforts are all the more admirable because the villain is blackmailing the beautiful woman who is also the hero's love interest. In both cases she agrees, under protest and with great remorse, to set a trap for the hero. In their standard work *Politik och film* ['Politics and film'], Leif Furhammar and Folke Isaksson point out that this is a common theme in folklore: people are forced to help the villain, but they are released when the pressure exerted by the villain is removed.

---

32 Aldgate and Richards, *Britain Can Take It*, p. 59.
33 Ilja, 'En modern hjälte', *Idun*, 1943:30.
34 T. S., '"Mr. V," a British melodrama with Leslie Howard, opens at Rivoli', *The New York Times*, 13 February 1942.
35 See e.g. Murphy, *British Cinema and the Second World War*, p. 89; Chapman, *Past and Present*, p. 111.

Furhammar and Isaksson also draw attention to the fact that although *Pimpernel Smith* is not a religious film, it does tie into Christian mythology, knowledge of which was omnipresent in the early 1940s. This circumstance is likely to have caused viewers to draw parallels between Howard's character and Christ. Smith is literally a saviour figure to everyone he rescues. Like no one else, he is able to move between the evil Nazi sphere and his own idealistic one. As a professor, he teaches a circle of disciples who initially do not understand his greatness. It is only when they see his wounded hand that they realize his true identity. The wound is inflicted when Smith, disguised as a scarecrow, is targeted by a sharp-shooting German soldier who is guarding the concentration camp prisoners chosen to labour in the farm fields. After the shot is fired, the wounded Smith hangs as if crucified, his head leaning forward and down like in a Passion of Christ painting while blood drips from his hand. His resemblance to the Saviour recurs in the film's final scene with the promise that Smith will return (i.e. be resurrected).[36]

## Horatio Smith and Raoul Wallenberg

British propagandists planned for Leslie Howard to visit Sweden in June 1942 for a lecture tour. The plans had to be shelved, though, as Howard was busy directing a new feature film, *The First of the Few* (1942). This film biography of R. J. Mitchell, the successful designer of the Spitfire fighter plane, was an explicit propaganda product and highly regarded in Britain, where one writer called it 'one of the most inspiring British films ever made'.[37] That such a visit could have been very successful is evident from the many favourable comments about Leslie Howard and his films in the Swedish as well as the British press, both before and after his tragic death in 1943.[38] But although the cancelled visit was a setback, the

---

36 Furhammar and Isaksson, *Politik och film*, pp. 314–315. See also Aldgate and Richards, *Britain Can Take It*, p. 63.
37 'Leslie Howard is lost in air liner shot down by Nazis over Bay of Biscay', *The Daily Mirror*, 1 June 1943. *The First of the Few* was also very favourably received in Sweden; see Arne F, 'Farten ökar!' and 'Äreminne över två män och ett plan', both in *Filmjournalen*, 1943:48, 7; Artur Lundkvist, 'Spitfire', *Vi*, 1943:48; Carl Björkman, 'Filmkrönika', *Vecko-Journalen*, 1943:48, 30 and Miss Bio, 'Bäst i veckan', *Idun*, 1943:48, 4.
38 Stig Almqvist, 'Bränningar', 10; Stig A., 'Där brast ett ädelt hjärta', *Filmjournalen*, 1943:27; 'Sällsamma händelser kring Leslie Howard',

British Embassy in Stockholm had other ways of reaching out to politically and culturally influential Swedes. The British regularly organized film evenings to which they invited prominent residents of the Swedish capital as one way of marketing the British view of the ongoing global conflict. One example of this practice occurred following Germany's widely published destruction in June 1942 of the Czech mining community of Lidice in revenge for the murder of SS General Reinhard Heydrich. The newsreels and feature films produced in the aftermath of this deed were the main attraction at these embassy gatherings.[39] *Pimpernel Smith*, slightly abridged, fulfilled the same function in 1942, but it was only shown on a few occasions.

The German propaganda authorities exerted strong pressure for more German films and fewer Allied ones to be shown in Sweden. These demands were often met, particularly during the first years of the war when the German army appeared invincible. In the case of *Pimpernel Smith*, the German Minister for Public Enlightenment and Propaganda Joseph Goebbels not only wanted to prevent it from being shown in Swedish cinemas; he also demanded that embassy screenings of it should cease. The Swedish authorities complied.[40] However, they could not prevent a new copy of *The Scarlet Pimpernel* from being re-released in 1942 in the big film theatres. Almost without exception, the reviews were enthusiastic. *The Scarlet Pimpernel* had stood the test of time well, and Leslie Howard's elegant and humorous performance was a welcome return.[41] The German propaganda machine hence appears to have won a Pyrrhic victory. *Pimpernel Smith* was banned but widely discussed – according to a report in the Swedish evening papers in May 1945, as many as half a million Swedes managed

---

*Filmjournalen*, 1944:32; Ilja, 'En modern hjälte', *Idun*, 1943:30; Arne F, 'Dyre prins godnatt!', *Biografbladet*, 1942:25; Georg Svensson, 'Leslie Howard', *Bonniers Litterära Magasin*, 1943:6; –s, 'Leslie Howards och Noel Cowards filmer', *Filmjournalen*, 1944:1; Sam Forre, 'Ingenting öppnar våra ögon så som filmen', *Filmjournalen*, 1945:23, 8; Aldgate and Richards, *Britain Can Take It*, pp. 44–45.
39 Österberg, '"Eftervärldens dom har fallit hård"', p. 140. For a contemporary discussion about showing the forbidden films, see C. I., 'Förbjudna filmer', *Idun*, 1944:33, 6–7, 26.
40 Howard, *In Search of My Father*, pp. 117–119.
41 Reviews in *Aftonbladet, Arbetaren, Dagens Nyheter, Social-Demokraten, Stockholms Tidningen, Svenska Dagbladet*, all published 30 June 1942.

to watch the film illegally.[42] Even though access to *Pimpernel Smith* was restricted during the war years, it would not have been difficult for cinema audiences of the original Pimpernel film to draw parallels between revolutionary France and Nazi Germany.

As pointed out above, Raoul Wallenberg watched *Pimpernel Smith*, together with his sister Nina Lagergren, at one of the screenings that did take place before the ban. It is hardly surprising that Wallenberg took *Pimpernel Smith* and the outwardly gauche, but beneath the surface elegantly humorous and courageous, Horatio Smith to his heart. There is much to suggest that Wallenberg was quick to embrace Smith's bold efforts to save 'scientists, men of letters, artists, doctors' at any cost. Smith explains that for anyone who realizes that these are 'a few exceptional spirits' who contribute to the continued existence and progress of civilization, it is 'rather hard to stand by and see them destroyed'. To quote another line from the film, *Pimpernel Smith* is all about celebrating 'brains not brawn', with the message that wit goes hand in hand with bravery and moral courage.[43]

Wallenberg's letters contain several examples of his adherence to the ideals conveyed by Howard through Smith's character. In a letter of mid-October 1944 to Iver Olsen, Wallenberg's US 'employer', Wallenberg begins with an understatement worthy of a Pimpernel Smith: 'When I look back at the three months I spent here I can only say that it has been a most interesting experience and, I believe, not entirely without results.'[44] In December 1944 he summed up the situation in Budapest as 'risky and tense' with constant threats of violence, kidnapping, and sudden death. He described his own workload as 'almost superhuman'. The note's conclusion, however, exuded courage and confidence: 'On the whole, we are in good spirits and are enjoying the fight.'[45] According to another account,

---

42 'En halv miljon svenskar såg "Pimpernel Smith" illegalt', *Expressen*, 23 May 1945.
43 Homer Dickens, 'Leslie Howard became an international star by projecting the superiority of brain over brawn', *Films in Review*, April 1959; Aldgate and Richards, *Britain Can Take It*, pp. 60–62; Arie Vilner, '"Pimpernel" Smith (1941)', *The Objective Standard*, Fall 2019, 114–116; Neil McDonald, 'Leslie Howard, Propagandist and patriot', *Quadrant*, January–February 2015, 128–131.
44 Letter from Raoul Wallenberg to Iver Olssen [sic], Budapest 12 October 1944, RKA, Raoul Wallenberg, UD2018/05505, Vol. 1.
45 Raoul Wallenberg quoted in Levine, 'The Unfinished Story of a Swedish Hero', p. 54.

# The Scarlet Pimpernel

Wallenberg returned to the Swedish Legation very early in 1945 with shrapnel injuries, which did not seem to trouble him: '"It reminds me of a youthful adventure in the United States," he jokes. "But the risks were not actually so great there".'[46] Presumably he was referring to the episode some ten years earlier when he was threatened with a revolver by four men his own age, men who then robbed him and threw him into a ditch. Whether he was really afraid we do not know. His story as told to his mother, however, suggests a deliberate distancing from the danger. The robbers 'looked rather unpleasant'. After they had robbed him, he asked them to drive him and his luggage back to the main road. 'By this time they had become alarmed, perhaps because of my calmness, for I really didn't feel anxious at all; the whole time I thought it was rather interesting.' He added that the adventure had left him quite capable of jumping on a suburban train and reporting the incident to the police. Nor was there any question of him giving up hitch-hiking.[47] Leslie Howard would certainly have had no difficulty in portraying such lofty composure.

Horatio Smith and Raoul Wallenberg are alike in that they are both portrayed as saviours and leaders. Outwardly, Smith is as unlikely a hero as is Wallenberg with his architectural training: anything but spectacular in appearance and demeanour, he has an ability not to be frightened off by powerful, terrifying, and ruthless enemies.[48] The respective fates of the two men are equally significant. The finale of *Pimpernel Smith* is set in a railway station where von Graum plans to shoot Smith during an 'attempt to escape'. Before that, Smith manages both to disprove the German claim of having Aryan origins, which they had hoped the archaeological excavation would have proved, and to deliver a fiery speech in which he declares that the Nazis are doomed, saying that they have taken the first steps on the path of darkness from which there is no turning back.

When the film was being shot, the existence of concentration camps in Germany was a reality discussed in the Western press.

---

46 Derogy, *Fallet Raoul Wallenberg*, p. 169.
47 Letter from Raoul Wallenberg to Maj von Dardel, 27 June 1933, in Söderlund and Wallenberg (eds), *Älskade farfar!*, pp. 103–104. For a discussion about the same episode in reference to the interpretation of Philip Jackson's monument to Wallenberg in London, see Schult, *A Hero's Many Faces*, p. 122.
48 Schult, *A Hero's Many Faces*, p. 55.

Their presence is raised in the film when Smith and his students, under the guise of belonging to a then well-known German-American friendship association, carry out a daring rescue of Koslowski from a concentration camp.[49] While they were making the film, Howard and others were aware of the Nazis' racist policies but not of their consequences in the form of mass executions behind the front lines in the Soviet Union and the construction of extermination camps on Polish soil.[50] Charlie Chaplin's comment in his autobiography is telling: if he had known what was happening in Nazi Germany, he would not have included scenes from a concentration camp in *The Great Dictator*.[51] Joel Rosenberg has observed that we should be wary of believing that films can influence historical events when we look at them with the benefit of hindsight, but that some of them may still capture essential phenomena in their time. In a detailed and insightful analysis of *To Be or Not to Be*, he points out that its director, Ernst Lubitsch, succeeded in portraying the essence of Nazism, something many viewers in 1942 probably did not realize.[52] This reasoning may be applied to *Pimpernel Smith* as well. When it was filmed, the Holocaust as we know it today was unknown to many in the audiences. To latter-day viewers, this imparts prophetic overtones to Smith's words about the Nazis beginning their march to the abyss.

For Raoul Wallenberg, however, the Holocaust was a tragic reality whose terrible effects he tried to combat as best he could. The similarity is therefore to be found at the symbolic level. When Smith vanishes into the fog on the railway platform, posterity may view it as foreshadowing Wallenberg's disappearance virtually without trace. In 1957, a Swedish editorial writer stated that while Wallenberg's disappearance was a tragedy, his fate had unfortunately been all too common. In the Stalinist apparatus of terror, such disappearances were an everyday occurrence; and in such a case, it would by no means be certain that Wallenberg had been allowed to retain his identity. He might just as easily be listed in the Soviet records under the anonymous name of Smith, which

---

49 For the significance of this scene, see Eforgan, *Leslie Howard*, pp. 153–154. For Der Amerikanische Volksbund in contemporaneous film productions, see Zander, *Clio på bio*, pp. 120–123.
50 See Eforgan, *Leslie Howard*, pp. 159–161.
51 Chaplin, *My Autobiography*, p. 426. See Zander, 'Modernitetskritik i svartvitt', pp. 224, 227.
52 Rosenberg, 'Shylock's Revenge', pp. 237–238.

would make it practically impossible to say anything about his time in the Soviet Union.[53]

The similarity between the fictional Pimpernel Smith and the real-life Raoul Wallenberg is reinforced by the fact that Leslie Howard's death in 1943 is also to some extent shrouded in mystery. What is clear is that he was on a plane shot down by a German fighter off Gibraltar. One rumour claimed that the Germans believed Winston Churchill was on board, a belief the former Prime Minister mentioned in his post-war memoirs.[54] While the Germans could scarcely have possessed any such information, it has long been speculated that Howard had been sent on a secret mission to keep Spain out of the Second World War. If this was so, then preventing the completion of such a mission, combined with their knowledge of Howard's importance to the British propaganda effort, would have been the reason the Germans wanted him out of the way.[55] In her well-documented biography of Howard, Estel Eforgan firmly rejects the idea that the actor was a spy.[56] Whether the Germans were targeting Howard we will never know, but if they were it was probably because he was actively helping to shape public opinion. Through his explicitly anti-Nazi films, he certainly influenced many more people than Raoul Wallenberg.

### Pimpernel Smith, Svensson, and Raoul Wallenberg

The popularity of the Scarlet Pimpernel character remained high both during and after the Second World War. The head of the Swedish industrial company Bolinders, Birger Dahlerus, who had

---

53 'Raoul Wallenberg' (editorial), *Göteborgs-Posten*, 8 February 1957.
54 Churchill, *The Second World War*, p. 830.
55 Giles Tremlett, 'British film star was secret agent, claims author', *The Guardian*, 6 October 2008; Fiona Govan, 'Actor Leslie Howard kept Spain out of WWII, claims author', *The Daily Telegraph*, 6 October 2008. See also Howard, *A Quite Remarkable Father*, pp. 205–242. For Leslie Howard's great importance to Allied and especially British propaganda, see e.g. C. A. Lejeune, 'A symbol of England', *The New York Times*, 27 June 1943. Yet another aspect of Howard's last mission is found in Jimmy Burns's unconventional biography *Papa Spy: Love, Faith and Betrayal in Wartime Spain* (2009), which focuses on the author's father, Tom Burns, the press attaché at the British Embassy in Madrid, and intelligence operations in Spain during the Second World War. See also Jane Ridley's favourable review of *Papa Spy*, 'From Madrid with love', *The Spectator*, 21 October 2009.
56 Eforgan, *Leslie Howard*, pp. 126–139.

tried to bring about peace before the great madness broke out in 1939, was one of many individuals to be nicknamed the Scarlet Pimpernel. Another was the producer of *The Scarlet Pimpernel*, Alexander Korda. A few decades later, Michael Korda wrote about his uncle's stay in California after Britain had joined the Second World War, but before the US did so. Under the cover of an eccentric film mogul visiting the US film capital, Alexander Korda was to help ensure that British cinema would continue to be a successful export product despite the increasingly obvious patriotic elements, which were problematic in a neutral United States. Since it was not possible to reveal what his mission actually was, or that he had been sent out by Winston Churchill and the British government, there was a significant risk of his finding himself in hot water back home. The British public widely believed that it was unpatriotic to depart from British shores while the battle against the German forces was so fierce. It was also considered highly likely that American isolationists would attack Alexander Korda if he openly advocated that the United States should join the British in the fight against Nazi Germany. Another fear was that he would be seen as the agent of a foreign power and therefore fall into disfavour with US senators and be scrutinized by FBI agents. Worst of all would be if the Germans realized that his real purpose was to promote US participation in the war – in which case they would try to get rid of him. Michael Korda said that despite these obstacles and dangers, his uncle's choice was easy, because

> England had made him rich and famous and had offered him a place in its hierarchy of merit and fame. Now it had to be paid for. It was ironic that he had made *The Scarlet Pimpernel*, for he was about to play the role himself, in real life, and suffer the same torments.[57]

References to the Scarlet Pimpernel were the rule rather than the exception in wartime Scandinavia, above all in the Danish-Swedish border areas where both the war, in the form of the German occupation of Denmark, and the German persecution of Jews were more present than in many other parts of Raoul Wallenberg's homeland. The presence of risk-taking resistance men and women in German-occupied Denmark, and the contacts that Swedes had with them, invited comparisons with this hero in disguise. 'Motor-Larsson' and a man who went by the name 'Hot' (meaning 'Threat') transported

---

57 Korda, *Charmed Lives*, pp. 138–139, quotation p. 139.

both refugees and ammunition across the Sound, the strait called Öresund between Sweden and Denmark. Danish student Rigmor Schou recorded the sounds of the Resistance's sabotage actions on records, which were then smuggled to Britain and played on the BBC's European radio broadcasts. Businessman, publisher, and newspaperman Einar Hansen had moved from Denmark to Sweden in the 1920s and continued to maintain contacts across Öresund, sometimes by illegal means. He was a key figure in the escape of Danish Jews across Öresund in October and November 1943. The escape was made possible in part by the efforts of Danish fishermen such as Gilbert Lassen, who smuggled Jews from Denmark to Sweden in his boat, or by the bookbinder, reserve lieutenant, and resistance fighter Erling Kjær. Kjær managed to smuggle across more than 1,400 refugees, many of them Jews, before – following more than 140 noctural crossings of Öresund – being arrested, beaten, and sent to concentration camps in Germany, from which he was freed by the Swedish White Buses rescue mission in April 1945. What all these people had in common was that they were described as modern equivalents of the Scarlet Pimpernel and his successor, Pimpernel Smith – that is, they were the real-life Scarlet Pimpernels of the Second World War.[58]

International interest in the Pimpernel continued, too; it was, for instance, expressed in Truman Capote's spy tale 'Mr. Jones', a short story from 1945 containing obvious references to Orczy's *Pimpernel* novels.[59] However, the next time the Scarlet Pimpernel character appeared on the film screen it was not a success, despite the

---

58 Crick Holm, 'Öresunds Röda nejlika', *Se*, 1945:21, 12–13; Crick Holm, 'Röda nejlikan (Birger Dahlerius): "Ribbentrop var dramats bov"', *Se*, 1945:27, 6–8, 32; Princeps, '"Röda nejlikan" i Malmö', *Vecko-Journalen*, 1945:20, 20; M. G., 'Radions röda nejlika', *Röster i Radio*, 1945:24, 7, 38; '"Röda nejlikan" svensk vicekonsul', *Svenska Dagbladet*, 15 March 199; Modéer, *Patriot i gränsland*, pp. 25–29, 191–205; Conny Palmkvist, *Sundets röda nejlikor*, pp. 286, 364. The theme also recurs even when stories of heroic rescue actions are told from other parts of the world, such as in an article about the American who saved writers Franz Werfel and Heinrich Mann from the Germans after the fall of France in 1940: Anonymous, 'Amerikansk Pimpernel räddade Werfel', *Dagens Nyheter*, 14 September 1945, or in a text about Louise Boitard, who saved many Allied airmen from German imprisonment: Anonymous, 'Fransk "nejlika" förde flygare till gränserna', *Dagens Nyheter*, 11 April 1946.

59 Dilworth, 'Truman Capote's "MR. JONES" and THE SCARLET PIMPERNEL', pp. 71–72.

seemingly good prospects after Alexander Korda had teamed up with the successful US film producer Samuel L. Goldwyn. The fact that the financing for *The Elusive Pimpernel* (1950) had been secured was not very significant as Michael Powell, who directed the film together with Emeric Pressburger, felt justifiably thwarted when Margaret Leighton was cast as the leading lady against his wishes. Nor were his plans to turn *The Elusive Pimpernel* into a musical welcomed. Not even the new leading man David Niven, who had previously starred opposite Leslie Howard in *The First of the Few* (which Howard had directed), was enthusiastic, but he was compelled to accept the job for contractual reasons. The film's fate was sealed when Korda and Goldwyn fell out, with the result that the latter refused to pay his share, leading to legal repercussions. The film was only released in the United States several years later in a black-and-white version entitled *The Fighting Pimpernel*. The bright Technicolor production and the light-hearted touch could not conceal the fact that the many controversies and compromises had resulted in a film that did not live up to its predecessor by a long chalk. *The Elusive Pimpernel* attracted few viewers and was a financial disaster.[60]

The Pimpernel's continued appeal on the film screen became clear to Swedish cinemagoers that same year, 1950, when they again had the opportunity to see Edvard Persson. He was one of the most popular Swedish actors of the time, and in his film career he came to personify the down-to-earth, patriarchal farmer of southern Sweden. In *Pimpernel Svensson*, he plays Anders Svensson – a man who, like Leslie Howard's Pimpernel of the 1940s, has a very common surname, as Svensson can be said to be the Swedish equivalent of Smith. Svensson's quiet and secure life as a farmer is shattered when he learns that his sailor nephew Ville is being held prisoner in the Soviet-occupied northern German city of Stettin. After arriving in Germany, Svensson manages to communicate with the Soviet authorities by way of singing, whereupon he makes contact with Ville while wearing a Soviet general's uniform he has 'borrowed'. His escape plan succeeds, but by then Anders has become such a good friend of the Soviet soldiers that they have voluntarily arranged for Ville to receive his release papers. Waiting for Anders on his return are his nephew's anxious and grateful wife and mother plus an equally impressed local population, who confer the grand nickname of Pimpernel Svensson on Anders.

---

60 Perry, *The Great British Picture Show*, p. 151.

From *Pimpernel Svensson* we can draw several conclusions. First, the film's plot is in stark contrast to the then ongoing, and fruitless, negotiations with the Soviet authorities concerning Raoul Wallenberg. Other Swedes had also disappeared without a trace. They included a number of sailors who had been on board ships that had disappeared in the Baltic Sea in 1947 and 1948. It could not be ruled out that some of these men had been imprisoned in the Gulag; they were consequently included in a formal question submitted in the Swedish Parliament, the Riksdag, in 1964. In that question, representatives of the centre-right opposition called on the Social Democratic government to seek information about what had happened to Swedes who had disappeared in Soviet captivity.[61]

Second, it was by no means a given that all cinemagoers would watch a film featuring Edvard Persson with the tense Swedish-Soviet relationship in mind. Instead, they might identify with his character's willingness to solve problems and reach consensus, even when he was unable to communicate in the traditional manner. A few years earlier, Persson had combined an acclaimed concert tour of the Swedish settlement regions in the United States with filming *Jens Månsson in America* (1947). Jens, played by Persson, inherits an estate in the United States from a brother on condition that he finds and obtains the approval of the third brother, who also lives there. One major problem is that Jens knows no English. However, with the aid of a helpful compatriot who cheerfully leaves his job as a waiter in New York to assist him, combined with the fact that most people they encounter are Swedish descendants who still speak Swedish, the mission is crowned with success.[62] In *Pimpernel Svensson* there are certainly no Swedish speakers in Soviet uniform, but in the world of popular culture there were no obstacles to the hope that with the help of wine, women, and song it would be possible to communicate with the mighty neighbour to the east. This would make it possible to bring home Swedes who had been caught up in the Second World War or its wake.

Third, the film stories of the Scarlet Pimpernel and Pimpernel Smith were obviously very popular in Sweden. When *Pimpernel Smith* finally opened in cinemas in 1945, it was given as good reviews as *The Scarlet Pimpernel* had received three years earlier

---

61 Ohlin, *Bertil Ohlins memoarer 1940–1951*, pp. 74–76.
62 Wallengren, *Welcome Home, Mr Swanson*, pp. 140–143.

and has continued to receive.[63] Prominent cultural figures such as Georg Svensson, editor of the prestigious cultural magazine *Bonniers Litterära Magasin*, and his famous fellow writer Artur Lundkvist were among those who praised Leslie Howard's acting and the film's intelligent and ironic scenes, which 'hid a fine energy beneath the seemingly light approach to the topic'.[64] Other typical reviews praised 'a solidly made film' and expressed 'bubbling delight' at the 'most witty and insightful film made during the war years'.[65] *Pimpernel Smith* became a long-running hit in Swedish cinemas and won the approval of the general public as a whole. It was therefore not surprising that a Swedish film was made on the assumption that the audience knew the story of the Scarlet Pimpernel and Howard's portrayals of the theme.

It is clear, then, that *Pimpernel Svensson* evoked the popularity of the British films. However, this connection also brought with it great responsibility. Ahead of the premiere on 31 August 1950, the Swedish comedian and writer Erik Zetterström, better known by his pen name of Kar de Mumma, noted that many audience members

---

63 See e.g. 'Röda nejlikan', *Röster i Radio*, 1963:16, 22; Karin Michal, 'I kväll visar TV legendariska "Nejlikan" – Leslie Howard i klassisk roll', *Aftonbladet*, 30 June 1963; Henning Sten, '"Röda nejlikan" – en äventyrsfilm i TV', *Expressen*, 30 June 1963; 'Röda nejlikan – än en gång', *Röster i Radio*, 1971:7; Björn Norström, 'Alla älskar "Röda nejlikan"', *Expressen*, 5 February 1971; Björn Norström, 'Leslie Howard gjorde Röda Nejlikan odödlig', *Expressen*, 26 July 1984; Anne Hedén, 'Han räddar aristokraterna från giljotinen', *Aftonbladet*, 16 July 1989; Bernt Eklund, 'Klassiskt äventyr med fräck ädling', *Expressen*, 16 July 1989.
64 Georg Svensson in *Bonniers Litterära Magasin*, 1945:6, 517; Artur Lundkvist, 'Filmkrönikan', *Ord & Bild*, 1945, p. 334; the quotation comes from the latter source; Artur Lundkvist, 'Pimpernel Smith', *Vi*, 1945:22, 29. See also Yngve Kernell's favourable report in *Idun*, 1945:23, 4.
65 T. H–n., 'Premiär: Pimpernel Smith', *Expressen* and '–hn' in *Arbetaren*, both 23 May 1945. See also the reviews in *Dagens Nyheter, Morgon-Tidningen, Stockholms Tidningen, Svenska Dagbladet*, all 23 May 1945 and *Sydsvenskan*, 10 July 1945. The favourable views have persisted over the years; see also 'Humor och elegans vapen mot nazismen', *Dagens Nyheter*, 22 November 1964; Alf Montan, 'Humorn hans vapen', *Expressen*, 21 November 1964; 'En nejlika bland nazister', *Röster i Radio*, 1964:48; Torsten Jungstedt, 'Vad är engelsk humor?', *Röster i Radio*, 1971:12, 14; Lars Löfstrand, 'Pimpernel Smith', *Expressen*, 17 September 1977; Elisabeth Melander, 'Filmen som gjorde nazisterna rasande', *Aftonbladet*, 17 September 1977; Torsten Jungstedt, 'På mångas begäran: Pimpernel Smith', *Röster i Radio & TV*, 1977:38, 20–21.

would still have fond memories of Leslie Howard's portrayals of the Scarlet Pimpernel and Pimpernel Smith. Many of them would surely welcome Edvard Persson's efforts to carry on this legacy, but there was an undeniable risk that the film would seem like a remake of *Camille*, in which an unknown amateur actor had attempted Greta Garbo's signature role.[66]

Kar de Mumma's fears were well grounded. The filming of *Pimpernel Svensson* had been fraught with difficulties, including disagreements between the lead actor and the scriptwriter, Åke Ohlmarks, who was also a well-known translator and religious historian. As a result, almost all the scenes were filmed in two versions, one based on Persson's wishes and the other adhering to the script.[67] The fact that Persson usually had to give in was an indication that his heyday was over. This was also reflected in the film's mixed reception among critics. Some reviewers did praise Persson's vocal performances, with lyrics that were better than in many of his other films. The well-known film critic Bengt Idestam-Almquist, better known as Robin Hood, thought it was both an entertaining story and one of the best popular comedies for years.[68] Another reviewer reacted against the ridiculous opening and sentimental ending, but appreciated that a Pimpernel from southern Sweden had picked up on 'the fact that people like to see Russians being cheated'.[69] Others drew attention to 'the Pimpernel's remarkable naivety and the sluggish action' and the total lack of credibility. This was only partly compensated for by the fact that the film appeared to be a fantasy story, and that the music worked well as a form of communication when language misunderstandings otherwise dominated.[70] Some critics went beyond mild censoriousness. Amateurish elements and the film's political stance – or rather lack of one – led one reviewer to dismiss the film as not even managing to be offensive.[71]

---

66  Kar de Mumma, 'Svensson i ryska zonen m. fl. nöjen', *Svenska Dagbladet*, 30 August 1950.
67  Richter, *Edvard Persson*, pp. 242–244.
68  Robin Hood (Bengt Idestam-Almquist) in *Stockholms Tidningen*. See also the pseudonyms Filmson in *Aftonbladet*, Nils Beyer in *Morgon-Tidningen* and –hn in *Arbetaren*, all published 31 September 1950; and –eis– in *Sydsvenskan* and O. Bull in *Skånska Dagbladet*, both 5 September 1950.
69  Trannel, 'Rio och Rex: *Pimpernel Svensson*', *Arbetet*, 5 September 1950.
70  Jerome, 'Saga: Pimpernel Svensson', *Dagens Nyheter*, 31 August 1950.
71  Mikael Katz, 'Pimpernel Svensson', *Expressen*, 31 September 1950.

His colleague in the Communist newspaper *Ny Dag* expressed a similar opinion, branding the film 'unprecedentedly naive'.[72] A reviewer in the leading conservative daily *Svenska Dagbladet* was of a similar mind, saying that in *Pimpernel Svensson* 'idiocy reaches sublime heights'.[73] The film received a similar judgement after a screening in New York. The fact that it had a running time of 90 minutes baffled *The New York Times* critic because its plot was so thin, although he did admit that, judging from their cheerful responses, the cinemagoers – many of whom had Swedish roots – had no objections.[74]

*Pimpernel Svensson* was thus not one of Edvard Persson's most successful films, but it still reached a fairly large audience. It was based on a typical dimension that contributed greatly to Persson's long-lasting popularity: a lively carnival spirit combined with a consensus message. A typical example is a line from the film praising the Soviet general Vlasov: if more commanders had been like him, war and misery would not have been necessary. 'This', writes the film scholar Kjell Jerselius, 'is a recurring pathos in Edvard Persson's films: everyone may be converted, and all problems may be solved if only the parties can meet over a drink and get to know one another and speak their minds in pleasant company.'[75] That the humour in the Swedish version was less like British elegance and irony and more like popular burlesque comedy has to do with the great difference between Persson's image and Howard's. As a patriarchal father figure, the former came to embody the calm, confident, and food-loving southern Swede, who sometimes had an edgy relationship with Swedishness but was nonetheless securely grounded in it. For a long time, Persson embodied this culture as effectively as Howard personified the typical ideal of Englishness.

---

72 The pseudonym Fors in *Ny Dag*, 31 September 1950. See also Armand in *Göteborgs Handels- och Sjöfartstidning*, 3 October 1950 and *Variety*, 11 February 1953.
73 The pseudonym Lill in *Svenska Dagbladet*, 31 September 1950. The unfavourable views have dominated on later broadcast dates; see e.g. Lars Bergström, 'Pimplande Persson', *Expressen*, 22 July 1990.
74 Wallengren, *Welcome Home, Mr Swanson*, p. 144.
75 Jerselius, *Hotade reservat*, pp. 97–99, 175–179, quotation p. 98.

## From black to 'red' Pimpernel: Harald Edelstam as an emulator of Raoul Wallenberg

The above review suggests that there were, and are, strong links between the Scarlet Pimpernel, Pimpernel Smith, Leslie Howard, and Raoul Wallenberg, particularly in symbolic terms and on several levels. In 1947, when the search for Wallenberg was repeatedly discussed in the Swedish public sphere, one writer claimed that 'in certain English circles' there was a desire for a new Scarlet Pimpernel who, with the help of 'some bold collaborators', would go behind the Iron Curtain and free the Swede who in many respects personified the Scarlet Pimpernel.[76]

Mia Leche Löfgren, a Swede who actively helped refugees, was an outspoken critic of the restrictive Swedish refugee policy in the late 1930s and early 1940s. Like Leslie Howard's Pimpernel Smith, she emphasized the difficulties faced by German scientists who did not comply with Nazi decrees, and she was angry that so few Swedish academics were willing to help them.[77] While she had little good to say about scientists, businessmen, and politicians who were united in their opposition to more generous policies on refugees in Sweden, her admiration for Raoul Wallenberg was all the greater. Learning about his achievements in Budapest was 'like reading an adventure novel or reliving the Scarlet Pimpernel in the guise of Leslie Howard. Here is the same inexhaustible goodness of heart, paired with an almost gleeful ingenuity, and the daring Swede also harbours a fair measure of the roguish Swedish Viking spirit.'[78] Writing a year later, she returned to the idea that this Swedish lad had 'something of the old Viking blood in his veins'. This time she did not mention Howard, but in describing Wallenberg, the qualities she listed were very much associated with the Scarlet Pimpernel and Pimpernel Smith. The Swede, she wrote, had acted audaciously, with a boldness approaching the foolhardy, because in Budapest he 'loved danger, which he actively pursues, and in addition he relished bluffing when something could be gained with a bluff'.[79]

---

76 '"Röd nejlika" kan befria Wallenberg?', *Provinstidningen Dalsland* and *Söderhamns Tidning*, 25 August 1947.
77 Löfgren, *Hård tid*, pp. 23–28.
78 Mia Leche Löfgren, 'Vi kan ej slå oss till ro med Wallenbergs försvinnande', *Göteborgs Handels- och Sjöfartstidning*, 17 July 1947.
79 Mia Leche Löfgren, 'Dubbelbottnad avsikt', *Göteborgs Handels- och Sjöfartstidning*, 8 June 1948.

The association between the Scarlet Pimpernel and Raoul Wallenberg was also raised in connection with the premiere of Eric Åkerlund's play *Raoul* at Malmö City Theatre in 1983. One reviewer pointed out that there were not only similarities in terms of saving innocent people from tyrannical regimes. In Lars Humble's portrayal of the Swedish diplomat, Leslie Howard's character had been given a new lease of life. Wallenberg was not only portrayed as an intelligent, upper-class adventurer in general terms. He also had the ability to elegantly insult a guest by the way he poured wine or served dishes in an unconventional order. 'Raoul Wallenberg almost certainly borrowed some traits from his old film hero', was the conclusion.[80]

Nor is it surprising to discover that Wallenberg has repeatedly been likened to a modern-day Scarlet Pimpernel outside Sweden as well. The comparison is reinforced by the fact that 'elusive', a word closely associated with Baroness Orczy's hero, has also been used to characterize the Swedish diplomat.[81] It is hence no surprise that the Scarlet Pimpernel story has been applied to other individuals who went to great lengths to save Jews and others during the war years. For instance, Oskar Schindler has repeatedly been described as 'the "Scarlet Pimpernel" of the Second World War'.[82] In connection to the defeat of France in 1940, Charles Howard, the 20th Earl of Suffolk, succeeded in bringing industrial diamonds, heavy water, and a number of French scientists from Paris to England. Harold Macmillan, later Conservative Prime Minister from 1957 to 1963, was Charles Howard's contact during the Second World War. In retrospect, Macmillan noted that meeting 'a mixture between Sir Francis Drake and the Scarlet Pimpernel was something altogether out of this world'.[83] Varian Fry, an American who helped hundreds of writers and artists escape the Germans and their allies, is known as 'the American Pimpernel'.[84] Another example is the priest Hugh

---

80 Maria Schottenius, 'Raoul Wallenberg som charmig äventyrare', *Aftonbladet*, 14 February 1983.
81 Smith, *Lost Hero*, p. 92. See also Ellie Tesher, 'Is "Scarlet Pimpernel" still alive?', *Toronto Star*, 20 October 1979; Alan Patient, 'The Swedish Pimpernel', *The Listener*, 20 March 1980; 'Hunting the Pimpernel', *The Daily Telegraph*, 2 May 1980 and Bauer, *Jews for Sale?*, p. 234.
82 Crowe, *Oskar Schindler*, p. 541.
83 Harold Macmillan, *The Blast of War 1939–1945*, p. 102.
84 That the Scarlet Pimpernel story is still well known in Britain is clear, for example in the fact that the main British title of Andy Marino's book about

O'Flaherty, who was active in the Vatican from 1943 to 1945. During that time, he hid downed bomber crews and escaped prisoners of war while also helping the Italian Resistance, all while the SS was working to stop him. His fate was the subject of a 1983 television film. The title was a given: *The Scarlet and the Black*.[85]

The history-cultural chain of the Scarlet Pimpernel does not end there; it can easily be extended to include Harald Edelstam, 'the ambassador turned Pimpernel'.[86] A member of the Swedish aristocracy, he first trained to become an officer alongside his friend and colleague Per Anger. Unlike Wallenberg, Edelstam made working for the Swedish Foreign Office (Utrikesdepartementet, UD) his career. He had his first posting during the Second World War. During his time at the Swedish Legation in Berlin, he reacted to the fact that so little was being done by Swedes when Jews came asking for protection. He was soon transferred to Norway, where he acted to rescue Norwegian Jews and Resistance fighters. His often very bold rescue actions led to Edelstam being given the honorary name of 'the Black Pimpernel', an appellation which has since been applied to Nelson Mandela.

The action that made Edelstam famous occurred when he was ambassador to Chile. The Swedish government supported President Salvador Allende, who was overthrown in a military coup on 11 September 1973. Edelstam soon began working to provide protection for those persecuted by the junta's military and police. His efforts saved hundreds of left-wing sympathizers from torture, imprisonment, or execution.[87] His unorthodox methods aroused

---

Varian Fry is *American Pimpernel*. In the United States, by contrast, it was instead called *A Quiet American: The Secret War of Varian Fry*, a reference to Graham Greene's famous 1955 novel *The Quiet American*.

85 At the time when the TV drama was broadcast, criticism of the Vatican was intense. Investigations had shown that the Catholic Church was doing too little to stop what was happening. In some local cases Catholic priests had even encouraged the genocide, and after 1945 the Vatican had protected and helped perpetrators escape. Because the TV drama was set in the Vatican, it instead gave the impression that Catholic Church workers were generally involved in rescue operations, which probably contributed to the Vatican's permission for CBS to film on location in the Vatican, according to Arthur Unger in 'Mini series dramatizes quiet acts of heroism in Nazi-occupied Rome', *The Christian Science Monitor*, 1 February 1983.

86 Kristen Bjørnkjær, 'Ambassadøren der blev pimpernel', *Information*, 25 September 2007.

87 Lindahl, 'Harald Edelstam', pp. 374–395; Edelstam, *Janusansiktet*, pp. 151–164, 426–445.

the displeasure of the new rulers, who made him *persona non grata* and deported him.

Edelstam was also far from universally appreciated at the UD. One of the highest-ranking officials there, Wilhelm Wachtmeister, was frustrated over Edelstam's acting without paying any attention to instructions from the UD. Instead, it was his own humanitarian passions plus strong support from the student left – the invisible Black Pimpernel was said to have turned radically 'red' – that drove him: 'He behaved like some kind of miniature Raoul Wallenberg', was Wachtmeister's grim assessment.[88] Upon Edelstam's return home, however, the tone was different. He was warmly welcomed, especially by the Chilean refugees who had come to Sweden. Within a generally radical social climate, his meeting in 1974 with Cuban leader Fidel Castro was described as an encounter between 'two heroes of the people'.[89] Another comparison was made between Wallenberg and Edelstam as examples of men of duty who did not hesitate to depart from the rules and overstep their authority in order to save lives.[90] And when journalist Eric Sjöquist published *Affären Raoul Wallenberg* in 1974, his colleague Bang (Barbro Alving) wrote a very favourable review of the book in which she asked why Swedish diplomats in Moscow had been so feeble in their actions: in the late 1940s and 1950s, there was 'not a shadow of a Harald Edelstam in the Swedish Embassy'.[91]

The favourable reviews of the early 1970s have been echoed on subsequent occasions when Edelstam has been praised, sometimes in his own right, sometimes in connection with other role models such as Raoul Wallenberg.[92] The similarities between Wallenberg's

---

88 Wachtmeister, *Som jag såg det*, p. 179. See also the chapter 'Mumrikarnas hämnd' in Fors, *Svarta nejlikan*, pp. 326–328. Edelstam was also controversial in subsequent posts, including when he was mediator between the Philippines and Malaysia over a disputed area in Borneo and when he was Swedish ambassador to Afghanistan; see Edelstam, *Janusansiktet*, pp. 376–379; Karlsson, *Ett utrikes liv*, pp. 77, 79.
89 'Två folkhjältar i Havanna', *Vecko-Journalen*, 1974:6, 35. See Lindahl, 'Harald Edelstam', p. 392.
90 Hemming Sten, 'Raoul Wallenberg' (interview with Gunnar Möllerstedt), *Expressen*, 22 February 1974.
91 Barbro Alving, 'Sveket mot Raoul Wallenberg', *Expressen*, 20 September 1974.
92 See e.g. Kjell Wigers, 'Vi är olika värda ända in i döden', *Expressen*, 9 September 2013; Ola Larsmo, 'Därför borde det anses som "osvenskt" att vara nationalist', *Dagens Nyheter*, 28 January 206; Jan Eliasson, José

and Edelstam's deeds were particularly emphasized at the premiere of the Swedish-Danish-Mexican production of *The Black Pimpernel* (2007), where it was stated that they had become role models 'when risking their lives and/or careers to save thousands of unknown people from imprisonment, torture, and death'.[93] It is worth adding that both men were allegedly targets of German assassination attempts during the Second World War.[94] However, the attempt to present Edelstam as a 1970s version of the Scarlet Pimpernel did not do him any good at the time. For example, Wachtmeister repeated his criticism of Harald Edelstam almost verbatim in a debate with Edelstam's son Erik, which was published in conjunction with the Swedish premiere of *The Black Pimpernel*.[95]

Erik Edelstam was critical not only of the UD's treatment of his father but also to some extent of the film itself, although he was its leading defender.[96] He stressed that while *The Black Pimpernel* was a work of fiction, it was also an attempt to portray a hero in the same way that Raoul Wallenberg and Oskar Schindler had been depicted in *Good Evening, Mr. Wallenberg* and *Schindler's List*.[97] Edelstam senior's kinship with both the Scarlet Pimpernel and Raoul Wallenberg was also stressed in a scene in which the

---

Goni Carrasco and Eva Zetterberg, 'Låt den 6 oktober bli en dag till minnet av Zaida Catalán', *Dagens Nyheter*, 8 March 2020; Per Kudo, 'Den gråtande ambassadören blottlägger UD:s blinda fläck', *Svenska Dagbladet*, 21 June 2020.

93 Cordelia Edvardson, 'Världen behöver alla sina hjältar', *Svenska Dagbladet*, 22 November 2007. Other tributes to Edelstam include one made by Isabel Allende in an interview with Ole Hoff-Lund in *Svenska Dagbladet*, 11 September 2007 and Wolfgang Hansson, 'Räddade – av den svenske rebellen' (interview with Carolina Hultgren), *Aftonbladet*, 14 September 2007; Åke Lundgren, 'Svarta nejlikan räddade mitt liv' (interview with Carolina Hultgren), *Expressen*, 15 September 2007; Ana Martinez, 'Vi behöver fler Edelstam', *Expressen*, 19 September 2007, and Ola Larsmo, 'Är nationalism osvenskt?', *Dagens Nyheter*, 5 June 2008. The link between Raoul Wallenberg and Harald Edelstam had been made earlier, including by Pierre Schori; see Jonas Sima, 'Pierre Schori berättar i TV i kväll: "Jag grät när jag såg Wallenberg-filmen"', *Expressen*, 7 October 1990.

94 Lindahl, 'Harald Edelstam', p. 381.

95 Wilhelm Wachtmeister, 'Jag ifrågasätter Edelstams omdöme', *Expressen*, 15 September 2007.

96 Erik Edelstam, 'Pappa räddade liv – blev mobbad på UD' and 'Era skildringar av pappa är pinsamma', *Expressen*, 11 and 16 September 2007.

97 Mats Fors, 'Filmen är en fiktion', *Expressen*, 12 September 2007.

Chile of the early 1970s is complemented by one of his memories of a rescue operation of Jews during the Second World War. The biography of Edelstam published two years later was structured in a similar way. Its author, Mats Fors, focused mainly on Norway from 1942 to 1944 and Chile in 1973, which had consequences for the overall narrative.[98] In other words, 'the Norway and Chile events sit on opposite ends of a thin seesaw that is in danger of cracking', claimed one reviewer, who also pointed out that neither Edelstam nor Norwegian Resistance fighters have published a written account of the Swedish diplomat's exploits in Norway. The result was that Fors had difficulty integrating the protagonist into the larger sequence of events there.[99]

Edelstam's status as a hero was not greatly helped by *The Black Pimpernel*. It attracted few viewers to Swedish and Chilean cinemas, perhaps because the story of Edelstam never 'gets under the surface of the material', as one reviewer put it.[100] Unsurprisingly, the Swedish press compared the film to *Good Evening, Mr. Wallenberg*, to the disadvantage of *The Black Pimpernel*. Film critic Mats Johnson recalled the complexity that Stellan Skarsgård had brought to Wallenberg in the former film and said it was completely lacking in *The Black Pimpernel*.[101] Recurring complaints were that the chopped-up chronology made it difficult to follow the plot and that the choice of Michael Nyquist in the lead role was less than successful. One reviewer summed up his cinema visit by saying that 'The only image that lingers on the retina is that of a greying playboy on a history-less Tintin adventure in a foreign land'.[102]

Edelstam's inability to match Wallenberg's level is not only, or even mainly, related to the reception of a film about him.

---

98 Fors, *Svarta nejlikan*, passim.
99 Tommy Gustafsson, review of Fors, *Svarta nejlikan: Harald Edelstam – en berättelse om mod, humanitet och passion*, *Historisk Tidskrift*, 2011:2, 407–409.
100 Gunnar Rehlin, 'The Black Pimpernel', *Variety*, 29 October 2007.
101 Mats Johnson, 'Svarta nejlikan', *Göteborgs-Posten*, 13 September 2007.
102 Michael Tapper, 'Svarta nejlikan (2)', *SydSvenska Dagbladet, Snällposten*, 13 September 2007. For similar views see Jeanette Gentele, 'Otydligt om Chilekuppen', *Svenska Dagbladet*, 13 September 2007; Susanne Sigroth-Lambe, 'Svårgreppbar nejlika', *Upsala Nya Tidning*, 13 September 2007; Jan-Olov Andersson, 'Chilekuppens svenske hjälte', *Aftonbladet*, 14 September 2007; and Eva af Geijerstam, 'Svarta nejlikan', *Dagens Nyheter*, 14 September 2007. For an extensive discussion of the film's format, contents, and reception, see Gustafsson, 'The Black Pimpernel', pp. 18–26.

# The Scarlet Pimpernel

One important difference in how posterity views the two men is that rescuing Chilean leftist activists does not have the same exalted position in history culture as does rescuing Jews during the Second World War. In addition, Edelstam outlived his mission and did not die until 1989, which does not fit in with the heroic ideal, as few heroic role models live to the age of 76. A further explanation is that Edelstam was, and remained, a diplomat. Wallenberg, as we know, did not have this background, and he was not given a chance to choose to continue on this path. Throughout his career, Edelstam had the reputation of being a black sheep in the diplomatic fold and was a sharp contrast to the 'mummies at the UD', to quote *The Black Pimpernel*'s director, Ulf Hultberg.[103] Edelstam undeniably shared this activist approach with Wallenberg. The problem in the creation of the former's heroic image is that while he remained something of a rebel, he still remained within the diplomatic corps, which he was both distanced from and distanced himself from.

That this corps is not associated with heroic deeds has been made clear, if not before, then certainly in conjunction with the broadcast of the Swedish drama documentary series *Diplomaterna* ['The diplomats'] on Swedish public service television in the spring of 2009. Scenes from exclusive parties, beach shots of a UD official surrounded by scantily clad women, and racist remarks made by him and his colleagues during a Nigerian state visit to Sweden resulted in outraged comments about 'gin & tonic drifters'.[104] Rebuttals of this television portrayal were offered in response. The UD's defence lawyers stressed that hard-working civil servants make up the core of the Swedish diplomatic service, adding that working for poor pay and with little support from the Swedish Government Offices, they try to defend Swedish interests around the world.[105] Other commentators drew a distinct line between

---

103 Karoline Eriksson, 'Hur var det att filma på plats i Santiago?' (interview with Ulf Hultberg), *Svenska Dagbladet*, 11 September 2007. See also Fors's statement on p. 27 in *Svarta nejlikan* that Edelstam's life had 'a shimmer of drama and adventure that was lacking in the more sedate but far more successful careers of many of his colleagues at the UD'.
104 Gunilla Kinn, 'Gin & tonic-glidarna ger UD dåligt rykte', *Expressen*, 9 February 2009; Mats Carlbom, 'Tv-serie om diplomaterna upprör', *Dagens Nyheter*, 4 March 2009; Barbro Hedvall, 'UD: Var är omdömet?', *Dagens Nyheter*, 5 March 2009.
105 Karin Arbsjö, 'UD diskuterar åtgärder efter SVT:s serie', *Sydsvenskan*, 3 March 2009; Jan Eliasson, Rolf Ekéus and Sven Hirdman, 'Verklighetsförfalskning

worshipping idols and heroes on the one hand and diplomats on the other. To the extent that there were any exceptions, they were Edelstam acting the part of the Scarlet Pimpernel in Santiago de Chile in 1973 and Raoul Wallenberg – although the latter was, as one Swedish journalist asserted in sweeping terms, 'more CIA agent than diplomat'.[106]

These comments can certainly be seen as a media storm in teacup, but they can and should be regarded in a wider context. In the light of revelations and debates about Sweden's lack of strict neutrality during both the Second World War and the Cold War, there is a great need to remember those Swedish diplomats who did follow in the footsteps of the Scarlet Pimpernel. One of the most striking expressions of this position is the art-works displayed in the Southern Connecting Room in the Riksdag (Parliament) building in Stockholm. An accompanying written text says that they aim to remind us of 'the need for humanity, yesterday and today', with a starting point in three Swedes who personified these qualities: Raoul Wallenberg, Folke Bernadotte, and Harald Edelstam. Although the three men are given equal space in the text, there is no doubt that Wallenberg is the primary example of the theme which permeated the commemorative year dedicated to him in 2012, namely that 'one man can make a difference'.[107]

\*

There is much to suggest that the tale of the aristocrat who hid behind a guileless facade and risked his life to save others – a story which remained very popular for most of the twentieth century – is no longer so viable today. The Scarlet Pimpernel

---

av Sveriges Television', *Dagens Nyheter*, 5 March 2009; Mats Carlbom, 'Jag förstår alla inom UD som känner sig kränkta' (interview with State Secretary for Foreign Affairs Frank Belfrage), *Dagens Nyheter*, 8 March 2009. See also Ulf Zander, 'Ett fredsälskande folk: Diplomaternas historielösa självbild sitter djupt rotad', *Sydsvenskan*, 2 March 2009. The debate continued independently following a proposal to close the Swedish Consulate in New York; see e.g. Urban Ahlin and Jan Eliasson, 'Sverige backar in i framtiden', *Svenska Dagbladet*, 26 April 2009 and 'New York?, New York?' (editorial), *Sydsvenskan*, 27 April 2009.

106 Staffan Heimerson, 'Hasse Ericson går igen och UD-männen är rasande', *Aftonbladet*, 15 March 2009.

107 'One person can make a difference: An introduction to the works of art in the Southern Connecting Room', www.riksdagen.se/globalasse

novels are no longer being published in such large print runs as they used to be, and no new films about him have been made for decades. Nevertheless, the comparison between the fictional Scarlet Pimpernel and the real Raoul Wallenberg is relevant, not only, or even mainly, because the latter was inspired by Leslie Howard's *Pimpernel Smith*. The Swedish historian Kristian Gerner has captured the link between the two heroes with great perspicacity. His starting point is that Wallenberg may also have seen the film *The Petrified Forest* (1936), which starred Leslie Howard as a disillusioned, roaming British writer. After taking out a life insurance policy, with the waitress at a coffee shop in a godforsaken Arizona slum as its beneficiary, he allows himself to be shot by a gangster, whereupon the waitress is able to train and become the artist she has long dreamed of being. Howard's and Wallenberg's deeds are certainly of very different kinds, but

> the film hero Leslie Howard played the role of 'Wallenberg' even before Raoul Wallenberg became Saint Wallenberg. Spiteful historians have insinuated that Wallenberg was trying to play the hero but was merely an insignificant cog in a larger machine. However, he was not a dandy pretending to be a film hero. He wanted to save – and succeeded in saving – many lives. The reality surpassed the fiction. Raoul Wallenberg became the Scarlet Pimpernel. The declaration of sainthood came when Raoul Wallenberg was designated by Yad Vashem as one of 'The Righteous Among the Nations'.[108]

---

ts/15.-bestall-och-ladda-ned/informationsmaterial/en-manniska-kan-gora-skillnad-eng.pdf (accessed 21 January 2022).
108 Kristian Gerner, 'Helgon och agent', *Judisk Krönika*, 2012:4, 24.

# Chapter 4
# Raoul Wallenberg and Sweden: from bone of contention to brand

Asked when the Swedish Foreign Office (Utrikesdepartementet, UD) will have paid off its debt to Raoul Wallenberg caused by its delayed action in the immediate post-war years, the Swedish diplomat and former Minister for Foreign Affairs Jan Eliasson replied: 'Never.'[1] The debt remains despite the process of coming to terms with what had been Sweden's policy at that time, plus the apology made in 2001 by Sweden's then Prime Minister Göran Persson to Wallenberg's family.[2] This pattern is a familiar product of the official politics of memory since the turn of the last century, according to which past wrongs are publicly held up to legal scrutiny. Heads of state, usually born after the wrongs occurred, have apologized to the victims and their families in the hope of achieving closure and reconciliation. On the basis of modern moral values, and with the Second World War as the main hurdle, political leaders have bowed their heads and begged survivors for forgiveness.[3]

The list of Swedes who deserve a modern-day apology could be made longer. The wealthy entrepreneur Axel Wenner-Gren, who in addition to his business activities had attempted to broker peace in the summer of 1939, was blacklisted three years later by the British and US governments for his supposed inappropriately good relationships with Nazi luminaries. No evidence that Wenner-Gren was a German spy has ever been presented, even though the material collected on him in US archives eventually became almost as extensive as the UD's Swedish files on Wallenberg. The diplomat

---

1 Ricki Neuman, 'Raoul Wallenberg är hemma igen' (interview with Jan Eliasson and others), *Svenska Dagbladet*, 10 June 2010.
2 See e.g. '"Vi måste fortsätta söka efter sanningen": Göran Persson bad Wallenbergs anhöriga om ursäkt', *Aftonbladet*, 12 January 2001.
3 See e.g. Karlsson, *Europeiska möten med historien*, pp. 269–280.

Leif Leifland, who had good insights into both cases, noted a similar 'anxious evasiveness' on the part of Swedish decision-makers vis-à-vis the great powers, irrespective of whether they were located in the West or the East. He stressed that this comparison should not be carried too far: after all, the reprehensible actions of Sweden's coalition government in the Wenner-Gren case did not have such fatal effects as the Swedish passivity in the Wallenberg case probably had in the immediate post-war years.[4]

The case of Wallenberg also differs from that of Wenner-Gren, and most others, in that the vanished diplomat has been discussed with considerable continuity in Sweden. For a long time it was an infected bone of contention in domestic politics, the main issue being how neutral Sweden should relate to its powerful neighbour and superpower to the east, the Soviet Union. Swedish politicians and UD representatives failed to persuade Soviet and Russian politicians to initiate and, after the dissolution of the Soviet Union, to fully support an investigation into the Wallenberg case. In retrospect, the official Swedish reaction to the Soviet capture of Wallenberg, especially from 1945 to 1947, had obvious shortcomings. It cannot be ruled out that the feeble action in the first few years after his disappearance led to neglected opportunities to secure his release.

That conclusion was also reached by the government-appointed commission of enquiry which presented its extensive findings in 2003. The enquiry's chairman, civil servant and Liberal politician Ingmar Eliasson, expressed doubts about the report's blunt title: *Ett diplomatiskt misslyckande* ['A failure of diplomacy']. His biography suggests that he favoured a title more in line with that proposed by Bertil Ohlin, also a member of the Liberal Party and its leader from 1944 to 1967, who in 1975 described the early actions as regards the Wallenberg case of those in charge of Sweden's foreign policy as 'a serious mistake'. The other members of the Eliasson commission supported the title 'A failure of diplomacy' because it was important to 'call a spade a spade'. The then Minister for Foreign Affairs Anna Lindh, who was assassinated the year the enquiry was published, made no attempts to defend her party colleague and predecessor as Foreign Minister, Östen Undén, whose actions were heavily criticized in the enquiry. In retrospect but in the same

---

[4] Leifland, *Svartlistningen av Axel Wenner-Gren*, pp. 9, 15, 17, 55–58, 253–254.

spirit, the then Prime Minister Göran Persson, like Lindh a Social Democrat, stated that although he had not apologized until 2001, he had repeatedly expressed regret for the Swedish authorities' actions in the Wallenberg case. Nor did any other politician object to the commission's findings. Instead: 'This report was placed on file without debate', Eliasson noted, some ten years later.[5]

The admission, however, was extremely belated. As we shall see, previously published White Papers had presented a totally different picture of Sweden's actions. The longstanding unwillingness to come to terms with this narrative has probably contributed to a still lingering frustration. Susanne Berger, an American scholar based in Germany, is one of those commentators who have repeatedly criticized Swedish politicians, from the early post-war period up to the present time, for not making enough of an effort to get the leaderships of the Soviet Union and then Russia to reveal once and for all the truth about what happened to Wallenberg. Berger argues that no Swedish government has attempted to exert sufficient pressure on the Soviet and Russian leaders to grant access to important, still classified information. She firmly rejects the idea that the Wallenberg mystery cannot be solved.[6]

---

5 Eliasson, *Jag vet var jag kommer ifrån*, p. 297; Eliasson et al., *Ett diplomatiskt misslyckande*, passim. Bertil Ohlin's assessment of the official handling of the Wallenberg case is found in his 1975 autobiography, *Bertil Ohlins memoarer 1940–1951*, p. 72, and Göran Persson's conclusion is in Fichtelius, *Aldrig ensam, alltid ensam*, p. 309. See also Palmklint and Larsson (eds), *Raoul Wallenberg*. For reactions to the last-mentioned see e.g. 'Regeringen ville tro på humanitet' and 'Undfallenhet mot Sovjet röd tråd för Sverige', both published in *Upsala Nya Tidning*, 1 April 2001. Some of the reactions to the enquiry led by Eliasson, which also noted the diplomatic failure, include Dan Nilsson, 'Wallenberg ett politiskt fiasko', *Svenska Dagbladet*, 5 March 2003; Erik Magnusson, 'Ministrar kritiseras för Raoul Wallenbergs öde', *Sydsvenskan*, 5 March 2003; Barbro Hedvall, 'En makalös inkompetens', *Dagens Nyheter*, 6 March 2003; Hans Wolf, 'Ett mänskligt misslyckande', *Dagens forskning* 2003:7, 16. The enquiries also attracted international attention; see e.g. 'Wallenberg panel says Sweden should have pressed Moscow more', *The New York Times*, 13 January 2001 and 'Panel suggests Swedes did not do enough to save Wallenberg', *Los Angeles Times*, 13 January 2001.

6 Berger, 'Raoul Wallenberg and the Complexities of Historic Truth'; Berger, 'Stuck in Neutral'. See also Susanne Berger, 'UD offrade Raoul Wallenberg', *Dagens Nyheter*, 17 December 2000; Susanne Berger, 'Don't mention the war', *Dagens Nyheter*, 1 February 2006; Susanne Berger, 'Svensken i Korpus 2', *Dagens Nyheter*, 23 January 2007; Susanne Berger and

Berger has certainly pointed out many flaws in the Swedish actions, but the analysis should not stop there. In a discussion about historical justice and comparisons between the historian and the judge, Martin Wiklund points out that it is important to try to understand the actors of that time on the basis of their operating conditions. That, however, does not prohibit the making of overall moral and ideological judgements. In a scenario where history is on trial in a court-like situation, justice may, for the historian, 'function as a normative ideal that favours impartiality without implying indifference or value neutrality'.[7] But if and when history is used as a moral yardstick, this balancing act becomes difficult because a particularly tricky question is *whose* morality is at issue – that of the historical actors, or our own moral perceptions in the early twenty-first century? As mentioned at the beginning of this book, it is unavoidable for history to be a dual thought process. This process is what 'gives meaning to the past, on the basis of both the values of that time and our later moral horizon', states Klas-Göran Karlsson.[8] In other words, the Wallenberg case does include moral aspects, but it would be unfortunate if conclusions about it were to be dominated by moralizing in hindsight. It is thus a matter of singling out – as was done in 'A failure of diplomacy' – inadequate actions of diplomat Staffan Söderblom and Minister for Foreign Affairs Östen Undén *and* of placing these actions in the context of the early post-war period in order to better understand why the two men acted as they did. Such contextualization may, for example, provide clues as to why Raoul Wallenberg was not initially granted the same elevated position as another Swedish humanitarian role model, Folke Bernadotte, who, like Wallenberg, made his most important contributions during the final stages of the Second World War.

The ensuing history-cultural explanations embody a degree of divergence. Some are closely associated with Raoul Wallenberg whereas others are bound up with Swedish domestic and foreign

---

Lorraine Borgolini, 'När individens rättigheter står mot statens intressen', *Judisk Krönika*, 2007:4, 19–23; Susanne Berger, 'Sätt press på Ryssland', *Sydsvenskan*, 11 May 2008; Susanne Berger, 'Obesvarade frågor', *Judisk Krönika*, 2009:5, 19–20; 'Interview: Historian Susanne Berger on the fate of Raoul Wallenberg', RadioFreeEuropeRadioLiberty, 12 August 2012 (rferl.org) (accessed 3 January 2022). See also 'The Wallenberg cover-up' (editorial), *The Wall Street Journal*, 11 November 1985.

7 Wiklund, 'The Ideal of Justice and its Significance for Historians as Engaged Intellectuals', pp. 44–62, quotation p. 54.

8 Karlsson, *Europeiska möten med historien*, p. 385.

policies and with general trends in the West, especially regarding the view of the Holocaust. As stated above, the explanations do not excuse the wait-and-see approach of Söderblom, Undén, and other actors; but they do help to shed an explanatory light on their handling of the Wallenberg case.

## Trying to understand the Holocaust

Media reports of the Holocaust's effects were published both in Sweden and in other countries while the genocide was ongoing. Protests against Nazi racial policy were expressed while the Second World War was still raging. As mentioned in the Introduction, these often appeared in Jewish publications, but texts about what was happening were also published in daily newspapers from 1942 onwards.[9] In neutral Sweden, articles about pogroms and persecutions also appeared in some of the major newspapers from 1938 onwards.[10] Even so, it should be emphasized that the Holocaust as we know it today was still largely unknown to the general public when the Second World War was entering its final stages. International research has highlighted the obstacles to these reports becoming widely known because they were often given a low profile in the newspapers, not least because the combined message of these unimaginable reports was not a good fit with prevailing views about journalism. Reporters assigned to writing about the war were expected to report news of a kind germane to established narratives. When news of mass persecution and mass murder began to leak out, journalists were simply not equipped for writing about it. Besides, these reports of the incredible and the unimaginable had to compete for attention with reports of wartime events, refugee flows, and day-to-day news.[11]

Because of the low impact of previous attempts, the people assigned to report from the liberated concentration camps in Germany in the spring of 1945 realized that they would have to do so in new ways. True, the text and photo reports from Bergen-Belsen, Dachau, and other camps had sent shock waves around the

---

9 See e.g. Marcus Ehrenpreis, 'Där de eviga ljusen släcktes: Personliga minnen från förstörda församlingar', *Judisk Tidskrift*, 1944:1, 1–6. See also Tydén, 'Att inte lägga sig i', pp. 125–137.
10 See e.g. Rudberg, *The Swedish Jews and the Holocaust*, pp. 188–200.
11 Kalb, 'Introduction: Journalism and the Holocaust, 1933–1945', pp. 5–12; Leff, *Buried by the Times*, passim.

world, but the strong reactions did not necessarily reflect a general understanding of what had happened, or what had been the motives behind the Nazi extermination policy.[12] Attempts to draw attention to the persisting antisemitism in Sweden led to long debates in the Swedish Parliament, the Riksdag, about legislating against anti-Jewish propaganda. One Riksdag member praised Sweden's official policy of neutrality but criticized 'the official moral neutrality', which meant that too few Swedes protested against lingering antisemitism. Others argued that persecution of Jews was a specifically German phenomenon and had no counterpart in Sweden.[13] In 1947, the tense situation between the British and Jews in Palestine in the immediate post-war years, the difficulties experienced by Jewish refugees seeking new homelands, the pogroms in Poland, and other examples of persistent antisemitism made one writer warn that nothing had been learned. Active evil had been replaced 'by a cold-blooded lack of action that is almost equally frightening'.[14]

The early post-war discussions demonstrate that information is not the same as knowledge. During the Second World War, there had been obvious problems for Jews and non-Jews alike in converting information about the genocide into an understanding of what was really going on, and to what extent. These difficulties persisted in the early post-war years, partly as a result of a reluctance among survivors to talk about their experiences or, among those who were willing, to attract attention. Information that had reached Allied and neutral governments during the war years was often not made public. Another difficulty was understanding the scale of the mass murder that was happening. For example, in 1942 the Swedish diplomat Göran von Otter received a detailed account of the Nazi genocide from Kurt Gerstein, who had joined the SS with the aim of finding out for himself what was going on. The information was

---

12 Zelizer, *Remembering to Forget*, chapter 5. For analyses of these photos in the Swedish press see Max Liljefors, *Bilder av Förintelsen*, pp. 100–104; Liljefors and Zander, 'Det neutrala landet Ingenstans', pp. 220–224; Zander, 'To Rescue or be Rescued', pp. 357–358; Holmila, *Reporting the Holocaust in the British, Swedish and Finnish Press, 1945–50*, pp. 37–45.
13 Marcus Ehrenpreis, 'Sveriges antijudiska kampförbund' and 'Mot antijudisk hetspropaganda' (republication of the Riksdag statements of 29 January and 9 April 1946), *Judisk Tidskrift*, 1946:1, 1–6 and 1946:4, 93–104.
14 Mia Leche, 'Vår gemensamma skam', *Judisk Tidskrift*, 1947:10, 276–278, quotation p. 276. See also Anne-Marie Lundström, 'Nazismen som tidssjukdom', *Samtid och Framtid*, 1946:5, 300–307.

passed on to staff at the UD, but no one there or in the Swedish government took any immediate action to pursue the matter. This inertia was due to a combination of reasons, including the difficulty of verifying Gerstein's information, an unwillingness to contribute to what might be an example of 'atrocity propaganda', and political conflicts over whether or not Sweden should make any official protests against Germany.[15]

This lack of interest was not total. For example, Bo Enander and Franz Arnheim published a book entitled *Så härskade herrefolket* ['How the master race ruled'] immediately after the end of the war, a book which included accounts of the course and consequences of the Holocaust.[16] The Nuremberg Trials of 1945 to 1946 were also significant as they dealt with the Nazi genocide for the first time in a non-Jewish context. One aspect of the trials was the supplying of detailed historical background information about entrenched antisemitic prejudices. During the proceedings the prosecutors also repeatedly referred to the mass murders of Jews and, although less frequently, also of Roma. In addition, US lawyers highlighted the mass executions performed by the *Einsatzgruppen* death squads on the Eastern Front in the first phase of the Holocaust. However, the lawyers had not yet grasped the difference between the concentration camps, where life was certainly brutal and many people died, and the extermination camps on Polish soil, where the aim was the industrial mass murder of as many Jews and 'undesirables' as possible. During the Nuremberg Trials, the stated aim was to concentrate on the Nazi plan to launch a war of aggression. Even though there were recurring accounts of abuses of the Jews, these were not given the status of a separate category of crime but were classified under 'crimes against humanity' or 'war crimes'. None of the lawyers was able to situate the Nazi crimes against the Jewish people as part of the overall Nazi ideology, whose very foundation was antisemitism.[17]

---

15 Koblik, *The Stones Cry Out*, pp. 79–115, 141–165; Zetterberg, 'Staffan Söderblom', p. 266; Åmark, *Främlingar på tåg*, pp. 175–199.
16 Enander and Arnheim, *Så härskade herrefolket*, passim. The book attracted the attention of a number of contemporary reviewers, see e.g. Ragna Aberstén-Schiratzki's review in *Judisk Tidskrift*, 1945:6, 189–191 and Lena Kaplan, 'Utrotningen av Europas judar – en översikt', *Judisk Krönika*, 1945:5–6, 73–80. See also Kvist Geverts, 'Tracing the Holocaust in Early Writings in Post-War Sweden', pp. 139–161.
17 Marrus, 'The Holocaust at Nuremberg', pp. 5–41. See Levy and Sznaider, *The Holocaust and Memory in the Global Age*, pp. 57–95.

## Wallenberg and Sweden

The encounter with grievously sick and exhausted women in refugee camps made a strong impression on a number of writers. Their texts told Swedish readers about the urgent requirements associated with rehabilitating people who had been subjected to so much cruelty. It was a major challenge to integrate them into Swedish society, not least because of the hostilities that re-emerged, for instance when Jewish women were harassed by Catholic Poles who had themselves been victims of Nazism but who were still antisemites.[18] One of the many Swedes who became involved in assisting the humanitarian effort – work that was severely tested when tens of thousands of survivors of the extermination and concentration camps arrived in Sweden in the spring of 1945 – was the influential Social Democratic politician and reformer Alva Myrdal. She argued that the physical presence of the victims of Nazi genocidal policies helped to awaken Swedes once and for all to the consequences of the ideal of a society freed from what Hitler and his followers had termed 'subhumans' unfit to live. In the summer of 1945, she wrote: 'Finally, the stench, the hunger, the agony from the German concentration camps have come crashing even into our Swedish consciousness.'[19]

Even so, this close contact with survivors did not automatically produce insights into what had been happening outside the safety of Sweden. The reception of the refugees alternated between considerateness and thoughtlessness. The reporting focused at least as much on the high quality of modern Swedish aid efforts as on the horrors that the new arrivals had endured.[20] The apparent reactions of the alleged perpetrators dominated in the Swedish press, but less attention was paid to the crimes they were acused of, including the Holocaust. As Finnish historian Antero Holmila has noted, as the crimes of individual perpetrators were being highlighted there was simultaneously an intense debate, also raging in the immediate post-war years, about whether it was reasonable to speak of a collective German guilt. There was no lack of comments about the extermination of Jews, but these were, to all intents and purposes, excusively associated with Germany

---

18 Giloh, 'En humanitär tiger', pp. 90–98; Tora Nordström-Bonnier, 'För oss är kriget inte vunnet', *Expressen*, 22 June 1945.
19 Alva Myrdal, 'Barbarernas offer och straff', *Judisk Tidskrift*, 1945:7, 202.
20 Zander, 'Efterskrift' (2005), pp. 227–233; Zander, 'Dire Strait?', pp. 221–247.

and Nazism.[21] Remarks that antisemitism was a widespread phenomenon and that '[t]he Jewish question is the common shame of every country and every people' were among the exceptions.[22]

It was thus rare in Sweden for commentators to raise aspects of complicity or passivity. Instead, the press coverage of the Nuremberg Trials emphasized that Swedes had also suffered during the war and were therefore victims of Nazism, too.[23] In the following years, however, scores were settled with individuals who had sided with the Nazis. Historian Johan Östling stresses that these experiences of Nazism took on great importance in post-war Sweden. One way in which this development was expressed was through total or secondary stigmatization. The former was applied to individuals who were branded as 'Hitler's Swedish lackeys', and who continued to defend Nazism after the war ended in 1945. Secondary stigmatization mainly affected cultural figures, such as the literary critic Fredrik Böök and the singer and actress Zarah Leander, both of whom had more or less openly embraced the German cause. The stigma of Nazism also affected the historian of ideas Erich Wittenberg. In a high-profile debate in the late 1940s and 1950s, his application for an associate professorship was rejected despite his extensive scholarly output. Wittenberg represented German national conservatism and philosophical idealism. Consequently, he was associated with Nazism and the danger of its return. That he had firmly denounced Nazism on multiple occasions, and that as a Jew he had been forced to abandon his academic career in Germany and flee to Sweden in 1935, did not help his cause. At that time, fear of remnants of the Nazi ideology – in the Wittenberg case in the form of guilt by association – was stronger than any Swedish solidarity with victims of the Holocaust.[24]

One reason why the Holocaust did not play a prominent role in the Nuremberg Trials, or in post-war societies in general, was the continuing lack of adequate words to describe what had happened.

---

21 Holmila, *Reporting the Holocaust in the British, Swedish and Finnish Press, 1945–50*, pp. 89–106; Antero Holmila, '"A Hellish Nightmare"', pp. 163–187.
22 Mia Leche, 'Vår gemensamma skam', *Judisk Tidskrift*, 1947:10, 276–278, quotation p. 278. For a similar perspective but with an American starting point see Henry Morgenthau, 'De indirekt ansvariga för utrotningen av 6.000.000 judar', *Judisk Krönika*, 1947:10, 181–186.
23 Tydén, 'Att inte lägga sig i', pp. 143–144.
24 Östling, *Sweden After Nazism*, pp. 138–145, 148–150.

'Genocide' was launched in 1944, but it took a number of years for the term to become widely established. Similarly, 'Holocaust' as a concept associated with the Nazi genocide was only adopted in the late 1950s. It came into wider use after the US television drama of the same name made its triumphant progress around the world in 1978–1979. As in other Western countries, the *Holocaust* television series engendered a large number of articles when it was shown on Swedish television in the spring of 1979. Only a few of these addressed aspects of the Holocaust related to Sweden, such as Swedish refugee policy before and during the Second World War, or the witness accounts that had reached Swedish ears early on. Most of the writers perceived the Holocaust as a historical phenomenon associated solely with Nazism and Germany.[25] With a few exceptions, it was not until the 1990s that questions about Sweden's actions prior to and during the Second World War began to be debated, the main ingredients being criticism of the restrictive refugee policies and the pragmatic policies of negotiation and neutrality – policies to which critics have referred as policies of yielding or adaptation.[26]

## In the shadow of Folke Bernadotte

In Swedish history culture, events such as the efforts to feed the starving Greek population in 1941–1942 or the actions of the 'Warsaw Swedes', who served as couriers for the Polish Resistance in order to spread information about the Holocaust, have only gained attention on a few occasions, or only in the early twenty-first century. From an early stage, the spotlight has primarily focused on Folke Bernadotte and Raoul Wallenberg. One indication to that effect is that these two role models have repeatedly been discussed together. It has been said that Bernadotte and Wallenberg became acquainted before the war when both men were working in the United States.[27] However, their link was an indirect one and was connected with a 1944 proposal to send Bernadotte as a Red Cross representative to protect Jews in Hungary. Instead, the task was assigned to Valdemar Langlet, with whom Wallenberg later collaborated.[28]

---

25 Zander, '*Holocaust* at the Limits', pp. 277–283.
26 Zander, *Fornstora dagar, moderna tider*, pp. 443–455. See Åmark, *Att bo granne med ondskan*, pp. 291–297.
27 Rudolph Philipp, 'Lever Raoul Wallenberg – människokärlekens partisan?', *Året Runt*, 1947:25, 9.
28 Bauer, *Jews for Sale?*, p. 232; Runberg, *Valdemar Langlet*, pp. 44–45.

One important difference between the respective situations of the two men was that the Wallenberg case was coloured from the outset by the realities of the Cold War, including Sweden's fragile relations with the new superpower of the Baltic Sea region, the Soviet Union. By contrast, Bernadotte was initially an unproblematic figure. This 'man of destiny', who in the final stages of the war had enjoyed 'the confidence of both sides', had bravely ventured into the wolf's lair and negotiated with the egregious SS chief Heinrich Himmler in order to carry out 'this magnificent humanitarian operation, which is a credit to the Swedish name'.[29] After the end of the war, Bernadotte published several best-selling pieces in which he recounted his memories of meetings with Himmler and of the perilous rescue operations in northern Germany in the spring of 1945. Admittedly, protests were heard early on that Count Bernadotte was highlighting his own efforts at the expense of other Red Cross workers. Another dilemma was Bernadotte's favourable attitude towards SS General Walter Schellenberg, whom Jacob Wallenberg had contacted in 1944 to ask him to protect Raoul Wallenberg from his hardline and ruthless SS colleagues in Budapest.[30] In his introduction to the general's posthumously published autobiography, the British historian Alan Bullock acerbically observed: 'On certain subjects Schellenberg maintains a discreet silence'.[31] Nor did Bernadotte acknowledge the involvement in, or at least the extensive knowledge of, the mass murder of Jews that a man in Schellenberg's position would have had. Bernadotte's testimony during the Nuremberg Trials largely adhered to the SS general's story that his had been the voice of reason that had worked on Heinrich Himmler and Ernst Kaltenbrunner until they had agreed to release prisoners from the concentration camps. Folke Bernadotte's endorsement of such a historical narrative was controversial to the highest degree.[32]

---

29  Hugo Björk, 'Folke Bernadotte, ödets man, har båda parters förtroende', *Stockholms Tidningen*, 2 May 1945; Ragna Abersteén-Schiratzki, 'I människokärlekens tjänst' (review of Folke Bernadotte's *Slutet*), *Judisk Tidskrift*, 1945:8, 243.
30  Carlberg, *Raoul Wallenberg*, p. 268.
31  Alan Bullock, 'Introduction' to Walter Schellenberg's *The Schellenberg Memoirs*, p. 13.
32  On Folke Bernadotte's favourable attitude towards Schellenberg see Deland, *En godtycklig historia*, pp. 16–17. Schellenberg went back to a story that resembled the one he had used in Nuremberg; it is found, e.g., in an edited

The fact, however, remained: Bernadotte had brought back victims of the Nazi regime who were successfully being cared for in Sweden. This 'proved' that Swedish hospitals and their staff were among the best in the whole world. The rescue operation gave the Swedish public authorities support for their argument that Swedish humanitarian efforts, which had been widely publicized in the aftermath of the First World War with Elsa Brändström as the figurehead, had not been a one-off event. As the rest of Europe lay in ruins, Swedes – members of the royal family as well as 'ordinary' nurses and bus drivers – had shown that they were prepared to leave their war-spared homeland and risk life and limb to save some of the people who were in desperate straits. As a lauded friend of peace, Folke Bernadotte continued to attract great attention in the context of his Middle East mediation mission, and even more so after Jewish terrorists had assassinated him in Jerusalem in 1948. There was much praise for his efforts in Sweden, and tributes kept pouring in from the rest of the world, too.[33]

One reason why Bernadotte's contributions were so highly lauded at home had to do with the people he saved. Historian Mikael Byström has noted that there was a hierarchy in the view of refugees, a hierarchy based on geographical proximity and ethnicity. Those arriving from neighbouring countries were given the warmest welcome, although sometimes an ambivalence was expressed even about them. Both in speeches in the Swedish Parliament and in newspaper articles, for example, commentators distinguished between 'ordinary Danes' and 'Danish Jews'. The former were accorded the highest status.[34] Most of the people who initially arrived on the White Buses were originally from Denmark and Norway. The Hungarian Jews that Wallenberg had rescued were not as visible in Sweden.

## Neutrality as an ideal

During the Second World War, Sweden's objective was to stay out of the conflict at all costs. This goal was one reason why neutrality

---

version in Heydecker and Leeb, *The Nuremberg Trial*, pp. 43–50, and in *The Schellenberg Memoirs*, pp. 428–454.
33 Zander, 'Efterskrift' (2005), pp. 227–233; Zander, 'To Rescue or be Rescued', pp. 362–364. The phenomenon where victims create heroes is found in many other countries; see further Karlsson, *Med folkmord i fokus*, pp. 36–37.
34 Byström, *En broder, gäst och parasit*, passim.

was highly valued, both as a concrete policy and as an ideal. The Swedish enthusiasm for peace and neutrality can be traced back to the eighteenth century, but it was given a boost by the two world wars. Reports from the horrific battles of 1914–1918 served as an effective antidote to the message of activists who wanted Sweden to join the war on Germany's side.[35] The hope of being able to stay outside once again guided Swedish foreign policy throughout the Second World War. This approach was later labelled 'small-state realism'. The policy pursued under the leadership of Per Albin Hansson was characterized by constant attempts to 'promote the desire for peace at the expense of the desire for resistance'.[36] In practice, this entailed making concessions to whichever warring party happened to be the strongest at the time. In the early years of the war, that meant that Germany could often dictate the terms. Towards the end of the war, the situation was radically different. Sweden's priority then was to improve its foreign-policy relations with the Allies and, not least, with the Soviet Union. The latter had been strained ever since the Finnish Winter War of 1939–1940, when, with the exception of the pro-Moscow Communists, Swedes had sympathized with Finland.

This new orientation not only affected Sweden's handling of the Wallenberg case; perhaps the most obvious consequence was the highly controversial extradition of the Balts in 1945–1946. Sweden's coalition government of the war years had been replaced by a Social Democratic one. Most of the centre-right commentators opposed a far-reaching extradition to the Soviet Union of the Baltic, Soviet, and German soldiers who were currently in Sweden. So, too, did Social Democratic Minister for Foreign Affairs Östen Undén in the initial internal discussions in his party. He changed sides, however, and more than anyone else he became associated with the Swedish decision that most of the interned soldiers – more than the number required under international law – would be shipped east. Undén categorized the Soviet Union as a nation fully governed by the rule of law, whereas 'political maturity was not particularly prominent' in the Soviet-occupied Baltic states. Sweden's future Prime Minister Tage Erlander expressed a similar view, saying that both the British and the Soviets had a sincere ambition to create a lasting peace, which contrasted sharply to the aggressive policies

---

35 Zander, *Fornstora dagar, moderna tider*, pp. 137–144; Sturfelt, *Eldens återsken*, pp. 185–218.
36 Johansson, 'Neutrality and Modernity', p. 165.

pursued in Germany during Hitler's time in power.[37] These and similar statements contrasted sharply with the fate that awaited most of those extradited, who were either executed or shipped off to the Gulag.

The notion that Sweden was a northern utopia that had been spared the horrors of war was reinforced during the Second World War. Christian Günther, Minister for Foreign Affairs in the war-time coalition government, argued that neutrality could primarily be understood as a nation's obligation to be impartial in relation to warring parties; but an even more important aim was to ensure that the country's own territory was protected: under no circumstances should it become a theatre of war or a base for military operations by a foreign power.[38] To be sure, the fact that Sweden had escaped the horrors of war might arouse the envy of less fortunate people and even lead to 'despondent anxiety or unhealthy self-flagellation'. In the future, too, it was of the utmost importance to try to help the less fortunate. Nevertheless, the priority remained self-evident: 'Like every individual, a people may have duties to others; but first and foremost it has obligations to itself, to its own population, its country, its past, and its future.'[39]

Only a few months later, however, Günther expressed doubts as to whether the emphasis on Swedish distinctiveness and the praise of Swedish neutrality might have gone too far. If the country continued to stress its own particular merits, there was a real danger that Swedes would not be in step with the rest of the world once the war was over.[40] There is much to suggest that his warning fell on deaf ears, though. On returning home, Swedes who had experienced the effects of the war were surprised at how little the worldwide conflict had affected their compatriots. This observation was confirmed by a study conducted in the summer of 1944. Most respondents said that although the war had brought some restrictions and limitations, familiar routines had governed their day-to-day existence.[41] Foreign observers were also surprised at the Swedish state of innocence and outsidership. In 1943 Kurt Erich

---

37 Herbert Tingsten, 'Östen Undén', *Dagens Nyheter*, 15 August 1948; Hägglöf, *Berätta för Joen*, p. 196; Berge, *Det kalla kriget i Tidens spegel*, p. 46.
38 Günther, *Tal i en tung tid*, p. 121.
39 Günther, *Tal i en tung tid*, pp. 147–148.
40 Günther, *Tal i en tung tid*, pp. 162–164.
41 Johansson, 'Neutrality and Modernity', pp. 170–171.

Suckert, who wrote under the pseudonym Curzio Malaparte, had travelled from the warring Soviet Union to peaceful Sweden. His semi-documentary *Kaputt*, published the following year, sharply contrasted the horrors of the Eastern Front with a summery Stockholm. In the Swedish capital, he had become aware that even educated and generally well-informed Swedes with an elevated standing in society displayed little insight into what was happening elsewhere in Europe.[42]

A few months after the war ended in Europe, the American journalist Demare Bess reported from Stockholm. She began her article by recounting a meeting she had had with a friend and fellow countryman, an army officer who had recently visited Sweden for the first time. Her friend was impressed by the Swedish standard of living, which differed markedly from that of war-torn Europe and in some respects surpassed that of the United States. This fact bothered him. The Swedes had got off far too lightly compared to other countries which had been occupied and/or fought against Hitler's armies. Writing for an American readership, Bess went on to qualify this harsh verdict. Sweden had essentially pursued a foreign policy like those of other smaller nations such as the Netherlands, Belgium, Denmark, and Norway. However, they had had geography against them, whereas Sweden had benefited from skilful diplomacy and a lot of luck. She admitted that there was some justification for American criticism of Sweden for its excessive accommodation with Germany in the early years of the war, but this had to be set against the sanctuary that both US bomber crews and Danish Jews had enjoyed in this bastion of peace.[43]

The Swedish public was also able to learn about the partly contrasting US and Swedish perspectives on Swedish foreign policy during the Second World War. The Harvard historian Bruce Hopper, who had been in Sweden from 1941 to 1942, published an article in the Social Democratic magazine *Tiden* ['The time'] in connection with the end of the war in Europe. He criticized the Swedish government's failure to acknowledge that the transit of German soldiers through the country constituted 'a violation of its neutrality that had been accepted under the threat of force majeure'. Otherwise he praised the fact that politicians, the press, and the Swedish people had preserved 'the moral climate of neutrality' as well as being

---

42 Malaporte, *Kaputt*, pp. 18–20.
43 Demaree Bess, 'The Swedes are out to get business', *The Saturday Evening Post*, 22 September 1945.

willing to help refugees. Hopper's main argument was that while Sweden 'had been a very important lung for a suffocated Europe', it was a small state that depended on a functioning balance of power. When that balance was destroyed in the early years of the war, with Germany as the dominant power, Sweden's neutrality had also been lost and was only restored in 1943.[44]

Although this criticism was mild, the response from the economist, Social Democrat, and editor of *Tiden*, Gunnar Myrdal, was unequivocal. He stressed that Sweden had a good conscience and its inhabitants had nothing to reproach themselves for. In his 'peculiar article', featuring an outside expert's 'cold analysis', Hopper had not taken sufficient account of the fact that Sweden had 'by and large skilfully played our role and safeguarded our interests without harming those of others'. There had been no lack of courage and risk-taking. The Swedish concessions to Nazi Germany had been 'unavoidable' and no greater 'than necessity demanded'.[45] Sweden's Minister for Foreign Affairs made himself the spokesman of a similar view: 'The intrinsic value that Undén primarily perceived in the policy of neutrality was the neutral state existing as an oasis beyond the world conflict', summarizes historian Sten Ottosson.[46]

Sweden's prevailing foreign policy continued to be defended in *Tiden*, where issues related to the nation's neutral position in a polarized Cold War climate were regularly discussed during the immediate post-war decades.[47] This stance helped ensure that neutrality and its visual expressions, such as soldiers standing on guard somewhere in Sweden, continued to be widely accepted in the decades that followed. It has been aptly said that in modern Sweden, memories of war were consigned 'down to the dark and fearful cellars of the subconscious'.[48] Thus, with the exception of the immediate post-war years, when participation in Western or Nordic defence cooperation was being discussed, the Swedish ideal of neutrality persisted largely unchallenged throughout the following decades. One consequence of this was that Sweden was

---

44 Bruce Hopper, 'Sverige – en studie i neutralitetspolitik', *Tiden*, 1945:3, 271–280, quotations pp. 275, 279.
45 Gunnar Myrdal, 'Neutraliteten och vårt samvete', *Tiden*, 1945:5, 257–270, quotations pp. 258, 260.
46 Ottosson, *Den (o)moraliska neutraliteten*, p. 206.
47 Berge, *Det kalla kriget i Tidens spegel*, passim.
48 Sturfelt, 'Utanför krigskartan', p. 164.

repeatedly portrayed as a nation periodically surrounded, trapped, and squeezed between competing great powers and disparate social systems. The Second World War had taught Sweden the need for far-reaching flexibility and the necessity of adapting to prevailing realities and buying time, for instance by making use of influential figures such as Marcus Wallenberg, who had been sent to negotiate with the Western Allies and had helped to avert an emerging conflict with Britain early in the war.[49]

The rhetoric aimed at the outside world both during and after the Second World War was dominated by an emphasis on Sweden's continued independence in the form of neutrality and non-alignment. As Undén explained, it also involved representing a policy of independence according to which Sweden could stand for freedom and democracy and criticize anti-democratic forces. The dilemma was that such statements must not collide with Sweden's non-aligned foreign policy, which was based on friendship with all other nations whatever their form of government. Accordingly, the 1948 Social Democratic Party Congress resulted in two separate statements: one in which the Congress 'supported the government's policy of being friends with all [and] one in which it declared how deeply it detested some of those friends'.[50] One consequence of this foreign-policy balancing act was a long period of caution in Sweden's relations with the two superpowers, but it also resulted in a distanced view of much of Europe. Post-war changes in how Swedish foreign policy was regarded saw strict neutrality giving way to a more active, and occasionally activist, perspective on the outside world. Sweden's growing international involvement was only marginally directed at its immediate neighbourhood and the rest of Europe and all the more at newly independent nations in Africa and Asia. It was felt that unifying Sweden's far-off foreign policy and aid policy could offer greater opportunities for both a political reorientation and a distancing from the alliance politics that dominated close at hand in Europe.[51]

Although this may seem paradoxical at first glance, the ideal of neutrality could be applied to Folke Bernadotte and Raoul Wallenberg. At an early point in time, it became the established

---

49 Hägglöf, *Det kringrända Sverige*, pp. 223–255.
50 Molin, *Omstridd neutralitet*, p. 23.
51 Boheman, *Tankar i en talmansstol*, pp. 201–207; Åselius, *Vietnamkriget och de svenska diplomaterna*, passim.

view that they were special and profoundly honourable because they had voluntarily left Sweden for risky missions in war-torn Europe. Although neutrality was highly valued, their achievements were appreciated because they had chosen to forgo the tranquillity of life at home in order to help people in need. Texts about Wallenberg's case repeatedly emphasized that he, as a Swede taking an active part in war-torn Hungary, had increased Soviet suspicion. The Soviets found it unlikely that Wallenberg would have left safe, neutral Sweden for brutal Budapest merely to save human lives. As already pointed out, the Soviet secret service believed this claim was a cover for espionage activities.[52] An editorial in the newspaper *Arbetet* in 1957 sums up this mindset well: 'Wallenberg's fate stands forth in all its tragedy as symbolic of small, neutral, humanitarian-focused Sweden's contribution to the Second World War.' The writer concluded that the Swedish diplomat had been part of the conflict but had persevered with his peaceful humanitarian mission.[53]

Sweden's non-combative modern history thus created the setting for a narrative of progress characterized by the idea that neutrality was not only a legal and security-orientated concept; it also encompassed aspects of culture, emotion, and mentality. Neutrality developed into an ideal for the past, the present, and the future. Perceived as the foundation of Swedish modernity and Swedish prosperity, neutrality – as aptly summarized by historian Alf W. Johansson – became 'a state of mind'.[54]

### Raoul Wallenberg in the wake of the Second World War

*Se* ['Look'] was Sweden's first picture magazine, founded in 1938 and inspired by the US magazines *Life* and *Look* and the British *Picture Post*. The cover of the first issue in August 1945 featured Margit Symo, 'a fiery dancer of genuine Hungarian descent',

---

52 Philipp, *Raoul Wallenberg*, p. 157; Per Anger, 'Kampen för Raoul Wallenberg', *Svensk Tidskrift*, 1992:8–9; Per Anger, 'Varför ryssarna tog Raoul Wallenberg', *Svensk Tidskrift*, 1992:1. The fact that Wallenberg left safe, neutral Sweden to save Hungarian Jews to whom he owed nothing was mentioned by Georg Klein in an interview with Gabi Gleichmann in *Judisk Tidskrift*, 1985:2, 9.
53 'Wallenbergs öde', *Arbetet*, 8 February 1957.
54 Johansson, 'Neutrality and Modernity', p. 170. See also Stråth, 'The Swedish Image of Europe as the Other', pp. 362–377; Liljefors and Zander, 'Det neutrala landet Ingenstans', pp. 209–242.

kneeling and aiming a bow and arrow at an unknown target. It was particularly striking that she did so without a stitch on her body. But it was not just her beauty, background as a dancer and film actress, or willingness to take off her clothes that made *Se*'s editors want to put her on the cover. She was, readers were informed, none other than Hungary's answer to the First World War spy Mata Hari. Because Symo was liked by the Germans and skilfully kept on good terms with them, she had on several occasions managed to convey information to the Swedish Legation in Budapest about where and when pogroms against the city's Jews would take place. The 'beautiful photo reportage' did indeed mention Raoul Wallenberg, but only in passing: according to Symo, his disappearance might be explained by his being murdered by the Nazis.[55]

On the one hand, it is tempting to regard the report on Symo as a one-off piece with an unpleasant aftertaste. The mass murder of Budapest's Jews became the backdrop for Symo's peripheral rescue contribution, whose truth was impossible to prove but which gained its 'news value' from the combination of female spy and nudity. Attention, both in text and pictures, focused entirely on the cheerfully posing nude dancer who had been 'a saving angel' in Budapest. The interview with Symo, who later became a well-known actress in West Germany, was spiced up with details of her dramatic escape to Sweden aboard a Red Cross ship carrying prisoners of war, and with the plans for her forthcoming 'show film'. The film would present her as the Swedish-Hungarian equivalent of another exotic, sensual, and 'ethnic' figure, the musical star Carmen Miranda.

On the other hand, the story about Symo adheres to a pattern. Wallenberg's achievements – and disappearance – became known in the spring of 1945. In a large double-spread article in *Dagens Nyheter* on 6 March 1945, a Hungarian who had made his way to Sweden via an adventurous journey through Germany told Swedish readers about a 'Swedish feat in Hungary'. His detailed account had great credibility, asserted the journalist who conducted the interview. The highest praise was due to Valdemar Langlet and Raoul Wallenberg, and in particular the latter's efforts to save human lives. The writer stressed that Wallenberg had received sterling assistance at the Legation, but his indomitable will, and his ability to 'take the bull by the horns' in order to persuade the Arrow Cross leaders to respect the Swedish protective passports issued

---

55 'Nakendansös och räddande ängel', *Se*, 1945:31, 16–17, 31.

to Jews, was admirable, not least given that he had received death threats and that 'armed gangsters' had been sent out to impede or even prevent his work. The tribute continued the next day in a shorter version, with a correction, as Wallenberg had been given the title of attaché instead of secretary to the Legation.[56] An article in *Expressen*, a daily newspaper founded as late as 1944, also extolled Wallenberg's efforts. A brief presentation began by saying that he was undoubtedly 'a clever lad' who had saved thousands of Jews 'from death and concentration camps'. The writer went on to sketch some milestones in his career and concluded by saying that he was 'known as a pleasant young man'. A longer article in the same paper also praised his contribution. His achievements implicitly contributed to spreading Swedish goodwill, as manifested in the many thank-you messages from all over the world addressed to his mother. At the same time, the journalist expressed concern that Wallenberg had disappeared without a trace. The latest news was undeniably bleak. The possibility that he was still alive 'must be regarded as doubtful'.[57]

The arrival in Stockholm in April that same year of the Swedish envoy Ivan Danielsson and his colleagues was another reminder of the Swedish efforts in Budapest. Before coming home they had been taken from the Hungarian capital to Moscow. At first their return did not direct any attention to Wallenberg's situation. Instead, when one of those rescued was given the opportunity to speak, she expressed great gratitude for the way everyone at the Swedish Legation had been protected in Hungary, which had resulted in her being able to come to 'that paradise of peace and light called Sweden'.[58]

In May, *Se* published a photo reportage under the headline 'The Budapest Legation – a stronghold in battle'. The opening text included a description of the Swedish endeavour to rescue Budapest's Jews, albeit without going into the practical details, and of the fierce battle against the antisemitic Arrow Cross members who had entered the Legation on Christmas Eve. The ensuing photo spread, featuring photographs of one of 'those who were there'

---

56 'Svensk bragd i Ungern: Kapplöpning med judetåg mot gränsen' and 'Den svenska hjälpen i Ungern', *Dagens Nyheter*, 6 and 7 March 1945.
57 'Tack från hela världen till Wallenbergs mor', *Expressen*, 7 March 1945; Magnus, 'En duktig grabb', *Expressen*, 8 March 1945.
58 Vera Forsberg, 'Ungerskt inferno', *Vi*, 1945:11, 11–12. See Hägglöf, *Berätta för Joen*, pp. 160–161 and Britt-Marie Mattsson, *Neutralitetens tid*, p. 30.

in the autumn of 1944, portrayed the Legation staff's vulnerable situation during the city's last months in German hands and 'how even the diplomats had to defend themselves with weapons in their hands against fighting desperados'.[59] The individuals named in *Se*'s photo reportage were Lars G:son Berg, Margareta Bauer, and the Save the Children representative Asta Nilsson, called 'Budapest's angel'.[60] As in previous articles, the focus lay on the Swedish Legation's collective work, although the efforts of Ivan Danielsson, Wallenberg, and Per Anger did receive special mention.

Not surprisingly, the best-informed accounts were to be found in Jewish periodicals such as the British *The Jewish Chronicle* and the Swedish *Judisk Krönika* [the title also means 'Jewish chronicle']. During the war, writers for these journals provided well-informed accounts of the ongoing genocide, stating where, how, and to what extent it was occurring. It was in these magazines, which had a much smaller readership than many daily newspapers and weeklies, that the fullest descriptions of the work done by Wallenberg and the other Budapest Swedes were published. *Judisk Krönika* also drew attention to the significance of a letter from King Gustaf V to Admiral Miklos Horthy, in which the Swedish King made it clear to the Hungarian head of state what the consequences would be after the war if no action was taken to halt the deportations of Hungarian Jews. The writer also highlighted the Red Cross efforts in the spring of 1945.[61]

At the end of 1946, the issue of Raoul Wallenberg's disappearance was discussed in the Riksdag, the Swedish Parliament, for the first time. It was brought up again the following year, but at that point there was still no sign of the great dissatisfaction with the government's actions that soon came to characterize the case.[62] Articles about Wallenberg were published fairly regularly in newspapers and magazines in the immediate post-war years, and public demonstrations in his memory were held at irregular intervals in the late 1940s. In 1947, Riksdag members Bertil von Friesen, Ture Nerman, and Vilhelm Lundstedt nominated Wallenberg for the Nobel Peace Prize. Supporters of the nomination included Albert Einstein, but

---

59 'Budapestlegationen – en fästning i strid', *Se*, 1945:21, 16–19.
60 'Budapests ängel', *Vecko-Journalen*, 1945:12, 5.
61 'Plight of Budapest survivors: Swedish officials saved thousands of Jews', *The Jewish Chronicle*, 23 March 1945, p. 9; bM, 'Sveriges stora insats vid räddningen av judar', *Judisk Krönika*, 1945:5–6, 96–97.
62 Villius and Villius, *Fallet Raoul Wallenberg*, pp. 54–57.

it did not win the approval of the Swedish government, which was necessary if a candidate was to be considered.[63] That same year, some of the people involved in trying to discover his fate founded a Raoul Wallenberg Committee. In the years that followed he was portrayed as 'the spiritual monument' whose 'noble features' personified a Swedish humanitarian tradition.[64] Soon after it became known that he had been abducted by Soviet troops, meetings were arranged with the main aim of putting pressure on Minister for Foreign Affairs Östen Undén and staff at the UD to discover his fate in Soviet hands and to secure his release and return to Sweden. One such meeting in the Stockholm Concert Hall in the summer of 1948 was estimated to have attracted about 1,000 people.[65] It is therefore incorrect to assert that there was a lack of public debate in Sweden from 1945 onwards and that an active rejection of commemorative efforts resulted in 'more than 30 years of near silence' about Wallenberg and his achievements.[66]

From time to time, indeed, the Wallenberg affair – or case, as it came to be called – gained a particularly prominent place in the Swedish public sphere. Wallenberg's relatives, as well as politicians, commentators, and journalists periodically returned to the topic of what he had achieved during the Second World War and what had happened to him since. He was certainly missing, and possibly dead, but this 'agent of love for humanity' and his contribution were still fondly remembered.[67] Wallenberg continued to be a

---

63 Anders Örne, 'Dialog om fredspriset', *Vecko-Journalen*, 1947:43; Sjöquist, *Raoul Wallenberg*, p. 195; Stewart McBride, 'Raoul Wallenberg – the hero of the Holocaust', *The Christian Science Monitor*, 24 July 1980.
64 Mia Leche, 'Fredshjälte i mörk tid', *Göteborgs Handels- och Sjöfartstidning*, 9 February 1957; 'Raoul Wallenberg' (editorial), *Göteborgs-Posten*, 8 February 1957; 'Wallenberg, Sovjet och Sverige' (editorial), *Dagens Nyheter*, 8 February 1957.
65 See e.g. 'Raoul Wallenbergs gärning', *Judisk Tidskrift*, 1946:7, 216–218; M. E. (Marcus Ehrenpreis), 'Raoul Wallenberg: Ett brev', and Hugo Valentin, 'En partisan i mänsklighetens tjänst: Anförande vid Konserthusmötet den 11 jan. 1948', *Judisk Tidskrift*, 1948:1, 1–6.
66 Schult, 'Whose Raoul Wallenberg is it?', p. 775. See also Kaplan and Schwarz, 'Raoul Wallenberg in Israel', p. 18.
67 'Raoul Wallenberg – "agent för människokärlek"', *Expressen*, 8 February 1957 and 'Raoul Wallenberg', *Göteborgs Handels- och Sjöfartstidning*, 8 February 1957. See also the statement by Leif Cassel, Riksdag member and Vice President of the Conservative Party, who after the Soviet declaration that Wallenberg was dead called him 'a martyr … in the service of

symbol, declared Mia Leche Löfgren some ten years after his disappearance, because he 'was a hero of peace, a figure of light in a dark and evil time'.[68]

The Wallenberg case not only left its mark on political discussions in the Riksdag and the op-ed pages of newspapers. In the 1960s and 1970s, the authors Maj Sjöwall and Per Wahlöö enjoyed great success with their police-detective novels, which contained recurring elements of social critique. When they located part of the plot of their 1966 novel *The Man Who Went Up in Smoke* in what they regarded as a friendly and open Budapest, far removed from Cold War notions of a brutal and repressive Communist-run Hungary, it was a short step to a reminder of what had happened in the city some twenty years earlier. When policeman Martin Beck agrees to find a missing man, the Swedish State Secretary instructs him on the importance of history not repeating itself. The last thing Sweden needs, the novel's politician asserts, is yet another Wallenberg case.[69]

As we know, however, remembrance always walks hand in hand with oblivion. The closely related question is therefore whether or not people and events in the past have obtained the recognition and the posthumous reputation that they deserve.[70] In the early years of the twenty-first century, the endeavour of Valdemar Langlet and his wife, Nina, to rescue Jews in Budapest has attracted some attention, but Langlet has also been categorized as 'one of the forgotten ones'.[71] However, the Langlets were by no means totally ignored after the war. One example is a 1979 series of television programmes entitled *När kriget kom* ['When the war came'], in which one episode dealt with the Langlets' efforts in Budapest in 1944–1945. The episode did not appeal to television reviewer Kerstin Hallert, whose main objection was that some relevant aspects had been downplayed. To begin with, there was a tendency to highlight the Langlets' contributions at the expense of Raoul Wallenberg, because it was implied

---

humanity' and added: 'We shall never forget him'; *Arbetet*, 8 February 1957, and the description of him as 'humanity's martyr' in *Göteborgs Handels- och Sjöfartstidning*, 9 February 1957.

68 Mia Leche, 'Fredshjälte i mörk tid', *Göteborgs Handels- och Sjöfartstidning*, 9 February 1957.
69 Tapper, *Snuten i skymningslandet*, p. 194; Lesser, *Scandinavian Noir*.
70 Paul Ricoeur, *Memory, History, Forgetting*, pp. 86–90.
71 Runberg, *Valdemar Langlet*. See also Sjöquist, *Dramat Raoul Wallenberg*, pp. 250–252; Levine, *Raoul Wallenberg in Budapest*, pp. 212–249, which describes Langlet and Carl Ivan Danielsson as 'the forgotten Swedes'.

that the latter only assisted Jews with business connections and/or relatives in Sweden, whereas the Langlets wanted to save all those in need, whatever their ethnicity and status. Hallert found it upsetting that Wallenberg, who, unlike the Langlets, 'had been left behind', was only mentioned in a concluding interview with Per Anger. Hallert was also indignant that the programme producer, Sonja Pleijel, who was known for her 'anything but anti-Soviet attitude', and the rest of the programme crew had neglected to present how the Soviets had conducted themselves – conduct that had been particularly reprehensible in the Wallenberg case.[72] Pleijel countered by observing that while Valdemar and Nina Langlet had indeed been able to return and had been helped, unlike Raoul Wallenberg, they had soon been forgotten. It was in order to highlight their achievements to the public that the programme focused on their actions rather than on Wallenberg's.[73]

## The failure of diplomacy

While the Second World War was still going on, not many people in Sweden outside the UD knew what Raoul Wallenberg and his colleagues at the Swedish Legation were doing in Budapest. One of those who did know, and who did his best to stay updated, was the diplomat Sven Grafström. Like Wallenberg, he has been remembered in the historical narrative for his courageous actions during the Second World War. During the German attack on Poland in 1939, Grafström had evacuated diplomats and other foreign nationals from Warsaw under difficult circumstances. While Wallenberg was carrying out his mission in Budapest, Grafström was stationed at the UD in Stockholm. His diaries, which were considered to contain so much sensitive information that they remained unpublished for 34 years, show that even UD staff had difficulty in obtaining information. On 29 December 1944, he wrote that Danielsson had gone into hiding and Wallenberg was being persecuted by the Arrow Cross. However, this information did not come from the Swedish Legation, because contact with Budapest had been broken. Instead,

---

72 Kerstin Hallert, 'Inte ett ord om Wallenberg ...', *Svenska Dagbladet*, 22 September 1979.
73 Sonja Pleijel, 'Makarna Langlet, Raoul Wallenberg och ett program i televisionen', *Svenska Dagbladet*, 14 October 1979. See also K. S., 'Ställ inte Wallenberg och Langlet mot varandra', *Svenska Dagbladet*, 21 October 1979.

the information came from a German source.[74] Lennart Petri, who took over the investigations about Wallenberg in 1946, noted that it was only in July 1945 that he gained access to 'a detailed account of what had happened in Budapest'.[75] In other cases, too, it proved difficult to clarify what had happened to other missing persons in Budapest, as well as in other parts of Eastern Europe that had come under Soviet control.[76] For example, a meeting between a Swedish UD official and the Finnish ambassador at the end of the war in Europe revealed how hard it was to obtain reliable information. Not only was the fate of the Swedes who had been operating in Berlin unclear. The Swiss chargé d'affaires in Budapest had disappeared as well. Also, there was still no information about what had happened to Wallenberg after he had '"saved himself" by going across to the Russians'. The frustration was not lessened by the fact that Swedish enquiries to Soviet officials continued to go unanswered.[77]

The difficulties in obtaining information did not improve significantly after the war in Europe ended. Later estimates suggest that as many as 40 million people had become displaced persons. Many of them were living in dire circumstances while trying to discover the fate of missing family members, relatives, and friends, often to no avail.[78] In Eastern Europe, these problems were compounded by the deportations carried out by the Soviet security police. In Hungary alone, 750,000 civilians were sent to temporary camps before being transported to the Gulag to join hundreds of thousands of their compatriots captured by the Red Army on the Eastern Front.[79] It was thus hard to obtain information about people who had disappeared for various reasons during the war. This was particularly

---

74 Ekman (ed.), *Sven Grafström: Anteckningar 1938–1944*, p. 625. For the handling of the diaries, see Thorsell, *Mein lieber Reichskanzler!*, pp. 309–319.
75 Petri, *Sverige i stora världen*, p. 181.
76 See e.g. letter from Folke Bernadotte to Rickard Lindström, 9 May 1945; letter from Rickard Lindström to Folke Bernadotte, 31 July 1945; letter from Andre Leicht to Folke Bernadotte, 6 October 1945, RA, Svenska Röda Korset I, Folke Bernadottes arkiv, Greve Folke Bernadotte af Wisborg 1943–1945, Vol. 6. See also Hägglöf, *Berätta för Joen*, p. 167.
77 Gripenberg, *Dagbok 1945–1946*, p. 121.
78 Wyman, *DPs: Europe's Displaced Persons, 1945–1951*, pp. 15–37; Jähner, *Aftermath*, pp. 38–41.
79 Applebaum, *Gulag*, p. 432; Szita, *The Power of Humanity*, pp. 103–105.

true of Budapest, where Wallenberg was one of several Swedes who had disappeared. However, the Swedish diplomat was not just an ordinary displaced person. He had been sent on an official mission, he had diplomatic status, and he had friends and acquaintances who had contacted the Swedish authorities for answers but had received no clarification as to whether there was any information about him at the UD or any other Swedish authority. The frustration at the difficulty of obtaining information through official channels caused at least one of Wallenberg's relatives, who lived in Denmark, to contact Folke Bernadotte, who was Vice Chairman of the Swedish Red Cross, in July 1945, to ask about the possibility of travelling to Budapest in order to make enquiries on the spot.[80] Valdemar Langlet, who had remained in the Hungarian capital after its capture by the Red Army, was also unable to obtain credible information. It could not be ruled out that Wallenberg, who had been declared an outlaw by the Arrow Cross in December 1944, had been lured into a trap, but rumours suggested that he might just as easily have been abducted to Germany as to the Soviet Union. That Wallenberg might have been murdered by the Arrow Cross or abducted by the Germans were scenarios repeatedly mentioned as possibilities by Swedish-Soviet contacts in the immediate post-war years.[81]

## An alley cat among the purebreds

A Swedish diplomat who had been a member of the pro-socialist 'red gang' of young radicals within the UD in the 1960s and 1970s later wrote a retrospective account eulogizing his boss, Per Anger. Not only had Anger supported them through thick and thin; the fact that he and Wallenberg had acted largely outside the rules and protocols in Budapest also made him appear more of a revolutionary than the gang members were.[82] This view echoes a common description of Wallenberg, Anger, and Valdemar Langlet, who

---

80 Letter from Consul A. Jöhncke to Folke Bernadotte, 27 July 1945, RA, Svenska Röda Korset I, Folke Bernadottes arkiv, Greve Folke Bernadotte av Wisborg 1943–1945, Vol. 5. Whether or not the trip was made is not evident from the source material.
81 Langlet, *Kaos i Budapest*, pp. 143–144; Runberg, *Valdemar Langlet*, p. 36; Derogy, *Fallet Raoul Wallenberg*, p. 205–208; Eliasson et al., *Ett diplomatiskt misslyckande*, pp. 248–250, 263–266.
82 Åselius, *Vietnamkriget och de svenska diplomaterna*, pp. 175–176.

had all acted outside the normal boundaries in an exceptional manner and had courageously defied authority both among their own ranks and in their opponents'.[83] That Wallenberg, who was a dynamic and, in many ways, unconventional individual, was not a trained diplomat but had become one ad hoc owing to the mission he undertook in 1944, plus the fact that he came from a country with a conformist culture, further helped to highlight the distance between him and the professional diplomats.[84] His attire – he is said to have arrived in Budapest wearing a windbreaker, a simple hat, and a rucksack – was unlike that of a diplomat, as was his unwillingness to deal with 'all kinds of bureaucracy'.[85] Wallenberg's actions provoked many of his fellow diplomats. A number of them opined that he had broken the unwritten rules of how a diplomat should behave.

In 1949, Lars G:son Berg assessed Wallenberg's record in his book *Boken som försvann: Vad hände i Budapest*. Withdrawn for unclear reasons, the book was republished in 1983. Berg's assessment was retained in the Swedish reissue but edited out in the 1990 English-language version, entitled *The Book That Disappeared: What Happened in Budapest*. Berg stressed that Wallenberg's contributions had been enormous but also noted that his colleague's tendency to go to extremes had been problematic. Wallenberg's actions had forced the head of mission, Ivan Danielsson, to take measures he did not want to take; besides, said Berg, they had contributed to UD officials in Stockholm receiving a less than accurate description of what was happening in the Hungarian capital. Berg's ambivalent attitude was expressed as follows: 'I admire Raoul more than any other human being. That is not to say that I always approved of all his actions in Budapest, which might sometimes have been downright dangerous for purely Swedish interests.'[86]

Wallenberg's stubborn and idealistic drive to succeed was certainly laudable because it helped to save many Jews. However,

---

83 See Hughes-Hallett, *Heroes*, pp. 5–6; Holbrooke, 'Defying Orders, Saving Lives', pp. 135–138; Schult, *A Hero's Many Faces*, pp. 248–249.
84 Berger, 'Missed Opportunities?', p. 74.
85 Philipp, *Raoul Wallenberg*, p. 81; Lévai, *Raoul Wallenberg, hjälten i Budapest*, p. 39; Anger, *With Raoul Wallenberg in Budapest*, pp. 49–50; Per Anger, 'Raoul Wallenberg', *Judisk Tidskrift*, 1985:12, 6.
86 Berg, *Boken som försvann*, p. 14. For reasons why the book was withdrawn, see Hasselbohm, 'Vad hände sedan?', pp. 194–196.

# Wallenberg and Sweden

in retrospect it has been claimed that he kept acting foolhardily, egotistically, and ruthlessly. This was particularly true of his deliberate bypassing of his boss, Danielsson, who advocated a less defiant policy towards the Germans and the Hungarian Arrow Cross.[87] Such unconventional and controversial behaviour probably contributed to Wallenberg's not being well regarded by the officials of the government ministry charged with finding him and securing his release. To Wallenberg, acting outside protocol was probably of minor importance, because he did not primarily regard himself as a Swedish diplomat. His main activity was humanitarian, and he was in Hungary on behalf of the War Refugee Board. One result may well have been that the UD did not regard Wallenberg as 'one of its own' and therefore assigned lower priority to his case.[88]

## Soviet smokescreens

There are several other likely explanations for the lack of interest and concrete action in the Wallenberg case. One is linked to the messages received by Staffan Söderblom and others from the Soviet Deputy Minister of Foreign Affairs Vladimir Dekanozov, who had a background in the Soviet secret service and close ties with NKVD chief Lavrentiy Beria. In response to an enquiry about Wallenberg, Dekanozov informed Söderblom that the Swedish Legation was safe in the western part of Budapest and measures had been taken to protect Wallenberg. A similar reassuring message was conveyed by the Soviet ambassador to Sweden, Alexandra Kollontay. Over a number of years she had established good contacts among the Swedish elite, including with several members of the Wallenberg family, whom she had met in the early 1930s. When she assured UD staff in Stockholm in January 1945 that Wallenberg was in safe Soviet custody, it was therefore a highly credible statement. She was probably unaware of the Soviet leadership's reasons for arresting him. Her continued enquiries with Moscow about his fate caused irritation and may have been the reason why she was not allowed to remain in the ambassadorial post in Stockholm. The likelihood of her being kept in the dark, combined with her reassuring

---

87 Eliasson et al., *Ett diplomatiskt misslyckande*, pp. 313–318 and the texts cited there; Jangfeldt, *The Hero of Budapest*, pp. 329–330.
88 Eliasson et al., *Ett diplomatiskt misslyckande*, pp. 206–208, 317–321, 340–346.

message, probably contributed to several months passing without any Swedish request being made that the Soviet authorities should return Wallenberg to his homeland without delay.

It was not until the end of April 1945 that Staffan Söderblom contacted Dekanozov again. By then, a reply with a different content had begun to take shape. The Soviets maintained that Wallenberg had had contact with Red Army soldiers; however, he had soon driven off in a car and had then died somewhere in Hungary under unclear circumstances.[89] Another Soviet tactic was to avoid responding to Swedish enquiries. This silence was one reason why UD staff continued to seek answers from Moscow through official channels, trying to interpret Soviet actions (as well as the lack of them) as best they could. At the same time, however, they began to search elsewhere for clues to Wallenberg's disappearance, in particular via more or less credible witnesses who claimed to have information about him.[90]

Reasons of a partly different nature have to do with financial considerations. One of these was tied to Swedish-Soviet trade relations and what was known as the 'billion-kronor loan'. Back in the early 1920s, the Social Democrats had suggested making a loan to the Soviet Union, but the proposal was rejected by the Riksdag. So was a similar proposal ten years later, after Marcus Wallenberg the Elder had warned of too great a risk and too low an interest rate. In 1944, Swedish-Soviet financial negotiations resumed again. The idea that these talks would have led to Stalin ordering the kidnapping of Raoul Wallenberg in order to exert pressure on the Swedish government was dismissed by the commission of enquiry into his case. The notion has since been revived by historian Peter Axelsson, though. He does not dismiss the possibility that one relevant factor while Stalin and Söderblom were discussing Wallenberg in Moscow in 1946 was indeed the concurrent negotiations over the billion-kronor loan by Sweden's Social Democratic government, a government whose motives in this regard were political rather than

---

89 Eliasson et al., *Ett diplomatiskt misslyckande*, pp. 187–307; Matz, 'Sweden, the United States, and Raoul Wallenberg's Mission to Hungary in 1944', pp. 97–101; Matz, 'Cables in Cipher', pp. 347–350; Ratuszniak, 'Contact between Alexandra Kollontai and the Wallenberg Family (1930–1945)', pp. 65–83; Vaksberg, *Aleksandra Kollontay*, pp. 300–305.
90 Matz, '"All Signs Indicate that Gestapo Agents Murdered Him"', pp. 148–173; Johan Matz, 'Analogical Reasoning and the Diplomacy of the Raoul Wallenberg Case 1945–7', pp. 582–606.

financial. If it had transpired that the missing Swede was sitting imprisoned in the Soviet Union, the billion-kronor loan would have been politically impossible; moreover, the scheme would have denigrated the reputations of its main proponents.[91]

Another financial aspect of Wallenberg's disappearance which has been used to explain the feeble and belated Swedish response is based on a story launched soon after his disappearance. The tale claimed that he was carrying a large sum of money and that the fuel tank of his Studebaker was filled with gold and gemstones belonging to Jews who wanted to save their valuables from the plundering Arrow Cross, Germans, and Russians.[92] This story, which has popped up intermittently, has in recent years been dismissed as Soviet propaganda, not least because such a scenario invited the conclusion, favourable to the Soviets, that Wallenberg had been murdered as part of a robbery in Hungary.[93] This conclusion is very reasonable, but it needs to be placed in the context of accusations made against Swedish embassy personnel in the years around the end of the war. A handful of them were accused of having acted for their own benefit by trading on the black market or exploiting vulnerable individuals. The UD took these accusations seriously. If Wallenberg had turned out to have been guilty of a similar crime, it would probably have been difficult to go on the offensive against Moscow.

## Lobbying by Wallenberg's relatives and US proposals

Even after the Soviet abduction of Wallenberg, American interest in his case was considerable. When Swedish newspapers printed articles about the Swedish diplomat's activities in Budapest, the articles became the subject of diplomatic correspondence.[94]

---

91 Peter Axelsson, 'Raoul Wallenberg's fate and a Swedish billion kronor credit to the Soviet Union', www.rwi-70.de/raoul-wallenberg-fate-and-a-swedish-billion-kronor-credit/ (accessed 20 March 2022).
92 See, for instance, Werbell and Clarke, *Lost Hero*, pp. 199–202; Jangfeldt, *The Hero of Budapest*, pp. 289–290; Jangfeldt, *En rysk historia*, pp. 435–439; Bengt Jangfeldt, 'Raoul Wallenberg and the question of the Jewish valuables', www.rwi-70.de/raoul-wallenberg-and-the-question-of-the-jewish-valuables (accessed 12 February 2022).
93 Matz, 'Foreign Policy Analysis', pp. 424–427; Matz, 'Did Raoul Wallenberg Try to Leave Budapest in January 1945 with Jewelry?', pp. 17–41.
94 Herschel Johnson, 'War Refugee Board, DCG-1142', Stockholm, 7 March 1945 and the message from Iver C. Olsen to Brigadier General William

Wallenberg's achievements were also reported to American readers. In April 1945, *The New York Times* published an article that highlighted his actions and also discussed his abrupt and unexplained disappearance from the Hungarian capital.[95] By all accounts, the brothers Marcus and Jacob Wallenberg were keen to gain clarity about Raoul's disappearance, but Wallenberg's half-brother, Guy von Dardel, was extremely active. He tried to win US support for Wallenberg's cause by travelling to the United States in the spring of 1947, hoping to meet Harry S. Truman to gain his support in the search for Wallenberg. No such meeting with the President materialized, but von Dardel did write a number of letters to high-ranking Americans and managed to get a letter published in *The Washington Post*.[96] In addition, Wallenberg's mother worked behind the scenes to gain support from influential Americans. In late November 1946, Maj von Dardel wrote a letter to Eleanor Roosevelt in which she stressed that thousands of Hungarian Jews had been saved by her son, who had worked on behalf of both 'the swedish king and the american president [sic]'. Maj von Dardel was keen for her letter to be published, so that the American public could help shape opinion in favour of Raoul Wallenberg and his release. Another hope she had was that Eleanor Roosevelt might consider chairing an American Raoul Wallenberg Association.[97]

Most of Maj von Dardel's hopes remained unfulfilled, but after two months Eleanor Roosevelt forwarded the letter to the US State Department and to Andrei Gromyko, the Soviet Union's UN ambassador and later long-time Minister of Foreign Affairs. George Warren, the US adviser on refugee affairs, was careful to express his admiration for Wallenberg's achievements but added that according to the last report of October 1945, the Swede had left Budapest for Debrecen in March of that year, after which all traces had ceased. Warren's comment was: 'It does not appear that any official action

---

O'Dwyer, 'Swedish Achievements in Budapest', Stockholm, 12 March 1945, RKA, Raoul Wallenberg, UD2018/05505, Vol. 1.
95 'Jews in Hungary helped by Swede', *The New York Times*, 26 April 1945.
96 Letter from Guy von Dardel to Eleanor ('Mrs. Franklin D.') Roosevelt, 8 May 1947, FDRML, ergen1866.pdf (marist.edu); Guy von Dardel, 'Raoul Wallenberg's secret mission', *The Washington Post*, 25 April 1947.
97 Letter from Maj von Dardel to Eleanor Roosevelt, 21 February 1947, FDRLM, ergen1367.pdf (marist.edu); Gersten, *A Conspiracy of Indifference*, pp. 95–96.

can be taken until some clue as to his whereabouts is received.[98] Soviet records of correspondence between the Soviets and the Americans indicate that the von Dardel visit did not go unnoticed, but no directives came from Moscow about possible countermeasures.[99] Unsurprisingly, Gromyko's reply to Eleanor Roosevelt was non-committal. He had forwarded Maj von Dardel's letter to the Soviet Consulate General 'for taking appropriate measures'.[100]

Guy von Dardel's lobbying may have contributed to the hope-inducing expressions of admiration for Wallenberg's achievements that came from Americans in the public sphere. One of the world's most widely circulated magazines, the *Reader's Digest*, extolled the Swedish diplomat. He had been snatched away from those he had rescued, which was both a tragedy and the basis of a legend.[101] In an article in *The Boston Globe* and in a letter to the former Secretary of Commerce Henry Wallace, the influential newspaper and radio journalist Dorothy Thompson appealed to Wallace for help to find out what had happened to Wallenberg. Thompson further affirmed that the US government would do everything in its power to clarify the fate of the Swede who had heeded Franklin D. Roosevelt's plea for humanitarian action in a desperate situation. She was convinced that there had been some kind of mistake which the Soviet authorities would surely be willing to rectify.[102]

Wallace did as Thompson asked him, but he received no answer from the Soviets.[103] Thompson was not content to urge Wallenberg's cause in the press. Twice in 1947, she appealed to Eleanor Roosevelt and asked her to contact Stalin. The former First Lady made it clear that she had no influence over the Soviet leadership and that she could do nothing beyond what she had

---

98 Letter from George Warren to Eleanor Roosevelt, 21 February 1947, FDRLM, ergen1367.pdf (marist.edu).
99 Matz, 'The Konnov/Mikhailov/Barourskii espionage crises', pp. 35–36.
100 Letter from Andrei A. Gromyko to Eleanor Roosevelt, March 19 1947, FDRLM, ergen1367.pdf (marist.edu). See also Gersten, *A Conspiracy of Indifference*, pp. 95–98.
101 Ralph Wallace, 'Raoul Wallenberg, hero of Budapest', *The Reader's Digest*, July 1947, pp. 96–100.
102 Dorothy Thompson, 'An open letter to Henry Wallace by Dorothy Thompson', *The Boston Globe*, 18 April 1947; Letter from Dorothy Thompson to Henry Wallace, 18 April 1947, FDRLM, ergen1866.pdf (marist.edu).
103 Matz, 'The Konnov/Mikhailov/Barourskii espionage crises', p. 36.

already done in contacting Gromyko.[104] That same year, Elisabeth Bailey – the wife of Roger Bailey, one of Raoul Wallenberg's architecture instructors from the University of Michigan – contacted Guy von Dardel and told him that she had informed the Senator for Michigan, Arthur Vanderberg, about the case.[105] Vanderberg in turn contacted diplomat Dean Acheson, who was then Deputy Secretary of State and became Secretary of State two years later. Acheson replied that the US government would like to exert pressure on its Soviet counterpart, but to do so required the initiative of the Swedish authorities. He sent a similar reply to Guy and Maj von Dardel, who had written to both him and Vanderberg.[106]

### Östen Undén, Staffan Söderblom, and the Raoul Wallenberg case

When Iver Olsen reported to the War Refugee Board in 1944, he noticed a tension between the UD and Wallenberg, who had 'jumped in with too big a splash'. The latter's energetic efforts did not appear to be appreciated by the people who preferred traditional diplomatic methods, but those methods had not helped the vulnerable Jews. One US commentator predicted that the Swedish diplomat would not be met with gratitude back home despite the help he had given.[107] This turned out to be essentially true. While Wallenberg was still operating in Budapest, John Pehle, who headed the effort at the War Refugee Board, had written to thank the Swede for the great work he had done.[108] Representatives of the War Refugee Board continued to display a strong involvement

---

104 Gersten, *A Conspiracy of Indifference*, pp. 98–100.
105 Letter from Elisabeth J. Bailey to Guy von Dardel, 2 April 1947, TNYPL, Rudolph Philipp Papers on Raoul Wallenberg, Box 1.
106 Letter from Arthur Vanderberg to Dean Acheson, 4 April 1947. Letter from Dean Acheson to Arthur Vanderberg, 23 April 1947, TNYPL, Rudolph Philipp Papers on Raoul Wallenberg, Box 1; Sjöquist, *Raoul Wallenberg*, p. 137; Matz, 'The Konnov/Mikhailov/Barourskii espionage crises', p. 35.
107 Letter from Iver Olsen to John W. Pehle, 10 August 1944, quoted in Eliasson et al., *Ett diplomatiskt misslyckande*, p. 146. See also Werbell and Clarke, *Lost Hero*, p. 44; Gann, *Raoul Wallenberg*, p. 72.
108 Letter from J. H. Pehle to Raoul Wallenberg, Washington D.C., 12 December 1944, RKA, Raoul Wallenberg, UD2018/05505, Vol. 1 as well as in RKA, Raoul Wallenberg, UD2001/00009, Vol. 61. See also Erbelding, *Rescue Board*, pp. 229–230.

on Wallenberg's behalf. They requested – and received – help from the US Embassy in Moscow in their attempts to uncover Wallenberg's fate.[109] However, it took several months before the US decision-makers ultimately responsible for Wallenberg, Secretary of State Edward Stettinius and Secretary of the Treasury Henry Morgenthau Jr, were informed. The US offer to assist in the investigation was not sent to the Swedish Foreign Minister but to Staffan Söderblom, the Swedish ambassador in Moscow. He, in turn, did not pass on the US requests for Swedish pressure in the matter to Stockholm. He also dismissed the offers of US assistance made by the US ambassador in Moscow, Averell Harriman, 'and not even politely', as one later commentator acerbically observed.[110]

Foreign Minister Östen Undén also remained cool when it came to contacts with Western countries. In a 1947 meeting with representatives of the then newly formed Wallenberg Committee, he expressed strong doubts that a Soviet minister could possibly be making untrue statements. He further questioned whether the Committee members would have been equally suspicious if the opposite party had been the United States. Other participants in the meeting dismissed this comparison because the United States was a democratic country that offered opportunities for monitoring and follow-up.[111]

Evidently Undén was not personally influenced by the shift from German towards American influence that had taken place in Sweden after the Second World War, particularly in cultural respects. In the early years of the war, he had made a name for himself as an independent truthteller who paid little heed to tactical considerations; one example is provided by his repeated objections to the German transit transports through Sweden. This, then, was a man who 'operated above

---

109 Herschel Johnson to Secretary of State. No. 1251, Stockholm, 4 April 1945; Letter from George L. Warren to William O'Dwyer, Washington D.C., 8 May 1945; Cable to Harriman, Moscow, from Department and War Refugee Board (undated); Edward Stettinius, Outgoing Telegram, 9 April 1945, Letter from William O'Dwyer to Edward Stettinius, 12 April 1945; Herschel Johnson to Secretary of State, 7 June 1945, RKA, Raoul Wallenberg, UD2018/05505, Vol. 1.
110 Steinhouse, *Wallenberg Is Here!*, p. 290. See also Eliasson et al., *Ett diplomatiskt misslyckande*, pp. 272–274; Matz, 'Sweden, the United States, and Raoul Wallenberg's Mission to Hungary 1944', pp. 101–108; Gersten, *A Conspiracy of Indifference*, p. 90.
111 Petri, *Sverige i stora världen*, p. 188; Villius and Villius, *Fallet Raoul Wallenberg*, pp. 59–60.

party affiliations'.[112] His position within the Social Democratic movement was a powerful one, and he had the support of the Prime Minister, Tage Erlander, who regarded him as the most astute member of the government.[113] He also won the appreciation of many women Social Democrats during the divisive internal battle over whether or not Sweden should become a nuclear-weapons nation. Like Erlander, Undén supported the Social Democratic Women's League, which campaigned for a 'no' vote.[114] Despite recurring criticism of how he handled the 1945 to 1946 extradition of the Balts and the Wallenberg case, his time as Minister for Foreign Affairs between 1945 and 1962 was often portrayed in a favourable light. In 1969, when the newspaper *Expressen* named the most important Swedes of the twentieth century – a list, incidentally, which did not include either Folke Bernadotte or Raoul Wallenberg – Undén was accorded the honorary title of 'Mr. Neutrality'.[115] When his biography was written some 15 years later, renewed emphasis was placed on his achievement in steering a free Sweden between the East and the West. The author did not conceal his admiration for the former Foreign Minister; the biography was intended to be a tribute to a Swedish politician of international stature.[116]

While he was Minister for Foreign Affairs, Undén's critics argued that he was by no means neutral. A few years after the war, the eminent Swedish publicist and political scientist Herbert Tingsten made it clear why his earlier appreciation of Undén had turned into its opposite. Tingsten's criticism was not softened when he learned of the minister's more or less favourable statements about North Korea and East Germany or his willingness to vouch for Soviet excuses regarding what had happened to Raoul Wallenberg.[117]

---

112 Johansson, *Herbert Tingsten och det kalla kriget*, p. 182; Möller, *Östen Undén*, pp. 208–223. See von Heland, *Optimismens och besvikelsens år 1922–1952*, pp. 175–176, 214, 218.
113 Erlander (ed.), *Tage Erlander: Dagböcker 1963–1964*, p. 139.
114 Nancy Eriksson, *Nancy Eriksson minns*, pp. 121, 155, 161, 226.
115 'Herr Neutralitet', *Expressen*, 9 November 1969.
116 Möller, *Östen Undén*, p. 576. See Thede Palm, 'Vem var Östen Undén', *Svensk Tidskrift*, 1986:7–8, 381–385.
117 (Herbert Tingsten), 'Undén – en studie i grått', *Dagens Nyheter*, 15 August 1948; Tingsten, *Mitt liv*, p. 207; Arvid Fredborg, 'Oppositionen och utrikespolitiken', *OBS!* 1948:16, 28.

One possible explanation for Undén's statements is that they might have been uttered as part of the internal struggle over foreign policy which took place in Sweden in the immediate post-war years. A number of diplomats and senior military officers, as well as Liberal and Conservative politicians, were critical of Undén and desired a relaxation of the policy of neutrality so as to enable a rapprochement with the Western powers. Undén vigorously opposed such proposals.[118] Instead, his policy was one of demonstrably distancing Sweden from the United States. One result of this was that the US proposals concerning Wallenberg did not initially meet with any Swedish interest.[119] At the same time, just as Olof Palme did later, Undén declared that non-aligned Sweden was not engaged in 'inciting hatred of the Soviet Union'. In this respect he was aligning himself with an optimistic view of the neighbour to the east that was held by many Swedes in the immediate post-war years. This attitude lasted longer in Sweden than in many other Western countries, and it was particularly apparent in those who were in charge of Sweden's foreign policy. It is therefore not surprising that official Sweden wanted neither 'anti-Americanism nor anti-Sovietism'.[120]

In the world of the popular press in the 1950s, pairs of opposites dominated: good-evil, democracy-dictatorship, development-underdevelopment and freedom-oppression. With a few exceptions, the United States was associated with the positive concepts and the Soviet Union with the negative ones.[121] In the political debate, in which the Wallenberg case was a recurring bone of contention, the division was less clear-cut. The fact that Rolf Sohlman, a Swedish diplomat with many years of experience in Moscow and an expert on Russia, was on good terms with Undén invited criticism, both within the UD and in the public debate. Such objections often went hand in hand with claims that Undén was 'too apt to listen to Soviet views'.[122] There is

---

118 Molin, 'Neutralitetens dolda kris (1948–49)', pp. 74–86.
119 Villius and Villius, *Fallet Raoul Wallenberg*, pp. 52–53; Rosenfeld, *Raoul Wallenberg*, pp. 145–152; Bierman, *Righteous Gentile*, pp. 186–191.
120 Ahlmark, 'Att avslöja diktaturen', p. 19; Wahlbäck, 'Raoul Wallenberg och synen på Sovjet 1944–47', p. 255.
121 Salomon, *En femtiotalsberättelse*, p. 49.
122 Jarring, *Utan glasnost och perestrojka*, p. 25 and his diplomat colleagues Petri, *Sverige i stora världen*, pp. 269, 287, 291, 295, 329–331, 334–335, 339, and Wachtmeister, *Som jag såg det*, p. 77. See also Karlsson, *Vår man i Moskva*, pp. 20–25; Kronvall, 'Rolf Sohlman', pp. 274–275, 279–292, 299–300.

reason to maintain that a foreign-policy duel was fought throughout the initial post-war decades. This duel took place partly inside the UD between pro-Western officials – a majority – in one corner and Undén and his supporters in the other,[123] and partly in newspaper columns, with Undén and Tingsten as the main adversaries. Against the anti-Communism expressed primarily by Tingsten stood an 'anti-anti-Communism', which was particularly conspicuous in the Social Democratic press.[124]

Unlike Undén, Söderblom had gained a reputation for being accommodating towards German demands even while the Second World War was still going on. Undén's critics argued that because Sweden's relations with the Soviet Union were severely strained, it was an unfortunate move to appoint a German 'collaborationist' as ambassador to Moscow. This rumour reached Soviet politicians, and according to this view of history, it raised obstacles to Söderblom during his time as Sweden's envoy in Moscow from 1944 to 1946. There, too, he pursued a policy of accommodation. His colleague Sven Grafström wrote acidly that Söderblom had first genuflected to the south and then to the east.[125] Söderblom feared that like his predecessor in the post, Vilhelm Assarsson, he, too, would be deported owing to the frosty relations between Sweden and the Soviet Union.[126] The lawyer and author Omi Söderblom draws a somewhat different picture in a comprehensive and well-written 2021 study of her great-uncle Staffan Söderblom and the Wallenberg case. In certain respects, the book – based on new source material – was written with the intention of not assuming a defensive position in her kinsman's favour. Nevertheless, her book is in many ways a vindication of Staffan Söderblom, a career diplomat held in high esteem by Per Albin Hansson and Östen Undén. He was a key player in the great efforts to keep Sweden out of the Second World War, and he helped to obtain free passage through the Soviet

---

123 Zetterberg, 'Sven Grafström', pp. 339–344; Bergquist, 'Lennart Petri', pp. 402–403.
124 Johansson, *Herbert Tingsten och det kalla kriget*, pp. 181–203; Molin, *Omstridd neutralitet*, pp. 19–45. See also Ahlmark, 'Att avslöja diktaturen', p. 19; Bjereld, *Hjalmarsonaffären*, pp. 93–96; Ottosson, *Den (o)moraliska neutraliteten*, pp. 205–209, 225–230.
125 Ekman (ed.), *Sven Grafström: Anteckningar 1938–1944*, p. xix.
126 Pieter Tham, 'Skulle jag ha kallat Stalin mördare?' (interview with Staffan Söderblom), *Vecko-Journalen*, 1980:8, 19; Eliasson et al., *Ett diplomatiskt misslyckande*, pp. 149–151; Bokholm, *Tisdagsklubben*, p. 340.

Union for Swedes and other Nordic residents while the fighting was still going on. The blackening of his character, intensified by the link 'between the mythologizing of Wallenberg and the brutalization of Söderblom', is due in no small part to a smear campaign led by Grafström, a campaign which resulted in a 'political stigmatization'. That it took hold and persisted was not least due to the fact that Söderblom's continued strong involvement in the Wallenberg case contrasted with Undén's palpable lack of interest.[127]

While this more nuanced depiction of Söderblom is welcome, there are nevertheless good reasons to examine his time as ambassador in Moscow. His policy has been likened to a bridge-building project geared to achieving wide-ranging cooperation between Sweden and the Soviet Union. What Söderblom did not realize was that the Soviet Union was busily constructing a power empire within Europe. In this process, good relations with Sweden were not high on the agenda. Söderblom nonetheless tried to achieve good relations with the authorities in the Kremlin. Among other things, this attitude meant that he downplayed the plundering and other brutal actions committed by Soviet troops in Budapest and Berlin.[128] In his memoirs, Per Anger recalled Söderblom's words in this spirit when Wallenberg's colleagues and other Swedes from the Legation in Budapest reached Moscow in April 1945: 'Remember – not one harsh word about the Russians!'[129] In recent times, Söderblom's actions – with their obviously unfavourable consequences for the investigation into Wallenberg's disappearance – have hence been categorized as 'passive' and 'remarkable' by Swedish officialdom.[130]

In interviews conducted 35 years after his meeting with Stalin, Söderblom insisted that in a meeting with 'the top man' – which was to be regarded as 'an unusual favour' – it would have been unwise to make accusations against the Soviet authorities. It was of paramount importance to keep the door open for further negotiations and 'to say nothing that might aggravate the situation'.

---

127 Söderblom, *Söderblom och Wallenbergaffären*, pp. 57–68, 234–268, 311–318, quotation p. 373.
128 Zetterberg, 'Staffan Söderblom', pp. 250–273. See also Pieter Tham, 'Skulle jag ha kallat Stalin mördare?' (interview with Staffan Söderblom), *Vecko-Journalen*, 1980:8, 19–20, and Eliasson et al., *Ett diplomatiskt misslyckande*, pp. 152–159, 335–336, 373–377.
129 Anger, *With Raoul Wallenberg in Budapest*, p. 146.
130 Eliasson et al., *Ett diplomatiskt misslyckande*, p. 81.

The main aim was not to provoke the Soviet authorities.[131] However, the fact remains that what Söderblom said to Stalin actually weakened the Swedish negotiating position. In the spring of 1945, a rumour had spread that Wallenberg had been killed by Nazi sympathizers in Budapest.[132] In his meetings with Soviet politicians and officials, Söderblom espoused this view. He told them he was convinced that Wallenberg had 'fallen victim to an accident or to bandits' in Budapest. In June 1946 Söderblom raised the matter with Joseph Stalin, whose 'voice and look gave the impression of a friendly attitude towards his visitors'. The Swedish ambassador's sympathetic description of the Red Tsar in his report to his colleagues in Stockholm had the same tone as his account of the meeting during which Söderblom informed the Soviet leader of his own conviction that Wallenberg had been killed in Hungary.[133] Söderblom added that it was probable that 'the Soviet-Russian military authorities have no accessible information about Wallenberg's further fate'. It was hardly surprising that the Soviet replies to the Swedish enquiries about Wallenberg stated that the Swedish diplomat was not in their country.[134]

Furthermore, the Swedish government never considered suggesting an exchange of individuals. Switzerland had found itself in a similar situation when two people from its Legation in Budapest were detained by the Red Army. There were two Soviet fighter pilots in Switzerland, and so the idea of an exchange was raised. Discussions took place within the Swiss Foreign Ministry as to whether such an exchange was compatible with the principles of international law and extradition law, but finally an agreement between the Swiss and the Soviets was negotiated towards the end of 1945. The exchange took place the

---

131 Pieter Tham, 'Skulle jag ha kallat Stalin mördare?', *Vecko-Journalen*, 1980:8, 18, 20 and Kaa Eneberg, 'Ryssarna fick ej provoceras' (interview with Staffan Söderblom), *Dagens Nyheter*, 1 February 1980. See also Ingmar Lindmarker, 'Staffan Söderblom minns mötet 1946: "Stalin lovade undersöka fallet Raoul Wallenberg"', *Svenska Dagbladet*, 27 January 1980.
132 Philipp, *Raoul Wallenberg*, p. 11.
133 S(taffan) Söderblom, 'Ang. audiens hos Stalin', 18 June 1946, RA, Utrikesdepartementets arkiv, Hp 1 Er, 18 June 1946, No. 430, and RKA, Raoul Wallenberg, UD2018/005505, Vol. 48.
134 Quoted from Möller, *Östen Undén*, p. 276. See also 'UD-problemet Wallenberg' (editorial), *Dagens Nyheter*, 1 February 1980; Eliasson et al., *Ett diplomatiskt misslyckande*, pp. 299–304; Petersson, *Med Moskvas ögon*, pp. 30–32.

following year.[135] Similar exchanges, this time involving spies, later occurred between Italy and Denmark respectively on the one side and the Soviet Union on the other. Swedish embassies monitored similar cases. The Swedish diplomat Gunnar Hägglöf tried to interest Undén in a similar Swedish action, but he was told that 'Sweden does not want to engage in any "human trafficking".'[136] When Per Anger again raised the idea in the late 1950s, Undén's response was similar: 'Swedish governments do not do that sort of thing.'[137]

## Rudolph Philipp and the Wallenberg campaign

Although Raoul Wallenberg's achievements and fate were repeatedly highlighted in the daily press and weekly magazines during the immediate post-war period, silence mostly prevailed at the official level. The few and half-hearted efforts by politicians and diplomats to discover the fate of the missing Swedish diplomat have been summed up as 'too little, too late'.[138] In addition, it took time before his actions was officially recognized in Sweden. On Gustaf VI Adolf's 70th birthday in November 1952, Wallenberg was awarded the Illis Quorum medal for his humanitarian work in Budapest, with the added comment that the award was not posthumous.[139]

---

135 'Procès Verbal-rectifie', Bern, 28 December 1945; Lage Olsson, 'Wallenbergärendet', 23 May 1995, RKA, Raoul Wallenberg, UD2001/00009, Vol. 52; 'Schweizerische Politik in Sachen Harald Feller und Max Meier', Bern, 27 June 1995; Kerstin Olsson, 'Wallenbergärendet', 4 July 1995, RKA, Raoul Wallenberg, UD2001/00009, Vol. 53; Jan Lundvik, 'Promemoria: Hur kan Moskva tänkas ha uppfattat det svenska agerandet i Raoul Wallenberg-ärendet?' 9 June 2000, RKA, Raoul Wallenberg, UD2018/005505, Vol. 22.
136 'Rapport från Kungliga svenska beskickningen i Bern till Hans Excellens Herr Ministern för Utrikes Ärenden', Bern, 24 September 1945, RKA, Raoul Wallenberg, UD2018/005505, Vol. 1; Gunnar Hägglöf, 'När Wallenbergarkivet öppnas ...', *Svenska Dagbladet*, 7 December 1979.
137 Per Anger, 'Raoul Wallenberg', *Svensk Tidskrift*, 1984:4, 509. See also Anger, *With Raoul Wallenberg in Budapest*, p. 154; Möller, *Östen Undén*, p. 278.
138 Eliasson et al., *Ett diplomatiskt misslyckande*.
139 Freed, 'Humanitarianism vs. Totalitarianism', pp. 503–528. See also Arne Ruth, 'A casualty of pragmatism and passivity', *The Washington Post*, 7 January 2001. Nor did Valdemar Langlet receive any significant recognition from official Sweden in the immediate post-war years; see further Runberg, *Valdemar Langlet*, pp. 63–66.

For reasons to which we shall return, it took a few more decades before he was honoured with monuments in Sweden.[140]

Judging from Undén's diary entries, he was satisfied with the efforts made in the immediate post-war period to discover Wallenberg's fate. In the course of the investigation he became convinced that Wallenberg was dead, a view that Gustaf VI Adolf said he shared at a meeting in 1959.[141] It should be noted that Undén changed his position about Wallenberg's fate over time. Following Stalin's death in 1953, after initially telling people who worked close to him that the missing Swede was probably dead, he began to harbour hopes that Wallenberg might still be alive. After the Soviet announcement in 1957 that Wallenberg had died of a heart attack, Undén told his staff that it was probably true.[142] Outwardly, however, he maintained the official Swedish position that the missing Swede could still be a Soviet prisoner.

In the wake of Nikita Khrushchev's 'secret' speech in 1956 in which he attacked Stalin, hopes rose of learning more about the Gulag prisoners, who had been non-persons during the Red Tsar's time in power.[143] Many people still assumed that Wallenberg was alive, and a number of those who displayed the greatest commitment to his case had only been active in Sweden for a few years. The first director of the Raoul Wallenberg Aid Committee was Eugen Reiz, who was born in Hungary in 1883 and held a doctorate in cultural history from the University of Kraków. He had subsequently worked in Germany but had fled after Hitler's rise to power in 1933 and arrived in Sweden in 1938. As well as helping the Hungarian refugees who came to Sweden in the last year of the war, until his death in January 1947 Reiz was a driving force when it came to obtaining information about Wallenberg's fate. Another leading figure was the Austrian-Jewish journalist Rudolph Philipp. He had been a volunteer fighter in the First World War, was politically active, and was involved in trade unions during the interwar period before fleeing to Sweden in the late 1930s, where he mainly

---

140 See Schult, *A Hero's Many Faces*, p. 66.
141 Molin (ed.), *Östen Undén: Anteckningar 1918–1952*, pp. 191, 350, 394; Molin (ed.), *Östen Undén: Anteckningar 1952–1966*, pp. 418, 431–432, 478, 586.
142 Berger, 'Missed Opportunities?', p. 78.
143 Jarring, *Rikets förhållande till främmande makt*, pp. 50–51; Gerner, 'Konsekvenser för den svenska utrikespolitiken', p. 79; Petersson, *Med Moskvas ögon*, p. 33.

earned his living as a fencing instructor.[144] Philipp was the first to write a book, published in 1946, about Wallenberg's achievements in Budapest. In his book as well as in subsequent publications, Philipp levelled scathing criticism at the actions of the Swedish government and the UD.[145]

Wallenberg's relatives had established a good rapport with Philipp during the interviews on which his book was based. Wallenberg's stepfather Fredrik and his half-brother Guy von Dardel arranged for the book to be translated into English, then distributed it in manuscript form to the World Jewish Congress, and tried unsuccessfully to have it published by an American publisher.[146] Reviews of the book in the Swedish press varied. In addition to describing it in less than flattering terms as a 'sensational book', critics pointed out that the first person to draw attention to Wallenberg was not a Swede. Even so, it was clear to them that Philipp was the right man for the job. 'He is a whole Ministry for Foreign Affairs in himself', proclaimed one reviewer, adding that Philipp had written a book that no Swede could have managed to write.[147]

In the autumn of 1946, Philipp lent the Swedish government the materials on which his book was based. From statements he made at the time, representatives of the government had been convinced by his conclusion that Wallenberg was still alive.[148] A few months

---

144 Carlberg, *Raoul Wallenberg*, p. 455.
145 Philipp, *Raoul Wallenberg*, pp. 158–169; Rudolph Philipp, 'Lever Raoul Wallenberg – människokärlekens partisan?', *Året Runt*, 1947:25, pp. 8–9, 33–34; Rudolph Philipp, 'Vad UD underlåtit göra för Raoul Wallenberg', *OBS!* 1951:7, pp. 5–8; Rudolph Philipp, 'Raoul Wallenberg lever', *Vi*, 1955:2, pp. 7–11.
146 Letter from Dr Oscar Karbach to Fredric von Dardel, 25 November 1946; letter from Guy von Dardel to Howard Moorepark, 27 April 1947, TNYPL, Rudolph Philipp Papers on Raoul Wallenberg, Box 1.
147 Ivan Oljelund, 'Död eller levande?', *Upsala*, 24 March 1947; Karl Kern, 'En humanitetens hjälte', *Skånska Socialdemokraten*, 1 December 1946. See also Mia Leche Löfgren, 'Vi kan ej slå oss till ro med Wallenbergs försvinnande', *Göteborgs Handels- och Sjöfartstidning*, 17 July 1947 and 'Sympativåg över hela landet för en av fredens hjältar', *Svenska Dagbladet*, 16 July 1947. The term 'sensational book' comes from 'Kring Wallenberg' (editorial), *Expressen*, 18 July 1947. See also Eliasson et al., *Ett diplomatiskt misslyckande*, pp. 431–435.
148 'Fallet Wallenberg: Regeringen tror på mina bevis, säger Philipp', *Arbetet*, 1 December 1946; 'Regeringen har sett Wallenbergsmaterial', *Göteborgs Handels- och Sjöfartstidning*, 2 December 1946.

later, hope increased that an answer would come from Moscow. Prior to Folke Bernadotte's visit to the Soviet capital, the head of the Soviet Red Cross had responded to an inquiry from Bernadotte about Wallenberg.[149] As was the case with Stalin's promise to Söderblom that there would be further investigation, no answer materialized after the visit.

Shortly thereafter new findings were presented. Albert Szent-Györgi, a Hungarian who had been awarded the Nobel Prize in Medicine in 1937 for the discovery of vitamin C, had been forced into hiding in Budapest because as a resistance fighter he had helped Jews flee the country. He was given sanctuary at the Swedish Legation. His son-in-law Györgi Libik worked as Per Anger's driver and was one of the last people to see Wallenberg before he was taken into Soviet custody. Szent-Györgi was part of a delegation of Hungarian politicians that travelled to Moscow in May 1945, where, like Söderblom, he conducted negotiations with Soviet politicians. Even there and then, Szent-Györgi concluded that there was no Soviet antipathy towards Wallenberg. However, he believed that the missing Swede had met his fate as someone hunted and hated by both the Arrow Cross and the Germans. He maintained this opinion until his death in the United States in 1986.[150]

Szent-Györgi's standpoint attracted general attention when he and his compatriot, the publicist Jenő Lévai, who had been rescued by and worked with Elsa Brändström after the First World War and been helped by Wallenberg during the Second World War, spoke out in the summer of 1947 about Wallenberg's last days in Budapest. Lévai had previously written a book about the Angel of Siberia and had been commissioned by the Hungarian Wallenberg Committee (founded in 1945 but already dissolved by this time) to write a book about Wallenberg. Both Szent-Györgi and Lévai argued that the most likely explanation was that the Swedish diplomat had been killed by Germans or the Arrow Cross, as he was unlikely to have been offered any protection by the Soviets. Lévai referred to a study performed by the Hungarian authorities which he had seen. Among the tens of thousands of Hungarians who had returned

---

149 'Raoul Wallenbergs öde inför rödakorskonferens', *Aftonbladet*, 5 May 1947; 'Ryske rödakorschefen söker Raoul Wallenberg', *Morgon-Tidningen*, 14 May 1947.

150 Anger, *With Raoul Wallenberg in Budapest*, pp. 94–108; Söderblom, *Söderblom och Wallenbergaffären*, pp. 209–211.

from captivity in the Soviet Union, no one had seen or heard of the Swede. However, this conclusion met with stiff opposition, as did statements about 'how easy it was to die in Hungary' for anyone who was there in January 1945.[151]

## The debate becomes heated

One example of the explosive power of Wallenberg's case occurred in July 1947, when the Stockholm branch of the Swedish section of the International Women's Federation for Peace and Freedom, whose members had early on become engaged in trying to discover Wallenberg's fate, invited Lévai and Szent-Györgi to an evening of discussion about the Swedish diplomat's disappearance. The meeting, which was reported even by newspapers based outside Stockholm and with very varied ideological affiliations, had a dramatic beginning when it became clear that Szent-Györgi would not participate because he had gone abroad. Lévai did appear, but after reading out his speech translated into Swedish, he made it clear that the extensive material he had collected over two and a half years, comprising thousands of pages and hundreds of witness accounts, could only be examined by specialists. When Lévai dismissed people who were working to prove a preconceived hypothesis, it was obvious that he was referring to Rudolph Philipp, who was also present. Philipp's response was that Lévai was lying 'from beginning to end'. After noisy reactions from the audience, Lévai promised to present evidence to an impartial delegation within 36 hours. Before leaving the meeting to travel to Oslo, he presented the documentary find he had made in Budapest: a draft of a Nansen Plan for Hungary allegedly written by Wallenberg. This was rejected by Wallenberg's fellow diplomat Lars G:son Berg, who had been present at the opening of the bank vault in Budapest where Wallenberg's belongings had been stored. No document concerning a Nansen Plan had been found there, and there was doubt that the draft referred to by Lévai had even been written by a Swede. Like Philipp, G:son Berg argued against Lévai's claim that the Arrow Cross or the Germans had murdered

---

151 *Ny Dag*, 17 September 1947. See also '10.000-tals ha utfrågats om Wallenberg', *Trelleborgstidningen*, 18 July 1947; 'Gåtan olöst om Wallenberg: Wallenbergkännare går till attack', *Provinstidningen Dalsland*, 18 July 1947; Eric Sjöquist, *Raoul Wallenberg*, p. 95; and Brink, *Raoul Wallenberg i dagspressen under kalla kriget*, pp. 22–23.

Wallenberg, saying that this would have been virtually impossible 'after he had come under the protection of the Russians'.[152] The meeting became 'a heated debate in the otherwise peaceful Women's Federation premises' and ended with 'a gentle but determined women's deputation which departed immediately' in order to renew contact with Lévai.[153]

In the wake of the meeting Philipp received praise. Some of those who believed that the answers to the questions about Wallenberg were to be found in Moscow lauded Philipp for his great commitment and comprehensive efforts. Not everyone was satisfied, though. Philipp's critics questioned his failure to present clear evidence for his thesis.[154] An editorial writer for one of the leading evening newspapers had not realized that Philipp was Austrian but described him as a compatriot of Lévai. It must, the writer continued, 'be regarded as almost macabre that these Hungarians should sit here in Stockholm and air their internal antipathies in public'. What added to the bitter aftertaste was that this was a deeply tragic event which had preoccupied and tormented the Swedish people for over two years, 'causing bitter disappointment to all the official investigators'.[155]

Undeterred, Philipp renewed his attack on Lévai. Like Lévai, Philipp had interviewed a number of people in Budapest who had followed Wallenberg's activities from close quarters. They had distanced themselves from Lévai because they feared what his information, published in a Hungarian book, might lead to as the Soviet Union further tightened its grip on Hungary. Philipp said

---

152 'Philipp: Raoul Wallenberg levde ännu vid jultiden 1946', *Göteborgs Handels- och Sjöfartstidning*, 19 July 1947; 'Dokumentfynden ökar mystiken kring Wallenberg', *Dagens Nyheter*, 19 July 1947.
153 'Dokumentfynden ökar mystiken kring Wallenberg', *Dagens Nyheter*, 19 July 1947. See also 'Wallenberg dog i Ungern tror Szent-Györgyi', *Arbetet*, 18 July 1947; 'Bevisen i Wallenbergaffären granskas i offentlig dispyt', *Arbetaren*, 18 July 1947; 'Ord-duellen Wallenberg torkar in: Den utmanade har rest hem', *Aftonbladet*, 18 July 1947; 'Wallenberg var ryssarnas fånge', *Arbetaren*, 19 July 1947; 'Wallenberg-bevis under diskussion', *Göteborgs Handels- och Sjöfartstidning*, 18 July 1947.
154 'Levai vill inte visa dokument om Wallenberg', *Arbetet*, 19 July 1947. Philipp disputed the information because he had been very eager to present the documents but had not received the UD's permission to present all the documents regarding the case: 'Wallenberg-historien: Prat om värdelöst papper förhindrade upplysningar', *Arbetaren*, 21 July 1947.
155 'Kring Wallenberg', *Expressen*, 18 July 1947.

that this was one of several reasons why they had no confidence in the Hungarian Wallenberg Committee.[156]

The controversial nature of the assertion that Wallenberg was dead is also shown by the fact that the Swedish publisher removed the section in the Hungarian edition in which Lévai implied that Wallenberg had died in Budapest. He was asked to write a new version with an ending in which the Swedish diplomat disappears into the unknown. The change did not go unnoticed. The fact that Lévai laconically and abruptly ended his tale on 17 January, Wallenberg's last day in the Hungarian capital, and did not report on the investigations into what had happened thereafter 'must be interpreted by the Swedish reader as a necessary and forced political consideration', one reviewer asserted.[157] Another writer stressed that the main reason the book was worth reading was 'not the merit of the author but that of the subject'. A particularly serious matter was the way in which the Swedish translation had been 'fiddled and tampered with by means of changes and omissions' because there were people in Sweden with knowledge of 'Raoul Wallenberg's subsequent fate' that collided with Lévai's claims. Despite the changes made to the Swedish edition, the message from the Hungarian original was still clear, and this satisfied the Soviet authorities. That was less than surprising, since '[t]he person who thinks that anyone can sit in Hungary and write anything other than what suits the Soviet power can cast the first stone'.[158] Despite such devastating criticism, the first two Swedish editions of the book quickly sold out. But after pressure from Rudolph Philipp and Maj von Dardel, among others, the book was withdrawn and the third edition pulped.[159]

---

156 Mia Leche-Löfgren, 'Vi kan ej slå oss till ro med Wallenbergs försvinnande', *Göteborgs Handels- och Sjöfartstidning*, July 17 1947; 'Spåren av Wallenberg slutar på Budapestgata', *Morgon-Tidningen*, 17 July 1947; 'Nansenaktion till Ungerns hjälp: Raoul Wallenbergs sista projekt', *Svenska Dagbladet*, 18 July 1947; 'Philipp: Raoul Wallenberg levde ännu vid jultiden 1946', *Göteborgs Handels- och Sjöfartstidning*, 19 July 1947.
157 T. Hln, 'Dokument om Raoul Wallenberg', *Dagens Nyheter*, 13 July 1948.
158 Mia Leche Löfgren, 'Dubbelbottnad avsikt', *Göteborgs Handels- och Sjöfartstidning*, 8 June 1948.
159 Sjöquist, *Raoul Wallenberg*, p. 195. Jenő Lévai's original text, in which he dismissed accusations that Wallenberg had been removed from Budapest by the NKVD, was printed in an English edition that was published in 1988; Lévai, *Raoul Wallenberg*, p. 218.

New information in October 1947 suggesting that Wallenberg was still alive revived the issue of his disappearance.[160] Philipp continued to pursue the matter, renewing his attacks on those who, like the Hungarian Vilmos Böhm, claimed – 'even though they knew better' – that the Germans had killed Wallenberg.[161] It soon became clear that Philipp was the strong man of the Wallenberg campaign. As time passed, he gained the approval of people who shared his view that the Swedish government was doing too little in the matter, not least because his demands were reasonable in that it was the Soviet Union that was accountable for whatever had happened to Wallenberg, and because – unlike the Swedish government – his starting point was not one of doubt.[162]

## Philipp vs. pro-Moscow Communists

In 1945, Philipp made his voice heard in earnest in his new homeland when he published a quasi-autobiography that was very much a showdown with the Czech shoe king Tomáš Bata and his system of exploitation. Under this system, workers became co-owners, but without any obvious benefits as they were encouraged to compete against each other in pursuit of higher production goals while being held responsible for any losses the company might incur.[163] Anyone who took a stand alongside the workers in an explicit critique of a capitalist exploitative system might be expected to garner sympathy from the left. This was by no means a given, though. Ten years earlier, Charlie Chaplin had that exact experience when his film *Modern Times* went from being a project cherished by leading Soviet cultural politicians to a cautionary tale, as his critique of the machine society ran counter to the large-scale investment in heavy industry in the Soviet Union.[164] Philipp, too, had previously been on good terms with influential Communists in Moscow. His criticism of Bata led to him being made a guest of

---

160 See e.g. 'Raoul Wallenberg var i livet för blott några månader sedan', *Svenska Dagbladet*, 21 October 1947; 'Återigen Raoul Wallenberg', *Arbetaren*, 22 October 1947; 'Raoul Wallenberg', *Stockholms Tidningen*, 22 October 1947.
161 Rudolph Philipp, 'De ungerska "reskamraterna"', *OBS!* 1951:3, 61.
162 See e.g. Mia Leche, 'Raoul Wallenberg än en gång', *Göteborgs Handels- och Sjöfartstidning*, 26 January 1951.
163 Philipp, *Skor, svett och tårar*, passim.
164 Zander, 'Modernitetskritik i svart-vitt', pp. 217–218.

honour in the Soviet capital, but the outcome of his elevation was unexpected. At first there had been a consensus that the Bata system was an example of capitalist predation, but the Soviet Communists adopted the basic idea that workers should be encouraged to compete against one another, with prizes for the most successful, regardless of whether they were producing women's stockings or tractors. Inspired by Bata, the Soviet Union introduced 'shock workers', called *udarniki*, who wore a badge of honour like a medal on their chests. Although Philipp was paid for a new edition of his critical book on the Bata system, it was withdrawn a few weeks later. Nor did the film, intended for export only and with a final scene showing the Soviet flag flying over Bata factories, see the light of day.[165]

For Swedish pro-Moscow Communists, this type of criticism was not welcome, and that mindset also coloured their attitude in the Wallenberg case. In the Communist daily paper *Ny Dag*, it was therefore Jenő Lévai's opinion that prevailed. The newspaper's writers sympathized with the idea that Wallenberg had been murdered by the Arrow Cross, which meant that the Soviet Union had nothing to do with his disappearance. Confidence in the authorities in Moscow was also expressed by *Ny Dag*'s reproducing an argument from the Soviet magazine *Novoye Vremya*. The gist of that argument was that people from 'reactionary circles' were exploiting 'the tragedy of Raoul Wallenberg' with the aim of disseminating propaganda against the Soviet Union.[166] *Ny Dag*'s readers were left in no doubt that Rudolph Philipp was one of these reactionaries, and '[his] book, based on hearsay and rumour and dictated by counter-revolutionary fervour', found no favour with the newspaper's reviewer.[167] This censorious tone was echoed when the Riksdag debated Wallenberg's disappearance in

---

165 Philipp, *Skor, svett och tårar*, pp. 348–352. Philipp continued to talk about his former employer, Bata. He repeatedly warned of what he saw as the shoe manufacturer's anti-union policies; see e.g. Ivan Oljelund, 'Framstående kapitalister', *Sölvesborgs-Tidningen*, 16 July 1962; Lars Lundkvist, 'Så arbetade det multinationella företaget: De gjorde en toppaffär på samhällets bekostnad', *Arbetet*, 8 December 1970.
166 *Ny Dag*, 17 September 1947; *Ny Dag*, 3 February 1948. See also Brink, *Raoul Wallenberg i dagspressen under kalla kriget*, pp. 22–23, 26.
167 'Wallenbergrykten avslöjas', *Ny Dag*, 18 July 1947. For a critique of this standpoint, see 'I dag', *Göteborgs Handels- och Sjöfartstidning*, 19 July 1947.

May 1951. 'The international trickster Philipp' was one of those who continued to write 'abusive letters' as part of an anti-Soviet propaganda campaign.[168] It is worth noting that such views were not only expressed in *Ny Dag*. For example, an editorial writer in the Liberal newspaper *Expressen* criticized both Philipp and Lévai and 'the competition' between them in their unsavoury struggle over the truth about Wallenberg's fate.[169]

For a couple of decades Philipp held a prominent position in the public sphere, claiming time and again that Wallenberg was alive and no effort should be spared to free him. Together with Maj von Dardel and others, he wrote an open letter to Sweden's Prime Minister in March 1951. The group welcomed a public enquiry announced by Tage Erlander and expressed their good will by explaining that they wanted to avoid the issue becoming subjected to party politics. They had therefore persuaded members of the centre-right opposition not to push the matter any further, so that the government could pursue its efforts to trace the missing Swede in peace. However, they stressed that one thing was already clear: evidence existed according to which the Soviet Union was responsible for Wallenberg's disappearance.[170] In April 1953, encouraged by the testimony of the freed Italian diplomat Claudio de Mohr plus the death of Stalin about a month earlier, Philipp expressed the hope that the Kremlin authorities would do away with their earlier mistakes so that Sweden could have 'one of her finest sons' back.[171]

The silence from Moscow persisted but Philipp stubbornly maintained his belief that Wallenberg was alive. In 1955, he said that it was wrong to call the Wallenberg case a mystery, as there were numerous testimonies from prisoners who stated that they had either shared a cell with Wallenberg or had had contact with him via tapping. Several returning prisoners from the Soviet Union, of

---

168 'Svindelkampanjen om Raoul Wallenberg inför riksdagen', *Ny Dag*, 23 May 1951.
169 'Kring Wallenberg', *Expressen*, 18 July 1947.
170 Maj von Dardel, Yngve Schartau, Birgitta de Vylder-Bellander, and Rudolph Philipp, 'Öppet brev till statsministern', *Arbetaren*, 5 March 1951. See also 'Raoul Wallenberg blev fängslad av ryska NKVD', *Sölvesborgs-Tidningen*, 16 January 1951.
171 'Nya ryska makthavarna ger Wallenberg fri?', *Arbetaren*, 24 April 1953; 'Raoul Wallenbergs öde', *Trelleborgstidningen*, 24 April 1953; and 'Pressopinionen', *Göteborgs Handels- och Sjöfartstidning*, 15 January 1955.

various nationalities, recounted stories of a man called Wallenberg whose conduct was exemplary even in prison and who had instilled courage in them. Their narratives strengthened Philipp's conviction that the missing Swede was not a forced labourer but rather a privileged prisoner of the state. That view also formed the starting point for the application by Sweden's ambassador to Moscow, Rolf Sohlman, which underwent an important change before it was sent to Marshal Voroshilov. Maj von Dardel did not wish to ask for a 'pardon' for Wallenberg, as that would be tantamount to admitting that he had committed crimes against the Soviet Union. Instead of 'pardon', it was 'justice' that should be demanded. However, there had been no response to the request. The combative Philipp argued that one factor contributing to the weak response from Moscow was that the official Swedish proposals were too cautiously presented. When the Speaker of the Riksdag's Second Chamber, Gustaf Nilsson, had met with Bulganin and Voroshilov, Ambassador Sohlman had been hovering 'like a nursemaid by his side'. That had prevented Nilsson from speaking freely, and as a result his intervention had been ineffective.[172] Likewise, it was a recurring problem that the people in charge of Sweden's government and its foreign policy did not react strongly enough against the 'agents and provocateurs' who served the Soviets by spreading false information about what had happened in Budapest in 1944–1945, and who also helped to discredit serious witnesses that had recently come forward.[173]

When, in 1957, the Soviets presented information to the effect that Wallenberg had died in the Lubyanka prison in 1947, Philipp was quick to speak out. The document was 'a web of fabrications'. It was his firm conviction that Wallenberg was alive, and therefore the fight for his release would continue.[174] Philipp continued to be

---

172 'UD har entydiga bevis att Wallenberg lever', *Arbetaren*, 16 November 1955; 'Ryssarna misstolkar Sohlmans artighet i fallet Wallenberg', *Arbetet*, 16 November 1955; 'Rättvisa och ej nåd begärd för Wallenberg', *Provinstidningen Dalsland*, 16 November 1955.
173 'UD utan civilkurage i Tomsen-affären', *Göteborgs Handels- och Sjöfartstidning*, 10 August 1956; 'Ryssbesked om Wallenberg får besk kommitté-kritik', *Provinstidningen Dalsland*, 26 April 1957.
174 Rudolph Philipp: '"Wallenberg lever: Kampen fortsätter"', *Göteborgs-Posten*, 8 February 1957; 'En väv av påhitt – och dåliga påhitt', *Göteborgs-Posten*; 'Svensk vitbok nu angelägen', *Upsala Nya Tidning*; 'Wallenberg-aktionen: "Vi vet att Raoul levde betydligt senare ..."', *Stockholms Tidningen*, all published on 8 February 1957.

troubled by Östen Undén's reluctance to exert further pressure. He also criticized those who, for reasons of realpolitik, defended the Minister for Foreign Affairs' initial wait-and-see position in relation to the Wallenberg case.[175] However, after the news from Moscow that Wallenberg had died in 1947, some of Philipp's most persistent critics were neutralized. Writers in *Ny Dag* dealt as best they could with the news from the Kremlin, among other things by blaming 'international businessmen' who had spread all sorts of stories about the missing diplomat, stories which had resulted in the Swedish government's investigators repeatedly being led astray. The leader of the Swedish Communist Party, Hilding Hagberg, commended Wallenberg. His achievements had been exemplary, as anti-fascists in all countries agreed. The news of his death was therefore bitter, but it also demonstrated a Soviet determination to 'liquidate post-war mistakes and ensure the most comprehensive democratization and safeguarding of the laws as well as of the rights of the people'.[176] While unwavering loyalty to the authorities in Moscow persisted, the writers in *Ny Dag* stopped asserting Soviet innocence; instead, they were more than willing to support Soviet Minister of Foreign Affairs Andrei Gromyko in 1957 when he declared that as far as the Soviets were concerned, the Wallenberg affair was closed.[177] Nor did the *Ny Dag* journalists see any further reason to write about Philipp.

In conjunction with discussions about new witness accounts, both in the early and late 1950s, Philipp maintained his conviction that the Swedish diplomat was still in Soviet custody. One new development was that he toned down his criticism of the leaders of Sweden's foreign policy. That, however, was the calm before the storm. Philipp was one of the driving forces when, in February 1951, the Wallenberg campaign – together with several other organizations, some of which were women's federations and associations – presented the Swedish government with a letter demanding that it was high time not only to request Soviet investigations, but also to express an unambiguous demand to Moscow that Wallenberg must be returned to Sweden. A similar message was conveyed in a magazine article by Philipp in early 1951, in which he

---

175 'Svårt återkomma till Sovjet säger UD i Wallenbergaffären', *Göteborgs Handels- och Sjöfartstidning*, 26 April 1957.
176 'Beskedet om Raoul Wallenberg' (editorial) and Hilding Hagberg, 'Sanningen är bitter för oss alla', *Ny Dag*, 8 February 1957.
177 'Gromyko: Wallenberg-affären avslutad!', *Aftonbladet*, 19 February 1957.

claimed to present the truth about Wallenberg – a truth which, by implication, was not necessarily recognized by members of Sweden's government and UD officials.[178] Philipp's activities were probably one reason why the question about what the Swedish government and the UD had achieved in the Wallenberg case was raised in the Riksdag in February 1951.[179] The tone was further sharpened in the winter of 1951–1952, when Philipp repeatedly accused Erlander, Undén, and State Secretary Folke Thunborg of incompetence and tardiness in the matter. He also claimed that Hungarian witnesses who had testified that they had seen Wallenberg alive after he had been declared missing by the Soviets had ended up in trouble. The witnesses' statements were particularly sensitive for the Hungarian Communist regime. Owing to the carelessness of UD officials, the Hungarian police had arrested these witnesses soon after the police became aware of them, whereupon the witnesses were forced to withdraw their statements under threat.[180]

Peace was finally made between the UD and Wallenberg's relatives, and the latter handed over the material they had collected, including through Philipp, to the UD. A year later, however, outraged accusations were again heard in the public debate. Against the express wishes of the Swedish government, representatives of the Wallenberg campaign wanted to publish a classified exchange of notes between Sweden and the Soviet Union. Simultaneously, Philipp renewed his attack on UD officials who were, in his opinion, spreading a malicious rumour that Wallenberg had been guilty of misconduct in Budapest.[181] By the late 1950s, the language was much milder. Then Philipp was pleased that a Justice of the Supreme Court of Sweden had agreed with him in recognizing the truthfulness of some of the witness accounts of the returned Gulag prisoners. This was a great advantage, because '[n]othing is more alien to me than to seek conflict

---

178 Rudolph Philipp, 'Sanningen om fallet Raoul Wallenberg', *Allt*, 1951:1; 'Regeringen uppmanas kräva R. Wallenbergs hemsändande', *Arbetaren*, 26 February 1951.
179 'Interpellation: Fru Gärde Widemar ang. redogörelse för efterforskningarna efter Raoul Wallenberg', *Riksdagens protokoll. Andra kammaren*, No. 8, Tuesday 27 February 1951.
180 'Raoul Wallenberg lever trots allt!', *Aftonbladet*, 12 January 1951; Rudolph Philipp, 'Vad UD underlåtit göra för Raoul Wallenberg', *OBS!* 1951:7.
181 See e.g. Ronnie Olsson, 'Erlanders hemliga samtal om Wallenberg', *Aftonbladet*, 25 May 1982.

with those in power in Sweden. We depend as much on the goodwill of the Swedish Government Offices as on that of the Kremlin'.[182] This affable tone had previously been the exception rather than the rule. In 1945, Philipp had politely debated with Tage Erlander about the police and their degree of impartiality in Swedish society.[183] When they met again a few years later, to discuss Raoul Wallenberg, the tone was much more hostile. One of the people who accessed tape recordings from the meetings described Philipp as 'terribly harsh in his criticism of the Swedish Foreign Office's actions', and notes from the meetings give the same impression, with Philipp repeatedly and unhesitatingly interrupting Erlander and other representatives of the government and the UD.[184] In his autobiography, the Prime Minister diplomatically referred to Philipp as the Wallenberg family's 'energetic collaborator'.[185] Erlander's diary entries contained different and much less polite descriptions. In these, the Prime Minister accused Philipp, 'the family's well-intentioned evil spirit', of writing 'mendacious articles' and of constantly derailing the conversations between them with his 'idiotic and vicious attacks'. Erlander also described Philipp, and his 'ally' Arvid Fredborg, a Conservative journalist who in 1943 had published the strongly Third Reich-critical book *Bakom stålvallen* [English edition: *Behind the Steel Wall, A Swedish Journalist in Berlin 1941–43*], as 'ruthlessly manipulative'. After Khrushchev's resignation in 1964, Erlander wrote that a new leader might provide new opportunities. It was a modest hope. On one point, though, he was quite clear: 'Philipp will be phoning like a madman.'[186]

---

182 'Rudolph Philipp: Bevisningen är bindande', *Göteborgs Handels- och Sjöfartstidning*, 30 May 1959.
183 Tage Erlander, 'Polisen och demokratin', *Tiden*, 1945:3, pp. 146–150; Rudolph Philipp, 'Polisen och samhället', *Tiden*, 1945:3, pp. 151–155.
184 Eric Sjöquist, 'När världen upptäckte Raoul Wallenberg', *Expressen*, 16 January 1981. See also Sjöquist, *Dramat Raoul Wallenberg*, pp. 118–127 and Valfrid Paulsson, 'Sammanfattning av statsministerns samtal med fru von Dardel den 18 juni kl. 16.00–17.00', RKA, Raoul Wallenberg, UD2018/005505, Vol. 30.
185 Erlander, *1955–1960*, p. 294.
186 Erlander (ed.), *Tage Erlander: Dagböcker 1945–1949*, p. 150; Erlander (ed.), *Tage Erlander: Dagböcker 1950–1951*, p. 211; Erlander (ed.), *Tage Erlander: Dagböcker 1961–1962*, p. 46; Erlander (ed.), *Tage Erlander: Dagböcker 1963–1964*, p. 275; Erlander (ed.), *Tage Erlander: Dagbok 1965*, p. 73. See also Erlander (ed.), *Tage Erlander: Dagböcker 1955*, p. 170.

Östen Undén and his colleagues at the UD joined Philipp's critics. Arne S. Lundberg, who had been the lead man in charge of the Wallenberg case for a number of years, complained in the early 1950s that it was difficult to establish well-functioning cooperation between the Swedish government and Wallenberg's immediate family. Lundberg strongly advised against any assertive diplomatic measures, such as the presentation of a démarche to the authorities in Moscow, and also defended the need for secrecy. Philipp's presence made this necessity far harder to ensure, he said, because experience showed that sooner or later he would publish, in a more or less distorted form, conversations that had been held behind closed doors.[187] Sven Grafström joined in the lament, describing Philipp as a 'complete hysteric who had found easily duped victims in Raoul Wallenberg's despairing mother and his half-brother Guy von Dardel'.[188] Among Grafström's colleagues, words such as ill-judged, nervous, unbalanced, aggressive, and suspicious were used to describe Philipp, although his deep knowledge of Central European affairs won grudging recognition.[189] Anyone who challenged the notion that Wallenberg was alive in Soviet captivity ran the risk of being accused by Philipp of doing 'Moscow's bidding', which was not popular.[190] Nor did Queen Louise of Sweden, who admittedly possessed no formal influence, have much confidence in Philipp.[191] He, in turn, continued to have limited confidence in the Swedish authorities' handling of the Wallenberg case, as again became evident in connection with Erlander's proposal in 1965 for a new White Paper about the exchange of notes between the UD and Moscow. Philipp argued that such a White Paper was counterproductive because it signalled that the case was closed, which meant that Wallenberg no longer fulfilled the function of a prominent prisoner of state and a potential bargaining chip. Philipp argued forcefully that handling the case in such a way was irresponsible, which ultimately meant that the Swedish government

---

187 Arne S. Lundberg, 'PM', 19 and 26 November 1951; Arne S. Lundberg, 'Till Wallenberg-aktionen', November 1951; Arne S. Lundberg, 'P.M.' 22 July 1953, RKA, Raoul Wallenberg, UD2018/005505, Vol. 1.
188 Ekman (ed.), *Sven Grafström: Anteckningar 1945–1954*, pp. 782–783. See also Möller, *Östen Undén*, pp. 277–278.
189 Petri, *Sverige i stora världen*, p. 185. See also Villius and Villius, *Fallet Raoul Wallenberg*, pp. 57–58; Bierman, *Righteous Gentile*, p. 202.
190 Ehrenstråle and Ehrenstråle, *Sju dagar i oktober 1947*, p. 120.
191 Palmstierna, *Fjädern i min hand*, p. 194.

bore as much responsibility for Wallenberg's imprisonment as did the Kremlin.[192]

## The fight for Raoul Wallenberg continues

In the late 1940s, one writer criticized the raw force and brutality of the Soviet Union, which was abundantly obvious in the Wallenberg case. Even the Swedish authorities did not escape the criticism unscathed. Those in charge of Sweden's foreign policy were described as individuals who caused no anxiety in the Kremlin.[193] Similar criticisms continued to be made, and they were justified. Disagreements about the Wallenberg case existed at the Swedish government level, within the UD, and at the royal court. One commentator said that overall, 'it was difficult for individuals within the UD administration to assert themselves in the Wallenberg affair'.[194] Per Anger later expressed a similar opinion. He had been put in charge of the Wallenberg case in 1949. As he stated in 1979, he became increasingly critical of the Swedish government's mode of action. After a number of confrontations with Erlander and Undén, he resigned the position as the government's spokesman in favour of increased involvement with the Wallenberg Committee. When he spoke out in the early 1980s, his verdict was harsh: 'the lost years' after the war ended had been characterized by 'unimaginably lame and very-nearly-lame attempts to get to the bottom of the matter'.[195]

These high-level tensions may be glimpsed in political memoirs as well. Carl-Fredrik Palmstierna, a baron, courtier, historian, and close acquaintance of Maj and Guy von Dardel, was both criticized and applauded for his eagerness – expressed in his autobiography *Fjädern i min hand* ['The feather in my hand'] – to point to problematic conditions in 1970s Sweden in general, and the Swedish unwillingness to put pressure on the Soviet authorities in the

---

192 '"Sverige bär ansvar för Wallenberg-fallet": Kritik mot Erlander', *Göteborgs Handels- och Sjöfartstidning*, 2 July 1965.
193 'Raoul Wallenberg', *Arbetaren*, 29 April 1949.
194 Sjöquist, *Raoul Wallenberg*, p. 106.
195 Anger, *With Raoul Wallenberg in Budapest*, pp. 149–155; Dag Lindberg, 'Här räddade han tiotusenden ur dödsmaskinen' (interview with Per Anger), *Vi*, 1982:19, 10. See also Anger, 'Raoul Wallenberg', *Svensk Tidskrift*, 1984:4; Per Anger, 'Kampen för Raoul Wallenberg', *Svensk Tidskrift*, 1992:8–9; Rolf H. Lindblom, 'Raoul Wallenbergs öde', *Svensk Tidskrift*, 1992:6.

Wallenberg case in particular.[196] Palmstierna had tried in vain to influence Gustaf VI Adolf to assume an active role and demand an answer as to what had happened to the missing diplomat. Palmstierna said that Dag Hammarskjöld reacted coldly to a similar suggestion because the UN Secretary-General was caught up in 'that blasted Foreign Ministry esprit de corps!' Nor was Palmstierna successful when, in 1966, he urged the prominent Social Democrat Alva Myrdal to include Raoul Wallenberg in her speech on political prisoners in conjunction with the formation of the Swedish branch of Amnesty International.[197] Myrdal's party colleague Ulla Lindström, who was a minister from 1954 to 1964, did not share Palmstierna's view. In her autobiography *I regeringen* ['In the government'], she argued that official Sweden had done everything in the nation's power. She dismissed State Secretary for Foreign Affairs Arne S. Lundberg's special personal involvement in the matter, putting it down to Lundberg's allegedly having 'something of the Wild West novel and detective thriller in his nature: missing heroes and suspected spies arouse his particular interest, attract him irresistibly, it would seem'.[198]

Unsurprisingly, the recurring schisms led to occasionally tense contacts between the UD and Wallenberg's relatives in what could sometimes be an almost hostile atmosphere. Eric Sjöquist writes, 'a peculiar struggle was going on over Raoul Wallenberg – not primarily between Sweden and the Soviets, but between the official Swedish authorities and the private campaigns, including those conducted by the Wallenberg campaign and the von Dardel family, which were pushing for something to be done about the case'.[199] The latter were not content with exerting pressure but pursued their own ways of drawing attention to the case. These included helping to organize international hearings about Wallenberg's

---

196 See e.g. the favourably inclined Stig Ahlgren, 'Orosanden vid Gustaf VI Adolfs hov', *Svenska Dagbladet*, 24 September 1976 and the critical reviewers Jarl Torbacke, 'Då rev drottningen sönder Palmstiernas brev ...', *Expressen*, 28 September 1976, and Ruth Halldén, "Fjädern i min hand': En pinsam självbelåtenhet', *Dagens Nyheter*, 7 October 1976.
197 Palmstierna, *Fjädern i min hand*, pp. 191–198, 205–206, quotation p. 195.
198 Ulla Lindström, *I regeringen*, pp. 99–100.
199 Sjöquist, *Raoul Wallenberg*, p. 140; Sjöquist, *Affären Raoul Wallenberg*, p. 133. See also e.g. Petri, *Sverige i stora världen*, pp. 186–187; Villius and Villius, *Fallet Raoul Wallenberg*, pp. 59–67; Carl Persson and Anders Sundelin, *Utan omsvep*, p. 122.

disappearance and writing letters to American and Soviet leaders. These approaches and contact channels had not secured the prior approval of the Swedish government and the UD.[200]

## Raoul Wallenberg and Henry Kissinger

One consequence of the Wallenberg family's activity in the case was that leading Swedish politicians repeatedly expressed concern over initiatives beyond their control. One example can be found in the discussions that were held in 1952 after the Swedes believed for the first time – thanks to the testimony of the previously mentioned Claudio de Mohr – that they had firm evidence that Wallenberg had been taken to the Soviet Union in 1945. It was hoped that this information would lead to an opening in the talks with Moscow. Tage Erlander's concern about an unforeseen move at home is telling: 'Just as long as the relatives don't cause any trouble.'[201] Cooperation subsequently improved, but the mutual suspicion between the Swedish government and the UD on the one hand and Wallenberg's family on the other was still expressed on later occasions.[202]

One such incident occurred in 1973 and proved troublesome not only for the Swedish government but also for US Secretary of State Henry Kissinger. Maj von Dardel had asked the US government to raise the Wallenberg case in conjunction with the impending state visit of Soviet leader Leonid Brezhnev. Thomas R. Pickering, a young US State Department official who later became US ambassador to Russia and other countries, plus four other State Department officials suggested that the United States should support her appeal, not least because Wallenberg had been hired by the American Iver Olsen, and make an official enquiry to the Soviet authorities about the fate of the Swedish diplomat. Pickering's recommendation was not supported by his superior, Henry Kissinger.[203] Instead, Kissinger

---

200 See e.g. Göran Berg, 'Promemoria', 3 November 1980, RKA, Raoul Wallenberg, UD2018/005505, Vol. 2.
201 Erlander (ed.), *Tage Erlander: Dagböcker 1952*, p. 31. See Petri, *Sverige i stora världen*, p. 191.
202 See e.g. Erlander (ed.), *Tage Erlander: Dagböcker 1961–1962*, p. 50; letters from Guy von Dardel to Leif Leifland, 21 June and 30 November 1979, RA, Raoul Wallenbergkommitténs arkiv. E1:12 Korrespondens. Huvudserie 1979, I–M.
203 Bierman, *Righteous Gentile*, pp. 190–192; William Korey, 'Wallenberg and the undelivered letter', *The Christian Science Monitor*, 28 August 1995.

secretly contacted the UD to give advance notice of his response. He intended to contact Wallenberg's mother to express his sympathy, but also to tell her that it was not possible for the United States to pursue the case. It was a matter for the Swedish government and the Red Cross.[204] Leif Leifland, who worked on the Wallenberg case for a number of years, argued that the American reluctance to become wholeheartedly involved in the Swede's fate in the early 1970s was mainly because Kissinger did not want to jeopardize the chances of an agreement with the Soviet Union over the Middle East. The fact that Olof Palme had spoken out sharply against US foreign policy in general and the Vietnam War in particular was less important than 'relations with the other superpower and concern for peace in the Middle East'.[205]

The story of Maj von Dardel's letter became public in March 1979, just over a year after her death. Sven Strömberg, Swedish Radio's correspondent in London, had been granted permission to go through classified US documents. His findings were presented in a double-spread article in the Sunday supplement of the leading Swedish daily paper *Dagens Nyheter*, an article which attracted attention not only in Sweden. It was not long before the article was picked up by representatives of US intelligence. This is hardly surprising, because over the years Strömberg had commented on both Swedish and American efforts in the Wallenberg case. He stressed that high-ranking Swedish officials had rejected US invitations to cooperate in the matter both before and now, but he was even more critical of Kissinger's actions. Given that he had grown up in a family forced to flee Germany in 1938, a different reaction would have been expected and desirable. Kissinger, 'who at one time was persecuted as a Jew by the Nazis', should not have dismissed the possibility of discovering what had happened to Wallenberg out of hand. Strömberg's explanation of why Kissinger had ultimately

---

204 Message from Leif Leifland, 13 June 1973, RKA, Raoul Wallenberg, UD2001/00009, Vol. 1.
205 Leifland, *Frostens år*, pp. 153–155. For a similar conclusion see Eliasson, 'Vietnamkriget och de svensk-amerikanska förbindelserna', pp. 121–126; Pierre Schori, 'Olof Palme i världen', pp. 131–132. On the continued – and often sensitive – contacts between representatives of the Wallenberg committees, the UD, and Kissinger, see e.g. letters from Guy von Dardel to Per Anger, 18 May and 24 June 1979, RA, Raoul Wallenbergföreningens arkiv, E1:1. Korrespondens, Huvudserie 1979, A–H.

refused to endorse von Dardel's appeal was the American's critical view of Sweden's Vietnam policy.[206]

Whatever explanation was given for Kissinger's decision, we catch a glimpse of him as a modern equivalent of one of the foremost exponents of realpolitik: Klemens von Metternich. The Austrian diplomat features prominently in Kissinger's 1954 doctoral thesis, published three years later as *A World Restored: Metternich, Castlereagh and the Problems of Peace 1812–1822*. Robert D. Kaplan has convincingly argued that this book demonstrates the decisive influence that the Holocaust – as well as the feeble negotiating efforts of the British and French leaders vis-à-vis Adolf Hitler in the context of the Munich Agreement of 1938 – had on Kissinger's thinking about international relations. Anyone who is able to draw the lines from his analyses of early nineteenth-century diplomacy to the decisions he made during his time as US Secretary of State will gain insights into the principles of realism that Kissinger espoused through *A World Restored*. These principles include the belief that disorder is worse than injustice; that the idea that one's own side is morally superior to the other is misleading and harmful; and that stability is preferable to rapid change and demands for universal justice.[207] Given such a background, his decision in 1973 not to discuss Raoul Wallenberg with the Soviet authorities may be regarded as highly rational. Avoiding an issue that was sensitive for Soviet politicians and diplomats was 'a practical accommodation to reality, not a unique moral insight', to quote his favourable assessment of those diplomats who, after the devastating Thirty Years' War, negotiated the Peace of Westphalia in 1648 proceeding from

---

206 Sven Strömberg, 'Vietnamkritiken irriterade: Retad Kissinger stoppade aktion för Wallenberg', *Dagens Nyheter*, 18 March 1979. A similar conclusion was suggested by Jack Anderson in 'A missing Swedish diplomat's fate', *The Washington Post*, 30 June 1979. Strömberg's article also attracted attention in the US in other respects. Soon after being published it was translated by CIA employees: WALLENBERG, RAOUL VOL. 2_0044.pdf (cia.gov) (accessed 22 November 2021). Strömberg was also discussed within the CIA in 1980, when he was presumed to be a good possible contact, not least in connection with questions about Raoul Wallenberg's fate: 'Memorandum for C/INS', 23 April 1980, specialCollection/nwcda2/46/WALLENBERG, RAOUL VOL 3_0051, Nazi War Crime Disclosure Act, Records of the Central Intelligence Archive (CIA), National Archives.

207 Robert D. Kaplan, 'Kissinger, Metternich, and realism', *The Atlantic*, June 1999, www.theatlantic.com (accessed 23 November 2021).

their conviction of 'the necessity to come to an arrangement with each other', not on the basis of 'some sort of superior morality'.[208]

## Quiet diplomacy as a contentious domestic political issue

The main political objective in Sweden during the Cold War was that the country should continue its neutrality policy from the Second World War by means of strict non-alignment. The question of how this policy should be applied in practice sometimes led to disagreement, though. One example was the noisy discussions that erupted after Khrushchev suddenly and unexpectedly cancelled his state visit to Sweden in 1959. The leader of the Swedish Conservative Party, Jarl Hjalmarson, had opposed the visit from the outset and renewed his attack on the Social Democratic government. As a result of his criticism, Hjalmarson was excluded from the Swedish delegation representing Sweden at the United Nations that year. The official Soviet explanation for the cancellation of the state visit was anti-Soviet agitation. That the Wallenberg case was part of this agitation is clear from an internal Soviet report. It stressed that from the outset, the centre-right opposition in Sweden had used the Wallenberg affair to conduct 'anti-Soviet propaganda'.[209]

Continually fuelling the domestic debate over Raoul Wallenberg were recurring Soviet moves and witness accounts that reached UD staff in an irregular stream from the end of the war and for half a century thereafter. These utterances reached the public sphere as well, which was not something that might have been taken for granted. As a result of the lack of clarity and evidence about Wallenberg, a great deal of attention was paid to people who claimed to have seen or met the Swedish diplomat. One early statement came from Stella Kuylenstierna-Andrassy, a Swede who had married into one of Hungary's most influential families, writing about her experiences of the turbulent war years in Hungary and her dramatic escape from the Red Army in 1945. One of the stops along the way was 'Hungary's most beautiful city', Sopron, where she maintained that Wallenberg had set up an office. According to some accounts he had been killed in bombing raids on the city,

---

208 Henry Kissinger, *World Order*, p. 3.
209 Gerner, 'Konsekvenser för den svenska utrikespolitiken', pp. 80–81. See also Bjereld, *Hjalmarsonaffären*, pp. 97–112 and Jarring, *Rikets förhållande till främmande makt*, pp. 47–48.

whereas other rumours claimed that he had been taken as a Soviet prisoner to the nearby Cseklész Castle following the occupation of the area by the Red Army at the end of March 1945.[210]

Some three decades later, Britt and Hans Ehrenstråle claimed something completely different. Hans Ehrenstråle was a Swedish diplomat who had been a successful mediator in Greece in 1944 and had carried out humanitarian work in France, Italy, Yugoslavia, and Poland in the years after the war ended. During the last-mentioned mission, partisans had taken the Ehrenstråles to a badly wounded and exhausted man. Although it was not possible to identify him, they thought it highly likely that the man in question was Raoul Wallenberg, who had been brought to the area on prisoner transport.[211] The fact that this Polish trail was presented by two highly respected people with considerable international experience helped to make it impossible 'despite all the peculiar circumstances, to dismiss their story out of hand'.[212] In practice, however, both explanations were rejected, but there were many other trails to follow.

After the tentative start, the UD began a very extensive effort in the 1950s, much of which was carried out in secret. All of the 136 volumes pertaining to the Wallenberg case that have been made public contain investigations with witnesses, conducted with source-critical accuracy in accordance with the rules and guidelines that characterize practitioners of the historical past. All leads and suggestions were dealt with and followed up. Turning them into evidence was extremely difficult, partly because there was a need to preserve the safety of individuals. This was the case, for example, with a Polish contact who was active in dissident circles and had already been subjected to reprisals by the Polish Communist regime.[213] Some informants acted in good faith but provided

---

210 Kuylenstierna-Andrassy, *Pustan brinner*, pp. 136–140. See also Jan Kuylenstierna, 'Tog ryssarna Raoul Wallenberg i ungerska staden Sopron i mars 45?', *Aftonbladet*, 14 February 1951.
211 Ehrenstråle and Ehrenstråle, *Sju dagar i oktober 1947*, pp. 98–111.
212 'En döende i en lada i Polen i oktober 1947 ... Wallenberg?', *Expressen*, 27 April 1980. 'Förklaring från Rudolph Philipp', *Arbetaren*, 15 February 1951; Maj von Dardel, Guy von Dardel, Birgitta de Vylder-Bellander, Rudolph Philipp and Yngve Schartau, 'Wallenbergaffären', *Aftonbladet*, 16 February 1951
213 Percy Westerlund, 'Wallenberg-ärendet', 11 March 1980, RKA, Raoul Wallenberg, UD2001/00009, Vol. 10.

dubious information, while others freely invented. However, a large number of consistent reports, often based on information obtained through tapping on prison walls and water pipes or conversations between prisoners, left little doubt that Wallenberg had been, and possibly still was, in Soviet captivity. A steady stream of such witness accounts came in the wake of the repatriation, starting in the 1950s, of German prisoners of war, as well as people of other nationalities who had also been imprisoned in the Gulag. A number of these statements were raised at irregular intervals during the investigative process.[214] Despite this comprehensive endeavour, however, the ministers responsible could do nothing more than refer to previous investigations – all of which had been fruitless – when attention paid to these witness accounts led to questions being asked in the Riksdag.[215]

Prison guards have repeatedly come forward with more or less fanciful stories.[216] In some cases the witnesses' credibility was considered to be high, but there were other complicating factors. The information that Wallenberg had died in a Soviet prison as early as 1945 or 1946 was hard to verify. The source was a KGB agent who had defected to Britain and whose identity had to be kept secret because his family was still living in the Soviet Union. When the former agent was eventually interviewed by UD staff, his testimony still seemed credible despite some contradictions, but the chances of having it verified were basically non-existent.[217]

Other witnesses who either claimed to have met Wallenberg after 1945, but outside the Soviet Union, or who claimed to have had direct or indirect contact with him in prisons and prison camps were

---

214 See e.g. Martin Hallqvist, 'Anteckningar om tyska fångar', 3 October 1990, RKA, Raoul Wallenberg, UD2018/005505, Vol. 10.
215 Section 1, Svar på interpellation ang. Efterforskningarna efter Raoul Wallenberg m.m., *Riksdagens protokoll. Andra kammaren*, No. 14, 3 April 1964; Section 6, Ang. Raoul Wallenbergs öde, *Riksdagens protokoll*, No. 85, 20 May 1974.
216 The latter also include very loose speculations that the death of the heir to the Wallenberg empire, Marc 'Boy-Boy' Wallenberg, was not suicide but rather revenge from the Soviet security service aimed at his father, Marcus Wallenberg; this is argued by Bo J. Theutenberg in *Dagbok från UD: Volym 5 (1986–1988)*, 2020, pp. 391–392.
217 Sven Julin, 'Gordijevskij om Raoul Wallenberg', Memorandums, 13 and 14 January 1986; Sven Julin, 'Raoul Wallenbergvittnet Gordijevskij', Memorandum, 20 January 1986; Sven Julin, 'Brittiska frågor om Raoul Wallenbergärendet', Memorandum, 28 February 1986; Sven Julin,

easy to dismiss at an early stage. For example, around 1970 a traumatized German nurse did not think it unlikely that she had treated Wallenberg, but it turned out that she had been working in places where he had never been. Nor did it take long to reject the claim made by a Hungarian resident of Rome who relayed a compatriot's claim that Wallenberg had been observed in Kyiv in the late summer and autumn of 1947, or that of a Hungarian who firmly asserted that he was the last person to see Wallenberg in Budapest at a time four weeks after his disappearance. The former German prisoner of war who 'liked to talk about his memories in theatrical terms', while clearly appearing to pay no attention to detail, was dismissed almost immediately, as was the woman who claimed that Raoul Wallenberg – who had allegedly acquired an alias, whereupon he had lived and worked in Tallinn – was her father. Another person who came forward was certainly 'not a pleasant acquaintance', and his account was probably 'another Wallenbergian will o' the wisp'; but nevertheless, the story was recorded and researched before it, too, could be disputed.[218]

No testimony was dismissed immediately, but suspicion ran high from the outset about the fairly incoherent information offered by a certain 'Mr Budapest'. A similar reaction met the man who had waited for decades before establishing contact with the UD, not least because the diplomat who interviewed him was surprised that while he had a crystal-clear memory of having seen a sign bearing the name 'Raoul Wallenberg' in a Gulag camp, he had no idea that the man was Swedish. A former Gulag prisoner in exile in Israel revealed, as soon as the Swedish diplomat who had come to interview him stepped through the door of his Tel Aviv home, that

---

'Britterna, Gordijevskij och Raoul Wallenberg', Memorandum, 10 April 1986; Sven Julin, 'Gordijevskijs vittnesmål om Raoul Wallenberg', Memorandum, 29 May 1986; Sven Julin, 'Gordijevskij om Raoul Wallenberg', Memorandum, 15 December 1986, Lars-Åke Nilsson, 'G:s vittnesmål', 9 January 1987, RKA, Raoul Wallenberg, UD2018/005505, Vol. 2.

218 See e.g. Per Anger, 'P.M. ang. Raoul Wallenberg', 16 October 1950, RKA, UD2018/005505, Vol. 28; S. Lundström, 'Strängt förtroligt. PM', 28 May 1957; Per Anger, 'P.M. ang. Raoul Wallenberg', 16 October 1950, RKA, UD2018/005505, Vol. 8; Per Anger, 'P.M. ang. Raoul Wallenberg', 16 October 1950, RKA, UD2018/005505, Vol. 9; Lars Fredén, 'Wallenbergärendet', 23 September 1991, RKA, Raoul Wallenberg, UD2001/00009, Vol. 40; Lars Grundberg, 'Tallinns Raoul Wallenberg', 14 November 1991, RKA, Raoul Wallenberg, UD2001/00009, Vol. 41.

he had never met the missing Swede. The supposed witness had come forward because he wanted company, if only for a few hours. Another informant emphasized his own credibility by proclaiming that he had no interest whatsoever in the reward offered by the Swedish state to anyone who could provide clues in the Wallenberg case. That did not prevent him from enclosing his account number in his next letter to the UD.[219]

Other witnesses remained relevant for a relatively long period of time – sometimes for decades – even in cases where they appeared at an early stage to be 'liars' or 'pathological individuals' who had already exhibited 'psychological peculiarities ... at an early stage in Russian captivity'.[220] The same held true of witnesses who were *de facto* exposed as liars, such as the exiled Polish Jew Abraham Kalinski. A handwriting analysis showed that he had forged a letter from a doctor in Vladimir Prison stating that Wallenberg was alive after 1947.[221] In accordance with established practice, UD officials continued to conduct a dialogue with the Pole even after he unilaterally broke a vow of secrecy in the late 1970s and continued to elaborate on his claims, as when he asserted in 1985 that Wallenberg had died of pneumonia as late as February that year.[222] The conclusion was that he was 'an intellectually confused and emotionally unstable person with what appears to be a manifest need to play a prominent role in the matter of

---

219 See e.g. letter from Per Anger to Leif Leifland, 2 November 1976, RKA, Raoul Wallenberg, UD2001/00009, Vol. 2; letter from R. James Balfour to G(östa) Brunnström 22 April 1970; Gösta Brunnström to Leif Leifland, 'Raoul Wallenbergs försvinnande' 30 April 1970, RKA, UD2018/005505, Vol. 1; 'Polemik kring Wallenbergvittne', RKA, UD2001/00009, Vol. 36; Anders Troedsson, 'Vittnesmål om Raoul Wallenberg i fångläger i Permoblasten 1960–1965: intervju med Grigoriy Svjets, den 11 juni 2005', RKA, UD2018/005505, Vol. 25.

220 The assessment of the Austrian Otto Schöggl was first made in 1958, but his testimony was still being considered possibly viable in 1986; see Sven Julin, 'Raoul Wallenbergvittnet Otto Schöggl', 1 October 1986, RKA, UD2001/00009, Vol. 25.

221 See e.g. Abraham Kalinski, 'Wallenberg levde 1957: öppet brev till KGB-chefen', *Göteborgs-Posten*, 2 February 1980. See Sven Julin to Sven Hirdman, 'Raoul Wallenberg', report, 3 July 1985 and Sven Julin, 'Wallenbergvittnet Kalinski', Memorandum, 10 September 1985, RKA, Raoul Wallenberg, UD2001/00009, Vol. 24.

222 Sven Hirdman, 'Samtal med Kalinski om Raoul Wallenberg', Memorandum, 22 December 1978, RKA, Raoul Wallenberg, UD2018/005505, Vol. 10;

Raoul Wallenberg'.[223] Because such statements were made in secret, in accordance with the policy of quiet diplomacy, it was difficult for representatives of the Swedish government and the UD to repudiate these accounts publicly. After Kalinski had been interviewed several times in 1979, one journalist argued that his testimony was 'strong' and credible.[224] Following Kalinski's appearance on the Swedish television news programme *Aktuellt*, another journalist, accepting the story that Wallenberg was still imprisoned in the Soviet Union, complained that no representative of the Swedish government had listened to the Polish refugee before.[225]

Occasionally the witness accounts led to Swedish requests to Moscow for the information to be investigated. The answer was practically always the same: since it had been established that Wallenberg had died in July 1947, there was no need for new investigations.[226] UD officials did not give up. When opportunity arose, they sought to gain new clues in the Wallenberg case via informal contacts in the Soviet Union. For example, Tage Erlander discussed the issue with Hjalmar Mehr, then a member of the

---

Bengt Friedman, 'Strängt förtroligt', 2 January 1979 and Sven Hirdman, 'Raoul Wallenberg', 4 January 1979, RKA, Raoul Wallenberg, UD2001/00009, Vol. 4; Lars-Åke Nilsson, 'Abraham Kalinski', 30 April 1979 and Sven Hirdman, 'Samtal med Kallinski i Wallenberg-ärendet', 22 May 1979, RKA, Raoul Wallenberg, UD2001/00009, Vol. 5; Lars-Åke Nilsson, 'Kalinskis brevkort', 26 March 1980, RKA, Raoul Wallenberg, UD2001/00009, Vol. 10; Magnus Faxén, 'Ryskspråkig New York-tidning uppger att Raoul Wallenberg dog i februari i år', 29 October 1985, RKA, Raoul Wallenberg, UD2001/00009, Vol. 24; Sven Hirdman, 'Wallenbergvittnet Kalinski', 24 August 1984; Björn Lyrvall, 'Wallenbergärendet: Kalinskys vittnesmål avskrives' 8 October 1991, RKA, Raoul Wallenberg, UD2001/00009, Vol. 41. The UD also informed American diplomats of Kalinski's lack of credibility; see letter from Rodney Kennedy-Minott to Frank Church, 7 May 1979, RA, Raoul Wallenbergföreningens arkiv, E 1:2. Korrespondens. Huvudserie 1979, I–M.
223 (Sven) Julin, 'Promemoria', 15 August 1985, RKA, Raoul Wallenberg, UD2001/00009, Vol. 24.
224 Anders Hasselbohm, 'Hennes far mötte Raoul Wallenberg' (interview with Anna Bilder), *Vecko-Journalen*, 1979:10. See also Jens Thomsen, 'Da jeg første gang så Wallenberg', *Berlingske Tidende*, 28 May 1979.
225 Bengt Hansson, 'En kväll fylld av bra underhållning', *Göteborgs-Tidningen*, 27 January 1979.
226 (Sverker) Åström, 'Sjöborgsutredningen', 30 January 1959; Rolf Sohlman, 'ang. Raoul Wallenberg nr 187', RKA, Raoul Wallenberg, UD2018/005505, Vol. 1.

Stockholm City Council. Because of his Jewish origins, Mehr had become aware of the Nazi genocide early on and had helped to receive Jewish and Baltic refugees.[227] In 1954 he travelled to the Soviet Union to study its attitude towards the disabled, of whom there were many after the war. He also met the writer Ilya Ehrenburg. The latter had worked as a war correspondent and had paid close attention to the horrific fate of the Soviet Jews. Before Mehr left Sweden, Arne S. Lundberg asked him to sound out the Soviet position on the Wallenberg case.[228]

The approach adopted by Sweden's Social Democratic governments may be summarized as quiet diplomacy combined with the exertion of concrete pressure in conjunction with Swedish-Soviet state visits. Prime Minister Tage Erlander's commitment, like that of Undén, appears to have been weak at first, but there are many indications that the Prime Minister gradually became increasingly involved.[229] In conjunction with the 1965 White Paper, he claimed that he had worked on the case every week for ten years.[230] Erlander repeatedly raised the matter with the Soviet leaders. During these talks he stressed that the matter might seem small from the Soviet point of view but that it was 'large and important' for Sweden. An answer to the question might help to remove an 'irritant' in relations between the two countries.[231] Prior to Nikita Khrushchev's impending but later cancelled state visit in 1959, Erlander and Mehr discussed the advisability of writing a letter to the Soviet leader. Maj von Dardel also wrote a letter to Khrushchev prior to his scheduled visit. Erlander perceived clear domestic political advantages from writing a letter and presenting it together with the letter from Wallenberg's mother, as it would show that the diplomatic effort was not only being conducted in secret. However, he was strongly advised against such an action by Lundberg, as it would make further diplomatic negotiations more difficult. Instead,

---

227 Erlander (ed.), *Tage Erlander: Dagböcker 1963–1964*, p. 235; Björn Elmbrant, *Stockholmskärlek*, pp. 64–78.
228 Elmbrant, *Stockholmskärlek*, pp. 109–111.
229 Wilhelm Agrell, 'Handslag i det tysta', *Sydsvenskan*, 23 September 2011.
230 K. G. Michanek and Eric Sjöquist, 'Wallenbergaffären gav Erlander ingen ro', *Expressen*, 17 September 1965.
231 Erlander, *1955–1960*, pp. 298–306. See also Harrison, *Jag har ingen vilja till makt*, pp. 495–499. For the Soviet viewpoint see Gerner, 'Konsekvenser för den svenska utrikespolitiken', pp. 77–80; Petersson, *Med Moskvas ögon*, pp. 35–36, 107–108.

the matter was dealt with by the presentation of an official Swedish note to the Soviet government.[232]

The famous Swedish physician Nanna Svartz (1890–1986) became the subject of biographies and eulogies in the early twenty-first century, writers focusing on her skill as a doctor and medical researcher, on her becoming Sweden's first female professor at a state university, and on her exposing the unfortunate consequences of the fact that women who pursued careers were still primarily responsible for the family and home. It is rarely, if ever, mentioned that Svartz became a central figure in the Wallenberg case in the second half of the 1950s and early 1960s because of reports that Wallenberg was being held in a mental hospital.[233]

The Swedish-Soviet negotiations were given new impetus after Svartz asked her Soviet colleagues whether any of them knew anything about Wallenberg. The Soviet physician A. L. Myasnikov contacted her during a conference in Stockholm in 1954, and at a subsequent meeting with her in Moscow he added more detail to his statement that Wallenberg was being held in custody. While in the Soviet capital she also encountered Vladimir Semyonov, whom she had known since the early 1940s. At that time he had been working under Madame Kollontay, who, after developing a serious illness, had been treated and cured by Svartz in what was described as something of a miracle.[234] These ties of friendship may have contributed to Semyonov's initial confirmation of Myasnikov's statement, with the addition that Wallenberg was not in good health. The Soviet diplomat presumably realized that he had gone too far. When Svartz tried to reach him the following day, she was informed that he had gone to Africa and would not return for a number of weeks. Svartz, who was a colleague of Fredrik von Dardel at the Karolinska Institute in Stockholm and a good friend of Erlander, shared this new information, which she considered highly credible, with the Prime Minister. In 1961 Erlander wrote to Khrushchev demanding Wallenberg's release. When Rolf Sohlman delivered the letter to the Soviet leader, Khrushchev brusquely dismissed both the Swedish ambassador and the hope that there was any new information to consider. However, the issue

---

232 Erlander (ed.), *Tage Erlander: Dagböcker 1959*, pp. 123, 136, 146.
233 See Gunilla Bolinder, *A Tribute to the Memory of Nanna Svartz 1890–1986*, pp. 6–56; Gunilla Lindberg, *Starka kvinnor som fört Sverige framåt*, pp. 202–215.
234 Vaksberg, *Aleksandra Kollontaj*, pp. 293–294.

lived on. When Minister for Foreign Affairs Torsten Nilsson met Khrushchev in May 1963, the latter denied knowledge of Nanna Svartz and added that there would have been no reason for the Soviet Union not to hand over Wallenberg if he had still been alive, but that this was not the case.[235] Less than a year later, talks in which the Wallenberg question was the main issue were held in Sweden between Gromyko and Erlander. The Soviet Minister for Foreign Affairs maintained that the information Svartz had received in 1961 was based on a misinterpretation. When Svartz again contacted Myasnikov in the mid-1960s, both by letter and at a meeting with him and two officials from the Soviet Ministry of Foreign Affairs, he also agreed with the explanation that a linguistic misinterpretation had occurred. This amended version scarcely improved Swedish-Soviet relations, and it posed a severe challenge to the friendship between Erlander and Svartz.[236] The 'misinterpretation' did not do away with the allegations that Wallenberg was a prisoner in a Soviet mental hospital. On the contrary, such assertions continued to be made in the decades that followed.[237]

The fairly good atmosphere that had prevailed at the meeting between Nilsson and Khrushchev in 1964 had mostly evaporated a year later when the Soviet leader arrived in Sweden on a state visit. He was greeted by bold placard headlines from the tabloid *Expressen*, demanding in both Russian and Swedish: 'Where is our fellow countryman? Where is Raoul Wallenberg?' Bilingual headlines reappeared inside the newspaper atop double-spread articles describing Wallenberg's contributions in Budapest, reportage from the streets

---

235 Erlander (ed.), *Tage Erlander: Dagböcker 1961–1962*, pp. 26–28, 30, 32, 35, 38–39, 47–50; Leif Belfrage, 'P.M.', 7 February 1961, RKA, Raoul Wallenberg, UD2001/00009, Vol. 17; Svartz, *Steg för steg*, pp. 213–215; Nilsson, *Människor och händelser i Europa*, pp. 269–273; Persson and Sundelin, *Utan omsvep*, pp. 124–129; Pierrejean and Pierrejean, *Les secrets de l'Affaire Raoul Wallenberg*, pp. 234–236; Carlberg, *Raoul Wallenberg*, pp. 528–537.
236 Letter from A. L. Myasnikov to Nanna Svartz, 29 April 1964; Eric Virgin, 'PM', 27 March 1965; 'P.M. angående statsminister Erlanders samtal med ministerpresident Kosygin den 11 juni 1965 angående Wallenbnergfrågan', RKA, Raoul Wallenberg, UD2018/005505, Vol. 30; Hans Hederberg, 'Så kändes det att höra honom 'tyda' vårt samtal', *Aftonbladet*, 17 September 1965; Erlander (ed.), *Tage Erlander: Dagbok 1965*, pp. 28, 63, 73; Harrison, *Jag har ingen vilja till makt*, p. 711.
237 See e.g. Mark Lippold, 'Wallenberg lever på mentalsjukhus', *KvällsPosten*, 11 September 1979.

where he had walked while still a free man, and speculation about his fate after he had been taken into custody by Soviet personnel.[238] Together with Nilsson, Erlander again confronted Khrushchev with the information regarding Wallenberg in Soviet custody, but the negotiations did not lead to a breakthrough. The Soviet leader firmly maintained that he could not be held responsible for the crimes that had taken place under Stalin's rule, when thousands of people had disappeared without a trace into prisons and prison camps. He had nothing new to add. Pursuing the case could not be regarded as anything other than a component in the Cold War, and it risked leading to a marked deterioration in relations between Sweden and the Soviet Union. Moreover, the Soviets found it difficult to understand that the Swedish government was poisoning relations between the countries by stubbornly pursuing the disappearance of just one man when millions of Soviet citizens had perished in a war in which Sweden had not participated. The mood was not helped by Khrushchev's dismissal of King Charles XII, who had invaded Russia in the early eighteenth century when Sweden was a Great Power in Europe. Charles XII was certainly no longer such a key figure in the Swedish historical narrative as he had been before the Second World War. Even so, the Soviet leader's disparagement of Sweden's warrior king, followed by an audacious parallel between the ill-fated (for Sweden) war of that time – which had effectively ended in Sweden's defeat after losing the Battle of Poltava in 1709 – and present-day Swedish aggression against the Soviet Union, was not appreciated by Khrushchev's Swedish hosts. Initially perceived as a joke, his statement soon became 'something oddly thick, clumsy, and unpleasant'.[239]

The Soviet attitude hence led to discord on the Swedish side. For three years, Nanna Svartz had kept her story secret. As a result of Khrushchev's lies and unwillingness to discuss the matter, she was prepared to make it public but was persuaded not to by Olof Palme. Leading Social Democrats were also frustrated, partly owing to

---

238 *Expressen*, 21 June 1964. See also Wrigstad, *Så här var det*, p. 115.
239 Sven Erlander, *Tage Erlander. Dagböcker 1963–1964*, p. 234; 'Raoul Wallenberg' (editorial), *Göteborgs-Posten*, 8 February 1957; 'Vitboken' (editorial), *Stockholms Tidningen*; 'Chrusjtjov på sverigebesök: Jag tänker inte avlägga räkenskap för stalintiden', *Arbetet*; 'Chrusjtjov irriterad över frågande om Wallenberg', *Göteborgs Handels- och Sjöfartstidning* and 'Jag vill inte sitta här och bli förhörd, sa Krusse', *Expressen*, all published 17 September 1965. See also Petersson, *Med Moskvas ögon*, pp. 36–38.

Khrushchev's uncooperativeness and partly because the Soviets did not understand the demands made by Swedish domestic opinion on the Swedish government over the Wallenberg case.[240] Wallenberg's relatives and other activists in the Wallenberg campaign were not the only critics of the Swedish government's policy. True, there were times when the opposition parties did not object to the official policy.[241] However, more often than not centre-right politicians submitted questions to be raised in the Riksdag and engaged with the case in other ways, often demanding greater transparency and a tougher approach to the Soviet Union. A number of them probably agreed with the acerbic non-socialist editorial writer who, in the wake of the state visit, criticized the cautious Social Democrats in the government, who eulogized Swedish ideals of neutrality but who were unable to put Khrushchev up against the proverbial wall because they assumed that '[t]he sunshine of the dictator must be regarded as a gift of grace and takes on an extra glow when compared to his thunder'.[242]

## Is Raoul Wallenberg still alive?

Wallenberg's disappearance engaged many Swedes, thereby guaranteeing it a continued central place in the Swedish public sphere. By the beginning of the 1950s, 1.6 million Swedes had already signed a petition to Joseph Stalin demanding to know what had happened to Wallenberg. At the same time, Stig Dagerman, by that time acclaimed as a novelist and fearless journalist who had written in-depth reports about the suffering in Germany in the year after the end of the war, published one of his daily texts. These were known collectively as 'Dagsedlar', with the implication of 'a slap in the face'. Writing in verse, Dagerman criticized the Swedish government's appeasement of Soviet rulers and also a more general Swedish unwillingness to

---

240 Rosenfeld, *Raoul Wallenberg*, pp. 153–157. See also Nilsson, *Människor och händelser i Europa*, pp. 269–273 and Lindström, *Och regeringen satt kvar!*, pp. 64, 229.
241 Erlander (ed.), *Tage Erlander: Dagböcker 1953*, p. 90.
242 'I dag', *Göteborgs Handels- och Sjöfartstidning*, 20 May 1963. See also K. G. Michanek, 'Ohlin kontaktar Erlander i dag: Vi vill veta allt om Wallenberg', *Expressen*, 18 September 1965; Ohlin, *Bertil Ohlins memoarer 1940–1951*, pp. 72–76; Nilsson and Åsbrink, *Stjärna på liberal himmel!*, pp. 261–278.

stand up for humanitarian values. In the name of neutrality (he wrote caustically), the Swede pulls down his hat and covers his ears to avoid seeing and hearing the victims of dictatorships. He believed that this Swedish lack of backbone was manifested in the wake of the incident known as the Catalina affair, involving the disappearance of a Swedish Air Force DC3 that was gathering signals intelligence in the direction of the Soviet Union and the subsequent shooting-down by Soviet fighter jets of a Catalina plane sent out to find out what had happened to the DC3. Dagerman wrote sarcastically that the Swedish authorities did not take a stand to honour the memory of their fellow countrymen who had been killed, but instead ducked for cover behind Sweden's policy of neutrality. He added that this stance had also affected Raoul Wallenberg, who had been left to his fate by a passive Foreign Minister and by many of his compatriots who had said as little as possible about the missing Swede. Dagerman's socially critical writings gained an extended lifespan when some of his thousand or so daily verses, including those cited above, were printed in a collected volume. The first edition was published in 1954, the year Dagerman passed away, and the book has been reprinted fairly regularly up to the present day.[243]

When Folke Bernadotte's hero status was questioned in the 1950s by historian Hugh Trevor-Roper, the response from the UD was an official White Paper alongside outraged articles in the Swedish press in which virtually all writers, regardless of their ideological affiliation, defended the Swedish count of royal lineage.[244] The UD also initiated a White Paper on Raoul Wallenberg. One reason was to demonstrate that, despite the Soviet authorities' declaration that he had died in 1947, a great deal of effort had been and was still being made to clarify the matter. In a radio commentary in February 1957 (also published in the White Paper of the same year), the man in charge of the case, Arne S. Lundberg, emphasized the sheer amount of material and number of names of individuals that formed part of the investigation: 'The file must be the largest in the UD's archives.' The investigation carefully recorded the many twists and turns of the Swedish-Soviet contacts. However, there was no self-criticism

---

[243] Stig Dagerman's daily texts about Wallenberg and the Catalina plane that had been shot down were originally published in the Syndicalist newspaper *Arbetaren*, on 12 December 1951 and 7 October 1952 and have been reprinted in Dagerman, *Dagsedlar*, pp. 52, 64.

[244] Zander, 'Med andra ögon', pp. 89–90.

## Wallenberg and Sweden 173

of the UD's handling of the case. On the contrary: answering the rhetorical question of whether more could have been done at an early stage, the answer was no, because 'no countries, not even the great powers', had been successful in recovering prisoners accused of espionage.[245]

The comments about the enquiry made it clear that views about the Swedish operations and the Soviet response were largely divided along party-political lines. At the same time, the pro-Moscow Swedish daily newspaper *Ny Dag* expressed its admiration for a forward-thinking Soviet Union, which the paper contrasted sharply with the villainous United States.[246] This attitude marked a pivot by the newspaper with regard to the Wallenberg case. For a decade, the paper had dismissed the idea that he had been or still was a Soviet prisoner, but now the paper asserted that both the Swedish and the Soviet people had previously been deceived by the Soviet security services under the loathsome Beria.[247] However, this view met with objections from other quarters. In the conservative journal *Svensk Tidskrift*, the editorial writer wondered whether everything that could have been done had in fact been done. The investigation itself was welcome, but it should have been undertaken earlier. The writer also wondered why so much effort had initially been put into enquiring about Danielsson and other diplomats from the Legation in Budapest, whereas clarification of what had happened to Wallenberg had been viewed as less urgent. The writer also focused a spotlight on Söderblom and Undén's slowness to act: 'unfortunately, the possibility exists that this attitude on the part of the UD has had disastrous consequences'.[248]

Internal criticism was almost completely absent from the report published by the UD in 1965. This was not surprising, as the Social

---

245 Arne Lundberg, 'Radiokommentar framförd i Sveriges radios programpunkt "Dagens eko" den 7 februari 1957', in *Raoul Wallenberg: Dokumentsamling jämte kommentarer rörande hans fångenskap i Sovjetunionen*, pp. 9, 13. For a defence of the efforts by the UD and Lundberg, see 'Wallenberg' (editorial), *Stockholms Tidningen*; 'Raoul Wallenberg' (editorial), *Göteborgs Handels- och Sjöfartstidning*; 'Svar från Kreml' (editorial), *Expressen*, all published on 8 February 1957.
246 Salomon, *En femtiotalsberättelse*, p. 49.
247 'Besked om Raoul Wallenberg: Avled för tio år sedan' and 'Beskedet om Raoul Wallenberg' (editorials), both in *Ny Dag*, 8 February 1957. See 'Ny Dag och Wallenberg', *Dagens Nyheter*, 9 February 1957.
248 'Raoul Wallenberg död?' and 'Dagens frågor: Dokumenten i Wallenbergaffären', *Svensk Tidskrift*, 1957, quotation p. 159.

Democratic Party leadership was aware of the high domestic political price if the Swedish government appeared feeble and submissive to its powerful neighbour to the east.[249] Consequently, Tage Erlander maintained that the Swedish government 'had left no clue unexplored, however tenuous it may have seemed. We have used every opportunity to raise the matter diplomatically or through personal contacts. An intensive examination of all the material and the detailed internal deliberations has always been taking place.'[250] The comments included disappointment that the existing material had not led to more results. 'Darkness continues to loom just as frighteningly over the fate of the Swedish diplomat', but it would be even worse if the enquiry led to the end of the efforts. Closing the case would be nothing less than 'a dishonourable end'.[251] There was also frustration that the enquiry had led to more questions than answers.[252] This time, however, the opposition's criticism was more circumspect. The editorials of some of the major newspapers expressed support for Erlander's affirmation that no stone had been left unturned in the hunt for Wallenberg, albeit with the added comment that Sweden had acted too sluggishly and tardily in the first few years.[253]

Another contentious issue was the credibility of the information supplied by Nanna Svartz and some released Gulag prisoners to the effect that Wallenberg was still alive. Support for that view came from a number of US writers who presented 'enough anecdotal evidence' and also from a number of Swedes, including Wallenberg's colleagues from Budapest, Lars G:son Berg and

---

249 See e.g. Lindström, *Och regeringen satt kvar!*, p. 230. See 'Vitboken', *Arbetet*, 17 September 1965 and 'Raoul Wallenberg' (editorial), *Dagens Nyheter*, 17 September 1965.
250 Tage Erlander, 'Inledning', in *Raoul Wallenberg: Dokumentsamling rörande efterforskningarna efter år 1957*, p. 8.
251 'Dagens frågor', *Svensk Tidskrift*, 1965:6 and 'Levande begraven' (editorial), *Göteborgs Handels- och Sjöfartstidning*, 17 September 1965.
252 'Avslöjande vid kongress: "Svårigheter med språket"', *Dagens Nyheter*, September 17 1965; 'Vitboken om Raoul Wallenberg lämnar många frågor utan svar', *Sydsvenskan*, 17 September 1965. See also Villius and Villius, *Fallet Raoul Wallenberg*, pp. 129–137.
253 'Raoul Wallenberg' (editorial), *Dagens Nyheter*, 17 September 1965; 'Obarmhärtig ny vitbok i Wallenbergaffären' (editorial), *Sydsvenskan*, 17 September 1965; 'Wallenbergs öde – ett tragiskt slut', *Aftonbladet*, 17 September 1965; 'Fallet Raoul Wallenberg', *Upsala Nya Tidning*, 17 September 1965.

Per Anger. The latter held on to the view that Wallenberg was alive until proven otherwise well into the 1990s.[254]

In the Swedish government's private internal discussions, however, doubts were expressed that the Swedish diplomat was still living, even though there might be grounds for taking Svartz's story seriously. What was there to suggest that the Soviet authorities would admit their mistake and send back 'a wreck of a human being', wondered one minister. She found it far more believable that they had preferred to close the case once and for all by administering a lethal injection to a patient who had become a foreign-policy liability.[255]

Doubts were also expressed in the Swedish public sphere, primarily in connection with what was considered a lack of credibility in the version presented by Svartz. The historian Hans Villius and his wife Elsa raised source-critical objections in accordance with the principles of the historical past. They advised that it was important to approach the problem objectively: 'If you become too emotionally involved, you risk having the facts obscured and locking yourself into the human tragedy'.[256] What they objected to was that all manner of vague stories claiming that Wallenberg was alive were given more credence than the Soviet death certificate stating that he had died on 17 July 1947. To be sure, the question of the certificate's authenticity was not settled, but relying on accounts that 'seemed credible' was not good enough. Instead, witness narratives 'must contain information which makes it clear *beyond doubt* that they are true'. The Villiuses maintained this conclusion in a book, *Fallet Raoul Wallenberg* ['The Raoul Wallenberg case'], which was published in 1966 and received considerable attention.[257] They reaffirmed their views more than ten years later, when the Georgian Simon Gogoberidze came to play a part in the Wallenberg enquiry. He was another in a long line of unreliable

---

254 Anger, *With Raoul Wallenberg in Budapest*, p. 168; Berg, *The Book That Disappeared*, pp. 234–235; von Dardel, *Raoul Wallenberg*, pp. 94–107. See also Steinhouse, *Wallenberg Is Here!*, p. 291; Rosenfeld, *Raoul Wallenberg*, pp. 153–169; Smith, *Lost Hero*, pp. 124–138; 'WWII savior of Jews reportedly spied for U.S.', *The Los Angeles Times*, 5 May 1996.
255 Lindström, *Och regeringen satt kvar!*, pp. 63–64.
256 Hans Villius, 'En evig gåta?', *Röster i Radio-TV*, 1965:5, 17.
257 Villius and Villius, 'Misstro och trovärdighet i fallet Wallenberg', *Dagens Nyheter*, 30 September 1965, and the same authors' *Fallet Raoul Wallenberg*, 1966, p. 137 and 'Vad hände Raoul Wallenberg? Vad vi vet

witnesses, a phenomenon which has placed the vanished Swede 'on one occasion in Verkhneuralsk in Siberia, on another in Butyrka Prison in Moscow, on another in a mental hospital, and on yet another in Vladimir'.[258] Wallenberg's half-brother Guy von Dardel reacted strongly, saying that the Villiuses all too casually dismissed testimony that could well be credible. They had no way of knowing whether Wallenberg was still alive or not. A mere suspicion that this might be so should spur renewed efforts to obtain clarification from the Soviets.[259] He was supported by Svartz, who questioned the authenticity of the death certificate and argued that there were indications that Wallenberg was still alive.[260] The Villiuses maintained their view and pointed to a large number of contradictions between the witness statements. The fact that so many people were prepared to disregard these could only be explained by wishful thinking: 'One wishes that the man who did so much to save people from death should not himself have fallen victim to it, but still be alive'.[261]

The last word had not yet been spoken, though. Together with others 'with some knowledge of the facts', and on the basis of the oral witness statements, Carl Fredrik Palmstierna was convinced that Raoul Wallenberg had been alive at least into the early 1960s. Acting on this contention, he launched a frontal attack on the then-dominant view among Swedish historians in the early 1970s. Their focus on source-critical methods was often pursued 'ad absurdum': 'If a lie was printed but existed at the same time as the event, it was assigned a higher value than a source that was passed down orally and was in this sense a later one', he wrote, aiming his remarks at the Villiuses. The line of argument they had trumpeted

---

och vad vi nästan vet', *Kulturens Värld* 2009:1, 31–32. They received support from e.g. the journalist and author Ivar Harrie; see his article 'Gåtan Wallenberg', *Expressen*, 9 February 1966.
258 Villius and Villius, 'Samma otillförlitliga vittnesmål: Raoul Wallenberg dog 1947', *Dagens Nyheter*, 3 March 1979.
259 Guy von Dardel, 'Makarna Villius och Raoul Wallenberg', *Sydsvenskan*, 3 February 1966. For a similar standpoint see von Dardel, *Dagbok*, 1972.
260 Nanna Svartz, 'Wallenberg-ärendet alltjämt en öppen fråga', *Svenska Dagbladet*, 9 March 1966.
261 Elsa Villius and Hans Villius, 'Önsketänkande om Wallenberg', *Stockholms Tidningen*, 11 February 1966. See also the same authors' 'Professor Svartz på djupt vatten' and Sven Wahlström, 'Professor Svartz' språkliga misstag', both in *Aftonbladet*, 19 March 1966.

in 1966 was a textbook example of an approach to history which he firmly rejected.[262]

The sensitive question of whether or not Raoul Wallenberg was still alive also led to exchanges of views within the American public sphere. In *Lost Hero: The Mystery of Raoul Wallenberg*, the Swedish-born rabbi Frederick E. Werbell and the author and historian Thurston Clarke placed great faith in the information conveyed by Nanna Svartz. They also claimed that her enquiries had resulted in Wallenberg being taken from the mental hospital to remote Wrangell's Island. They did not take a stand as to whether his life had ended there, but they argued that by the mid-1960s both Erlander and Svartz had concluded that Wallenberg was dead. In the light of the information available in the early 1980s, they agreed with this conclusion.[263]

Lena Biorck Kaplan, President of the Raoul Wallenberg Committee of the United States, reacted strongly. She stressed that such a conclusion had no support from either Erlander or Svartz and ran counter to 'much evidence, well beyond 1965, that Wallenberg is languishing deep within the bowels of the Soviet Union'. Unfounded assertions about the Swede's death were unfortunate for many reasons, not least because it 'does an injustice to the thousands of people of good will throughout the world who are working day and night for Raoul Wallenberg's release'.[264]

## The Gulag in the Swedish cultural debate

The polarized Cold War climate was very much in evidence in the cultural debate in many Western countries. Particularly fierce battles raged over Robert Conquest's *The Great Terror* (1968) and the works of Alexander Solzhenitsyn. In both cases, the focus was on the Communist terror apparatus and its catastrophic effects on millions of people. Solzhenitsyn's novels in particular helped to spark a debate in the West about Soviet society. His partly first-hand depiction of the Soviet camp system, *The Gulag Archipelago*, was written over a ten-year period from 1958 to 1968 and was published in the West in 1973–1975. It attracted

---

262 Carl-Fredrik Palmstierna, *Bränn dessa brev*, pp. 79, 242. See also Palmstierna, *Fjädern i min hand*, pp. 204–205.
263 Werbell and Clarke, *Lost Hero*, pp. 238–257.
264 Lena Biorck Kaplan, 'Raoul Wallenberg', *The New York Times*, 14 March 1982.

a great deal of attention and led to a large number of opinion pieces in the West, not least because Solzhenitsyn stressed that the terror system, which clashed badly with slogans of equality and justice, was a well-integrated part of Soviet Communism. In one of the first reviews of *The Gulag Archipelago* in the West German press, the influential historian Joachim Fest made it clear that with his book Solzhenitsyn had turned the radical notion that the Russian Revolution of 1917 was a victory for good morals upside down. One consequence occurred in France, where the encounter with Solzhenitsyn's insider perspective led to the abandonment of Communism by a large number of left-wing intellectuals.[265] In the United States, *The Gulag Archipelago*, coupled with Solzhenitsyn's forced exile in 1974, also attracted attention and became part of the political debate. The Democratic Senator Henry M. Jackson was an outspoken anti-Soviet and liberal 'cold warrior' who advocated increased military buildup, a greater focus on human rights, and allowing Soviet Jews to emigrate. He found Solzhenitsyn's shocking testimony from the Soviet labour camps to be further evidence of that nation's inability to comply with human rights. This view was also endorsed by other dissidents such as the nuclear physicist Andrei Sakharov. After Solzhenitsyn emigrated to the US in 1976, he repeatedly sided with Jackson when the latter criticized Richard Nixon, Henry Kissinger, Gerald Ford, and Jimmy Carter over a succession of years for appeasing the Communist rulers in the Kremlin.[266]

Jackson's recurring criticism of US leaders' policy towards the Soviet Union in the early 1970s became known as 'the Solzhenitsyn Affair'. A Swedish Solzhenitsyn Affair was playing out at the same time, based on the awarding of the 1970 Nobel Prize in Literature to the Soviet novelist. By then he had been classified as a 'non-author' in the Soviet Union, and he feared – with good reason – that he would be stripped of his Soviet citizenship if he left the country to accept the prize in Stockholm. A suggestion that Solzhenitsyn could receive the award at an official gathering at the Swedish Embassy in Moscow was not implemented. Criticism of the Swedish government and of Gunnar Jarring, the Swedish ambassador in Moscow, was harsh, and it was voiced on both sides of the

---

265 Elisa Kriza, *Alexander Solzhenitsyn*, p. 115.
266 Bloodworth, 'Senator Henry Jackson, the Solzhenitsyn Affair, and American Liberalism', pp. 69–77; Martin, 'The Sakharov-Medvedev Debate on Détente and Human Rights', pp. 146–162.

Atlantic, leading Olof Palme to defend the Swedish position both in the Swedish media and in *The New York Times*. Although the comparison was not always explicit, the implication of the objections was that Social Democratic governments were characterized by a submissiveness towards Soviet rulers, regardless of whether the issue was the disappearance of Raoul Wallenberg or the Nobel Prize to Aleksandr Solzhenitsyn.

Another controversial aspect was that Solzhenitsyn's books invited comparisons between the Nazi and the Soviet Communist camp systems. On the occasion of the 1976 international hearing named after the scientist, dissident, and Nobel Prize winner Andrei Sakharov, Simon Wiesenthal stressed that it was relevant to compare Nazism and Stalinism. Wiesenthal, who had lived and worked in the Soviet Union from 1939 to 1941, and who encountered Soviet prisoners of war in German concentration camps during the subsequent war years, had gained early insights into both the German and the Soviet terror apparatuses and saw a 'tremendous similarity ... between these two totalitarian states – the Nazi and the Soviet – in the treatment of prisoners'. However, he had been so preoccupied with tracking down Nazi criminals that he had had no opportunity to 'deal with the crimes committed in the misused name of socialism'.[267] It was no long stretch to apply similar comparisons to Raoul Wallenberg. For example, such comparisons were made in Kati Marton's book about Wallenberg in the early 1980s – a book that contrasted his Western humanism, which involved a defence of law and rights, logical arguments, and common sense, with the Nazis' 'useless, mindless extermination' of Jews, which was marked, as in Stalin's realm, by terror and informers. Arriving in the Soviet Union was not like coming to any other country, but to another planet.[268]

The Swedish debate about the *Holocaust* television series not only discussed the Nazi genocide. One commentator said that it was regrettable that the Soviet camp system had not been the subject of a similar series, because there was still silence about 'the Russian Holocaust'.[269] The silence had not been universal, though. Journalist Edward af Sandeberg, who had been arrested after the final battle for Berlin and sent to the Gulag, was a recurring

---

267 Wiesenthal, 'Deklaration av Simon Wiesenthal', p. 15.
268 Marton, *Wallenberg*, pp. 128, 174.
269 John-Erik Janson, 'Den ryska förintelsen går fortfarande fri', *Göteborgs-Posten*, 2 July 1979.

subject of newspaper articles in the post-war years. It was clear that he and other Swedes had been taken to the Soviet Union, but there was great frustration at the lack of response to Swedish enquiries.[270] Unlike Wallenberg, af Sandeberg was released. On his return he announced that he had come across a Romanian in the Soviet camp system who in turn claimed to have met Raoul Wallenberg in February 1946.[271] That message was passed on to the UD, but it was not the one that made the headlines. Instead, considerable attention was given to af Sandeberg's 'outrageous allegations' that Swedish Legation secretaries in Berlin, Hamburg, Dresden, and Vienna had engaged in black-market trading.[272] Such accusations had been made by Communists in the past, but this did not endear af Sandeberg to the left. In *Nu kan det sägas* ['Now it can be said'], he recounted his experiences of the Red Army's advance into Berlin, his captivity in the Soviet Union, and the NKVD's great influence on Soviet domestic and foreign policy.[273] Such accounts encountered vigorous opposition in pro-Moscow newspapers. They dismissed both Edward af Sandeberg and Rudolph Philipp as writers of falsehoods, adding that af Sandeberg, alternately referred to as 'the Nazi editor' and 'Goebbels' newsman', was not to be trusted because he was still coloured by Nazi German values.[274]

At the same time as the debate over Wallenberg's disappearance was going on in the summer of 1947, one of the most widely read Swedish weekly magazines ran a serial about a farmer's son from the Swedish province of Jämtland who had been a prisoner in the Gulag for four years. Similar reports were published at irregular intervals over a ten-year period in Swedish magazines.[275] The year

---

270 'Sovjet svarar ej på frågor om svenskarna', *Arbetet*, 4 January 1946; 'Svenska hem från ryskt krigsfångeläger', *Arbetaren*, 4 January 1946.
271 'Raoul Wallenberg alltjämt i livet', *Göteborgs Handels- och Sjöfartstidning*, 28 June 1946; 'Raoul Wallenberg alltjämt vid liv', *Söderhamns Tidning*, 28 June 1946; 'R. Wallenberg efterforskas på nytt av UD', *Svenska Dagbladet*, 29 June 1946.
272 See e.g. 'Anklagelserna mot Berlinlegationen', *Svenska Dagbladet*, 29 November 1946; 'Skojare fick 'diplomattjänst': UD-slarv i Wallenbergaffären', *Dagstidningen*, 3 August 1956.
273 af Sandeberg, *Nu kan det sägas*, passim.
274 'Göbbels nyhetsman berättar om Moskva', *Arbetartidningen*, 7 July 1946; *Ny Dag*, 17 September 1947.
275 Ragnar Rudfalk, 'Jag var Stalins fånge', parts I, II, and III, *Året Runt*, 1947:33, 34 and 35. See also e.g. Willy Strzelewicz, 'Robotarnas tragedi:

1949 saw the publication of a Swedish translation of Soviet defector Viktor Kravchenko's influential book *I Chose Freedom*, in which he described Stalin's purges and the NKVD's reign of terror and incarceration.[276] Another book that was translated into Swedish was Unto Parvilahti's memoir of almost a decade of imprisonment in the Gulag. Parvilahti, who had volunteered for the Waffen-SS, was arrested in 1944 and handed over to the Soviet Union in the spring of 1945, together with 20 other Finnish citizens who were holders of Nansen passports, at the initiative of Finnish Communist Minister of the Interior Yrjö Leino. In *Berijan tarhat: Havaintoja ja muistikuvia Neuvostoliitosta vuosilta 1945–1954* (published in the UK as *Beria's Gardens: Ten Years' Captivity in Russia and Siberia* and in the United States as *Beria's Gardens: A Slave Labourer's Experiences in the Soviet Utopia*), which was also translated into several other languages, including Swedish, Parvilahti described the prison system and his encounters with fellow unfortunates from different countries. He also portrayed life in Vladimir Prison, where other Gulag prisoners claimed to have met Wallenberg. It was a prison that had housed many notable prisoners and where the diet was better and vermin control more effective. Despite the few bright spots, the book was a scathing condemnation of the Soviet regime's cover-up of abuses and terror directed at its own population.[277]

Reactions to Parvilahti's book were marked by accusations that he had participated in and documented mass executions and had also committed other crimes during the Second World War. In the court case held in Helsinki in the autumn of 1958, which was described alternately as a case of defamation and a case of denazification, he went on the counterattack.[278] One commentator discussed the Soviet camp system only in passing but devoted all the more space to the apologetic comments Parvilahti repeatedly

---

Tyska koncentrationsläger – och ryska', *Samtid och Framtid*, 1948:8, 395–399; Klaus Ackermann, 'Straffångarnas armé', *Samtid och Framtid*, 1951:8, 490–492; Susanne Leonhard, 'Det ryska folket och NKVD', *Samtid och Framtid*, 1952:8, 452 and Osvald Harjo, 'Mina 13 år i ryska slavläger', *Folket i Bild*, 1957:26.

276 Kravtjenko, *Jag valde friheten*. See also Ahlmark, 'Att avslöja diktaturen', pp. 18–21; Karlsson, *Europeiska möten med historien*, pp. 140–141, 147–150.

277 Parvilahti, *Berias gårdar*, especially pp. 83, 191, 414–419.

278 Lars Bruun, 'Kränkt finländsk SS-man i kamp för "denazifiering"', *Svenska Dagbladet*, 25 November 1958.

expressed, with the aim of portraying the soldiers who fought in the Waffen-SS as brave and, with a few exceptions, innocent of war crimes.[279] Another writer instead stressed how the Finnish authorities had cravenly and submissively complied with Soviet directives. The extradition of Parvilahti and others with him on unclear grounds was indefensible, said this writer, as were the Soviet slave camps, which demonstrated 'the appalling indifference to human beings that characterizes the Communist system'.[280]

Robert Conquest's book *The Great Terror* also received mixed reviews, gaining supporters among anti-Soviet commentators while being dismissed as US Cold War propaganda by left-leaning writers. In addition, in the immediate post-war period, Herbert Tingsten, who had abandoned his life as a political scientist to become editor-in-chief of the daily newspaper *Dagens Nyheter*, regularly pointed to the similarities between Nazism and Communism.[281] Such comparisons were also made in connection with the trial of Adolf Eichmann in 1961 and, above all, in Hannah Arendt's totalitarian analysis of this bureaucrat and mass murderer, whose 'I obeyed orders' defence could be found in most dictatorships.[282] The argument met with resistance. True, Leonid Brezhnev's Soviet society was hardly progressive, but at a time of strong left-wing sympathies, it was still something of a model among left-wing intellectuals, who did not at all appreciate talk of the Gulag and terror. Ever since its foundation, the Soviet Union had been defended by left-wing intellectuals, who travelled there and admired the new society. Even many people who had never been to Communist Eastern Europe defended the system there. For most people who pursued their ideals in the East, Solzhenitsyn was not a role model but rather an example of a regressive reactionary. His criticisms of Soviet abuses were relativized and trivialized by means of comparing or equating them with the drawbacks of Swedish society. Solzhenitsyn, who was awarded the Nobel Prize for Literature in 1970 and driven into exile in 1974, also had defenders, but the attacks were such that reactions to his novels were described as 'hate propaganda' a few years into

---

279 Jörn Donner, 'Fascister och andra finländare', *Arbetet*, 19 January 1959.
280 Per-Olof Karlsson, 'Pinsam historia', *Dagens Nyheter*, 27 January 1959.
281 Ahlmark, 'Att avslöja diktaturen', pp. 13–16.
282 Arendt, *Eichmann in Jerusalem*, passim. See Erwin Leiser, 'Kring fallet Eichmann', *Tiden*, 1961:6, 343–344.

the 1970s. In this context, the film and theatre director Alf Sjöberg referred to the 'icy wind of neo-Stalinism'.[283] Solzhenitsyn's interest in Wallenberg was indirectly revealed in the former's book *The First Circle*, which appeared in Swedish translation in 1969. A central figure in the book is the Soviet Minister of State Security and head of the military police in Soviet-occupied territories, Viktor Abakumov. His name had been frequently mentioned in connection with the 1957 White Paper. At that time, the Soviet authorities had labelled Abakumov – who had fallen into disgrace after Stalin's death and was executed in 1954 – a high-handed executioner.[284] Thanks to Solzhenitsyn's novel, Björn Nilsson, a journalist at one of Sweden's most widely read tabloids, began to wonder whether it might be time to learn more about Abakumov. The Soviet minister had certainly been known to enrich himself at the expense of prisoners, but he had managed to escape reprisals until his execution in 1954. And – most importantly – he had been the person responsible for Wallenberg's fate in Soviet captivity.[285]

---

283 Cordelia Edvardson, 'Alf Sjöberg: I dag måste vi stå upp för våra värden!' (interview with Alf Sjöberg), *Vecko-Journalen*, 1974:5, 12–13; 'Ord som piskor', *Vecko-Journalen*, 1974:3, 35. For a more recent analysis of the Swedish Solzhenitsyn debates, see Gerner and Karlsson, 'På tvärs mot tidsandan?', pp. 114–133. See also Tapper, *Snuten i skymningslandet*, pp. 194–195.
284 See e.g. 'Berias hantlangare framme', *Arbetartidningen*, 8 February 1957; 'Wallenberg dog i Ljubljankafängelset: Sverige fortsätter med undersökningarna', *Arbetet*, 8 February 1957; 'Raoul Wallenberg dog 1947: Beriaminister får skulden', *Dagens Nyheter*, 8 February 1957; 'Berijaman får skulden: Svensk vitbok publiceras', *Arbetet*, 8 February 1957; 'Wallenberg död i ryskt skräckfängelse' and 'Märkligt att Sovjet lägger ansvaret på egna myndigheter', *Göteborgs-Posten*, 8 February 1957; 'Svar från Kreml' (editorial), *Expressen*, 8 February 1957; 'Wallenberg' (editorial) and 'Lundberg: Spionmisstankarna grundlösa', both in *Stockholms Tidningen*, 8 February 1957; Hans Wattrang, 'Stalin gav Beria lagskydd avrätta folk i hemlighet', *Expressen*, 8 February 1957; 'Avrättad Berija-man utpekad som skyldig', *Göteborgs Handels- och Sjöfartstidning*, 8 February 1957; 'Wallenberg förde stor förmögenhet med sig', *Stockholms Tidningen*, 9 February 1957.
285 Björn Nilsson, 'Sanningen om Wallenberg?', *Expressen*, 13 November 1969. On Abakumov see Rayfield, *Stalin and his Hangmen*, pp. 382–383, 399–403, 416–417, 421–422, 433–436, 440–444. See also Eliasson et al., *Ett diplomatiskt misslyckande*, pp. 365–367.

One motivating factor was the witness statements that Wallenberg had been sent to one of the camps of the Gulag archipelago, a phenomenon which had become well known thanks to Solzhenitsyn's novels. Perhaps further witness accounts from the Gulag might help dispel the fog regarding 'this brave man's fate', and once and for all 'prove that the explanation of his death in 1947 was fabricated', wrote Simon Wiesenthal.[286] Of particular interest was Solzhenitsyn's mention of one Erik Arvid Andersson, a Swedish 'billionaire's son' who makes a brief appearance in the second part of *The Gulag Archipelago*. When the author saw a photograph of Wallenberg, however, he could not recall anyone with that appearance in the prison-camp system, and neither he nor anyone else could explain who was hiding behind the name Erik Arvid Andersson.[287] That did not stop him from involving himself in the Wallenberg case. On the basis of his own experience, Solzhenitsyn attested that it was possible to survive in the Gulag for 25–30 years. He applied this conclusion to Wallenberg, whom he included in the category of Gulag prisoners who had endured the most and suffered in silence decade after decade.[288] The Swedish diplomat could therefore still be alive, said Solzhenitsyn, and he called for an international opinion to shed light on the case.[289] As will be seen in the next chapter, his wish was soon granted.

Solzhenitsyn's statement also contributed to renewed optimism in Sweden. The legendary journalist Barbro Alving, better known as Bang, had been involved in the Wallenberg case for some time,

---

286 Wiesenthal, 'Deklaration av Simon Wiesenthal', p. 17.
287 Letter from Lennart Westerberg to Gunnar Jarring, Moskva, 16 October 1970, RKA, Raoul Wallenberg, UD2018/005505, Vol. 1; 'Vem är svensken i fånglägret som Solzjenitsyn skriver om i sin senaste bok?' *Aftonbladet*, 31 December 1973; 'Solzjenitsyn: Min Andersson inte Wallenberg', *Dagens Nyheter*, 25 February 1974. See also von Dardel, *Dagbok*, 1972; Fredriksson, *Alexanders kurir*, p. 141.
288 Solzhenitsyn, *Warning to the West*, p. 20.
289 Other accounts, such as the one about the Hungarian András Toma, who was locked into a Soviet mental hospital in 1947 and discovered 53 years later, also contributed, at least up until about 1990, to continued hopes that Wallenberg was still alive. In contrast, one individual who knew about conditions in the Gulag, the Soviet diplomat Arkady Shevchenko, who defected to the United States, expressed strong doubt in the mid-1980s that Wallenberg could still be alive; see Ulf Hjertonson's account to Sven Julin on 1 September 1985 of a lunch meeting with Shevchenko, RKA, Raoul Wallenberg, UD2001/00009, Vol. 24.

and she was one of those who drew attention to Solzhenitsyn and his statements about the missing diplomat.[290] There was also a great commotion after Solzhenitsyn had visited Maj von Dardel and expressed his support for her struggle and his belief in the witness statements that her son was still alive.[291] Solzhenitsyn could be associated with Wallenberg in other, and indirect, ways as well. After more than a year's work, television producer Gunnar Möllerstedt's three-part documentary programme on Wallenberg was broadcast on Swedish television in 1974. In an interview prior to the premiere, Möllerstedt made it clear that viewers hoping for a solution to the mystery would be disappointed, as there were still a large number of unanswered questions. Several of the leading Swedish politicians who might have been able to answer them, including Tage Erlander, Torsten Nilsson, and Olof Palme, declined to take part. What Möllerstedt was able to demonstrate unequivocally, though, was how the Swede had become a pawn in a game between the great powers, a game in which Sweden had no reason to participate. Not only Soviet abuses needed to be brought to light; the same applied to the negligence of Swedish officials. On the latter point, Möllerstedt called for Sweden not to shy away from pillorying a system that demanded a never-ending flow of victims, of whom Raoul Wallenberg was one and Aleksandr Solzhenitsyn another.[292]

## Continued quiet diplomacy

During his time as one of Erlander's right-hand men Olof Palme had already been working on the issue of Wallenberg's disappearance, for example in conjunction with the Swedish state visit to the Soviet Union in 1956 and the publication of the White Paper on the Wallenberg case in 1965. While he was Prime Minister, the Wallenberg case was also one of the most important issues that Palme dealt with. In unofficial contexts, he had already stated – back in the 1960s – that he considered it probable that Wallenberg was dead. During a meeting between Palme and Maj and Fredrik von Dardel in February 1970, on the occasion of the twenty-fifth anniversary of Wallenberg's disappearance, the von Dardels

---

290 Arnborg, *Krig, kvinnor och gud*, pp. 406–407.
291 Eric Sjöquist, 'Vi måste rädda Raoul', *Expressen*, 13 December 1974.
292 Henning Sten, 'Raoul Wallenberg' (interview with Gunnar Möllerstedt), *Expressen*, 22 February 1974.

remained critical of the Swedish government's failure to make any new progress, even though they were certain that Soviet authorities continued to tell untruths. Palme retorted that he had worked hard to obtain an answer about what had actually happened to Wallenberg in Soviet captivity, but had had no reason to reconsider the conclusion reached in 1965 to the effect that it was unrealistic to expect any reconsideration by the Soviets.[293] This was probably the reason why Palme did not raise the issue of his fellow countryman's disappearance during negotiations with Alexei Kosygin in 1976.[294]

In a letter to the Prime Minister in the spring of 1973, Maj von Dardel commented tartly that he had 'time and again made headline-grabbing statements about abuses in various other countries, statements in which you tend not to mince your words'. These contrasted sharply with his habit of being 'very quiet about a Swede named Raoul Wallenberg'.[295] Palme was not completely silent, though. For example, in 1985 he paid tribute to Raoul Wallenberg and Folke Bernadotte in a speech at Stockholm's synagogue to mark the fortieth anniversary of the end of the Second World War. Wallenberg's 'heroic activities' in particular were worthy of all attention imaginable. Palme stressed that the Swedish government had left no stone unturned in trying to find out what had happened to Wallenberg and that this work would continue: 'We owe it to Raoul Wallenberg.'[296]

The Swedish-Jewish community appreciated the Prime Minister's tributes to Bernadotte and Wallenberg but found it remarkable that Palme never once mentioned Israel. This was particularly problematic given that, in a speech three years earlier, he had equated the extermination of Jewish children during the Second World War with the suffering of Palestinian children during the Israeli invasion of Lebanon.[297] Nor did Palme's declaration of the importance

---

293 Leif Leifland, 'Förtrolig: Ang. besök av överdirektör och fru von Dardel hos statsminister Palme den 3 februari 1970', RKA, Raoul Wallenberg, UD 2018/05505, Vol. 1.
294 See Marton, *Wallenberg*, p. 208.
295 Letter from Maj von Dardel to Olof Palme, 21 March 1973, RKA, Raoul Wallenberg, UD2001/00009, Vol. 2.
296 Palme, 'Andra världskriget', pp. 315–316.
297 See e.g. Jackie Jakubowski, 'Olof Palme talar till Sveriges judar', *Judisk Krönika*, 1985:3, 2. After Palme's murder it became clear that his embrace of PLO leader Yassir Arafat and unwillingness to support the state of Israel

of continued efforts in the Wallenberg case convince the latter's relatives. They insisted that the approach led by Palme – amounting to attempts to exert a quiet influence on the Soviet leaders – had not been successful, and nor was it desirable.[298]

The Social Democrats had been in power almost continuously since 1932 until they lost the Riksdag elections in 1976. After that loss, the policy regarding the Wallenberg case changed, at least at first. Quiet diplomacy increasingly gave way to public actions. The Minister for Foreign Affairs, Centre Party member Karin Söder, visited Wallenberg's parents and promised them that the UD would do everything possible to discover the truth about their son's fate. However, the measures adopted by the new centre-right government resembled those of the previous Social Democratic government; and proposals put forward by centre-right politicians for a new White Paper or a citizens' commission of enquiry, which had been presented in the Riksdag but had not been supported by the Social Democratic government, failed to gain support after the transfer of power in 1976.[299] The Liberal Party politician Per Ahlmark had taken an interest in the Wallenberg case as a journalist and debater, but in his new role as deputy Prime Minister he was soon criticized for keeping too low a profile. Similar criticism was levelled at his party colleague Ola Ullsten. As Minister for Foreign Affairs in January 1979, he presented a note to the Soviet government requesting Wallenberg's release. A few months later he demanded that Soviet authorities reopen the investigation into Wallenberg's fate, which caused irritation in Moscow.[300] The strained relations may have contributed to Ullsten's not mentioning the missing Swede when he met Alexei Kosygin during a state visit to the Soviet Union in 1980.[301] At the European security conference in Madrid in 1981

---

had not been appreciated by Jews living in the Nordic region, in contrast to his fight against racism and injustice and his demonstrated responsiveness to Jewish viewpoints; see Lars Dencik, 'Han var vår vän' and Ivar Müller, 'Till minnet av Olof Palme', *Judisk Krönika*, 1986:2, 3.

298 Östberg, *I takt med tiden*, pp. 182, 230–231.
299 Riksdag proposal 1975/76:1145 and documents in RKA, Raoul Wallenberg, UD2001/00009, Vol. 2.
300 Letter from Jan Lundvik to Leif Leifland, 'Strängt förtroligt', 6 September 1979, RKA, Raoul Wallenberg, UD 2018/05505, Vol. 4.
301 Eric Sjöquist, 'Nytt sensationsvittne – nu kräver regeringen: Släpp Raoul Wallenberg!', *Expressen*, 26 January 1979; Eric Sjöquist, 'Nya intressanta uppgifter om Wallenberg', *Expressen*, 29 August 1979; 'Ullsten

and the conference on human rights in Geneva the following year, Swedish delegates did mention the Wallenberg case, but they did so almost in passing and following pressure, especially from Canadian and American politicians.[302] Thus the members of the centre-right government also failed to gain clarity about Wallenberg, and with a few exceptions, their policy did not deviate in practice from that of their Social Democratic predecessors.[303]

By contrast, a noticeable shift occurred in the political literature. Books by and about Social Democratic politicians who were active in the 1940s, 1950s, 1960s, and 1970s frequently mentioned Wallenberg and the search for him. True, some non-socialist, particularly Liberal, politicians did act at the national level to encourage continuing efforts both to search for and to honour the missing diplomat.[304] However, he was rarely or never mentioned when their party colleagues, such as Ola Ullsten, Gösta Bohman, Thorbjörn Fälldin, and Karin Söder, who held important ministerial posts after 1976, later wrote or were interviewed about their political experiences. There is much to suggest that the doubts about Wallenberg's continued existence that were evident during Palme's years as Prime Minister persisted, and perhaps even increased, during his successors' time in government.

## The Swedish effort measured by American standards

Stig Bergling was a Swedish intelligence officer arrested by Israeli security police in 1979 on suspicion of spying for the Soviet Union. He confessed almost immediately. In connection with his trial, he proposed an exchange between Sweden and the Soviet Union, in which he would be one party and Raoul Wallenberg the other. An overview study of the Swedish intelligence apparatus states that the proposal received no response, either from the Swedish judiciary

---

i krav till Kosygin: Undersök nya uppgifterna i fallet Raoul Wallenberg', *Göteborgs-Posten*, 29 August 1979; 'Gjorde du fiasko i Moskva, Ullsten?', *Göteborgs-Tidningen*, 31 May 1980.

302 Handling of the cases appears in a number of documents in RKA, Raoul Wallenberg, UD2018/005505, Vol. 2.

303 Eric Sjöquist, 'När världen upptäckte Raoul Wallenberg', *Expressen*, 16 January 1981.

304 Nilsson and Åsbrink, *Stjärna på en liberal himmel!*, pp. 266–277; Ahlmark, *Det öppna såret*, pp. 364, 374, 377; Wästberg, *I tidens skugga*, pp. 286–287, 296, 312.

or from the Soviet authorities.[305] This is only partly true, though. The Liberal minority government led by Ola Ullsten thought it was worth a try. Senior representatives at the UD questioned the scheme but attempted to implement it as best they could. Embassy staff in Moscow made enquiries but the response from the Soviet liaison officers was cool, not least because the official position was that Wallenberg had died in 1947.[306] When the attempt became public in Sweden a year later, criticism was fierce. Failing to inform the Swedish security service, which had uncovered Bergling's spying, and bypassing the legal entities responsible for trying Bergling's case had been serious mistakes. Social Democratic ministers with previous experience of the Wallenberg case also questioned the kind of informal contacts that the Ullsten government had attempted. Such human trafficking at the highest level had never happened when they were in power, they said.[307] By this time, the trial against Bergling was over and he had been given a life sentence. He nevertheless maintained his view that an exchange would have been possible. In the early 2000s he claimed, on vague grounds, that Wallenberg had still been alive at least until 1989.[308]

Repeated criticism has been directed at the Swedish government for not following the example of the Swiss, who soon after the end of the war succeeded in having citizens of theirs in Soviet captivity released in exchange for Soviet citizens whom they

---

305 Frick and Rosander, *Bakom hemligstämpeln*, p. 301.
306 Leif Leifland, 'Promemoria: Utväxling Wallenberg-Bergling?', 19 September 1979; (Jan) Lundvik, 'Re: Wallenberg', 21 September 1979; (Jan) Lundvik, 'Re: Wallenberg', 26 September 1979; (Leif) Leifland to (Jan) Lundvik, 'Raoul Wallenberg', 12 October 1979, RKA, Raoul Wallenberg, UD2018/005505, Vol. 1. See also Ingmar Lindmarker, 'UD protesterade mot utväxlingsplan', *Svenska Dagbladet*, 2 September 1989.
307 Kaa Eneberg, 'Klart övertramp som riksdagen borde undersöka', *Dagens Nyheter*, 13 June 1980; Ingmar Lindmarker, 'Sovjet avvisade utväxling' and Omar Magnergård, 'Regeringen stod utanför', both in *Svenska Dagbladet*, 13 June 1980; Leif Brännström, 'Förklara dig Ullsten: Advokaten till attack i spionfallet', *Expressen*, 5 July 1980; 'Wallenberg-affären: "HD bör höra Ullsten"', *Göteborgs-Posten*, 3 August 1980; Sune Olsson, 'Utbytet obekant för Säpo', *Svenska Dagbladet*, 6 August 1980. See also Per Nygren, 'Spionen som kom in från värmen', *Göteborgs-Posten*, 8 October 1987; Sjöquist, *Dramat Raoul Wallenberg*, pp. 133–139; Carlberg, *Raoul Wallenberg*, pp. 573–574.
308 Stig Bergling, 'Wallenberg levde 1989', *Aftonbladet*, 12 January 2001.

had detained.[309] However, the idea had come up in Sweden from time to time. Exchanges like the one Bergling wanted had occasionally been proposed from the 1950s onwards. In 1965, for example, talks about an exchange were held between Swedish diplomats and a 'person who represented the Eastern bloc'. The idea was that Wallenberg would have been traded for the Swedish air-force officer Stig Wennerström, who had been given a life sentence a year earlier for spying for the Soviets.[310] The negotiations fell through, but the idea of an exchange arose again in the years around 1980. The new attention then being focused on Wallenberg had led to a debate in the American media over Sweden's policy regarding him. In early 1983, an influential conservative columnist named George Will sharply criticized the Swedish government's handling of the Wallenberg case. Will argued that the Swedish politicians in charge had been afraid of the Russians and still were.[311] Sweden's ambassador to the United States, Wilhelm Wachtmeister, stressed that the Swedish government had done and was still doing everything in its power to ascertain the missing diplomat's fate.[312] Wachtmeister was supported in the debate by the US writer, Erik Fredriksen. He argued that Sweden's actions during most of the Second World War were highly regrettable, but the rescue of the Danish Jews in the autumn of 1943 plus the Red Cross efforts in 1945 were proof that Sweden had not just hidden behind its neutrality.[313] Other US commentators took up the Wallenberg case, either to point out that the United States was also not blameless in its handling of the case or to wholeheartedly support Will.[314]

---

309 Gunnar Hägglöf, 'När Wallenbergarkivet öppnas ...', *Svenska Dagbladet*, 12 December 1979; Mikael Holmström, 'Invit utväxla Wallenberg nonchalerades', *Svenska Dagbladet*, 3 January 2001; Krister Wahlbäck, 'Undéns tystnad offrade Wallenberg', *Dagens Nyheter*, 13 January 2001.
310 Persson and Sundelin, *Utan omsvep*, pp. 129–132; Sven Fredrik Hedin, 'Utväxlingen', *Göteborgs-Tidningen*, 5 January 2000.
311 George F. Will, 'A question for Andropov: Where is Raoul Wallenberg?', *The Washington Post*, 6 January 1983; George F. Will, 'Wallenberg and Sweden's shame (cont'd)', *The Washington Post*, 16 January 1983.
312 Wilhelm Wachtmeister, 'Letters to the editor', *The Washington Post*, 7 January 1983; Wilhelm Wachtmeister, 'Letters to the editor', *The Washington Post*, 18 January 1983.
313 Erik Fredriksen, 'Letters to the editor: Raoul Wallenberg and Sweden (cont'd)', *The Washington Post*, 23 January 1983.
314 David Neal, 'We need a Wallenberg – to save Wallenberg', *The Washington Post*, 29 January 1983; Peter Hartsock, 'Letters to the editor: Raoul

Some of the debaters who argued that Swedish authorities had done too little to find out about Wallenberg noted that in a long series of missed opportunities, the most recent one had occurred less than a year and a half earlier. In conjunction with the grounding of the Soviet submarine U 137 in Swedish waters in October 1981, these commentators had proposed trading the Soviet submarine crew for Wallenberg or at least for definitive Soviet information that he was no longer alive. They were not alone: Swedes all over the country phoned newspaper editors with the exact same suggestion. Members of the Swedish Raoul Wallenberg Association publicly delivered a similar message when they demonstrated outside the Soviet embassy in Stockholm.[315] The idea of an exchange was also discussed at the UD. Diary notes from the crisis meetings that were held while the submarine was still aground reveal that a few voices had called for the Swedish government to abandon its long-held precautionary principle. However, the most influential figures at the UD considered that responding to one crime (the detention of Wallenberg) with another (using the submarine and its crew as hostages) was incompatible with Sweden as a state governed by the rule of law.[316] In contrast to the position he had held in 1979, Ola Ullsten, who was Minister for Foreign Affairs during the submarine

---

Wallenberg and Sweden (cont'd)', *The Washington Post*, 23 January 1983; George F. Will, 'Wallenberg and Sweden's shame (cont'd)', *The Washington Post*, 16 January 1983; Joan W. Sacarob and Abraham Cooper, 'Letters to the editor: Sweden and Wallenberg (cont'd)', *The Washington Post*, 14 January 1983.

315 Marika Liljequist, 'Sovjet firar – utan svenskar', *Expressen*, 5 November 1981; Omar Magnergård, 'Ubåt 137 – en svensk mardröm', *Svenska Dagbladet*, 27 December 1999.

316 'Hård svensk linje kan stoppa Sovjets gränskränkningar', interview by Lars Christiansson with Arkady Shevchenko, *Svenska Dagbladet*, 30 June 1985. On Shevchenko see Lars Christiansson, 'Sjevtjenko var FN:s biträdande generalsekreterare', *Svenska Dagbladet*, 30 June 1985. On the UD's follow-up of the interview, see Sven Julin to Ulf Hjertonsson, 'Raoul Wallenberg' 16 July 1985, Ulf Hjertonsson to Sven Julin, 'Raoul Wallenberg' 1 September 1985 and Sven Julin, 'Arkadij Sjevtjenkos uppgifter om Raoul Wallenberg', Memorandum, 15 August 1985, RKA, Raoul Wallenberg, UD2001/00009, Vol. 24; Evabritta Wallberg (ed.), Lennart Ljung, *Överbefälhavare Lennart Ljungs tjänstedagböcker 1978–1983: Vol. 1*, p. 189; Theutenberg, *Dagbok från UD: Volym 1*, p. 42; Theutenberg, *Dagbok från UD: Volym 4*, pp. 208–212. See Hirdman, 'Sverige och ubåtskränkningarna', p. 152.

crisis, argued that it was unethical to demand the exchange of Soviet citizens for a Swede. In addition to the moral and legal problems, informal contacts with people who had good insight into the Soviet power apparatus supplied the same answer as that given in connection with the Bergling case: Wallenberg was no longer alive, and so there was no counterparty for an exchange.[317]

In retrospect, Wachtmeister believed that Will and his allies had made a mistake when bringing the U 137 into the picture. If the Swedish government had used the Soviet submarine crew as prisoners and pawns, it would have violated both moral and legal principles. This argument was likely to be well received in the United States because at that time American embassy personnel were still being held hostage in Iran. Wachtmeister was hopeful that he had emerged victorious, at least judging by reactions in Washington political circles. Mounting a defence against Will had been of paramount importance because '[i]f such an accusation were allowed to stand unchallenged, our reputation in America would be damaged'.[318] By all accounts, however, the damage had already been done. In the international literature about Wallenberg, it became more the rule than the exception to view him as a victim of Swedish neutrality and associated Swedish cowardice in the nation's contacts with the Soviet Union.[319]

## The new Russian openness and Raoul Wallenberg

As successive Social Democratic and centre-right governments failed to clarify the Wallenberg case, it became less and less important as a domestic political controversy. There was certainly still frustration, though, when the issue was raised in the Riksdag in the late 1980s.

---

317 On the pressure exerted to use the grounded Soviet submarine in a trade for Wallenberg, see a large number of documents in RKA, Raoul Wallenberg, UD2001/00009, Vol. 14 and 16 plus UD2018/005505, Vol. 2. Wallenberg and the U 137 were also linked in other contexts. One Swedish hope was that because the Soviet authorities had admitted, after being pressured, that they had captured the Swedish diplomat and had shot down a Swedish DC 3 over international waters, they might admit more widespread violations; see Bodström, *Mitt i stormen*, pp. 267, 275.
318 Wachtmeister, *Som jag såg det*, pp. 282–283, quotation p. 282.
319 Marton, *Wallenberg*, p. 214; Yahil, 'Raoul Wallenberg – His Mission and His Activities in Hungary', pp. 7–9; Rosenfeld, *Raoul Wallenberg*, pp. 126–144; Steinhouse, *Wallenberg is Here!*, p. 290. See also Leonard Shapiro, who speaks of 'Swedish cowardice' in 'A Good Man' (review

A representative of the Conservative Party praised the fact that Social Democratic Prime Minister Ingvar Carlsson had once again raised the matter with Soviet authorities but regretted that Sweden had never submitted a formal request for Wallenberg's return.[320] The diary entries from 1986 of the then Conservative Party leader Ulf Adelsohn mention an extensive presentation of the Raoul Wallenberg case with historical flashbacks by Ingvar Carlsson. Between the lines, it is clear that the two party leaders had very modest hopes of a Soviet response to new Swedish enquiries.[321] At the same time, Wallenberg's international fame was a double-edged sword. On the occasion of his seventieth birthday, the Israeli Parliament, the Knesset, held an extraordinary session to extol the Swede's achievements. However, no official representative of Sweden attended, probably as a result of explicit Swedish criticism of the Israeli government for its policy regarding Palestine.[322]

A few years later, the situation was different when the memory of Wallenberg offered new opportunities for Swedish international diplomacy. When Prime Minister Ingvar Carlsson visited the United States in 1987, he chose to discuss existing Swedish-American schemes of cooperation. He also agreed with Ronald Reagan's eulogy over the rather short-lived Swedish colony in Delaware, whose three-hundred-and-fiftieth anniversary was the following year. In his reply Carlsson refrained from mentioning Wallenberg by name but he surely noted the goodwill associated with the missing Swede, who was, in Reagan's words, now 'a citizen of both our countries' and thereby 'a bond between us', as well as 'an inspiration to our peoples'.[323] The Israelis also again praised Wallenberg when Sweden's Minister for Foreign Affairs

---

of John Bierman's *Righteous Gentile: The Story of Raoul Wallenberg, Missing Hero of the Holocaust*, The New York Review of Books, 5 November 1981. For similar opinions held by Swedes see Ingmar Lindmarker, 'Raoul Wallenberg och likgiltigheten', *Svenska Dagbladet*, 4 August 1982 and Eric Sjöquist's interview with Per Anger, 'Sveriges svek mot Raoul Wallenberg', *Expressen*, 18 October 1985.

320 Section 2, Svar på fråga 1987/88:302 om Raoul Wallenbergs öde, *Riksdagens protokoll*, 1987:88:67, 11 February 1988.
321 Adelsohn, *Partiledare*, p. 364.
322 Ahlmark, *Det öppna såret*, p. 204.
323 Ronald Reagan and Ingvar Carlsson, 'Remarks at the Welcoming Ceremony for Prime Minister Ingvar Carlsson of Sweden: September 9, 1987', *Ronald Reagan: Public Papers of the Presidents of the United States, 1987*, Book II, pp. 1002–1004, quotation p. 1003.

Sten Andersson travelled there to inaugurate Raoul Wallenberg Street in Tel Aviv in 1990, a visit that gave him the opportunity to discuss the Middle East issue with representatives of both Israel and the PLO.[324]

The huge global shifts that occurred during the second half of the 1980s and led to the end of the Cold War and the dissolution of the Soviet Union had effects on the Wallenberg case. UD staff believed there was little likelihood that Wallenberg was still alive. To continue pursuing the issue without new and convincing material would place considerable strain on Swedish-Soviet relations.[325] When the Wallenberg case was nevertheless again raised in 1986 there was evident frustration among the Swedish diplomats working on it, who made attempts to forestall the same routine replies that they and their colleagues had received in 1957, 1965, and 1979. They did not hesitate to point out that continued Soviet lack of interest could well lead to worsened relations between the two countries.[326] That the Soviet Union's new leader Mikhail Gorbachev was signalling change and greater openness was noted, but the UD initially viewed these new signals with some scepticism. The tentative character of the actions taken by diplomats was not lost on those who argued that the previous patterns of guarded contacts with the powerful country in the East were being repeated, and that there was much to show that the UD was hoping that 'the whole thing would fizzle out'.[327]

The following years, however, did lead to one concrete change: the collapse of the Soviet Union in 1991 increased access to archives inside Russia. The availability of new documents certainly meant that the issue of Swedish subservience to the Soviet Union in the

---

324 Andersson, *I de lugnaste vatten ...*, pp. 384–385.
325 Mikael Westerlind, 'Samråd om Wallenberg-ärendet', Memorandum, 27 February 1985, RKA, Raoul Wallenberg, UD2018/005505, Vol. 2.
326 Peter Osvald, 'Vårt fortsatta agerande gentemot Sovjetunionen i Wallenberg-frågan: Några tänkbara alternativ', Memorandum, 25 September 1986, RKA, Raoul Wallenberg 2018/005505, Vol. 2; Peter Osvald, 'Wallenberg-frågan', Memorandum, 9 October 1986, RKA, Raoul Wallenberg, UD2001/00009, Vol. 27.
327 Kenne Fant, 'TF, UD och Raoul Wallenberg', *Svenska Dagbladet*, 10 November 1988. See also a letter from metalworker Henrik Unné to Pierre Schori, 10 November 1988, RKA, Raoul Wallenberg, UD2001/00009, Vol. 32 and a letter from Pierre Schori to Per Anger, 27 June 1989, RKA, Raoul Wallenberg, UD2018/005505, Vol. 2.

# Wallenberg and Sweden

Wallenberg case came up for discussion again.[328] In addition, Swedish historians were divided as to how the Soviet documents concerning Wallenberg, in particular the death certificate from 1947, were to be interpreted.[329] The question of whether this document was credible was an old one, but between the lines of the debate it became clear that there were very limited possibilities of finding new answers. Outside academia, however, there was no lack of people expressing renewed Swedish optimism: now the Soviet archives would be opened, they hoped, and they would reveal the answers to the Wallenberg case.[330] Support for such hopes also came from the Russian side; for instance, it was manifested in the way Boris Pankin expressed himself in the early 1980s versus the early 1990s. Soon after he replaced Aleksandr Yakovlev in 1983 as Soviet ambassador to Sweden, Pankin was invited to dinner at the home of Johan 'Joja' and Lena Bonnier in the company of a number of representatives of the newspapers *Dagens Nyheter* and *Expressen*, of whose boards the host was a member. In his welcoming address to Pankin, Joja Bonnier began not by referring to the Soviet submarine recently stranded in Swedish waters but rather by demanding: 'What have you done with Raoul Wallenberg?' Towards the end of the dinner Pankin gave a speech of thanks in which he referred back to the initial question, but then claimed that he had forgotten what it was.[331]

In 1991, a year after Pankin had left his post in Sweden, he claimed that he had personally pursued the Wallenberg case

---

328 See e.g. Anders Sundelin, 'Sverige har agerat undfallet: Nya dokument och nya röster om Raoul Wallenberg', *Dagens Nyheter*, 7 June 1994; Leif Leifland, 'Erlander aktiv', *Dagens Nyheter*, 18 June 1994; Anders Sundelin, 'Rätt och fel', *Dagens Nyheter*, 22 June 1994.

329 Rolf Karlbom, 'Mortifikation som juridiskt och historiskt problem', *Historisk tidskrift*, 1993:2, pp. 300–304; Helene Carlbäck-Isotalo, 'Källäget i Ryssland kräver nya ansatser i forskningen om sovjetisk historia', *Historisk tidskrift*, 1994:1, 98–100; Rolf Karlbom, 'Sovjetforskning eller skönmålning?' and Helene Carlbäck-Isotalo, 'Arkivdokument kontra fria fantasier: Wallenbergfallet färdigdiskuterat?', *Historisk tidskrift*, 1994:4, 630–636.

330 Ingmar Lindmarker, 'Sovjet ändrar ton om Wallenberg', *Svenska Dagbladet*, 5 September 1987; Leif Andersson, 'Nu kan vi få klarhet i svenska "affärer"', *Arbetet*, 26 August 1991.

331 Joja Bonnier and Boris Pankin's speeches at the dinner are discussed in the legendary journalist Bo Strömstedt's autobiography *Löpsedeln och insidan*, p. 364.

internally even before glasnost and perestroika had become the new watchwords. In his autobiography he regretted Wallenberg's fate and sharply criticized the Soviet powers responsible for the Swede's abduction.[332] Whether Pankin had any significant influence on the case is unclear, but there was a noticeable change in attitude in the Soviet Union and Russia in the years around 1990. One unambiguous example of the new tone was the message from Eduard Shevardnadze, the Soviet Union's Minister of Foreign Affairs from 1985 to 1090, to his Swedish counterpart. In 1989, Shevardnadze regretted what had happened 'during a tragic period' in Soviet history at a time when many other people had also been harmed, and he affirmed that the Soviets also wanted the truth to come out.[333] This was also the hope of Wallenberg's relatives, who received an invitation to Moscow that same year. They hoped that the new openness, and new individuals at the top of the security service, would unearth new information, but none was forthcoming. They were, however, presented with some of Wallenberg's personal belongings.[334]

Towards the end of his life, Andrei Sakharov raised the issue of Raoul Wallenberg with Aleksandr Yakovlev, a politician, diplomat, and historian who was a driving force behind the glasnost and perestroika reforms, but to no avail.[335] Sakharov's widow Yelena Bonner declared soon after her husband's death in 1989 that she no longer had any hopes that Wallenberg was still alive. She concluded that the information that he had died in 1947 was correct.[336]

---

332 Pankin, *De sista hundra dagarna*, pp. 221–222, 226–231.
333 Martin Hallqvist, 'Raoul Wallenberg: Promemoria', 6 September 1991, RKA, Raoul Wallenberg, UD2001/00009, Vol. 40.
334 See e.g. Leif Andersson, 'Återfick Raoul Wallenbergs pass', *Arbetet*, 17 October 1989; Per Anger, 'Raoul Wallenberg i dag', *Svensk Tidskrift*, 1990:7, 408–410; Sture Olsson, 'Han kan lösa gåtan Raoul Wallenberg', *Aftonbladet*, 24 August 1991; Leif Andersson, 'Nya dokument släpps idag?', *Arbetet*, 4 September 1991; Anne-Marie Forsell, 'Wallenberg försökte skicka telegram hem', *Arbetet*, 6 September 1991; Thomas Hamberg, 'Här satt Wallenberg', *Arbetet*, 27 November 1991. See also Gitta Sereny, 'A legend that refuses to die', *The Times*, 7 July 1989, and Serge Schmemann, 'After the Soviet Union: Soviet files show K.G.B. cover-up in the disappearance of Wallenberg', *The New York Times*, 28 December 1991.
335 Sakharov, *Moscow and Beyond*, p. 50.
336 Thomas Hamberg, 'Jelena Bonner övertygad om att Wallenberg dog -47', *Arbetet*, 13 October 1990.

Another dissident, the then recently released Ukrainian Catholic activist Josyp Tereya, declared in 1987 – after 24 years in Soviet camps, prisons, and mental hospitals – that Wallenberg might indeed be alive, but if so it was unlikely that the Soviet authorities would release him.[337] However, just because there was much to suggest that Wallenberg had been killed, or was a lost cause even if he was still alive, this did not mean that there was any consensus as to why he had ended up as a prisoner in the Soviet Union and what had happened to him there. A report by the Soviet defector Oleg Gordievsky to the effect that Wallenberg had been executed because he refused to be recruited as a Soviet agent circulated in the debate, but it was viewed with suspicion by professional historians. They disagreed on why Wallenberg had been arrested, though.[338]

This debate occurred at a time when the view of modern Swedish history was undergoing a major shift. The discussion centred not only on the less-than-desirable aspects of the welfare state but also on the policy of neutrality, or rather the deviations from it. Consequently, the Second World War came back into focus in the 1990s, but no longer with reference to such aspects as ersatz coffee, wood-gas cars, and stalwart soldiers standing guard somewhere in Sweden. This coming to terms with the shortcomings of neutrality, which also included a heated debate about the White Buses and Folke Bernadotte's hero status, coincided with two other processes.[339] From the early 1990s onwards, Sweden made a U-turn as its leading politicians paved the way for Swedish membership of the European Union. It thereby became increasingly important for Sweden to 'write itself into' the broader European historical narrative. At the same time, the Holocaust was becoming internationalized. Around the year 2000, Sweden played an increasingly important role in this process through the international activities

---

337 Janice Middleton, 'Soviet dissident says Raoul Wallenberg is alive', *The Ottawa Citizen*, 29 October 1987.
338 Jan-Olof Bengtsson, 'Wallenberg sköts', *iDAG*, 17 October 1990; 'Kan man lita på en f d dubbelagent?' (editorial) and Carl-Fredrik Wingquist, 'Wallenberg föll offer för ett djävulskt spel' (interview with Bernt Schiller), *iDAG*, 18 October 1990; Rolf Karlbom, 'Varför greps Raoul Wallenberg?', *iDAG*, 29 October 1990; Bernt Schiller, 'Spekulationer eller fakta om Wallenberg?', *iDAG*, 19 November 1990. See also Per Anger, 'Varför ryssarna tog Raoul Wallenberg', *Svensk Tidskrift*, 1992:1.
339 Zander, 'To Rescue or be Rescued', pp. 365–368. See also Wagrell, '*Chorus of the Saved*', pp. 142–146.

of the Living History information initiative, which was created in order to increase public knowledge of the Holocaust.[340]

The then Prime Minister, Social Democrat Göran Persson, was one of the initiators of Living History in 1997. Partly as a result of its activities, the official Swedish stance underwent a major change in the late 1990s. In 1998, artist and Holocaust survivor Lenke Rothman's monument *Att minnas – den goda gärningen* ['To be remembered – the good deed'], which is dedicated to Raoul Wallenberg, was inaugurated in the Riksdag. At the ceremony, Conservative Party leader Carl Bildt focused on modern Swedish history. In contrast to the Swedish policy of appeasement during the Second World War, he highlighted Wallenberg's achievements.[341]

Bildt has aptly been described as Olof Palme's ideological polar opposite.[342] When the Stockholm International Forum on the Holocaust was held in 2000, with its focus on remembrance, research, and education, it became clear that Bildt and Göran Persson shared the same views, at least regarding Raoul Wallenberg. One prominent feature of the conference was a ceremony in memory of Wallenberg. In his inaugural address to the conference, Persson emphasized the contrast between Sweden's actions during the Second World War, which in some respects had been less than honourable, and the heroic efforts of the Swedish diplomat. That Sweden must come to terms with the dark chapters of its past was a position Persson returned to several times during his ten years as Prime Minister (from 1996 to 2006), although he was also on several occasions an outspoken defender of Sweden's policy during the Second World War.[343]

---

340 Levy and Sznaider, *The Holocaust and Memory in the Global Age*, and Karlsson, *Med folkmord i fokus*. For a more extensive discussion about Living History and its importance in Swedish domestic and foreign policy see Karlsson, 'History in Swedish Politics – the "Living History" Project', pp. 145–162 and Karlsson, 'The Holocaust as Politics and Use of History', pp. 241–254.
341 Schult, *A Hero's Many Faces*, pp. 170–189. See also Rothman, *Hågkomsten, hyllningen och respekten för Raoul Wallenbergs gärning i Budapest*.
342 Mattsson, *Neutralitetens tid*, p. 74.
343 Persson, 'Opening Address by the Prime Minister of Sweden', p. 30. See also e.g. Persson, *Min väg, mina val*, p. 253. See Zander, 'To Rescue or be Rescued', p. 373.

## Innocently imprisoned then and now

The ambivalent attitude towards quiet diplomacy has reappeared from time to time over the past half century. In addition to widespread criticism of such an approach to politics, cases frequently occurred which invited comparisons with Wallenberg's. The Swedish government chose not to raise the case of Dagmar Hagelin, a young Swedish woman murdered in 1977 by Alfredo Astiz, an officer in the Argentine military junta, at a 1980 UN conference in Geneva on human rights. Ola Ullsten, then Minister for Foreign Affairs, acknowledged the similarities in how Swedish governments many years apart had dealt with Raoul Wallenberg and Dagmar Hagelin, mainly by arguing that the cases did not benefit from publicity. However, he did not believe that the government of which he was a member bore any responsibility for this quiet diplomacy. The people who had withheld information from the public about Swedes who had come to grief in foreign countries were 'UD men'.[344]

In the 2000s, there were some cases where Swedish diplomats and politicians did succeed in securing the release of Swedes by working quietly. One example is the case of Annika Östberg, who was transferred from a prison in the United States to Sweden after many years of pressure. However, her case was problematic. Quiet diplomacy has largely been associated with the innocently convicted, whereas Östberg was imprisoned in the Unites States for almost 28 years, convicted as an accomplice in two murders, which were committed by her then boyfriend.[345] In the early

---

344 Eric Sjöquist, 'Sverige tar inte upp fallet Hagelin i FN', *Expressen*, 23 February 1980. Nina Lagergren believed that there were major similarities between Raoul Wallenberg's disappearance and the murder of Dagmar Hagelin in that Swedish governments contented themselves with unsatisfactory answers from the perpetrators; Ingolf Kiesow, 'Krav på domstolsförfarande om Raoul Wallenberg', 8 June 1983, RKA, Raoul Wallenberg, UD2001/00009, Vol. 19. For articles on quiet diplomacy in general, see e.g. Peter Kadhammar, 'Sten Andersson hemligstämplar allt', *Expressen*, 5 August 1990; 'Tyst diplomati bäst diplomati' (editorial), *Arbetet*, 6 July 1991. See also Sten Andersson, 'Den tysta diplomatin', *Arbetet*, 27 July 1991, and Carl Bildt, 'Missbrukat begrepp', *Arbetet*, 5 August 1991.
345 Henrik Bredberg, 'Inhumana USA, humana Sverige', *Sydsvenskan*, 8 April 2009; Josef el Mahdi, Tobias Olsson and Sofia Strandberg, 'Lång kampanj bakom flytten', *Svenska Dagbladet*; Oisín Cantwell, 'Hon framställs som

2010s, criticism of quiet diplomacy was mainly associated with the case of Swedish journalists Martin Schibbye and Johan Persson, who were arrested in July 2011 after they had illegally entered the conflict-ridden Ogaden region in Ethiopia, and their Swedish-Eritrean colleague Dawit Isaak, detained in Eritrea since 23 September 2001. In November 2005 quiet diplomacy bore fruit for Isaak, but his time in freedom only lasted two days. Since then, renewed diplomatic efforts to secure his release have failed.[346] A recurring point of view has been that there is a potential ethnic factor in these modern examples of quiet diplomacy: several commentators have argued that if Isaak, and the Swedish-Chinese writer and publisher Gui Minhai, who went missing in Thailand in 2015 and later turned up in Chinese custody, had had a different skin colour and 'typical' Swedish names, the outcome of the negotiations with the regimes in Eritrea and China would have been different.[347]

At first, the Isaak case attracted limited attention in the Swedish media. From the autumn of 2002, however, articles began to multiply, and in 2005 the Swedish media began to seriously focus the spotlight on him.[348] One factor that contributed to the high profile of his case was that the UD's actions were inconsistent with the high ideals that have characterized Swedish foreign policy. While Isaak was sitting in prison, Sweden had given aid to Eritrea – money that might, in a worst-case scenario, have been used to build new prisons where more innocent people would be behind bars. The fact that the EU was still sending money, originally at Sweden's

---

oskyldig – det är hon inte', *Aftonbladet*; Stefan Wahlberg, 'Annika Östberg är ingen nationalhjälte', *Metro*; 'Ett lyckligt slut' (editorial), *Skånska Dagbladet*, all published on 9 April 2009.

346 Wilhelm Agrell, 'Handslag i det tysta', *Sydsvenskan*, 23 September 2011; Urban Löfqvist, 'Regeringen agerade för sent – och för lite', *Expressen*, 18 October 2011; Anders Göransson, 'Ex-diplomat: För sent för en "tyst" lösning', *Metro*, 19 October 2011. On the differences between the Isaak case and the Schibbye-and-Persson case, see Hanne Kjöller, 'Känsligt läge för protester', *Dagens Nyheter*, 7 October 2011. Schult, 'Whose Raoul Wallenberg is it?', pp. 773, 780 and 786–787, mentions both the anniversary year of 2012 and the discussions about quiet diplomacy in connection with Wallenberg och Isaak but without linking the two phenomena.

347 Anders Q. Björkman, 'Hög tid att larma och stå i', *Svenska Dagbladet*, 17 October 2016.

348 Kaaström, 'Dawit och tystnaden', p. 33–45; Wolfgang Hansson, 'Svenske Isaak är i hans våld', *Aftonbladet*, 11 December 2005.

# Wallenberg and Sweden

initiative, did not help matters.[349] In addition, one of the most intense phases in the highlighting of Isaak's case coincided with Sweden's presidency of the Council of the European Union in 2009. Critics argued that Sweden's Minister of Foreign Affairs Carl Bildt should accept the consequences of the failure of quiet diplomacy and exert strong pressure on the Eritrean government.[350] Simultaneously, Sweden's four largest newspapers launched a campaign calling for the Swedish journalist's release, culminating in the presentation of over 200,000 signatures to Eritrea's chargé d'affaires in Stockholm in May 2009.[351] Later that year Dawit Isaak was awarded the Tucholsky Prize, named after the German author and anti-Nazi Kurt Tucholsky.[352] In November 2009, more than 90 Swedish newspapers published an article by historian and author Peter Englund on the subject of freedom of expression and Dawit Isaak, to the accompaniment of many comments, most of which were favourable.[353] In the spring of 2010, newly accessed facts revealed the appalling conditions under which Isaak was forced to live in prison.[354]

---

349 See e.g. Lars Adaktusson, 'Svårbegripligt agerande i fallet Dawit Isaak', *Svenska Dagbladet*, 14 January 2009; Peter Landelius, 'Sverige räcker inte till', *Sydsvenskan*, 13 March 2009; Ewa Stenberg, 'Kan vi tro på tyst diplomati?', *Dagens Nyheter*, 29 March 2009; Oscar Julander, 'Diktatorn erkänner tortyren', *Aftonbladet*, 19 April 2009; Mats Bergstrand, 'Kampanjen för Isaak', *Dagens Nyheter*, 21 April 2009; Bengt Braun and Anders Nordström, 'Kampen för Dawit är kamp för demokratin' and Agneta Lindblom Hulthén, Ola Larsmo, Mats Söderlund, Ulrika Knutson and Anna Serner, 'Vi slutar inte kämpa!', both in *Expressen*, 3 May 2009.
350 Jesper Bengtsson, 'Skicka Carl Bildt till Eritrea', *Aftonbladet*, 6 February 2009.
351 Wolfgang Hansson, '209,963: Släpp Isaak!', *Aftonbladet*, 5 May 2009.
352 Marcus Boldemann, 'Dawit Isaak får Tucholskypriset', *Dagens Nyheter*, 15 November 2009.
353 Peter Englund's article was given different headlines in different newspapers, e.g. 'Åtta år i helvetet', *Aftonbladet*; 'Frige det fängslade ordet!', *Dagens Nyheter*; 'Dawits brott var att han yttrade sig', *Metro*; 'Åtta år i mörker', *Sydsvenskan*; 'Åtta år är en lång tid', *Svenska Dagbladet*, see also Sara Ullberg, 'Hedrad att få skriva om Dawit Isaak' (interview with Peter Englund), *Skånska Dagbladet*, all published on 18 November 2009; Rakel Chukri, 'Vad gör vi? Vad gör du?', *Sydsvenskan*, 19 November 2009.
354 Ewa Stenberg, 'Så lever Dawit Isaak som fånge nr 36' and Björn Wiman, 'Slå på sökarljuset: Nu vet vi var Dawit Isaak finns', both in *Dagens Nyheter*, 7 April 2010; Patrick Ekstrand, 'Ingen kommer levande därifrån', *Metro*, 7 April 2010; Maria Sundén Jelmini, 'Dawit Isaak hålls i bojor dygnet runt', *Svenska Dagbladet*, 8 April 2010.

The Eritrean response was a vague promise of a trial.[355] Just over a year later came the tenth anniversary of Isaak's imprisonment, which was widely publicized. At the same time unconfirmed reports circulated that he had died in prison.[356]

This last statement invited comparisons between the tragic fates of Wallenberg and Isaak. A number of people committed to finding answers to what happened to Wallenberg have written about Isaak as well. They have adopted a political-pedagogical use of history, stressing the similarities between then and now rather than the differences. For example, historian Mattias Hessérus ignored the concrete differences between Sweden's contacts with the Soviet Union during the Cold War and those with Eritrea in the twenty-first century. Instead, he emphasized the similarities between the diplomatic failure in the Wallenberg case and the inadequate foreign-policy-orientated handling of Isaak's case. Both situations revealed the political limitations of quiet diplomacy and the curtailment of the media's power. When nothing is said in official contexts, the media are helpless, as it is hard for them to report on silence. This last aspect was thought-provoking. It is frightening that 'the logic that long characterized the Raoul Wallenberg case now seems to be repeating itself in the handling of Dawit Isaak', Hessérus wrote.[357]

A similar application of the political-pedagogical use of history occurred in an article by the diligent Wallenberg researcher Susanne Berger and the journalist and publicist Arne Ruth in Sweden's largest daily newspaper, *Dagens Nyheter*. They wrote that the UD had not learned its lesson from the Wallenberg case; instead it repeated similar mistakes. The 'smokescreen' that Swedish diplomats put out in 2009 was 'exactly the same' as that used to cover up uncomfortable facts about Wallenberg. Berger and Ruth mainly reacted to Isaak's being without legal representation, but also to the vagueness of the UD's actions. They argued that the maintenance of business

---

355 Carl V. Andersson, Sofia Johansson and Daniel Siksjö, 'Dawit kan få rättegång', *Expressen*, 15 April 2010.
356 'Dawit Isaak – tio år utan framgång' (editorial), *Ystads Allehanda*, 15 August 2011; Lars Adaktusson, 'Tyst diplomati har inte hjälpt Dawit', *Metro*, 13 September 2011; Charlotta Friborg, 'Dags att visa ledarskap, Carl Bildt', *Östgöta Correspondenten*, 23 September 2011.
357 Mattias Hessérus, 'Wallenbergaffären går igen i fallet Isaak', *Svenska Dagbladet*, 24 March 2009. See also Schult, 'Whose Raoul Wallenberg is it?', pp. 787–788.

relations with the dictatorship of Eritrea was a sign that the Raoul Wallenberg tragedy risked being repeated.[358] In another context, it was pointed out that the Swedish government both then and now had offered credit and aid to the Soviet and Eritrean dictatorships but without demanding Wallenberg's and Isaac's freedom in exchange.[359] Wilhelm Agrell pointed out that one essential difference between the Wallenberg and Isaak cases was that while the former soon gained a tireless advocate in Rudolph Philipp, Isaak has not been represented by an equally stubborn defender. But Agrell has also noted a number of structural similarities in the handling of the two cases, despite the change over time which has meant that 'over the years, in terms of its foreign policy Sweden has walked the not very long road from anxious neighbour of a great power to a quiet and well-groomed small state that finally gets to sit at the grown-ups' table'.[360]

Dawit Isaak's imprisonment has also been discussed in recent years, notably in 2021, the twentieth anniversary of his detention. Many of the objections are recognizable, such as criticism of the UD's initially feeble commitment and the shortcomings of quiet diplomacy.[361] One of the most striking examples was an advertisement from Reporters Without Borders with quotations regarding ongoing efforts to secure Isaak's release. The quoted statements came from three Swedish Foreign Ministers, summed up as '20 years of big words and quiet diplomacy' with zero results.[362] The criticism was met with a defence of 'the patient consular and political work',[363] together with the hope of indications that the

---

358 Susanne Berger and Arne Ruth, 'Dawit Isaak riskerar bli en ny Raoul Wallenberg', *Dagens Nyheter*, 18 November 2009. See also Susanne Berger, 'Det kan fallet Wallenberg lära oss om Dawit Isaak', *Dagens Nyheter*, 26 January 2011. On Swedish business contacts with Eritrea see Åke Wredén, 'Svensk guldjakt i Eritrea', *Dagens Nyheter*, 9 April 2010.
359 Adaktusson, *Världens bästa story*, pp. 277–278.
360 Wilhelm Agrell, 'Handslag i det tysta', *Sydsvenskan*, 23 September 2011.
361 Martin Liby Troein, 'Dawit Isaak: Det duger inte med tyst diplomati', *Dagens Nyheter*, 23 September 2021; Kurdo Baksi, Ulrika Hyllert, and Grethe Rottböll, 'Låt inte Dawit tillbringa ännu en födelsedag i en hemsk cell', *Svenska Dagbladet*, 27 October 2021; Helena Giertta and Kurdo Baksi, 'Den hotade yttrandefriheten', *Dagens Nyheter*, 15 December 2021.
362 'Regeringen arbetar med oförminskad kraft', advertisement from Reporters Without Borders, *Sydsvenskan*, 27 September 2021.
363 Margot Wallström, 'Diplomatiska metoder', *Dagens Nyheter*, 30 September 2021.

Eritrean regime was on the ropes, which might pave the way for Isaak's release.[364]

The big difference compared to ten years earlier was that the Raoul Wallenberg case was no longer an object of comparison. Instead, it was generally contemporary people who were mentioned – both other innocently imprisoned people and famous Swedes who could potentially influence those in power in the dictatorships that kept Swedes imprisoned without judicial review.[365] When there was an occasional historical reference, it was to a person who, like Wallenberg, was regarded as a role model in the spirit of the Scarlet Pimpernel: Nelson Mandela.[366]

One history-cultural insight is that it is rarely possible to isolate people and events and relegate them to a distant 'then'; sooner or later, present-day aspects intrude. The question of what lessons we have *actually* learned from the Wallenberg case and how they influence Swedish policy today, for example in connection with Dawit Isaak, once again brings out the relevance of the inadequate diplomatic and political handling of the Wallenberg case. But regardless of whether Wallenberg is used as a positive or a negative example, his present-day position as a role model is rarely questioned. The post-war Raoul Wallenberg has gone from being a festering and ideologically charged bone of contention to being a strong Swedish brand, but this development depended on the Swedish diplomat attracting international attention in the 1970s and 1980s, with the United States as the hub.

In addition to the American interest in Raoul Wallenberg, other nations' actions have also had a major impact on the Swedish history of the Wallenberg case. Unsurprisingly, various ways of relating to the Soviet superpower characterized the debate in the first post-war decades. Subsequently, the end of the Cold War, Sweden's membership of the EU, and the growing international interest in the Holocaust, which has found expression in many different ways, have been of great significance. However, the

---

364 Johan Karlsson Schaffer, 'Dagarna är räknade för Eritreas diktator', *Svenska Dagbladet*, 23 September 2021; Erik Esbjörnsson, 'Det politiska kaoset skapar öppningar i fallet Dawit Isaak', *Dagens Nyheter*, 23 September 2021.
365 Kurdo Baksi, 'Höj din röst för Dawit Isaaks frigivande, Alexander Isak', *Svenska Dagbladet*, 2 April 2022.
366 Jens Littorin, 'ÖIS manifesterar för Dawit Isaak: Han är vår Mandela', *Dagens Nyheter*, 23 September 2021.

external influence needs to be complemented by the view of the past in Sweden, a view which has influenced the conception of Raoul Wallenberg and the memory of him to at least as great an extent.

In the decades following the end of the Second World War, a combination of a historical and practical past dominated in Sweden, although the latter concept should be seen as particularly robust in this context. The 'then' of the Second World War and the 'now' of the Cold War merged into an explanatory model represented by both politicians and professional historians. In accordance with small-state realism, a relatively small nation like Sweden had to make repeated concessions regarding its non-alignment and neutrality in order to preserve its independence. Another concurrent factor was that an earlier domestic admiration for Sweden as an imperial power in the Baltic Sea during the seventeenth and early eighteenth centuries was increasingly outcompeted by a more up-to-date historiography combined with an optimistic view of the future. Admittedly, attention was paid to the Holocaust itself and to the survivors who now and again made their presence felt in the public sphere.[367] It was rare, however, for this dark chapter to feature prominently in depictions of and debates about the Second World War, and even rarer for there to be discussions about the ways in which Sweden was part of this history. This was compounded by a confusion of concepts, as some of the Communists and Syndicalists who had been interned in labour camps because they were considered a security risk afterwards claimed that they had been in concentration camps. In their interpretation of the war years, they depicted themselves as a kind of resistance fighters in contrast to the establishment. Folke Bernadotte and Raoul Wallenberg, who were rarely named in these contexts, were implicit exceptions to a politically 'brown' standpoint according to which royalty and business leaders had generally sympathized with Adolf Hitler's Germany.[368]

During the 1990s, this viewpoint became widely adopted as people increasingly came to terms with Sweden's modern history. There was one important difference, though. In retrospect, it is obvious that the focus on the morally charged issues of Swedish modern history paved the way for an important change. The earlier intermittent interest in the Holocaust was replaced by recurring

---

367 See e.g. Wagrell, '*Chorus of the Saved*', pp. 315–332.
368 Östling, 'The Rise and Fall of Small-State Realism', pp. 134–140; Zander, 'In a Land of Dreams', pp. 455–478.

discussions of its significance during the Second World War, for posterity, and in a Sweden which during this decade became part of the EU.[369] Raoul Wallenberg's shifting status during this same period can be illustrated with a few telling examples. Against the background of the continuing great American interest in the missing Swede – an interest still evident at this time in the form of ceremonies and tributes – a translated volume of letters written by and to Raoul Wallenberg was published, as well as several new books about him and his fate; one Swedish journalist and US correspondent asked why the Swedish efforts to pay tribute to him were still rather few and half-hearted.[370]

A few years later, in conjunction with the first of three big conferences in Stockholm – a conference which was also a highly publicized national and international event in the Swedish information campaign about the Holocaust – the same journalist argued that Prime Minister Göran Persson should *not* talk about Folke Bernadotte and Raoul Wallenberg. They were already well known and extensively used to demonstrate Swedish contributions during the Second World War. Instead, in line with the many cases of coming to terms with the past, he should talk about the dark sides of Sweden's modern history which included antisemitism, racism, and a restrictive refugee policy before and during the early years of the war.[371]

## In memory of Raoul Wallenberg

Just like other history cultures, Swedish history culture is by no means clear-cut. The early twenty-first century has seen Swedish society come to terms with the past, but also attempts to include the dark chapters in the grand narrative. Calls are still being made for dealing with the dark sides of modern Swedish history, but they are fewer in number and lack the intensity of the 1990s. At that time, it was a common criticism that Folke Bernadotte had exaggerated his own importance in saving thousands of concentration-camp prisoners during the last months of the war. A charge levelled against the Count was that he failed to mention the Danes and

---

369 Karlsson, 'The Uses of History and the Third Wave of Europeanisation', pp. 38–55; Karlsson, 'Tell Ye Your Children ...', pp. 79–94.
370 Staffan Thorsell, 'Är det någon som bryr sig i Sverige?', *Expressen*, 17 January 1995.
371 Staffan Thorsell, 'Om detta borde han berätta', *Expressen*, 10 January 2000.

Norwegians who had played a decisive role in preparing the White Buses operation. Over time this criticism has subsided, though, and in recent decades Bernadotte has regained popularity.[372] A similar development occurred regarding the view of non-alignment and neutrality: over time, the debates of the 1990s have led to a sense of pride that these reckonings have taken place.

That Swedes are considered to have come to terms with old sins once and for all has opened the door to a revival of the view of Sweden as a model moral country. It fits better into such a context to cite Wallenberg's achievements as a neutral Swede in Budapest in 1944–1945 than to dwell on the long and sorrowful aftermath of his disappearance. As part of integrating Wallenberg into a good narrative of Swedish modern history, he has been placed in the ranks of successful Swedes such as Alfred Nobel and Dag Hammarskjöld.[373] Wallenberg was also awarded four medals in the 1980s and 1990s; and in 1987, along with Folke Bernadotte and Dag Hammarskjöld, he became the subject of a postage stamp under the collective title 'In the service of humanity'.[374] To put it another way, Wallenberg's rescue efforts in Hungary have become increasingly important as the Holocaust has been given an ever-more prominent position in Swedish history culture. This does not amount to saying that the diplomatic failure has been entirely shut away in a cupboard. The link between Wallenberg and quiet diplomacy is not made as often as it used to be, but it still surfaces now and then. The fact that Vladimir Putin has been caught out in strategic power lies over the past two decades has gained renewed topicality following the Russian attack on Ukraine in February 2022. Swedish writers have reminded us that such lies are nothing new in Soviet and Russian history; among many other examples, Soviet denials and half-truths have run like a central thread through the Raoul Wallenberg case.[375]

---

372 See the journalist Herman Lindqvist's tribute in 'Himmlers mage öppnade för Bernadottes bussar', *Aftonbladet*, 21 August 2011, and Per T. Ohlsson's 'När Malmö var räddningen', plus the subsequent debate between Ohlsson and Rolf Tufvesson, 'Niels Christian Ditleff är inte bortglömd', *Sydsvenskan*, 18 and 26 September 2011.
373 The link between Nobel, Wallenberg, and Hammarskjöld was made by Kenne Fant in Curt Carlsson, 'Kenne Fant sprider PR i USA för Nobel och den svenska modellen', *Arbetet*, 31 October 1993.
374 Liljefors and Zander, 'Det neutrala landet Ingenstans', pp. 235–236.
375 See e.g. Ingrid Carlberg, 'När den strategiska lögnen upphöjs till statsreligion', *Dagens Nyheter*, 28 February 2022.

A narrative that has been 'corrected' can still invite debate, however. This was demonstrated, for example, in connection with the Raoul Wallenberg Room at the Army Museum, the first permanent Wallenberg exhibition in Sweden, which opened in January 2009. The author, critic, and journalist Kaj Schueler saw the exhibition as 'a beautiful memorial to Wallenberg' that was informative but not intrusive.[376] A different reviewer felt that the Second World War was missing from the exhibition and noted the conspicuous absence of Nazis, Arrow Cross members, and Jews. 'The staging is almost demonstratively low key', said this commentator, arguing that the exhibition conveyed material for a legend of a Swedish saint more than for a universal tale of a hero.[377]

That there are differences of opinion over how history should be understood and interpreted is not surprising. However, such disagreements are often swept under the carpet when it is time for anniversaries and commemorative years. While world wars, genocides, disasters, and other significant events tend to have a strong impact on people for a long time and contribute to new and alternative interpretations, anniversary celebrations and commemorative events are of a different nature. Their purpose is rather to reinforce established notions of the past, and of the ways in which that past relates to developments now and to the future.[378]

The 2012 commemorative year highlighted Raoul Wallenberg as a Swedish brand. It was also a kind of countermeasure aimed at Hungarian Prime Minister Viktor Orbán, who at the same time had signalled his desire to draw attention to Wallenberg – not primarily in connection with the persecution of Jews then and now, though, but rather as part of a far-right offensive.[379] Even so, solemn speeches in Wallenberg's honour were not a guarantee of success, as was demonstrated by the reactions to the presence of Iran's ambassador, which constituted a problem given that the country's then President, Mahmoud Ahmadinejad, had a reputation as a

---

376 Kaj Schueler, 'Utställning med budskap', *Svenska Dagbladet*, 25 January 2009.
377 Lars Linder, 'Mer helgon än hjälte', *Dagens Nyheter*, 6 February 2009. Eva Bäckstedt said in 'Hjältar lockar till samtal', *Svenska Dagbladet*, 3 March 2009, that 'the Wallenberg Room is neither grand nor original, but it is informative'.
378 Sjöland, *Historia i magasin*, p. 56; Zander, 'Raoul Wallenberg – en förebild i tiden?', pp. 119–121.
379 Interview with Olle Wästberg, 5 November 2021.

Holocaust denier. Swedish opinion shapers also criticized Sweden's Minister for Foreign Affairs Carl Bildt for not officially denouncing the measures taken by the national-conservative Viktor Orbán and his populist Fidesz party with a view to moving away from democracy and freedom of expression.[380]

Bildt explained that the figure of Raoul Wallenberg which formed in the lead-up to and during the centenary celebrations of his birth on 4 January 1912 was an exemplary historical personage and therefore offered an opportunity to learn from history. Accordingly, his achievements were worthy of emulation, and the focus should hence not be on his time in Soviet captivity but on his achievements in Budapest.

One visible indication that reconciliation had finally been achieved was the partial rededication of Gustav and Ulla Kraitz's bronze briefcase, originally part of the Hope monument outside the UN building in New York. Located outside the offices of the UD on a black granite bench, the case bearing the initials *R.W.* can be interpreted as meaning that Raoul Wallenberg is once and for all accepted as a Swedish diplomat on a fully equal basis, and that his colleagues' failure to bring him home from the Soviet Union is a closed chapter.[381]

---

380 Zander, 'Raoul Wallenberg – en förebild i tiden?', p. 127.
381 See Johan Hellekant, 'Nytt minne för Wallenberg', *Svenska Dagbladet*, 16 April 2012.

# Chapter 5
# The Americanization of Raoul Wallenberg

In the mid-1980s, the Jewish-American composer Leonard Bernstein was working on a multilingual opera that would 'be about half a century of learning nothing'.[1] The beginning of the performance would be set in Austria two months before the Anschluss. Other settings were to include Łodz and Lyon during the Second World War. The final stop would be a cell in the Gulag with one of the opera's main characters: Raoul Wallenberg. Working on the opera was demanding. With the catastrophic history of the twentieth century in general, and the Holocaust in particular, in mind, Bernstein described 'the *exhaustion*, physical and emotional, of living through it, then and now'.[2] The burden was too heavy to bear; at his death in 1990, the opera remained unfinished.

Had Bernstein been able to complete his project, he would have joined an already longstanding post-war tradition of references to the Holocaust in art music. It is therefore no surprise that others have taken up the baton and set Wallenberg's life and fate to music in recent decades. The fruits of this musical interest in the Swedish diplomat include the musical *Wallenberg*, staged in New York in 2010, and three operas: *Wallenberg*, premiered in Dortmund in 2001; *Raoul*, premiered in New York in 2008; and *Raoul Wallenberg – saknad* ['Raoul Wallenberg – missing'], a work composed by Inger Wikström that was first performed in 2018.

Forms of expression that are considered to be art music are characterized by their combination of concrete and abstract elements. Memories of and references to the Holocaust can therefore be

---

1 Mark Segal, 'Bernstein's many missions' (interview with Leonard Bernstein), *The Australian Jewish Times – The Jerusalem Post International Edition*, 5 September 1985.
2 Leonard Bernstein quoted in Baber, *Leonard Bernstein*, p. 223.

manifested in a less clear-cut manner than they are in prose and moving images. This creates 'a broader and possibly more expansive interpretive space'.[3] By contrast, the reactions to *Raoul* were straightforward. The German Michael Kunze, known as a successful music producer and writer of musicals, had written the libretto. The composer was Gershon Kingsley, who had fled Berlin for Palestine in 1938 at the age of 15. Later he emigrated to the United States, where he became a pioneer in electronic music and a musical composer of everything from religious hymns and soundtracks to advertising jingles. Kingsley's main focus on Wallenberg's last days in Budapest is evident in the musical, which features the characters of Iver Olsen, Per Anger, Winston Churchill, and Joseph Stalin. *Raoul* draws on the spreading rumours in the Hungarian capital, which convinced some people that Wallenberg was working for the Germans and others that he was a US spy. In interviews prior to *Raoul*'s German premiere in Bremen in 2018, Kingsley admitted that his friends' prediction had come true: they had said he would have 'a tough time' with this work. Both the public and the critics objected to flaws in the musical craftsmanship, oversimplifications of the plot, a palpable poverty of ideas, some overly obvious adaptations to the present day, the 'comic-book dialogue', and 'the generally hysterical tone and heavy-handed symbolism'. If opera was to be used for *Vergangenheitsbewältigung* – coming to terms with the past – then *Raoul* was not a suitable work.[4]

*Wallenberg*, with music by Estonian Erkki-Sven Tüür and libretto by German playwright Lutz Hübner, is set mainly in Budapest, where Wallenberg is fighting the Germans led by Adolf Eichmann. A key theme is that without a relevant narrative, a role model like Wallenberg has difficulty in asserting himself or herself, but also that there is a danger that the legend and myth around the person may create a one-dimensional figure. The opera's first act focuses on Wallenberg's departure for Budapest and his activities in the Hungarian capital. He is portrayed as an altruistic figure who is grappling with feelings of doubt and inadequacy. In the

---

3 Rosengren, '"Massaker-musik" och bortglömt minne', p. 187.
4 Derek Scally, 'Holocaust opera fails to strike the right note with public', *The Irish Times*, 25 February 2008; Sigrid Schuer, 'Gershon Kingsleys Oper "Raoul" in Bremen', *Die Welt*, 3 March 2008; Hartmut Lück, 'Vergangenheitsbewältigung im Musical: Geht das? "Raoul" von Gershon Kingsley im Bremer Schauspielhaus', *Neue Zeitschrift für Musik*, Vol. 169, No. 2, March–April 2008, 75.

second act the historical context is less evident. His imprisonment in the Gulag is the starting point for how the historical Wallenberg fell victim to the myth of him as an almost superhuman hero and role model.

In the first act, Eichmann predicts that Wallenberg will be the loser of the drama. All that will remain is the hero's halo and a portrait bust, but neither is of any practical use to the Swede. Wallenberg and Eichmann have been the main antagonists regardless of where the opera has been performed. The production staged in Tallinn in 2007 by the Russian opera director Dmitry Berman was more in keeping with Tüür's vision of how it should be staged than others. The audiences and critics responded very favourably, even though the Estonian version of *Wallenberg* was coloured both by the tragic story and by a highly charged present-day context. The opera premiered in the shadow of the internationally publicized controversy over the Bronze Soldier, the statue of a Red Army soldier which – despite vigorous protests from Estonia's Russian minority – was moved from central Tallinn to a war cemetery on the city's outskirts, plus a concurrent debate over the decoration of the roof of the opera building. It had been redesigned during the Communist era and decorated with socialist-realist motifs of happy peasants and welcoming Red Army soldiers. Demands were made to the effect that these should also be relocated farther away, but they were not heeded.

In an interview, Tüür declared *Wallenberg* to be his most overtly political piece, mainly because he wished to use the fate of the Swedish diplomat to dramatize 'the two evil regimes of the twentieth century'.[5] The Tallinn production featured a striking difference in how the Nazi and the Soviet evils were portrayed. Perhaps owing to the tense situation between Estonians and Russians in Estonia, the opera's Soviet prison guards were made to appear harmless, in sharp contrast to the German soldiers. The latter were traditionally portrayed as exuding harshness and ruthlessness, qualities reinforced by their black leather uniforms, modern-style riot helmets, and *Star Wars*-like laser sabres. By contrast, their Soviet counterparts were cheerful comrades in glittering red uniforms.

---

5 Burkhard Schäfer, 'Künstler sollen politisch sein' (interview with Erkki-Sven Tüür), *Die Zeit*, 21 November 2008. See also Maxim Reider, 'An Estonian experience' (interview with Erkki-Sven Tüür), *The Jerusalem Post*, 9 January 2015.

During his time as head of drama and opera in Dortmund, the English director John Dew commissioned operas about the gay-rights activist Harvey Milk, the West German Chancellor Willy Brandt, and Raoul Wallenberg. Dew argued that these men, by virtue of their deeds, showed kinship with the fictional opera heroes of old. In one interpretation of Dew's attitude, one enthusiastic Swedish reviewer of the premiere screening of *Wallenberg* declared that the protagonist 'deserves to be immortal. Like an Elvis, like a Lady Di. He is needed'.[6] Other reviewers were also favourable, but with some reservations. One theme with variations was the discrepancy between the historical Wallenberg's stature and the opera tenor's vain attempt to portray the greatness of his role model.[7] Other unfavourable comments noted shortcomings in both music and libretto and observed that the finale was 'grossly irreverent'.[8]

The 'Wallenberg Circus' that filled every square inch of the stage did not invite any approving comparisons with post-war celebrities. Instead, the message was that Wallenberg's posthumous fame was a worse prison than the Soviet one, and that in this process it is not Communism but US popular culture that is the great culprit. This line of thinking was highlighted with the help of the opera's Elvis Presley figure, who asserted that Graceland was as effective an incarceration for him as the Gulag was for Wallenberg. The stage was then invaded by Mickey Mouse and other Disney characters, US astronauts, naval officers, and President Ronald Reagan, who was seen signing the document making Wallenberg an honorary US citizen; the President is nothing more than a puppet under the control of Eichmann's ghost. As the drama draws to a close Wallenberg again comes on stage, but this time in the form of a gymnast tasked with portraying the Swedish diplomat as the Jesus of our time: they both died for our sins.[9]

---

6 Leif Aare, 'En bejublad världspremiär i Dortmund: Operan "Wallenberg" fokuserar på humanisten och arbetsnarkomanen Raoul Wallenberg', *Dagens Nyheter*, 7 May 2001.
7 Tanja Schult, 'Raoul Wallenberg on Stage – or at Stake?', pp. 135–137.
8 Ingo Hoddick, 'Mythos der Moderne: "Wallenberg" von Erkii-Sven Tüür in Dortmund uraufgeführt', *Neue Zeitschrift für Musik*, Vol. 192, No. 4, August 2001, p. 69; Mary Ellen Hutton, 'Tüür's "Wallenberg" stinging, timeless and an operatic cyber-first', *American Record Guide*, September–October 2008.
9 Ulf Zander, 'Wallenberghyllan: Hjälten som opera', *Sydsvenskan*, 15 October 2007.

In the opera, Wallenberg remains a selfless role model who risks his life to save others. However, he is also a victim both of Stalin's dictatorial rule and of the phenomenon that has been disparagingly labelled as a Holocaust-Hollywood industry. What Tüür and Hübner did not take into account was that this popular-culture industry, which the concept's originators criticized, is an important prerequisite for Wallenberg's heroic status. Without the great interest of the film and television industry in the figure of Wallenberg from the late 1970s onwards, there would have been far less likelihood of him becoming the lead character in operas.

To refer again to the theories of Henry Rousso, these productions may be regarded as a few of the many examples of cultural bearers of the memory of Raoul Wallenberg. But what different kinds of characteristics distinguish these cultural reminders of the lost Swede? And how exactly did Wallenberg go from being a politically problematic reminder in Sweden of a man who disappeared in the powerful neighbouring country to being a globally relevant symbol? One factor that is of great importance in the present chapter is the Americanization that Wallenberg underwent from the late 1970s onwards. Modern scholarship has repeatedly discussed an 'Americanization of the Holocaust'. One of the hallmarks of this Americanization is the existence of many American Holocaust scholars, a number of whom made pioneering contributions in the field during the 1950s and 1960s. Another is a growing American-Jewish interest in the Nazi genocide, with the aim of strengthening Jewish identity at a time of increasing secularization. Other scholars have stressed that this Americanization is an inevitable element in making the Holocaust relevant in a multiethnic and multicultural United States, while still others have equated Americanization with a universalization of the Holocaust. One distinctive feature of this process is that the genocide committed by the Nazis and their allies during the Second World War is portrayed as one in a series of repressions and persecutions by authoritarian regimes.[10]

Critics of the Americanization of the Holocaust argue that its most distinctive feature is the ongoing and increasing commercialization of this genocidal history, as expressed mainly through novels and feature films set in concentration and extermination camps.

---

10 Mintz, *Popular Culture and the Shaping of Holocaust Memory in America*, pp. 34–35, 80–82, 97–102, 149–153; Linenthal, *Preserving Memory*, pp. 49, 255.

In the latter case, this Americanization has been associated with adaptations to values that are central to an US ideological tradition, such as freedom, equality, individualism, and innocence.[11] Those who criticize the Americanization of the Holocaust argue that even if these values may be considered acceptable, what is far worse is that their extension entails vulgarization while involving a profit motive, as manifested in sentimentality and happy endings because '[p]opularizers of the Holocaust have tended to look for cheap grace, for easy sources of consolation. They have sought to minimalize evil or severely limit its implications'.[12]

However, the Americanization of the Holocaust is far more multifaceted than that. First, US representations of the Holocaust are far more varied than this hostile attitude suggests. Second, views of the Holocaust in the United States have undergone a number of shifts since the end of the Second World War. As in many other places, the US view of the Holocaust in the early post-war decades often differed from the one that has come to dominate in recent decades.[13] As Klas-Göran Karlsson has pointed out, there is also another less value-charged and more analytical aspect of this Americanization:

> When the Holocaust is Americanized, the starting point is that the representation and meaning of the genocide changes when it is adapted to broadly held American values and is thereby integrated into American history culture. Conversely, this means that the Holocaust just as inevitably leaves its mark on this history culture.[14]

From this reasoning it follows that certain aspects of Raoul Wallenberg came to be emphasized, partly because they corresponded well with American attitudes but also because the Swedish diplomat's actions left their mark on American society. The American outrage at Sweden's feeble actions on his behalf, as detailed in the previous chapter, is one side of this coin. The edifying and individualistically conceived television series *Wallenberg: A Hero's Story*, to which we shall return shortly, is the other.

---

11 Rosenfeld, 'The Americanization of the Holocaust', pp. 122–125, 130–135.
12 Berenbaum, *After Tragedy and Triumph*, p. 13.
13 Fermaglich, *American Dreams and Nazi Nightmares*, pp. 1–23.
14 Karlsson, *Europeiska möten med historien*, pp. 315–316, quotation p. 316.

## An emerging international interest

Among the Hungarians, and especially the Jews who fled the country at the end of the war, Wallenberg was remembered. The same was true among many of those forced to flee by the 1956 Hungarian crisis.[15] As noted earlier, American interest was initially much in evidence, but it gradually waned. However, references to Wallenberg and his achievements were still being made throughout the 1950s, especially in Jewish radio programmes and magazines.[16] Wallenberg's deeds were highlighted from time to time in daily newspaper articles in various countries, often written by people with personal knowledge of his activities in Budapest. The trial of Adolf Eichmann in Jerusalem in 1961 featured briefings on the places where the German SS officer and his associates had operated during the war. In the account of the Holocaust in Hungary, Wallenberg was described as a particularly courageous individual, 'a man of sterling qualities' whose actions had resulted in his becoming '[t]he main target of [Eichmann's] venom'.[17] The Swedish White Papers of 1957 and 1965 also made echoes in the West.[18] For example, the first one received attention in the Swiss daily newspaper *Neue Zürcher Zeitung*.[19] One reader of that article was a man named Carl Lutz. Like Wallenberg, he had issued protective passports to save as many Jews as possible. His superiors disapproved, however, and after the end of the war they berated him for having exceeded his authority. The article about his missing diplomat colleague prompted Lutz to write to a member of the Swiss government. His aim was to persuade his government to exert pressure on the Soviet leaders, but his appeal fell on stony ground. Lutz also failed to win personal recognition. At the same time, he tried in vain to

---

15 Schult, *A Hero's Many Faces*, p. 67; Schult, 'Whose Raoul Wallenberg is it?', pp. 773–774.
16 Diner, *We Remember with Reverence and Love*, p. 261 and note 31 on p. 447.
17 *The Trial of Adolf Eichmann*. Vol. 1, Sessions No. 6–8, p. 107.
18 For the international press coverage see 'Ryska Wallenbergbeskedet ger eko i utländsk press', *Expressen*, 8 February 1957; 'Alla anständiga människor känner raseri och äckel', *Dagens Nyheter*, 9 February 1957; and 'UD begär besked även om Wallenbergs sekreterare', *Göteborgs-Posten*, 9 February 1957.
19 'Der Fall Wallenberg: Weißbuch des schwedischen Außenministeriums', *Neue Zürcher Zeitung*, 14 March 1957.

gain international support for his own nomination for the Nobel Peace Prize, citing his efforts to save Budapest's Jews as the main justification.[20]

One close associate of Wallenberg's was Per Anger, who regularly monitored what was written about his missing colleague in Sweden and internationally. When Heiner Lichtenstein, later founder of the West German Raoul Wallenberg Association, published a book about the Swedish diplomat in 1982, Anger was quick to respond. While he appreciated that a German was taking an interest in Wallenberg, the problem was a number of inaccuracies in the book. For example, Lichtenstein claimed that Wallenberg had left Budapest for a trip to Stockholm in the autumn of 1944. Anger found this statement completely erroneous. Having been in daily contact with Wallenberg, he could attest that his colleague had not left Hungary during the period in question. For the same reason Anger also dismissed the report that Wallenberg had met with Joel Brand, who had been involved in an attempt to exchange Jews for lorries. Anger stressed that Brand was entirely unknown to the Swedes at the Legation in Budapest.[21]

The situation when Anger wrote his letter differed dramatically from the circumstances that prevailed when Lutz appealed to his government or, for that matter, a mere couple of years before. Relatives and members of the Wallenberg campaign had worked hard for a long time to bring Wallenberg to general attention on the other side of the Atlantic, but with little result. In Sweden there were regular articles about Wallenberg every time negotiations with the Soviet Union arose. On the international stage, the Wallenberg case was followed by a limited though often well-informed crowd.[22] One cause of the relative silence about Raoul Wallenberg during the period from 1965 to 1978 was the lack of any new and credible

---

20 Letter from Charles Lutz to Max Petitpierre, 26 March 1957, YVA, Charles Lutz Collection. See also Klibanski, 'The Archives of the Swiss Consul General Charles Lutz', pp. 357–359, and Tschuy, *Dangerous Diplomacy*.
21 Letter from Per Anger to Heiner Lichtenstein, 1 September 1982, YVA, Heiner Lichtenstein Collection. Yehuda Bauer, who has researched German-Jewish negotiations, has not found any link between Brand and Wallenberg either; see Bauer, *Jews for Sale?*
22 In a letter to Per Anger, 29 November 1972, for instance, Eric Sjöquist writes about the well-informed Wallenberg contacts he has found in Spain, England, West Germany, and Israel; see RKA, Raoul Wallenberg, UD2001/00009, Vol. 1.

evidence about his fate in the Soviet Union. As we have seen, the information supplied by the Jewish Polish exile Abraham Kalinski was revealed as unreliable by people who had the opportunity to subject his claims to close scrutiny. Consequently, those claims did not result in any new answers from the Soviets.

Nevertheless, it was around 1980 that the history-cultural turning point regarding Wallenberg occurred. At this point in time, information was published to the effect that Soviet politicians might have been prepared to discuss Wallenberg's release at an early stage, but had met with no clear response from the Swedish Foreign Office (Utrikesdepartementet, UD). The disclosure resulted – yet again – in a considerable number of articles about Swedish dereliction of duty in the immediate post-war years.[23] Alongside these articles, there was criticism of the way in which Swedish officialdom was seen to respond in a wait-and-see manner to the growing international interest.[24] These objections did not lead to any change of course by the Swedish government and the UD, though. Well into the mid-1980s, senior representatives felt that it was not appropriate, or indeed possible, to exert pressure on the US government to take up the Wallenberg case.[25]

Elsewhere in the West things were different. How are we to understand that Raoul Wallenberg became a hero to the broad mass of humanity at this time? One reason for this renewed interest, a reason to which considerable importance has been attached, was the death of Wallenberg's mother and stepfather in 1979.[26] The Nazi-hunter Simon Wiesenthal, who had begun to take an interest in the Swedish diplomat as early as 1971 and who had kept in contact with the UD on the case, noted a marked increase of attention around 1980. Wiesenthal contributed to this increase, among other things by lobbying for Wallenberg to

---

23 Börje Heed, '5 gånger svek UD Raoul Wallenberg', *Aftonbladet*, 31 January 1980; Ingmar Lindmarker, 'Uppgifter i hemliga Wallenberg-dokumenten: "Ryssarna var beredda att förhandla om frigivning"', *Svenska Dagbladet*; Olof Santesson, 'UD-problemet Wallenberg', *Dagens Nyheter*; Inger Viklund-Persson, 'Stalin lovade ta sig an Wallenbergfallet', *Göteborgs-Posten*, all published on 1 February 1980.
24 Anders Hasselbohm, 'Jag skäms över Sverige', *Vecko-Journalen*, 1979:27, 2.
25 'Svar av utrikesminister Sten Andersson på fråga av Hadar Cars om Raoul Wallenbergs öde', 24 October 1985, question no. 1985/86:106 (in the Riksdag); RKA, Raoul Wallenberg, UD2001/00009, Vol. 24.
26 Yahil, 'Raoul Wallenberg – His Mission and His Activities in Hungary', p. 8.

be awarded the Nobel Peace Prize.[27] Demonstrations were held outside Soviet embassies to mark the thirty-fifth anniversary of the Swede's disappearance. Demands for pressure to be exerted on the Soviet government were made both by Wiesenthal and by more or less well-known Americans and Canadians, who wrote to Swedish Prime Minister Ullsten calling for renewed Swedish pressure on the Soviet authorities and demanding that Sweden boycott the 1980 Olympic Games in the Soviet capital.[28] Of even greater significance was the international Wallenberg hearing held in Stockholm in 1981. Old and new reports about his imprisonment in the Soviet Union were presented there in an attempt to shed light on his fate.[29]

In addition, more and more international politicians engaged with the issue. Israeli Prime Minister Menachem Begin requested clarification of what had happened to the Swede, as did US President Jimmy Carter. The latter was probably spurred on by domestic critics, who maintained that US leaders had been uninterested in the Holocaust and had therefore remained passive both during the Second World War and in the immediate post-war decades.

---

27 See e.g. letter from Simon Wiesenthal to Henry Jackson, 12 February 1975; Jan Lundvik, 'Raoul Wallenberg', 29 March 1978; Jan Lundvik, 'Simon Wiesenthal om Raoul Wallenberg', 30 March 1978, RKA, Raoul Wallenberg, UD2001/00009, Vol. 3.

28 See e.g. letter from Robert C. Metcalf to Ola Ullsten, 11 April 1980; letter from Steve M. Jacobs to Ola Ullsten, 14 April 1980; letter from Frederic M. Fine to Ola Ullsten, 15 April 1980; letter from Meta Hopper to Ola Ullsten, 20 April 1980; letter from John L. Burton to Ola Ullsten, 22 April 1980; letter from Marc C. Hoffman to Ola Ullsten, 23 April 1980; letter from H. Levinson to Ola Ullsten, 29 April 1980; letter from Phyllis Winston to Ola Ullsten, 1 May 1980, RKA, Raoul Wallenberg, UD2018/005505, Vols. 1 and 2. See also Lillemor Stridsberg, 'Pressen stark på Sovjet inför OS', *Göteborgs-Posten*, 16 January 1980; Knud Wilhelmsen, 'Nazi-jægeren: boykot Olympiaden i Moskva', *Jyllands-Posten*, 14 February 1980.

29 Letter from Simon Wiesenthal to Marcus Wallenberg, 31 May 1978; letters from Simon Wiesenthal to Nina Lagergren and Carl-Fredrik Palmstierna respectively, 26 February 1979; and the exchange of letters between Guy von Dardel and Simon Wiesenthal, 2 and 9 July 1979, RA, Raoul Wallenbergföreningens arkiv E1:3. Korrespondens. Huvudserie 1979, N–Ö. For Simon Wiesenthal's involvement in the Wallenberg case, see Wiesenthal, *Justice Not Vengeance*, pp. 184–195, and Pick, *Simon Wiesenthal*, pp. 233–238. See also Stefan Meisel, '35 år är nog', *Judisk Krönika*, 1980:1–2, 23; Eric Sjöquist, 'Idrottsfolk! Kräv Raoul Wallenberg utlämnad innan ni reser till OS i Moskva!', *Vecko-Journalen*, 1980:3, 12–13.

US scholars had long debated whether their country's leadership, with President Franklin D. Roosevelt at the head, had done enough to stop the Holocaust. One critic, Arthur D. Morse, went so far as to label the US (and British) responses to what had been going on for a long time as bordering on apathy. He did, however, approve of the War Refugee Board and its activities in Budapest, as well as the efforts of Wallenberg. Morse argued that it was the War Refugee Board and its resources that made his work possible. In return, Wallenberg's deeds were essential when it came to legitimizing the very existence of the organization.[30] Henry L. Feingold reasoned along similar lines when he stressed the Swedish and Swiss efforts to rescue Jews in Hungary, although these efforts could not conceal the fact that 'the rescue operation in Hungary was a failure'. The task he left to future historians was to assess how much greater this failure would have been had representatives of the Roosevelt administration not initiated the War Refugee Board in 1944.[31]

However, criticism of American actions during the Second World War was not the only reason why Wallenberg was now repeatedly referred to in the United States. He was a perfect fit for that country during the Cold War of the 1970s and 1980s, at a time when attitudes towards totalitarianism caused people to view Nazism and Soviet Communism as birds of a feather. The reborn American Wallenberg Committee and other committed Americans exerted pressure on increasingly interested American politicians.[32] In 1979 two influential senators, Frank Church and Daniel Patrick Moynihan, helped to launch a committee to work for Wallenberg's release. American enthusiasm for Wallenberg gained official status in 1979, when the US government presented an award to Nina Lagergren in recognition of Raoul Wallenberg's achievements in Budapest. At the same time, US Secretary of State Cyrus Vance revealed that his country had officially become involved in the Wallenberg case. Both Carter and Vance had made official

---

30 Morse, *While Six Million Died*, p. 371.
31 Feingold, *The Politics of Rescue*, p. 294.
32 See e.g. Bierman, *Righteous Gentile*, p. 12; George Barany, 'A Hero Remembered', *Slavic Review*, 1983:4, 657; and letter from Rachel Oestreicher Haspel (the chair of the American Wallenberg Committee) to the diplomat Mark Palmer, 30 September 1985, RKA, Raoul Wallenberg, UD2001/00009, Vol. 24; letter from Edward M. Kennedy to Lina Massie, 23 April 1979, RA, Raoul Wallenbergkommitténs arkiv. E1:2, Korrespondens. Huvudserie 1979, I–M.

representations to the Soviet government.[33] Other politicians, such as the Democrats Claiborne Pell and Thomas Lantos, plus his wife, Annette – the latter two of whom were Hungarian Holocaust survivors – supported the proposal to make Raoul Wallenberg an honorary American citizen. The Lantoses were a driving force in the matter of Wallenberg, and around 1980 they attracted unprecedented attention. One result of their efforts was the resurrection of a Wallenberg Association in Sweden. They also helped Nina Lagergren and Guy von Dardel in their attempts to establish contact with US politicians, with the express aim of getting them to become actively involved in exerting pressure on the Soviet – and Swedish – authorities.[34]

One highlight of this international attention was that in 1981, the US Congress almost unanimously – of the 398 who voted, only two did not support the initiative – approved the proposal to make Raoul Wallenberg an honorary American citizen. In the early 1980s Guy von Dardel moved to sue the Soviet state. He turned to Morris Wolff, a lawyer specializing in international law. Wolff had some difficulty in gaining the ears of some of Reagan's advisers, but he did meet with a powerful response from the House Foreign Affairs

---

33 See e.g. letter from Guy von Dardel to Per Anger, 24 June 1979, RA, Raoul Wallenbergföreningens arkiv, E1:1. Korrespondens, Huvudserie 1979, A–H; Jimmy Carter and Annette Lantos, 'Raoul Wallenberg, October 19, 1979', *Jimmy Carter: Public Papers of the Presidents of the United States. 1979. Book II*, pp. 1887–1888; Shuart and Berliner, 'Jimmy Carter Conference – Town Meeting', p. 481.

34 Nadine Brozan, 'Mystery surrounds fate of Swede who saved Jews', *The New York Times*, 4 August 1979; Alan Cline, 'Her search for war hero gets support from Carter', *San Francisco Examiner & Chronicle*, 14 October 1979; Jean Merl, 'Swede kept thousands of Jews safe from Hitler', *Los Angeles Times*, 14 April 1980; Stefan Meisel, 'Svensk förening för Raoul Wallenberg', *Judisk Krönika*, 1979:4, 12; Vera Brodin, 'Raoul Wallenberg-förening bildad', *Dagens Nyheter*, 4 September 1979; Staffan Hultman, 'Svensk Raoul Wallenberg-förening bildad: Ökad chans nå klarhet', *Göteborgs-Posten*, 4 September 1979. On the Lantoses' contributions in the American Wallenberg Committee see Schult, *A Hero's Many Faces*, pp. 71–73. See also undated letter from Nina Lagergren to Henry M. Jackson, Daniel P. Moynihan, Claiborne Pell, and Stuart Eizenstat; letter from Ebba von Eckermann to Nina Lagergren, 15 June 1979 and letter from Guy von Dardel to Claiborne Pell, 23 August 1979, RA, Raoul Wallenbergföreningens arkiv, E1:2. Korrespondens, Huvudserie 1979, I–M, plus letter from John L. Burton to Ola Ullsten, 22 April 1980, RA, Raoul Wallenbergföreningens arkiv, E1:4. Korrespondens, Huvudserie 1980, A–K.

Committee. He could also rely on support from the Lantoses and Claiborne Pell. The collaboration between Wolff and von Dardel resulted in the latter's filing a high-profile lawsuit against the Soviet Union in a US court in February 1984. The suit demanded Soviet clarification about Wallenberg's fate, 83 million dollars in compensation, and – most importantly – the release of the Swedish diplomat, as the lawsuit proceeded from the presumption that he was still alive. Not surprisingly, Moscow provided no new information on the matter. Nor was there any Soviet reaction after a US judge ruled in October 1985 that the Soviet Union had violated international law in arresting Wallenberg. Despite the lack of response from the Kremlin, the lawsuit helped to focus renewed attention on the Swedish diplomat both in the United States and elsewhere.[35]

Wallenberg became an honorary citizen of Canada in 1985 and of Israel in 1986. A year later he was honoured by the World Jewish Congress. During the 1980s, monuments began to be erected in his memory, and streets and squares were named after him, some of them directly linked to places with a Holocaust connection. Examples include the trees dedicated to Wallenberg on the road in the Yad Vashem Museum in Jerusalem that honours the Righteous Among the Nations. The United States Holocaust Memorial Museum in Washington D.C. is located at 100 Wallenberg Place. Since the turn of the millennium, criticism and frustration have been expressed that individual cities do *not* have any location named after Wallenberg.[36]

As a result of this fresh attention, Wallenberg committees were established in a number of countries.[37] Another consequence was a renewed and greatly intensified cooperation between the Swedish and the American Wallenberg Committees. The extensive correspondence in the Raoul Wallenberg Association's archives bears witness to a reawakened optimism.[38] This was also evident in the

---

35 Morris Wolff, *Whatever Happened to Raoul Wallenberg?*
36 Tom R. Schulz, 'Es ist der Held unserer Zeit', *Die Welt*, 11 May 2001.
37 See e.g. letter from Guy von Dardel to Per Anger, 24 June 1979, RA, Raoul Wallenbergföreningens arkiv, E1:1. Korrespondens, Huvudserie 1979, A–H; letter from Nina Lagergren to Arne Melchior, 26 September 1979, RA, Raoul Wallenbergföreningens arkiv, E1:2. Korrespondens, Huvudserie 1979, I–M.
38 See the extensive exchange of letters primarily between Swedish and American interested parties from late spring 1979 to 1980 in NRA, Raoul Wallenbergkommitténs arkiv. E:1–5. Korrespondens.

# The Americanization of Wallenberg 223

press coverage of the case. In the wake of the findings presented in the White Papers of 1957 and 1965, a number of writers had argued that while there was no certain evidence that Wallenberg was dead, Swedes must be prepared to accept that this was the case.[39] Wallenberg's relatives and their supporters disagreed. As seen earlier, Nanna Svartz's testimony had sparked renewed hope that in spite of everything, Wallenberg might still be alive.[40]

Around the same time as American interest in Raoul Wallenberg was growing, Elsa and Hans Villius resumed their criticism of unreliable informants who claimed to have met or heard of Wallenberg after 1947.[41] Such objections still fell on deaf ears among most of those who were involved in the case, people who hoped that now it had become a major international political issue, the missing Swede could be found and returned. One striking example is a multi-page article published in the early 1980s and supplemented by a map of the Soviet Union on which all the places where witnesses claimed to have met or seen Wallenberg were marked.[42] During the 1970s and 1980s witnesses claimed to have seen him alive with their own eyes, or they asserted that they knew he was still a prisoner in a camp or prison.[43] The actor, film director, and writer Kenne Fant dedicated *R*, a 1988 documentary novel based on the premise that Raoul Wallenberg was still alive in 1986 and was recalling episodes from

---

39 I. Pe., 'Wallenbergs öde' (editorial) and 'Föga hopp att svensken är vid liv', *Arbetet*, 8 February 1957; 'Raoul Wallenberg död?' (editorial), *Upsala Nya Tidning*, 8 February 1957; Mia Leche, 'Fredshjälte i mörk tid', *Göteborgs Handels- och Sjöfartstidning*, 9 February 1957; 'Raoul Wallenberg' (editorial), *Göteborgs-Posten*, 17 September 1965; 'Levande begraven' (editorial), *Göteborgs Handels- och Sjöfartstidning*, 17 September 1965; Staffan Mats, 'Raoul Wallenberg – 25-årig gåta: Räddade tiotusentals judar från gasdöden i Auschwitz', *Skånska Dagbladet*, 24 January 1972.
40 See e.g. 'Min son lever!', *Aftonbladet*, 8 February 1957; 'Wallenberg, Sovjet och Sverige' (editorial) and 'Wallenbergs mor: Raoul är inte död. Vi ger ej upp hoppet', *Dagens Nyheter*, 8 February 1957; 'Fallet Raoul Wallenberg' (editorial), *Upsala Nya Tidning*; 'Raoul Wallenberg på sjukhus i Moskva 1961', *Göteborgs Handels- och Sjöfartstidning*; 'Hon är säker på att han levde -61', *Expressen*; 'Bomb i vitbok om Wallenberg: han levde 1961!', *Arbetet*, all published 17 September 1965.
41 Villius and Villius, 'Raoul Wallenberg dog 1947', *Dagens Nyheter*, 3 March 1979.
42 Eric Sjöquist, 'Gåtan Raoul Wallenberg', *Expressen*, 15 March 1981.
43 Eric Sjöquist, 'Sensationellt vittne! Jag såg Wallenberg torteras', *Expressen*, 30 September 1973; Anders Hasslebohm, 'Jag heter Raoul, inte Paul',

his long life, to the '73-year-old Soviet dissident Danylo Shumuk, who, like Raoul Wallenberg, has been imprisoned for more than 42 years'.[44] A few years later, in a Canadian newspaper, Per Anger maintained that believing that his colleague from Budapest was still alive was not mere wishful thinking. Of course, Soviet prisoners lived in harsh conditions, but they were forced to live healthily, eating food with little fat, and having no access to alcohol or tobacco. A prisoner was simply not permitted to die. The Swedish actress and human-rights activist Sonja Sonnenfeld stated along the same lines that: 'I don't say he could still be alive today. I say I know he is alive. We want to know his fate, but that's not enough. We also want him free.'[45]

The Swedes who had been working for decades both to clarify Wallenberg's fate and to secure his release received help from abroad in the 1980s. When the BBC journalist John Bierman initially heard the story of the missing diplomat, he doubted its veracity. He was equally puzzled that no Westerner outside Scandinavia had as yet written anything substantial about Wallenberg. Bierman took on the task, and in 1981 he published the book *Righteous Gentile: The Story of Raoul Wallenberg*. Before that, he had produced a documentary film in the 'Man Alive' series, entitled *Missing Hero: Raoul Wallenberg* (1980). In the film, Bierman interviewed the Romanian Jew Leizer Bergher / Lazar Berger. After the Soviet Union had occupied Bessarabia, the Romanian had been transported eastwards, imprisoned, and then forced to fight in a Soviet penal battalion before being re-imprisoned. He remained in the Gulag camp and prison system until 1978, after which he emigrated to Israel. In conversations with Israelis and Swedish diplomatic staff

---

*Vecko-Journalen*, 1978:15, 10–13; Anders Hasslebohm, 'Wallenberg satt på Wrangelön 1962', *Vecko-Journalen*, 1978:16, 20–23; Martin Seiff, 'Begin wants Carter to ask Soviets: Is Wallenberg still alive', *The Jerusalem Post*, 14 June 1979; Michael Kernan, 'Phantom prisoner: Searching for a hero of the Holocaust', *The Washington Post*, 20 July 1979; Nadine Brozan, 'Mystery surrounds fate of Swede who saved Jews', *The New York Times*, 4 August 1979; Peter Hoffer, 'Nytt vittnesmål: Raoul Wallenberg ledde hungerstrejk i fängelse', *Göteborgs-Posten*, 9 December 1979; Eric Sjöquist, 'Raoul lever!', *Expressen*, 18 January 1987.
44 Kenne Fant, *R*, p. 5. Danylo Shumuk was released in 1987 after 42 years in Soviet, Polish, and German prisons and camps. He then he moved to Canada before returning in 2002 to Ukraine, where he died two years later.
45 Glenn Frankel, 'Searching for the truth and Raoul Wallenberg', *The Vancouver Sun*, 5 October 1991.

he variously claimed not to have met Wallenberg, or that they had been in the same prison together until the severely ill Swede had died in 1964. In the film Bergher said he had only heard of Wallenberg. The main reason for Bergher's inclusion in the documentary about Wallenberg, despite his contradictory information, seems to be Bierman's desire to inform viewers that it was possible to survive 34 years in Soviet camps.[46] Similar hopes were held by a number of Israeli members of the Rescue Wallenberg Committee of Jerusalem, which claimed in 1989 that Wallenberg had been a patient in a Moscow hospital two years earlier.[47] Chairwoman of the Raoul Wallenberg Committee of the United States Rachel Oestricher Bernheim did not say where her role model had gone after that, but even when she had first become involved in the Wallenberg case in 1981, she had refused to accept the claim that he had died in 1947. She has since maintained this position.[48]

The US citizen journalist Harvey Rosenfeld predicted that the newly awakened commitment to the Swede's cause around 1980 would in all likelihood mean that '[t]he case of Raoul Wallenberg will not go away'.[49] Behind the scenes, US politicians were making cautious overtures to Soviet and Swedish politicians.[50] In the Swedish public sphere, there was uncertainty about how far the United States was prepared to go and what the Soviet reaction

---

46 Göran Jacobsson, 'Vittnesuppgifter om Wallenberg av Lazar Berger', 20 January 1980; (Torsten) Örn, 'Re: Lazar (Leon Berger)', 24 January 1980; Lars-Åke Nilsson, 'Promemoria: Vittnesmål i Wallenberg-ärendet', 30 January 1980, RKA, Raoul Wallenberg, UD2001/000009, Vol. 9; Maria Karagianis, 'Reporter chronicles the story of Raoul Wallenberg, a war hero', *The Boston Globe*, 8 October 1981.
47 'Israeli group rejects Soviet claim that Raoul Wallenberg is dead', *Montreal Gazette*, 3 June 1989.
48 Robin Finn, 'Taking time to recognize a new age of heroes' (interview with Rachel Oestreicher Bernheim), *The New York Times*, 13 November 2001.
49 Harvey Rosenfeld, 'Where is Raoul Wallenberg?', *The New York Times*, 17 January 1981.
50 See e.g. enquiry from the chairman of the US Senate Committee on Foreign Relations Frank Church to Leonid Brezhnev, 23 October 1979, RA, Raoul Wallenbergkommitténs arkiv. E1:1, Korrespondens. Huvudserie 1979, A–H; letter from Edward M. Kennedy to Lina Massie, 23 April 1979 and letter from Sherrod McCall to Guy von Dardel, 10 July 1979, RA, Raoul Wallenbergkommitténs arkiv. E1:2, Korrespondens. Huvudserie 1979, I–M; and Ewerlöf, 'Wallenberg i MR-kommissionen', 17 and 20 February 1981, RKA, Raoul Wallenberg, UD2001/00009, Vol. 13.

would be.[51] Either way, it was argued that it was important to act quickly, or it would definitely be too late. When a Swedish tabloid conducted a phone-in about whether Wallenberg might still be alive, it added the follow-up questions 'if so, where and how?'[52] As Guy von Dardel wrote to Henrik Beer at the Red Cross headquarters in Switzerland, the renewed attention paid to Wallenberg not only benefited the search for von Dardel's half-brother, but also many other forgotten prisoners in the Soviet Union.[53]

The revived international, and especially American, interest in Raoul Wallenberg in the late 1970s should be regarded in the light of a change in attitude towards the Holocaust. From the end of the war until the early 1960s, the Holocaust had left little trace in American history culture. When the atrocities of the Second World War were discussed, the dominant topic was the massacre of thousands of Polish officers at Katyn. At the Nuremberg trials, Germany had been blamed, but persistent suspicions that the guilty party was actually the Soviet secret service helped to keep the issue alive. After all, during the Cold War Nazi Germany had been supplanted by a new totalitarian enemy: the Soviet Union. In addition, West Germany was an important Western ally, a circumstance which also helped to dampen the already meagre efforts

---

51 Ingmar Lindmarker, 'Wallenberg supermaktsfråga', *Svenska Dagbladet*, 9 September 1979.

52 Heed, '5 gånger svek UD Raoul Wallenberg'; Ulf Brandell, 'Är Raoul Wallenberg i livet?', *Svenska Dagbladet*, 12 February 1978; Anders Hasselbohm, 'Hennes far mötte Raoul Wallenberg' (interview with Anna Bilder), *Vecko-Journalen*, 1979:10; Harald Wigforss, '"Fallet Wallenberg" en kamp mot klockan', *Skånska Dagbladet*, 15 February 1979; Anders Hasselbohm, 'Ryssarna ljuger fortfarande om Raoul Wallenberg', *Dagens Nyheter*, 24 March 1979; Ingmar Lindmarker, 'Är det önsketänkande att Wallenberg lever?', *Svenska Dagbladet*, 4 February 1980; Gabi Gleichmann, 'Vi måste utgå från att han lever', *Expressen*, 17 January 1985; Berit Johansson, 'Lever Wallenberg?', *Borås Tidning*, 17 January 1985; Eric Sjöquist, 'Wallenberg lever!', *Expressen*, 18 October 1985. See also Guy von Dardel and Nina Lagergren, 'Raoul Wallenbergs humanitära insats och kampen för att få honom åter', undated text sent to *Dagens Nyheter* but not published; RA, Raoul Wallenbergföreningens arkiv, E1:1. Korrespondens. Huvudserie 1979, A–H.

53 Letter from Guy von Dardel to Henrik Beer, 14 December 1979, RA, Raoul Wallenbergkommitténs arkiv. E1:1, Korrespondens. Huvudserie 1979, A–H.

to draw attention to the Nazi genocide.[54] McCarthyism likewise increased fears of new outbreaks of the antisemitism that had been strongly entrenched in the United States until the outbreak of the Second World War. With the exception of *The Diary of Anne Frank*, books about antisemitism and the Holocaust rarely reached a wider audience. The new medium of television first dramatized Wallenberg's actions in Budapest in 1957, but the programme was not widely publicized, and in general the Nazi genocide was still rarely a topic in television and film. The Eichmann trial, which was the first judicial process to be broadcast on US television, temporarily raised awareness, but it did not lead to any breakthrough on a broad front.[55]

One important cause of the growing interest in the Holocaust was the tense situation in the Middle East. In the context of the 1967 Six-Day War and the 1973 Yom Kippur War, Israel emerged as a vulnerable and exposed nation in need of American support. Perhaps – so the drastic warning went – the destruction of the Jews had not been averted by the fall of the Nazis, but merely postponed.[56] Around 1980, too, representatives of various political camps were drawing parallels between the situation in 1940s Europe and that in the contemporary Middle East. The plausibility of such analogies was questioned, but the comparisons between then and now nevertheless helped the Holocaust to become much more widely known.

In his study of the role of the Holocaust in the United States, Peter Novick has emphasized that silence predominated until the mid-1960s. This was mainly due to the difficulty for survivors to speak about the tragedy or, when they did speak out, a reluctance to listen among the rest of the population, who preferred to focus on memories of American triumph rather than on the tragedy of the Holocaust. When American Jews celebrated the three-hundredth anniversary of the arrival of the first Jews to the United States in 1954, there was no mention whatsoever of the tragedy that had occurred only a decade or so earlier.

---

54 For an early Swedish analysis, see Erik De Laval, 'Nürnberg och Katyn', *Samtid och Framtid*, 1947:7. See also Jick, 'The Holocaust', pp. 304–311.
55 Shandler, *While America Watches*, pp. 122–127, note 55, p. 274; Doneson, *The Holocaust in American Film*, pp. 13–107; Torgovnick, *The War Complex*, pp. 62–63.
56 Novick, *The Holocaust in American Life*, pp. 103–203; Morgan, *Beyond Auschwitz*, pp. 79–90.

In the following decades, American Jews gradually shifted their position. Previously, they had mostly discussed internal Jewish affairs, but Jewish newspapers and magazines increasingly presented topics with greater universality. Simultaneously, the general understanding of the Holocaust became increasingly associated with Jews as the largest group of victims owing to the Nazis' antisemitic obsession. There were certainly still considerable political, cultural, and religious differences between Jewish right-wing and left-wing groups, but there was at least one unifying link: 'there was something for everybody in the Holocaust'. Novick stresses that this shift cannot be reduced to changes in the political sphere alone. One determining factor was the transformation in the late 1970s of the Holocaust from being a predominantly Jewish memory to being an American one.[57]

This shift in attitude, as well as the question of when the memory of the Holocaust took shape in the United States, has been the subject of much debate. Critics of Novick have pointed to other possible explanations, such as a decline in antisemitism and racism in US society at that time, the desire of older Jews to help ensure the survival of the memory of the Holocaust, and the successful efforts of Jewish intellectuals, scholars, and artists, all of whom contributed to giving this genocide a more prominent position, for example in universities and the media, and in film and on television.[58]

## Raoul Wallenberg and the mass media

A key history-cultural explanation for the growing interest in the Holocaust in the years around 1980 is the impact of the television series *Holocaust* (1978). Although it was heavily criticized by parts of the establishment, it was a public success, and it changed the status of the Holocaust in one stroke from a subject that had been researched to some degree but with little impact on the

---

57 Novick, *The Holocaust in American Life*, pp. 103–203, 209–211, quotation p. 184. See also Jick, 'The Holocaust', pp. 313–318; Cole, *Selling the Holocaust*, pp. 9–12.

58 For a nuancing of the assertions that the silence about the Holocaust dominated in the decades after the Second World War, see Diner, *We Remember with Reverence and Love*, passim; Alm, 'Holocaust Memory in America and Europe', pp. 500–504. For a critique of Novick's *The Holocaust in American Life* see Herf, 'How and Why Did Holocaust Memory Come to the United States?', pp. 457–474.

general public. As more than half the population in many countries followed the tragic fate of the Weiss family from the late 1930s to the end of the Second World War, the Nazi genocide received unprecedented attention. In its wake came questions about what had happened to those individuals who had dared to stand up to the Nazis in order to save the Jews. Nina Lagergren's visit to the United States in 1979 met with great interest from US journalists. Through their questions, the younger journalists revealed that they had little knowledge of the Wallenberg case, 'yet they were deeply moved and eager to find out more', said Lagergren. More and more Americans had discovered Wallenberg and regarded him as one of the greatest heroes of the Second World War.[59] But what lay behind this surge of interest after 34 years of dormancy? Lagergren was sure of the answer: 'As far as I can tell it is thanks to the television series *Holocaust*. ... The same thing happened in Germany and England, where committees for the liberation of Wallenberg were also formed'.[60]

One of the driving forces behind the American Wallenberg Committee, the aforementioned Annette Lantos, confirmed this conclusion at a subsequent press conference. She believed it was an advantage that the television drama had only focused on a few individuals. Like many others, she engaged more when confronted with the courage and goodness of a few people rather than with large-scale and anonymous depictions of the Nazi mass murder. Lantos also called for some kind of sequel to *Holocaust*, which should focus on Wallenberg. His story must be told over and over again, and it was important that new generations heard about the Swedish hero, preferably in the form of a film or television series.[61] She and others who were involved in trying to discover Raoul Wallenberg's

---

59 Elenore Lester and Frederick E. Werbell, 'The lost hero of the Holocaust', *The New York Times*, 30 March 1980; Stewart McBride, 'Raoul Wallenberg – the hero of the Holocaust', *The Christian Science Monitor*, 24 July 1980.

60 'Raoul Wallenbergs syster i tårar: "Jag vet att min bror lever"', *Expressen*, 25 July 1979. Nina Lagergren and Guy von Dardel also stressed the importance of the television series in 'Raoul Wallenbergs humanitära insats och kampen för att få honom åter', an undated text sent to *Dagens Nyheter* but not published; RA, Raoul Wallenbergföreningens arkiv, E 1:2. Korrespondens. Huvudserie 1979, I–M.

61 'Raoul Wallenbergs syster i tårar: "Jag vet att min bror lever"', *Expressen*, 25 July 1979. See also the report from Pierre/EW to UD 25 July 1979, RKA, Raoul Wallenberg, UD2001/00009, Vol. 6; letter from Kerstin Hallert to

fate probably harboured the same hope that was expressed once a television series about the Swede had become a reality: a narrative told in moving images would make even more people interested in the missing diplomat and thereby act as a catalyst for finding a solution, once and for all, to the mystery of what had happened to him after January 1945.[62]

Ronald Reagan, who had followed his presidential predecessor in advocating Wallenberg's becoming an honorary American citizen and who had signed the bill making it law in October 1981, looked forward to a television drama about the Swede's actions in Budapest. With his acting background, Reagan often referred to films as role models and reference points that had a bearing on current issues. Unsurprisingly, Wallenberg's tragic fate reminded Reagan of a movie: it worked dramaturgically and was 'a script that fascinated Reagan and that he mastered to the full', writes journalist Staffan Thorsell of the President's penchant for discussing Wallenberg with Swedish political leaders visiting the White House.[63]

For Reagan, the step between politics and religion was a short one. Consequently, he frequently referred to the Bible, a text which supplied the answers to virtually every problem and challenge. As a product of Judeo-Christian tradition, he repeatedly turned to representatives of Jewish organizations, not least to stress the importance of remembering the Holocaust in order to guard against totalitarian regimes such as that of the Nazis.[64] He included Raoul Wallenberg in such contexts on a number of occasions. The memory of the missing Swede, whose achievement was 'of biblical proportions',[65]

---

Nina Lagergren, 19 March 1979, RA, Raoul Wallenbergföreningens arkiv, E 1:1. Korrespondens. Huvudserie 1979, A–H; and 'Boken om Wallenberg – en väckarklocka', *Svenska Dagbladet*, 30 October 1984.

62 Ann Hodges, 'Miniseries may serve as catalyst for solving Wallenberg mystery', *The Houston Chronicle*, 7 April 1985.
63 Thorsell, *Sverige i Vita huset*, p. 241. See also Jan Lindström, 'I USA hyllas han som en hjälte', *Expressen*, 18 October 1985 and Schult, *A Hero's Many Faces*, p. 67. For an in-depth analysis of the links between film and politics in Ronald Reagan's thinking see Rogin, *Ronald Reagan, the Movie, and Other Episodes in Political Demonology*, passim.
64 Edel, *The Reagan Presidency*, pp. 1–8.
65 Ronald Reagan, 'Remarks on Signing a Bill Proclaiming Honorary United States Citizenship for Raoul Wallenberg of Sweden. October 5, 1981', *Ronald Reagan: Public Papers of the Presidents of the United States. 1981*, p. 890.

## The Americanization of Wallenberg

was invoked by Reagan both during meetings with representatives of Jewish communities and at ceremonies to honour the victims of the Holocaust or those who had survived the genocide.[66]

The President regularly reminded his audience of the link between Wallenberg's actions and the Soviets' responsibility for his disappearance. He was helped by the decision of Congress to make the Swede an honorary American citizen, as it stipulated that the President should 'ascertain from the Soviet Union Wallenberg's whereabouts'.[67] When Reagan spoke at the European Parliament in Strasbourg to mark the fortieth anniversary of the end of the Second World War, Wallenberg was a self-evident topic, but this time Reagan refrained from linking him with Soviet repression. This did not prevent him from harshly attacking Soviet foreign policy and Communism as a form of government, which caused a number of MEPs to start booing and several of them to leave the room in protest.[68] Some of the disgruntled parliamentarians may also have agreed with the critics who had reacted strongly to the President's actions a few days earlier. Following months of intense pressure, he had decided to visit a concentration camp in conjunction with his state visit to West Germany, but he also joined West German Chancellor Helmut Kohl in honouring fallen soldiers at the Bitburg war cemetery, where a number of Waffen-SS soldiers who might have been suspected of helping to shoot and kill unarmed Americans during the 1944 Battle of the Bulge were buried.

Given this general context, Reagan and his advisers almost certainly realized that the story of the diplomat who had disappeared in the Soviet Union would be a highly useful tool in the ongoing Cold War. They must surely also have known that the

---

66 Ronald Reagan, 'Remarks at a White House Ceremony Commemoration on the Day of Remembrance of the Victims of the Holocaust. April 20, 1982', *Ronald Reagan: Public Papers of the Presidents of the United States. 1982. Book I*, p. 496; Ronald Reagan, 'Remarks at a White House Meeting with Jewish Leaders. February 2, 1983' and 'Remarks to the American Gathering of Jewish Holocaust Survivors. April 11, 1983', *Ronald Reagan: Public Papers of the Presidents of the United States. 1983. Book I*, pp. 174, 525.
67 'Wallenberg Citizenship', *Congress and the Nation. Volume IV. 1981–1984*, p. 144.
68 Ronald Reagan, 'Address to a Special Session of the European Parliament in Strasbourg, France. May 8, 1985', *Ronald Reagan: Public Papers of the Presidents of the United States. 1985. Book I*, pp. 581–588.

Nazi genocide had made a powerful impact on the general public – although with a few decades' delay – owing to the success of the television series about the tragic fate of the Weiss family in the late 1970s. The Americanization of much of the world in the second half of the twentieth century has been a prime example of how successful soft power can be. When he launched the concept, its originator, the political scientist Joseph S. Nye, could look back on several decades of soft-power instruments which had helped to spread desirable values. As he noted, the importance of soft power cannot be overestimated. Various forms of popular culture have often effectively contributed to their recipients voluntarily reconsidering ingrained values.[69]

This is not to claim that culture – ranging from its most popular forms of expression to avant-garde experiments aimed at the few – is at the service of those in power. From installations and happenings to music, films, and television programmes, there are plenty of examples that have inspired protests and other forms of resistance. It is equally clear that the importance of television series such as *Roots* and *Holocaust*, in drawing attention to past injustices that had sometimes received limited attention before, must not be underestimated. These cultural manifestations have thereby become part of a history-cultural processing in the form of a kind of collective therapy. This reasoning may be applied to the dual trauma expressed in the visual representations of Raoul Wallenberg, to which we shall return shortly. On the one hand, these representations proceeded from the deep wound inflicted by the Holocaust, above all on the perception of Western civilization, with complex and longstanding repercussions. And on the other, they highlighted Wallenberg's disappearance, which was hence expanded from being a family tragedy and the subject of a Swedish domestic political controversy to being a tragic tale that touched the hearts of millions of viewers.

## Wallenberg as a television series

In the first half of 2010, both Wallenberg and the above-mentioned Jan Karski were the subjects of 'commemorative years', during which their wartime contributions were respectively linked to modern Swedish and Polish foreign and refugee policies.

---

69 Nye, 'Soft Power', pp. 153–171.

# The Americanization of Wallenberg

Even before this, there had been similarities with regard to interest in these two prominent figures. Karski, who lived in exile in the United States for many years, had already attracted considerable attention there and in Canada during the Second World War for his *Story of a Secret State*, published in 1944. In the decades that followed, however, his efforts to raise awareness of the Holocaust received scant attention. They came in for renewed interest in the 1980s, though. That was partly because Elie Wiesel drew attention to Karski's efforts, but even more influential was the Pole's participation in Claude Lanzmann's documentary *Shoah* (1985).[70] Similarly, there is an obvious link between the media attention paid to Wallenberg and the public's interest in him. This has been evident in Sweden ever since the 1960s, albeit on an initially rather modest scale. One illustrative example is the historian Hans Villius, who began to take an interest in Wallenberg after leaving academia to work for Swedish broadcasting. One of his first television programmes was about the missing Swede. Together with his wife, Elsa, Villius again focused on Wallenberg – in book form in 1966, and then again in television programmes in the 1990s.[71]

Generally speaking, the media coverage intensified in connection with major articles about Wallenberg or screenings of documentary films and television programmes about his fate. Such attention in turn led to articles about his actions in Budapest and about the UD's handling of the case, as well as to descriptions of the Soviet prison and camp system.[72] Besides, newspaper or magazine reports and television programmes encouraged people throughout the Western world, who were fascinated by Wallenberg's story, to contact Swedish politicians and diplomats. Another result was that new witnesses came forward.[73] It was also significant that

---

70 Zander, 'Remembering and Forgetting the Holocaust', pp. 203–209.
71 Ludvigsson, *The Historian-Filmmaker's Dilemma*, pp. 121, 143, 167, 171–172, 314, 333. The Villiuses' television programme was noticed in diplomatic circles; see e.g. 'Conversation Between Ambassador Parsons and Foreign Office Director for Political Affairs, Ambassador Hichens-Bergström, on February 5, 1965', RKA, Raoul Wallenberg, UD2001/00009, Vol. 6.
72 See e.g. Hans Villius, 'En evig gåta?' and Sven Wallmark, 'Så arbetade ryska fångbyråkratin', both in *Röster i Radio & TV*, 1965:5, 17, 39, 43; Sune Örnberg, 'Raoul Wallenberg', *Vecko-Journalen*, 1974:10, 10–11, 48.
73 Letter from John Cottor to Gunnar Jarring, 18 March 1970; Letter from William B. Macomber, Jr to Edward Kennedy, 29 April 1970; Letter from Barbara Chicoyne to Ola Ullsten, 1 May 1980; Letter from

diplomats found themselves working in partly new circumstances. Citing the example of British foreign policy, Yoel Cohen has observed that the practice of diplomacy changed as the supply of information increased. Since the 1970s, the media and diplomacy have interacted in many different ways. One result is a challenge to the belief that diplomacy can and should take place in secrecy. Cohen argues that through their coverage, the media help to shape foreign policy by influencing both decision-makers and the population they represent in a democracy.[74]

Historical novels set in wartime Budapest, as well as films and television programmes – especially documentaries – about Wallenberg, were regularly read and watched by politicians and diplomats, who analysed and commented on them.[75] In addition, UD staff around the world had to get used to the fact that both documentary and feature films about Raoul Wallenberg aroused a large response. The staff of the Swedish embassy in a country where a Wallenberg programme was shown almost always received spontaneous reactions from the public after the broadcast. Swedish embassy staff around the world soon began ordering information leaflets and folders about Wallenberg in order to satisfy people's curiosity about the Swede's achievements.[76] In 1987, one of the

---

Edward Schneider to Ola Ullsten, 1 May 1980, RKA, Raoul Wallenberg, UD2018/005505, Vol. 1. See also Derogy, *Fallet Raoul Wallenberg*, p. 241.

74 Cohen, *Media Diplomacy*, p. 156.

75 See e.g. Erlander (ed.), *Tage Erlander: Dagbok 1965*, pp. 20–21; (Carl) Lidbom, 'Wallenberg', 29 November 1982, RKA, Raoul Wallenberg, UD2001/00009, Vol. 18; Örjan Berner, 'Raoul Wallenbergärendet', 16 November 1989, RKA, Raoul Wallenberg, UD2018/005505, Vol. 3; Lage Olson, 'Jane Horney, Alexander Pavlov och Raoul Wallenberg', 27 February 1995, RKA, Raoul Wallenberg, UD2018/005505, Vol. 12; Jan Lundvik, 'Raoul Wallenberg: István Újszásy', 7 July 1999, RKA, Raoul Wallenberg, UD2018/005505, Vol. 20; 'Translation of Foreign Press Release, February 8, 1965' and 'Press Reaction on TV Program on Wallenberg Case' (undated), RKA, Raoul Wallenberg, UD2018/005505, Vol. 36.

76 See e.g. 'Pressmeddelande måndagen den 8 februari 1965', RKA, Raoul Wallenberg, UD2001/00009, Vol. 6; Bengt Borglund, 'Raoul Wallenberg uppmärksammas i TV', 29 March 1978, RKA, Raoul Wallenberg, UD2001/00009, Vol. 3; 'Brittisk publicitet om Raoul Wallenberg', 24 March 1980, RKA, Raoul Wallenberg, UD2001/00009, Vol. 9; Wilhelm Wachtmeister, 'Raoul Wallenberg', Washington, 21 March 1981, RKA, Raoul Wallenberg, UD2001/00009, Vol. 13; Lind, 'Wallenberg-filmen', 26 May 1982 and Ingolf Kiesow, 'Raoul Wallenberg i tyska medier', Bonn, 6 July 1982, RKA, Raoul Wallenberg, UD2001/00009, Vol. 16; [Lars

most widely circulated publications in the series 'UD informerar' was published on the theme of Raoul Wallenberg. The 50-page report, complemented with documents and photographs, dealt with the man, his deeds, his disappearance, and the search for him. The text was translated into English as soon as possible.[77] No wonder *Holocaust* was cited as an important factor when, in the mid-1980s, the UD was briefing its staff on the status of the Wallenberg case in the United States.[78] *Holocaust* also sparked a number of further television series about the Second World War and/or the Holocaust, such as *Playing for Time* (1980) and *Winds of War* (1983).[79]

Fifteen years before *Holocaust*'s triumphal march across the West there had been plans for a feature film about Raoul Wallenberg, directed by Arne Mattsson and – it was hoped – with Max von Sydow in the leading role. The intention to make it a co-production between the Swedish film company Sandrews and a Communist film group in Budapest raised eyebrows, as did the uncertainty about how the film would end. Another obstacle was that Wallenberg's mother did not give her permission. Nor did Sweden's Minister for Foreign Affairs Torsten Nilsson, who was upset at claims he had been in favour of the project at an early stage.[80]

As mentioned earlier, the situation in the United States in the early 1980s was different. Events honouring Wallenberg in Los Angeles at that time were attended by a number of film stars. In addition, representatives of the film and television industry showed interest in Annette Lantos's request for a Wallenberg story presented on the large or small screen, despite the failure of

---

Hedström, 'Raoul Wallenberg', Canberra, Australia, 17 April 1985; Wilhelm Wachtmeister, 'Wallenberg-filmen', 13 March 1985; Magnus Faxén, 'Tribute to Raoul Wallenberg', 15 March 1985; Magnus Faxén, 'Tribute to Raoul Wallenberg', 9 May 1985, RKA, Raoul Wallenberg, UD2001/0 0009, Vol. 23; Sven Julin, 'Raoul Wallenberg', Memorandum, 11 October 1985 and interpellation 1985/86:33 from Conservative Party member Per Stenmarck to Sten Andersson, 17 October 1985, RKA, Raoul Wallenberg, UD2001/00009, Vol. 24. See also Per Anger, 'Raoul Wallenberg', *Svensk Tidskrift*, 1984:4, 197.

77 Wallenberg, *UD informerar; Raoul Wallenberg*.
78 Sven Julin, 'Raoul Wallenbergefterforskningarna: Inför kabinettssekreterarens besök i New York 1985-03-14', Memorandum, 5 May 1985, RKA, Raoul Wallenberg, UD2001/00009, Vol. 23.
79 See e.g. Doneson, *The Holocaust in American Film*, pp. 194-195.
80 'Raoul Wallenberg skulle bli en film med ungersk hjälp', *Göteborgs Handels- och Sjöfartstidning*, 8 August 1964.

the first four attempts, including a proposed feature film starring the Swedish actors Per Mattsson and Max von Sydow. Another suggestion for a future Wallenberg film was well received at the 1980 Cannes Film Festival, but it also fell through.[81] A third plan focused on Jon Voight, who was contracted to play the role of the Swedish diplomat in a film based on John Bierman's then newly published book *Righteous Gentile: The Story of Raoul Wallenberg*. Even though the script was ready to go, nothing else happened. One of the main reasons why the Voight production was cancelled was that the film company did not believe the drama would appeal to the all-important teenage audience.[82]

Such doubts, though, were soon dispelled by several successfully completed projects. In the United States, interest reached a peak in 1985 on the fortieth anniversary of Wallenberg's disappearance. The American Wallenberg Committee moved to premises near the UN building in New York and launched a new campaign. Music concerts were given in Wallenberg's honour, streets were named after him, and a special room dedicated to him was set up in the New York Public Library.[83] That year also saw the premiere of the four-hour, two-episode NBC and Paramount television series, *Wallenberg: A Hero's Story*. It is significant that the first clips from it were shown at a banquet initially intended for an exclusive

---

81 Letter from John Berenyi to Nina Lagergren, 10 June 1980, RA, Raoul Wallenbergföreningens Arkiv. E1:4. Korrespondens. Huvudserie 1980, A–K; Betty Skawonius, 'Avhopp från Feuer', *Dagens Nyheter*, 16 January 1982; 'Per Mattsson', *Dagens Nyheter*, 2 March 1982.

82 'Jon Voight as "Raoul Wallenberg"', *Variety*, 6 May 1981; Mary Lou Cooper, 'Salute to a hero', *Los Angeles Times*, 24 November 1981; Stephen Farber, 'NBC doing Wallenberg's fight for Jews', *The New York Times*, 16 July 1984; Arnold Mann, 'Lamont Johnson, crunches and *Wallenberg*', *Emmy Magazine*, March/April 1985, p. 6; Edwin McDonell, 'Publishing: The Swedish hero who disappeared', *The New York Times*, 25 September 1981. See also Olle Tunberg, 'Wallenberg-manifestation', 30 November 1981 and related material, RKA, Raoul Wallenberg, UD2001/00009, Vol. 14.

83 Magnus Faxén, 'Artister och författare hyllar Raoul Wallenberg', Memorandum, 23 May 1985, RKA, Raoul Wallenberg, UD2001/00009, Vol. 23; Magnus Faxén to Pierre Schori, 'Re: Wallenberg-kommittén i USA står på egna ben och startar ny kampanj', Memorandum, 20 August 1985; letter from Rachel Oestreicher Haspel to Pierre Schori, 21 August 1985; letter from Rachel Oestreicher Haspel to Mark Palmer, 30 September 1985, RKA, Raoul Wallenberg, UD2001/00009, Vol. 24.

gathering of 250 people. However, because American interest in Wallenberg was still great, the Sheraton Centre in Manhattan was filled to capacity. By the end of the evening the festively dressed guests, some 40 of whom were people Wallenberg had rescued, had not only watched clips from the series but had also listened to speakers who included Elie Wiesel, Senator Daniel Patrick Moynihan, Per Anger, Nina Lagergren, and Henry Kissinger. Unlike in the early 1970s, no sensitive US-Soviet negotiations were at stake. Accordingly, the former US Secretary of State spoke at length about Wallenberg as a man who went beyond the conventions of diplomacy in an exemplary way in order to save human lives, with the result that he 'will serve as an example for our period'. The many tributes were not just empty words. Before the evening was over, the dinner guests had donated half a million dollars to a study centre about the Swede at the New York Public Library.[84]

*Wallenberg: A Hero's Story* was filmed in 1984 in Stockholm as well as in Zagreb in what was then Yugoslavia, because the television company was not permitted to film in Hungary. The series was released in the United States in early April 1985 but Swedish viewers had to wait until October of that year. The director was Lamont Johnson, who had spent a long career in television working mainly on docudramas based on historical events. The script was written by Gerald Green, who had had great success with his screenplay for *Holocaust*, which he had also adapted into a best-selling novel.[85] The lead role was played by Richard Chamberlain, who had made his breakthrough in 1961 as Dr Kildare in the television series of the same name and who had appeared in several films in the 1960s and 1970s. By 1980 he had become the uncrowned king of epic television series, 'the Robert Redford of the living room', with hits such as *Centennial* (1978–1979), *Shogun* (1980), and *The Thorn Birds* (1983) to his credit.[86] Physically he did not look much like

---

84 Carol Lawson, 'A tribute to a hero, Raoul Wallenberg', *The New York Times*, 15 March 1985.
85 Alan L. Gansberg, 'Johnson to Yugoslavia for "Wallenberg"', *The Hollywood Reporter*, 19 July 1984; Ron Kreuger, 'Lamont Johnson completes "Wallenberg" for NBC', *Screen International*, 23 February 1985; Arnold Mann, 'Lamont Johnson, crunches and *Wallenberg*', *Emmy Magazine*, March/April 1985, pp. 6–8, 54. On Gerald Green see Zander, '*Holocaust* at the Limits', pp. 267–268.
86 Charles Higham, 'Richard Chamberlain: Kildare to Hamlet', *The Saturday Evening Post*, April 1974, pp. 70–71, 110–114; Donald Chase, 'Richard

Wallenberg, but the producers presumably hoped that viewers would reach the same conclusion as Tibor Vayda, who had escaped the Arrow Cross terror regime in 1944 thanks to Wallenberg. He noted that Chamberlain 'had the same kind of presence and sympathy' as the heroic Swede.[87] Other actors included the internationally well-known Swedes Lena Olin and Bibi Andersson, the latter in the role of Maj von Dardel. Per Anger contributed as the narrator.[88]

The narrative structure of *Wallenberg: A Hero's Story* resembled the very successful structure used for *Holocaust* and before that for *Roots*, ABC's drama about slavery in the United States. The latter had been a hit in 1977 and had thereby paved the way for television series in historical settings. The television companies' recipe for success was to focus on a few real and/or fictional individuals for whom the audience would feel sympathy or antipathy. These characters' fates were then used to illustrate the 'grand narrative'. This method was particularly obvious in the hero's story in the television drama. Mostly for dramaturgical reasons, many of the people who had helped Wallenberg in Budapest, or done similar work there, were excluded or had to settle for a peripheral role.[89] Still, the focus on Wallenberg did not preclude brief appearances in the television series by representatives of the Hungarian Resistance and other role models in the diplomatic corps, such as Carl Lutz.

---

Chamberlain: Beyond romance', *The Saturday Evening Post*, March 1983, pp. 52–55; Aljean Harmetz, 'Richard Chamberlain's mini-series mastery', *The New York Times*, 1 May 1988; Lynn Elber, '5 questions: Richard Chamberlain', *The Record*, 26 June 1998.

87 Lynn Simross, 'Holocaust survivors record act of heroism: Eyewitness recalls Raoul Wallenberg's exploits during war', *The Los Angeles Times*, 7 April 1985.

88 When the television series was shown, meetings were held at which Bibi Andersson read aloud from Maj von Dardel's then newly published book *Raoul*; 'Boken om Raoul Wallenberg – en väckarklocka', *Svenska Dagbladet*, 30 October 1984; 'Metanela', *Svenska Dagbladet*, 31 January 1985.

89 See Lamont Johnson's arguments about the streamlining he felt obliged to make in *Wallenberg: A Hero's Story* in Arnold Mann, 'Lamont Johnson, crunches and *Wallenberg*', *Emmy Magazine*, March/April 1985, pp. 6–7. See Zander, '*Holocaust* at the Limits', p. 275, and Zander, *Clio på bio*, p. 35.

## Historical and poetic truths

In addition to the patent relevance of *Wallenberg: A Hero's Story* to the present book, both the structure of the series and the reactions to it illustrate a long-standing conflict associated with the contradiction between the historical and the practical past. On the one side are advocates of historical truth and objectivist ideals, who argue that the requirements of historical scholarship must also be applied to historical products that possess clear fictional elements. The argument is that there is a link between historical reality and its representation, with the implication that all history conveyed in a moving-image format should be presented in manner similar to written academic texts. The core of this approach is the (fault) finding of discrepancies between the results presented by historians and deviations from these in films or television series. Proponents of this view may indeed acknowledge the importance of such films as *Holocaust* and *Wallenberg: A Hero's Story*, but with one caveat: they were 'important, if flawed, vehicles for educating the ... public'.[90]

On the other side stand the advocates of poetic truth. They stress that the story must indeed be true, but on the basis of different criteria. The design of the dramaturgy is of the utmost importance, and there should be a narrative structure with a clear beginning, middle, and end. The result is a distillation of historical events. Similarly, the choice of actors, the consideration given to traditional genre elements, and adaptation to the attitudes and fashions prevailing at the time of filming are more important than the types of complex and multivalent analyses of the past that form the hallmark of historical scholarship. Simplifications, a reduced number of actors, and romantic elements characterize many historical television and film productions, all with the aim of getting the audience to become involved in the drama and to experience the actors as believable in their roles. With such a method, what appears to be a historical inaccuracy can in fact be a deliberate anachronism inserted to clarify the plot, or as a nod to a sophisticated audience. In other words, emotional credibility trumps historical realism because creators of film and television dramas strive to appeal to the audience's 'melodramatic imagination'. If the result is successful, the viewers of the film or television

---

90 Berenbaum, *After Tragedy and Triumph*, p. 6.

programme consider it to be more credible than other historical representations, mainly because this type of presentation of the past is directly linked to events and values of their own time. This approach has traditionally dominated among representatives of the film and television industry, although it has not prevented them from stressing that various dramas are 'based on' or 'inspired by' actual historical events.[91]

It should be emphasized that the division between historical and poetic truth is not always easy to maintain. Just over a year after the end of the war, the Hungarian Jew Miklós Nyiszli published his testimony from Auschwitz-Birkenau, where he had performed autopsies on the bodies of twins on whom German doctors had carried out brutal experiments. Right up until today his book has been considered highly credible, but it has also provoked debate because of his ambivalent portrayal of Josef Mengele, the 'Angel of Death', who was one of the main perpetrators of the medical 'research' which cost the lives of thousands of camp inmates. Moreover, in the light of recent decades of research on Auschwitz-Birkenau, a number of observations in Nyiszli's eyewitness account have been justifiably called into question. This revelation of some inaccuracies has not prevented *Auschwitz: A Doctor's Eyewitness Account* from being an important source of inspiration for the American and Hungarian feature films *The Grey Zone* (2001) and *Son of Saul* (2015) respectively.[92] The fact that we still have limited knowledge about the prisoners who were in the so-called Sonderkommando, and who were forced to perform some of the worst tasks in the death camp, is a separate issue. Viewers of these harrowing films are forced to grapple with fundamental existential and moral questions rather than trying to determine what is true, false, or not yet verified. In this way, the viewer is invited to struggle with very difficult issues which have rarely been accorded any significant space in traditional historiography.[93]

A more problematic encounter between historical and poetic truth characterizes *Atlantic Crossing* (2020). Produced for an international audience, this Norwegian television series focuses on the wartime exile of the Norwegian Crown Princess Märta in

---

91 Zander, *Clio på bio*, pp. 11–39; Creeber, *Serial Television*, pp. 27–28.
92 Zander, 'Efterskrift' (2022), pp. 213–226.
93 Kim Salomon, 'Visuell rapport från ett inferno', *Respons*, 2016:2, 12–13.

the United States. Contributing to the controversy created by the series was the suggestion of a romantic relationship between her and President Franklin D. Roosevelt, as well as several scenes in which the Crown Princess was said to have inspired a number of his important policy decisions, including the Lend-Lease Act, which allowed US exports of war materiel without departing from the country's neutrality that prevailed until the Japanese attack on Pearl Harbor on 7 December 1941. The lead actress Sofia Helin defended the series, arguing that at least since Shakespeare's day, history had been drawn with the aid of poetic truth. She added that in this particular case, suspicion of this kind of liberal treatment of the historical facts was complemented by a critical gender aspect: it was mainly men who objected to the portrayal of a strong and independent woman.[94]

To some extent the Norwegian historian Trond Norén Isaksen, who wrote a book about Crown Princess Märta's exile in the United States, agreed with the latter criticism. Earlier commentators had found it difficult to acknowledge the Crown Princess's important diplomatic role. Isaksen also distanced himself from critics who failed to take account of the differences between writing scholarly history and filming a fictional drama. The most serious flaw with the television series, he said, was not that the romance rumours were based solely on contemporary gossip aimed at damaging the President. What was worse was the fact that the series departed significantly from

> the historical truth, while its creators were sending a contradictory message by insisting on the one hand that the series was fiction and on the other that it was based on six years of research, and that in any case parts of what the viewers got to see were true.[95]

For filmmakers, poetic truth has mostly trumped historical truth, but since the last decades of the twentieth century, manifestations of 'retrovision' have characterized much historical representation in film and television. Using 'retrovision' as a starting point, there has been a willingness on the part of filmmakers to 'demythologise the past, gazing back sometimes with horror at its violence and oppression ... and sometimes with nostalgia for lost innocence

---

94 Maria Brander, 'Norska kritiken mot Sofia Helins nya serie – nu slår hon tillbaka', *Expressen*, 1 February 2021.
95 Trond Norén Isaksen, 'Sant och falskt om prinsessan i Vita huset', *Svenska Dagbladet*, 31 January 2021.

and style'.[96] Such films, combined with changing ideals of scholarship among professional historians, have helped to make the divide less clear-cut. Much evidence suggests that in the West in the twenty-first century, the opposing positions of the advocates of historical and poetic truth have become less uncompromising as well as less frequent. However, their survival has been aided by lingering knee-jerk reactions from historians who find it difficult to perceive the value of poetic realism, combined with recurring promises from film and television producers that audiences will be given historical realism and authenticity when in fact the shows' main determinants are found in other motives, and these contradictions have helped to keep these opposing positions in existence.[97] They were very much alive when *Wallenberg: A Hero's Story* was broadcast throughout the Western world in 1985.

## Making a difference

As the screenwriter Gerald Green pointed out in an interview, one important difference between *Holocaust* and *Wallenberg: A Hero's Story* was that while the former series portrayed fictional characters set within actual historical events, *Wallenberg: A Hero's Story* was based on a real person, and the story about him was true. Green also discussed the boundaries between historical and poetic truths. For reasons of space, he had been forced to exclude dramatic events, such as when Wallenberg, in a rowboat, searched for possible survivors of a massacre in the icy Danube River. Green conceded that he had sometimes been forced to deviate from the historical sequence of events in order to make the television drama work. In his defence, he argued that writers have been combining real people with fictional ones ever since the days of Homer. *Wallenberg: A Hero's Story* deviated from this pattern in that all the characters were based on people in real life. Green was therefore very confident ahead of the television screening, and he was not particularly anxious that experts in the field would be able to accuse him of any crucial inaccuracies.[98]

---

96 Cartmell and Hunter, 'Introduction: Retrovisions', p. 2.
97 Zander, *Clio på bio*, especially pp. 11–39; Hughes-Warrington, *History Goes to the Movies*, passim.
98 Elenore Lester, 'The scene: Wartime Budapest. The hero: Wallenberg', *The New York Times*, 7 April 1985.

One contributing reason for the great impact of television series like *Holocaust* and *Roots* was their scope. Their large number of episodes made it possible to gradually and slowly accustom viewers to the horrors that these history lessons illustrated with moving images.[99] The link between actual historical facts and the educational aspect was of great importance for the success of these series. It was hoped that the Wallenberg series would attract the attention of teachers, many of whom had been spurred on by *Roots* and *Holocaust* to include the topics of slavery and the Holocaust in their history classes. A series about Wallenberg might similarly pave the way for lessons about him and his achievements. If this happened, children would be likely to watch *Wallenberg: A Hero's Story* with their parents, guaranteeing large audiences. The series was watched in an estimated 17 million American homes, with an average of three viewers per household, totalling about 40 million viewers. Thus, a significant number of Americans did follow Wallenberg's fate, but they were far from the 120 million or so who had watched *Holocaust* in 1978.[100]

The narrative begins in Sweden, where Raoul Wallenberg is celebrating Midsummer with his relatives. His frustration at sitting on the sidelines while the war is happening around him is palpable. He therefore does not hesitate when he is asked if he would carry out a mission in Hungary to save as many of that country's Jews as possible from the Holocaust. The rest of the story unfolds in Hungary until his disappearance in January 1945.

One scene that was crucial in making viewers understand the hero's great commitment to the cause of the oppressed occurs before Wallenberg begins his mission in Budapest. *Wallenberg: A Hero's Story* draws on a recurring pattern in films and television series: the hero's awakening when he is confronted with the concrete effects of the Holocaust. Viewers of *The Eagle Has Landed* (1976) come to sympathize with German Colonel Kurt Steiner (Michael Caine) as he risks his life and career in an attempt to help a Jewish woman. Steiner helps her to escape from a train, presumably destined for an extermination camp, but to no avail as she is shot dead by SS guards. The Colonel then demonstratively distances

---

99 Creeber, *Serial Television*, p. 28.
100 See NBC and Paramount's advertising materials for *Wallenberg: A Hero's Story* plus Sven Julin, 'Raoul Wallenberg', 9 May 1985, RKA, Raoul Wallenberg, Vol. 23.

himself from the guards and their commander, which condemns him and his subordinates to the risky mission of trying to assassinate Winston Churchill.[101]

Another well-known example is how a German (actually a Sudeten German) moves from cooperating with the SS, more or less unthinkingly, to following his conscience and trying to save as many Jews as possible. The beginning of Oskar Schindler's (Liam Neeson) transformation in *Schindler's List* is the key scene when he witnesses German troops brutally emptying the Kraków ghetto of Jews. In *Wallenberg: A Hero's Story* and *Good Evening, Mr. Wallenberg* (1990), good Germans are mostly conspicuously absent, but in both cases the hero's awakening takes place at a railway station. It is when Wallenberg sees trains packed with Jews heading for the extermination camps, and how Jews trying to escape are mercilessly gunned down by German guards, that he fully realizes what is happening.

The strong link between the Holocaust and train transports is present in popular-culture depictions of Adolf Eichmann as well.[102] A scene involving trains is also the setting where the tension in *Wallenberg: A Hero's Story* reaches its climax. The first part of the drama culminates in a cliffhanger. Witness accounts of how Wallenberg acted at the Józsefváros railway yard differ: some accounts stress that many of the Jewish employees of the Swedish

---

[101] At times it has also been possible to link to the Nazi genocide in order to distinguish between brutal Nazis and dutiful, honourable Germans. The reversal has been illustrated by a comparison between the films *Went the Day Well?* (1942) and *The Eagle has Landed* (1976). Despite their plot differences, they both revolve around undercover German commando raids in enemy territory. In the former, produced in Britain while memories of the Blitz were still fresh and feelings of hatred, revenge, and bitterness dominated among Britons, the village inhabitants are all heroic and self-sacrificing, whereas the enemy Germans show their worst sides. In contrast, the roles are reversed in *The Eagle Has Landed*. The rural Britons of 1976 are narrow-minded, and their behaviour makes it easier for German spies with roots in South Africa and Ireland. The American soldiers are incompetent. Both Americans and British people are contrasted with the self-sacrificing, anti-Nazi German paratroopers. The latter are unmasked because they wear German uniforms under the Polish camouflage. Their German characteristics are revealed after one of them nobly sacrifices his life to save two children; MacKenzie, 'Nazis into Germans', pp. 83–91.

[102] See Zander, 'I våldets virvelvind', p. 318; Zander, 'Heroic Images', pp. 129–130.

Legation handed out protective passports to people in the railway carriages, whereas others maintain that it was Wallenberg himself who did most of the work. According to the latter narrative, he also managed to rescue people who lacked protective passports without the Hungarian gendarmes daring to intervene.[103] The television team picked up a dramatic story told by Sandor Ardai, one of Wallenberg's drivers in Budapest. Ardai said that Wallenberg had not only entered the railway carriages but had also jumped up onto one of them, a carriage which was filled with Jews, and tossed in protective passports to the passengers. The situation had become very threatening, because Wallenberg ignored German officers' orders to climb down from the railway-carriage roof while German guards and Arrow Cross men were simultaneously shouting at him and shooting over his head.[104] The cliffhanger ending of the first episode constitutes an adaptation of Ardai's story where German guards have Wallenberg in their rifle sights without him showing any sign of giving in. Viewers are left with the suggestion that he is prepared to die to save lives. The next episode begins with this crisis being averted.

## Wallenberg and the Baroness

There is evidence that Wallenberg met the Hungarian Minister of Foreign Affairs Baron Gabor Kemény on at least two occasions, including when the latter harboured hopes that the Swedish diplomat would convey a more presentable depiction of the new Arrow Cross-led Hungarian government to his superiors in Stockholm. Wallenberg also collaborated with the Foreign Minister's beautiful and wealthy wife, Elisabeth Kemény-Fuchs, who was the daughter of an Austrian baron and an Italian countess. Elisabeth had led a sheltered life, but she had also been brought up in a spirit of internationalism, whereas her husband was a convinced antisemite, mainly focused on the Hungarian fatherland. It has subsequently been claimed that the Baroness only became aware of her husband's antisemitic beliefs after their marriage. Her new-found insight, combined with witnessing the persecution of Jews, led her to cooperate with Wallenberg, with the goal

---

103 Lajos, 'Raoul Wallenberg i muntliga källor', pp. 253–254; Per Anger, 'Raoul Wallenberg', *Judisk Tidskrift*, 1985: 2, 7.
104 Cornelius, *Hungary in World War II*, pp. 341–342.

of influencing her husband and other Arrow Cross members to stop the ongoing mass murder.[105] When Gabor Kemény defended himself at the People's Tribunal in Budapest in 1946, he pointed to his meetings with Wallenberg and how they had worked together to save Jews. However, there were far more charges against him, and so he was sentenced to death and hanged.[106]

It has been argued that the Baroness 'appears to have [played] a decisive role in a critical situation for Wallenberg'.[107] A similar conclusion is drawn in Frederick E. Werbell and Thurston Clarke's *Lost Hero* (1982), in which they examine his contacts with the Keménys. Of particular significance are the Baroness's efforts – combined with those of Wallenberg and others – to try to influence her husband and other Arrow Cross members to stop the mass murder of Jews.[108] Werbell and Clarke emphasize that concrete negotiations on the issue did occur. They also relate that when the Baroness left Budapest, several diplomats came to the railway station to bid her farewell. Among them was Wallenberg, carrying a bouquet of flowers. The authors write that the Baroness and Wallenberg became 'very attached to each other' during the month or so that they worked together. Werbell and Clarke say that it is not clear whether the two became romantically involved, but they do cite a second-hand witness according to whom they had 'become very, very close'.[109]

In his original script Gerald Green had kept the friendship on a purely platonic level, but it became more intense after being reworked by the producers, who reasoned that the rules of the game are different in commercial television series and films set in historical contexts. In such films and series, a love theme is practically a

---

105 Telegram from the legation staff in Budapest from Danielsson to the UD in Stockholm, 22 October 1945, in Schattauer (ed.), *Räddningen*, p. 205. See also Schiller, *Varför ryssarna tog Raoul Wallenberg*, p. 75; von Dardel, *Raoul*, p. 16; Andrew Handler, *A Man for All Connections*, pp. 96–100; Marton, *Wallenberg*, pp. 101–108; Lester, 'Raoul Wallenberg', pp. 151–152; Sröbinger, *Das Rätsel Wallenberg*, pp. 168–170. Some scholars have claimed she had Jewish roots, which she strongly denied; Streissguth, *Raoul Wallenberg*, 2001, p. 65; Werbell and Clarke, *Lost Hero*, pp. 75–78.
106 Stone, *Hungary*, p. 161.
107 Sjöquist, *Affären Raoul Wallenberg*, p. 60.
108 Werbell and Clarke, *Lost Hero*, pp. 75–79, 93–99.
109 Werbell and Clarke, *Lost Hero*, p. 113. The rumour that the relationship was a love affair is also mentioned in Smith, *Lost Hero*, pp. 83–84.

requirement, and the producers' solution was to 'upgrade' the friendship to a romance. They seized on the book publisher's invitation to perceive a degree of truth in the rumours that the Swedish diplomat and the beautiful baroness had powerful feelings for each other. The resulting depiction was of a budding romance, including a tearful and flower-filled farewell in a railway carriage when they meet for the last time as Elisabeth leaves Budapest. Green felt no bitterness at the alteration to his script, as the audience needed a counterweight to the Holocaust. He emphasized that Wallenberg had indeed given the Baroness roses when she left Budapest.[110]

This invented romance was one reason why the creators' assertion that their series kept essentially close to the truth was challenged, and this in turn led to defensive arguments. Lamont Johnson – who characterized Baron Kemény as 'charming, romantic and [a] fascist' and his wife as a delightful woman – said before the premiere that as part of his research he had visited Elisabeth Kemény-Fuchs in France, implying that he did so to obtain her true version of events.[111] Green admitted that although the series was true to historical facts, one element was 'somewhat fanciful'. He was aware that it was highly unlikely that Raoul Wallenberg and Elisabeth Kemény-Fuchs had a relationship that extended beyond friendship, not least because the Baroness was well known to be attached to her husband and was six months pregnant when she met the Swedish diplomat for the first time.[112]

---

110 Elenore Lester, 'The scene: Wartime Budapest. The hero: Wallenberg', *The New York Times*, 7 April 1985.
111 Tom Shales, 'Crusty, pugnacious "Wallenberg" director made NBC film his way', *The Los Angeles Times*, 5 April 1985; Nancy Mills, 'Raoul Wallenberg – The Swedish Savior', *San Francisco Examiner & Chronicle*, 7 April 1985. In interviews related to the television film, Elisabeth Kemény strongly denied the rumours of a romance, not least because she was already married and pregnant; see Sjöquist, *Raoul Wallenberg*, p. 61, Sjöquist, *Dramat Raoul Wallenberg*, p. 29. It can be added that a romantic theme was also prominent in John Bierman's biography of Wallenberg, but in that case the object of the protagonist's tender feelings was Jeanette von Heidenstam, to whom Wallenberg (Bierman claims) proposed prior to his departure for Budapest; Bierman, *Righteous Gentile*, pp. 22–23. See also Schult, *A Hero's Many Faces*, p. 52.
112 Elenore Lester, 'The scene: Wartime Budapest. The hero: Wallenberg', *The New York Times*, 7 April 1985; Jangfeldt, *The Hero of Budapest*, p. 213.

With a touch of humour, the real-life female protagonist asserted that in her youth she had been more beautiful than the admittedly pretty actress Alice Krige, who portrayed her in the series. Her amusement was less evident when she commented on the liberties she felt the television producers had taken. Like many other women in the diplomatic colony she had been attracted by Wallenberg's charm, courage, and gentlemanliness, but she firmly denied the rumours of a romance. In fact, she had initially considered suing the broadcaster, but for unspecified reasons she had decided against it.[113]

## Wallenberg versus Eichmann

Although this romance is significant in relation to the requirements of the genre, and hence to the design of the television series, it cannot compete in importance with the duel between Raoul Wallenberg and Adolf Eichmann. Overall, their on-screen struggle fits into long-established narrative patterns and rhetorical devices. The Lithuanian historian Linas Eriksonas argues that all narratives, whether fictional or scholarly, are distinguished by the fact that they always require a hero and an antagonist.[114] That the encounter between these two strong personalities forms a climax in *Wallenberg: A Hero's Story* was already emphasized in the press material distributed before the premiere. The two men were destined to confront each other: 'Wallenberg and Eichmann ... must finally meet', reads the doom-laden text.[115] The dramatic

---

113 Eric Sjöquist, 'Jag tänkte stämma filmbolaget', *Expressen*, 15 October 1985. She also denied the rumours of a romance in an interview with Sara Callen a year later: 'Oral History Interview with Elizabeth Fuchs', 15 May 1986, USHMM, https://collections.ushmm.org/search/catalog/irn508629 (accessed 3 September 2021).
114 Eriksonas, *National Heroes and National Identities*, pp. 23–24, 37–38. See also Niklas Qvarnström, 'Tankeväckande blunder: Den moderna mytologin behöver både hjältar och monster', *Sydsvenskan*, 17 December 2008. Another aspect of the narrative perspective has been suggested by literary scholar Jerome Thale, who drew attention to the fact that the narrator in Joseph Conrad's *The Heart of Darkness* (1902) and in F. Scott Fitzgerald's *The Great Gatsby* (1925) also plays the role of hero in these novels; see Thale, 'The Narrator as Hero', pp. 69–73.
115 'Wallenberg: The Lost Hero', press material from ITV Network, Yorkshire Television, BFI issued prior to the UK premiere of *Wallenberg: A Hero's Story*. The encounter between Wallenberg and Eichmann also plays an important role in several other history-cultural depictons of

climax which the meeting between the diplomat and the SS officer entailed was duly praised by a number of critics.[116] That the television series includes a confrontation between Wallenberg and Eichmann is as unsurprising as the above-mentioned suggested romance between Wallenberg and Elisabeth Kemény. I shall return later to the significance of the dinner party at which the two adversaries measure their strength against each other. For the moment, we may conclude that the scene was included not only for dramaturgical reasons, but also as a result of the history-cultural shifts that led to Eichmann and Wallenberg becoming household names in the post-war period.

Whereas it took until around 1980 for Wallenberg to become internationally known, Eichmann achieved notoriety because of his trial in 1961. He had previously been named during the Nuremberg trials as one of the driving forces behind the Holocaust. His role in determining Nazi policies during the Second World War was limited, but as an organizer his importance cannot be overestimated.[117] Although he never advanced beyond a rank corresponding to that of lieutenant-colonel, the trial in Jerusalem made him one of the best-known Nazis, with the step-by-step revelation of his role as a planner of the genocide. This also meant that equally ruthless 'desk murderers', such as Edmund Veesenmayer, who helped to organize the extermination of Croatian and Serbian Jews in the Balkans in 1941–1944 and who worked closely with Eichmann in Budapest, were once and for all overshadowed by him. Veesenmayer, who was tried in the so-called Ministries Trial, also known as the Wilhelmstrasse Trial, in Nuremberg in 1949, was sentenced to twenty years in prison but only served two.

The Eichmann trial was covered by the media in a number of Western countries, and it brought renewed attention to the Holocaust in newspapers and on radio and television.[118] While many of these reports had a limited lifespan, philosopher Hannah

---

Wallenberg; see Schult, *A Hero's Many Faces*, p. 56. See also Arne Lapidus, 'Nazistbödeln som var Wallenbergs motståndare', *Expressen*, 17 October 1985.
116 See e.g. Tone, 'Wallenberg: A Hero's Story', *Variety*, 17 April 1985.
117 Conot, *Justice at Nuremberg*, pp. 257–259, 261; Holmila, *Reporting the Holocaust in the British, Swedish and Finnish Press, 1945–50*, pp. 102–105.
118 Wagrell, '*Chorus of the Saved*', pp. 267–300.

Arendt's reports from the trial remained controversial for a long time after it had ended. Criticized for downplaying the role of antisemitism in the implementation of the Holocaust, she won support for another facet of her coverage: Arendt argued that Eichmann was not a diabolical killer; instead, he had been a passive cog in the Holocaust machinery – just one desk murderer among many.[119]

One contemporaneous analysis was based on the assertion that Eichmann could not stand 'the smell of blood' but found pleasure in 'adding up the numbers of the dead and ... monitoring the transports from all the occupied areas to the death camps'.[120] Such perspectives may be complemented with British historian David Cesarani's debunking of earlier perceptions of Eichmann's time in Budapest as a 'high point' in his career, because he supposedly enjoyed unfettered powers there. The unit he commanded was in fact only one of several SS units in the Hungarian capital, and they worked against one another on a regular basis. Eichmann's 'success' in exterminating Budapest's Jews was mainly due to the strong support he received from Hungarian gendarmes, from high-ranking politicians who were also antisemites, and from Arrow Cross members, whose political influence increased during 1944. His efforts, however, were not appreciated by Himmler, who sometimes advocated a continuation of the genocide and sometimes wished to use the Jews of Hungary as part of attempts to achieve a separate peace with the Western Allies. As the realization grew among senior SS officers that it was only a matter of months before Germany would be brought to its knees, a rift developed between on the one hand Himmler, Walter Schellenberg, and Kurt Becher, who had been sent to Budapest by the head of the SS, and on the other the individuals who wanted to continue the mass murder of Jews. Those individuals were primarily led by Ernst Kaltenbrunner, who commanded the Gestapo and the SD, the intelligence agency of the SS and the Nazi Party, and was deeply involved in implementing the Holocaust. Eichmann sympathized with the latter approach and therefore continued to push for the Jews in Hungary to be sent to extermination camps or forced on death marches. Eichmann, who was heavily intoxicated and acted erratically at the end of his time in Budapest, came into conflict with Becher, who opposed further deportations of Jews. Both were summoned to a meeting in Berlin

---

119 Arendt, *Eichmann in Jerusalem*, especially pp. 21–55, 246–279.
120 Erwin Leiser, 'Kring fallet Eichmann', *Tiden*, 1961:6, 344.

with the head of the SS. What was said at that meeting is a matter of debate, but it is highly likely that Eichmann was reprimanded, and he was not highly regarded by Himmler in the following months either.[121]

In the autumn of 1958, legal proceedings against Erich Koch began in Warsaw. Before the war, he had made a name for himself in Nazi Germany as an expert on Eastern Europe, and during the war he had held high-ranking command positions over areas in Poland, Ukraine, and the Baltic states. In these capacities, he had been responsible for the deportation and mass murder of Jews and Poles. Put on trial, he varied his defence. At times he denied having committed crimes, at others he claimed he was only obeying orders, and all the time he referred to his severe lung disease, which had weakened him, although this did not prevent him from posing sharp questions and making long, meandering statements.[122] This pattern was largely repeated during the Eichmann trial a few years later. Hannah Arendt struggled to reconcile two images. On the one hand, a long line of witnesses described heinous crimes for which Eichmann was responsible. On the other hand, like the accused and ailing Koch, Eichmann was not at all the same man that he had been during the war years. The court did not comply with Simon Wiesenthal's suggestion that Eichmann be allowed to appear in the SS uniform so intimately associated with his atrocities. Instead, it was a pitiful man with a constant cold who sat wearing an ordinary suit on the accused's bench in a glass cage built especially for the trial. The only way Arendt could come to terms with this dilemma was to regard the SS officer as a textbook example of the banality of evil.[123]

This concept has become a commonplace in the wake of the Eichmann trial. It has also found its way into the film and television industry, though not without attendant problems. How can one of history's worst criminals, who is outwardly an ordinary and anything but cinematically charismatic bureaucrat with digestive problems, be represented in an interesting and dramatically effective

---

121 Cesarani, *Becoming Eichmann*, pp. 159–199. See also Schmid, 'Vorwort', p. 23, Levai, *Eichmann in Hungary*, pp. 80, 101, 103, 126–128, 136, 142; Carlberg, *Raoul Wallenberg*, pp. 328–329.
122 Jörn Donner, 'Den dödsdömde fången i Warszawa', *Bonniers Litterära Magasin*, 1959:5, 394–399.
123 Arendt, *Eichmann in Jerusalem*, pp. 54, 252. See also Cesarani, *Becoming Eichmann*, pp. 346–349.

manner? A recurring compromise has been a split between portrayals of the post-war Eichmann who was captured and put on trial and portrayals of the officer who had hundreds of thousands of lives on his conscience. The audience is thus confronted with a contrast between Eichmann's post-war ordinariness and images of a confident, ruthless, and power-hungry upwardly aspiring individual, who experienced the high point of his life while Budapest was literally collapsing around him.[124]

The historical Eichmann has repeatedly been a source of inspiration in films and television series, *Inglourious Basterds* (2009) being a well-known example. Unlike in the film with the almost identical title in the United States, *The Inglorious Bastards* (*Quel maledetto treno blindato*, 1978), the Holocaust is central in Quentin Tarantino's later version. In the Italian 'original', violent acts against Germans are generally legitimized by the atrocities they committed during the Second World War. In the later version, by contrast, the Nazi genocide of 'subhumans' is at the core of the film, and it is the implicit reason why American Jews and German anti-Nazis pursue a cruel revenge on German soldiers in France. The Holocaust is introduced as early as the opening scene, when a French farmer is forced to reveal where he has hidden Jews. The man who demands this information is SS officer Hans Landa, played by the Austrian actor Christoph Waltz, who won an Oscar for best supporting male actor. In Waltz's interpretation, Landa is akin to Eichmann in that he lays the groundwork for his interrogation breakthrough with arguments about duty and precise statistics. From underneath the bureaucratic and superficially benevolent SS officer, however, a very different person soon emerges. Apart from smoking an absurdly large pipe and not shying away from ordering the execution of defenceless people, he also turns out to be well educated and a good linguist, but above all an unscrupulous, manipulative, and ruthless 'Jew hunter'. His lightning-quick transitions between charm and polite friendliness on the one hand and cunning and ruthless brutality on the other have more in common with the kind of film Nazis whose origins go back to the propagandistic feature films of the Second World War than with the Eichmann depicted by Arendt: a 'paper-pusher' in the form of a zealous but colourless bureaucrat.[125]

---

124 See Zander, 'I våldets virvelvind', pp. 310–313, 316–319.
125 Gonshak, *Hollywood and the Holocaust*, pp. 207, 309–310.

In the television series *Holocaust*, the SS member Erik Dorf (Michael Moriarty) is based on a number of people, including the SS officer Otto Ohlendorf, who ordered the execution of 90,000 Jews, and Adolf Eichmann. The latter also appears as a character in the series, initially as a mentor to Dorf. In *Holocaust* the aim was to use Dorf as an example of a 'desk perpetrator', a genocidal killer who was also a loving family man leading a 'normal' life alongside his murderous activities. Ohlendorf in particular was an apt example. Outwardly he was a far cry from his SS colleague Ernst Kaltenbrunner, who, with his fencing scar and hatchet-faced profile, fitted the stereotypical image of a cold-blooded mass murderer. The contrast was striking when Ohlendorf spoke: he 'was small of stature, young-looking, and rather comely. He spoke quietly, with great precision, dispassion, and apparent intelligence.' The question that begged to be answered was how he could have committed the atrocities he described so detachedly and analytically. One person who saw him testify at the Nuremberg trials described him as 'ice-cold'; another perceived him as a Nazi version of Dr Jekyll and Mr Hyde.[126] The difficulty of dealing with the ambiguity displayed by Ohlendorf led one US psychiatrist to categorize him as a perverted sadist and madman, whereas one of his compatriots and colleagues instead marvelled at how a man 'of such integrity and incorruptibility could have commanded an *Einsatzgruppe*'.[127]

In *Holocaust*, the fictional character Dorf personified both Dr Jekyll and Mr Hyde, but the latter's acts of madness were replaced by murders carried out at a distance. The Ohlendorf-inspired SS officer filled the role of a person who was capable of behaving like Eichmann, but who was not in fact the infamous mass murderer. The creators of the series argued that it was unlikely that their audience would feel any sympathy for Eichmann in the role of husband and father. By contrast, Dorf could evoke sympathy, though with obvious limitations.[128] This characterization was far ahead of its time. To be sure, this type of 'desk killer' did appear in research into the Holocaust, but this was the first

---

126 Taylor, *The Anatomy of the Nuremberg Trials*, p. 248.
127 Conot, *Justice at Nuremberg*, p. 233.
128 Zander, '*Holocaust* at the Limits', p. 272; Torgovnick, *The War Complex*, p. 63. Ohlendorf's testimony during the Nuremberg trials received some of the most extensive contemporary news coverage; see Holmila, *Reporting the Holocaust in the British, Swedish and Finnish Press, 1945–50*, pp. 83–84, 104, 114.

time such a person had been portrayed in a fictional narrative with broad impact.[129] That the character lacked predecessors proved not to be a problem. Swedish film scholar Erik Hedling argues that this sharply defined but still believable portrayal of Dorf and some of the other architects of the Holocaust, beyond 'traditional and grotesque film monsters', formed a significant contribution to the success of the series.[130]

Hedling's American colleague Annette Insdorf has noted that the use of the same actors in similar roles is an effective technique by film and television makers, but that it also raises the question of the role of authenticity in film and television productions. The danger is that audiences will associate historical figures with well-known television and film faces rather than with those actual historical figures whom the actors represent.[131] In 1985, British actor Kenneth Colley was best known as an admiral in the Imperial Navy space fleet in the *Star Wars* films. A few years later he portrayed Paul Blobel, an SS officer who, like Eichmann, had many lives on his conscience, in another successful television series: *War and Remembrance* (1988). Viewers acquainted with Colley's previous acting roles were less than surprised to find him playing the role of Eichmann in *Wallenberg: A Hero's Story*. The Eichmann portrayed in this series is a good example of 'the cinematic Nazi' character, a personage who is usually 'simply presented as evil' and depicted in such a manner that the audience is not encouraged to identify with him or her.[132] It is highly likely that the creators of the Wallenberg series drew on the image Eichmann presented of himself in post-war exile in Argentina, when he was not interested in appearing as a grey bureaucrat, and on the accounts of witnesses who supplied their own picture of the SS officer. At his trial in Jerusalem in 1961, witnesses described how he could appear sympathetic in meetings with Jewish leaders, but only up to a point. When his wishes were not granted, his politeness swiftly turned to threats and contemptuous outbursts.[133] In *Wallenberg: A Hero's Story*, Eichmann as portrayed by Colley first appears in a scene in which he alternately

---

129 Bartov, *The 'Jew' in Cinema*, p. 206.
130 Erik Hedling, 'Förintelsen som melodram', *Sydsvenskan*, 19 June 2008.
131 Insdorf, *Indelible Shadows*, p. 25.
132 Kerner, 'On the Cinematic Nazi', pp. 203–204.
133 See e.g. witness Lindenstrauss during Session No. 15 in *The Trial of Adolf Eichmann*, pp. 234–235, and Bettina Stangneth, *Eichmann Before Jerusalem*, pp. 32–33, 48–50.

threatens and praises the leaders of Budapest's Jewish Council. Nothing bad will happen to them if they will just provide him with Jewish workers, he promises. But his true self emerges only a few moments later. As he leaves the room, he learns that the Hungarian regent Miklós Horthy has halted a train to Auschwitz with a record number of Jews on board. As the ominous music reaches its climax, a furious Eichmann shouts: 'We refuse to be stopped! We will keep on going until we have weeded out every damned Jew in Hungary!'

During Eichmann's trial, it was suggested that he had been an upstart, lacking in both common sense and good manners and that he had remained that way. From a West German perspective it was easy to attribute a 'Koofmichs-Mentalität' to him.[134] The first word's affinity with a minor 'Kaufmann', or merchant, had long invited the description of Koofmichs as hedonistic individuals willing to do anything to satisfy their desire for gold and material objects. In a similar vein, one of the journalists who studied Eichmann during his trial in Jerusalem in 1961 suggested that his stiff bow to the judge showed that he had never learned how to behave in 'better-class society'. Even his use of language gave him away: he was a half-educated man trying to appear cultured.[135] Subsequent portrayals of him have repeatedly included his complaints that he did not receive the appreciation he deserved during the war years, but also his lack of higher education and his brutal image. Another common element has been his hostility to aristocrats and his particular loathing of Admiral Horthy. Yet another frequent theme has been that the war provided great opportunities for ruthless bureaucrats.[136] This perspective was pushed to its extreme in *Eichmann* (2008). In one scene in the film, set in Jerusalem during the pre-trial interviews, Eichmann brags to the Israeli lead interrogator about all the beautiful women, thoroughbred horses, and top-quality liquor that he, a simple man, was able to enjoy during the Second World War, thanks to his position of power in the Third Reich.

People close to Wallenberg described him as an 'anti-snob', as evidenced by the fact that despite his privileged position he did not want to be given any advantages because of his origins, and that in the United States he had sometimes hitchhiked in order

---

134 Schmid, 'Vorwort', p. 9.
135 Meyer Levin, 'Eichmann's two worlds', *The Jewish Chronicle*, 23 June 1961.
136 Zander, 'I våldets virvelvind', pp. 303–320.

to come to know people he would never otherwise have met.[137] Quite a radically different picture appears in a number of British and American biographies and articles about Wallenberg. These state that he was not only a member of an aristocracy in the figurative sense – a financial aristocracy – but also claimed that he was of noble birth, which is a common characteristic of many heroic figures.[138] That he was part of the Wallenberg family probably had a concrete significance at that time. In the early 1960s, Alva Myrdal claimed off the record that it would have been impossible for her or others close to her to carry out the mission in Budapest. The reason was not that they lacked the necessary personal qualities, but that they were all too left-wing. By contrast, Raoul Wallenberg had been suitable owing to his high social position.[139]

The producer of *Wallenberg: A Hero's Story* was the seasoned Dick Berg, one of the pioneers of made-for-TV films and series. He drew on the idea of Wallenberg's 'aristocratic' origins and their significance when he argued that until Budapest, Wallenberg's life had been meaningless. He had mostly been a burden to his family, Sweden's equivalent of the Rockefeller dynasty. In the Hungarian capital, though, everything had fallen into place. Despite moments of despair, he was a humorous and hope-inducing man who had found the meaning of his own life in saving that of others.[140] This characterization was manifested in the finished production, above all in the contrast between Eichmann's brusque manner and Wallenberg's well-bred gentlemanly character. A similar sequence opens the already mentioned book by Frederick E. Werbell and Thurston Clarke, *Lost Hero: The Mystery of Raoul Wallenberg*,

---

137 Schreiber, 'The Heroic Life and Tragic Fate of Raoul Wallenberg', pp. 4–5.
138 Brown, *Courage*, pp. 83–84; Rosenfeld, *Raoul Wallenberg*, pp. 19, 24; Gibbon, *A Call to Heroism*, p. 168; Holbrooke, 'Defying Orders, Saving Lives', p. 137; Kershaw, *The Envoy*, p. 53; Gitta Sereny, 'A legend that refuses to die', *The Times*, 7 July 1989. Marcus Ehrenpreis characterized Wallenberg as 'that Swedish nobleman' in 'Raoul Wallenberg: Ett brev', *Judisk Tidskrift*, 1948:1, 1. On the connection between heroes and aristocrats, see Hughes-Hallett, *Heroes*, p. 10, and – with a special focus on Wallenberg – Schult, *A Hero's Many Faces*, p. 53.
139 According to the *Dagens Nyheter* journalist Ulf Brandell's diary notes from 25 August 1962; see Brandell, *Dagbok med DN*, p. 167.
140 Stephen Farber, 'NBC doing Wallenberg's fight for Jews', *The New York Times*, 16 July 1984. On Dick Berg's film and television career, see Dawn Chmielewski, 'Dick Berg dies at 87; television and film writer and producer', *Los Angeles Times*, 3 September 2009.

which, in the words of the authors, focused on Wallenberg the man and which therefore contains a lot of dialogue and a straightforward storyline.[141] This structure was perfect for fictionalization, and it was on this book that Green mainly based his script.[142] The encounter between Eichmann and Wallenberg also appears in an expanded and more streamlined version in *Wallenberg: A Hero's Story*. In the 'Arizona' nightclub, Eichmann offers Wallenberg and Per Anger champagne. At first they chat politely, but Eichmann's poorly concealed motives lead the Swedish diplomats to conclude that some Germans seem more interested in wiping out the Jews and profiting from that bloody business than in fighting the war. Eichmann in turn comments sharply that aristocrats like Wallenberg can change professions as they like and engage in diplomacy whenever they fancy doing so. The dialogue's implicit message is that Eichmann has only borrowed his position at the top of society. Behind his facade of duty and loyal obedience lurks an unscrupulous, unchristian bribe-taker, an ill-mannered upstart who is willing to free a small number of Jews for a large number of dollars. Conversely, the 'aristocrat' Wallenberg's exalted social position is taken as given.[143] That impression is reinforced by his aforementioned romance with a Hungarian noblewoman and the fact that – after his decisive awakening when he is confronted with the victims of the Holocaust – he does not change significantly. In this way, he is like the heroes in the novels of old who are constantly challenged and tested but do not evolve.

*Wallenberg: A Hero's Story* is thus above all a television series about the great hero and his powerful antagonist. Their struggle can be likened to a moral power struggle between the forces of good and evil, as described in the prologue to the US lawyer Carl L. Steinhouse's *Wallenberg is Here!*

> Two men of the same generation, dedicated to their respective tasks, but with widely disparate backgrounds, nurturing, environment and education, arrived in Budapest in 1944, fated to be locked in a great historical battle for human lives. The German, Adolph Eichmann, was determined to exterminate the Jews; the Swede, Raoul Wallenberg, was committed to frustrating that goal. The casual observer might reasonably conclude the contest to be

---

141 Werbell and Clarke, *Lost Hero*, pp. ix–xi, 3–5.
142 On Green's dependence on this book, see Elenore Lester, 'The scene: Wartime Budapest. The hero: Wallenberg', *The New York Times*, 7 April 1985.
143 Werbell and Clarke, *Lost Hero*, pp. 3–4, 28.

one-sided, the German backed by the determined leaders, military might and ruthlessness of the Third Reich, and the Swede supported only by certainty of his moral position, his ingenuity, wits, nerve and diplomatic standing, and American funds. Such a casual observer, however, couldn't have been more wrong.[144]

Wallenberg's struggle is thus morally irreproachable, but in all concrete respects virtually hopeless, which makes his efforts all the more admirable. In such a context, it is not a question of making the television series' viewers feel any sympathy for Eichmann. On the contrary: portraying a thoroughly evil, ruthless, unscrupulous, and powerful Eichmann makes his opponent's feats all the greater. That Eichmann is a very dangerous and powerful man is patent in almost every scene he appears in, but it is underlined in his encounters with Wallenberg. It is evident, for instance, when the German visits the Swedish Legation. The Jews working there all have Swedish protective passports, but they are also fully aware of who Eichmann is and what he is capable of. He tries to counteract this by pointing out his great tolerance. Wallenberg receives him politely, but makes fun of him the second he leaves.

We have seen that the demands and needs placed on a functioning fictional product are far from always consistent with the established historical facts. Wallenberg and Eichmann undeniably knew of each other's existence while they were operating in Budapest. A number of popular accounts state that they met for dinner and negotiations. However, Wallenberg was not interested in haggling with Eichmann, who may have feared that the Swede was well connected with SS men such as Kurt Becher or even perhaps SS chief Heinrich Himmler. The result was that Eichmann threatened Wallenberg, whose car was rammed by a German lorry a short time later. Wallenberg is said to have then gone to Eichmann, who expressed his regret at the accident while not ruling out further assassination attempts. In both cases this information comes from Wallenberg's associates Lars G:son Berg and Göte Carlsson, but it has not been confirmed by other sources. It is actually highly doubtful whether these meetings even occurred, and if there was a dinner it is more likely that Wallenberg shared it with Becher.[145]

---

144 Steinhouse, *Wallenberg is Here!*, p. ix.
145 Berg, *The Book That Disappeared*, pp. 13–16. See also Villius and Villius, *Fallet Raoul Wallenberg*, pp. 42–43; Schiller, *Varför ryssarna tog Raoul Wallenberg*, pp. 83–84, 190; Kovacs, *Skymning över Budapest*, pp. 134–135; Carlberg, *Raoul Wallenberg*, pp. 305–306.

This has not prevented negotiations between Eichmann and Wallenberg from being retold over and over again in various contexts, from biographies with scholarly ambitions via newspaper articles to literature written for children and young adults, starring the Swedish diplomat.[146]

Throughout *Wallenberg: A Hero's Story*, the Swede's heroic status is reinforced by the way he deals with the duty-bound Eichmann. The confrontation reaches its dramatic climax at a dinner party, when the Swedish diplomat's moral superiority is proved once and for all. The contrast is striking between the superficially civilized context of two gentlemen chatting over a glass of brandy and the subject of their conversation. Wallenberg asks how many Jews Eichmann has murdered: is it four, five, or six million? Eichmann replies that whatever the number, it is a praiseworthy achievement. He declares that he will go to his grave proud of his work, having done his duty and cleansed Europe of its Jews.[147] In his defiant response, Wallenberg says he will do everything in his power to ensure that his dinner companion goes to meet his maker as soon as possible. He further scoffs that Eichmann is beginning to talk like a soldier for a change. After all, the SS officer's career has been mostly technical, not to say administrative. Wallenberg adds scornfully that Eichmann is a man who has had to be content with routing trains but who has never fully succeeded in filling the

---

146 Adrup, 'Bjöd Eichmann på middag', *Dagens Nyheter*, 13 January 1980; Andres Küng, *Raoul Wallenberg*, pp. 35–40; Ahlander, *Raoul Wallenberg*, pp. 54–58; A. M. Rosenthal, 'Ich bin Wallenberg', *The New York Times*, 9 April 1987; Sjöquist, *Raoul Wallenberg*, pp. 46–50; Linnéa, *Raoul Wallenberg*, pp. 109–112; Lester, 'Raoul Wallenberg', p. 155; Nicholson and Winner, *Raoul Wallenberg*, p. 48; Brown, *Courage*, pp. 76–77; Kershaw, *The Envoy*, pp. 117–120; Skoglund, *A Quiet Courage*, pp. 88–91. See also György Konrád, 'On Wallenberg', *The Hungarian Quarterly*, Autumn 1998, in which the encounter is rewritten such that Wallenberg is forced to 'drink a toast with the devil himself'. In the world of fiction, Eichmann and Wallenberg's simultaneous presence in Budapest has inspired even more elaborate stories. In the novel *Safe Houses* (1984) by British-American writer Lynne Alexander, a Hungarian woman living in the United States searches for the vanished Raoul Wallenberg, convinced that he is her father. The reader is faced with the possibility that her father could equally well have been Eichmann.
147 This comment probably stems from a remark purportedly made during the Nuremberg trials by SS officer Dieter Wislicent, who was executed in 1948; see further in Klein, *Jag återvänder aldrig*, pp. 39–41.

quotas. The SS officer is forced to answer, which further reinforces Wallenberg's heroic status. As a fearless and effective rescuer, he has helped to ensure that the bureaucrat in a SS uniform has not fully succeeded in completing his ruthless task.

## Saving the ghetto

From the end of 1944 onwards, thousands of Jews who escaped the extermination campaign found themselves in Budapest's ghettos, both the one that came to be known as the small or international ghetto in the 13th district, with almost 40,000 inhabitants, and another ghetto in the 7th district, where nearly 70,000 people were obliged to reside. As we shall see, there are several possible explanations for that. However, ambiguity and alternative sequences of events do not fit well with on-screen historical dramas. The rescue of the ghetto (only one is mentioned) is also an important event in *Wallenberg: A Hero's Story*. For the members of the television team, though, it was less interesting to address the competing versions of the relevant sequence of events, but instead crucial to ensure that Raoul Wallenberg was given a decisive role.

It makes sense to start with examining the choices that the series creators – more or less actively – made by relating them to historical accounts of the Budapest ghetto in December 1944 and January 1945. To begin with, the continued fierce German resistance on both the Eastern and Western fronts in the final months of 1944 – as exemplified by the Battle of the Bulge and the defence of Budapest – makes it clear that Hitler was still trying to achieve military success in order to divide the Allies while the Holocaust continued unabated. Given this situation, the fact that most of the Jewish inhabitants of the Budapest ghettos were spared by a decision made on 16 January 1945 has puzzled historians of the war.

Among the individuals who made huge efforts to save the ghetto were Lajos Stöckler and Miksa Domonkos, both of whom were members of the Jewish Council. Still, they were obliged to negotiate as best they could while seeking support from representatives of neutral states.[148] A number of scholars have attributed a decisive importance to Domonkos, saying that it was

---

148 Kovacs, *Skymning över Budapest*, p. 292.

he who persuaded the Germans to protect the ghetto from the Arrow Cross death patrols.[149] For the creators of the television series, however, assigning an essential role to the Jewish leaders was not germane to their endeavour; they desired to supplement Wallenberg's heroic mission with yet another feat: the rescuing of Budapest's ghetto. That notion might be referred to as poetic licence concerning the truth. Many scholars have expressed doubts, pointing out that by that time Wallenberg was in Soviet captivity. This also means that the long-held contention that Wallenberg saved tens of thousands, perhaps even a hundred thousand, Jewish lives is not correct, as it includes those trapped in the ghetto; that is unlikely, as Wallenberg had no influence whatsoever on the Soviet military leadership, which was by then in control of developments.[150]

Still others have stressed the decision made by Karl Pfeffer-Wildenbruch, a member of Himmler's staff and a Waffen SS general, who was badly wounded during the fighting in Budapest but survived and spent ten years in Soviet captivity. He dismissed claims that Wallenberg had persuaded him to continue issuing *Schutzbriefe* to the ghetto residents in order to protect them from the Arrow Cross, claiming instead that he alone had protected the Jews. He also questioned the possibility that Himmler had ordered the ghetto to be spared in order to facilitate the negotiations for the release of Jews in exchange for money, gold, and diamonds that were underway between Himmler's emissary, the SS officer Kurt Becher, and the Jewish lawyer Resznő or Rudolf Kasztner, who, in retrospect, has been regarded as either a Nazi accomplice or as a man who was trying to save as many Jews as possible by any means necessary, including trying to trade human lives for money, goods, and military equipment. Kasztner's defence lawyers stressed that he had certainly negotiated with SS officers, but that was quite different from having collaborated with them.[151] In his version, Kasztner claimed that the ghetto had already been saved on 8 December 1944 because he – with Wallenberg's help – had persuaded Gerhard

---

149 See e.g. Smith, *Lost Hero*, p. 97; Lester, 'Raoul Wallenberg', p. 156.
150 See e.g. Braham, *The Politics of Genocide. Vol. 2*, pp. 872–876; Åmark, *Förövarna bestämmer villkoren*, pp. 273–279.
151 Schmid, 'Vorwort', pp. 11–29 and Landau, 'Nachschrift', pp. 337–348. See also Levai, *Eichmann in Hungary*, pp. 190–201.

Schmidhuber to protect the ghetto.[152] This explanation has been questioned on good grounds, as most evidence suggests that it was designed to give Becher – with whom Kasztner had been in close contact during the final months that the Germans still controlled Budapest – an alibi at the Nuremberg trial. When Kasztner testified, he firmly maintained that Becher was not guilty of war crimes. On the contrary, Becher had tried to persuade Himmler to stop the mass murder of Jews in Hungary.[153]

Another individual who has been assigned a key role is Gerhard Schmidhuber. The Major General, who has been wrongly labelled as an SS general in several books, was the commander of the 13th Panzer Division. He was also the supreme commander of the German forces in Hungary during the fighting against the Red Army until he was killed in Budapest on 11 February 1945, just two days before the German forces in the city surrendered to the Soviets. Schmidhuber is said to have feared that Jewish resistance to German troops would escalate if Arrow Cross members were permitted to launch a bloodbath. At the same time, he would have preferred to see the Hungarian antisemites fighting Soviet soldiers rather than massacring men, women, and children.[154] In the early 2020s, this scenario became topical again in Hungary, where initiatives to mount a plaque in Budapest in memory of Schmidhuber led to fierce debate.[155]

The plot of *Wallenberg: A Hero's Story* implies that the heroic Wallenberg is by no means able to save the ghetto on his own. In Werbell and Clarke's book on which the television series was based, the Swedish diplomat is the saviour of the ghetto, because the Soviet soldiers who liberated it encountered thousands of Jews holding Swedish passports. Although the Arrow Cross had been trying to kill Wallenberg for some time, he continued his work, saying that his life was that of a single individual, but that here it was a matter of saving thousands of lives. As the story goes,

---

152 Kastner, *Der Kastner-Bericht über Eichmanns Menschenhandel in Ungarn*, pp. 247–261.
153 Bogdanor, *Kasztner's Crime*, pp. 226, 251.
154 Ungváry, *The Siege of Budapest*, pp. 217, 302–303; Aronson, 'The West, the *Yishuv*, and the Rescue Debate Regarding Slovakia and Hungary', pp. 432–434.
155 'A historical debate on a controversial topic: Germans and Russians in Budapest, 1944–1945', *Hungarian Spectrum*, 15 February 2020, https://hungarianspectrum.org/tag/gerhardschmidhuber/ (accessed 20 January 2022).

though, he is unable to monitor the resolution of the ghetto drama, because by then he is being interrogated by Soviet officers. Instead, it is the Hungarian police officer Pál Szalai who – referring to Wallenberg – persuades Schmidhuber to call off the Arrow Cross plans to raid the ghetto.[156]

Such a scenario would, however, have been inadequate in a television series that uses every available means to highlight Wallenberg's heroism and his importance as the single most important saviour of Hungary's Jews. What follows instead is a scene that most closely resembles the description according to which the Swedish diplomat – either at a meeting in mid-January or via a letter – informed Schmidhuber that if he allowed the pogrom to go ahead, he would not be considered a soldier after the war but a war criminal.[157] In the television series, the by then exhausted Wallenberg asks Schmidhuber, played by Charles Brauer, to promise him on all he considers holy that the remaining Jews in the Budapest ghetto will be spared – a request honoured by the German officer.

### Raoul Wallenberg between fact and fiction: the reception of the television series

The not always straightforward distinction between the actual Second World War and latter-day representations of it was highly topical 40 years after the war ended. A Swedish-produced drama documentary about Jane Horney, a Swede accused of spying, was broadcast concurrently with *Wallenberg: A Hero's Story*. Horney was probably executed in January 1945 by members of the Danish Resistance, who assumed she was a

---

156 Werbell and Clarke, *Lost Hero*, pp. 153–155. See also Joszef Szekeres, *Saving the Ghettos of Budapest in January 1945*, passim, and Kershaw, *The Envoy*, p. 141. Giorgio Perlasca has questioned this version. In an interview with Linda G. Kuzmack in 1990, he claimed that Pál Szalai had exaggerated his own importance and that, unlike him, Wallenberg had not been directly involved in saving the ghetto; see 'Oral History Interview with Giorgio Perlasca', USHMM, http://collections.ushmm.org/search/catalog/irn504674 (accessed 3 September 2021).

157 Lévai, 'Aus welchen Gründen überlebte das Budapester Ghetto', p. 114. According to one version, Wallenberg supposedly informed Schmidhuber that he personally would witness against the general in a future war-crimes trial if the Arrow Cross were allowed to destroy the ghetto; see Smith, *Lost Hero*, pp. 96–97.

German spy. In Denmark, the documentary about her aroused powerful feelings, which led to death threats against several members of the Swedish film crew and the temporary suspension of the broadcast.[158]

At the same time the US television series *Winds of War*, based on Herman Wouk's hit novels, was being broadcast. Whereas the makers of the Jane Horney documentary claimed to be telling a true story, the US series mixed real people and events from the Second World War with invented human stories. The aim was to give the impression of historical authenticity. For example, the climax of the series, the Japanese attack on Pearl Harbor, was filmed on the same date 40 years after it had actually happened. The interplay between fact and fiction was reinforced by 'what happened next' articles, in which the actions of the novel's characters during the Second World War and the Holocaust were presented as if they were the lives of real people.[159] In an interview, Jane Seymour – one of the main characters in the sequel, *War and Remembrance* – stressed the great effort that had gone into creating authenticity. Part of the series had been filmed on location in the camps at Auschwitz. She said that some extras who had been prisoners there during the war years had broken down 'because they found it all so realistic'. For her, it was only a short step to describing the series as 'an excellent history lesson' that showed children the high price humanity had to pay for war and racism.[160]

The relationship between the Budapest of 1944–1945 and the reproduction of events there 40 years later also shaped the reactions to *Wallenberg: A Hero's Story*. The focus lay on the issue of whether the exploits of a real historical hero could – and should – be recast in the form of fiction in order to illustrate something as 'monumentally horrendous' as the Holocaust. As with the reception of *Holocaust*, a conflict existed between the crowd-pleasing effect

---

158 Ahnfeldt-Mollerup, 'Historien som nyhed', pp. 65–85. The question was also whether *Wallenberg: A Hero's Story* would be broadcast on Danish television, which first occurred in March 1998; see Nikulin (ed.), *Raoul Wallenberg i den danske presse*, pp. 48–49, 128.

159 Gittan Mannberg, 'Kärlek och äventyr i skuggan av ett krig', *Röster i Radio & TV*, 1985:34, 7–8, 16; K. G. Björkman, 'Slutet på "Krigets vindar"', *Aftonbladet*, 19 October 1985; 'Så gick det sen i "Krigets vindar"', *Aftonbladet*, 20 October 1985; Peter Svensson, 'Fortsättningen du inte får se', *Expressen*, 20 October 1985.

160 Gunnar Rehlin, '"Natalie" förändrade hennes liv. Jane Seymour berättar om sin roll i "Krig och hågkomst"', *iDAG*, 18 October 1990.

of a television series and negative criticisms of it.[161] Like the public's reaction to the Weiss story, the response to the Wallenberg narrative was not clear-cut. American critics debated the difficulties of addressing the Nazi genocide in television form, but their conclusions differed. Some were impressed by an engaging narrative about how a heroic few fought against all odds when the agents of evil were both ruthless and many more in number.[162] One reviewer found the (overly) obvious conflict between good and evil to be the main problem in television series about the Holocaust in general and in *Wallenberg: A Hero's Story* in particular. With a few exceptions, said this critic, the main figures in the narrative were reduced to one-dimensional characters. Ambivalence and complexity were at best hinted at, but they were often completely absent.[163]

In an otherwise very favourable appraisal, the *New York Times* television reviewer John J. O'Connor, who was also a pioneer in the field of film-and-history research, criticized the romance between Wallenberg and Baroness Kemény. The main problem was that the love story was only hinted at via meaningful glances and other devices that 'the producers obviously believe [are] required for [a] mass audience'. On top of this, the historical truth was stretched to the limit, or the people who made the series simply crossed the line.[164] Similar views appeared in assessments by Swedish critics. It was certainly good that more Swedes had the opportunity to learn more about what their compatriot had achieved in Budapest, but the producers could have left out the romantic episode. The series would have benefited from the inclusion of other, more dramatic sequences from the real-life Hungarian drama, said critics; instead, everything became 'rather banal in an American manner'.[165] In the

---

161 Zander, '*Holocaust* at the Limits', pp. 260–270.
162 Gus Stevens, 'TV-movie tells Wallenberg's story in 2 parts', *The Tribune*, 5 April 1985; John Voorhees, '"Wallenberg" miniseries takes a satisfying look at heroism', *The Seattle Times*, 7 April 1985; John J. O'Connor, 'TV review: Story of Wallenberg being shown in 2 Parts', *The New York Times*, 8 April 1985.
163 Arthur Unger, '"Wallenberg": disappointing treatment of a heroic and inspiring story', *The Christian Science Monitor*, 29 March 1985.
164 John J. O'Connor, 'TV review: Story of Wallenberg being shown in 2 Parts', *The New York Times*, 8 April 1985. See also 'Formula merchants are milking the mini-series', *The New York Times*, 5 May 1985.
165 Disa Håstad, '"En försvunnen hjälte": Romantiserat om Raoul Wallenberg', *Dagens Nyheter*, 15 October 1985. See also Lars Åhrén, 'Wallenbergserien saknar människor', *Göteborgs-Tidningen*, 16 October 1985.

same spirit the series was described as 'deodorized', mainly because the victims had allegedly become placeholder characters whereas Wallenberg was portrayed more like a film hero than a man of flesh and blood. In short, '[r]eality ... was sidelined'.[166]

Swedish reviewers repeatedly pointed out that Americans had a greater need for heroic stories and that these tended to be exaggerated. The Swedish connection to the subject matter nevertheless helped create a sympathetic attitude towards the US television drama. For example, buyers at Swedish Television had purchased the series even before filming began, a measure with few if any precedents.[167] In the wake of its screening on Swedish television, a number of critics were inspired by the portrayal of Wallenberg. Feeling pride in being Swedish, they added that 'it is pleasing that this man is finally being celebrated as the hero he was'.[168] In conjunction with a pre-screening at a television trade fair in Monte Carlo in February 1985, at which the audience was only shown clips from the series, one Swedish critic present stated that the Wallenberg-Chamberlain combination was irresistible.[169] This opinion was reiterated in conjunction with the screening of *Wallenberg: A Hero's Story*. The drama was saved by the fact that Chamberlain worked 'with small means, without Hollywood stereotypes and exaggerations' in combination with a realistic depiction of the horrific events of the Holocaust. One of the most approving Swedish reviewers said that this made it possible to overlook the ahistorical flirtation.[170] Although it was impossible to ignore the confounding of historical facts with contrived romance and other 'TV-like cosmetics', the series did serve its purpose. By focusing on a middle-class family, the *Holocaust* series had enabled viewers to grasp the Holocaust, whereas *Wallenberg:*

---

166 Inga-Lill Valfridsson, 'Gråtmild Wallenberg', *Aftonbladet*, 16 October 1985.
167 'Chamberlain spelar Raoul Wallenberg', *Svenska Dagbladet*, 17 August 1984.
168 Lasse Råde, 'Wallenberg-dramat', *Göteborgs-Tidningen*, 15 October 1985. See also Lars Åhrén, 'Wallenbergserien saknar människor', *Göteborgs-Tidningen*, 16 October 1985; Jan Lindström, 'I USA hyllas han som en hjälte', *Expressen*, 18 October 1985.
169 Hemming Sten, 'Lovande TV-serie om Wallenberg', *Svenska Dagbladet*, 14 February 1985.
170 Hemming Sten, 'Tacksamhet för Wallenbergfilmen', *Svenska Dagbladet*, 17 October 1985.

*A Hero's Story* showed what 'a true hero' had achieved in order to save as many people as possible.[171]
Per Anger and others who had been with Wallenberg in Budapest were frequently interviewed in connection with the television series, both in newspapers and in the current-affairs television programme broadcast after the final part of *Wallenberg: A Hero's Story*. The theme of that programme was the question of whether Wallenberg was still alive. Other coverage before and during the television series dealt with the scale of the Wallenberg rescue efforts, the recent US court ruling that the Soviet Union had violated international law by arresting Wallenberg, and the UD's handling of the case, focusing on the initial ham-fisted and hesitant approach to the Soviet leaders. A recurring message was that the official Swedish treatment of Wallenberg was anything but heroic, because he had been sacrificed on the altar of realpolitik, i.e. neutrality.[172]
Per Anger also commented on *Wallenberg: A Hero's Story*. He pointed out that the depiction of his and Wallenberg's actions in Budapest was mostly historically correct but that the reality had been far worse. However, he quite understood that it was not

---

171 K. G. Björkman, 'En äkta hjälte', *Aftonbladet*, 15 October 1985.
172 Lars Brusling, 'De undgick förintelsen: "Man känner igen många scener"' (interview with Georg and Eva Klein) plus Hans and Elsa Villius, 'UD och spelet om Wallenberg', *Röster i Radio & TV*, 1985:41, 6–10; Anita Hansson, 'Wallenberg som TV-hjälte', *Aftonbladet*, 13 October 1985; Anita Hansson, 'Wallenberg lever' (interview with Per Anger), *Aftonbladet*, 15 October 1985; 'Ännu en gång: Lever Wallenberg?', *Dagens Nyheter*, 16 October 1985; Görel Söderberg, 'Magasinet om Raoul Wallenberg: "Han får aldrig glömmas"', *Svenska Dagbladet*, 16 October 1985; Eric Sjöquist, 'Per Anger hjälpte till rädda judar i Budapest: Wallenberg lever!', *Expressen*, 16 October 1985; Bosse Händel, 'Verkligheten var mycket grymmare' (interview med Per Anger), *Göteborgs-Tidningen*, 16 October 1985; Kristina Kamp, 'Raoul räddade mig undan förintelsen' (interview with Kate Wacs), *Aftonbladet*, 16 October 1985; 'Domstol: Brott att gripa Raoul', *Aftonbladet*, 17 October 1985; Lasse Råde, 'Raouls egen bild!', *Göteborgs-Tidningen*, 17 October 1985; Eric Sjöquist, 'Vi har sett Wallenberg – så gick det efter filmen', *Expressen*, 17 October 1985; Lars Åhrén, 'En väckarklocka för svenska UD', *Göteborgs-Tidningen*, 17 October 1985; Anders Hasselbohm, 'Wallenbergs chef utpekad som nazist', *Aftonbladet*, 18 October 1985; Eric Sjöquist, 'Sveriges svek mot Raoul Wallenberg' (interview med Per Anger), *Expressen*, 18 October 1985; Eric Sjöquist, 'Palme frågar Gorbatjov om Wallenberg', *Expressen*, 19 October 1985; 'Raoul Wallenberg – ställ krav, Olof Palme' (editorial), *Expressen*, 20 October 1985.

possible to depict the full barbarity of the situation in Budapest at that time, that the producers had taken certain liberties such as including an imaginary ball, and that they had not been able to refrain from the fictional romance between Wallenberg and Baroness Kemény, which had outraged Wallenberg's relatives. Anger admitted that he had been a little apprehensive prior to the screening he had attended in London with Lamont Johnson and others. When he came out of the cinema, however, he had been calm, because Wallenberg's achievements had been 'portrayed in the right way'. Of course there was cause for objections, as some things were 'rather unreal' and some of the actors bore little resemblance to their real-life originals. However, the overall impression was good, and he therefore responded to concerned fellow Swedes by saying that the result could have been much worse because it was important to realize that this was 'a Hollywood product'. Anger also saw the value of experimenting with historical reality on this point, as the fictional love story demonstrated that Wallenberg had possessed strong emotions like any other human being.[173]

## A Swedish Wallenberg film for an international audience

That Hollywood products were not toothless became clear when *Wallenberg: A Hero's Story* was shown on Greek television (ERT). Afterwards, criticism was aimed at the fact that the hints at the role played by the Soviet Union had been cut out. The issue became a matter for the UD, which was puzzled by this change. Sweden's ambassador in Athens questioned why Greece as a NATO member would want to protect Soviet rulers. Officially, it was asserted that the Greek version had been shorter than the original owing to the removal of a résumé. However, things were not quite that simple. According to privately obtained information, the Soviet Embassy had contacted Greek television because *Wallenberg: A Hero's Story* was being shown on 7 November, the anniversary of the Russian Revolution. ERT's management felt that they should meet the Soviet authorities half-way, but they did not want to cut the series

---

173 Ingmar Lindmarker, 'Wallenbergs gärning skildrad på rätt sätt', *Svenska Dagbladet*, 6 February 1985; Leif Bergström, 'Raoul Wallenberg, amerikansk tv-film: En svensk hjältesaga', *Svenska Dagbladet*, 18 March 1985; Eric Sjöquist, 'Jag tänkte stämma filmbolaget', *Expressen*, 15 October 1985; Bo Händel, 'Verkligheten var mycket grymmare', *Göteborgs-Tidningen*, 16 October 1985.

itself. Their choice was to fade and black out the screen during the film's final credits. Whether this information, given 'confidentially', was correct was never clarified. A looming diplomatic crisis between Greece and Sweden was averted after Greek promises that the television series was still complete and that a full-length re-run would be broadcast in the near future.[174]

At about the same time, plans were again launched for a Swedish Wallenberg film aimed at an international audience. The initiators were Kenne Fant, who had personally researched the Wallenberg case, plus Klas Olofsson, who was CEO of the Swedish Film Institute, and the film producer Katinka Faragó. In 1987 Olofsson and Faragó read the proofs of *R* (1988), Fant's documentary novel about Wallenberg, and bought the film rights to it. Fant claims in his autobiography *Nära bilder* ['Close-up pictures'] that it was his book that formed the basis of the Swedish-Hungarian film *Good Evening, Mr. Wallenberg*, which had the rarely used subtitle in Swedish *En passionshistoria från verkligheten* ['A passion story from reality'].[175] Faragó paints a different picture. She had originally hoped to bring in Hungarian director István Szabó – known for *Mephisto* (1981) and *Hanussen* (1988), both films about men who had come under the Nazi spell – but he was too busy to take on the job of director. Kjell Grede was then asked. He had recently succeeded with a feature film called *Hip Hip Hurrah!* (1987), a collective biography of the Scandinavian artists who had lived and worked in the village of Skagen in northern Denmark in the last decades of the nineteenth century under the collective name of 'the Skagen Painters'. Grede hesitated at first, but then accepted the job because he felt that 'the film needed to be made'. He rejected *R* as a screenplay, though, and after reading up on the subject he wrote the script himself.[176]

---

174 See the documents about 'the Wallenberg film', i.e. *Wallenberg: A Hero's Story*, from 13, 14, 15, 25, 27 and 29 November and 2 and 12 December 1985, RKA, Raoul Wallenberg, UD2001/00009, Vol. 24.
175 Fant, *Nära bilder*, p. 291.
176 Kristoffersson and Faragó, *Katinka och regissörerna*, pp. 129–131. See also Ricki Neuman, 'Kjell Grede: Att göra upp med sin historia' (interview with Kjell Grede), *Judisk Krönika*, 1990:4, 27 plus Ulf Zander, interview with Kjell Grede, 7 July 2010. In the credits the question about the authorship of the script is solved with the line of text: 'With thanks to Kenne Fant who gave us the impulse to make the film.' Contemporary newspaper reports combined the information: Fant's documentary novel was the

Because Stellan Skarsgård played the lead role, as he had done in *Hip Hip Hurrah!*, several writers drew parallels with Grede's previous film. There was a significant dissimilarity, however. The focus on Wallenberg's last three weeks in Budapest demanded a different style and approach. 'In "Hip Hip Hurrah!" I painted so much light that the sorrow became visible. Now I have to paint so much sorrow that the light becomes visible', he explained during the filming.[177] In this process a documentary approach had never been an option, nor had extending the time span to a point in time after Wallenberg's disappearance. On the contrary, 'all the questions about Wallenberg's fate in the Soviet Union [had begun] to transform him into a statue, a pile of dry leaves, a pawn in a political game of hypothesizing and creating saint-like figures.' In contrast to this stood the goal of portraying Wallenberg the man.[178] In Budapest, Skarsgård had personally experienced the memory of the Swedish diplomat away from the grand tributes. Much of the film was shot in the former ghetto, which was still the home of Jews who had lived through the Second World War. The actor described how old ladies invited him for coffee and reached out to touch him because his portrayal of Wallenberg brought back memories for them. Meeting these survivors convinced him that the most important task was 'to be true to those people and to their lives'.[179]

Grede's description of Wallenberg as a complex individual who had dark elements but who was a figure of light worth emulating left its mark on the film, and it was repeatedly commented on. With its dialogue in several languages, *Good Evening, Mr. Wallenberg* was filmed on location in Budapest with the help of Hungarian actors and film workers. The film has some similarities with both

---

backbone of the script written by Grede; see e.g. Anna Broberg and Lotta Svedborg, 'Svensk storfilm om Raoul Wallenberg', *Aftonbladet*, 27 August 1988; Tore Ljungberg, 'Kjell Grede filmar igen: Budapest oslagbart', *Göteborgs-Posten*, 24 November 1988; Jan-Olov Andersson, 'Skarsgård blir Wallenberg', *Aftonbladet*, 21 July 1989 and Georg Cederskog, 'Livtag på Grede och Skarsgård', *Dagens Nyheter*, 26 September 1990. In Klas Viklund's interview with Kjell Grede, the director emphasizes the large amount of research he did when writing the script.

177 Per Ahlmark, 'På jakt efter Raoul Wallenbergs ansikte' (interview with Kjell Grede), *Expressen*, 1 October 1989.
178 Anders Hansson, 'Grede vill visa människan Wallenberg' (interview with Kjell Grede), *Göteborgs-Posten*, 23 September 1990.
179 Larry Gross, interview with Stellan Skarsgård, *BOMB*, Summer 1998, p. 38.

*Pimpernel Smith* and *Wallenberg: A Hero's Story*. As pointed out above, the latter includes a key scene that occurs on a railway platform. In a close analysis of a similar scene in *Good Evening, Mr. Wallenberg*, Richard Raskin has noted that there are obvious differences between Leslie Howard's Pimpernel Smith and Stellan Skarsgård's Raoul Wallenberg, notably in that the latter never uses disguises or aliases. More interesting, however, are the similarities, especially the ways in which the protagonists relate to their opponents.

> The use of bullying and insults, of a constant stream of threats and blame, keeping the adversary on the defensive at every turn and never letting him capture the initiative, the verbal and gestural flourish, the hammering away with an elaborative pretext, the perfect or near perfect timing of efforts coordinated with the confederates, etc.[180]

In addition, there are a number of similarities between *Wallenberg: A Hero's Story* and *Good Evening, Mr. Wallenberg*. The pattern recurs in scenes of the hero's awakening as he is confronted with the Holocaust, and the sequence of events is much the same. However, it is a very different Wallenberg that Skarsgård portrays. In Chamberlain's version, Wallenberg energetically accepts the mission in Stockholm and implements it in Budapest in the same style. He strides the stage as a tireless, joking, and defiant figure. In *Good Evening, Mr. Wallenberg* the protagonist more resembles the description repeatedly given in the 1970s by Márton Vörös, who had worked for the Swedish Red Cross in southern Hungary from 1944 to 1945 and was well-disposed towards Sweden. The background was that in December 1944, Wallenberg had only managed to save 300 people from the so-called international labour battalions, whereas 17,000 others had been deported to concentration camps in western Hungary, where most of them died of typhus or were tortured to death by the Arrow Cross. This failure plagued Wallenberg; he appeared haggard and hunched: 'It was a tired and very sorrowful man who stood before me. I saw that he had not even taken the time to shave, and this accentuated the pallor of his face even more.'[181]

---

180 Raskin, 'From Leslie Howard to Raoul Wallenberg', p. 9.
181 Vörös, *Även för din skull ... Svenska Röda Korset i Ungern i världskrigets dagar*, p. 41; Staffan Tjerneld, 'Nya rön om Raoul Wallenberg: 'Redan då var Wallenberg en gammal och hopsjunken man", *Expressen*, 18 June 1972. Werbell and Clarke included Vörös's account in *Lost Hero* (p. 114),

Skarsgård displays such traits even at an early stage during his meeting with the rabbi in Stockholm. In this version, Wallenberg is a doubter. He does not believe in God, politics, or ideologies. 'I'm mediocre', he adds. The fact that he chooses to go ahead anyway may be regarded as an expression of courage, because he confronts his fear both of external threats and of the experience of his own inadequacies.[182] For Peter Cohen, who directed the documentaries *The Story of Chaim Rumkowski and the Jews of Łódź* (1982) and *The Architecture of Doom* (1989), Skarsgård's Wallenberg drew attention to an interesting theme in the film: a banality of goodness. The problem, Cohen argued, was that this theme was not followed up but had to take a back seat as naked violence took over.[183]

The violence of Budapest is undeniably ever-present in *Good Evening, Mr. Wallenberg*, and it leaves its mark on the protagonist. In the Hungarian capital, he shows signs of exhaustion, irritation, inadequacy, and fear. He cannot sleep, and his shoes are too tight. The explanation for his behaviour lies in the fact that arbitrary violence has a more important function and is far more present in *Good Evening, Mr. Wallenberg* than in *Wallenberg: A Hero's Story*. While Chamberlain's Wallenberg stays essentially the same, Skarsgård's portrait of the Swedish diplomat shows that it was impossible to remain unaffected by the tragic events in Budapest. To become legendary under such conditions – as Wallenberg did – comes at a very heavy price.

When Kjell Grede passed away in December 2017, a recurring conclusion in tributes to him was that *Good Evening, Mr. Wallenberg* was his greatest work.[184] This was no after-the-fact construction. True, the focus on the Swedish martyr's struggle and downfall did not draw huge audiences to the cinemas, but the praise was all the more abundant. Those involved in the Wallenberg case expressed

---

but unlike much else in their book it did not make it into the script of *Wallenberg: A Hero's Story*, probably because it was directly contrary to Chamberlain's portrayal of Wallenberg.

182 See Bauhn, *The Value of Courage*, pp. 40–41.
183 Peter Cohen in Kaj Schueler, 'Att gestalta helvetet' (conversation between Peter Cohen, Erland Josephson, and Elisabeth Sörenson), *Judisk Krönika*, 1990:6, 16.
184 Helena Lindblad, 'Helena Lindblad minns regissören Kjell Grede', *Dagens Nyheter*; Anna Ångström, 'Kjell Grede sa: "Är du bra på att skratta?"', *Svenska Dagbladet*; Maria Domellöf-Wik, 'Känslostarka ögonblick blev till bildpoesi', *Göteborgs-Posten*, all published 17 December 2017.

their approval. The film would certainly help to shine the spotlight once again on the ham-fisted Swedish handling of Wallenberg's disappearance.[185] Swedish film critics stressed that it had been a long time since a domestic film had spoken such an internationally viable language while preserving its integrity.[186] A few writers and commentators did object to what they regarded as overly apparent literary elements, excessively obvious and crudely drawn scenes, and an inability to capture Wallenberg's personal development over time. Another objection was that the director had lacked emotional distance from the complex subject, and that this lack of distance had brought sentimental elements into the film. However, most of those who voiced criticism were also careful to highlight the film's strengths.[187]

Foreign reviewers generally agreed with the favourable comments.[188] *Good Evening, Mr. Wallenberg* was abundantly rewarded at the Swedish Guldbagge ('Golden Beetle') Awards gala in 1991. It was named Film of the Year by the Swedish Film Critics Association, came in for a good deal of attention when screened in Hungary, won acclaim at the Berlin International Film Festival, and

---

185 Erik Magnusson, 'von Dardel inför filmpremiären: Filmen gagnar Raouls sak' (interview with Guy von Dardel), *Sydsvenskan*, 5 October 1990; Jonas Sima, 'Pierre Schori berättar i tv i kväll: "Jag grät när jag såg Wallenberg-filmen"', *Expressen*, 7 October 1990.

186 Monika Tunbäck-Hansson, 'Kjell Gredes film om Wallenberg: Skakande och trovärdig', *Göteborgs-Posten*, 5 October 1990. See also Jan Aghed, 'Trovärdigt om Wallenberg', *Sydsvenskan*, 5 October 1990.

187 Lasse Bergström, 'Wallenberg som sömnlös desperado', *Expressen*, 5 October 1990; Anders Olofsson, 'Regissör drabbad av sitt verk', *Chaplin*, December 1990, pp. 348–349; Kaj Schueler, 'Att gestalta helvetet' (conversation between Peter Cohen, Erland Josephson and Elisabeth Sörenson), *Judisk Krönika*, 1990:6, 15–17. For one rare highly critical review, see Carl-Eric Nordberg, 'God afton, herr Wallenberg', *Vi*, 1990:43.

188 Hagnut Brockmann, 'Virtuoser Psychokrimi und unfaßbare Realität', *Volksblatt*, 21 January 1991; Christopher Boyer, 'Ein Opfer ist kein richtiger Mensch', *Die Tageszeitung*, 21 February 1991; Dieter Strunz, 'Wettbewerb: "Guten Abend, Herr Wallenberg"', *Berliner Morgenpost*, 21 February 1991; Sabine Carbon, 'Guten Abend, Herr Wallenberg', *Der Tagesspiegel*, 21 February 1991; Stephen Holden, 'A quiet hero lost at end of the war', *The New York Times*, 23 April 1993; Mary Houlihan-Skilton, 'Wallenberg: Portrait of unlikely hero', *The Chicago Sun-Times*, 11 June 1993; Ron Weiskind, 'Action hero', *Pittsburgh Post-Gazette*, 27 May 1994, plus the review in the American film industry's magazine *Variety*, 29 October 1990.

was nominated for an Oscar for Best Foreign Language Film. In a self-critical comment, Grede said that he had failed to show that the Holocaust was not just a historical phenomenon, but that variants of it still existed.[189] Many people disagreed with this view. Reviewers of the film repeatedly commented that Grede's audacity in depicting, in a realistic manner, how the vulnerable Wallenberg reveals his weaknesses but still keeps on battling was both more effective and more interesting than the usual cinematic hero portraits. The director had thereby 'in a very remarkable way [turned] history into the present', because he poses 'crucial questions' to us through his film.[190] That, too, was the starting point when the film was shown in schools in subsequent years, not infrequently with Grede himself as introducer and discussion leader.[191]

### The businessman as the role model of a new age

Psychologists Ashton D. Trice and Samuel A. Holland have studied ideals of masculinity on the basis of some 70 American films from the early 1920s to the late 1990s. They conclude that a changing view of masculinity leads to new heroic roles. Until the end of the Second World War, traditional soldier heroes dominated, but then the complex anti-hero emerged. From the 1980s onwards, they perceive a development in which superheroes appear again alongside depictions of the 'ideal man' in the role of the dunce.[192]

This analysis may be usefully applied to Skarsgård's Wallenberg and the depiction of Oskar Schindler in *Schindler's List*. Both Wallenberg and Schindler have a background as businessmen, which is of great importance in these films. Their professional category had long been unfavourably portrayed in popular culture, especially after the recurring economic crises of the 1920s and 1930s. Since those times, the world of business and its players had been depicted in increasingly muted colours. For example, the image of the businessman as a profiteer and/or lecherous libertine

---

189 Ricki Neuman, 'Kjell Grede: Att göra upp med sin historia' (interview with Kjell Grede), *Judisk Krönika*, 1990:4, 28.
190 Margareta Norlin, 'Verklighetens Wallenberg', *Aftonbladet*, 5 October 1990.
191 Jan Söderlind, 'Se varulven i ögat: Kjell Gredes uppmaning till Aranässkolans elever', *Arbetet*, 14 May 1991. See also Viklund, 'Kjell Grede: Använd filmupplevelsen!'
192 Trice and Holland, *Heroes, Antiheroes and Dolts*, passim.

was common in British films during Margaret Thatcher's leadership of the UK from 1979 to 1990. Amoral financial sharks have also come back into fashion in the early 2020s, in television series such as *Billions* and *Succession*.[193]

Exceptions include portrayals of capitalists who, after life-changing experiences, realize that life offers much more than successful business transactions, and who then put their new insights into practice and start leading richer lives for the benefit of both themselves and those around them. It is within this latter tradition that the 1990s film representations of Schindler and Wallenberg belong. Their respective backgrounds as experienced businessmen turn out to be a prerequisite for their heroic actions. The factual historical starting point is that in practical terms, the SS ran the Holocaust industry as a profitable business enterprise. Himmler wanted SS personnel to be incorruptible and exemplary, but the prioritization of financial profit-making led to recurrent elements of corruption and bribery within the organization.[194]

Against such a background, the films portray Schindler and Wallenberg as possessing superb 'people skills'. They know how to negotiate and establish business contacts with individuals both high and low. They know what women fall for, and who might be swayed into benevolence by a bottle of brandy or two. Lars G:son Berg writes that 'Wallenberg knew how much easier it is to bring a difficult transaction to a successful end after an abundance of good food and precious wines.' Both he and Schindler had acquired that insight before the war, and it was thanks to their skilful application of it that they were able to carry out their life-saving missions while the world was on fire.[195] Descriptions of Wallenberg in the immediate post-war years as 'a partisan in the service of humanity' should be viewed against this backdrop. The word 'partisan' was

---

193 Hedling, 'Krämare, profitörer och libertiner', pp. 213–254; John Lynch, 'Därför kan vi inte få nog av fiktiva finansmän', *Svenska Dagbladet*, 27 November 2021.
194 Allen, *The Business of Genocide*, pp. 128–164. See also Crowe, *Oskar Schindler*, p. 344.
195 Berg, *The Book That Disappeared*, p. 20. See also Anita Hansson, 'Wallenberg som TV-hjälte', *Aftonbladet*, 13 October 1985. On Schindler and Wallenberg's skills as businessmen and negotiators, see also Derogy, *Fallet Raoul Wallenberg*, p. 85; Anger, *With Raoul Wallenberg in Budapest*, pp. 49–50; Einhorn, *Handelsresande i liv*, p. 173; Crowe, *Oskar Schindler*, pp. 138–140; and Klein, *Jag återvänder aldrig*, pp. 99–100.

in vogue in the immediate post-war period, as a result of the successful resistance struggle of Soviet and Yugoslav partisans against the German occupiers. In Wallenberg's case, the word signalled that he had acted as a guerrilla fighter. The partisan is distinguished by the fact that he – or she – does not fight according to established conventions. It was argued that Wallenberg possessed none of the qualities necessary to succeed in traditional combat, because he 'lacked even that toughness that characterized so many men in the Resistance'.[196] This view of his lack of military ability is largely plucked out of thin air, though. His military service in Sweden was certainly associated with some problems, but he consistently received good reports and high marks.[197] Remarks to the effect that he was not suited to 'traditional combat' should instead be considered as a characteristic contained in the portrayal of Wallenberg as being essentially different from the many military men whom he more or less voluntarily confronted in Hungary. To be sure, he had brought a revolver to Budapest in order to feel braver, but it was never used.[198] In retrospect, that was no coincidence, as he was so much more adept when drastic situations demanded the use of unconventional weapons. He also displayed great personal valour. As an unarmed man in a violent place, he was 'without legal protection, left at the mercy of ... well-armed desperadoes who no longer felt any respect for either God or Satan as they saw their doom approaching'.[199] This relationship was captured in another typically worded dramatic description from the early post-war years of 'how, with a white piece of paper in his hand, he defeated the Arrow Cross devil who was armed to the teeth'.[200] As Per Anger noted in retrospect, Wallenberg's ability to play different roles contributed to his success. He could be formal when necessary, but also harsh in his dealings with Germans as he did not hesitate to bellow at them in their own language.[201]

---

196 Hugo Valentin, 'En partisan i mänsklighetens tjänst: Anförande vid Konserthusmötet den 11 jan. 1948', *Judisk Tidskrift*, 1948:1, 3–6. See also Philipp, *Raoul Wallenberg*, pp. 13, 117.
197 Lars Brink, *När hoten var starka*, pp. 156–160, 163, 174–192.
198 Anger, *With Raoul Wallenberg in Budapest*, p. 50; Per Anger, 'Raoul Wallenberg', *Judisk Tidskrift*, 1985:2, 6.
199 Philipp, *Raoul Wallenberg – kämpe för humanitet*, p. 19.
200 Lévai, *Raoul Wallenberg, hjälten i Budapest*, p. 260.
201 Carlberg, *Raoul Wallenberg*, p. 302.

In recent popular-culture contexts, Schindler and Wallenberg constitute a different type of partisan. In particular, Wallenberg, as portrayed by Skarsgård, has realized that it is useless to fight the men of darkness with weapons in the manner of a traditional hero. This role model of the new era is adept at exploiting contacts and interpreting information. Nor does he hesitate to lie, bribe, and bluff to save more Jewish lives. Above all, he is equipped with courage and the other qualities necessary to negotiate successfully with dangerous representatives of totalitarian regimes.[202]

The similarities between Spielberg's Schindler and Grede's Wallenberg should not be stretched too far, though. Steven Spielberg took pains to portray Oskar Schindler (Liam Neeson) and the German camp commandant Amos Goeth (Ralph Fiennes) as ambivalent and complex characters whose personalities comprised both light and dark traits. One of Spielberg's sources of inspiration was the classic film *Citizen Kane* whose protagonist, modelled on several US newspaper magnates but with William Randolph Hearst as the most obvious inspiration, is an ambivalent character who acts both exemplarily and reprehensibly. The films' Kane and Schindler both practise the art of pretence: whereas the former excels in fake news, the latter is concerned with 'the presentation' as expressed by 'his ability to create a successful business by first creating the image of one'.[203]

Despite the similarities, the tone of the two films also differs significantly. The feel-good emotion that the celebration of the heroic Schindler was intended to evoke, despite the difficult subject matter, does not exist in *Good Evening, Mr. Wallenberg*. Numerous films and television series on the theme of the Holocaust highlight the contrast between a virtuous, deep-rooted German culture and the barbarity of the ongoing mass murder. A callous genocidal individual like Reinhard Heydrich (David Warner) in *Holocaust* may certainly be a gifted pianist, and plastic surgery can hide a person's true identity, but a beautiful voice is recognizable even if the facial features are different, which in *Phoenix* (2014) leads to treacherous revelations of betrayal and greed both during and after the war. However, a classical work may also act as a link

---

202 Another example of the same narrative tradition is Paul Rusesabagina (Don Cheadle) in *Hotel Rwanda* (2004); see Zander, 'Heroic Images', pp. 130–131.
203 Joshua Hirsch, *Afterimage*, p. 145.

between music lovers, regardless of whether one is a Jew on the run and the other an officer in the German army, as occurs in Roman Polanski's *The Pianist* (2002). Both *Schindler's List* and *Good Evening, Mr. Wallenberg* feature scenes of German officers playing classical music on confiscated pianos. One crucial difference is that in *Good Evening, Mr. Wallenberg*, the officer plays badly.[204] And – as distinct from Neeson's Schindler – for Skarsgård's Wallenberg a quiet post-war existence is not a realistic option. A return to an idyllic Sweden would end in futility and unreality. In the film's hindsight, his sole remaining option is, in the words of film critic Anders Olofsson, 'to step out through the back door of history and merge with his own myth'.[205]

The protagonist himself is not the only non-traditional character in *Good Evening, Mr. Wallenberg*. The antagonist also differs from those in most other films about the Holocaust. He displays kinship with the perpetrator in *Music Box*, also from 1990. In many ways, this film makes references to the legal proceedings against John 'Ivan' Demjanjuk in the 1980s, which highlighted the fact that Eastern Europeans who had participated in genocide had been able to obtain sanctuary in the United States on condition that they had been explicit anti-Communists. While most of *Music Box* is set in Chicago, Second World War Hungary is never far away.[206] For American star lawyer Ann (Jessica Lange), the trial of her beloved father, Michael 'Mike' Laszlo (Armin Mueller-Stahl), is traumatic. Although she manages to get her father acquitted, the exhibits and testimony presented to the court contribute to her growing conviction that her father is actually identical to the man who, under the name of Miska, committed horrific crimes in Budapest in 1944–1945. At an overarching level, *Music Box* conveys an insight similar to that championed by Christopher Browning two years later in the acclaimed book *Ordinary Men*: namely that genocide

---

204 Insdorf, *Indelible Shadows*, pp. 267–268; Zander, 'Den slingrande vägen från Auschwitz', pp. 306–307; Zander, *Clio på bio*, pp. 204–205, 215. The discrepancy between beautiful music and the Holocaust had been used as early as 1949 in the Czechoslovak film *Distant Journey*, in which children in the ghetto in Theresienstadt (Terezin) rehearse a performance of Giuseppe Verdi's *Requiem* for Adolf Eichmann's visit; Avisar, *Screening the Holocaust*, p. 58.
205 Anders Olofsson, 'Regissör drabbad av sitt verk', *Chaplin*, December 1990, p. 349.
206 Jordan, *From Nuremberg to Hollywood*, pp. 129–144.

requires the participation of foot soldiers who are willing, or can be persuaded, to do the dirty work.

For similar reasons, Eichmann appears just twice in *Good Evening, Mr. Wallenberg* and then only in passing. Even so, he is an ever-present threat. Eichmann is the person the Jews are always talking about, even after he has left Budapest. On a visit to Eichmann's empty luxury villa, Wallenberg's Hungarian-Jewish chauffeur shoots at the SS officer's Christmas tree to mark that Eichmann belongs to the past, whereas he himself represents what is to come. However, this faith in the future is revealed to be deceptive, and Wallenberg reacts strongly against the focus on Eichmann. What would happen if there were an Eichmann in every stairwell, he asks indignantly, adding that if the SS man disappears there will still be fanatical Arrow Cross men around who wish the Jews dead at least as much as the *Obersturmbannführer* does. The Swede's outburst is based on his experience that Hungarians often prove willing to help the Germans and are sometimes even more brutal in hunting down Jews, whether the latter are in protected 'Swedish houses' or not. While Grede's film team has not entirely distanced itself from the popular-culture iconography associated with Wallenberg and Eichmann, the Swedish diplomat as depicted by them is most successful when he has been transformed into a heroic myth. A Jewish man tells his grandchildren about how Wallenberg met Eichmann over dinner, and how he won a complete moral victory over the SS man by virtue of his arguments.[207]

### Raoul Wallenberg in moving images: universalism, Americanization, nationalization

The historian Lawrence Baron has drawn attention to a number of contradictions between the Holocaust as a historical event and how it has subsequently been portrayed. Unsurprisingly, the theme has changed over time. Nor is it in any way peculiar that differences exist between generations, with older people generally preferring more 'realistic' depictions whereas younger ones find it easier to relate to more recent additions to the genre. Examples of

---

207 Kjell Grede claimed in an interview prior to the film premiere that he had received confirmation that Wallenberg and Eichmann had eaten dinner together but that he chose not to include the event (directly) in the film; see Elisabeth Sörenson, 'Filmen Kjell Grede inte kunde avvisa', *Svenska Dagbladet*, 3 April 1990.

these additions in the early twenty-first century are cases in which the inherently tragic story can function as the starting point for gallows humour, or wishful thinking about how things might have turned out differently. Baron also notes that many professional historians have been doubtful about, or outright dismissive of, fictionalizations based on 'generic formulas of epic struggles between good heroes and evil villains' or on the 'imposing [of] edifying endings on an unmitigated tragedy'. Focusing, as in *Schindler's List*, on Holocaust survivors has also been criticized by historians because the 'fortunate exceptions' risk obscuring the fact that an overwhelming majority of those subjected to the horrific concretization of Nazi racial policy also fell victim to it. Baron argues that such objections, together with more widespread exhortations not to attempt to represent the Holocaust at all, do not measure up. Because it was human beings who planned and carried out the Holocaust, with the result that other human beings resisted or were killed, the Holocaust is an event that cannot be placed outside history; it must remain a part of it. Rather than dismissing the vast array of representations that the Holocaust has generated outright, we should use them as objects for analyses that do not only shed new light on the Holocaust as a historical event. To an even greater degree, these representations may lead us to a better comprehension of how the Nazi genocide has been understood by different generations. In addition, studying them shows us the possible lessons and moral meanings that might be extracted from it in the form of different types of fictionalization.[208]

One interesting outcome in terms of history culture is the radical transformation that has occurred in descriptions of escaping the Nazi genocide. After the war, Jewish survivors of the Holocaust described themselves as remnants – individuals who had been torn from their roots or avoided the slaughter. The implication was that they were the remains of a residual ethnic group. By contrast, narratives from the late twentieth century onwards have had an undertone that has been labelled 'triumphant', because it places the emphasis on survival and the survivors.[209] Another aspect is that films and television series are based on the idea that we make history, rather than that we are history. As Deborah Cartmell and

---

208 Baron, *Projecting the Holocaust into the Present*, pp. viii–ix, 1–5, quotation p. 2. See Wulf Kansteiner, 'Entertaining Catastrophe', pp. 144–146; Cole, *Selling the Holocaust*, pp. 87–94.
209 Wendy Lower, *The Ravine*, p. 138.

I. Q. Hunter have noted, professional historians have 'typically shown the individual dwarfed by the past' because they are part of a 'blind and relentless machinery of historical process'. The basic approach in popular literature, film, and television is radically different, in that it 'asserts that people energetically influence history'.[210] In such a context, it is obvious that individuals such as Oskar Schindler and Raoul Wallenberg have formed appropriate role models. They have been both necessary and desirable in order that we may extract some encouraging messages from the catastrophic, and therefore by definition unfavourable, mental image of the Holocaust.[211]

In the early 1980s, American-produced television series about the Holocaust were characterized by an emphasis on survival, glorification, and suspense. With the public success of *Holocaust*, the 'survivor paradigm' described by Baron became widely prevalent. Particularly in the United States, Israel, and West Germany, the theme of individuals risking their own lives to save a few of the many millions condemned to die by German racial policy fell on fertile ground. In keeping with this paradigm, those who, like Wallenberg, were not Jews but who saved many of them came to be likened to 'lights in the great darkness'.[212]

The British historian Tony Kushner adds to this picture by pointing out that those who look back on the Holocaust from a safe distance often do so with the belief that had they been alive in the 1940s they would not have been perpetrators, and hopefully not victims either. At the same time, genocides and persecutions continue to be part of our everyday life today. In such a morally contradictory situation, there is a risk that it becomes difficult to connect with the Holocaust other than in the form of 'fascination at its sheer horror or by taking glib inspiration from the two-dimensional representation of its canonized non-Jewish heroes such as Oskar Schindler and Raoul Wallenberg'.[213] Kushner's conclusion can be supplemented with another line of reasoning, which sheds light on the continuing admiration for those non-Jews who saved Jews from the Holocaust. True, the missing Swede cannot

---

210 Cartmell and Hunter, 'Introduction: Retrovisions', p. 2.
211 See Levy and Sznaider, *The Holocaust and Memory in the Global Age*, pp. 131–207 and Schult, *A Hero's Many Faces*, p. 75.
212 Grunwald-Spier, *The Other Schindlers*, p. 13; Per T. Ohlsson, 'I skuggan av Wallenberg', *Sydsvenskan*, 29 July 2012.
213 Tony Kushner, '"Pissing in the Wind"?', pp. 60–61, quotation p. 61.

tell his story, any more than millions of Holocaust victims can, but because he ensured the survival of thousands of doomed individuals, his story has become an important and recurring aspect of the survivor paradigm. It has been further bolstered by a number of interviews with some of those he rescued, published to coincide with the screening of the television series about him in the United States.[214]

## Back to Budapest

Historical dramas on film and television are usually expensive productions. As pointed out above, there is a great need to relate to the values that prevailed at the time of filming, even in those cases where the productions are based on or inspired by actual events from the past, such as Wallenberg's actions in Budapest in 1944–1945. Overall, we can also conclude that the creations of *Wallenberg: A Hero's Story* and *Good Evening, Mr. Wallenberg* were closely tied to the surge of interest in the Holocaust that began with the screening of the *Holocaust* series in the West in 1978–1979, and that culminated in the years around the turn of the millennium. Similarly, it is obvious that both productions focus on well-known figures, not least Adolf Eichmann, and on themes such as the struggle between good and evil. Despite these similarities, it is too much of a simplification to ascribe general validity to these similar – and in some respects superficial – expressions of an almost all-encompassing universalist and/or Americanized way of describing and understanding the Nazi genocide. The film and television scholar Glen Creeber makes an important point about dramas set in historical settings, dramas such as *Roots* and *Holocaust* and, we might add, *Wallenberg: A Hero's Story* and *Good Evening, Mr. Wallenberg*. Creeber stresses that the people behind productions of this kind 'are extremely conscious and sometimes even self-conscious about the way in which they are representing history, offering a version of the past that is implicitly aimed at and constructed for a contemporary, frequently nationally based, mass audience'.[215]

---

214 See e.g. Lynn Simross, 'Holocaust survivors record act of heroism: Eyewitness recalls Raoul Wallenberg's exploits during war', *The Los Angeles Times*, 7 April 1985; James H. Tolpin, 'Memory of Raoul Wallenberg refreshed by tv miniseries', *Sun Sentinel*, 9 April 1985.

215 Creeber, *Serial Television*, p. 23.

If we view these types of productions as possessing the potential to be relevant to both international and national audiences, it is clear that many considerations contribute to the way in which the history of the Holocaust in Hungary is portrayed on screen. For example, the Italian broadcaster RAI's television series *Perlasca – An Italian Hero*, also called *Perlasca – The Courage of a Just Man* (2002), helped to make Giorgio Perlasca known outside Italy, while also becoming an element of an ongoing domestic debate about the legacy of Fascism and Italian guilt. That Perlasca had begun to distance himself from Fascism even before the outbreak of the Second World War, and that he – along with Carl Lutz, Raoul Wallenberg, and others – made major efforts to rescue Jews, helped him to become an Italian equivalent of Oskar Schindler. The television series brought 'the good Italian' to life.[216]

The national interpretative patterns become even more evident in a comparison between *Perlasca – An Italian Hero / Perlasca – The Courage of a Just Man* and the Spanish-produced *The Angel of Budapest* (2011). Both television series are set in roughly the same period, but it is not only their protagonists who differ. The latter production focuses not on Perlasca, but on the Spanish diplomat Ángel Sanz Briz and his issuing of over 5,200 Spanish identity documents to Hungarian Jews. It is not just the fact that the encounters between Perlasca and Sanz Briz are portrayed in radically different ways. Whereas in the Italian version Perlasca more or less co-opts the Spanish Legation in order to enable more rescue operations, in the Spanish version he humbly asks for protection. Even with its emphasis on Perlasca as the good Italian and its concealment of the Fascist context, the Italian series named after him clearly has a different tone and emphasis. It features failures, violence, and brutality, in contrast to the Spanish production, in which most of the people being persecuted are rescued by a thoroughly good representative of Christian – and Spanish – values.[217]

*Wallenberg: A Hero's Story* was created at the transition point between, on the one hand, films and television series which – in the wake of the Vietnam War and the Watergate scandal – challenged notions of both a glorious past and present-day successes, and, on the other hand, the Reagan era's nationalistic desire for revenge,

---

216 Perra, 'Legitimizing Fascism through the Holocaust?', pp. 95–109.
217 Serfőző, 'Angel Sanz Briz and Giorgio Perlasca', pp. 257–273.

manifested on cinema and television screens.[218] Anyone who saw Richard Chamberlain's Wallenberg need not be surprised for one second that the real Wallenberg was awarded the honorific designation of 'Righteous Among the Nations'. By acting selflessly and fearlessly in a highly dangerous situation, the fictional version of the US-funded Swede linked back to 'the good war myth'. This myth had been established during Franklin D. Roosevelt's presidency, when his speeches continually alluded to values and vocabulary that revived the notion of American exceptionalism: the United States was 'God's chosen nation', as well as 'a righteous nation opposing evil in the world'.[219] Such a self-image, according to which American virtues without exception stand in stark contrast to Nazi German ones, had led the United States to join in the struggle to defeat Hitler and his followers once and for all. Against such a backdrop, *Wallenberg: A Hero's Story* reflected a long-influential American view that the Holocaust makes clear

> what it means *not* to be American. Unlike blacks and Native Americans, the Jews did not suffer in the United States but can see it as the place of their rebirth, which makes Holocaust memory less suited for criticism of this country than the memory of the sufferings of these other groups.[220]

*Good Evening, Mr. Wallenberg* is one of a small number of Swedish-funded films and television series connected to the Holocaust. It fits into an overall pattern in the period from the immediate post-war years up until our own 2020s, a period during which Swedish film and television productions set against the backdrop of the Second World War are easily counted. The productions that do exist usually feature themes rooted in the war years as well as a strong ability to survive, such as outsidership, soldiers on guard, and the defence of national independence – the audience success of the 1973 television series *Någonstans i Sverige* ['Somewhere in Sweden'] constituting a prime example.[221]

Kjell Grede's starting point was radically different and is best described as a moral use of history in the course of which previously

---

218 Zander, *Clio på bio*, pp. 83–117.
219 Zietsma, '"Sin Has No History"', p. 534.
220 Alm, 'Holocaust Memory in America and Europe', p. 506.
221 Zander, 'World War II at 24 Frames a Second – Scandinavian Examples', pp. 207–225; Zander, 'På vakt eller på krigsstigen?', pp. 23–41; Hedling, '*Somewhere in Sweden*', pp. 237–251.

concealed wrongs come to the surface. In this case, it was not least the transition period, which encompassed the fall of the Berlin Wall and the end of the Cold War, that fuelled debates about the past. The fact that Grede and his film crew had received the Hungarian authorities' blessing to film *Good Evening, Mr. Wallenberg* on the spot was a major breakthrough, as these events formed a shameful chapter in Hungary's history. Engagements with aspects of Swedish history were significant as well. These were sparked in part by much-debated books about Sweden and the Holocaust by the US historian Steven Koblik, and the Swedish journalist Maria-Pia Boëthius's book about Sweden and the Second World War, *Heder och samvete* ['Honour and conscience']. In Sweden there had long been a reluctance to deal with the dark shadows of the Second World War, something the director described as being typically Swedish: 'We Swedes know everything – but have not experienced anything.' One concrete aspect of such an attitude, he continued, was that the next generation was being duped. Rather than being conveyed via complex figures such as Wallenberg, the history of the Second World War was retold in black and white by placing heroes and villains like Winston Churchill and Adolf Hitler in the foreground. Grede's opinion did not prevent him from categorizing Wallenberg 'as one of the few heroes of the Second World War, a person who transcends limits set by others, who saves thousands of lives, at constant risk to his own'.[222]

*Good Evening, Mr. Wallenberg* was a sign of its time. True, it did not reach a large international audience, but it did constitute a response to the international attention paid to Wallenberg. Then, as now, neutrality and non-alignment were no longer self-evident Swedish tenets. It hence seemed to be more than a coincidence that a film was made in which the protagonist is a Swede who voluntarily – and at great cost – becomes an active participant who makes a difference in one of the darkest chapters of the Second World War. Wallenberg as portrayed by Skarsgård thereby anticipated the events of the 1990s. As a new member of the European Union, Sweden retroactively wrote itself into the Second World War. A few years later, via the Living History Forum, Sweden became an

---

222 Ricki Neuman, 'Kjell Grede: Att göra upp med sin historia' (interview with Kjell Grede), *Judisk Krönika*, 1990:4, 26–28. On the Swedish debates about the Second World War and the Holocaust, see Zander, *Fornstora dagar, moderna tider*, pp. 445–455 and Zander, '*Holocaust* at the Limits', pp. 277–283.

international actor in terms of information and education about the Holocaust as well as in relation to the late twentieth- and early twenty-first-century memory politics of commemoration, which so often related to, or emanated from, that genocide.

From this reasoning, it follows that every country and every period will have the Wallenberg, Schindler, Perlasca, Sanz Briz, or other role model from the past who is relevant to the moment, but who also belongs within the framework set by national history cultures and international trends on how the Holocaust can and should be represented. If the planned new Swedish television series about Raoul Wallenberg comes to fruition, we may reasonably assume that we will recognize him and his deeds. It is equally certain that the motives for his actions in Second World War Budapest will be adapted to the values of the 2020s.

# Chapter 6
# The immortalized Raoul Wallenberg

In February 2022, one of Sweden's leading daily newspapers published an interview with Jeanette Gustafsdotter, the Social Democratic government's Minister for Culture and Democracy. Conducted by the playwright, author, and cultural journalist Stina Oscarson, the interview attracted much attention in the following few days, mainly because of the newly appointed Minister's many vague and contradictory answers. One of them came after Oscarson queried how Gustafsdotter felt about the iconoclastic demonstrations of recent years, with statues being toppled from their pedestals because the exalted historical figures did not fit in with today's values. The Minister replied that on the one hand it was correct to remove a statue if the immortalized individual had violated human rights, but on the other hand she was adamant that 'we should not erase history'.[1]

As Oscarson noted, one problem in this context was that politicians need to find solutions to this kind of dilemma by translating lofty slogans about human rights into concrete policies. Gustafsdotter probably had difficulty answering the question

---

1 Stina Oscarson, 'Stina Oscarson till kulturministern: Varför duckar du?', *Svenska Dagbladet*, published on *SvD*'s website on 10 February and in the printed paper on 13 February 2022. See also Adam Cwejman, 'Medieanpassade politiker lär sig inte tänka', *Göteborgs-Posten*, 11 February 2022; Magdalena Andersson, 'Kulturministern har kronisk nybörjarotur', *Expressen*, 11 February 2022; Nina Solomin, 'Kulturministern tycks bara brinna för en sak', *Svenska Dagbladet*, 17 February 2022; Elina Haimi, 'Kulturministern hade fått frågorna i mycket god tid' (interview with Stina Oscarson), *Svenska Dagbladet*, 17 February 2022; Olle Svenning, 'Oscarson avslöjar även sin egen inkompetens', *Aftonbladet*, 17 February 2022; Ida Ölmedal, 'Det duger inte, kulturministern!', *Sydsvenskan*, 20 February 2022.

because she perceived no relevant difference between today's values and the era of the nineteenth and early twentieth centuries, when memorials were being erected every five minutes on the basis that those worthy of remembrance represented the nation or some value associated with it. While defending human rights and/or opposing slavery could certainly be examples of such values, they were by no means the most highly prioritized ones.

The Minister was subsequently credited with a phenomenon known as 'Schrödinger's statue', to the effect that 'it is just as right to remove objectionable art as to leave it standing'.[2] What she captured with her ambiguous reply – albeit unintentionally – was the inherent dilemma linked to statues and monuments. They have rarely, if ever, been apolitical. Before their models are cast in bronze or carved in stone, the proposals and models are the subject of heated discussions, which result in compromises and sometimes even conflicting symbols in the same monument. During the last decades of the nineteenth century and the first decades of the twentieth, there were attempts to make the final form of a monument rise above the debates that had preceded its ceremonial dedication. Once the drapery had been removed from the statues made of durable materials, the intention was to demonstrate that the individual(s) or thing they depicted represented eternal values. In the original and educative meaning of the word 'didactics', the proponents of monuments from the late eighteenth to the early twentieth century stressed the social benefit of these exalted role models. The idea was that they would serve as enduring textbooks. The edifying and unambiguous messages conveyed via the statues would actively contribute to making the viewers better citizens.[3]

As history has repeatedly shown, however, values are rarely eternal. One result is that the ideals of what constitutes a good citizen have shifted over time and space. Today's democratic societies do not prize either the one-dimensional soldier heroes of the past or totalitarian ideologies and their aesthetic ideals. Consequently, the monument genre has fallen out of favour compared with the obsession with statues that prevailed around the turn of the last century. The fact that monuments were an important tool in the service of nationalist rulers, whether in democracies or

---

2 Erik Helmerson, 'Ministern borde se "Vita huset"', *Dagens Nyheter*, 19 February 2022.
3 Zander, 'Läroböcker i sten' and sources cited there, p. 109.

dictatorships, contributed to the decline in the genre's reputation. In addition, the potential of statues to influence people has been downplayed, at least in Western democracies. One history-cultural explanation is that in today's society, other channels such as film, television, and the internet have the greatest impact when it comes to communicating the past. The declining popularity of monuments is probably also a result of changing ideals of art and artists. It is true that hard-to-interpret symbols and messages have often been part of monuments, but – for the didactic reasons mentioned above – the main message has almost always been obvious. The monuments of the nineteenth and early twentieth centuries aimed to freeze time, to transform the depicted person or thing into symbols that all citizens had the same image of and relationship to. In the twentieth century, the trend went in a different direction. Modern art theorists usually reject the idea that art can or should be described as a uniform and coherent phenomenon. A common objective in art today is to challenge the viewer's expectations with works that are complex and ambiguous in both form and content.[4]

One history-cultural lesson is that monuments, like the people and events they commemorate, may retain their symbolic meanings; but they may lose them, too, or acquire new ones. The result may be that bronzed role models are permitted to remain standing unchallenged, even though they represent values that are no longer considered relevant.[5] Other monuments become politically activated and reinterpreted. The result has been that some statues are highly visible while also becoming anonymous anomalies in modern democracies. Others are controversial from the outset or may be given new functions, though rarely as creatively as when the German artist and curator Christian Jankowski, as part of the art project *Heavy Weight History* (2013), enlisted Polish wrestlers to try lifting monuments in Warsaw. The fact that many of the statues that were erected when Poland was a Communist nation were easy to topple – unlike, for example, the statue of Ronald Reagan, who is regarded as the politician who guaranteed Poland's most recent national independence – was appreciated by the wrestlers and audiences alike. The conclusion was not so obvious when

---

4 See e.g. Drucker and Cathcart, 'The Hero as a Communication Phenomenon', especially pp. 112–124, and von Osten, 'Producing Publics – Making Worlds!', p. 259.
5 Klas Rönnbäck, 'En amputerad historia', *Ord & Bild*, 2008:4, 59.

monuments commemorating the Holocaust proved impossible to dislocate, because they illustrated a history that involved both Christian and Jewish Poles as well as Germans in a complex and still contentious context.[6]

The philosopher Susan Neiman reminds us that '[i]f monuments are values made visible, it's likely you ignore the ones around you. Values are most visible when they're under threat'.[7] With this in mind, it is clear why some monuments have been forgotten at one point in time only to become highly controversial the next. Among many examples are Sweden's kings from the country's era as a Great Power, which in retrospect fit poorly with the self-image of a peace- and neutrality-loving nation, and the Confederate generals of the American Civil War, who, apart from their military successes, have increasingly come to be seen as representatives of a system of slavery and white supremacy that continues to make its presence felt in the United States. Another illustrative example is the Bronze Soldier of Tallinn. To many Estonians, this monument was a reminder of the lengthy Soviet occupation, and its city-centre location interrupted the line of monuments and memorials marking the struggle of Estonians for freedom and independence. By contrast, many Russians in Estonia associated the statue with the Red Army's dearly bought victory over Nazi Germany in 1941–1945. Yet another challenge for the Russian minority in Estonia was the design of the basement of the nearby Museum of Occupations and Freedom in Tallinn. Statues of Soviet dignitaries, many of them mutilated, still stand there today next to the public toilets. Members of the Russian-speaking population of Estonia objected to both these developments, saying that, like the move of the Bronze Soldier to a military cemetery on the outskirts of Tallinn, the placement of the statues in the museum basement was an insult to the history associated primarily with the Soviet Union and its main successor state, Russia.[8]

## Holocaust memorial places and non-places

A way of dealing with the memory of the Holocaust has been, and still is, to erect monuments. One purpose has been to pay tribute

---

6 Zander, 'The Footprints Frighten Me', pp. 86–89.
7 Neiman, *Learning from the Germans*, p. 266.
8 Burch and Zander, 'Preoccupied by the Past', pp. 53–73; Zander, 'Läroböcker i sten', pp. 122–123.

to and honour the people who saved Jews and others whom the Nazis considered 'undesirable'. However, the events of the Second World War, and the Holocaust in particular, made it impossible for many artists to continue 'to affirm an unproblematic continuity between the past and the present, between history and identity', as the Swedish art historian Max Liljefors has observed.[9] Some monuments erected to the memory of the victims of the Nazi genocide do draw on well-established forms of representation. Many depictions of the Holocaust are dominated by a small number of motifs and symbols, such as mothers and children, barbed wire, people filled with fear and anguish or indomitable resistance, references to the Old Testament or crucifixions, and variations on the theme of the struggle between good and evil.[10]

Other artists have approached the Holocaust with the aim of challenging the prevailing conventions. The resulting 'counter-monuments' are, on the one hand, based on the original functions of conventional monuments, which may be summed up as the objectives of classical antiquity according to which monuments should commemorate, remind, and teach. On the other hand, the designers of counter-monuments have sought to create contrasts to conventional monuments. Applying different design languages and technical solutions, they want to demonstrate the voids left by the victims of the Second World War in urban and cultural landscapes. The artists also accept that this will happen at the expense of their works' visibility.[11] Works such as these, produced mainly during the 1980s, were part of the *Vergangenheitsbewältigung* – the work of coping with the past – that has been a key feature in West Germany and the unified Germany at least since the 1970s.

At the same time as new perspectives have emerged in the arts, traditional needs and functions have remained strong. This is particularly true of the spotlighting of figures such as Oskar Schindler and Raoul Wallenberg. However, both the people who helped to save their fellow human beings from genocide and the places where the mass murders took place are associated with oblivion as well as remembrance. As James Young has pointed out, at the end of the war the concentration and extermination camps were places linked with violence and death, but they themselves could

---

9 Liljefors, 'The Interplay of Memory and Amnesia', p. 48.
10 Amishai-Maisels, *Depiction and Interpretation*, pp. 131–242.
11 Young, *The Texture of Memory*, pp. 27–48.

not speak. Although the camps remained as constant reminders in the landscape, the memory of them faded. Deliberate work was required to re-establish the links between then and now.[12] Such attempts at collective remembrance have not guaranteed continued attention, though. The coverage of the Nuremberg Trials of 1945–1946 emphasized the importance of Auschwitz on a number of occasions. However, the camp lost influence as a symbol of Nazi genocide in the West until the 1960s. This was mainly due to its having been liberated by the Red Army, whereas British and American encounters with the packed concentration camps in Germany meant that continued attention was being paid after 1945 to the media-famous concentration camps of Bergen-Belsen, Buchenwald, and Dachau.[13] Over time, though, Auschwitz has increasingly become the dominant symbol of Nazi genocide. Whereas the other extermination camps were pulled down by the Nazis to conceal what had happened there, Auschwitz was left in a relatively undamaged state after the war. Moreover, during the Cold War there were various political and ideological reasons in both Eastern and Western Europe for making Auschwitz a central memorial site, which required not only the re-creation of the camp but also reprioritization and new construction.[14] The result is that Auschwitz is now a concrete place and a symbol which has been given the function of summing up the Holocaust: '"Auschwitz" is to the "Holocaust" what "Graceland" is to "Elvis"', as Tim Cole described the history-cultural significance of the camp.[15]

It is partly because of Auschwitz's near-iconic status that those aspects of the Holocaust which did not occur in camps have had difficulty asserting themselves in post-war history culture. In the former Soviet Union, at least 1.5 million Jews and other Soviet citizens were executed by the *Einsatzgruppen* that followed on the heels of the regular German troops during their invasion of the Soviet Union. Some of the sites of these mass murders have received greater attention in recent years, but many of them remain suppressed, reduced to 'non-places' or 'trauma sites' of memory, to use the

---

12 Young, *The Texture of Memory*, p. 119.
13 Holmila, *Reporting the Holocaust in the British, Swedish and Finnish Press, 1945–50*, pp. 21–24, 104.
14 See e.g. Novick, *The Holocaust in American Life*, pp. 63–66, 93–94, 122; Shandler, *While America Watches*, pp. 11–13, 16–18; Cole, *Holocaust City*, pp. 221–223.
15 Cole, *Selling the Holocaust*, p. 98.

terminology of historian Dominick LaCapra.[16] The importance of continuing to search for and draw attention to such sites is obvious, given that the perpetrators both carried out physical murders and went to great lengths to erase many of the victims from written sources and thus from memory. The sites of actual extermination, regardless of whether they are now infamous and well-known extermination camps such as Auschwitz-Birkenau or an overgrown ravine in Ukraine, should be highlighted in the future in order to counteract the extermination policy of the perpetrators. Research and education are important components of such work, as are the construction and maintenance of monuments and memorials.[17]

## Holocaust monuments and Wallenberg statues

The story of Wallenberg and monuments encompasses – using the terminology of Henry Rousso – personal, cultural, and official memorials, and these have not necessarily had to have any geographical connection with the places where he has since been remembered and celebrated. More than 30 monuments have been erected in his honour in a dozen countries. Tanja Schult's review in *A Hero's Many Faces: Raoul Wallenberg in Contemporary Monuments* (2009) illustrates that monuments to Wallenberg are not constructed according to a uniform template. He has been portrayed as a rescuer, diplomat, prisoner, and victim, personifying desirable qualities such as courage, humanity, and hope.[18]

In a number of cases, the artists' own experiences have made powerful contributions to the design of the artworks. Gustav Kraitz was a student at the Hungarian Royal Drawing School and Art Teachers' College in Budapest at the same time as Wallenberg was operating in the city. At the end of the war, Kraitz was captured by Soviet troops and sent as a prisoner to the Soviet Union. After five years, he returned to Hungary but became disillusioned with the Communist dictatorship. Kraitz managed to escape to Sweden in 1956. He included points of contact between himself and Wallenberg in the monument *Hope*.[19]

---

16 LaCapra, *History and Memory after Auschwitz*, p. 10.
17 See Lower, *The Ravine*, p. 20.
18 Schult, *A Hero's Many Faces*, passim.
19 Eva Dandanelle, 'Kraitz gestaltar hoppet', *Konstperspektiv*, 2001:1, 34–36; Mattias Karlsson, 'Gustav Kraitz: Skapar för FN och Malmö', *Sydsvenskan*, 30 March 2006.

Created by Kraitz, together with his wife Ulla, the artwork was inaugurated in New York in 1998. *Hope* is an example of how monuments must be placed in both their spatial and temporal contexts. When Dag Sebastian Ahlander, then Swedish cultural attaché in New York, had the idea of trying to put Sweden on the map in the city, Raoul Wallenberg was his first choice. That Ahlander received a large and fairly rapid response was due not least to the process analysed in the previous chapter. Wallenberg, by then well known, conveyed laudable human qualities while constituting a good Swedish example with which many Americans were familiar, and to which they responded favourably.[20] It did not hurt that the successful businessman Marcus Storch – son of Gilel Storch, who did much to save Jews at the end of the Second World War and who had chaired the Swedish branch of the Jewish World Congress – made a substantial donation.[21] The monument, with features such as pillar-like stone obelisks that resemble traditional elements of the genre, also brings to mind fire-damaged chimneys. Other key features were paving stones taken from the Jewish ghetto in Budapest plus a bronze briefcase bearing Wallenberg's initials. A tangible reminder of his activities as a diplomat, the briefcase also reminded viewers that his efforts to rescue persecuted people had been a result of negotiations at his desk as well as of hands-on rescue operations in railway stations, in protected houses, and elsewhere.[22]

The placement of the work in the immediate vicinity of the UN building facilitated understanding of the monument's dual message. Although *Hope* is based on the tragedy that occurred in Budapest in 1944–1945, it also expresses the hope that this history will not be repeated and that we will have a brighter future. It may be a coincidence, but the message that it is vital to be prepared to fight evil, as Wallenberg was, is reinforced by the fact that a work of art depicting St George's battle against the dragon is located opposite *Hope*. As we shall see in greater detail later, the latter symbol has been used before to represent Wallenberg's fight against the Nazis.

---

20 Ahlander, 'The History of the Monument', pp. 9–11, and the interview with Dag Sebastian Ahlander by Ulf Zander, 14 April 2004. See also Schult, *A Hero's Many Faces*, pp. 203–219.
21 Annie Maccoby Berglof, 'Lasting monuments', *The Financial Times*, 1 October 2011.
22 David Finn, *Hope*, pp. 9–11.

Another sculpture that has been in the immediate vicinity of the UN building since 1988 is Swedish artist Carl Fredrik Reuterswärd's *Non-Violence*, also known as *The Knotted Gun*. The titles are apt given that the work's revolver is unusable because its barrel has been tied in a knot. As the German cultural writer Thomas Steinfeld has stated, the sculpture can be read as a symbol of non-violence with particular relevance to Sweden, given the country's 200-year history of peace together with a foreign policy that has for long periods been conducted under the slogans of non-alignment and neutrality. The placement of the work outside the UN building is also a reminder of the post-war Swedish combination of neutrality and internationalism, which has been manifested not least in a strong involvement in supranational organizations, including the United Nations and its sub-organizations.[23]

This interpretation may be complemented on the basis of the spatial proximity between *Hope* and *Non-Violence*. With Wallenberg as a telling example, it has been possible for Sweden to combine aspects contained in both works of art: the ideals of neutrality and peace, and at the same time active participation in the Second World War. It is also easy to recall the oft-repeated depiction in words and images of Raoul Wallenberg as a man who did have a revolver at hand in wartime Budapest, but who chose to fight his enemies using different and inherently non-warlike weapons, and who did so with great success.

The present chapter is not a survey that claims to cover most of the large number of Wallenberg monuments that exist in many parts of the world. For such a review, the interested reader is referred to the above-mentioned doctoral thesis by Tanja Schult. Her comprehensive analysis of monuments dedicated to Raoul Wallenberg has both breadth and depth, with a particular focus on their art-historical and cultural-historical aspects. In what follows I will draw on many of her findings, but also complement them with political-ideological and history-cultural perspectives, using two Hungarian and two Swedish Wallenberg monuments as points of departure. Unlike previous researchers in the field, I have been able to benefit from the Swedish archival material on the Wallenberg case, which was classified for a long time, and which frequently includes issues and problems related to Wallenberg monuments.

---

23 Thomas Steinfeld, 'Det neutrala Sverige var en fredlig zon i en hejdlöst våldsam värld', *Dagens Nyheter*, 24 April 2022.

## Wallenberg as a snake killer

A common conclusion drawn by adherents of the Polish-British historian Isaac Deutscher is that the majority of Jews who were active Communists in post-war Eastern Europe abandoned their Jewish identity, either voluntarily or under duress, to become 'non-Jewish Jews'.[24] A relevant factor here is that during the period between the world wars, which was characterized by growing anti-Jewish sentiment, some Jews in Hungary had concluded that rallying behind Communist slogans was a new and implicitly better opportunity to become integrated into Hungarian society. The question is, however, whether this was merely a matter of a shift in identity. Jews in the Communist Party could to some extent combine political involvement with Jewish issues, the latter regularly being couched in Communist linguistic terms. According to this idiom, 'the Jewish question' was intimately connected with capitalism. The conclusion was therefore that the demise of capitalism as a social system would entail the evaporation of Jewish vulnerability. Such a forward-looking approach attracted many Jews who, unsurprisingly, looked back on the past with horror. Their support of a Hungary which was at least on the surface freed of antisemitism and the persecution of Jews, nationalism, and class antagonism, constituted a total identification with the Party and the 'movement'.[25]

For István Szirmai, who made his political career in the Hungarian Communist Party, this meant willingly endorsing the official position, which included a radical criticism of Zionism. His reluctance to openly discuss the Holocaust and Jewish issues unrelated to Zionism was probably not only, or even primarily, an expression of his having become a 'non-Jewish Jew'. Rather, recurring post-war elements of antisemitism, also noticeable within the Communist Party, were a recurring reminder of his Jewish origins, whether he wished it or not.[26]

Many aspects of the Jewish presence in Hungary are certainly gone forever. As in many other parts of Europe, Jewish architects exerted a great influence on the urban landscape in Budapest and many other Hungarian cities. One reason why the Jewish elements are hard to spot is that they were concrete expressions of

---

24 Deutscher, 'The Non-Jewish Jew', pp. 25–41.
25 Kovács, 'The Jewish Question in Contemporary Hungary', pp. 210–212.
26 Bohus, 'István Szirmai between Communism and Zionism', pp. 409–426.

a Jewish bourgeoisie who worked hard to be recognized for their contributions as Hungarian citizens. In view of this ambition, it is instead buildings and places associated with Jewish identity and religious practice that are conspicuous in today's cityscape. The former ghetto in Budapest is now a memorial site, equipped with monuments and information signs.[27]

The traces of Raoul Wallenberg have become very evident, too. In guidebooks to the Hungarian capital, locations of his activities and also monuments and memorials to him are listed as must-see sights.[28] This was not always the case. Wallenberg is a concrete example of how Jewish history and the memory of the Holocaust were controversial elements in Hungarian historiography before and after the Communists came to power in 1948. A few years later, a show trial was prepared to 'prove' that Wallenberg had not been taken to the Soviet Union. It claimed that he had instead been murdered in Budapest by 'cosmopolitan Zionists'. The trial was in line with Stalin's then ongoing anti-Zionist offensive. The leading Jewish figures of László Benedek, Miksa Domonkos, and Lajos Stöckler, as well as Pál Szalai and Károly Szabó, who had been among the last to meet Wallenberg before his disappearance, were arrested and tortured to ensure that they provided information in line with the anti-Jewish interpretation. Owing to Stalin's death in March 1953, the execution of NKVD chief Lavrenity Beria in December that same year, and the de-Stalinization that followed their deaths, the trial was cancelled. Domonkos died shortly afterwards. Stöckler suffered life-long injuries from the torture he had endured.[29]

The show trial was followed by a general oblivion imposed by the Communist rulers, both with regard to Wallenberg himself and in respect of many of the buildings and places in Budapest where the Holocaust had taken place. In the Soviet version of the Great Patriotic War, it was mainly Soviet citizens who had fallen victim to Nazism. This idea had consequences for views of the Holocaust. As in other parts of Soviet-dominated Eastern Europe, Jews – including

---

27 Cole, *Holocaust City*, pp. 226–244; Frojimovies, Komoróczy, Pusztai, and Strbik, *Jewish Budapest*, pp. 3–17, 42–49, 105–113, 468–476.
28 See e.g. Nylén, *Budapest bortom turiststråken*, pp. 83–94.
29 Szita, *The Power of Humanity*, pp. 138–140; Károl Szábo, 'Show trial preparations 1953 in Budapest', Searching for Raoul Wallenberg, www.raoul-wallenberg.eu/testimony/show-trial-preparations-1953-in-Hungary (accessed 27 January 2020).

those who had lived in the Soviet Union and been murdered by the Germans and their allies – were excluded from the narrative of the Nazi genocide, so as not to distract attention from Soviet suffering. Nor was the fact that Wallenberg had been seen in the company of Soviet soldiers before his disappearance mentioned in the text of an official monument.[30]

These decrees contrasted with proposals and contributions made in the early post-war years. Many of the Jews who had survived the persecutions in Hungary were keen to keep the memory of Wallenberg alive. One concrete and early expression of this desire was the painting of his portrait, which now hangs in the Swedish National Portrait Gallery at Gripsholm Castle near Stockholm. In Budapest a plaque was set up with a text commemorating his achievements, and a street was named after him. Survivors also arranged a memorial concert in 1946. At this time, too, another Swede who took part in the rescue operations, Valdemar Langlet, called for a monument in honour of Wallenberg in the Hungarian capital.[31] In September 1945, the Swedish press reported that such a monument was being planned.[32] The background was that some of the city's Jews, who had started a collection for a Wallenberg monument, had commissioned the sculptor and art professor Pál Pátzay to design one. He had hidden Jews during the war, and while in Budapest he had met Wallenberg, who saved him and his friends from deportation to an extermination camp.[33] Eager to pay tribute to Wallenberg, he accepted the assignment. The work, called *The Snake Killer*, was inspired by French and Italian neoclassicism, contained references to St George and the dragon, and portrayed an energetic, muscular, and naked man in bronze. He is fighting a symbolic battle against evil, represented in the monument by a snake, which he tramples down with his left foot and holds in a firm grip with his left hand while he is in the process of striking a blow at the head of the beast with the

---

30 Henry Kamm, 'Wallenberg: Statue rises in Budapest', *The New York Times*, 15 April 1987; Cole, *Holocaust City*, p. 233. For a comprehensive discussion of the unwillingness to discuss the Jewish victims of the Holocaust in Soviet-dominated Eastern Europe, see Karlsson, *Med folkmord i fokus*, pp. 38–41.
31 Langlet, *Verk och dagar i Budapest*, p. 149.
32 'Raoul Wallenberg får staty i Budapest', *Göteborgs Handels- och Sjöfartstidning*, 28 September 1945.
33 For his contributions to saving Jews during the Second World War, Pátzay was honoured as a 'Righteous Among the Nations' by Yad Vashem in 1998.

weapon he holds in his right hand. An inscription on the pedestal states that the man fighting the snake is Wallenberg.[34]

In his 1948 biography of Wallenberg, Jenő Lévai predicted that the inauguration was imminent. The statue would 'bear witness to future generations about this great son of the Swedish nation and about his legendary work – the rescue of hundreds of thousands of human lives. The monument will stand there on the banks of the Danube, proclaiming that without his work the waves of the Danube would have carried with them tens of thousands more mutilated corpses.'[35] However, it turned out that Lévai's assurance was premature. Owing to Wallenberg's disappearance, the Swedish diplomat was a much more sensitive subject in Moscow than in Budapest. The three-metre-high monument was placed in Szent István Park, where Jews had been taken for sorting during the 1944 deportations.[36] But it was never unveiled. The Communists in Hungary had been working for years to weaken other parties. Applying methodical 'salami tactics', they undermined their political opponents bit by bit.[37] In 1949, the Communists finally gained the upper hand. The result was a far greater readiness to accommodate Soviet wishes. One of these was that reminders of Wallenberg were not desirable, and even less so when the artist involved was regarded by the Communists as a liberal-minded Social Democrat. The night before the inauguration ceremony the statue disappeared. Witnesses reported that it was dismantled with the help of horses and ropes, probably on the orders of the Hungarian secret police who wanted to demonstrate their loyalty to the Soviet Union.[38]

In 1953 the monument reappeared in front of a medical facility in Debrecen, but the inscription had been removed. However, the memory of the original monument remained alive. For example, a picture of it together with a portrait of Wallenberg adorned

---

34 Where nothing else is stated, the interpretation of the monument is based on Schult, *A Hero's Many Faces*, pp. 81–95. It has been repeatedly asserted that the snake bore swastikas on its head – information which Schult denies.
35 Lévai, *Raoul Wallenberg, hjälten i Budapest*, pp. 259–260.
36 Langlet, *Kaos i Budapest*, pp. 51–55.
37 Hägglöf, *Det andra Europa*, pp. 156–158.
38 Jan Gerd, 'Wallenbergs minne lever i Ungern', *Bohuslänningen*, 29 March 1979; Fowkes, 'Monumental Sculpture in Post-War Eastern Europe, 1945–1960', pp. 24–25, 40–45, 201.

the stationery of the Israeli Raoul Wallenberg Committee.[39] The Swedish press referred repeatedly to Pátzay's artwork, often in combination with photographs of his model, complete with the inscription citing Wallenberg's achievements.[40] In conjunction with the Soviet crushing of the 1956 uprising in Hungary, a Swedish editorial writer suggested that even though there was no statue of Wallenberg, it was not hard to imagine a different kind of monument inspired by his achievements: 'That monument we see before us, that monument we can erect through actions undertaken in the spirit of Raoul Wallenberg. The opportunity is offered in the form of aid to Hungary, the scene of Wallenberg's humanitarian efforts.'[41]

## 'A monument never without flowers'

In Hungary, with its vivid memories of the devastation the country had suffered in the final years of the Second World War and during the 1956 uprising, there was a great need to commemorate role models from the past from the late 1980s onwards. This need was particularly evident with regard to those individuals who had not been elevated to a pedestal, or who had been forced down from one during the Communist era. One illustrative example is the case of Imre Nagy, head of government during the Hungarian Revolution. After the 1956 uprising, he became *persona non grata* in Hungary. He was rehabilitated in 1989 and his remains reburied on 16 June 1989 with full honours in the presence of 100,000 Hungarians on the thirty-first anniversary of his execution. The next step was the erection of a monument to his memory. The commission went to Támas Varga, son of Imre Varga. That Nagy had been invisible in Hungarian history for more than 30 years probably contributed to

---

39 Such stationery can be found in RA, Raoul Wallenbergföreningens arkiv, E1:1. Korrespondens, Huvudserie 1979, A–H.
40 See e.g. Rudolph Philipp, 'Lever Raoul Wallenberg – människokärlekens partisan?', *Året Runt*, 1947:25, 9; Rudolph Philipp, 'Raoul Wallenberg lever', *Vi*, 1955:2, 9; Hugo Valentin, 'En partisan i mänsklighetens tjänst: Anförande vid Konserthusmötet den 11 jan. 1948', *Judisk Tidskrift*, 1948:1, 6; 'Alla anständiga människor känner raseri och äckel', *Dagens Nyheter*, 9 February 1957; Ivar Harrie, 'Gåtan Wallenberg', *Expressen*, 9 February 1966; Jan Gerd, 'Wallenbergs minne lever i Ungern', *Bohuslänningen*, 29 March 1979; Mats Svensén, 'Wallenberg-statyn blev varumärke för läkemedel', *Vi*, 1984:37, 12–13.
41 'Raoul Wallenberg', *Göteborgs-Posten*, 8 February 1957.

making abstract or allegorical representations of him seem unsuitable. Instead he was depicted life size, standing on a bridge. At the time of its inauguration the monument was placed in Martyrs Square, near the Parliament and also near the obelisk dedicated to the Red Army soldiers who had liberated Budapest. Tellingly, Nagy's back was turned to the latter memorial.[42]

However, the story did not end there and then. As early as 2012 representatives of the Fidesz-led government proposed moving the monument, but they had to withdraw their proposal following protests. Seven years later they made a new attempt. Under the pretext of restoring Martyrs Square to the condition it had been in from 1934 until the 1944–1945 battles, including a replica of the monument which had then stood in commemoration of those who had died during Béla Kun's short-lived 1919 republic, the Nagy monument was moved in December 2018. Some six months later it was quietly re-erected a kilometre or so from Martyrs Square.[43]

Domestic role models were not the only ones to re-enter Hungarian history culture during the new openness of the 1980s and especially the decade's second half. It was not long before Raoul Wallenberg also came up for discussion, even though Kati Marton, a US journalist with Hungarian roots, has firmly argued that Wallenberg was a non-person in Hungary at the beginning of the decade. To support her assertion, she has cited the fact that no official Hungarian enquiry had ever been made to clarify what had happened to Vilmos Langfelder, who, in addition to being Wallenberg's chauffeur, was a Hungarian citizen.[44]

However, the officially sanctioned oblivion was not all-encompassing. Although the monument in tribute to Wallenberg did not materialize after the end of the war, he was not forgotten in Hungary during the Communist era. In 1978 Péter Bacsó made a film about Wallenberg, but the Hungarian authorities banned screenings of it.[45] While visiting Hungary the following year, a Swedish journalist asked a worker in the Debrecen factory if he knew who the statue outside the factory represented. The answer was: 'If there had been a name on the statue, no one would have

---

42 James, *Imagining Postcommunism*, pp. 148–149.
43 Ábraham Váss, 'The relocation of Imre Nagy's statue draws controversy', *Hungary Today*, 8 January 2019; Ábraham Váss, 'Imre Nagy's statue silently unveiled in its new location', *Hungary Today*, 6 June 2019.
44 Marton, *Wallenberg*, pp. 210–211.
45 Szita, *The Power of Humanity*, p. 145.

thought about who he is. But now that there is no name, everyone knows who the statue represents. That man is a hero.'[46] Five years later, when staff at the Swedish Embassy in Budapest visited addresses in the city associated with Wallenberg, there was a strong response. People in the buildings usually knew about the Swedish diplomat's activities and were happy to talk about events they remembered or had heard about from others.[47] At the beginning of the 1980s, the Hungarian historian János Pótó began researching what had happened to *The Snake Killer*. Around the same time, information began to circulate that Hungarian diplomats had admitted that the statue in Debrecen depicted Wallenberg.[48] John Bierman's biography of Wallenberg, which includes a passage about Pátzay's monument and its removal, was published in 1985 in an underground *samizdat* version, most copies of which were confiscated by the Hungarian security police.[49]

At the same time, signs of a new openness were emerging. In 1984, for instance, a street in Budapest was named after Wallenberg. Prior to the meeting of the Lutheran World Federation in Budapest that same summer, it was announced that the Swedish diplomat's disappearance would be on the agenda. This did indeed happen, and church leaders raised the issue with representatives of the Hungarian government.[50] In conjunction with this meeting in Budapest David W. Preus, who was an American bishop and vice-president of the Federation, planned to lay a wreath in Wallenberg's

---

46 Jan Gerd, 'Wallenbergs minne lever i Ungern', *Bohuslänningen*, 29 March 1979.
47 Thomas Palme, 'Besök på Wallenberg-adresser i Budapest', Memorandum, 21 November 1984, RKA, Raoul Wallenberg, UD2001/00009, Vol. 22.
48 *The Guardian*, 1 September 1986. See also 'Raoul Wallenbergs staty i Debrecen', 1 September 1980, RKA, Raoul Wallenberg, UD2001/00009, Vol. 25.
49 Thomas Palme, 'Beslag av Wallenbergbok i Budapest', 23 May 1985, RKA, Raoul Wallenberg, UD2001/00009, Vol. 23; Sven Julin, 'Bok om Raoul Wallenberg', 5 July 1985, RKA, Raoul Wallenberg, UD2001/00009, Vol. 24. See also Bierman, *Righteous Gentile*, pp. 283–284; Szita, *The Power of Humanity*, p. 146.
50 'Kyrkor väntas ta upp Raoul Wallenbergs fall', *Svenska Dagbladet*, 24 July 1984; Richard Swartz, 'Lutherska världsförbundet: Ungrare splittrar öst', *Svenska Dagbladet*, 26 July 1984; 'Lutheraner frågar om Wallenberg', *Svenska Dagbladet*, 27 July 1984; Richard Swartz, 'Sverige talade om Wallenberg', *Svenska Dagbladet*, 2 August 1984; 'Wallenberg – ein Beispiel', *Napról Napra*, 2 August 1984.

memory in a private capacity. When this became known, other participants wished to take part in the ceremony, to which Preus agreed. However, the bishop soon realized that such a demonstration would be too sensitive to the Hungarian authorities, and he therefore cancelled the official memorial service. Instead, he laid a wreath at the plaque honouring Wallenberg's memory in the street named after him.[51]

1984 was also the year when a movement emerged with the aim of influencing the authorities to return *The Snake Killer* to its original location to mark the fortieth anniversary of Wallenberg's disappearance. The magazine *Historia* published a lengthy article recounting the history of the monument in late 1940s Budapest. The article was followed by a proposal in the influential daily *Magyar Nemzet* to return the statue to Budapest as a 'worthy gesture'. Nor was it long before Wallenberg was honoured by representatives of the Hungarian regime in front of both domestic and foreign guests at a rally commemorating the mass deportations of Jews carried out by the Germans and their Hungarian allies in 1944.[52] The Swedish press cited a 'well-informed source' in the Hungarian capital. The anonymous speaker suggested that the renewed interest in Wallenberg, and in particular the articles about the missing statue of him, was 'a kind of trial balloon' aimed at testing how far the Soviet authorities were willing to permit a history to be made visible that they had traditionally been unwilling to acknowledge. It soon became clear that the time was not yet ripe. This first Hungarian attempt won no support from the Soviet politicians in the Kremlin.[53]

Meanwhile the thaw in Hungary paved the way for another monument. Nicolas M. Salgo, who served as US ambassador to Hungary from 1983 to 1986, wanted to promote the erection of a monument to Wallenberg's work in Budapest. Salgo was a Hungarian Jew who had left Hungary in 1933. He had moved first to Switzerland, then to Sweden, and then to the United States.

---

51 'Wallenbergmöte avlyst' and 'Minnesplakett inte monument', *Svenska Dagbladet*, 4 and 5 August 1984.
52 Richard Swartz, 'Ungern hedrar Wallenbergs minne', *Svenska Dagbladet*, 17 May 1984; Szita, *The Power of Humanity*, p. 145.
53 Richard Swartz, 'Statyn till Budapest? Ungern vill hylla Wallenberg', *Svenska Dagbladet*, 5 May 1984; Eric Bourne, 'Soviets quash a Hungarian proposal to honor Wallenberg', *The Christian Science Monitor*, 8 May 1984.

A collector of Hungarian art, he had been married to a Swede and was well acquainted with Wallenberg's story. In 1985 he asked his friend, the Pátzay student Imre Varga, if he would dare to create a monument to Wallenberg. The artist's previous works included a large monument to Béla Kun's short-lived Hungarian Soviet Republic of 1919. According to Salgo, Varga was a community-minded but apolitical artist who enjoyed considerable artistic and political prestige in Hungary. When, in the early 2000s, Varga looked back to the creation of the Wallenberg monument, he claimed that he had agreed to do the commission almost immediately after being asked.[54] The contemporaneous diplomatic material presents a partly different picture, though. According to those papers, Varga was initially hesitant but soon showed interest in the project, whereupon he prepared a proposal for a monument. When the sketch was finished Salgo contacted Thomas Palme, who worked at the Swedish embassy in Budapest from 1981 to 1986, in order to gain his support. The American ambassador, who was on good terms with Ronald Reagan, was sure that the US President would favour the idea, but Salgo was reluctant to seek his overt support, as it would risk scuppering the whole project.[55]

Looking back 27 years later, Thomas Palme portrayed the process of putting Varga's monument in place as being fast and smooth. It had not taken long to go from Salgo's discussions with the Wallenberg family and the mayor of Budapest, through the enlistment of Varga, to the Swedish government's approval of the monument's inauguration.[56] But diplomatic correspondence from the mid-1980s paints a different picture. The many foreign-policy complications predicted by diplomat Jan Eliasson, later a Social Democratic Minister for Foreign Affairs, resulted in a decision

---

54 Eric Sjöquist, *Dramat Raoul Wallenberg*, p. 231, and Schult, *A Hero's Many Faces*, p. 157, base their information on interviews with the artist in the first decade of the twenty-first century.

55 Ragnar Dromberg, 'Wallenberg restitutus?', secret report to Jan Eliasson, 5 March 1986, Ragnar Dromberg, 'Wallenberg restitutus – än en gång' 21 May 1986, RKA, Raoul Wallenberg, UD2001/00009, Vol. 26; Ragnar Dromberg, 'Ungerska Wallenbergmonumentets tillkomst m.m.' 3 May 1989, RKA, Raoul Wallenberg, UD2001/00009, Vol. 33. See also Éva Hajdú, 'The Wallenberg Memorial in Budapest', *The New Hungarian Quarterly*, Autumn 1987, pp. 115–117; Andraás Kö, 'Mindig diszíti virág: Szobor születése', *Mai Nap*, 10 March 1989.

56 Thomas Palme, 'Monument med historia', *Svenska Dagbladet*, 29 April 2012.

not to support Salgo.⁵⁷ The Swedes were aware of how sensitive the Wallenberg issue was for Hungarian-Soviet relations. 'Adding stones to the Hungarian burden would ... serve no one', a Swedish diplomat noted, but the Swedes continued to monitor the progress of the statue project closely.⁵⁸

During a visit to Moscow, Varga approached Mikhail Gorbachev's staff and requested permission to erect a Wallenberg monument. The response was favourable, but on one condition: the monument must not contain any references to Wallenberg in the Soviet Union. The artist received financial support from Peter Wallenberg, a relative of Raoul's, and travelled to Sweden to select suitable blocks of stone.⁵⁹ This was not the first time that a Swedish quarry had been utilized by an Eastern European artist. Almost 40 years earlier, the sculptor Nathan Rapoport had received help from the Jewish Agency in Stockholm to select stone blocks for the 1943 Warsaw Uprising monument he was working on at the time. The stone blocks, which ironically had originally been commissioned by his German fellow artist Arno Becker for a monument to Adolf Hitler's victories, were, like the bronze centrepiece Rapoport had completed in Paris, sent by sea for onward transport to Warsaw. The reason was that he feared that if the 90 components were transported by land, there was an evident risk that they would be seized by Soviet soldiers. The smuggled sections were then assembled before the monument was inaugurated on 19 April 1948.⁶⁰

Similar concerns emerged in the 1980s. As a result of the country's longstanding financial crisis, the Communist Party under János Kádár, Prime Minister of Hungary during 1956–1958 and 1961–1965 and General Secretary of the Communist Party during

---

57 Jan Eliasson, 'Wallenberg', 23 May 1986, RKA, Raoul Wallenberg, UD2001/00009, Vol. 26.
58 Julin, 'Raoul Wallenberg', 14 January 1985. See also Vidar Hellners, 'Wallenberg', document no. 204, 12 October 1984; Vidar Hellners, 'Wallenberg', 14 January 1985, RKA, Raoul Wallenberg, UD2001/00009, Vol. 22, and Ragnar Dromberg, 'Nytt minnesmärke över Raoul Wallenberg i Budapest', Memoranda 10, 13, and 14 April 1987; Ragnar Dromberg, 'Nya Raoul Wallenbergmonumentet', 5 and 7 May 1987 and 'Invigning av monumentet över Raoul Wallenberg', 12 May 1987, RKA, Raoul Wallenberg, UD2001/00009, Vol. 28.
59 Letter from Wilhelm Wachtmeister to Peter Wallenberg, 15 May 1986 and W[ilhelm] Wachtmeister, 'Ang. Raoul Wallenberg monument i Budapest', 19 June 1986, RKA, Raoul Wallenberg, UD2001/00009, Vol. 26.
60 Young, *The Texture of Memory*, pp. 168–170.

1956–1988, began negotiations with the United States on increased economic cooperation. One obvious challenge in this context was not to annoy party colleagues in Moscow. While Western popular culture was gaining a foothold in Hungary in the 1970s and 1980s, the United States was still the nation's main enemy in official propaganda. In a situation where the two countries had been continuously and cautiously approaching each other – with the result that Hungary was one of the most favoured of the Soviet Union's satellite states in Washington D.C., while the confrontational rhetoric of the Cold War continued to make itself felt at regular intervals – Salgo chose to play it safe.[61] The US Embassy was the recipient of the Wallenberg statue in Hungary, as it was unclear whether the local authorities would grant their permission. As a last resort, the monument was to be erected on the Embassy grounds and be visible through the fence. The site was already home to a Hungarian statue of a US general who had played a prominent role in the First World War. Salgo had acquired the statue from the Hungarian state on the promise that it would be transported to the United States, but had no intention of taking the work out of the country. Like the possible future Wallenberg statue, it stood on the Embassy grounds 'waiting for better times'.[62]

The turning point came when János Kádár was invited to Sweden on an official state visit. He was concerned about the questions that Swedish politicians and journalists might ask about Wallenberg's fate. At this time, Salgo renewed his offer to donate a Wallenberg monument. The local Hungarian politicians were still unsure of Moscow's attitude, but that mattered less when Kádár began to show interest in the project. However, this did not rule out further obstacles, such as a ban on mentioning the Varga monument in the *Magyar Nemzet* newspaper.[63]

The original plan to place the monument in Szent István Park on the Pest side, the intended site of *The Snake Killer*, was shelved. A proposal for a location on Margaret Island, opposite Szent István Park, also failed to gain approval. Varga realized that some local dignitaries still wanted to delay or derail the project, and that

---

61 Borhi, *Dealing with Dictators*, pp. 327–357.
62 Ragnar Dromberg, 'Wallenberg restitutus?', secret report to Jan Eliasson, 5 March 1986, RKA, Raoul Wallenberg, Vol. 26. See also Schult, *A Hero's Many Faces*, pp. 157–158.
63 Sjöquist, *Dramat Raoul Wallenberg*, p. 230; Schult, *A Hero's Many Faces*, p. 158.

continued demands for a central site would play into their hands. He therefore accepted a less central location on the Buda side.[64] The site proved to be an inspired choice, as the remote location was reminiscent of a lost hero.[65] It was claimed that Wallenberg's abandoned and destroyed car had been found close by three weeks after his disappearance.[66] In an interview, Varga indirectly made it clear that the peripheral location was not important because the monument was 'never without flowers'.[67]

Varga's monument is located in a green area beside a busy street. It consists of two separate upright granite blocks with Wallenberg standing between them. Seen from the side, the blocks conceal an older man, wearing a simple coat with a raised collar, trousers, and shoes. The clothing invites the interpretation that it is a prisoner from the Gulag camps who is represented. Varga thus broke his promise to exclude allusions to Wallenberg's Soviet fate. Behind the prisoner, on the other side of the bisected granite blocks, Pátzay's *The Snake Killer* is engraved in gold. It serves as a reference both to that monument, which at that time was still 'disappeared', and to Wallenberg's achievements in Budapest during the war. Even the title *The New Raoul Wallenberg Monument* served as a reminder of the non-existence of *The Snake Killer* in Budapest in 1987. In this way, Varga used his monument to honour both Wallenberg and Pátzay. The reference to *The Snake Killer* also created a contrast. It reminds viewers that in his youth Wallenberg was capable of opposing both the Germans and the antisemitic Arrow Cross. By contrast, the older man in prison clothes is powerless and abandoned. Although it is unlikely that Wallenberg survived for any length of time in the Soviet prison and camp system, he is nevertheless depicted as an old man, suggesting a lengthy imprisonment.[68]

---

64 Andraás Kö, 'Mindig diszíti virág: Szobor születése', *Mai Nap*, 10 March 1989, RKA, Raoul Wallenberg, UD2001/00009, Vol. 30. See also Schult, *A Hero's Many Faces*, pp. 158–159. Some years later, an American complained over the peripheral location, which he felt was a poor reflection of Wallenberg's contribution; see 'Budapest ghetto', *The New York Times*, 5 July 1992.
65 Cole, *Holocaust City*, p. 235.
66 Bierman, *Righteous Gentile*, p. 201; Rosenfeld, *Raoul Wallenberg*, p. xxii; Schult, *A Hero's Many Faces*, p. 159.
67 Andraás Kö, 'Mindig diszíti virág: Szobor születése', *Mai Nap*, 10 March 1989, RKA, Raoul Wallenberg, UD2001/00009, Vol. 30.
68 Schult, *A Hero's Many Faces*, pp. 160–165.

Tanja Schult points out that to Varga, Wallenberg is a new Moses. Like the biblical figure the Swede is a link between God and the people, albeit in a secularized form. The gesture being made by the figure of Wallenberg and the bisected block of granite suggest Moses parting the Red Sea and helping the Jews to escape captivity in Egypt. Moses saved his people from slavery; Wallenberg, although not Jewish himself, helped Jews to escape the Holocaust. The comparison can be taken one step further. Moses never reached the Holy Land, and his burial site is unknown. Wallenberg never returned either, and his final resting place is unknown too. The analogy between Moses and Wallenberg has also been used by others who have written about the missing Swede, including Annette Lantos, who referred to Wallenberg as 'our Moses from the North'.[69]

In connection with the filming of *Good Evening, Mr. Wallenberg*, Per Anger said that 'Hungary has become for us a gateway to Eastern Europe and the Soviet Union'.[70] For him, it must have felt special that Hungary was the very nation that opened up in the late 1980s, as its capital was so closely linked to his and Wallenberg's efforts in 1944–1945. However, the Hungarians did not want any Nordic link to be present at the inauguration, whose low-key nature instead signalled discomfort with a historical memory, as did the anonymous rededication of the Imre Nagy monument in the summer of 2019. A request from the Swedish ambassador Ragnar Dromberg to give a brief speech met with solid resistance from the Hungarian government. There was a great risk, came the reply, that both official relations between Sweden and Hungary and Dromberg's activities in Budapest would be damaged. The main stumbling block was that through its 'alliance loyalty' to the Soviet Union, Hungary fully accepted the Soviet version of Wallenberg's death. A Swedish speech was likely to challenge this version, with consequences for Hungarian-Soviet relations.[71] The topic's political sensitivity was also evident from the fact that the opening ceremony was toned down and lacked a speech from anyone representing

---

69 Schult, *A Hero's Many Faces*, p. 165.
70 'Raoul Wallenbergs öde blir TV-film i Ungern', *Svenska Dagbladet*, 27 April 1989.
71 Ragnar Dromberg, 'Ang. invigningen av Raoul Wallenbergmonumentet', 15 May 1987, RKA, Raoul Wallenberg, UD2001/00009, Vol. 28. See Sten Strömholm to Martin Hallqvist, 'Wallenberg: Jenő Fock', 16 February 1990, RKA, Raoul Wallenberg, UD2001/00009, Vol. 36.

Sweden, which Nina Lagergren reacted to. She asked whether 'the government intended to accept this treatment'. The response from the Swedish Foreign Office (Utrikesdepartementet, UD) was that Ambassador Dromberg 'couldn't very well impose a Swedish speech against the wishes of the Hungarians'.[72] The monument was unveiled on 2 May 1987, a week before Kádár travelled to Sweden. It was a 'small and discreet affair' attended by senior party officials plus a few invited foreign guests, including Salgó and Dromberg. The situation was similar just over two years later on the occasion of George Bush's state visit to Budapest. The US President stated some years later that he had paid tribute to the Swede's achievements at the monument, but it had been a modest event. The issue of Wallenberg's disappearance was still so sensitive in US-Soviet relations that Bush refrained from giving a speech at the new monument.[73] Nonetheless, Varga's Wallenberg monument has been described as a symbol of the approaching end of the Cold War and a renewed interest in the Holocaust in Hungary.[74]

## The *Snake Killer*'s return

Imre Varga's Wallenberg monument was so much more than a memorial because its installation signalled that it was now possible to discuss previously taboo topics.[75] A Hungarian Wallenberg Committee was founded in the late 1980s with the stated aim of seeking clarity about Wallenberg's fate.[76] Around 1990, Hungarian

---

72 Sven Julin, 'Raoul Wallenberg', Memorandum, 19 May 1987, RKA, Raoul Wallenberg, UD2001/00009, Vol. 28.
73 'Interview with Members of the White House Press Corps. July 13, 1989', *George Bush: Public Papers of the Presidents of the United States. 1989. Book II*, p. 953; George Bush, 'Remarks at the Simon Wiesenthal Center Dinner in Los Angeles, California. June 16, 1991', *George Bush: Public Papers of the Presidents of the United States. 1991. Book I*, p. 678.
74 Cole, *Holocaust City*, p. 236. See also Ragnar Dromberg, 'Nya Raoul Wallenberg-monumentet invigt' and 'Kring invigningen av nya Wallenberg-monumentet', 20 May 1987, RKA, Raoul Wallenberg, UD2001/00009, Vol. 28; Henry Kamm, 'Wallenberg: Statue rises in Budapest', *The New York Times*, 15 April 1987 and Jackson Diehl, 'Hungary to honor Swede who saved Jews: New statue of Wallenberg to be dedicated next month nearly 40 years after Holocaust', *The Washington Post*, 28 April 1987.
75 Carl G. Ströhm, 'Das Denkmal für Wallenberg ist mehr als nur Erinnerung', *Die Welt*, 28 April 1987.
76 Szita, *The Power of Humanity*, p. 150.

politicians began to make statements that were clear departures from the previous line. For most of the post-war period the Holocaust had been a non-topic in Hungary, but now for the first time came official denunciations of wartime antisemitism and regrets about the fate of the Jews in 1944–1945. In the same breath, the Holocaust was described as the most shameful event in human history.[77] For example, a commemoration of the victims of the Holocaust was held in the Hungarian Parliament in 1989, with Giorgio Perlasca among those present.[78] In 1989, too, Imre Varga's *Memorial of the Hungarian Jewish Martyrs* was inaugurated in the courtyard of the great synagogue in Pest.[79] The interest in the Holocaust was matched by an equally strong continuing interest in Wallenberg. A new edition of Jenő Lévai's book on Wallenberg was published in 1988. Another commemorative plaque to Wallenberg was inaugurated in 1989. His activities in Budapest were also the subject of newspaper and magazine articles plus radio and television programmes. In April 1989, a symposium on human rights was held in Budapest in the presence of Per Anger. The Hungarian Central Bank also minted 270 gold and silver coins in Wallenberg's honour, with the proceeds designated for charitable purposes.[80]

---

77 Braham, *The Politics of Genocide*, Vol. 2, pp. 1346–1359, especially p. 1358.
78 'Minnesstund i parlamentet över judeförföljelserna', RKA, Raoul Wallenberg, UD2001/00009, 11 May 1989, Vol. 33.
79 Cole, 'Turning the Places of Holocaust History into Places of Holocaust Memory', pp. 282–283.
80 Gárdos Miklós, 'Ércalak a fasorban: Raoul Wallenberg tragédiája "Amikor beborul feletted az ég"', *Magyarország*, 1988:25; László Gyurkó, 'In memoriam R.W.', *Tükür*, 10 May 1988; articles in *Magyar Nezmet* and *Nepszabadsag*, 25 August 1988; Roger Gartoft, 'Ny minnestavla i Budapest med Wallenberganknytning', 19 February 1988, and Ragnar Dromberg, 'Raoul Wallenbergs halvsyskon på besök i Budapest', 4 May 1988 and Ragnar Dromberg, 'Ny ungersk minnestavla, TV- och radioprogram', 7 August 1989, RKA, Raoul Wallenberg, UD2001/00009, Vol. 30; Ragnar Dromberg, 'Nyutgåva av ungersk 'klassiker' om Raoul Wallenberg', 29 August 1988, and Ragnar Dromberg, 'Nytryck av ungersk bok från 1948 om Raoul Wallenberg', 14 September 1988, RKA, Raoul Wallenberg, UD2001/00009, Vol. 31; Ragnar Dromberg to Vollrath Tham, 'Raoul Wallenberg-symposium i Budapest', 18 April 1989; Ragnar Dromberg, 'Ungerska Raoul Wallenberg-föreningen', 19 April 1989, RKA, Raoul Wallenberg, UD2001/00009, Vol. 32; Ragnar Dromberg, 'Ny ungersk minnestavla, TV- och radioprogram', 7 August 1989, RKA, Raoul Wallenberg, UD2001/00009, Vol. 33 and 'Ädel Wallenbergpeng', *Arbetet*, 2 February 1990.

As late as 1986, senior representatives of the Hungarian government had made it clear that the monument in Debrecen would not be returned to Budapest.[81] A few years later, the Hungarian Raoul Wallenberg Association resumed efforts to move the statue to Szent István Park in the Hungarian capital. One initial problem was that the director of the pharmaceutical company Biogal, outside whose entrance the statue had stood since 1953, was not prepared to surrender his company's monument. He felt it was an excellent allegory of humanity's struggle against disease. That made it a suitable brand for the company, even though the snake, which represents evil in the monument, traditionally has a favourable symbolic significance in medicine and healing. He added that the monument in Debrecen was in any case a memorial to Wallenberg, as he had been on his way to that city when he was arrested in 1945. It was also pointed out that with the inauguration of Varga's statue in 1987, Budapest now already had a monument.[82]

A smaller replica of *The Snake Killer* was erected in Budapest in 1989.[83] It was not until July 1998 that a breakthrough occurred in the negotiations for the original. By that time, a statue committee had been formed with the aim of re-inaugurating Pátzay's monument at its original location in the near future. Following negotiations with Debrecen's municipal politicians and Biogal's management, a decision was made to produce a replica. Thanks to donations from the City of Budapest, Hungarian and Swedish companies, and private individuals, the plan was put into action. On 18 April 1999, more than half a century after the original inauguration was to have taken place, the statue was unveiled. Those who dropped the curtain were the Mayor of Budapest Gabor Demszky, who was also a Wallenberg champion, and the poet and writer György Somlyo, who had included Wallenberg in his novel *Rampa* (1984, German translation *Die Rampe* 1988) set in the Second World War concentration camps.[84]

---

81 Krister Wahlbäck, 'Wallenberg-statyn i Ungern', 29 January 1986, RKA, Raoul Wallenberg, UD2001/00009, Vol. 25.
82 Article in *HVG*, 30 January 1999.
83 Nylén, *Budapest bortom turiststråken*, p. 90.
84 Staffan Carlsson, 'Invigning av Raoul Wallenbergstaty', 6 May 1999, RKA, Raoul Wallenberg, UD2001/00009, Vol. 68; Szita, *The Power of Humanity*, p. 157. On Somlyo see Gyorgy Gomori, 'Gyorgy Somlyo: Hungarian poet with a European voice', *The Guardian*, 8 June 2006.

## Reconciliation, but with reservations

The complexity of post-Communist Hungarian history culture is demonstrated by the fact that it has not been self-evident to combine the renewed interest in the Holocaust in the 1990s with a self-critical approach to the persecution of the country's Jews in 1944–1945. Alexandra Kowalski described the view of the Holocaust in Hungary after 1990 as contradictory – an apt description. Whereas memories of the Holocaust were rarely mentioned before 1990, ambivalence has been noticeable after that date: on the one hand there has been a desire to commemorate the genocide in the public sphere, but on the other there has been a reluctance to render the memory of it visible.[85]

The reconciliations with past historical narratives which characterize the moral use of history have thus been selective in Hungary; in addition, they have been actively opposed by influential forces. Since the early 1990s, the extreme right and neo-Nazism have been a force to be reckoned with in Hungary and the rest of Eastern Europe. Antisemitism and anti-Romani sentiment have been commonplace in these movements, both in word and deed. Right-wing extremists have expressed a desire to return to what is believed to have been good national unity and an exemplary combination of nationalism and religion during the period 1919–1944. Central to this nostalgia is an admiration for Admiral Horthy. In accordance with his last wishes, his remains were brought from Portugal – where he had lived in exile from 1949 until his death in 1957 – back to Hungary, and were buried there in 1993, after the last Russian soldier had left the country. The right-wing nationalist striving to rehabilitate Horthy has continued with undiminished vigour ever since.[86]

Another leading figure of the right-wing movement is Pál Teleki, but his legacy has been debated. In the early 2000s, there was a fierce battle over whether he should be honoured with a statue in Budapest. His supporters usually cited the situation that had preceded his suicide in April 1941. During his second term as Prime Minister during 1939–1941, Teleki strove to balance the prevailing pro-German foreign policy against a pro-British orientation.

---

85 Kowalski, 'The Wandering Memorial', p. 216.
86 Gerner, 'Hungary, Romania, the Holocaust and Historical Culture', pp. 242–243.

The issue came to a head when Germany attacked Yugoslavia. The choice was between joining Germany and remaining aloof, thereby risking a German invasion. The first option won. Teleki regretted the decision in a letter to Admiral Horthy, whereupon he shot himself. His action has been seen as a sacrifice and an honourable attempt to save the Hungarian nation from participating in a disastrous war. The other side of the coin is that Teleki represented an antisemitic policy. A traditional conservative, he had little time for Hitler, but the two men shared a disparaging view of Jews, which under Teleki's rule manifested itself in anti-Jewish legislation that paved the way for subsequent ghettoization and deportations.[87] As a result of the protests Tibor Rieger's statue of Teleki was not installed in Budapest but in Balatonboglár, which had been a Hungarian refuge for thousands of Polish refugees during the Second World War. Two monuments to him were also erected in 2020 in Poland, one in Kraków and the other in Skierniewice, where he is portrayed alongside Charles de Gaulle, Polish leader Józef Piłsudski, and the President of the post-First World War independent but short-lived Ukraine, Simon Petlura, on the grounds that in 1920, during his first term as Hungarian Prime Minister, Teleki had provided the Poles with ammunition and supplies, thereby contributing to their victory over Soviet-Russian forces.[88]

In the final stages of the war, Admiral Horthy went from being a prisoner of the Germans to being incarcerated by the Allies. That the latter considered him a war criminal puzzled him. In his view, he was the mastermind of a Hungarian resistance to Nazi Germany. In the end, the Allies did not put him on trial, but his plea of Hungarian innocence has recurred at irregular intervals.[89] One occasionally successful strategy has been to place the entire burden of blame for the genocide committed against Jews in Hungary on Adolf Eichmann. It is claimed that he was the one who imposed the transition on Hungarians from disliking Jews to killing them en masse. That transition was concretely orchestrated by a seizure of power without which the Holocaust in Hungary

---

87 Hanebrink, 'The Memory of the Holocaust in Postcommunist Hungary', pp. 261–263, 270–274.
88 See e.g. 'Protest gegen Entscheidung in Ungarn: Statue für Pál Teleki', www.hagalil.com/archiv/ 2004/02/Teleki.htm (accessed 20 April 2022); Péter Cseresnyés, 'Monument to former PM Teleki erected in Krakow', *Hungary Today*, 5 November 2020.
89 Sakmyster, *Hungary's Admiral on Horseback*, pp. 381–382.

would – it is implied – never have taken place, or at least not on such a devastating scale.[90]

Contributing to the survival of this notion is the direct or indirect support it has received from internationally recognized Holocaust specialists. The frequently expressed conclusion that the problems of Hungarian Jews began with the German invasion goes hand in hand with an underestimation of the importance of the strong antisemitic currents in Hungary during the interwar period and the Second World War.[91] It was this antisemitism that reached its tragic climax when the Germans began persecuting the Jews in 1944. Eichmann and his colleagues could then count on considerable assistance from the Hungarian police and 'ordinary Hungarians', with the result that virtually the entire Jewish population of rural Hungary and a considerable proportion of the capital's Jewish residents were deported to extermination camps, where the majority perished.

Furthermore, it is a history-cultural fact that there is a greater willingness in Hungary – as in the other countries of former Soviet-dominated Eastern Europe – to attach less importance to the German occupation during the Second World War than to the subsequent Soviet one. For example, conservative commentators have argued that the Second World War is not about Jews and genocide, an argument that has been made in the same breath as calls for greater attention to be paid to atrocities committed by Communist regimes. The historical narrative that has its main representatives among the far right has woven together anti-Communism, antisemitism, and 'a self-victimisation narrative viewing the West as a permanent threat to the authentic Hungarian values'.[92]

In Budapest, one of the most apparent signs of this prioritization is Terror Háza, the House of Terror, a privately funded

---

90 For an example of this historical narrative, see Korda, *Charmed Lives*, pp. 38–39. See Andrew Handler, *A Man for All Connections*, p. 109; Herczl, *Christianity and the Holocaust of Hungarian Jewry*, p. 183; Richard Swartz, 'Raoul Wallenberg litade på sin springpojke' (article about Wallenberg's young assistant Jonny Moser), *Svenska Dagbladet*, 25 February 2009.

91 Cole, *Holocaust City*, pp. 49–52; Lomax, 'Combatting the Ultra-Right in Hungary', pp. 328–331; Apor, 'Eurocommunism: Commemorating Communism in Contemporary Europe', pp. 233–246.

92 Trencsényi, '"Politics of History" and Authoritarian Regime-Building in Hungary', p. 173. See also Hanebrink, 'The Memory of the Holocaust in Postcommunist Hungary', p. 275.

museum of the 1939–1989 period, which enjoys public financial support and is sanctioned at the highest political level. Ten of the twelve rooms of this museum are devoted to the Soviet period, whereas the reign of terror by the Arrow Cross receives limited attention. The anti-Communist focus of the museum is not only manifested in the exhibition. The museum was inaugurated on 25 February 2002, the day established in June 2000 by the Fidesz party in memory of the victims of the Communist dictatorships, in order to 'offset' the Holocaust Memorial Day established by the previous socialist government. Violence, martyrs, and terror are recurring elements in the exhibition, but it is not always easy to distinguish between perpetrators and victims, a conclusion pronounced by the first director of the museum, who drew a parallel between those who committed crimes during the Holocaust and those who helped the Communists stay in power until 1990. Controversial comparisons between Fascism and Communism in the same spirit recur in the exhibition. A guiding principle has been the concept of 'double occupation', combined with a lack of perspectives explaining the historical roots of political terror, violence, and antisemitism in Hungary. Notably, the museum has usually had more visitors than the state-funded museum in Budapest, which opened in 2004.[93]

Even though the confrontation with Hungary's complicity in the Holocaust has been hesitant and somewhat slow in coming, there was, and still is, a continued appreciation of Wallenberg's achievements among many Jewish and Christian Hungarians. Tom Lantos's proposal in 1999 to make Wallenberg an honorary Hungarian citizen did not immediately gain traction, but in 2003 the Swedish diplomat was accorded that honour in Budapest. Two years later, on the occasion of the sixtieth anniversary of his disappearance, Wallenberg was commemorated in a ceremony at the Budapest Holocaust Memorial Center. Around the turn of the millennium, there was thus a powerful political desire to take a stand against domestic antisemitism, not least because it could be regarded as a latter-day echo of

---

93 Cole, *Holocaust City*, pp. 244–247; Blutinger, 'An Inconvenient Past', pp. 83–92; Gerner, 'Hungary, Romania, the Holocaust and Historical Culture', pp. 242–252; Julia Creet, 'The House of Terror and the Holocaust Memorial Centre', pp. 29–59; Hanebrink, 'The Memory of the Holocaust in Postcommunist Hungary', pp. 279–283; Trencsényi, '"Politics of History" and Authoritarian Regime-Building in Hungary', pp. 174–175.

the Arrow Cross movement.[94] Against this background, it is reasonable to consider the re-inauguration of *The Snake Killer* in Budapest as a stand by the young democracy's political establishment against the dark legacy of the Second World War. Tim Cole writes that the ceremony was 'nothing less than a self-conscious act of symbolic restitution, paid for by both private donors and the city authorities. Whilst it had not been possible to restore Wallenberg himself, here was the opportunity to restore the disappearing memorial that had assumed such importance as representative of the disappearing man.'[95] With the exception of a protest from the far-right party MIEP, there was total political unity, the other parties strongly opposing what they perceived as MIEP's antisemitic and anti-Wallenberg stance.[96] Moreover, the original *Snake Killer* was the product of a Hungary which, for a short time after the Second World War, had not been under the thumb of the Soviets. The reinstallation of Pátzay's monument linked pre-Communist and post-Communist Hungary. Such an approach invited the interpretation that the intermediate period had been an unfortunate parenthesis.

## A helping hand

May 1991 saw the first-ever official visit of a Swedish head of state to Hungary. According to media reports, the programme had a very tight schedule – with one exception. At Varga's monument to Wallenberg, the Swedish royal couple placed a bouquet and stopped to honour the Swede's achievements. Queen Silvia also visited the school named after Valdemar Langlet. 'We receive constant reminders of how alive [Wallenberg's and Langlet's] efforts remain', King Carl XVI Gustaf summarized.[97] These reminders continued to

---

94 Interview with Tom Lantos by Tibor Kis, published in *Nepszabadsag*, 2 June 1999. See also [Staffan] Carlsson, 'Raoul Wallenberg', 2 June 1999, RKA, Raoul Wallenberg, UD2001/00009, Vol. 68; 'In memoriam Raoul Wallenberg: Einweihung mit fünfzig Jahren Verspätung', *Budapester Zeitung*, 31 May 1999 and 'Hungary remembers Wallenberg 60 years after his disappearance', *The Jerusalem Post*, 18 January 2005.
95 Cole, *Holocaust City*, p. 238.
96 Articles from *Nepszabadsag*, 29 and 30 January 1999 and [Staffan] Carlsson, 'Ungern – högerextremistiska partiet MIEP protesterar mot upprättandet av Wallenbergstaty', 29 January 1999, RKA, Raoul Wallenberg, UD2001/00009, Vol. 67.
97 Ninni Jonzon, 'Wallenbergs staty fick Silvia att stanna upp', *iDAG*, 28 May 1991.

be made. Although the Swedish royal couple were not present in Budapest the following year, Raoul Wallenberg's eightieth birthday was honoured in a series of joint Swedish-Hungarian events.[98] The Holocaust and Raoul Wallenberg were also commemorated on several occasions in 1994 on the occasion of the fiftieth anniversary of the German occupation of Hungary and the subsequent persecution of the Jews.[99] The following year Per Anger received a Hungarian award and King Carl XVI Gustaf, in his capacity as Sweden's highest representative, was awarded the Hungarian Auschwitz Foundation Medal in recognition of the work done by Anger and Wallenberg, among others, during 1944–1945.[100]

Jan Lundvik, Sweden's ambassador to Hungary from 1994 to 1998, has subsequently attested to the great Hungarian interest in Raoul Wallenberg, expressed both by those saved by him and by other more recent admirers. One difficulty was to explain why Sweden had not honoured him publicly, but the 1998 inauguration of Lenke Rothman's monument to Wallenberg put that criticism to rest.[101]

A major reason why it took until the 1990s to inaugurate the first Swedish Wallenberg monument – Staffan Nihlén's *Pienza* (1993) in Malmö – was that according to tradition, monuments should not be erected to people who are still alive. Installing statues of Wallenberg was tantamount to acknowledging that he was dead, argued those who hoped he was still alive. Wanting to honour Wallenberg at 'his' University of Michigan, paying tribute to him in the Israeli Parliament, the proposals to name a hospital after him, and the erection of a memorial to him in Moscow are just four of many examples of well-intentioned efforts from the 1970s to the late 1990s that were halted either by the Swedish government or by Wallenberg's family. The reason was that words such as 'memory' and 'memorial', customarily used in these contexts,

---

98 'Firandet av Raoul Wallenbergs aatioaarsdag i Budapest', 31 July 1992, RKA, Raoul Wallenberg, UD2001/00009, Vol. 44.
99 Péter Bajtay, 'Ämne: händelser som rör Sverige i Holocaust-minnesåret', 16 February 1994, RKA, Raoul Wallenberg, UD2001/00009, Vol. 48.
100 Letter from President Árpád Göncz to Per Anger and reply letter from Anger to Göncz (both undated); Jan Lundvik, 'Ungerska Auschwitzstiftelsens medalj', 23 November 1995, RKA, Raoul Wallenberg, UD2001/00009, Vol. 55. See also Jan Lundvik, 'Tidningsartikel om Wallenbergs fotograf', 30 December 1994; [Jan] Lundvik, 'Artikel om Raoul Wallenberg', 3 January 1995, RKA, Raoul Wallenberg, UD2001/00009, Vol. 50.
101 Lundvik, 'My Undertaking Began On a Grey Autumn Day 1960', p. 14.

implied an admission that he was no longer alive.[102] For the same reason, Maj von Dardel appealed in 1947 for Pátzay's monument not to be erected in Budapest. Her arguments were, of course, quite different from those that justified the statue's removal. Rudolph Philipp wrote that she 'does not want some dead hero, she wants her son back'.[103] On the same grounds, Philipp said he had asked 'international organizations that wanted to erect a monument in Geneva to Raoul Wallenberg's achievements to shelve this idea'.[104] Similar answers were given by the UD to an American enquiry in the early 1980s, with the addition that official Sweden could not of course influence the decision.[105]

During a visit to Hungary in 1987, a member of the Supreme Court of Sweden, Ingrid Gärde-Widemar, who was then Chair of the Swedish Raoul Wallenberg Association, had asked Imre Varga if he would consider creating yet another memorial to Wallenberg, this time in Stockholm.[106] Varga welcomed the suggestion and met with Nina Lagergren in January 1988. However, she and her brother Guy von Dardel chose to reject the proposal for a Wallenberg monument by Varga in Stockholm.[107] Over time, this resistance to erecting monuments to Wallenberg in Sweden diminished. In August 1996, the Stockholm City Council decided to instruct the city's Cultural Committee to explore the possibility of erecting a Wallenberg monument at Nybroviken, a picturesque seaside location in central Stockholm close by the Royal Dramatic Theatre. In September 1997, a decision was made to launch and fund the project.[108]

---

102 These cases are dealt with in a large number of documents in RKA, Raoul Wallenberg, UD2001/00009, Vol. 1; RKA, Raoul Wallenberg, UD2018/05505, Vol. 1; RKA, Raoul Wallenberg, UD2018/05505, Vol. 2; RKA, Raoul Wallenberg, UD2018/05505, Vol. 19.
103 Rudolph Philipp, 'Lever Raoul Wallenberg – människokärlekens partisan?', Året Runt, 1947:25, 9.
104 Rudolph Philipp, 'Raoul Wallenberg lever', Vi, 1955:2, 8.
105 'Föreslaget Wallenberg-monument', 3 February 1982, RKA, Raoul Wallenberg, UD2001/00009, Vol. 15.
106 Ragnar Dromberg, 'Wallenberg-minnesmärke från Ungern till Stockholm? (Förslag om inbjudan el.dyl. till skulptören Varga)', 3 December 1987, RKA, Raoul Wallenberg, UD2001/00009, Vol. 29.
107 Ragnar Dromberg, 'Inget Wallenbergmonument i Stockholm – tills vidare', 9 February 1988, RKA, Raoul Wallenberg, UD2001/00009, Vol. 30.
108 Bo Wingren, 'Förslag ang. minnesmärke över Raoul Wallenberg', official statement, City of Stockholm Cultural and Sports Administration, 15 November 1998, RKA, Raoul Wallenberg, UD2001/00009, Vol. 67.

In 1998, Stockholm was the European Capital of Culture. One appropriate item on this event's agenda might be the inauguration of a Wallenberg monument, argued the members of the 'Working Group for a monument to Raoul Wallenberg's achievements', founded in January 1997 and led by Carmen Regnér. The idea was to donate the monument to the City of Stockholm. The issue was formally discussed but repeatedly postponed. By April 2008, it was clear that no consensus could be reached on the issue, not least because of resistance to the idea that a group of private individuals would have the right to determine the design of a memorial to Wallenberg. Another strong contributing factor was that the City of Stockholm had more or less simultaneously announced a competition for a Wallenberg monument among internationally recognized artists. In this situation, the Working Group approached authorities on the island of Lidingö, where Raoul Wallenberg had lived for a time as a young man, and offered them the statue. By contrast to the Stockholm reaction, the response from Lidingö was immediately favourable.[109]

The monument was soon finished. Back in 1993, Willy Gordon had created and presented a plaster model of an oversized man, implicitly Wallenberg, handing out protective passports. His proposal had found no favour with the politicians in Stockholm.[110] In connection with the work on producing a Wallenberg monument, his plaster model was talked about again, and this time it won the Working Group's approval. This is not surprising, as it was not the first time Gordon had made references to the Holocaust and to well-known Swedes in his works. He had come from Latvia to Sweden at the age of seven, subsequently studying art from 1940 to 1945. The war and the Nazi genocide had left their mark on him. Looking back, he stated that all the works he had created up to that point 'seemed trivial and meaningless'. One result was that the nature of his creative work changed. While he had certainly taken an interest in Jewish matters before, the Holocaust helped to change both the form and the content of his creations.[111] This was noted at the time. In 1945, the German-Swedish publicist and documentary filmmaker Erwin Leiser drew attention to Gordon's 'highly

---

109 Catharina Ingelman-Sundberg, 'Frågor kring Wallenbergstaty', and Omer Magnergård, 'Två monument reses över Raoul Wallenberg', *Svenska Dagbladet*, 3 and 10 May 1998. See also Schult, *A Hero's Many Faces*, p. 99.
110 Larsson and Åsbrink, *'Det är väl ingen konst'*, p. 15.
111 Gordon, *Willy Gordon*, pp. 9–34, quotation p. 24.

expressive art', in particular to the sketch for a monument entitled 'Freedom Composition'. It was, he wrote, 'a Jewish *j'accuse* against our era, a shocking indictment of humanity which did not stop the systematic extermination of the Jews that was proclaimed and carried out by the Nazis', but which nevertheless displayed faith in the future.[112] Leiser again referred to Gordon five years later, in connection with the monument at the cemetery of the Malmö Jewish Community honouring the 150 refugees who had been laid to rest there. Leiser said that the work, which had been realized, unlike 'Freedom Composition', displayed a significant maturity in the artist.[113]

Gordon subsequently produced a large number of public sculptures, including some dedicated to famous Swedes such as the Social Democratic pioneer Axel Danielsson (1973), the actor Erland Josephson (1976, 2006), the ballet choreographer Birgit Cullberg (1981), and the popular composer Evert Taube (1990). He was thus used to portraying people and often depicted highly stylized bodies. The four-metre-high monument *Raoul Wallenbergs gärning* (Raoul Wallenberg's Achievement), unveiled by the then Speaker of the Riksdag Birgitta Dahl on 28 May 1998, featured this same approach. Gordon was inspired by a photograph of Raoul Wallenberg taken at a railway station in Budapest. In it the Swede stands with his back to the camera, wearing a hat and overcoat and handing out protective passports. In Gordon's interpretation, the significance of Wallenberg's action is indirectly evident from the fact that the hands ready to receive the protective passports bearing Sweden's national emblem of the three crowns are larger than those of the Wallenberg figure. The focus is thus on the rescue work. However, because the bronze figure is headless the result is a de-individualization and anonymization which invited criticism.[114]

## Art, monument, or both?

The objections to Gordon's monument were a drop in the ocean compared to the debate that followed the announced competition for a Wallenberg monument in Stockholm. All six proposals, three from Swedish and three from foreign artists, were non-figurative. Most of

---

112 Erwin Leiser, 'Ung judisk skulptör', *Judisk Tidskrift*, 1945:12, 387–389.
113 Erwin Leiser, 'Willy Gordon', *Judisk Tidskrift*, 1950:5, 159–161.
114 Schult, *A Hero's Many Faces*, pp. 104–107.

the artists used the Jewish star as a basis for their monuments, with the exception of the winning entry, Kirsten Ortwed's *Hommage à Raoul Wallenberg*. The Danish sculptor had composed a group of twelve bronze sculptures combined with Wallenberg's signature, drawn in the ground directly adjacent to the sculptures. The difficulty, she argued, was to describe the complex and extremely serious situation of Wallenberg and the Jews in Budapest without succumbing to sentimentality. Her artistic solution to the problem was to use sphinx-like shapes. Dignified and serious, they could visually guide the viewer to think about Raoul Wallenberg's memory and the houses, streets, and railway freight carriages in Budapest where he had saved so many Jews.[115]

One of Ortwed's compatriots said that her Wallenberg monument was a fantastic challenge, which provoked questions about what sculptures are and what they can contribute.[116] The competition jury members and the City of Stockholm Art Council were also impressed by her non-figurative artwork and commissioned her to create a monument at Nybroviken in central Stockholm. Many residents of the capital dissented radically, though. Commentators, including Per Anger, argued that it would be better to honour Wallenberg with another monument.[117] Sonja Sonnenfeld, Chair of the Raoul Wallenberg Association, complained that Ortwed's tribute had nothing whatsoever to do with Wallenberg's achievements. The monument was 'loveless and unworthy'. The best outcome would be if it were not installed.[118]

Bo Wingren, Chair of the Stockholm Art Council, was somewhat sympathetic to the criticism, because the proposal was 'an artistic design that is very far from the traditional view of monuments'.[119]

---

115 Kirsten Ortwed, 'Motivering och tekniske uppgifter', 4 September 1998, RKA, Raoul Wallenberg, UD2001/00009, Vol. 67. Her explanation is also found in Ahlstrand (ed.), *Raoul Wallenberg*, pp. 10–11. On the jury's opinion of the other monument proposals, see Larsson and Åsbrink, *'Det är väl ingen konst'*, pp. 16–19.
116 Ole Nørling, 'Monument for Wallenberg', *Berlingske Tidende*, 24 October 2000.
117 Per Anger, Georg Klein, Jan Lundvik and Harry Schein, 'Hedra Raoul Wallenberg med ett annat minnesmärke', *Dagens Nyheter*, 2 January 1999.
118 Viktoria Myrén, 'Storbråk om Wallenbergs minnesmärke', *Aftonbladet*, 8 June 1999.
119 Viktoria Myrén, 'Storbråk om Wallenbergs minnesmärke', *Aftonbladet*, 8 June 1999.

The jury chair, author Per Wästberg, took a more assertive stance, saying that the era of traditional heroic displays was over and it was time to find new ways to celebrate heroes, including Wallenberg.[120] Similar wording was repeated in the jury citation. Wallenberg's achievements were too great and impossible to portray in a traditional form. What was needed was a monument that both 'liberated the imagination' and could be linked to concepts such as freedom and openness, as well as to character traits that were identifiable in Wallenberg: 'imaginative, unorthodox, improvisational, and in unceasing motion'.[121]

The monument was solemnly inaugurated in 2001, with King Carl XVI Gustaf, the then UN Secretary-General Kofi Annan, and other potentates in attendance. The debate continued to rage even after the ceremony. As before, there were two diametrically opposed views. Critics argued that Wallenberg's achievement was of such a nature that it had no Swedish equivalent. Therefore, it was important that his ability to take decisive action was 'translated' into a worthy monument, not into something resembling giant garden slugs or, as the economist Carl Hamilton put it in an often-quoted and controversial column, 'twelve half-chewed bits of liquorice, or frozen dog shit'.[122] The main problem, argued critics, was that there were no references to Wallenberg either as an individual or as a historical actor. Abstract art was not in itself a problem, but if future generations could not understand Wallenberg's endeavour on the basis of the monument, it did not fulfil its function. Ortwed's *Hommage* was undeniably art, but it did not work as a monument.[123]

---

120 Peter R. Meyer's documentary film *Raoul – och de 30 monumenten*, broadcast by Sveriges Television, 24 September 2001.
121 'Tävlingsjuryn för ett monument över Raoul Wallenberg: Juryns motivering för sitt beslut enligt protokoll den 23 oktober 1998', RKA, Raoul Wallenberg, UD2001/00009, Vol. 67.
122 Carl B. Hamilton, 'Hur hyllar vi våra döda?', *Aftonbladet*, 9 March 2002. See also Carl B. Hamilton, 'När finkonstnärer ger den stora Förklaringen', *Aftonbladet*, 8 March 2003, and Larsson and Åsbrink, '*Det är väl ingen konst*', pp. 19–20. The comparison between Ortwed's artwork and the giant slugs is from Peter Hansen, 'Konst och monument går inte ihop', *Svensk Tidskrift*, 2002:1, 12.
123 Morton H. Narrowe, 'Wallenberg-monument utan Wallenberg', *Judisk Krönika*, 2001:5, 9; Morton H. Narrowe, 'Konstverk eller monument?', *Judisk Krönika*, 2002:5, 41; Peter Hansen, 'Konst och monument går inte ihop', *Svensk Tidskrift*, 2002:1, 11–13. See also Ståhle, *Mellan konsten och publiken*, pp. 70.

There was an unspoken attitude as well: the idea that certain conditions must exist in order for there to be an encounter between a work of art and its viewer. As was the case a century ago, the monuments of today require the viewer to be familiar with the symbols and imagery used by the artist. For example, an American artistic effort during the Cold War failed in its purpose to strengthen Americans' sympathy for the United States and opposition to Communism. The failure occurred because most members of the audience did not possess the tools needed to decode the artworks, which turned the expected propaganda triumph into a fiasco.[124]

The bronze briefcase that is part of the Kraitzes' *Hope* monument, which stands by itself in a dozen locations around the world, and Ortwed's work invite similar interpretations: the abandoned briefcase and the collection of sphinxes with no self-evident centre convey a sense of emptiness and loneliness. Beyond the obvious contrast that one work is figurative and the other is not, there is another difference. The bronze briefcase is linked to Wallenberg because it bears the initials R.W. Ortwed's tribute offers no such assistance. It requires a willingness on the part of the viewer to accept the concept and try to interpret it on the basis of existing information, while knowing that there is no such thing as a key.[125] The monument's supporters argued that viewers who had a trained eye and an alert mind had ample opportunity to make associations with a variety of phenomena and approaches: Greek temple facades, Biblical references, simultaneous rest and movement, and the struggle between good and evil, life and death, in the form of rescue and flight versus ethnic mass murder. The fact that Ortwed's sculptures were at once both simple and enigmatic, opening up 'like Rorschach's inkblots' to a host of questions and interpretations, was a good thing. Ultimately, Ortwed undoubtedly did create a monument to one of the individuals who had done the most to save people from genocide. Her tribute was deliberately unorthodox, but it was nevertheless 'a sculptural parallel to Wallenberg's actions.'[126]

---

124 Bustow, 'The Limits of Modernist Art as a "Weapon of the Cold War"', pp. 68–80. See also Barbro Hedvall, 'Saknadens monument', *Dagens Nyheter*, 1 October 2008.v
125 Schult, *A Hero's Many Faces*, p. 276; Tanja Schult, 'Monument med mänskliga proportioner', *Svenska Dagbladet*, 27 January 2010.
126 Madeleine von Heland, 'Till minne av Raoul', *Moderna Tider*, November 2001, 28–30, quotation p. 30; Jakob Wamberg, 'Lang dags rejse mod rum', pp. 33–34; Eva Pohl, 'En anden frihed', *Berlingske Tidende*, 10 May 2002; Torben Weirup, 'Fra den nye verden', *Berlingske Tidende*, 25 June 2008.

The debate over Ortwed's Wallenberg monument illustrates the complex nature of commemoration: there is a confluence of past and present, and at the same time the connection between historical content and artistic form becomes conflicted. The monuments erected in honour of Raoul Wallenberg in Hungary, Sweden, and the United States hence imply that the history of the man is not merely the sum of his deeds in wartime Budapest and his fate in Soviet captivity. The way in which he is remembered in bronze and granite is also related to issues and values in contemporary societies, as well as to what we hope for – and fear – in the future.

**Plate 1** *Hope – a monument to Raoul Wallenberg*, by Gustav and Ulla Kraitz. Photo: Ulf Zander.

**Plate 2** *The Snake Killer*, by Pál Pátzay. Photo: Wikimedia Commons.

**Plate 3** *The New Raoul Wallenberg Monument*, by Imre Varga.
Photo: Wikimedia Commons.

**Plate 4** *Hommage à Raoul Wallenberg*, by Kristin Ortwed.
Photo: Bengt Oberger, Wikimedia Commons.

**Plate 5** *R. W. Briefcase*, by Gustav and Ulla Kraitz. Photo: Ulf Zander.

# Chapter 7
# The history-cultural Raoul Wallenberg

The interest in Raoul Wallenberg is not just due to the story itself – what he did during his life in general, and in Budapest during 1944–1945 in particular, and how he ended his days. The extraordinary story of his life has resulted in a multitude of history products. Their design and the reactions to them show that issues of how history is communicated, perceived, and received are an indispensable part of the story of Raoul Wallenberg.

Viewed in this way, the discussions about the Wallenberg monuments reviewed in the preceding chapter are not, as that chapter observed, merely expressions of different cultural ideals. They relate just as much to similarities and divergences between the history cultures and heroic ideals of different countries. Modern research has emphasized a change in the perception of heroes over the course of the twentieth century. Before that, role models were said to have achieved their exalted positions owing to their courageous, vigorous, and dedicated actions, usually in a situation of crisis or war.[1] 'Times of heroism are generally times of terror', wrote the nineteenth-century American essayist and philosopher Ralph Waldo Emerson.[2] To him, the links between heroism and violence were therefore self-evident. Heroism was intimately associated with manliness, daring, a mind shaped by military experience, and readiness to fight. Moreover, being heroic was not a rational and intellectual trait; rather, it was based on the emotions: 'heroism feels [but] never reasons', Emerson concluded. Furthermore, he linked heroism directly to what was right and proper and to the character of the hero; a role model must convey a sense of gravitas and credibility.[3]

---

1 Hook, *The Hero in History*, pp. 16, 157.
2 Emerson, *Character and Heroism*, p. 80.
3 Emerson, *Character and Heroism*, pp. 19, 56, 60–61, quotation p. 61.

A first challenge to the combination of masculinity, war, and heroism can be traced back to the First World War. An even greater strain was felt after the end of the Second World War. Millions of dead soldiers and civilians, plus millions more victims of the Nazi genocide policies, forced people to come to terms with old and new manifestations of aggressive nationalism, antisemitism, and racism.[4] One resulting question was whether the Second World War had had a sobering influence, or was there reason to fear a Hitler myth – that the 'master of Belsen and Buchenwald' would return as a revered hero? The implicit answer was that measures must be taken to prevent such a development.[5] But it was not only the obvious effects of the war in the form of death and suffering that contributed to the fading of the hero cult. Drawing on Evelyn Waugh's writings, literary scholar Richard York outlines a shift in perspective: in the rear-view mirror of the Second World War, acts of heroism were reduced to superficial and artificial phenomena constructed on the basis of prefabricated and manipulated ideals.[6] As a consequence of the 1939–1945 war, the ideals of warlike honour and unconditional self-sacrifice found it increasingly difficult to assert themselves in the post-war period, at least in the democracies of Western Europe. The war-inspired heroic ideal, preferably focusing on great men, lost much of its value and previous functions. The question was whether traditional heroes, who have the capacity to change the course of history single-handed, were compatible with modern democracies with their watchwords of inclusiveness, diversity, and equality.[7] In the West the answer has repeatedly been negative, with obvious consequences both for an increased

---

4 Hook, *The Hero in History*, p. 148; Schult, *A Hero's Many Faces*, pp. 48–50.
5 Per Helin, 'Vad är en hjälte?', *Idun*, 1945:30, 8, 19. See also Corrado Alvaro, 'Vår tids hjältedyrkan', *Samtid och Framtid*, 1949:2, 98–99. One concrete step away from the traditional heroic ideal was that the subject of history, in which the praise of national role models and a warlike past was a central feature, was given a reduced significance in the Swedish school system in the wake of Nazism and the Second World War; see further in Zander, *Fornstora dagar, moderna tider*, pp. 327–340 and Östling, *Sweden After Nazism*, pp. 172–192. The shift towards a new heroic ideal was not appreciated by everyone, however; see e.g. Greta Renborg, 'Vår tids hjälte', *Perspektiv* 1960:9, 404–407.
6 York, 'Evelyn Waugh's Farewell to Heroism', pp. 245–253.
7 Hook, *The Hero in History*, p. 158; Schult, *A Hero's Many Faces*, p. 49.

interest in various kinds of everyday heroes and regarding a change in attitude as to which people or events should be honoured by monuments, as well as the aesthetic ideals that should characterize their design. It is obvious that Raoul Wallenberg has been one of the individuals who have fitted in well with this process of change.[8] As we have seen, the difficulties in realizing Swedish monuments commemorating him were not related to any idea of his being unsuitable for immortalization.

This shift has been particularly obvious in Sweden, whose long peaceful history is well matched by a downplayed perception of heroism. 'Being the first person to set foot on the moon is no more heroic than taking care of your old mother and patiently waiting for better times that never come', is a statement along these lines.[9] The Social Democratic politician and then Sweden's Cabinet Secretary for Foreign Affairs, Pierre Schori, espoused this view in a television interview shortly after the premiere of *Good Evening, Mr. Wallenberg*. When asked if there were heroes today – that is, in 1990 – of the same kind as Raoul Wallenberg, he answered yes. However, Schori did not choose someone who had made self-sacrificing contributions in any of the world's conflict zones as an example substantiating his claim. Instead, he singled out a hard-working kindergarten teacher and a worn-out factory worker who kept on struggling as best they could in tough working conditions.[10]

How, then, do we explain the great attention paid to Wallenberg, Schindler, and others who were involved in rescue operations? One explanation is that they have become the heirs of the soldier heroes of the Second World War. It cannot be overlooked that Wallenberg was inspired by traditional heroic ideals similar to those of the warriors, or at least by the values that had guided Leslie Howard's suave heroes the Scarlet Pimpernel and Pimpernel Smith, who employed cunning and disguises rather than clenched fists and glistening weapons. When Wallenberg put on a uniform on various occasions, both he and others testified to a considerable enthusiasm

---

8 Schult, *A Hero's Many Faces*, passim.
9 Olav Wikström, 'Hjältar, finns dom?', *Moderna tider*, December/January 2000–2001, 62.
10 Per T. Ohlsson, 'Att må illa framför TV-n', *Sydsvenskan*, 9 October 1990. Around 1990, Wallenberg was presented as an anomaly in other contexts as well; see e.g. Micke Widell, 'Raoul – en osvensk hjälte', *Sydsvenskan*, 26 September 1990.

for firearms training and other warlike pursuits.[11] However, it was not for these actions that he became famous. Wallenberg and others who saved people from the ongoing genocide participated in the Second World War under different circumstances. Though caught up in the course of the war, they did nothing to reinforce it, instead striving to reduce its deleterious impacts. In a philosophical sense, it is not self-evident that courage as a virtue is associated with morality and goodness, but when the connection is made in the context of the Holocaust, the symbolic value becomes great.[12] In a time of Nazi darkness Wallenberg brought light and hope for a better future, in accordance with a simplified but nonetheless common dichotomy.[13] One consequence is that individuals who made heroic efforts to save people from the genocides of the Second World War have sometimes been equated with modern, vaguely defined everyday heroes, probably to indicate a distance from the heroic ideals of the past.[14]

## New times, new ideals

These ideals, of course, do not remain the same over time. As we have seen, *Wallenberg: A Hero's Story* and *Good Evening, Mr. Wallenberg* represent two different versions of the Swedish diplomat, the former linking to the hero worship of the past. The latter highlights the protagonist's doubts but his moral character is unimpeachable. By contrast, this is not the case with Oskar Schindler, who undergoes an inner journey from being a profit-hungry Nazi sympathizer to experiencing a growing commitment to the survival of the Jews. The British historian Simon Sebag Montefiore argues that such a perspective of change embodies a greater potential. From a selection of a hundred heroes, it is

---

11 Letter from Raoul Wallenberg to Amalia Wallenberg, 29 July and 17 September 1930, in Nylander and Perlinge (eds), *Raoul Wallenberg in Documents, 1927–1947*, pp. 26, 30; Philipp, *Raoul Wallenberg*, pp. 33–34.
12 See Bauhn, *The Value of Courage*, pp. 38–39; Schult, *A Hero's Many Faces*, pp. 300–301.
13 See e.g. Judith Weintraub, 'Amid Holocaust horrors, a bright light: To the protector of Budapest Jews, belated honor and remembrance', *The Washington Post*, 6 September 1990; Paul Hendrickson and Laurie Goodstein, 'What the death machine could not kill: When the world went dark, they provided light', *The Washington Post*, 22 April 1993.
14 See Lundgren, *I hjältens tid*, pp. 7–21.

hence not Wallenberg but Schindler who is Montefiore's main role model associated with the Holocaust. The latter is implicitly more interesting because, unlike the Swede, he is a complex person with eccentric, opportunistic, and even villainous characteristics. The fact that Schindler chooses to abandon a profitable business and instead proves willing to sacrifice everything to save as many Jews as possible from the Holocaust makes him a fascinating character.[15]

Even so, the warrior still enjoys heroic status in many history cultures and has repeatedly been employed in order to serve democracies. It has become clear that even democratic forms of government need role models in order to gain legitimacy. While over time Wallenberg became an increasingly obvious diplomatic failure in Sweden, he fulfilled an important function as a vanished but simultaneously almost ever-present hero in Cold War America. His example showed what kind of adversary the Soviet Union was, as not even the fact that he had made great efforts to save Jews from the Holocaust – a factor which gained an ever-increasing existential significance in the historical narrative and public debate – had saved him.

Despite a decline in American attention paid to Wallenberg, it is apparent that he is still an individual that counts, as evidenced for example by President Joe Biden's contributions to the celebration of his memory. That Biden supported making Wallenberg an honorary US citizen in 1981, and was a key figure behind the decision to posthumously award the Swede the Congressional Gold Medal in 2014, has repeatedly been cited to his credit. In the wake of the withdrawal of US forces from Afghanistan in 2021, though, a different note was sounded. The disappointed Middle East expert Michael Rubin used the retreat to draw a number of bold comparisons between the Holocaust in the past and US foreign policy in the present. The heroic deeds of the past were placed in opposition to today's cynicism and incompetence. The role models Oskar Schindler and Raoul Wallenberg contrasted sharply with a President whom Rubin labelled an 'anti-Wallenberg'.[16]

---

15 Montefiore stresses the similarities between Schindler and the protagonist in Charles Dickens's novel *A Tale of Two Cities* (1859); see further in Montefiore, *101 World Heroes*, pp. 281–282.
16 Michael Rubin, 'Biden praised Wallenberg but now betrays his legacy', www.aei.org/op-eds/biden-praised-wallenberg-but-now-betrays-his-legacy (accessed 7 January 2022).

The controversial elements of Varga's Wallenberg monument in Budapest, with its references to the ageing Wallenberg as a Gulag prisoner and to Pátzay's removed statue, helped to fuel criticism of the Communist exclusion of Wallenberg from Hungarian history. The renewed interest in Wallenberg also influenced the cautious reassessment of the Jewish catastrophe in Hungary in 1944–1945 that took place in the 1990s and early 2000s. That Tom Lantos, the Holocaust survivor who was a driving American force in honouring Raoul Wallenberg, was given a monument inaugurated in 2018 on the street that had been named after him in 2016 could be taken as evidence that the memory of the Holocaust is still being kept alive in Hungary. This is only partly true, though. Since then the trend has been in the direction of historical revisionism. The revived desire to place sole responsibility for the Holocaust on the German occupiers, thereby exonerating the Hungarians, has been manifested not least in connection with the monument on Budapest's Freedom Square that depicts a German eagle attacking the Angel Gabriel: a visualization of a blameless Christian Hungary. Erected in 2014, that monument has been controversial in both the Hungarian and the international press; in addition, the fence in front of it has regularly been covered by quotes and witness statements from the Hungarian Holocaust. Raoul Wallenberg has appeared in words and images as part of these protests against the rewriting of the Hungarian history of the Second World War.[17]

In Sweden, the situation was and remains different. Whereas coming to terms with Soviet Communism was not possible in Hungary until the glasnost of the 1980s, Raoul Wallenberg was a central feature of the Swedish Cold War debate. His disappearance in the Soviet Union and the Swedish government's conduct towards the Soviet authorities constituted an urgent domestic political issue from shortly after the end of the war until the 1980s. Most of the evidence indicates that by the time of the dissolution of the Soviet Union, the transformation of Wallenberg was in full swing.

---

17 Mark MacCinnon, 'Statue in Budapest based on Second World War evokes dark history', *The Globe and Mail*, 15 December 2014; Ingrid Carlberg, 'Raoul Wallenberg skulle bli bedrövad av historieförfalskningen i Ungern', *Dagens Nyheter*, 24 October 2021. For in-depth analyses of this development and the associated symbolism policies, see István Rév, 'Liberty Square, Budapest', pp. 607–623, and Pető, 'The Illiberal Memory Politics of Hungary', pp. 241–249.

In Sweden he went from being a divisive to a healing force that rose above political and ideological differences.

At the same time, debates were raging about Sweden's historical guilt, voiced as accusations of a neutrality that lacked substance and a strong pro-German bias during the Second World War. However, these debates do not seem to have had any profound effect on Sweden's self-image. The dark chapters were fairly unproblematically incorporated into the grand narrative. Historical realities have entailed a long period of peace in Swedish history. While the absence of war was by no means viewed as an unambiguously good thing in influential circles, at least until the First World War, peace and neutrality have been cherished concepts from the time of the Second World War onwards. Depictions of Swedish soldiers on guard and other images along the same lines have been very popular since the end of the war. By contrast, most of the warrior heroes of olden times who were at the heart of a historically orientated nationalism have been forgotten, or dismissed as embarrassing reminders of an era that people no longer want to acknowledge.[18]

As a result of this reorientation, the number of vertical and individualizing statues has decreased over the last 50 years or so. Swedish art historian Jessica Sjöholm Skrubbe has found an increasing number of horizontal artworks that convey messages of equality and collective exploits. In addition, an increasing number of modern monuments feature life-size individuals. These are not elevated on pedestals and plinths but are at the same level as the viewer, inviting us to see the depicted person as both a role model and an equal.[19] Another changed approach to public art is international, or at least Western. Miwon Kwon has drawn attention to the challenge to the 'art-in-public-places paradigm' of the 1960s and 1970s. This art often proceeded from abstract, modernist sculptures, which were in many cases enlarged versions of works by male artists found in museums or galleries. A recurring dilemma was that the artwork was not always in harmony with the site where it was installed, while another problem was the general public's indifference or hostility to public art. At best, the artworks functioned as a contrast to their surroundings; at worst they were symbols which appealed only to a knowledgeable and privileged

---

18 Zander, *Fornstora dagar, moderna tider*, passim; Liljefors and Zander, 'Det neutrala landet Ingenstans', pp. 209–242.
19 Sjöholm Skrubbe, *Skulptur i folkhemmet*, pp. 130–175.

few. As a reaction, more artists began to bridge the gap between art and utility, paying greater attention to the importance of specific sites to the design and size of their artworks and to the potential for interaction between public art and its audience. This should not be understood as a striving for harmony and conformity; in a number of cases, artists have very deliberately used their works to question the function and significance of public spaces, but they have also encouraged interaction between the creator of the work and people in the public space.[20]

It is in the light of such changes that the controversy surrounding Ortwed's sphinxes is best understood. In connection with her monument, it became clear that everyone agreed that Wallenberg should be honoured with a memorial, but where supporters saw an exemplary work of art, opponents saw one that was unworthy of the man to whom it was supposed to pay tribute. Between the lines of the critics' arguments, it was clear that they held fast to the idea that monuments should continue to fulfil their traditional function of being *exempla virtutis*, that is, portrayals of exemplary citizens whose deeds encourage emulation. The best way to present this in visual form was as heroic larger-than-life representations. After all, such monuments – mainly from the late nineteenth and early twentieth centuries – already stood at Nybroviken. The critics also argued that Ortwed's monument suffered from a potential democratic deficit, because the general public did not have the tools to decode it. Ortwed's defenders, on the other hand, maintained that the diversity of interpretation was a guarantee of democratic interaction, created in the encounter between monument and viewer. The sphinxes' low position, which enabled the visitor not only to study them from the side but also to move among them, was a clear break from the raised statue-heroes of the past, that is, the ideal attributed to Carl Hamilton and others. In Ortwed's words, it was about getting away from 'the man on the horse'.[21] That argument was in line with the jury citation, which included the statement that 'Raoul Wallenberg's own fate is too immense for the traditional forms of a monument'; therefore, the 'fragments, attempts, and moulds' in Ortwed's

---

20 Kwon, *One Place after Another*, pp. 56–99.
21 Eva Pohl, 'En anden frihed', *Berlingske Tidende*, 10 May 2002. See also e.g. Clemens Poellinger, 'Jaha, nu har det hänt: Wallenbergmonumentet är väck', *Svenska Dagbladet*, 25 April 2003. See also Schult, *A Hero's Many Faces*, pp. 240–242.

artwork supposedly created an appropriate link to the missing Swede's achievements.²²

## Raoul Wallenberg: a role model in and for our times?

Even if the era of equestrian statues is over in the realm of public art, role models such as Wallenberg still fulfil an important function. In such a context, the presumed major difference compared with a 'typical' American heroic ideal – a difference repeatedly asserted by Swedes in connection with *Wallenberg: A Hero's Story* and *Good Evening, Mr. Wallenberg* – is less than substantial. Wallenberg may not have been accorded an old-style type of elevated position in Swedish monuments, but he still invites heroic representations as someone who simultaneously represents neutral and humanitarian Sweden. As in representations of Oskar Schindler, the good deeds performed by the real-life Swedish Scarlet Pimpernel have often been portrayed in accordance with an important concept in American history culture: the lone hero who takes up the fight despite the odds against him. The creation of such heroic images has been reinforced by the contrast between active, masculine heroes and passive Jewish victims. Certainly, Jewish heroism and rebellion do appear, mainly though not exclusively in Israeli history culture, but they are rare in the stories about heroes during the Holocaust, such as Schindler and Wallenberg. The rescue and liberation of Jews has been an important part of national identity formation in a number of Western countries, and in such contexts the focus has been on the role models, those men and women who rescued Jews and others from the ongoing mass murder. To put it cynically, those individuals who were saved become the means to an end: national pride, channelled via the morally superior few who dared to take action against the Nazi Holocaust machinery.²³

Such a conclusion in no way diminishes Raoul Wallenberg's historic achievement in Budapest in 1944–1945. We can all behave heroically, but a person like Wallenberg, who has achieved the

---

22 Erik Lidén, 'Namnteckningen ska minna om Wallenberg', *Svenska Dagbladet*, 18 November 1998.
23 See Cole, *Selling the Holocaust*, pp. 82–83; Zander, 'To Rescue or be Rescued', pp. 370–374; Schult, *A Hero's Many Faces*, p. 75; Holmila, *Reporting the Holocaust in the British, Swedish and Finnish Press, 1945–50*, pp. 46–49.

status of a legend, embodies something more. Art historian John Lash notes that by always taking action to the best of his ability, thanks to which endeavour the role model constantly surpasses himself, the hero becomes an example for his group, for his nation, or even for all of humanity.[24] By this definition, Wallenberg is in all respects a role model in and for our times. Like other legendary figures he exceeded his own expectations and those of others, but this was in itself no guarantee of his post-war heroic status. So far, Raoul Wallenberg has demonstrated a considerable ability to survive. It has been possible to adapt his story to different contexts in different times and different places. There is much to suggest that his heroic deeds and tragic fate will remain alive in both the historical and the practical past. He will presumably have a central place in historical scholarship as well as in the public sphere as long as rejection of the Holocaust and of dictatorial oppression is a key element in the maintenance of democratic values. Beyond this proud banner, however, challenges remain. Using the UK as an example, David Cesarani has emphasized that the nation's history must be characterized by a sense of balance: it can and should highlight the British people's tenacious resistance to Nazism at the cost of many lives; but it must also draw attention to restrictive refugee policies prior to the outbreak of the Second World War, as well as to expressions of antisemitism.[25] Similarly, in a Swedish history of the Holocaust, Raoul Wallenberg's role in saving human lives and his tragic end in the Soviet Union should be nuanced: the story of the legend and hero who saves his country's honour through his deeds is well worth telling, but it should be accompanied by the less edifying aspects of Sweden and the Holocaust, as well as by the Swedish Foreign Office's (Utrikesdepartementet, UD's) few and clumsy attempts to discover his fate in the immediate post-war years.

A closely related and remaining challenge is the distinction that still exists between the historical and the practical past, which is highly evident with regard to the ways in which the Holocaust is interpreted. In line with analysts who have equated an Americanization with a trivialization of the Holocaust, David Cesarani's *Final Solution* depicts two very different Holocausts: one characterized by new research findings that are rarely reflected

---

24 John Lash, *The Hero*, p. 5.
25 Cesarani, 'Should Britain Have a National Holocaust Museum?', pp. 19–21.

in novels, textbooks, films, television series, or political speeches, and 'another' genocide which is conveyed by long-established narratives of good and evil, plus apparently simple links between the Holocaust of the past and the contemporary fight against antisemitism and xenophobia. There is no easy solution to this contradiction, but Hayden White's plea for self-reflection and the questioning of ingrained historical beliefs is a good starting point. The twentieth century is filled with events that are 'supposedly unimaginable, unthinkable, and unspeakable', and this has created an awareness of the limitations of the ways in which these events can be represented. White concludes that this means that events such as the Holocaust cannot be fitted into traditional ways of interpreting and understanding history.[26]

One way forward would be to allow the two ways of relating to the past to be subject to constructive criticism so that steps can be taken to make them complementary rather than contradictory. This means that history producers outside academia need to develop a greater understanding of the conditions that prevail in historical scholarship and that professional historians in general should become better at understanding other ways of communicating history, an understanding which would, for example, entail improved skills in analysing the characteristics of various genres and visual media. Given such insights, one of the things that become clear is that as memories fade, expectations are created with regard to monuments. They should make history timeless by dramatizing exemplary individuals and pivotal events in bronze and granite, so that their historical significance lives on into the future. But while these monuments are made of enduring materials, the messages they convey are children of the time in which they were born. Ralph Waldo Emerson famously and laconically observed that 'every hero becomes a bore at last', meaning that sooner or later the exalted individual becomes overexploited and irrelevant. As the first President of the United States, George Washington, went from being an exemplary figure to being associated merely with a monument that was both literal and figurative, elevated and seemingly faultless, he became increasingly difficult to identify with in the process.[27] Sooner or later, Raoul Wallenberg will

---

26 Hayden White, 'Historical Emplotment and the Problem of Truth', pp. 51–52.
27 See Fishwick, 'Did Anyone Ever See Washington Nude?', pp. 297–307.

face the same fate. From a history-cultural perspective, it is clear that monuments, as well as the heroes they depict, are doomed to oblivion if they do not provide answers to present-day questions. The history-cultural lesson, however, is that few role models last forever, any more than the monuments erected in their honour do. Ultimately, as Wallenberg's half-sister Nina Lagergren once said, it is better to teach children the importance of taking responsibility and standing up for human dignity than it is to erect monuments.[28]

## Tragedy, trauma, triumph

Many of the historical events discussed in this book have left such deep scars that they are best described as traumatic. There is good reason to distinguish between, on the one hand, individuals who suffer trauma as a result of a psychological and emotional reaction to an event or experience that they perceive as deeply disturbing and upsetting, and, on the other, collective constructions of trauma. In the latter case, historical events become a matter which may involve other people than those directly affected. This is, above all, true of the Holocaust, whose aftermath we are still grappling with. In the case of Raoul Wallenberg, the uncertainty about what happened to him meant that his immediate family had to live under severe psychological stress for many decades. The political battle over the Swedish government's actions with regard to gaining reliable information about his fate, a battle which raged with varying degrees of intensity in Sweden for decades, contributed to the ceaseless reopening of a wound that could not be healed while the Cold War lasted. A circumstance related to the latter phenomenon is that there is often a generational factor to be taken into account: some collective traumas either emerge, and are reinforced, or fade once the people who actually experienced the shocking events have passed away.[29]

The German sociologist Bernhard Giesen completes the picture by demonstrating that triumph and trauma can coexist or follow each other. He has pointed out that in the Western tradition,

---

28 Christian Brøndum, 'Idealisme er ikke nok', *Berlingske Tidende*, 3 May 2000.
29 Alexander, *Trauma: A Social Theory* and Alexander, Eyerman, Giesen, Smelser, and Sztompka, *Cultural Trauma and Collective Identity*, Berkeley, California: University of California Press 2004.

triumphant tales of heroes such as Raoul Wallenberg coexist in parallel with tragic role models. He also notes that stories of popular uprisings against tyrants have increasingly been replaced by an interest in collective trauma, exemplified by slavery, displacement, persecution, terror, and genocide. In addition, post-war debates in Germany illustrate how a trauma can first be nationalized, whereupon it has the potential to be both mythologized and made universally relevant.[30]

The fact that Raoul Wallenberg did not return from his mission in Hungary, and that we still do not know how he ended his days, has helped to keep his story alive. We can walk in his footsteps on the streets of Budapest, where street names, monuments, and cafés remind us that his legacy is by no means forgotten. From time to time we can watch and listen to stories about him at operas, in theatres, on television, or at the cinema. However, there is no location linked to his passing. Whereas over the past hundred years unidentified soldiers have been laid to rest in the graves of unknown soldiers, there is no final resting place for Raoul Wallenberg, who has gone down in history as anything but unknown. Given this background, the many portrayals of him may be said to fill a deeply felt human need for many of those who wish to mourn, remember, and honour him.

---

30 Giesen, *Triumph and Trauma*, passim.

# Bibliography

## Archives

### Israel

Yad Vashem Archive (YVA), Jerusalem
  Charles Lutz Collection, P 19/16
  Heiner Lichtenstein Collection, P 26/137

### Sweden

Government Offices Archives (RKA), Stockholm
  Raoul Wallenberg, UD2001/00009, Vols 1, 2, 3, 4, 5, 6, 9, 10, 13, 14, 15, 16, 17, 18, 19, 22, 23, 24, 25, 26, 27, 28, 29, 30, 31, 32, 33, 34, 36, 40, 41, 44, 48, 50, 52, 53, 55, 61, 67, 68.
  Raoul Wallenberg, UD2018/005505, Vols 1, 2, 3, 4, 8, 9, 10, 11, 12, 14, 16, 19, 20, 22, 25, 28, 30, 36, 48.
The National Archives (RA) Marieberg, Stockholm
  Raoul Wallenberg Association Archive, Correspondence, E: 1–4.
  Swedish Foreign Office [Utrikesdepartementet, UD] Archive, Hp 1 Er, 18 June 1946, No. 430.
The National Archives (RA) Arninge, Stockholm
  Swedish Red Cross I, Folke Bernadotte's Archive, Greve Folke Bernadotte af Wisborg 1943–1945, Vols 5, 6.

### The United Kingdom

British Film Institute Archive and Library (BFI), London
  Wallenberg: *The Lost Hero*, press material from ITV Network, Yorkshire Television 1985.

Bibliography                                                              339

## United States

The Franklin D. Roosevelt Presidential Library and Museum (FDRL), Hyde Park, New York
Eleanor Roosevelt Papers, General Correspondence, 1945–1948.
von Dardel, Guy.
Gromyko, Andrei 1946–1947.
The National Archives, Washington D.C.
Special Collection, Wallenberg, Raoul, Vol. 3, Nazi War Crime Disclosure Act, Records of the Central Intelligence Archive (CIA), Washington D.C.
The New York Public Library. Humanities and Social Sciences Library (TNYPL), New York
Rudolph Philipp Papers on Raoul Wallenberg, Box 1.
United States Holocaust Memorial Museum, Washington D.C.
Sara Callen, 'Oral History Interview with Elizabeth Fuchs', 15 May 1986, Accession Number: 1997.A.0441.8, RG Number: RG-50.462.0008 (Gift of the Gratz College Holocaust Oral History Archive), https://collections.ushmm.org/search/catalog/irn508629.
Linda G. Kuzmack, 'Oral History Interview with Giorgio Perlasca', 5 September 1990, Accession Number: 1990.446.1 | RG Number: RG-50.030.0178 (Gift of the Gratz College Holocaust Oral History Archive), https://collections.ushmm.org/search/catalog/irn504674.

## Official publications

*Congress and the Nation. Volume IV. 1981–1984. A Review of Government and Politics*, Washington D.C.: Congressional Quarterly Inc., 1985.
Eliasson, Ingemar et al., *Ett diplomatiskt misslyckande: Fallet Raoul Wallenberg och den svenska utrikesledningen*, Swedish Government Official Reports SOU, 2003: 18.
*George Bush. Public Papers of the Presidents of the United States. 1989. Book II – July 1 to December 31, 1989*, Washington D.C.: United States Government Printing Office, 1990.
*George Bush. Public Papers of the Presidents of the United States. 1991. Book I – January 1 to June 30, 1991*, Washington D.C.: United States Government Printing Office, 1992.
*Jimmy Carter. Public Papers of the Presidents of the United States. 1979. Book II – June 23 to December 31, 1979*, Washington D.C.: United States Government Printing Office, 1980.
Palmklint, Ingrid and Daniel Larsson (eds), *Raoul Wallenberg: Report of the Swedish-Russian Working Group*, Stockholm: Original documents published by the Swedish Foreign Office. New series II: 52, 2001.
*Raoul Wallenberg: Dokumentsamling jämte kommentarer rörande hans fångenskap i Sovjetunionen*, Stockholm: Ministry for Foreign Affairs, 1957.

*Raoul Wallenberg: Dokumentsamling rörande efterforskningarna efter år 1957*, Stockholm: Ministry for Foreign Affairs, 1965.
*Riksdagen: minutes. Second Chamber*, No. 8, February 1951, Stockholm: The Riksdag [Swedish Parliament], 1951.
*Riksdagen: minutes. Second Chamber*, No. 14, 3 April 1964, Stockholm: The Riksdag, 1964.
*Riksdagen: minutes*, No. 55, 22 January 1976, Stockholm: The Riksdag, 1976.
*Riksdagen: minutes*, No. 85, 20 May 1974, Stockholm: The Riksdag, 1974.
*Riksdagen: minutes* 1987:88:67, 11 February 1988, Stockholm: The Riksdag, 1988.
Ronald Reagan. *Public Papers of the Presidents of the United States. 1981. January 20 to December 31, 1981*, Washington D.C.: United States Government Printing Office, 1982.
Ronald Reagan. *Public Papers of the Presidents of the United States. 1982. Book I – January 1 to July 2, 1982*, Washington D.C.: United States Government Printing Office, 1983.
Ronald Reagan. *Public Papers of the Presidents of the United States. 1983. Book I – January 1 to July 1, 1983*, Washington D.C.: United States Government Printing Office, 1984.
Ronald Reagan. *Public Papers of the Presidents of the United States. 1985. Book I – January 1 to June 28, 1985*, Washington D.C.: United States Government Printing Office, 1988.
Ronald Reagan. *Public Papers of the Presidents of the United States. 1987, Book II – July 4 to December 31, 1987*, Washington D.C.: United States Government Printing Office, 1989.
*The Trial of Adolf Eichmann: Record of Proceedings in the District Court of Jerusalem*. Vol. 1, Jerusalem: State of Israel Ministry of Justice, 1992.

## Collections of letters and documents, and diaries

Adelsohn, Ulf, *Partiledare: Dagbok 1981–1986*, Stockholm: Gedins Förlag, 1988 [1987].
Brandell, Ulf, *Dagbok med DN: Ur dagböcker förda 1960–1962*, Stockholm: Trevi, 1976.
von Dardel, Fredrik, *Dagbok*, 1972, www.raoul-wallenberg.eu/wp-content/uploads/2012/05/1972/fvDdiary.pdf (accessed 21 June 2021).
von Dardel, Maj, *Raoul*, Stockholm: Rabén and Sjögren, 1984.
Ekman, Stig (ed.), *Sven Grafström: Anteckningar 1938–1944*, Stockholm: Royal Swedish Society for the Publication of Manuscripts Relating to Scandinavian History, 1989.
Ekman, Stig (ed.), *Sven Grafström: Anteckningar 1945–1954*, Stockholm: Royal Swedish Society for the Publication of Manuscripts Relating to Scandinavian History, 1989.
Erlander, Sven (ed.), *Tage Erlander: Dagböcker 1945–1949*, Hedemora: Gidlunds Förlag, 2001.

# Bibliography 341

Erlander, Sven (ed.), *Tage Erlander: Dagböcker 1950–1951*, Hedemora: Gidlunds Förlag, 2001.
Erlander, Sven (ed.), *Tage Erlander: Dagböcker 1952*, Hedemora: Gidlunds Förlag, 2002.
Erlander, Sven (ed.), *Tage Erlander: Dagböcker 1953*, Hedemora: Gidlunds Förlag, 2003.
Erlander, Sven (ed.), *Tage Erlander: Dagböcker 1955*, Hedemora: Gidlunds Förlag, 2005.
Erlander, Sven (ed.), *Tage Erlander: Dagböcker 1959*, Hedemora: Gidlunds Förlag, 2009.
Erlander, Sven (ed.), *Tage Erlander: Dagböcker 1961–1962*, Hedemora: Gidlunds Förlag, 2011.
Erlander, Sven (ed.), *Tage Erlander: Dagböcker 1963–1964*, Hedemora: Gidlunds Förlag, 2012.
Erlander, Sven (ed.), *Tage Erlander: Dagböcker 1965*, Hedemora: Gidlunds Förlag, 2013.
Gripenberg, G. A., *Dagbok 1945–1946*, Stockholm: Royal Swedish Society for the Publication of Manuscripts Relating to Scandinavian History, 2019.
Levai, Jenő (ed.), *Eichmann in Hungary: Documents*, Budapest: Pannonia Press, 1961.
Molin, Karl (ed.), *Östen Undén: Anteckningar 1918–1952*, Stockholm: Royal Swedish Society for the Publication of Manuscripts Relating to Scandinavian History, 2002.
Molin, Karl (ed.), *Östen Undén: Anteckningar 1952–1966*, Stockholm: Royal Swedish Society for the Publication of Manuscripts Relating to Scandinavian History, 2002.
Nylander, Gert and Anders Perlinge (eds), *Raoul Wallenberg in Documents, 1927–1947*, Stockholm: Banking & Enterprise, 2000.
Schattauer, Wolfgang (ed.), *Räddningen: Budapest 1944. Rapporter ur UD:s arkiv*, Stockholm: Fischer & Co, 1997.
Söderlund, Gustaf and Gitte Wallenberg (eds), *Älskade farfar! Brevväxlingen mellan Gustaf och Raoul Wallenberg 1924–1936*, Stockholm: Bonniers, 1987.
Theutenberg, Bo J., *Dagbok från UD. Volym 1. Högdramatik i UD. Ubåtar, protestnoter och annat (1981–1983)*, Stockholm: Stockholm Institute of International Law Arbitration and Conciliation, 2012.
Theutenberg, Bo J., *Dagbok från UD. Volym 4 (1981–1985). Ryska björnens järngrepp om Sverige*, Stockholm: Stockholm Institute of International Law Arbitration and Conciliation, 2018.
Theutenberg, Bo J., *Dagbok från UD. Volym 5 (1986–1988)*, Stockholm: Stockholm Institute of International Law Arbitration and Conciliation, 2020.
Wallberg, Evabritta (ed.), *Överbefälhavare Lennart Ljungs tjänstedagböcker 1978–1983. Vol. 1*, Stockholm: Royal Swedish Society for the Publication of Manuscripts Relating to Scandinavian History, 2010.

Wallenberg, Birgitte and Gustaf Söderlund (eds), *Letters and Dispatches 1924–1944. Raoul Wallenberg*, New York: Arcade Publishing, 1995 [1987].

## Interviews

Ahlander, Dag Sebastian, 14 April 2004.
Grede, Kjell, 7 July 2010.
Lagergren, Nina, 29 April 2008.
Wästberg, Olle, 5 November 2021.

## Booklets, pamphlets etc.

Ahlander, Dag Sebastian, 'The History of the Monument', in Jan Torsten Ahlstrand (ed.), *The Raoul Wallenberg Monument in New York*, Lund: Museum of Artistic Process and Public Art [Skissernas museum], 1998, pp. 9–11.
Ahlstrand, Jan Torsten (ed.), *Raoul Wallenberg: Minnesmärke i Stockholm. Sex tävlingsförslag av Bernard Kirschbaum, Franco Leidi, Lars Olof Loeld, Kirsten Ortwed, Christian Partos, Jaume Plensa*, Lund: Museum of Artistic Process and Public Art [Skissernas museum], 1999.
Ahlstrand, Jan Torsten (ed.), *The Raoul Wallenberg Monument in New York*, Lund: Museum of Artistic Process and Public Art [Skissernas museum], 1998.
Bolinder, Gunilla, *A Tribute to the Memory of Nanna Svartz 1890–1986*, Stockholm: Royal Swedish Academy of Engineering Sciences, 2016.
Larsson, Jan, *Swedish Portraits: Raoul Wallenberg*, Stockholm: The Swedish Institute, 1995.
Philipp, Rudolph, *Raoul Wallenberg – kämpe för humanitet*, Stockholm: Fredens Förlag, 1947.
*Raoul Wallenberg*, Stockholm: The Swedish Institute, 1988.
*Raoul Wallenberg – A Hero for Our Time*, New York: The Raoul Wallenberg Committee of the United States, 1985.
*Raoul Wallenberg-kalendern 2013*, Stockholm: The Living History Forum, 2013.
Rothman, Lenke, *Hågkomsten, hyllningen och respekten för Raoul Wallenbergs gärning i Budapest 1944*, Stockholm: Sveriges Riksdag, 1998.
*UD informerar; Raoul Wallenberg*, Stockholm: Norstedts 1987.
Wästberg, Per, *Om Raoul Wallenberg*, Stockholm: Public Art Agency Sweden, 1998.

## Daily newspapers

### Canada

*The Globe and Mail, Montreal Gazette, The Ottawa Citizen, Toronto Star, The Vancouver Sun.*

## Denmark

Berlingske Tidende, Information, Jyllands-Posten.

## Germany

Badische Zeitung, Berliner Morgenpost, Der Tagesspiegel, Die Tageszeitung, Volksblatt, Die Welt, Die Zeit.

## Hungary

Budapester Zeitung, Hungary Today, HVG, Magyar Nezmet, Mai Nap, Napról Napra, Nepszabadsag.

## Ireland

The Irish Examiner, The Irish Times.

## Israel

Haaretz, The Jerusalem Post.

## Sweden

Aftonbladet, Arbetaren, Arbetartidningen, Arbetet, Bohuslänningen, Borås Tidning, Dagens Nyheter, Dagstidningen, Expressen, Göteborgs Handels- och Sjöfartstidning, Göteborgs Morgonpost, Göteborgs-Posten, Göteborgs-Tidningen, iDAG, Metro, Morgon-Tidningen, Ny Dag, Östgöta Correspondenten, Provinstidningen Dalsland, Skånska Dagbladet, Skånska Socialdemokraten, Social-Demokraten, Söderhamns Tidning, Sölvesborgs-Tidningen, Stockholms Tidningen, Svenska Dagbladet, Sydsvenskan, Trelleborgstidningen, Upsala, Upsala Nya Tidning, Ystads Allehanda.

## Switzerland

Neue Zürcher Zeitung

## United Kingdom

The Daily Mail, The Daily Mirror, The Daily Telegraph, The Financial Times, The Guardian, The Independent, The International Herald Tribune, The Listener, The Manchester Guardian, The Observer, The Spectator, The Sunday Times, The Times.

## United States

The Boston Globe, The Chicago Sun-Times, The Christian Science Monitor, The Detroit News, The Houston Chronicle, The Los Angeles Times, The New York Sun, The New York Times, Pittsburgh Post-Gazette, The Record, The San Francisco Examiner & Chronicle, The Saturday Evening Post, The Seattle Times, Sun Sentinel, The Tribune, The Wall Street Journal, The Washington Post.

## Magazines and weekly publications

### Australia

The Australian Jewish Times – The Jerusalem Post International Edition, Quadrant.

### Hungary

The Hungarian Quarterly, The New Hungarian Quarterly, Magyarország, Tükür.

### Russia

Moscow News.

### Sweden

Allt, Axess, Biografbladet, Bonniers Litterära Magasin, Dagens forskning, ETC, Filmjournalen, Folket i Bild, Historisk tidskrift, Idun, Jorden Runt, Judisk Krönika, Judisk Tidskrift, Konstperspektiv, Kulturens Värld, Moderna tider, OBS!, Ord & Bild, Perspektiv, Populär Historia, Respons, Röster i Radio, Röster i Radio & TV, Samtid och Framtid, Scandia, Se, Svensk Tidskrift, Tiden, Vecko-Journalen, Vi, Året Runt.

### United Kingdom

The Jewish Chronicle, Screen International, Times Literary Supplement.

### United States

American Record Guide, BOMB, Emmy Magazine, The Explicator, Films in Review, Foreign Politics, The Hollywood Reporter, The Jewish Week, The New Yorker, The New York Review of Books, The Objective

# Bibliography

*Standard*, *The Reader's Digest*, *The Saturday Evening Post*, *Slavic Review*, *Time Magazine*, *Variety*.

## Websites

www.aei.org, www.theatlantic.com, www.britishcouncil.se, www.cia. gov, www.jdc.org, www.hagalil.com, www.hungarianspectrum.org, www.raoul-wallenberg.eu, www.regeringen.se, www.rferl.org, www.riksdagen.se, www.rwi-70.de, www.Soz-u-Kult.de, www.suite101.com, www.ui.se/utrikesmagasinet.

## Books and articles

Adachi, Agnes, *Child of the Winds: My Mission with Raoul Wallenberg*, Chicago: Adams Press, 1989.

Adaktusson, Lars, *Världens bästa story*, Stockholm: Ekerlids Förlag, 2011.

Agrell, Wilhelm, *The Shadows around Wallenberg: Missions to Hungary, 1943–1945*, Lund: Historiska Media, 2019 [2006].

Agrell, Wilhelm, *Venona: Spåren från ett underrättelsekrig*, Lund: Historiska Media, 2003.

Ahlander, Dag Sebastian, *Raoul Wallenberg: Hjälten som försvann*, Stockholm: Natur & Kultur, 2001.

Ahlmark, Per, 'Att avslöja diktaturen – Tingsten, nazismen och kommunismen', in Per Ahlmark et al., *Sovjetmyten i Sverige*, Stockholm: Timbro, 1992, pp. 11–27.

Ahlmark, Per, *Det öppna såret: Om massmord och medlöperi*, Stockholm: Timbro, 1997.

Ahlmark, Per, *Gör inga dumheter medan jag är död! Memoarer*, Stockholm: Bokförlaget Atlantis, 2011.

Ahnfeldt-Mollerup, Eline, 'Historien som nyhed – den offentlige debat om Jane Horney-serien', in Claus Ladegaard (ed.), *När medierne spinder historiens tråd*, Copenhagen: Akademisk Forlag, 1993, pp. 65–85.

Aldgate, Anthony and Jeffrey Richards, *Britain Can Take It: The British Cinema in the Second World War*, London and New York: I. B. Tauris, 1986.

Alexander, Jeffrey C., *Trauma: A Social Theory*, Cambridge: Polity Press, 2012.

Alexander, Jeffrey C., Ron Eyerman, Bernhard Giesen, Neil J. Smelser and Piotr Sztompka, *Cultural Trauma and Collective Identity*, Berkeley, California: University of California Press, 2004.

Allen, Michael Thad, *The Business of Genocide: The SS, Slave Labor, and the Concentration Camps*, Chapel Hill, North Carolina: University of North Carolina Press, 2002.

Alm, Martin, 'Holocaust Memory in America and Europe' (*Danish*) *Historisk Tidsskrift* 110.2 (2010), 494–524.

Åmark, Klas, *Att bo granne med ondskan: Sveriges förhållande till nazismen, Nazityskland och Förintelsen*, Stockholm: Bonniers, 2016 [2011].

Åmark, Klas, *Förövarna bestämmer villkoren: Raoul Wallenberg och de internationella hjälpaktionerna i Budapest*, Stockholm: Bonniers, 2016.

Åmark, Klas, *Främlingar på tåg: Sverige och Förintelsen*, Stockholm: Kaunitz-Olsson 2021.

Amishai-Maisels, Ziva, *Depiction and Interpretation: The Influence of the Holocaust on the Visual Arts*, Oxford: Butterworth-Heinemann, 1993.

Andersson, Lars M., Lars Berggren and Ulf Zander, 'Bilden som källa', in Lars M. Andersson, Lars Berggren and Ulf Zander (eds), *Mer än tusen ord: Bilden och de historiska vetenskaperna*, Lund: Nordic Academic Press, 2001, pp. 7–16.

Andersson, Sten, *I de lugnaste vatten …*, Stockholm: Tidens Förlag, 1993.

Anger, Per, *With Raoul Wallenberg in Budapest: Memories of the War Years in Hungary*, New York: Holocaust Library 1981 [1979].

Annan, Kofi, 'Introduction by Kofi A. Annan', in Ingrid Carlberg, *Raoul Wallenberg: The Heroic Life of the Man Who Saved Thousands of Hungarian Jews from the Holocaust*, London: MacLehose Press, 2015 [2012], pp. 13–15.

Apor, Péter, 'Eurocommunism: Commemorating Communism in Contemporary Europe', in Malgorzata Pakier and Bo Stråth (eds), *A European Memory? Contested Histories and Politics of Remembrance*, New York and Oxford: Berghahn Books, 2010, pp. 233–246.

Applebaum, Anne, *Gulag: A History*, New York: Anchor Books, 2004 [2003].

Arendt, Hannah, *Eichmann in Jerusalem: A Report on the Banality of Evil*, Harmondsworth: Penguin, 1992 [1963].

Arnborg, Beata, *Krig, kvinnor och gud: En biografi om Barbro Alving*, Stockholm: Bokförlaget Atlantis, 2010.

Aronson, Shlomo, 'The West, the *Yishuv*, and the Rescue Debate Regarding Slovakia and Hungary: Old and New Historiography', in David Bankier and Dan Michman (eds), *Holocaust Historiography in Context: Emergence, Challenges and Achievements*, New York and Oxford: Berghahn Books, 2008, pp. 421–434.

Åselius, Gunnar, *Vietnamkriget och de svenska diplomaterna 1954–1975*, Stockholm: Dialogos Förlag, 2019.

Asplund, Johan, *Tid, rum, individ och kollektiv*, Stockholm: LiberFörlag 1983.

Avisar, Ilan, *Screening the Holocaust: Cinema's Images of the Unimaginable*, Bloomington and Indianapolis: Indiana University Press, 1988.

Baber, Katherine, *Leonard Bernstein and the Language of Jazz*, Urbana, Chicago and Springfield: University of Illinois Press, 2019.

Barany, George, 'The Current Stage of Research on Raoul Wallenberg', in Randolph L. Braham and Attila Pók (eds), *The Holocaust in*

*Hungary Fifty Years Later*, New York: East European Monographs, 1997, pp. 567–598.

Baron, Lawrence, *Projecting the Holocaust into the Present: The Changing Focus of Contemporary Holocaust Cinema*, Lanham: Rowman & Littlefield Publishers, Inc., 2005.

Bartov, Omer, *The 'Jew' in Cinema: From* The Golem *to* Don't Touch My Holocaust, Bloomington and Indianapolis: Indiana University Press, 2005.

Bauer, Yehuda, 'Conclusion: The Holocaust in Hungary: Was Rescue Possible?', in David Cesarani (ed.), *Genocide and Rescue: The Holocaust in Hungary 1944*, Oxford and New York: Berg, 1997, pp. 193–209.

Bauer, Yehuda, *Jews for Sale? Nazi-German Negotiations, 1933–1945*, New Haven and London: Yale University Press, 1994.

Bauer, Yehuda, *Rethinking the Holocaust*, New Haven and London: Yale University Press, 2000.

Bauhn, Per, *The Value of Courage*, Lund: Nordic Academic Press, 2003.

Ben-Tov, Arieh, *Facing the Holocaust in Budapest: The International Committee of the Red Cross and the Jews in Hungary, 1943–1945*, Dordrecht: Martinus Nijhoff Publishers, 1988.

Berenbaum, Michael, *After Tragedy and Triumph: Essays in Modern Jewish Thought and the American Experience*, Cambridge: Cambridge University Press, 1990.

Berend, Iván T., 'The Road toward the Holocaust: The Ideological and Political Background', in Randolph L. Braham and Bela Vago (eds), *The Holocaust in Hungary: Forty Years Later*, New York: Columbia University Press, 1985, pp. 31–42.

Berg, Lars G:son, *Boken som försvann: Vad hände i Budapest*, Arboga: Textab Förlag, 1983 [1949].

Berg, Lars G[:son], *The Book That Disappeared: What Happened in Budapest*, New York and Los Angeles: Vantage Press, 1990 [1949].

Berge, Anders, *Det kalla kriget i Tidens spegel: En socialdemokratisk bild av hoten mot frihet och fred 1945–1962*, Stockholm: Carlssons Bokförlag, 1990.

Berger, Susanne, 'Missed Opportunities? The Swedish Handling of the Raoul Wallenberg Case', in Stefan Karner (ed.), *Auf den Spuren Wallenbergs*, Innsbruck, Vienna and Bolzano: StudienVerlag 2015, pp. 73–95.

Berger, Susanne, 'Raoul Wallenberg and the Complexities of Historic Truth', *The Wallenberg Bulletin, Autumn 2005*.

Berger, Susanne, 'Stuck in Neutral: The Reasons behind Sweden's Passivity in the Raoul Wallenberg Case', www.raoul-wallenberg.asso.fr/wallenberg_res/berger/stuck_25oct05.pdf, 2005 (accessed 12 November 2016).

Berger, Susanne and Vadim Birstein, 'Raoul Wallenberg and Mellaneuropeiska – Swedish economic "agents" in World War II', www.birstein.com 2017 (accessed 5 December 2021).

Bergquist, Lars, 'Lennart Petri', in Gunnar Artéus and Leif Leifland (eds), *Svenska diplomatprofiler under 1900-talet*, Stockholm: Probus Förlag, 2001, pp. 398–409.

Bergström, Ingvar, *Den symboliska nejlikan i senmedeltidens och renässansens konst*, Malmö: Allhems Förlag, 1958.

Berkhofer Jr, Robert F., *Fashioning History: Current Practices and Principles*, Houndmills, Basingstoke and New York: Palgrave Macmillan, 2008.

Bierman, John, *Righteous Gentile: The Story of Raoul Wallenberg, Missing Hero of the Holocaust*, Harmondsworth: Penguin Books, 1982 [1981].

Bjereld, Ulf, *Hjalmarsonaffären: Ett drama i tre akter*, Stockholm: Santérus Förlag, 1997.

Blomqvist, Anders E. B., 'Local Motives for Deporting Jews: Economic Nationalizing in Szatmárnémeti in 1944', *The Hungarian Historical Review* 4.3, 2015, 673–704.

Bloodworth, Jeff, 'Senator Henry Jackson, the Solzhenitsyn Affair, and American Liberalism', *The Pacific Northwest Quarterly* 97.2, Spring 2006, 69–77.

Blum, John Morton, *From the Morgenthau Diaries: Years of War 1941–1945*, Boston: Houghton Mifflin, 1967.

Blutinger, Jeffrey, 'An Inconvenient Past: Post-Communist Holocaust Memorialization', *Shofar* 29.1, Fall 2010, 73–94.

Bodström, Lennart, *Mitt i stormen*, Stockholm: Hjalmarson & Högberg, 2001.

Bogdanor, Paul, *Kasztner's Crime*, New Brunswick and London: Transaction Publishers, 2016.

Boheman, Erik, *Tankar i en talmansstol*, Stockholm: P. A. Norstedt & Söners Förlag, 1970.

Böhm, Tomas, 'Raoul's Childhood and Youth – A Psychological Perspective', in Karl Gabor (ed.), *Raoul Wallenberg: One Man Can Make a Difference*, Stockholm: The Jewish Museum in Stockholm, 2004, pp. 30–32.

Bohus, Kata, 'István Szirmai between Communism and Zionism: Discourses of Jewishness, Holocaust Memory, and Antisemitism in Postwar Hungary', in Jan Gerber, Philipp Graf and Anna Pollmann (eds), *Geschichtsoptimismus und Katastrophenbewusstsein: Europa nach dem Holocaust*, Göttingen: Vandenhoeck & Ruprecht, 2022, pp. 409–426.

Bokholm, Rune, *Tisdagsklubben: Om glömda antinazistiska sanningssägare i svenskt 30- och 40-tal*, Stockholm: Bokförlaget Atlantis, 2001.

Borhi, László, *Dealing with Dictators: The United States, Hungary, and East Central Europe, 1942–1989*, Bloomington and Indianapolis, Indiana: Indiana University Press, 2016.

Braham, Randolph L., 'The Holocaust in Hungary: A Retrospective Analysis', in Randolph L. Braham and Scott Miller (eds), *The Nazis' Last Victims: The Holocaust in Hungary*, Detroit: Wayne State University Press, 1998, pp. 27–43.

Braham, Randolph L., *The Politics of Genocide: The Holocaust in Hungary*, Vol. 1 and 2, New York: Columbia University Press, 1994.
Breitman, Richard, *Official Secrets: What the Nazis Planned, What the British and the Americans Knew*, New York: Hill and Wang, 1999.
Brent, Jonathan, *Stalins arkiv: Sökandet efter det Nya Ryssland*, Stockholm: Ekerlids Historia, 2009.
Brink, Lars, *När hoten var starka: Uppkomsten av en väpnad folkrörelse*, Gothenburg: Text & Bild Konsult, 2009.
Brink, Lars, *Raoul Wallenberg i dagspressen under kalla kriget*, Mellerud: Text & Bild Konsult, 2017.
Brown, Gordon, *Courage: Eight Portraits*, London: Bloomsbury, 2007.
Bullock, Alan, 'Introduction', in Walter Schellenberg, *The Schellenberg Memoirs: A Record of the Nazi Secret Service*, London: Andre Deutsch Limited, 1956, pp. 9–18.
Burch, Stuart and Ulf Zander, 'Preoccupied by the Past – The Case of Estonian's Museum of Occupations', *Scandia* 80.2 (2008), 53–73.
Bustow, Robert, 'The Limits of Modernist Art as a "Weapon of the Cold War": Reassessing the Unknown Patron of the Monument to the Unknown Political Prisoner', *Oxford Art Journal* 20.1 (1997), 68–80.
Byström, Mikael, *En broder, gäst och parasit: Uppfattningar och föreställningar om utlänningar, flyktingar och flyktingpolitik i svensk offentlig debatt 1942–1947*, Uppsala: Uppsala University, 2006.
Camargo, Leda Lucia, 'Preface: A Vision of Humanity and Responsibility', in Fábio Koifman and Jill Blonsky, *Two Diplomats and People in Need*, Stockholm: The Brazilian Embassy in Stockholm, 2014, pp. 5–11.
Campbell, Joseph, *The Hero with a Thousand Faces*, Princeton, New Jersey: Princeton University Press, 2004.
Carlberg, Ingrid, *Raoul Wallenberg: The Heroic Life of the Man Who Saved Thousands of Hungarian Jews from the Holocaust*, London: MacLehose Press, 2015 [2012].
Cartmell, Deborah and I. Q. Hunter, 'Introduction: Retrovisions: Historical Makeovers in Film and Literature', in Deborah Cartmell, I. Q. Hunter and Imelda Whelehan (eds), *Retrovisions: Reinventing the Past in Film and Fiction*, London and Sterling, Virginia: Pluto Press, 2001, pp. 1–7.
Cassirer, Ernst, *The Myth of the State*, New Haven and London: Yale University Press, 1961 [1948].
Cesarani, David, *Becoming Eichmann: Rethinking the Life, Crimes, and Trial of a 'Desk Murderer'*, Cambridge, Massachusetts: Da Capo Press, 2006 [2004].
Cesarani, David, *Final Solution: The Fate of the Jews 1933–49*, London: Pan, 2016.
Cesarani, David, 'Should Britain Have a National Holocaust Museum?', *The Journal of Holocaust Education* 7.3 (1998), 17–27.
Chaplin, Charles, *My Autobiography*, London: Bodley Head, 1964.

Chapman, James, *Past and Present: National Identity and the British Historical Film*, London: Bloomsbury, 2005.
Churchill, Winston S., *The Second World War: The Hinge of Faith*. Volume 4, Boston: Houghton Mifflin, 1950.
Cohen, Yoel, *Media Diplomacy: The Foreign Office in the Mass Communications Age*, London and Totowa, New Jersey: Routledge, 1986.
Cole, Tim, *Holocaust City: The Making of a Jewish Ghetto*, New York and London: Routledge, 2003.
Cole, Tim, *Selling the Holocaust: From Auschwitz to Schindler. How History is Bought, Packaged, and Sold*, New York and London: Routledge, 1999.
Cole, Tim, 'Turning the Places of Holocaust History into Places of Holocaust Memory: Holocaust Memorials in Budapest, Hungary, 1945–1995', in Shelley Hornstein and Florence Jacobowitz (eds), *Image and Remembrance: Representation and the Holocaust*, Bloomington and Indianapolis, Indiana University Press, pp. 272–287.
Conot, Robert E., *Justice at Nuremberg*, New York: Harper & Row Publishers, 1983.
Cornelius, Deborah S., *Hungary in World War II: Caught in the Cauldron*, New York: Fordham University Press, 2011.
Creeber, Glen, *Serial Television: Big Drama on Small Screen*, London: BFI Publishing, 2004.
Creet, Julia, 'The House of Terror and the Holocaust Memorial Centre: Resentment and Melancholia in Post-89 Hungary', in Conny Mithander, John Sundholm and Adrian Velicu (eds), *European Cultural Memory Post-89*, Amsterdam and New York: Rodopi, 2013, pp. 29–62.
Crowe, David M., *Oskar Schindler: The Untold Account of His Life, Wartime Activities, and the True Story Behind* The List, New York: Westview Press, 2004.
Dagerman, Stig, *Dagsedlar*, Stockholm: Federativs Förlag, 1960.
Danielsson Malmros, Ingmarie, 'Den historiska berättelsen i teori och praktik', in Klas-Göran Karlsson and Ulf Zander (eds), *Historien är närvarande: Historiedidaktik som teori och tillämpning*, Lund: Studentlitteratur, 2014, pp. 177–247.
von Dardel, Fredrik, *Raoul Wallenberg. Fakta kring ett öde: En sammanfattning*, Stockholm: Proprius Förlag, 1970.
Deák, István, *Essays on Hitler's Europe*, Lincoln, Nebraska: Nebraska University Press, 2001.
Deák, István, 'A Fatal Compromise? The Debate Over Collaboration and Resistance in Hungary', *East European Politics and Societies* 9.2 (1995), 209–233.
Deák, István, 'The Holocaust in Hungary', *The Hungarian Quarterly* 45 (Winter 2004), 50–70.

Deland, Mats, *En godtycklig historia: Om Sveriges behandling av tyska och svenska krigsförbrytare efter andra världskriget*, Stockholm: The Living History Forum, 2010.
Derogy, Jacques, *Fallet Raoul Wallenberg*, Malmö, Stuttgart and Zürich: Berghs, 1980.
Deutscher, Isaac, 'The Non-Jewish Jew', in Isaac Deutscher, *The Non-Jewish Jew and Other Essays*, London and New York: Oxford University Press, 1968, pp. 25–41.
Dilworth, Thomas, 'Truman Capote's "MR. JONES" and THE SCARLET PIMPERNEL', *The Explicator* 77.2 (2019), 71–72.
Diner, Hasia R., *We Remember with Reverence and Love: American Jews and the Myth of Silence after the Holocaust, 1945–1962*, New York and London: New York University Press, 2009.
Doneson, Judith E., *The Holocaust in American Film*, New York: Syracuse University Press, 2002.
Drucker, Susan J. and Robert S. Cathcart, 'The Hero as a Communication Phenomenon', in Susan J. Drucker and Robert Cathcart (eds), *American Heroes in a Media Age*, Cresskill, New Jersey: Hampton Press, 1994, pp. 1–13.
Dugan, Sally, *Baroness Orczy's The Scarlet Pimpernel: A Publishing History*, London and New York: Routledge, 2012.
Dwork, Debórah and Robert Jan van Pelt, *Auschwitz: 1270 to the Present*, New York and London: W. W. Norton & Company, 1996.
Edel, Wilbur, *The Reagan Presidency: An Actor's Finest Performance*, New York: Hippocrene Books, 1992.
Edelstam, Erik H., *Janusansiktet: Berättelsen om diplomaten Harald Edelstams liv och tid*, Stockholm: Carlssons Förlag, 2013.
Eforgan, Estel, *Leslie Howard: The Lost Actor*, London and Portland, Oregon: Vallentine Mitchell, 2010.
Ehrenstråle, Britt and Hans Ehrenstråle, *Sju dagar i oktober 1947*, Uppsala: Brombergs Bokförlag, 1980.
Einhorn, Lena, *Handelsresande i liv: Om vilja och vankelmod i krigets skugga*, Stockholm: Prisma, 1999.
Eliasson, Ingemar, *Jag vet var jag kommer ifrån: Stycken om mitt liv*, Stockholm: Bonniers, 2013.
Eliasson, Jan, *Ord och handling: Ett liv i diplomatins tjänst*, Stockholm: Bonniers, 2022.
Eliasson, Jan, 'Vietnamkriget och de svensk-amerikanska förbindelserna', in Erik Pierre and Ingmar Karlsson (eds), *Insikt och beslut: Studier tillägnade Leif Leifland*, Stockholm: Militärhistoriska Förlaget, 1991, pp. 121–126.
Elmbrant, Björn, *Stockholmskärlek: En bok om Hjalmar Mehr*, Stockholm: Atlas Förlag, 2010.
Emerson, Ralph Waldo, *Character and Heroism*, Amsterdam: Fredonia Books, 2002.

Emling, Shelley, *A Forgotten Hero: Folke Bernadotte, the Swedish Humanitarian Who Rescued 30,000 People from the Nazis*, Toronto: EVW Press, 2019.
Enander, Bo and Franz Arnheim, *Så härskade herrefolket*, Stockholm: Bonniers, 1945.
Eriksonas, Linas, *National Heroes and National Identities: Scotland, Norway and Lithuania*, Brussels: Peter Lang, 2004.
Eriksson, Nancy, *Nancy Eriksson minns*, Stockholm: Bonniers, 1985.
Erlander, Tage, *1955–1960*, Stockholm: Tidens Förlag, 1976.
Erbelding, Rebecca, *Rescue Board: The Untold Story of America's Efforts to Save the Jews of Europe*, New York: Anchor Books, 2019.
Fant, Kenne, *Nära bilder*, Stockholm: Norstedts, 1997.
Fant, Kenne, *R*, Stockholm: Norstedts, 1998.
Fayer, Joan, 'Are Heroes Always Men?', in Susan J. Drucker and Robert S. Cathcart (eds), *American Heroes in a Media Age*, Cresskill, New Jersey: Hampton Press, 1994, pp. 24–35.
Feingold, Henry L., *The Politics of Rescue: The Roosevelt Administration and the Holocaust, 1938–1945*, New York: Holocaust Library, 1970.
Fenyo, Mario D., *Hitler, Horthy, and Hungary: German-Hungarian Relations, 1941–1944*, New Haven and London: Yale University Press, 1972.
Fermaglich, Kirsten, *American Dreams and Nazi Nightmares: Early Holocaust Consciousness and Liberal America, 1957–1965*, Waltham, Massachusetts, 2006.
Fichtelius, Erik, *Aldrig ensam, alltid ensam: Samtalen med Göran Persson 1996–2006*, Stockholm: Norstedts, 2007.
Finn, David, *Hope: A Monument to Raoul Wallenberg*, Woodstock and New York: The Overlock Press, 2000.
Fishwick, Marshall W., 'Did Anyone Ever See Washington Nude?', in Ray B. Browne and Marshall W. Fishwick (eds), *The Hero in Transition*, Bowling Green, Ohio: Bowling Green University Popular Press, 1983, pp. 297–307.
Fleming, Michael, *Auschwitz, the Allies and Censorship of the Holocaust*, Cambridge and New York: Cambridge University Press, 2014.
Fors, Mats, *Svarta nejlikan: Harald Edelstam – en berättelse om mod, humanitet och passion*, Stockholm: Bokförlaget Prisma, 2009.
Fowkes, Reuben, 'Monumental Sculpture in Post-War Eastern Europe, 1945–1960', unpublished thesis, Essex 2002.
Fredriksson, Stig, *Alexanders kurir: Ett journalistliv i skuggan av det kalla kriget*, Stockholm: Carlssons Förlag 2011 [2004].
Freed, G. B. [G. Barany], 'Humanitarianism vs. Totalitarianism: The Strange Case of Raoul Wallenberg', *Papers of the Michigan Academy of Science, Arts and Letters* 46 (1961), 503–528.
Frey, David, *Jews, Nazis, and the Cinema of Hungary: The Tragedy of Success, 1929–44*, London and New York: I. B. Taurus, 2018.

Frick, Lennart W. and Lars Rosander, *Bakom hemligstämpeln: Hemlig verksamhet i Sverige i vår tid*, Lund: Historiska Media, 2004.
Frojimovies, Kinga, Géza Komoróczy, Viktória Pusztai and Andrea Strbik, *Jewish Budapest: Monuments, Rites, History*, Budapest: Central European University Press, 1999 [1995].
Furhammar, Leif and Folke Isaksson, *Politik och film*, Stockholm: PAN/ Norstedts, 1971.
Gann, Christoph, *Raoul Wallenberg: So viele Menschen retten wie möglich*, Munich: dtv, 1999.
Gerner, Kristian, *Centraleuropas historia*, Stockholm: Natur & Kultur 1997.
Gerner, Kristian, 'Fallet Raoul Wallenberg, Vilmos Böhm och Stalin', *Historielärarnas Förenings Årsskrift* 63 (2005), 69–77.
Gerner, Kristian, 'Hungary, Romania, the Holocaust and Historical Culture', in Klas-Göran Karlsson and Ulf Zander (eds), *The Holocaust on Post-War Battlefields: Genocide as Historical Culture*, Malmö: Sekel Förlag, 2006, pp. 225–259.
Gerner, Kristian, 'Konsekvenser för den svenska utrikespolitiken', in Per Ahlmark et al., *Sovjetmyten i Sverige*, Stockholm: Timbro, 1992, pp. 66–96.
Gerner, Kristian and Klas-Göran Karlsson, *Folkmordens historia: Perspektiv på det moderna samhällets skuggsida*, Stockholm: Natur & Kultur, 2005.
Gerner, Kristian and Klas-Göran Karlsson, 'På tvärs mot tidsandan? Solzjenitsyn och *Gulagarkipelagen* i den svenska 1970-talsdebatten', in Marie Cronqvist, Lina Sturfelt and Martin Wiklund (eds), *1973: En träff med tidsandan*, Lund: Nordic Academic Press, 2008, pp. 114–133.
Gersten, Alan, *A Conspiracy of Indifference: The Raoul Wallenberg Story*, Bloomington, Indiana: Xlibris, 2001.
Gerő, András, *Modern Hungarian Society in the Making: The Unfinished Experience*, Budapest: Central European University Press, 1997.
Gibbon, Peter H., *A Call to Heroism: Renewing America's Vision of Greatness*, New York: Grove Atlantic, 2002.
Giesen, Bernhard, *Triumph and Trauma*, London and New York: Routledge, 2004.
Giloh, Mordechai, 'En humanitär tiger: Alva Myrdals bidrag till flyktingmottagandet i Sverige 1945', in Mattias Hessérus, Karin Kvist Geverts, Pontus Rudberg and Malin Thor Tureby (eds), *Moderniteten som framgång och tragedi: En vänbok till Lars M Andersson om ett föränderligt 1900-tal*, Lund: Nordic Academic Press 2021, pp. 85–100.
Gluck, Mary, 'The Budapest Flâneur: Urban Modernity, Popular Culture, and the "Jewish Question" in Fin-de-Siècle Hungary', *Jewish Social Studies* 10.3 (Spring/Summer 2004), 1–22.
Gonshak, Henry, *Hollywood and the Holocaust*, Lanham, Boulder, New York and London: Rowman & Littlefield, 2015.

Gordon, Willy, *Willy Gordon*, Järna: Meta bokproduktion, 1976.
Grunwald-Spier, Agnes, *The Other Schindlers: Why Some People Chose to Save Jews in the Holocaust*, Briscombe Port: The History Press, 2010.
Günther, Christian, *Tal i en tung tid*, Stockholm: Bonniers, 1945.
Gustafsson, Tommy, 'The Black Pimpernel: The Biopic as a Mediator of the Past', *Film International* 6.5 (2008), 18–26.
Handler, Andrew, *A Man for All Connections: Raoul Wallenberg and the Hungarian State Apparatus*, Westport: Praeger, 1996.
Hanebrink, Paul, 'The Memory of the Holocaust in Postcommunist Hungary', in John-Paul Himka and Joanna Beata Michlik (eds), *Bringing the Dark Past to Light: The Reception of the Holocaust in Postcommunist Europe*, Lincoln and London: University of Nebraska Press, 2013, pp. 261–291.
Hardi-Kovacs, Gellert, *Hemligast av alla: C-byrån. Berättelsen om Sveriges hemliga underrättelse under andra världskriget*, Stockholm: Carlssons Bokförlag, 2022.
Harrison, Dick, *Jag har ingen vilja till makt: Biografi över Tage Erlander*, Stockholm: Ordfront Förlag, 2017.
Hasselbohm, Anders, 'Vad hände sedan?', in Lars G:son Berg, *Boken som försvann: Vad hände i Budapest*, Arboga: Textab Förlag, 1983, pp. 187–203.
Hedling, Erik, 'Krämare, profitörer och libertiner: Thatcherismen i brittisk 80-talsfilm', in Hans De Geer (ed.), *Skapare, skojare och skurkar: Företagaren i litteratur, film och konst*, Stockholm: Timbro, 1994, pp. 213–232.
Hedling, Erik, '*Somewhere in Sweden*: Quality Fiction and Popularized History in the World War II Television Series', in Marianne Stecher-Hansen (ed.), *Nordic War Stories: World War II as History, Fiction, Media, and History*, New York and Oxford: Berghahn Books, 2021, pp. 237–251.
von Heland, Erik, *Optimismens och besvikelsens år 1922–1952*, Stockholm: LTs Förlag, 1969.
Herczl, Moshe Y., *Christianity and the Holocaust of Hungarian Jewry*, New York and London: New York University Press, 1993.
Herf, Jeffrey, 'How and Why Did Holocaust Memory Come to the United States? A Response to Peter Novick's Challenge', in Jeffry M. Diefendorf (ed.), *Lessons and Legacies. Volume IV: New Currents in Holocaust Research*, Evanston, Illinois: Northwestern University Press, 2004, pp. 457–474.
Heydecker, Joe J. and Johannes Leeb, *The Nuremberg Trial: A History of Nazi Germany as Revealed through the Testimony at Nuremberg*, Cleveland and New York: The World Publishing Company, 1962 [1958].
Hirdman, Sven, 'Sverige och ubåtskränkningarna', in Erik Pierre and Ingmar Karlsson (eds), *Insikt och beslut: Studier tillägnade Leif Leifland*, Stockholm: Militärhistoriska Förlaget, 1991, pp. 147–155.

Hirsch, Joshua, *Afterimage: Film, Trauma, and the Holocaust*, Philadelphia: Temple University Press, 2004.
Holbrooke, Richard, 'Defying Orders, Saving Lives: Heroic Diplomats of the Holocaust', *Foreign Affairs* 86 (June 2007), 135–138.
Holbrooke, Richard, *To End a War*, New York: Random House, 1998.
Holmila, Antero, '"A Hellish Nightmare": The Swedish Press and the Construction of Early Holocaust Narratives, 1945–1950', in Johannes Heuman and Pontus Rudberg (eds), *Early Holocaust Memory in Sweden: Archives, Testimonies and Reflections*, Palgrave Macmillan, 2021, pp. 163–187.
Holmila, Antero, *Reporting the Holocaust in the British, Swedish and Finnish Press, 1945–50*, Houndmills, Basingstoke: Palgrave Macmillan, 2011.
Hook, Sidney, *The Hero in History: A Study in Limitation and Possibility*, London: Secker & Warburg, 1945.
Hughes-Hallett, Lucy, *Heroes: Saviours, Traitors and Supermen*, London: Harper Perennial, 2005.
Hughes-Warrington, Marnie, *History Goes to the Movies: Studying History on Film*, London and New York: Routledge, 2007.
Howard, Leslie Ruth, *A Quite Remarkable Father*, New York: Harcourt, Brace and Company, 1959.
Howard, Ronald, *In Search of My Father: A Portrait of Leslie Howard*, New York; St Martin's Press, 1981.
Hägglöf, Gunnar, *Det andra Europa*, Stockholm: P. A. Norstedt & Söners Förlag, 1981.
Hägglöf, Gunnar, *Det kringrända Sverige*, Stockholm: P. A. Norstedt & Söners Förlag, 1983.
Hägglöf, Ingemar, *Berätta för Joen: Mina år med ryssarna 1943–1947*, Stockholm: Norstedts Förlag, 1984.
Insdorf, Annette, *Indelible Shadows: Film and the Holocaust*, Cambridge: Cambridge University Press, 1989.
James, Beverly Ann, *Imagining Postcommunism: Visual Narratives of Hungary's 1956 Revolution*, College Station, Texas: Texas A&M University Press, 2005.
Jangfeldt, Bengt, *En rysk historia*, Stockholm: Wahlström & Widstrand, 2015.
Jangfeldt, Bengt, *The Hero of Budapest: The Triumph and Tragedy of Raoul Wallenberg*, London and New York: I. B. Taurus, 2014 [2012].
Jarring, Gunnar, *Rikets förhållande till främmande makt: Memoarer 1952–1964*, Stockholm: Bonniers, 1983.
Jarring, Gunnar, *Utan glasnost och perestrojka: Memoarer 1964–1973*, Stockholm: Bonniers, 1989.
Jerselius, Kjell, *Hotade reservat: Spelfilmerna med Edvard Persson*, Uppsala: Filmförlaget, 1987.

Jick, Leon A., 'The Holocaust: Its Use and Abuse within the American Public', *Yad Vashem Studies* 14 (1981), 303–318.

Johansson, Alf W., *Herbert Tingsten och det kalla kriget: Antikommunism och liberalism i Dagens Nyheter 1940–1952*, Stockholm: Tidens Förlag, 1995.

Johansson, Alf W., 'Neutrality and Modernity: The Second World War and Sweden's National Identity', in Stig Ekman and Nils Edling (eds), *War Experience, Self Image and National Identity: The Second World War as Myth and History*, Stockholm: The Bank of Sweden Tercentenary Foundation & Gidlunds Förlag, 1997, pp. 163–185.

Jordan, James, *From Nuremberg to Hollywood: The Holocaust and the Courtroom in American Fictive Film*, London and Portland, Oregon: Vallentine Mitchell, 2016.

Jähner, Harald, *Aftermath: Life in the Fallout of the Third Reich 1945–1955*, London: W. H. Allen, 2019.

Kaaström, Katrin, 'Dawit och tystnaden', in Johan Karlsson and Rickard Sjöberg (eds), *Dawit och friheten: Om den svenske samvetsfången och Eritreas inställda demokratisering*, Stockholm: Silc Förlag, 2004.

Kádár, Gábor and Zoltán Vági, 'Rationality or Irrationality? The Annihilation of Hungarian Jews', *The Hungarian Quarterly* 45 (Summer 2004), 32–54.

Kalb, Marvin, 'Introduction: Journalism and the Holocaust, 1933–1945', in Robert Moses Shapiro (ed.), *Why Didn't the Press Shout? American and International Journalism during the Holocaust*, Jersey City: Yeshiva University Press in association with KTAV Publishing House, 2003, pp. 1–13.

Kantsteiner, Wulf, 'Entertaining Catastrophe: The Reinvention of the Holocaust in the Television of the Federal Republic of Germany', *New German Critique* 30 (Autumn 2003), 135–162.

Kaplan, Nadan and Barry Schwarz, 'Raoul Wallenberg in Israel Recovered Memory and Mediocre Commemoration', *Holocaust Studies* 29.1 (2023), 116–140.

Karlsson, Ingmar, *Ett utrikes liv*, Lund: Historiska Media, 2021.

Karlsson, Klas-Göran, *Europeiska möten med historien: Historiekulturella perspektiv på andra världskriget, förintelsen och den kommunistiska terrorn*, Stockholm: Bokförlaget Atlantis 2010.

Karlsson, Klas-Göran, 'The Evil Twins of Modern History? Reflections on the Entangled History of Communism and National Socialism', in Klas-Göran Karlsson, Johan Stenfeldt and Ulf Zander (eds), *Perspectives on the Entangled History of Communism and Nazism: A Comnaz Analysis*, Lanham: Lexington Books, 2015, pp. 9–50.

Karlsson, Klas-Göran, 'Historiedidaktik: begrepp, teori och analys', in Klas-Göran Karlsson and Ulf Zander (eds), *Historien är nu: En introduktion till historiedidaktiken*, andra reviderade utgåvan, Lund: Studentlitteratur, 2009, pp. 23–70.

Karlsson, Klas-Göran, 'History in Swedish Politics – the "Living History" Project', in Attila Pók, Jörn Rüsen, and Jutta Scherrer (eds), *European History: Challenge for a Common Future*, Hamburg: Edition Körber-Stiftung, 2002, pp. 145–162.

Karlsson, Klas-Göran. 'The Holocaust in European Historical Culture', in Teresa Pinhero, Beata Cieszynka and Eduardo Franco (eds), *Ideas of Europe/Ideas for Europe: An Interdisciplinary Approach to European Identity*, Frankfurt: Peter Lang, 2012, pp. 427–440.

Karlsson, Klas-Göran, 'The Holocaust as a History-Cultural Phenomenon', in Martin L. Davies and Claus-Christian W. Sznejmann (eds), *How the Holocaust Looks Now: International Perspectives*, Houndmills, Basingstoke and New York: Palgrave Macmillan, 2007, pp. 85–96.

Karlsson, Klas-Göran, 'The Holocaust as Politics and Use of History – The Example of Living History', in Kurt Almkvist and Kay Glans (eds), *The Swedish Success Story?* Stockholm: Axel and Margaret Ax:son Johnson Foundation, 2004, pp. 241–251.

Karlsson, Klas-Göran, 'The Holocaust as a Problem of Historical Culture: Theoretical and Analytical Approaches', in Klas-Göran Karlsson and Ulf Zander (eds), *Echoes of the Holocaust: Historical Cultures in Contemporary Europe*, Lund: Nordic Academic Press, 2003, pp. 9–57.

Karlsson, Klas-Göran, *Med folkmord i fokus: Förintelsens plats i den europeiska historiekulturen*, Stockholm: The Living History Forum, 2008.

Karlsson, Klas-Göran, 'Tell Ye Your Children … The Twisted Swedish Road to Holocaust Recognition', *Scandinavian-Canadian Studies / Études Scandinaves au Canada* 23 (2016), 78–94.

Karlsson, Klas-Göran, 'The Uses of History and the Third Wave of Europeanisation', in Małgorzata Pakier and Bo Stråth (eds), *A European Memory? Contested Histories and Politics of Remembrance*, New York and Oxford 2010: Berghahn Books, pp. 38–55.

Karlsson, Mats, *Vår man i Moskva: En studie över den svenske ambassadören Rolf Sohlmans syn på Sovjetunionen och dess utrikespolitiska ambitioner 1947–1950*, Stockholm and Södertörn: The research programme called Sweden during the Cold War, working report No. 10, 1999.

Kerner, Aaron, 'On the Cinematic Nazi', in Oleksandr Kobrynskyy and Gerd Bayer (eds), *Holocaust Cinema in the Twenty-First Century: Memory, Images, and the Ethics of Representation*, New York and Chichester, West Sussex: Wallflower Press, 2015, pp. 203–219.

Kershaw, Alex, *The Envoy: The Epic Rescue of the Last Jews of Europe in the Desperate Closing Months of World War II*, Cambridge, Massachusetts: Da Capo Press, 2010.

King, Sol, 'In Tribute to Raoul Wallenberg', in *Sir Nikolaus Pevsner: Architecture as a Humane Art*, Ann Arbor: University of Michigan, 1973, pp. 5–12.

Kissinger, Henry, *World Order: Reflections on the Character of Nations and the Course of History*, London and New York: Allen Lane, 2014.
Klapp, Orrin E., 'The Folk Hero', *Journal of American Folklore* 61.1 (1949), 17–25.
Klein, Georg, *Jag återvänder aldrig: Essäer i Förintelsens skugga*, Stockholm: Bonniers, 2011.
Klibanski, Bronia, 'The Archives of the Swiss Consul General Charles Lutz', *Yad Vashem Studies* 15 (1983), 357–366.
Knight, Amy, 'The Selling of the KGB', *The Wilson Quarterly* 24.1 (2000), 16–23.
Koblik, Steven, *The Stones Cry Out: Sweden's Response to the Persecution of the Jews, 1933–1945*, New York: Holocaust Library, 1988.
Korda, Michael, *Charmed Lives: A Family Romance*, Harmondsworth: Penguin Books Ltd, 1980 [1979].
Kovács, András, 'The Jewish Question in Contemporary Hungary', in Randolph L. Braham and Bela Vago (eds), *The Holocaust in Hungary: Forty Years Later*, New York: Columbia University Press, 1985, pp. 55–74.
Kovacs, Gellert, *Skymning över Budapest: Historien om Raoul Wallenberg och kampen för människoliv 1944–45*, Stockholm: Carlssons Förlag, 2013.
Kowalski, Alexandra, 'The Wandering Memorial: Figures of Ambivalence in Hungarian Holocaust Memorialization', in Olivette Otele, Luisa Gandolfo and Yoav Galai (eds), *Post-Conflict Memorialization: Missing Memorials, Absent Bodies*, Cham: Palgrave Macmillan 2021, pp. 213–240.
Kravtjenko, Viktor, *Jag valde friheten: En sovjetämbetsmans personliga och politiska upplevelser*, Stockholm: Natur & Kultur, 1949.
Kristoffersson, Birgitta and Katinka Faragó, *Katinka och regissörerna: 125 filmer och 55 år bakom kameran*, Malmö: Bokförlaget Arena, 2008.
Kriza, Elisa, *Alexander Solzhenitsyn: Cold War Icon, Gulag Author, Russian Nationalist? A Study of the Western Reception of his Literary Writings, Historical Interpretations, and Political Ideas*, Stuttgart: ibidem-Verlag, 2014.
Kronvall, Olof, 'Rolf Sohlman', in Gunnar Artéus and Leif Leifland (eds), *Svenska diplomatprofiler under 1900-talet*, Stockholm: Probus Förlag, 2001, pp. 274–316.
Kushner, Tony, *The Holocaust and the Liberal Imagination: A Social and Cultural History*, Oxford and Cambridge, Massachusetts: Blackwell, 1994.
Kushner, Tony, '"Pissing in the Wind"? The Search for Nuance in the Study of Holocaust "Bystanders"', in David Cesarani and Paul A. Levine (eds), *"Bystanders" to the Holocaust: A Re-Evaluation*, London and Portland: Frank Cass, 2002, pp. 57–76.
Kuylenstierna-Andrassy, Stella, *Pustan brinner*, Stockholm: Natur & Kultur, 1948.

# Bibliography

Küng, Andres, *Raoul Wallenberg: Igår, idag*, Stockholm: Timbro, 1985.
Kvist Geverts, Karin, 'Tracing the Holocaust in Early Writings in Post-War Sweden', in Johannes Heuman and Pontus Rudberg (eds), *Early Holocaust Memory in Sweden: Archives, Testimonies and Reflections*, Cham: Palgrave Macmillan, 2021, pp. 139–161.
Kwon, Miwon, *One Place after Another: Site-Specific Art and Locational Identity*, Cambridge, Massachusetts and London: The MIT Press, 2004.
LaCapra, Dominick, *History and Memory after Auschwitz*, Ithaca and London: Cornell University Press 1998.
Laczó, Ferenc, 'From Collaboration to Cooperation: German Historiography of the Holocaust in Hungary', *The Hungarian Historical Review* 9.3 (2020), 530–555.
Lagercrantz, Olof, *Vårt sekel är reserverat åt lögnen: Artiklar 1938–1993 med några anslutande dagboksanteckningar*, Stockholm: Karneval Förlag, 2007.
Lagergren, Nina, 'Still, We Cannot Close This Chapter', in Karl Gabor (ed.), *Raoul Wallenberg: One Man Can Make a Difference*, Stockholm: The Jewish Museum in Stockholm, 2004, pp. 7–10.
Lajos, Attila, *Hjälten och offren: Raoul Wallenberg och judarna i Budapest*, Växjö: The Swedish Emigrant Institute, 2004.
Lajos, Attila, 'Raoul Wallenberg i muntliga källor', in Lars Berggren, Mats Greiff, Jesper Johansson, Johan Svanberg and Malin Thor (eds), *Samhällshistoria i fokus: En festskrift till Lars Olsson om arbete, migration och kultur*, Malmö: Big Bad Books, 2010, pp. 243–267.
Landau, Ernest, 'Nachschrift', in Rudolf Kastner, *Der Kastner-Bericht über Eichmanns Menschenhandel in Ungarn*, Munich: Verlag bei Kindler, 1961, pp. 337–348
Langer, Joakim and Pelle Berglund, *Constantin Karadja: Bara ett liv till*, Tyresö: Sivart Förlag, 2009.
Langlet, Nina, *Kaos i Budapest*, Vällingby: Harrier, 1982.
Langlet, Valdemar, *Till häst genom Ungern*, Stockholm: Wahlström & Widstrand, 1934.
Langlet, Valdemar, *Verk och dagar i Budapest*, Stockholm: Wahlström & Widstrand, 1946.
Larsson, Kaj and Brita Åsbrink, *'Det är väl ingen konst': Tycker skönandar, moralister, klottrare, lustigkurrar, hjältedyrkare, avgudadyrkare, stadsplanerare, barn, politiker, arkitekter, du och jag*, Stockholm: Carlssons Förlag, 2008.
Lash, John, *The Hero: Manhood and Power*, London: Thames & Hudson, 1995.
Leche Löfgren, Mia, *Hård tid*, Stockholm: Lars Hökerbergs Bokförlag 1946.
Leff, Laurel, *Buried by the Times: The Holocaust and America's Most Important Newspaper*, Cambridge, Massachusetts: Cambridge University Press, 2005.

Leifland, Leif, *Frostens år – Om USA:s diplomatiska utfrysning av Sverige*, Stockholm: Santérus Förlag, 1997.

Leifland, Leif, 'Lars-Åke Nilsson', in Gunnar Artéus and Leif Leifland (eds), *Svenska diplomatprofiler under 1900-talet*, Stockholm: Probus Förlag, 2001, pp. 441–460.

Leifland, Leif, *Svartlistningen av Axel Wenner-Gren: En bok om ett justitiemord*, Stockholm: Askelin and Hägglund, 1989.

Leijonborg, Lars, *Kris och framgång: Mitt halvsekel i politiken*, Stockholm: Ekerlids Förlag, 2018.

Lesser, Wendy, *Scandinavian Noir: In Pursuit of a Mystery*, New York: Farrar, Straus & Giroux, 2020.

Lester, Elenore, 'Raoul Wallenberg: The Righteous Gentile from Sweden', in Randolph L. Braham and Bela Vago (eds), *The Holocaust in Hungary: Forty Years Later*, New York: Columbia University Press 1985, pp. 147–160.

Lévai, Jenő, 'Aus welchen Gründen überlebte das Budapester Ghetto – als Einziges – die Ausrottung?', *Proceedings of the World Congress of Jewish Studies*. Vol. II, Jerusalem: World Union of Jewish Studies, 1972, pp. 99–115.

Lévai, Jenő, *Raoul Wallenberg: His Remarkable Life, Heroic Battles and the Secret of his Mysterious Disappearance*, Melbourne: WhiteAnt Occasional Publisher, 1988 [1948].

Lévai, Jenő, *Raoul Wallenberg, hjälten i Budapest*, Stockholm: Saxon and Lindström, 1948.

Levine, Paul, *From Indifference to Activism: Swedish Diplomacy and the Holocaust, 1938–1944*, Uppsala: Uppsala University, 1995.

Levine, Paul A., *Raoul Wallenberg in Budapest: Myth, History and Holocaust*, London and Portland, Oregon: Vallentine Mitchell, 2010.

Levine, Paul A., 'Raoul Wallenberg Was a Real Life Hero', in Karl Gabor (ed.), *Raoul Wallenberg: One Man Can Make a Difference*, Stockholm: The Jewish Museum in Stockholm, 2004, pp. 33–35.

Levine, Paul A., 'Raoul Wallenbergs uppdrag i Budapest: Bakgrund och motiv', in Lars M. Andersson and Karin Kvist Geverts (eds), *En problematisk relation? Flyktingpolitik och judiska flyktingar i Sverige 1920–1950*, Uppsala: Uppsala University, 2008, pp. 269–288.

Levine, Paul A., 'The Unfinished Story of a Swedish Hero', in Karl Gabor (ed.), *Raoul Wallenberg: One Man Can Make a Difference*, Stockholm: The Jewish Museum in Stockholm, 2004, pp. 36–57.

Levy, Daniel and Natan Sznaider, *The Holocaust and Memory in the Global Age*, Philadelphia: Temple University Press, 2006.

Lichtenstein, Heiner, *Raoul Wallenberg, Retter von hunderttausend Juden: Ein Opfer Himmlers und Stalins*, Cologne: Bund-Verlag, 1982.

Liljefors, Max, *Bilder av Förintelsen: Mening, minne, komprometteing*, Lund: Palmkrons Förlag, 2002.

Liljefors, Max, 'The Interplay of Memory and Amnesia: Sites of Memory in Europe and Africa', in Elna Svenle and Marika Wachtmeister (eds), *Förlust/Loss*, Knislinge: The Wanås Foundation, 2008, pp. 47–59.

Liljefors, Max and Ulf Zander, 'Det neutrala landet ingenstans: Bilder av andra världskriget och den svenska utopin', *Scandia* 75.2 (2003), 209–242.

Lindahl, Ingemar, 'Harald Edelstam', in Gunnar Artéus and Leif Leifland (eds), *Svenska diplomatprofiler under 1900-talet*, Stockholm: Probus Förlag, 2001, pp. 374–397.

Lindberg, Gunilla, *Starka kvinnor som fört Sverige framåt*, Hudiksvall: Winberg Citybook, 2005.

Lindström, Ulla, *I regeringen: Ur min politiska dagbok 1954–1959*, Stockholm: Bonniers, 1969.

Lindström, Ulla, *Och regeringen satt kvar! Ur min politiska dagbok 1960–1967*, Stockholm: Bonniers 1970.

Linenthal, Edward T., *Preserving Memory: The Struggle to Create America's Holocaust Museum*, New York: Columbia University Press, 2001.

Linnéa, Sharon, *Raoul Wallenberg: The Man Who Stopped Death*, Philadelphia and Jerusalem: The Jewish Publication Society, 1993.

Lomax, Bill, 'Combatting the Ultra-Right in Hungary: The Limitations of Liberalism', in Leslie C. Eliason and Lene Bøgh Sørensen (eds), *Fascism, Liberalism, and Social Democracy in Central Europe: Past and Present*, Aarhus: Aarhus University Press, 2002, pp. 318–332.

Lomfors, Ingrid, *Blind fläck: Minne och glömska kring Svenska Röda korsets hjälpinsats i Nazityskland 1945*, Stockholm: Bokförlaget Atlantis, 2005.

Lower, Wendy, *The Ravine: A Family, a Photograph, a Holocaust Massacre Revealed*, Boston and New York: Houghton Mifflin Harcourt, 2021.

Lozowick, Yaacov, *Hitler's Bureaucrats: The Nazi Security Police and the Banality of Evil*, New York and London: Continuum, 2002.

Ludvigsson, David, *The Historian-Filmmaker's Dilemma: Historical Documentaries in Sweden in the Era of Häger and Villius*, Uppsala: Uppsala University, 2003.

Lundgren, Svante, *I hjältens tid: Berättelser om mod och civilkurage under Förintelsen*, Stockholm: Sahlgren, 2006.

Lundvik, Jan, 'My Undertaking Began on a Grey Autumn Day in 1960', in Karl Gabor (ed.), *Raoul Wallenberg: One Man Can Make a Difference*, Stockholm: The Jewish Museum in Stockholm, 2004, pp. 11–15.

MacDonald, Robert H., *The Language of Empire: Myths and Metaphors of Popular Imperialism, 1880–1918*, Manchester and New York: Manchester University Press, 1994.

MacKenzie, S. P., 'Nazis into Germans: Went the Day Well? (1942) and The Eagle Has Landed (1976)', *Journal of Popular Film and Television* 31.2 (Summer 2003), 83–92.

Macmillan, Harold, *The Blast of War 1939–1945*, London: Macmillan & Co Ltd, 1967.
Magnusson, Hans, 'The Search for Raoul Wallenberg – A Personal View', in Stefan Karner (ed.), *Auf den Spuren Wallenbergs*, Innsbruck, Vienna and Bolzano: StudienVerlag, 2015, pp. 181–186.
Malaporte, Curzio, *Kaputt*, London: Alan Redman Limited, 1948.
Marino, Andy, *The American Pimpernel: The Man Who Saved the Artists on Hitler's Death List*, London: Arrow Books Ltd, 2000.
Marrus, Michael R., *The Holocaust in History*, London: Penguin Books, 1993 [1987].
Marrus, Michael R., 'The Holocaust at Nuremberg', *Yad Vashem Studies* 26 (1998), 5–41.
Martin, Barbara, 'The Sakharov-Medvedev Debate on Détente and Human Rights: From the Jackson-Vanik Amendment to the Helsinki Accords', *Journal of Cold War Studies* 23.3 (Summer 2021), 138–174.
Marton, Kati, *Wallenberg*, New York and Toronto: Random House, 1982.
Mattsson, Britt-Marie, *Neutralitetens tid: Svensk utrikespolitik från världssamvete till medgörlig lagspelare*, Stockholm: Forum, 2010.
Matz, Johan, '"All Signs Indicate that Gestapo Agents Murdered Him": Soviet Disinformation, the Katyn Massacre, and the Raoul Wallenberg Case, 1945–7', *The International History Review* 38.1 (2016), 148–173.
Matz, Johan, 'Analogical Reasoning and the Diplomacy of the Raoul Wallenberg Case 1945–7', *The International History Review*, 37.3 (2014), 582–606.
Matz, Johan, 'Did Raoul Wallenberg Try to Leave Budapest in January 1945 with Jewelry and 15–20 kg of Gold Hidden in the Gasoline Tank of his car? On Sensationalism in Popular History and Soviet Disinformation', *Journal of Intelligence History* 15.1 (2015), 17–41.
Matz, Johan, 'The Konnov/Mikhailov/Barourskii Espionage Crises of July–August 1947 and the Vyshinskii Note on Raoul Wallenberg', *Journal of Intelligence History* 17.1 (2018), 30–51.
Matz, Johan, *Stalin's Double-Edged Game: Soviet Bureaucracy and the Raoul Wallenberg Case, 1945–1952*, Lanham: Lexington Books, 2020.
Matz, Johan, 'Sweden, the United States, and Raoul Wallenberg's Mission to Hungary in 1944', *Journal of Cold War Studies* 14.3 (Summer 2012), 97–148.
Medoff, Rafael, *Blowing the Whistle on Genocide: Josiah E. DuBois, Jr, and the Struggle for a U.S. Response to the Holocaust*, West Lafayette, Indiana: Purdue University Press, 2009.
Melman, Billie, *The Culture of History: English Uses of the Past 1800–1953*, Oxford: Oxford University Press, 2006.
Milles, Ulrika, *Ensamvargar: Stig Ahlgrens 1900-tal – Manlighet, kärlek, litteratur*, Stockholm: Bonniers, 2019.
Mintz, Allan, *Popular Culture and the Shaping of Holocaust Memory in America*, Seattle and London: University of Washington Press, 2001.

Modéer, Kjell Å., *Patriot i gränsland: Einar Hansen – Entreprenör och mecenat*, Stockholm: Bokförlaget Atlantis, 2002.

Molin, Karl, 'Neutralitetens dolda kris (1948–49)', in Bo Huldt and Klaus Misgeld (eds), *Socialdemokratin och svensk utrikespolitik: Från Branting till Palme*, Stockholm and Gothenburg: The Swedish Institute of International Affairs, 1990, pp. 74–86.

Molin, Karl, *Omstridd neutralitet: Experternas kritik av svensk utrikespolitik 1948–1950*, Stockholm: Tidens Förlag, 1991.

Montefiore, Simon Sebag, *101 World Heroes: Great Men and Women for an Unheroic Age*, London: Quercus Books, 2007.

Morgan, Michael L., *Beyond Auschwitz: Post-Holocaust Jewish Thought in America*, Oxford and New York: Oxford University Press, 2001.

Morse, Arthur D., *While Six Million Died: A Chronicle of American Apathy*, New York: Abrams Press, 1967.

Murphy, Robert, *British Cinema and the Second World War*, London: Continuum, 2000.

Möller, Yngve, *Östen Undén: En biografi*, Stockholm: Norstedts 1986.

Neiman, Susan, *Learning from the Germans: Race and the Memory of Evil*, New York: Farrar, Straus and Giroux, 2019.

Neuman, Ricki, 'Wallenberg? Which One?', in Karl Gabor (ed.), *Raoul Wallenberg: One Man Can Make a Difference*, Stockholm: The Jewish Museum in Stockholm, 2004, pp. 17–18.

Nicholson, Michael and David Winner, *Raoul Wallenberg: Diplomaten som räddade 100 000 judar från koncentrationslägren*, Örebro: Libris, 1990 [1989].

Nikulin, Leon (ed.), *Raoul Wallenberg i den danske presse: Artikler og illustrationer*, Viby: Panorama, 2002.

Nilsson, Olle and Brita Åsbrink, *Stjärna på en liberal himmel! Ingrid Gärde Widemar, advokat, riksdagsledamot, första kvinnan i högsta domstolen*, Stockholm: Bokförlaget Atlantis, 2005.

Nilsson, Torsten, *Människor och händelser i Europa*, Stockholm: Tidens Förlag, 1978.

Novick, Peter, *The Holocaust in American Life*, Boston and New York: Houghton Mifflin, 1999.

Nye, Joseph S, Jr, 'Soft Power', *Foreign Policy* 80 (Autumn 1990), 157–171.

Nylén, Hasse, *Budapest bortom turiststråken*, Stockholm: Cessohiss, 2005.

Oakeshott, Michael, *On History and Other Essays*, Indianapolis: Indiana: Liberty Fund, Inc., 1999 [1983].

Ohlin, Bertil, *Bertil Ohlins memoarer 1940–1951: Socialistisk skördetid som kom bort*, Stockholm: Bonniers, 1975.

Östberg, Kjell, *I takt med tiden: Olof Palme 1927–1969*, Stockholm: Leopard Förlag, 2008.

von Osten, Marion, 'Producing Publics – Making Worlds! Om förhållandet mellan konstoffentlighet och motoffentlighet', in the special issue on 'Konst, makt, politik', *Kairos* 12 (2007), 239–261.

Österberg, Eva, *Tystnader och tider: Samtal med historien*, Stockholm: Bokförlaget Atlantis, 2011.
Österberg, Oscar, '"Eftervärldens dom har fallit hård". Lidice, Oradour och Sant'Anna i berättelser om andra världskriget', in Klas-Göran Karlsson and Ulf Zander (eds), *Katastrofernas århundrade: Historiska och verkningshistoriska perspektiv*, Lund: Studentlitteratur, 2009, pp. 133–162.
Östling, Johan, 'The Rise and Fall of Small-State Realism: Sweden and the Second World War', in Henrik Stenius, Mirja Österberg, and Johan Östling (eds), *Nordic Narratives of the Second World War: National Historiographies Revisited*, Lund: Nordic Academic Press, 2011, pp. 127–147.
Östling, Johan, *Sweden After Nazism: Politics and Culture in the Wake of the Second World War*, New York and Oxford: Berghahn Books, 2016 [2008].
Ottosson, Sten, *Den (o)moraliska neutraliteten: Tre politikers och tre tidningars moraliska värdering av svensk utrikespolitik 1945–1952*, Stockholm: Santérus Förlag, 2000.
Paldiel, Mordechai, *Saving One's Own: Jewish Rescuers during the Holocaust*, Lincoln: University of Nebraska Press, 2017.
Palme, Olof, 'Andra världskriget: Anförande i Stockholms Synagoga söndagen den 28 april 1985', in Olof Palme, *En levande vilja*, Stockholm: Tidens Förlag, 1987, pp. 314–319.
Palmkvist, Conny, *Sundets röda nejlikor: Hur svensk polis och Helsingörs syklubb räddade danska flyktingar under andra världskriget*, Stockholm: Forum Förlag, 2020.
Palmstierna, Carl-Fredrik, *Bränn dessa brev: Minnen från det ljusa 20-talet, det mörknande 30-talet och de stora katastrofernas år. Människor – miljöer 1921–1945*, Stockholm: Bonniers, 1973.
Palmstierna, Carl-Fredrik, *Fjädern i min hand: Minnen 1945–1973*, Stockholm: Bonniers, 1976.
Pankin, Boris, *De sista hundra dagarna: Sovjetunionens dramatiska upplösning*, Höganäs: Bokförlaget Bra Böcker, 1992.
Parvilahti, Unto, *Berias gårdar: Minnesbilder och iakttagelser från Sovjetunionen 1945–1954*, Stockholm: Natur & Kultur, 1958 [1957].
Patai, Raphael, *The Jews of Hungary: History, Culture, Psychology*, Detroit: Wayne University Press, 1996.
Perra, Emiliano, 'Legitimizing Fascism through the Holocaust? The Reception of the Miniseries *Perlasca: un eroe italiano* in Italy', *Memory Studies* 3.2 (2010), 95–109.
Perry, George, *The Great British Picture Show: From the Nineties to the Seventies*, Frogmor: Paladin, 1974.
Persson, Carl and Anders Sundelin, *Utan omsvep: Ett liv i maktens centrum*, Stockholm: Bokförlaget PAN/Norstedts, 1991 [1990].
Persson, Göran, *Min väg, mina val*, Stockholm: Bonniers, 2007.

Persson, Göran, 'Opening Address by the Prime Minister of Sweden at the Ceremonial Opening 26 January 2000', in *The Stockholm International Forum on the Holocaust: A Conference on Education, Remembrance and Research. Stockholm, Sweden, 26–28 January 2000*, Stockholm: Swedish Government Offices 2000, pp. 29–30.

Petersson, Bo, *Med Moskvas ögon: Bedömningar av svensk utrikespolitik under Stalin och Chrusjtjov*, Stockholm: Arena, 1994.

Pető, Andrea, 'The Illiberal Memory Politics of Hungary', *Journal of Genocide Research* 24.2 (2022), 241–249.

Petri, Lennart, *Sverige i stora världen: Minnen och reflexioner från 40 års diplomattjänst*, Stockholm: Bokförlaget Atlantis, 1995.

Pierrejean, Claudine and Daniel Pierrejean, *Les secrets de l'Affaire Raoul Wallenberg: Du juste de Budapest au premier martyr de la guerre froide*, Paris: L'Harmattan, 1998.

Philipp, Rudolph, *Raoul Wallenberg: Diplomat, kämpe, samarit*, Stockholm: Fredborg, 1946.

Philipp, Rudolph, *Skor, svett och tårar*, Stockholm: Axel Holmströms Förlag, 1945.

Pick, Hella, *Simon Wiesenthal: A Life in Search of Justice*, London: Weidenfeld & Nicolson, 1996.

Pihurik, Judit, 'Hungarian Soldiers and Jews on the Eastern Front, 1941–1943', *Yad Vashem Studies* 35.2 (2007), 71–102.

von Platen, Gustaf, *Resa till det förflutna: Lättsinne i allvarstid. Minnen. Del 1*, Stockholm: T. Fischer & Co 1993.

Plunka, Gene A., *Staging Holocaust Resistance*, New York: Palgrave Macmillan, 2012.

Ranki, Vera, *The Politics of Inclusion and Exclusion: Jews and Nationalism in Hungary*, New York and London: Holmes & Meier, 1999.

Raskin, Richard, 'From Leslie Howard to Raoul Wallenberg: the transmission and adaptation of a heroic model', *P.O.V.* 28 (December 2009), pov.imv.au.dk/Issue_28/POV_28cnt.html (accessed 25 May 2017).

Ratuszniak, Jan, 'Contact between Alexandra Kollontai and the Wallenberg Family (1930–1945)', *Zapinski Historyczne*, No. 3, 2017, zapiskihistoryczne.pl/files/issues/4ee30363bbce2e4ad7f21ddac369b97a_ZH_2017_3_04_ENG_Ratuszniak_N.pdf (accessed 18 June 2020).

Rayfield, Donald, *Stalin and his Hangmen: An Authoritative Portrait of a Tyrant and Those Who Served Him*, London and New York: Random House, 2004.

Rév, István, 'Liberty Square, Budapest: How Hungary Won the War', *Journal of Genocide Research* 20.4 (2018), 607–623.

Richter, Jan, *Edvard Persson*, Stockholm: Bonniers, 1974.

Ricoeur, Paul, *History, Memory, Forgetting*, Chicago and London: University of Chicago Press, 2006.

Rogin, Michael, *Ronald Reagan, the Movie, and Other Episodes in Political Demonology*, Berkeley, Los Angeles and London: University of California Press, 1988.

Roginskij, Arsenij and Nikita Ochotin, 'Die Archive des KGB. Ein Jahr nach dem Putsch', *Osteuropa* 67.11/12 (2017), 53–75.

Rosen, Robert N., *Saving the Jews: Franklin D. Roosevelt and the Holocaust*, New York: Thunder's Mouth Press, 2006.

Rosenberg, Göran, *Rabbi Marcus Ehrenpreis obesvarade kärlek*, Stockholm: Bonniers, 2021.

Rosenberg, Joel, 'Shylock's Revenge: The Doubly Vanished Jew in Ernst Lubitsch's *To Be or Not to Be*', *Prooftexts* 16.3 (September 1996), 209–244.

Rosenfeld, Alvin H., 'The Americanization of the Holocaust', in Alvin H. Rosenfeld (ed.), *Thinking about the Holocaust after Half a Century*, Bloomington and Indiana: Indiana University Press, 1997, pp. 119–150.

Rosenfeld, Harvey, *Raoul Wallenberg* (Revised Edition), New York and London: Holmes & Meier Publishers, 1995 [1982].

Rosengren, Henrik, '"Massaker-musik" och bortglömt minne: Förintelsen som minneskonstruktion i konstmusik', in Mattias Hessérus, Karin Kvist Geverts, Pontus Rudberg and Malin Thor Tureby (eds), *Moderniteten som framgång och tragedi: En vänbok till Lars M Andersson om ett föränderligt 1900-tal*, Lund: Nordic Academic Press, 2021, pp. 187–200.

Rousso, Henry, *The Vichy Syndrome: History and Memory in France since 1944*, Cambridge, Massachusetts and London: Harvard University Press, 1991.

Rubenstein, William D., *The Myth of Rescue: Why the Democracies Could Not Have Saved More Jews from the Nazis*, New York: Routledge, 1997.

Rudberg, Pontus, *The Swedish Jews and the Holocaust*, London and New York: Routledge, 2017.

Runberg, Björn, *Valdemar Langlet: Räddare i faran*, Bromma: Megilla Förlag, 2000.

Rüsen, Jörn, *Historische Orientierung: Über die Arbeit des Geschichtsbewusstseins, sich in der Zeit zurechtzufinden*, Cologne, Weimar and Vienna: Wochenschau Verlag, 1994.

Rüsen, Jörn, 'Holocaust Memory and Identity Building: Metahistorical Considerations in the Case of (West) Germany', in Michael Roth and Charles Salas (eds), *Disturbing Remains: Memory, History, and Crisis in the Twentieth Century*, Los Angeles: The Getty Research Institute, 2001, pp. 252–270.

Sachar, Howard M., *Dreamland: Europeans and Jews in the Aftermath of the Great War*, New York: Vintage Books, 2003.

Sakharov, Andrei, *Moscow and Beyond: 1986 to 1989*, New York: Alfred A. Knopf, 1991.

Sakmyster, Thomas, *Hungary's Admiral on Horseback: Miklós Horthy, 1918–1944*, New York: East European Monographs, Boulder, 1994.

Salomon, Kim, *En femtiotalsberättelse: Populärkulturens kalla krig i Folkhemssverige*, Stockholm: Bokförlaget Atlantis, 2007.

af Sandeberg, Edward, *Nu kan det sägas: Sanningen om min fångenskap i Sovjet och Berlins fall*, Stockholm: Saxon & Lindströms Förlag, 1946.

Schellenberg, Walter, *The Schellenberg Memoirs: A Record of the Nazi Secret Service*, London: Andre Deutsch Limited, 1956.

Schiller, Bernt, *Varför ryssarna tog Raoul Wallenberg*, Stockholm: Natur & Kultur, 1991.

Schmid, Carlo, 'Vorwort', in Rudolf Kastner, *Der Kastner-Bericht über Eichmanns Menschenhandel in Ungarn*, Munich: Verlag bei Kindler, 1961, pp. 11–29.

Schreiber, Penny, 'The Heroic Life and Tragic Fate of Raoul Wallenberg', in Penny Schreiber and Joan Lowenstein (eds), *Remembering Raoul Wallenberg: The University of Michigan Celebrates Twentieth-Century Heroes*, Ann Arbor: University of Michigan Press, 2001, pp. 1–19.

Schori, Pierre, 'Olof Palme i världen', in Peter Antman and Pierre Schori, *Olof Palme: Den gränslöse reformisten*, Stockholm: Tidens Förlag, 1996, pp. 123–194.

Schult, Tanja, *A Hero's Many Faces: Raoul Wallenberg in Contemporary Monuments*, Houndmills, Basingstoke and New York: Palgrave Macmillan, 2009.

Schult, Tanja, 'Raoul Wallenberg on Stage – or at Stake? Guilt and Shame as Obstacles in the Swedish Commemoration of their Holocaust Hero', in David Dean, Yana Meerzon and Kathryn Price (eds), *History, Memory, Performance*, Houndmills, Basingstoke: Palgrave Macmillan, 2015, pp. 135–152.

Schult, Tanja, 'Whose Raoul Wallenberg Is It? The Man and the Myth: Between Memory, History and Popularity', *Culture Unbound* 2.5 (2010), 770–796.

Serfőző, Éva, 'Angel Sanz Briz and Giorgio Perlasca: Competing Narratives of Heroism in Rescuing Hungarian Jews during the Holocaust in the Films *The Angel of Budapest* (2011) and *Perlasca: The Courage of a Just Man* (2002)', *Holocaust Studies* 27.2 (2021), 257–273.

Shalit, Erel, *The Hero and His Shadow: Psychopolitical Aspects of Myth and Reality in Israel*, Lanham, New York and Oxford: University Press of America, 1999.

Shandler, Jeffrey, *While America Watches: Televising the Holocaust*, New York and Oxford: Oxford University Press, 1999.

Shepherd, Naomi, *Wilfrid Israel: German Jewry's Secret Ambassador*, London: Weidenfeld & Nicolson, 1984.

Shuart, James M. and Herman A. Berliner, 'Jimmy Carter Conference – Town Meeting', in Herbert R. Rosenbaum and Alexej Ugrinsky (eds), *Jimmy Carter: Foreign Policy and Post-Presidential Years*, Westport, Connecticut and London: Greenwood Press, 1994, pp. 471–487.

Sjöholm Skrubbe, Jessica, *Skulptur i folkhemmet: Den offentliga konstens institutionalisering, referentialitet och rumsliga situationer 1940–1975*, Gothenburg and Stockholm: Makadam Förlag, 2007.
Sjöland, Marianne, *Historia i magasin: En studie av tidskriften Populär Historias historieskrivning och av kommersiellt historiebruk*, Lund: Lund University, 2011.
Sjöquist, Eric, *Dramat Raoul Wallenberg*, Stockholm: Norstedts, 2001.
Sjöquist, Eric, *Raoul Wallenberg*, Stockholm: Norstedts, 1985.
Skoglund, Elizabeth R., *A Quiet Courage: Per Anger, Raoul Wallenberg's Co-Liberator of Hungarian Jews*, Grand Rapids: Michigan: Baker Books, 1997.
Smith, Danny, *Lost Hero: Raoul Wallenberg's Dramatic Quest to Save the Jews of Hungary*, New York: HarperCollins Publishers, 2001 [1986].
Söderblom, Omi, *Söderblom och Wallenbergaffären: Nytt ljus i ett trauma*, Stockholm: Carlssons Bokförlag, 2021.
Solzhenitsyn, Aleksandr, *Warning to the West*, London: The Bodley Head, 1976.
Stangneth, Bettina, *Eichmann Before Jerusalem: The Unexamined Life of a Mass Murderer*, New York: Alfred A. Knopf, 2014.
Steinhouse, Carl L., *Wallenberg is Here! The True Story About How Raoul Wallenberg Faced Down the Nazi War Machine and the Infamous Eichmann and Saved Tens of Thousands of Jews*, Bloomington, Indiana: 1st Books Library, 2002.
Stone, Norman, *Hungary: A Short History*, London: Profile Books, 2020.
Strate, Lance, 'Heroes: A Communication Perspective', in Susan J. Drucker and Robert S. Cathcart (eds), *American Heroes in a Media Age*, Cresskill, New Jersey: Hampton Press, 1994, pp. 15–23.
Stråth, Bo, 'The Swedish Image of Europe as the Other', in Bo Stråth (ed.), *Europe and the Other and Europe as the Other*, Brussels, Berlin, Frankfurt am Main, New York, Oxford and Vienna: P.I.E.-Peter Lang, 2004, pp. 359–383.
Streissguth, Thomas, *Raoul Wallenberg: Swedish Diplomat and Humanitarian*, New York: Rosen Publishing, Inc, 2001.
Ströbinger, Rudolf, *Das Rätsel Wallenberg*, Stuttgart and Bonn: Burg Verlag, 1982.
Strömstedt, Bo, *Löpsedeln och insidan: En bok om tidningen och livet*, Stockholm: Bonniers, 1994.
Sturfelt, Lina, *Eldens återsken: Första världskriget i svensk föreställningsvärld*, Lund: Sekel Förlag, 2008.
Sturfelt, Lina, 'Utanför krigskartan: Första världskrigets svenska berättelser om neutralitet och modernitet', in Magnus Jerneck (ed.), *Fred i realpolitikens skugga*, Lund: Studentlitteratur, 2009, pp. 143–168.
Ståhle, Göran, *Mellan konsten och publiken*, Stockholm: Carlssons Förlag, 2010.

Sudoplatov, Pavel and Anatoli Sudoplatov, with Jerrold L. and Leona P. Schecter, *Special Tasks: The Memoirs of an Unwanted Witness – A Soviet Spymaster*, Boston, New York, Toronto and London: Little Brown & Company, 1994.
Svartz, Nanna, *Steg för steg: En självbiografi*, Stockholm: Bonniers, 1968.
Száraz, György, 'The Jewish Question in Hungary: A Historical Retrospective', in Randolph L. Braham and Bela Vago (eds), *The Holocaust in Hungary: Forty Years Later*, New York: Columbia University Press, 1985, pp. 13–30.
Szekeres, Joszef, *Saving the Ghettos of Budapest in January 1945: Pál Szalai, the 'Hungarian Schindler'*, Budapest: Budapest Archives, 1997.
Szita, Szabolcs, *The Power of Humanity: Raoul Wallenberg and his Aides in Budapest*, Budapest: Corvina, 2012.
Szita, Szabolcs, *Trading in Lives? Operations of the Jewish Relief and Rescue Committee in Budapest, 1944–1945*, Budapest: Central European University Press, 2005.
Tabori, Paul, *Alexander Korda*, London: Oldbourne, 1959.
Tapper, Michael, *Snuten i skymningslandet: Svenska polisberättelser i roman och film 1965–2010*, Lund: Nordic Academic Press, 2011.
Taylor, Telford, *The Anatomy of the Nuremberg Trials: A Personal Memoir*, New York: Alfred A. Knopf, 1992.
Thale, Jerome, 'The Narrator as Hero', *Twentieth Century Literature* 3.2 (1957), 69–73.
Thorsell, Staffan, *Mein lieber Reichskanzler! Sveriges kontakter med Hitlers rikskansli*, Stockholm: Bonniers, 2006.
Thorsell, Staffan, *Sverige i Vita huset*, Stockholm: Bonniers, 2015.
Tingsten, Herbert, *Mitt liv: Tidningen 1946–52*, Stockholm: Norstedts, 1963.
Torgovnick, Mariana, *The War Complex: World War II in Our Time*, Chicago: University of Chicago Press, 2005.
Trencsényi, Balázs, '"Politics of History" and Authoritarian Regime-Building in Hungary', in Niels F. May and Thomas Maissen (eds), *National History and New Nationalism in the Twenty-First Century: A Global Comparison*, New York and London: Routledge, 2021, pp. 171–189.
Trice, Ashton D. and Samuel A. Holland, *Heroes, Antiheroes and Dolts: Portrayals of Masculinity in American Popular Films, 1921–1999*, Jefferson, North Carolina and London: McFarland & Company, Inc., Publishers, 2001.
Tschuy, Theo, *Dangerous Diplomacy: The Story of Carl Lutz, Rescuer of 62,000 Hungarian Jews*, Grand Rapids: Eerdmans Publishing Company, 2000.
Tydén, Mattias, 'Att inte lägga sig i: Till frågan om Sveriges moraliska skuld till Förintelsen', in Lars M. Andersson and Mattias Tydén (eds), *Sverige*

*och Nazityskland: Skuldfrågor och moraldebatt*, Stockholm: Dialogos Förlag, 2007, pp. 123–147.

Ungváry, Krisztián, *The Siege of Budapest: One Hundred Days in World War II*, New Haven and London: Yale University Press, 2005 [1999].

Vaksberg, Arkadij, *Aleksandra Kollontaj: En biografi*, Stockholm: Norstedts, 1997.

Viklund, Klas, 'Kjell Grede: Använd filmupplevelsen!', in Klas Viklund (ed.), *Bilden av Förintelsen: Handledning för att se, analysera och diskutera filmer om nazism och motståndskamp*, Stockholm: Swedish Film Institute, 1998, pp. 27–33.

Villius, Elsa and Hans Villius, *Fallet Raoul Wallenberg*, Stockholm: Geber 1966.

Volkogonov, Dmitri, *Stalin: Triumph and Tragedy*, London: Weidenfeld and Nicolson, 1991 [1988].

Vörös, Márton, *Även för din skull ... Svenska Röda Korset i Ungern i världskrigets dagar*, Stockholm: Askild & Kärnekull, 1978.

Wachtmeister, Wilhelm, *Som jag såg det: Händelser och människor på världsscenen*, Stockholm: Norstedts, 1996.

Wagrell, Kristin, *'Chorus of the Saved': Constructing the Holocaust Survivor in Swedish Public Discourse, 1943–1966*, Linköping: Linköping Studies in Art and Science, 2020.

Wahlbäck, Krister, 'Raoul Wallenberg och synen på Sovjet 1944–47', in *Till en konstnärssjäl: En vänbok till Stig Ramel*, Stockholm: Bokförlaget Atlantis, 2002, pp. 239–258.

Wallengren, Ann-Kristin, *Welcome Home, Mr Swanson: Swedish Emigrants and Swedishness on Film*, Lund: Nordic Academic Press, 2014 [2013].

Wamberg, Jakob, 'Lang dags rejse mod rum: En introduktion til Kirsten Ortweds skulptur', in Jakob Wamberg, Lise Skytte Jakobsen, Per Jonas Storvse and Britta Töndborg, *Kirsten Ortwed: Full Length*, Copenhagen: The National Gallery of Denmark [Statens museum for kunst], 2008, pp. 8–36.

Wästberg, Olle, *I tidens skugga: Verksamhetsberättelse från 1945*, Stockholm: Ekerlids Förlag, 2022.

Weber, Cynthia, *International Relations Theory: A Critical Introduction*, London and New York: Routledge, 2005 [2001].

Wecter, Dixon, *The Hero in America: A Chronicle of Hero-Worship*, Ann Arbor: University of Michigan Press, 1966 [1941].

Werbell, Frederick and Thurston Clarke, *Lost Hero: The Mystery of Raoul Wallenberg*, New York: McGraw-Hill Book Company, 1982.

Wheeler, Douglas, 'And Who Is My Neighbor? A World War II Hero or Conscience for Portugal', *Luso-Brazilian Review* 26.1 (Summer 1989), 119–139.

White, Hayden, 'Historical Emplotment and the Problem of Truth', in Saul Friedländer (ed.), *Probing the Limits of Representation: Nazism and the*

'Final Solution', Cambridge, Massachusetts: Harvard University Press, 1992, pp. 37–53.
White, Hayden, *The Practical Past*, Evanston, Illinois: Northwestern University Press, 2014.
Wiesen, S. Jonathan, 'Overcoming Nazism: Big Business, Public Relations, and the Politics of Memory, 1945–50', *Central European History* 29.2 (1996), 201–226.
Wiesenthal, Simon, 'Deklaration av Simon Wiesenthal', in *Vittnen från GULAG: Internationella Sacharov-Hearingens dokument om förtrycket i Sovjet*, Lund: Foundation for Human Rights in Eastern Europe, 1976, pp. 14–18.
Wiesenthal, Simon, *Justice Not Vengeance: Recollections*, New York: Grove Weidenfeld, 1989.
Wiklund, Martin, 'The Ideal of Justice and its Significance for Historians as Engaged Intellectuals', in Stefan Berger (ed.), *The Engaged Historian: Perspectives on the Intersections of Politics, Activism and the Historical Profession*, New York and Oxford: Berghahn Books, 2018, pp. 44–62.
Wolff, Morris, *Whatever Happened to Raoul Wallenberg? The True story of Holocaust Hero Raoul Wallenberg and the Author's Efforts to Rescue him from Soviet Union Imprisonment*, Scotts Valley, California: CreateSpace Independent Publishing Platform, 2012.
Wrigstad, Per, *Så här var det*, Stockholm: Norstedts, 1979.
Wyman, David S., *A Race Against Death: Peter Bergson, America, and the Holocaust*, New York: The New Press, 2002.
Wyman, Mark, *DPs: Europe's Displaced Persons, 1945–1951*, Ithaca and London: Cornell University Press, 1998 [1989].
Yahil, Leni, 'Raoul Wallenberg – His Mission and His Activities in Hungary', *Yad Vashem Studies* 15 (1983), 7–53.
York, Richard, 'Evelyn Waugh's Farewell to Heroism', in Graham Gargett (ed.), *Heroism and Passion in Literature: Studies in Honour of Moya Longstaffe*, Amsterdam and New York: Rodopi, 2004, pp. 245–253.
Young, James E., *The Texture of Memory: Holocaust Memorials and Meaning*, New York and London: Yale University Press, 1993.
Zander, Ulf, *Clio på bio: Om amerikansk film, historia och identitet*, Lund: Historiska Media, 2006.
Zander, Ulf, 'Den slingrande vägen från Auschwitz: Om Förintelsens bilder och de eventuella sambanden mellan då och nu', *Scandia* 66.2 (2000), 283–319.
Zander, Ulf, 'Dire Strait? When the Holocaust Came to Sweden: A Regional Perspective', in Johannes Heuman and Pontus Rudberg (eds), *Early Holocaust Memory in Sweden: Archives, Testimonies and Reflections*, Cham: Palgrave Macmillan, 2021, pp. 221–247.
Zander, Ulf, 'Efterskrift', in Ben Shephard, *Befrielsen av Bergen-Belsen*, Lund: Historiska Media, 2005, pp. 219–233.

Zander, Ulf, 'Efterskrift', in Miklós Nyiszli, *Jag var Mengeles patolog: En läkares ögonvittnesskildring från Auschwitz*, Stockholm: Lind & Co, 2022, pp. 205–226.

Zander, Ulf, 'The Footprints Frighten Me: Visualisations of Borderline Events', in Patrick Amsellem (ed.), *Memory Matters*, Lund: Museum of Artistic Process and Public Art [Skissernas museum], 2018, pp. 86–102.

Zander, Ulf, *Fornstora dagar, moderna tider: Bruk av och debatter om svensk historia från sekelskifte till sekelskifte*, Lund: Nordic Academic Press, 2001.

Zander, Ulf, 'Heroic Images: Raoul Wallenberg as a History-Cultural Symbol', in Martin L. Davies and Claus-Christian W. Sznejmann (eds), *How the Holocaust Looks Now: International Perspectives*, Houndmills, Basingstoke and New York: Palgrave Macmillan, 2007, pp. 126–135.

Zander, Ulf, '*Holocaust* at the Limits: Historical Culture and the Nazi Genocide in the Television Era', in Klas-Göran Karlsson and Ulf Zander (eds), *Echoes of the Holocaust: Historical Cultures in Contemporary Europe*, Lund: Nordic Academic Press 2003.

Zander, Ulf, 'In a Land of Dreams: Left-Wing Politics and the Place of the Holocaust in Tage Erlander's Sweden', in Jan Gerber, Philipp Graf and Anna Pollmann (eds), *Geschichtsoptimismus und Katastrophenbewusstsein: Europa nach dem Holocaust*, Göttingen: Vandenhoeck & Ruprecht, 2022, pp. 455–478.

Zander, Ulf, 'I våldets virvelvind: Representationer av Adolf Eichmann i förintelsens historiekulturer', in Eva Österberg and Marie Lindstedt Cronberg (eds), *Våld: Representationer och verklighet*, Lund: Nordic Academic Press, 2006, pp. 303–322.

Zander, Ulf, 'Läroböcker i sten: Historiedidaktiska aspekter på monument och minnesmärken', in Klas-Göran Karlsson and Ulf Zander (eds), *Historien är nu: En introduktion till historiedidaktiken*, second revised edition, Lund: Studentlitteratur, 2008 [2004], pp. 107–129.

Zander, Ulf, 'Med andra ögon. Svensk historia i mötet mellan inhemsk och utländsk debatt', in Lars M. Andersson, Fabian Persson, Peter Ullgren and Ulf Zander (eds), *På historiens slagfält: En festskrift tillägnad Sverker Oredsson*, Lund: Sisyfos Förlag, 2002, pp. 75–95.

Zander, Ulf, 'Modernitetskritik i svart-vitt: Chaplin mellan kapitalism, kommunism och nazism', in Johan Dietsch, Klas-Göran Karlsson, Barbara Törnquist-Plewa and Ulf Zander (eds), *Historia mot strömmen: Kultur och konflikt i det moderna Europa*, Stockholm: Carlssons Förlag 2007, pp. 212–235.

Zander, Ulf, 'Oskar Schindler and Raoul Wallenberg – National, European and American Heroes', in Teresa Pinhero, Beata Cieszynka and Eduardo Franco (eds), *Ideas of Europe/Ideas for Europe, An Interdisciplinary Approach to European Identity*. Frankfurt: Peter Lang, 2012, pp. 443–454.

Zander, Ulf, 'På vakt eller på krigsstigen? Andra världskriget i svensk 2000-talstappning', in Erik Hedling and Ann-Kristin Wallengren (eds), *Den nya svenska filmen: Kultur, kriminalitet, kakofoni*, Stockholm: Bokförlaget Atlantis, 2014, pp. 23–41.

Zander, Ulf, 'Raoul Wallenberg – en förebild i tiden? Reflektioner kring ett jubileumsår', *Historielärarnas Förenings Årsskrift* 70 (2012), 118–131.

Zander, Ulf, 'Remembering and Forgetting the Holocaust: The Cases of Jan Karski and Raoul Wallenberg', in Krzysztof Kowalski and Barbara Törnquist-Plewa (eds), *The Europeanization of Heritage and Memories in Poland and Sweden*, Krakow: Jagiellonian University Press, 2016, pp. 189–211.

Zander, Ulf, 'Swedish Rescue Operations during the Second World War: Accomplishments and Aftermath', in Marie Louise Seeberg, Irene Levin and Claudia Lenz (eds), *The Holocaust as Active Memory: The Past in the Present*, London: Ashgate Publishing, 2013, pp. 165–185.

Zander, Ulf, 'To Rescue or be Rescued: The Liberation of Bergen-Belsen and the White Buses in British and Swedish Historical Cultures', in Klas-Göran Karlsson and Ulf Zander (eds), *The Holocaust – Post-War Battlefields: Genocide as Historical Culture*, Lund: Sekel Förlag, 2006, pp. 343–383.

Zander, Ulf, 'World War II at 24 Frames a Second – Scandinavian Examples', in Helle Bjerg, Claudia Lenz and Erik Thorstensen (eds), *Historicizing the Uses of the Past: Scandinavian Perspectives on History Culture, Historical Consciousness and Didactics of History Related to World War II*, Bielefeld: Transcript Verlag, 2011, pp. 207–225.

Zelizer, Barbie, *Remembering to Forget: Holocaust Memory through the Camera's Eye*, Chicago and London: University of Chicago Press, 1998.

Zetterberg, Kent, 'Staffan Söderblom', in Gunnar Artéus and Leif Leifland (eds), *Svenska diplomatprofiler under 1900-talet*, Stockholm: Probus Förlag, 2001, pp. 250–273.

Zetterberg, Kent, 'Sven Grafström', in Gunnar Artéus and Leif Leifland (eds), *Svenska diplomatprofiler under 1900-talet*, Stockholm: Probus Förlag, 2001, pp. 317–351.

Zietsma, David, '"Sin Has No History": Religion, National Identity, and U.S. Intervention, 1937–1941', *Diplomatic History* 31.3 (June 2007), 531–565.

## Films, television programmes, and monuments

### Feature films

*Casablanca* (Michael Curtiz, 1942).
*Diplomacy / Diplomatie* (Volker Schlöndorf, 2013).
*Distant Journey / Daleká Cesta* (Alfred Rádok, 1949)
*The Eagle Has Landed* (John Sturges, 1976).

*Eichmann* (Robert Young, 2007).
*The Elusive Pimpernel / The Fighting Pimpernel* (Michael Powell and Emeric Pressburger, 1950).
*The First of the Few / Spitfire* (Leslie Howard, 1942).
*Gone with the Wind* (Victor Fleming, 1938).
*Good Evening, Mr. Wallenberg / God afton, herr Wallenberg* (Kjell Grede, 1990).
*The Great Dictator* (Charles Chaplin, 1940).
*The Grey Zone* (Tim Blake Nelson, 2001).
*Hanussen* (István Szabó, 1988).
*Hero / Accidental Hero* (Stephen Frears, 1992).
*Hip, hip, hurra! / Hip Hip Hurrah!* (Kjell Grede, 1987).
*The Inglorious Bastards / Quel maledetto blindato* (1978).
*Inglourious Basterds* (Quentin Tarantino, 2009).
*Is Paris Burning? / Paris brûle-t-il?* (René Clément, 1966).
*Jens Mansson in America / Jens Månsson i Amerika* (Bengt Janzon, 1947).
*Mephisto* ((István Szabó, 1981).
*Modern Times* (Charles Chaplin, 1935).
*Music Box* (Costra-Gavras, 1990).
*The Petrified Forest* (Archie Mayo, 1936).
*Phoenix* (Christian Petzold, 2014).
*The Pianist* (Roman Polanski, 2002).
*Pimpernel Smith / Mr. V* (Leslie Howard, 1941).
*Pimpernel Svensson* (Emil A. Lingheim, 1950).
*The Scarlet Pimpernel* (Harold Young, 1934).
*Schindler's List* (Steven Spielberg, 1993).
*Son of Saul / Saul fia* (László Nemes, 2015).
*Svarta nejlikan / The Black Pimpernel / El Clavel Negro* (Ulf Hultberg, 2007).
*To Be Or Not To Be* (Ernst Lubitsch, 1942).
*Went the Day Well?* (Alberto Cavalcanti, 1942).

## Television series and films

*The Angel of Budapest / El ángel de Budapest* (Luis Oliveros, 2011).
*Atlantic Crossing* (Alexander Eik and Janic Heen, 2020).
*Billions* (Reed Morano et al., 2016–).
*Centennial* (Harry Falk et al., 1978–1979).
*Holocaust: The Story of the Family Weiss* (Marvin J. Chomsky, 1978).
*Perlasca – An Italian Hero / Perlasca – The Courage of a Just Man / Perlasca – Un eoro Italiano* (Alberto Negrin, 2002).
*Playing for Time* (Daniel Mann and Joseph Sargent, 1980).
*Roots* (Marvin J. Chomsky et al., 1977).
*The Scarlet and the Black* (Jerry London, 1983).

*Shogun* (Jerry London, 1980).
*Succession* (Adam McKay et al., 2018–)
*The Thorn Birds* (Daryl Duke, 1983).
*Wallenberg: A Hero's Story* (Lamont Johnson, 1983).
*War and Remembrance* (Dan Curtis, 1988).
*Winds of War* (Dan Curtis, 1983).

## Documentaries

*Diplomaterna* (Fredrik Undevik, 2009).
*Missing Hero: Raoul Wallenberg* (John Bierman, 1980).
*Raoul – och de 30 monumenten* (Peter R. Meyer, 2001).
*Shoah* (Claude Lanzmann, 1986).

## Monuments

*Ahead of the Battle of Warsaw*, Karola Badyny (2020), Skierniewice, Poland.
*Att minnas – den goda gärningen: Hågkomsten, hyllningen och respekten för Raoul Wallenbergs gärning i Budapest 1944*, Lenke Rothman (1997), Stockholm.
*Hommage à Raoul Wallenberg*, Kirsten Ortwed (2001), Stockholm.
*Hope*, Gustav and Ulla Kraitz (1998), New York.
*Imre Nagy*, Támas Varga (1996), Budapest, Hungary.
*Memorial for the Victims of German Occupation*, Párkanyi Raab Péter (2004), Budapest, Hungary.
*Memorial of the Hungarian Jewish Martyrs*, Imre Varga (1989), Budapest, Hungary.
*The New Raoul Wallenberg Monument*, Imre Varga (1987), Budapest, Hungary (copy in Tel Aviv, Israel) 2002.
*Non-Violence* or *The Knotted Gun*, Carl Fredrik Reuterswärd (1988), New York (and replicas in about 30 places around the world).
*Pál Teleki*, Tibor Rieger (2004), Balatonboglár, Hungary.
*Pál Teleki*, Stefan Dousa (2020), Kraków, Poland.
*Pienza*, Staffan Nihlén (1993), Malmö, Sweden.
*Raoul Wallenbergs gärning*, Willy Gordon (1998), Lidingö, Sweden.
*The Ronald Reagan Monument*, Władysław Dudek (2011), Warsaw.
*R. W. Briefcase*, Gustav and Ulla Kraitz (1998), Lund and several other cities.
*The Snake Killer* or *Wallenberg Memorial Statue*, Pál Pátzay (1949, original, 1999, replica), Budapest and Debrecen, Hungary.
*Tom Lantos*, Mamikon Yengibarian (2018), Budapest, Hungary.
*Wallenberg Memorial*, Philip Jackson (2005), London.

## Musical, operas, and stage play

*Raoul*, Erik Åkerlund (1983).
*Raoul*, Gershon Kingsley and Michael Kunze (2008).
*Raoul Wallenberg – saknad*, Inger Wikström (2018).
*Wallenberg*, Laurence Holzman, Felicia Needleman and Benjamin Rosenblut (2010).
*Wallenberg*, Erkki-Sven Tüür and Lutz Hübner (2001).

# Index

Whenever names occur both in the running text and in footnotes on the same pages, references to the latter have been omitted. In order to keep the index to reasonable proportions, newspaper articles and similar items have, with a few exceptions, not been included, nor have references to the author's own works.

Abakumov, Viktor 183
Acheson, Dean 134
Adachi, Agnes 4n5, 6n13
Adaktusson, Lars 203n359
Adelsohn, Ulf 193n321
Agrell, Wilhelm 35n83, 36–37, 40, 42n104, 56n16, 61n33, 63n42, 167n229, 200n346, 203
Ahlander, Dag Sebastian 259n146, 294
Ahlmark, Per 33n78, 137n120, 138n124, 181n276, 182n281, 187, 188n304, 193n322, 270n177
Ahnfeldt-Mollerup, Eline 264n158
Aldgate, Richard 67n4, 72n15, 72n19, 79n32, 81n38, 82n43
Alexander, Lynne 259n146
Allen, Michael Thad 275n194
Allende, Salvador 95
Alm, Martin 22n48, 228n58, 284n220
Alving, Barbro (Bang) 96, 184
Åmark, Klas 9–12, 15–17, 32n75, 55n15, 59n26, 61n33, 108n15, 111n26, 261n150

Americanization of the Holocaust 214–215
Amishai-Maisels, Ziva 291n10
Andersson, Bibi 238
'Andersson, Erik Arvid' 184
Andersson, Sten 194
*The Angel of Budapest* (2011), television series 283
Anger, Per 34, 62n38, 63, 65n49, 95, 119n52, 122, 127, 128n85, 139, 141, 144n150, 156, 164n218, 165n219, 175, 193n219, 194n327, 211, 217, 221n33, 222n37, 224, 234n76, 237–238, 245n103, 257, 267–268, 275n195, 276, 308, 310, 317, 321n117
antisemitism 52–58, 108
Applebaum, Anne 126n79
Ardai, Sandor 245
Arendt, Hannah 182n282, 249–252, 251n123
Arnborg, Beata 185n290
Arnheim, Franz 108
Aronson, Shlomo 262n154

Arrow Cross 56–57, 64–65, 120, 127, 129, 131, 144–145, 238, 245–246, 250, 261–263, 271–272, 276, 279, 307, 315–316
Åsbrink, Brita 171n242, 188n304
Åselius, Gunnar 127n82
Asplund, Johan 25n55
*Atlantic Crossing* (2020), television series 240–242
Auschwitz, Auschwitz-Birkenau 58, 240, 264, 292–293
*Auschwitz: A Doctor's Eyewitness Account* (1946) *see* Nyiszli
Avisar, Ilan 76n28, 278n204
Axelsson, Peter 130–131

Baber, Katherine 210n2
Bacsó, Péter 301
Bailey, Elisabeth 134
Barany, George 28n63, 220n32
Baron, Lawrence 279–281
Bartov, Omer 254n129
Bata, Tomás 148–149
Bauer, Yehuda 14, 55, 58n24, 111n28, 217n21
Bauhn, Per 272n182, 328n12
Becher, Kurt 250–251, 258–259, 261–262
Beer, Henrik 226
Begin, Menachem 219
Benedek, László 297
Ben-Tov, Arieh 29n65
Berenbaum, Michael 215n12, 239n90
Berend, Iván T. 53n9
Berg, Dick 256
Berg, Lars G:son 122, 128, 145, 174, 175n254, 258, 275
Berger, Lazar (Leizer Bergher) 224–225
Berger, Susanne 34n80, 61n33, 104–105, 128n84, 202–203
Bergling, Stig 188–190

Berglund, Pelle 32n76
Bergström, Ingvar 73n22
Beria, Lavrentiy 129, 173, 297
Berkhofer Jr, Robert F. 18n44
Berman, Dmitry 212
Bernstein, Leonard 210
Bernadotte, Folke 13, 26–27, 30, 100, 104–105, 111–113, 118, 126n76, 127, 136, 144, 172, 186, 197, 205–207
Bess, Demare 116
Biden, Joe 329
Bierman, John 137n119, 155n189, 158n203, 220n32, 224, 225, 236, 247n111, 302, 307n66
Bietz, Bertold 30
Biorck Kaplan, Lena 177
Bildt, Carl 9n21, 198, 199n344, 201, 209
Bjereld, Ulf 138n124, 161n209
*The Black Pimpernel* (2007), film 97–98
Blomqvist, Anders E. 8, 56n18
Bloodworth, Jeff 178n266
Blutinger, Jeffrey 315n93
Bogdanor, Paul 262n153
Bodström, Lennart 192n317
Boëthius, Maria-Pia 285
Boheman, Erik 61, 62, 118n51
Böhm, Vilmos 36–37, 148
Bohman, Gösta 188
Bohus, Kata 296n26
Boitard, Louise 87n58
Bokholm, Rune 138n126
Bonner, Yelena 196
Bonnier, Johan ('Joja') 195
Borhi, László 306n61
Bourke, Joanna 7–8
Braham, Randolph L. 53n10, 58n25, 261n150, 310n77
Brand, Joel 217
Brändström, Elsa 67, 113, 144
Brezhnev, Leonid 158
Brink, Lars 145n151, 276n197

# Index

Brown, Gordon 256n138, 259n146
Browning, Christopher 278
Bulganin, Nikolai 151
Burns, Jimmy 85n55
Bush, George 309
Bustow, Robert 323n124
Byström, Mikael 113

Campbell, Joseph 5
Capote, Truman 87
Carlberg, Ingrid 3, 4n7, 6–8, 15n37, 35, 64n45, 64n47, 65n51, 112n30, 143n144, 169n235, 189n307, 207n375, 251n121, 258n145, 276n201, 330n17
Carlsson, Ingvar 193
Carlsson, Göte 258
Carl XVI Gustaf, King of Sweden 316, 317
Carter, Jimmy 16, 178, 219–220, 221n33
Cartmell, Deborah 242n96, 280
*Casablanca* (1942), film 23
Cassel, Leif 123–124n67
Cassirer, Ernst 43n105
Catalina affair, the 172
Cathcart, Robert S. 23n49, 289n4
Cesarani, David 55, 56n16, 58n23, 250, 251n121, 251n123, 334–335
Chamberlain, Richard 237–238, 271, 272n181, 284
Chaplin, Charles 75, 84, 148
Chapman, James 79n35
Church, Frank 166n222, 220, 225n50
Churchill, Winston 85–86, 211, 244, 285
Clarke, Thurston 4n4, 131n92, 134n107, 177, 246, 256–257, 262, 263n156, 271, 271n181
Cohen, Peter 272
Cohen, Yoel 234

Cole, Tim 29, 228n57, 280n208, 292, 297n27, 298n30, 307n65, 333n23, 309n74, 310n79, 314n91, 315n93, 316, 333n23
Colley, Kenneth 254–255
Conot, Robert E. 249n117, 253n127
Conquest, Robert 177, 182
Cornelius, Deborah S. 57n22, 245n104
Creeber, Glen 240n90, 243n99, 282–283
Creet, Julia 315n93
Crowe, David M. 29n67, 94n82, 275n194, 275n195

Dagerman, Stig 171–172
Danielsson, Ivan 62n43, 63, 121–122, 124n71, 125, 128, 129, 173, 246n105
Danielson Marmros, Ingmarie 31n74
von Dardel, Guy 50, 132–134, 143, 155, 156–157, 158n202, 159n205, 162n212, 176, 221–222, 225n50, 226, 229n60, 318
von Dardel, Fredrik 50, 143, 157, 175n254, 176n259, 184n287, 185–186, 246n105
von Dardel, Maj 50, 67, 83n47, 132–134, 147, 150–151, 156–159, 162n212, 167, 185–186, 235, 238, 318
Deák, István 52n8, 57n19, 57n21–22
Dekanozov, Vladimir 129–130
Deland, Mats 112n32
Demszky, Gabor 311
Derogy, Jacques 67n2, 83n46, 127n81, 275n195
Deutscher, Isaac 296
Dew, John 213
Dilworth, Thomas 87n59

Diner, Hasia R. 216n16, 228n58
*Diplomaterna* (2009), TV drama documentary series 99
Domonkos, Miksa 260–261, 297
Doneson, Judith E. 227n55, 235n79
Dromberg, Ragnar 308, 309, 310n80, 318n106, 318n107
Drucker, Susan J. 23n49
DuBois, Josiah, Jr 59
Dugan, Sally 70, 71n14

*The Eagle Has Landed* (1976), film 243–244
Edel, Wilbur 230n64
Edelstam, Erik 97
Edelstam, Harald 95–100
Eden, Anthony 59
Eforgan, Estel 67n4, 72n16, 75n26–27, 76n28, 84n49–50, 85n56
Ehrenpreis, Marcus 61, 106n9, 107n13, 123n65, 256n138
Ehrenstråhle, Britt 155n190, 162
Ehrenstråle, Hans 155n190, 162
Eichmann, Adolf 56–58, 65, 182, 211–213, 216, 244, 248–260, 278n204, 279, 282, 313–314
Eichmann Trial 227, 249–252, 255
Einhorn, Lena 61n34, 62n40, 275n195
Eliasson, Ingemar 46n111, 103, 104
Eliasson, Jan 27, 34, 96n92, 100n105, 102, 103, 304, 305n57, 306n62
Elmbrant, Björn 167n227, 228
*The Elusive Pimpernel* (*The Black Pimpernel*, 1950), film 87–88
Emerson, Ralph Waldo 325, 335
Enander, Bo 108
Englund, Peter 201
Engzell, Gösta 63
entangled history 24–25
Erbelding, Rebecca 60n28
Eriksonas, Linas 248

Erlander, Tage 114, 136, 150, 153, 154, 158n201–202, 166–170, 171n241, 174, 185–186, 234n75

*A Failure of Diplomacy/Ett diplomatiskt misslyckande* (2003) 39n97, 45, 46n111, 61n33, 104n5, 127n81, 129n87–88, 130n89, 134n107, 135n110, 138n126, 139n128, 139n130, 140n134, 141n138, 143n147, 183n285
Fälldin, Thorbjörn 188
Fant, Kenne 194n327, 207n373, 223, 224n44, 269
Faragó, Katinka 269
Feingold, Henry L. 220n31
Fenyo, Mario D. 57n22
Fermaglich, Kirsten 215n13
Fest, Joachim 178
Fichtelius, Erik 104n5
Finn, David 294n22
Fishwick, Marshall W. 335n27
Fleming, Michael 58n24
Fors, Mats 96n80, 97n97, 98
Fowkes, Reuben 299n38
Frankfurter, Felix 59
Fredborg, Arvid 154
Fredriksen, Erik 190
Fredriksson, Stig 184n287
Frick, Lennart W. 189n305
Fry, Varian 94, 95n84
Furhammar, Leif 78–80

Gann, Christoph 134n107
Gärde-Widemar, Ingrid 318
Gerner, Kristian 21n46, 35n87, 37n91, 42n103, 101, 142n143, 161n209, 167n231, 183n283, 312n86, 315n93
Gerstein, Kurt 107–108
Gersten, Alan 132n97, 133n100, 134n104, 135n110

Gibbon, Peter H. 256n138
Giesen, Bernhard 336–337
Gluck, Mary 53n9
Goebbels, Joseph 81
Gogoberidze, Simon 175
Göncz, Árpád 40
Gonshak, Henry 252n125
*Good Evening, Mr. Wallenberg* (1990), film 29–30, 98, 244, 269–275, 277–279, 282, 284–286, 308, 327–328, 333
Gorbachev, Michail 194
Gordievsky, Oleg 163–164n217, 197
Gordon, Willy 319–320
Grafström, Sven 62, 125, 138–139, 155
*The Great Dictator* (1940), film 75, 84
Grede, Kjell 29, 269–274, 279n207, 284
Green, Gerald 237, 242–243, 246–247, 257
*The Grey Zone* (2001), film 240
Gromyko, Andrei 132, 133n100, 134, 152, 169
Grunwald-Spier, Agnes 281n212
Gulag 115, 126, 142, 153, 163–165, 177–185, 212–213, 224–225, 307, 330
*The Gulag Archipelago* (1973–75) 177–178
Gustafsdotter, Jeanette 287–288
Gustafsson, Tommy 98
Gustaf V, King of Sweden 57, 122
Gustaf VI Adolf, King of Sweden 141, 142, 157
Günther, Christian 115

Hagberg, Hilding 152
Hagelin, Dagmar 199
Hägglöf, Gunnar 118n49, 141, 190n309, 299n37
Hägglöf, Ingemar 115n37, 121n58, 126n76

Hallert, Kerstin 124–125, 229–230n61
Hamilton, Carl 322, 332
Hammarskjöld, Dag 26, 157, 207
Handler, Andrew 6n11, 9, 63n41, 246n105, 314n90
Hanebrink, Paul 53n10, 313n87, 314n92, 315n93
Hansen, Einar 87
Hardi-Kovacs, Gellert 34n80, 61n33
Harriman, Averell 135
Harrison, Dick 167n231, 169n236
Hasselbohm, Andreas 128n86, 166n224, 218n24, 226n52, 267n172
Hedling, Erik 254, 275n193, 284n221
Helin, Sofia 241
*Hero/Accidental Hero* (1992), film 24
Herczl, Moshe Y. 54n12, 57n21, 314n90
Herf, Jeffrey 228n58
Hessérus, Mattias 202
Himmler, Heinrich 58, 112, 250–251, 258, 262
Hirdman, Sven 38n95, 99n105, 165–166n221, 166n222, 191n316
Hirsch, Joshua 277n203
historical past 17–21, 66, 162, 175, 205, 239, 334–335
historical truth 15, 239–242, 277
history culture, history-cultural, uses of history 11–121, 25–33, 40–44, 95, 105–106, 202–206, 228–229, 248–249n115, 289–293, 314–315, 325–337
Hitler, Adolf 55, 75, 76, 160, 260, 285, 305
Hjalmarson, Jarl 161
Holbrooke, Richard 23, 24n50, 27, 32n77, 128n83, 256n138
Holland, Samuel A. 73n20, 274

Holmila, Antero 107n12, 109, 110n21, 249n117, 253n128, 292n13, 333n23
*Holocaust* (1978), television series 179, 228–229, 232, 235, 239, 253–254, 265, 267, 281–282
Holocaust 106–111
and Sweden 106–113
definition 110–111
in Hungary 54–58
reporting 106–107
Holocaust memory/consciousness 83–84, 109–111, 206–209, 227–228, 279–281
*Hommage à Raoul Wallenberg*, monument 321–324, 332–333
Hook, Sidney 325n1, 326n4, 326n7
Hopper, Bruce 116–117
Horthy, Miklós 10, 57, 63, 122, 255, 312–313
Horney, Jane 263–264
Howard, Charles, Earl of Suffolk 94
Howard, Leslie 68, 71–85, 90–93, 271, 327
Howard, Ronald 75n27, 81n40
Hübner, Lutz 211, 214
Hughes-Hallett, Lucy 128n83, 256n138
Hughes-Warrington, Marnie 242n97
Hull, Cordell 62n40, 64
Hultberg, Ulf 99
Hunter, I. Q. 242n96, 281

*Inglourious Basterds* (2009), film 252
Insdorf, Annette 76n28, 254, 278n204
Isaak, Dawit 200–204
Isaksen, Trond Norén 241
Isaksson, Folke 78–80
Israel, Wilfrid 74

Jackson, Henry M. 178
Jackson, Philip 29, 83n47
Jähner, Harald 126n78
James, Beverly Ann 301n42
Jangfeldt, Bengt 3, 6–7, 65n51, 67, 129n87, 131n92, 247n112
Jankowski, Christian 289
Jarring, Gunnar 137n122, 142n143, 161n209, 178–179, 184n287, 233n73
*Jens Månsson in America* (1947), film 89
Jerselius, Kjell 92
Jick, Leon A. 227n54, 228n57
Johansson, Alf W. 114n36, 115n41, 136n112, 138n124
Johnson, Herschel 62n37, 62n40, 64n48, 131n94, 135n109
Johnson, Lamont 237, 238n89, 247, 268
Johnson, Mats 98
Jordan, James 278n206

Kaaström, Katrin 200n348
Kádár, Gabor 57n19
Kádár, János 305–306, 309
Kalb, Marvin 106n11
Kalinski, Abraham 165–166, 218
Kállay, Miklós 55
Kaltenbrunner, Ernst 112, 250, 253
Kantsteiner, Wulf 280n208
Kaplan, Robert D. 160
Karlsson, Klas-Göran 11, 12, 21n46, 22n48, 24n51, 25n52–53, 102n3, 105, 113n33, 181n276, 183n283, 198n340, 206n369, 215, 298n30
Karadja, Constantin 32
Karski, Jan 59, 232–233
Kasztner, Resznő/Rudolf 261–262
Kemény, Gabor 245–247
Kemény-Fuchs, Elisabeth 245–249, 265, 268

# Index

Keneally, Thomas 29
Kerner, Aaron 254n132
Kershaw, Alex 6–7, 67n4, 256n138, 259n146, 263n156
Khrushchev, Nikita 2, 142, 154, 161, 167–171
King, Sol 6n14
Kingsley, Gershon 211
Kissinger, Henry 158–161, 178, 237
Kjær, Erling 87
Klein, Georg 28n62, 259n147, 275n195
Koblik, Steven 61n34, 108n15, 285
Koch, Erich 251
Kohl, Helmut 231
Kollontay, Alexandra 129, 130n89, 168
Konrád, György 259n146
Korda, Alexander 70, 86, 88
Korda, Michael 86, 314n90
Kosygin, Aleksei 186–187
Kovács, András 296n25
Kovacs, Gellert 258n145, 260n148
Kowalski, Alexandra 312
Kraitz, Gustav 209, 293–294, 323
Kraitz, Ulla 209, 294, 323
Kravchenko, Viktor 181
Krige, Alice 248
Kriza, Elisa 178n265
Kun, Béla 36–37, 53, 70, 301, 304
Küng, Andres 259n146
Kunze, Michael 211
Kushner, Tony 60n31, 281
Kuylenstierna-Andrassy, Stella 161–162
Kwon, Miwon 331–332

LaCapra, Dominick 292–293
Laczo, Fernec 56n17
Lagercrantz, Olof 26

Lagergren, Nina 6, 50, 67–68, 82, 198n344, 219n29, 220–221, 222n37, 226n52, 229, 230n61, 236n81, 237, 309, 318, 336
Lajos, Attila 4n6, 9–10, 12–16, 245n103
Langer, Joakim 32n76
Langfelder, Vilmos 33, 39, 301
Langlet, Nina 10, 124–125
Langlet, Valdemar 10, 54, 62–63, 120, 124–125, 127, 141n139, 298, 299n36, 316
Lantos, Annette 221–222, 229, 235, 308
Lantos, Tom (Thomas) 221–222, 315, 330
Lanzmann, Claude 233
Larsson, Daniel 34n28, 39n97, 104n5
Lauer, Koloman (Kálman) 52, 61, 65
Leche Löfgren, Mia 5, 93, 107n14, 110n22, 123–124, 143n147, 147n156, 148n162, 158, 223n39
Leff, Laurel 106n11
Leifland, Leif 35n86, 102–103, 158n202, 159, 165n219, 186n293, 187n300, 189n306, 195n328
Leiser, Erwin 319–320
Lester, Elenore 246n105, 259n146, 261n149
Lévai, Jenő 13n29, 57n22, 67n2, 128n85, 144–147, 251n121, 261n151, 263n157, 276n200, 299, 310
Levine, Paul 9–10, 12n26, 14–16, 62n44, 63n44, 65n49, 65n52, 82n45, 124n71
Levy, Daniel 108n17, 198n340, 281n211
Libik, Györgi 144
Lichtenstein, Heiner 9n21, 217

Liljefors, Max 107n12, 119n54, 207n374, 291, 331n18
Lindh, Anna 103
Lindmarker, Ingmar 36n10, 140n131, 189n306–307, 193n319, 195n330, 218n23, 226n51–52, 268n173
Lindström, Ulla 157, 171n240, 174n249, 175n255
Linenthal, Edward T. 214n10
Linnéa, Sharon 13n29, 67n2, 259n146
Lipke, Janis 32–33
Ljung, Lennart 191n316
Lomax, Bill 310n91
Lomfors, Ingrid 13n28
Louise, Queen of Sweden 155
Lower, Wendy 280n209, 293n17
Lozowick, Yaacov 58n23
Lubitsch, Ernst 75, 84
Ludvigsson, David 233n71
Lundberg, Arne S. 155, 157, 167, 172, 173n245
Lundgren, Svante 27n60, 328n14
Lundkvist, Artur 90
Lundvik, Jan 141n135, 187n300, 219n27, 234n75, 317, 321n117
Lutz, Carl 10–11, 28, 64, 216–217, 217n20, 238, 283

MacDonald, Robert H. 72n17
Macdonell, Archibald Gordon 75
MacKenzie, S. P. 244n101
Macmillan, Harold 94
Mairanovsky, Grigory 2
Mann, Heinrich 87n58
Marrus, Michael 8, 108n17
Märta, Norwegian Crown Princess 240–241
Martin, Barbara 178n266
Marton, Kati 27, 179, 186n294, 192n319, 246n105, 301
Mattsson, Britt-Marie 121n58, 198n342

Matz, Johan 37n92, 38, 39n96, 130n89, 130n90, 131n93, 133n99, 103, 134n106, 135n110
Medoff, Rafael 60n28
Mehr, Hjalmar 166–167
Melman, Billie 70n9, 71n12
Mengele, Joseph 240
Minhai, Gui 200
Mintz, Allan 214n10
Modéer, Kjell Åke 87n58
de Mohr, Claudio 150, 158
Molin, Karl 118n50, 137n118, 138n124
Möller, Yngve 136n116, 140n134, 141n137
Möllerstedt, Gunnar 185
Molotov, Vyacheslav 2
Montefiore, Simon Sebag 328–329
Morgan, Michael L. 227n56
Morgenthau, Henry, Jr 59–60, 110n22, 135
Morse, Arthur D. 14n33, 28n64, 220
Moynihan, Daniel Patrick 220, 221n34, 237
*Music Box* (1990), film 278–279
Murphy, Robert 79n35
Myrdal, Alva 109, 157, 256
Myrdal, Gunnar 117
Myasnikov, A. L. 168–169

Nagy, Imre 300–301
Nansen, Fridtjof 66–67
Neiman, Susan 290
Neuman, Ricki 13
neutrality, Swedish 113–119, 192
*The New Wallenberg Monument*, monument 303–309, 330
Nicholson, Michael 259n146
Nihlén, Staffan 317
Nikulin, Leon 264n158
Nilsson, Asta 67, 122
Nilsson, Björn 183
Nilsson, Gustaf 151
Nilsson, Olle 171n242, 188n304

# Index

Nilsson, Torsten 169–170, 171n240, 185, 235
Nordling, Raoul 32
*Non-Violence*, monument *see* Reuterswärd
Novick, Peter 227–228, 292n14
Nuremberg Trials 2, 108, 110, 249, 253, 292
Nye, Joseph S. 232
Nyiszli, Myklós 240
Nyquist, Michael 98

Oakeshott, Michael 17
O'Connor, John 265
Oestricher Bernheim, Rachel 225
O'Flaherty, Hugh 94–95
Ohlendorf, Otto 253
Ohlin, Bertil 89n61, 103, 104n5, 171n242
Olin, Lena 238
Olsen, Iver 34–35, 60–61, 82, 131n94, 134, 158, 211
Orbán, Viktor 208–209
Orczy, Emmuska 69–71, 73
Ortwed, Kirsten 321–324, 332
Oscarson, Stina 287
Östberg, Annika 199
von Osten, Marion 289n4
Österberg, Eva 25n54
Östling, Johan 110, 205n368, 326n5
von Otter, Göran 107
Ottosson, Sten 117n46, 138n124

Paldiel, Mordechai 29n65
Palme, Olof 137, 159, 170, 179, 185–187
Palme, Thomas 302n47, 49, 304
Palmklint, Ingrid 34n82, 39n97, 104n5
Palmkvist, Conny 87n58
Palmstierna, Carl-Fredrik 155n191, 156–157, 176, 177n262, 219n29
Pankin, Boris 195–196

Parádi, István 65
Parvilahti, Unto 181–182
Patai, Raphael 52n8
Pátzáy, Pál 298
Pehle, John 134
Pell, Claiborne 221–222
Perlasca, Giorgio 10, 28, 263n156, 286, 310
*Perlasca – An Italian Hero* (2002), television series 283
Perra, Emiliano 283n216
Perry, George 71n12, 88n60
Persson, Carl 157n199, 169n235, 190n310
Persson, Edvard 88–92
Persson, Göran 102, 104, 198, 206
Persson, Johan 200
Petersson, Bo 140n134, 142n143, 167n231, 170n239
Pető, Andrea 330n17
Petri, Lennart 126, 135n111, 137n122, 138n123, 155n189, 157n199, 158n201
Pfeffer-Wildenbruch, Karl 261
Philipp, Rudolph 13n29, 111n27, 119n52, 128n85, 140n132, 142–155, 162n212, 180, 199, 203, 276n196, 276n199, 300n40, 318, 328n11
Pick, Hella 219n29
Pickering, Thomas R. 158
*Pienza*, monument, *see* Nihlén
Pierrejean, Claudine 34n82, 169n235
Pierrejean, Daniel 34n82, 169n235
Pihurik, Judit 54n13
*Pimpernel Smith/Mister V* (1941), film 67–68, 74–84, 88–91, 101, 271, 327
*Pimpernel Svensson* (1950), film 88–92
poetic truth 239–242
Porter, Monica 7
Pótó, János 302

practical past 17–25, 66, 205, 239, 334–335
Preus, David W. 302–303

Ranki, Vera 53n9
Rapoport, Nathan 305
Raskin, Richard 68, 271
Rayfield, Donald 183n285
Reagan, Ronald 16, 193, 213, 230–231, 289, 304
Reiz, Eugen 142
Reuterswärd, Carl Fredrik 295
Rév, István 330n17
Richards, Jeffrey 67n4, 72n15, 72n19, 72n32, 81n38, 82n43
Ricoeur, Paul 124n70
Rogin, Michael 230n63
Roosevelt, Eleanor 132–134
Roosevelt, Franklin D. 57, 59, 60, 75, 133, 220, 241
*Roots* (1977), television series 232, 238, 243, 282
Rosander, Lars 189n305
Rosen, Robert N. 60n28
Rosenberg, Joel 84n52
Rosenfeld, Alvin H. 215n11
Rosenfeld, Harvey 6n14, 76n28, 137n119, 171n240, 175n254, 192n319, 225, 256n138, 307n66
Rosengren, Henrik 211n3
Rothman, Lenke 198, 317
Rotta, Angelo 10
Rousso, Henri 41, 214, 293
Rubin, Michael 329
Rubinstien, William 9
Rudberg, Pontus 106n10
Runberg, Björn 111n28, 124n71, 127n81, 141n139
Rüsen, Jörn 18, 22n47
Ruth, Arne 202

Sachar, Howard M. 53n10
Sakharov, Andrei 37n93, 179, 196
Sakmyster, Thomas 55n15, 313n89

Salomon, Kim 137n121, 173n246, 240n93
Salgo, Nicolas M. 303–306
af Sandeberg, Edward 179–180
Sanz Briz, Ángel 283, 286
*The Scarlet Pimpernel* (1934), film 68–69, 71–75, 77, 79, 86–87, 89–91, 327
Schellenberg, Walter 112, 250
Schibbye, Martin 200
Schiller, Bernt 258n145
Schindler, Oskar 25, 28–33, 94, 97, 274, 275n195, 281, 283, 286, 291, 327–329, 333
*Schindler's List* (1993), film 97, 244, 274–275, 277–278, 280
Schmidhuber, Gerhard 262–263
Schori, Pierre 97n93, 159n205, 194n327, 236n83, 273n185, 327
Schou, Rigmor 87
Schreiber, Penny 255n137
Schueler, Kaj 68n4, 208, 272n183, 273n187
Schult, Tanja 5, 6n14, 9n22, 15n37, 43n106, 44, 50n1, 52n7, 62n39, 65n49, 66n1, 67n2, 67n4, 83n47, 48, 123n66, 128n83, 142n140, 198n341, 200n346, 202n357, 213n7, 216n15, 221n34, 230n63, 247n111, 249n115, 256n138, 281n211, 293, 294n20, 295, 299n34, 304n54, 306n62, 63, 307n64, 307n66, 307n68, 308, 319n109, 320n114, 323n125, 326n4, 326n7, 327n8, 328n12, 332n21, 333n23
Schwartz, Nils 6–7
Semyonov, Vladimir 168
Serfösö, Eva 283n217
Serov, Ivan 1–3
Serova, Vera 1
Seymour, Jane 264

# Index

Shalit, Erel 44n108
Shandler, Jeffrey 227n55
Shevardnadze, Eduard 196
Shevchenko, Arkady 184n289
*Shoah see* Lanzmann
Shumuk, Danylo 224
Silvia, Queen of Sweden 316
Sjöholm Skrubbe, Jessica 331
Sjöquist, Eric 6n12, 52n7, 62n39, 67n2, 96, 123n63, 124n71, 134n106, 145n151, 147n159, 154n184, 156n194, 157, 167n230, 185n291, 187n301, 188n303, 189n307, 193n319, 199n344, 217n22, 219n29, 223n42, 223–224n43, 226n52, 230n63, 246n107, 247n111, 248n113, 259n146, 267n172, 268n173, 304n54, 306n63
Sjöwall, Maj 124
Skarsgård, Stellan 98, 270–272, 274, 285
Skoglund, Elizabeth R. 259n146
Smith, Danny 35n83, 261n149, 263n157
Smith, Ian Haydn 68
*The Snake Killer*, monument 298–303, 307, 311, 316, 330
Söder, Karin 187, 188
Söderblom, Omi 138–139
Söderblom, Staffan 105, 129–130, 138–140, 144, 173
Sohlman, Rolf 137, 151, 166n226, 168
Solzhenitsyn, Aleksandr 177–179, 182–185
Somlyo, György 311
*Son of Saul* (2015), film 240
Sonnenfeld, Sonja 224, 321
Soviet submarine, *see* U137
Ståhle, Göran 322n123
Stalin, Joseph 2, 38, 130, 139, 140, 142, 144, 171, 211, 297
Stangneth, Bettina 254n133

Steinfeld, Thomas 295
Steinhouse, Carl L. 135n110, 175n254, 192n319, 257–258
Stettinius, Edward 135
Stöckler, Lajos 260, 297
Stone, Norman 246n106
Storch, Gilel 294
Storch, Marcus 294
Stråth, Bo 119n54
Strömberg, Sven 159–160
Strömstedt, Bo 195n331
Sturfelt, Lina 117n48
Suckert, Kurt Erich 115–116
Sundelin, Anders 157n199, 169n235, 190n310
Svartz, Nanna 168–170, 174–177, 223
Svensson, Georg 90
Symo, Margit 119–120
Szabó, Károly 297
Szalai, Pál 263, 297
Szaras, György 52n8
Szekeres, Joszef 263n156
Szenes, Hanna 14
Szent-Györgi, Albert 144–145
Szirmai, Istvan 296
Szita, Szabolcs 57n19, 126n79, 297n29, 301n45, 302n49, 303n52, 309n76, 311n84
Sznaider, Natan 108n17, 198n340, 281n211

Tapper, Michael 124n69, 183n283
Tarantino, Quentin 252
Taylor, Telford 253n126
Teleki, Pál 312–313
Tereya, Josyp 197
Terror Haza, 'the House of Terror' 314–315
Thale, Jerome 248n114
Thompson, Dorothy 133
Thorsell, Staffan 126n74, 230
Thunborg, Folke 153
Tingsten, Herbert 115n37, 136, 138, 182

*To Be or Not To Be* (1942), film 75, 84
Torgovnick, Mariana 227n55, 253n128
Trencsényi, Balasz 314n92, 315n93
Trevor-Roper, Hugh 172
Trice, Ashton D. 73n20, 274
Tschuy, Theo 28n64, 217n20
Tüür, Erkki-Sven 211–212

U137, Soviet submarine 191–192
Ullsten, Ola 187–189, 191–192, 199, 219, 221n34, 233–234n73
Undén, Östen 103, 105, 114, 118, 123, 135–138, 141–142, 152, 155, 173
Ungváry, Krisztián 33n79, 65n50, 262n154

Vagi, Zoltán 57n19
Vaksberg, Arkadij 130n89
Vance, Cyrus 220
Vanderberg, Arthur 134
Varga, Imre 304–307, 310, 318, 330
Varga, Támas 300
Vayda, Tibor 238
Veesenmayer, Edmund 249
Villius, Elsa 4n7, 122n62, 135n111, 137n119, 155n189, 157n199, 174n252, 175–176, 223, 233, 258n145, 267n172
Villius, Hans 4n7, 122n62, 135n111, 137n119, 155n189, 157n199, 174n252, 175–176, 223, 233, 258n145, 267n172
Voight, Jon 236
Volkogonov, Dmitri 38
Voroshilov, Kliment 151
Vörös, Márton 271
Vrba, Rudolf 57, 62
*Vrba-Wetzler report see* Vrba *and* Wetzler
Vyshinsky, Andrey 37

Wachtmeister, Wilhelm 96, 97n95, 137n122, 190, 192, 234–235n76, 305n59
Wagrell, Kristin 197n339, 205n367, 249n118
Wahlöö, Per 124
Walde, Alfons 75
Wallace, Henry 133
*Wallenberg* (2001), opera 211–214
*Wallenberg – A Hero's Story* (1985), television series 16, 236–239, 242–269, 271, 282–284, 328, 333
Wallenberg, André Oscar 49
Wallenberg, Gustaf 50–52, 61n35
Wallenberg, Jacob (1746–1778) 49
Wallenberg, Jacob 52, 65n52, 112, 132
Wallenberg, Marcus 130, 132
Wallenberg, Peter 305
Wallenberg, Raoul Oscar 49–50
Wallengren, Ann-Kristin 89n62, 92n74
Waltz, Christoph 252
The War Refugee Board 58–62, 64, 129, 134–135, 220
Warren, George 132–133
Wästberg, Per 67n4, 188n304, 322
Weber, Cynthia 43
Wecter, Dixon 43n106
Wenner-Gren, Axel 102–103
Wennerström, Stig 190
Werbell, Frederick E. 4n4, 131n92, 134n107, 177, 229n59, 246, 256–257, 262, 263n156, 271–272n181
Werfel, Franz 87n58
Wetzler, Alfred 57, 62
White, Hayden 17, 335
Wiesel, Elie 233, 237
Wiesen, S. Jonathan 30n72
Wiesenthal, Simon 179, 184, 218, 219n27, 29
Wiklund, Martin 105
Wikström, Inger 210

Will, George 190, 191n314, 192
*Winds of War*, television serial 264
Wingren, Bo 318n108, 321
Winner, David 259n146
Wolff, Morris 221–222
Wyman, David S. 60n30
Wyman, Mark 126n78

Yahil, Leni 65n49, 192n319, 218n26

Yakovlev, Aleksandr 195–196
York, Richard 326
Young, Harold 70
Young, James E. 291–292, 305n60

Zetterberg, Kent 108n15, 139n128
Zetterström, Erik ('Kar de Mumma') 90–91
Zietsma, David 284n219